THE LETTERS OF PHILIP WEBB

THE PICKERING MASTERS SERIES

Philip Webb, by George Howard, c. 1875?

[*From the Castle Howard collection: reproduced by kind permission of the Hon. Simon Howard.*]

THE LETTERS OF PHILIP WEBB

Edited by
John Aplin

Volume I
1864–1887

LONDON AND NEW YORK

First published 2016
by Routledge
2 Park Square, Milton Park, Abingdon, Oxon OX14 4RN

and by Routledge
711 Third Avenue, New York, NY 10017

Routledge is an imprint of the Taylor & Francis Group, an informa business

Editorial material and selection © 2016 John Aplin; individual owners retain copyright in their own material

All rights reserved. No part of this book may be reprinted or reproduced or utilised in any form or by any electronic, mechanical, or other means, now known or hereafter invented, including photocopying and recording, or in any information storage or retrieval system, without permission in writing from the publishers.

Trademark notice: Product or corporate names may be trademarks or registered trademarks, and are used only for identification and explanation without intent to infringe.

British Library Cataloguing in Publication Data
A catalogue record for this book is available from the British Library

Library of Congress Cataloging-in-Publication Data
Webb, Philip, 1831–1915, author.
[Correspondence. Selections]
The letters of Philip Webb.
volumes cm
Contents: volume 1. Letters 1864–87 — volume 2. Letters 1888–98 — volume 3. Letters 1899–1902 — volume 4. Letters 1903–14.
  ISBN 978-1-84893-498-6 (Set) — ISBN 978-1-315-63964-2 (Set) — ISBN 978-1-138-76144-5 (vol. 1) — ISBN 978-1-138-76145-2 (vol. 2) — ISBN 978-1-315-64257-4 (vol. 2) — ISBN 978-1-138-76146-9 (vol. 3) — ISBN 978-1-315-64256-7 (vol. 3) — ISBN 978-1-138-76147-6 (vol. 4) — ISBN 978-1-315-64255-0 (vol. 4) 1. Webb, Philip, 1831–1915—Correspondence. 2. Architects—Great Britain—Correspondence. I. Aplin, John, editor. II. Title.
 NA997.W4A3 2016
 720.92—dc23
 2015035179

ISBN: 978-1-8489-3498-6 (Set)
eISBN: 978-1-315-63964-2 (Set)
ISBN: 978-1-1387-6144-5 (Volume I)
eISBN: 978-1-315-64258-1 (Volume I)

Typeset in Times New Roman
by Apex CoVantage, LLC

CONTENTS

VOLUME I 1864–1887

Preface	ix
Abbreviations and cue titles	xv
Introduction	xix

Letters 1864–1887	1

VOLUME II 1888–1898

Introduction	vii

Letters 1888–1898	1

VOLUME III 1899–1902

Introduction	vii

Letters 1899–1902	1

VOLUME IV 1903–1914

Introduction	vii

Letters 1903–1914	1
Index	319

PREFACE

I quite agree that they are literature, & I think that his letters are as fine a manifestation of his personality as his architecture, or anything else. There are masses of them in existence, & it would not be very easy to make a choice for publication.[1]

Editorial principles

The architect Philip Webb (1831–1915), co-founder with William Morris of the Society for the Protection of Ancient Buildings, was an important influence upon the emerging Arts and Crafts movement. This four-volume collection of letters comprises a comprehensive selection from his surviving correspondence, little of which has previously been published. As well as revealing the range of Webb's professional endeavours and the value he invested in a number of close friendships, the evidence presented in his letters confirms his position as a key member of the Morris circle.

It is unfortunate that, for many of Webb's buildings, few if any letters survive pertaining to their construction, although for some others a significant amount of material is available to show his typical ways of working. But important aspects of his professional practices, as well as his intellectual and emotional sympathies, also emerge in his private correspondence, and the legacy of his unswerving commitment to the preservation of our ancient building heritage is fully represented in the fascinating letters he drafted on behalf of the SPAB. As Sydney Cockerell suggested when writing to Webb's first biographer, W.R. Lethaby, there is something compelling and noble about Webb's writing, displaying a consistent thoughtfulness and integrity characteristic of the way in which he conducted all of his affairs.

The more than 1100 letters selected for inclusion have been newly transcribed, with the exception of a few published by John Brandon-Jones several decades ago, for which the originals have not been located, but which are too interesting to overlook. My aim has been to provide authoritative texts with a full scholarly apparatus in which the editorial interventions remain unobtrusive. Webb's alterations and deletions are therefore retained in full, as these often provide telling

PREFACE

information about the process of his thinking and (re)composition. As many of his letters survive only in their draft form, this is especially important. All deleted material is shown as ~~double crossed-through text~~, and insertions and second thoughts, wherever they are sited on the manuscript, are placed $^{\text{above the line, as superscript text}}$. Commonly used contractions and shortenings are not normally expanded, such as w$^{\underline{d}}$ and sh$^{\underline{d}}$, or wh. and 'tis, but occasionally, where the sense or context requires it, a word is filled out by employing editorial square brackets, such as in dim[ensio]$^{\underline{ns}}$. Webb used colons and semi-colons freely, where a full closure might make for clearer comprehension, and I have tended to rationalise these, converting a number to full stops in accordance with current usage.

Occasionally I have added missing apostrophes without comment, but I have not normally amended misplaced ones. In common with many literate Victorians, Webb often used an apostrophe to indicate possession as in 'your's' and it's', and these too I have left without comment. On the other hand, I have registered most spelling errors and archaic usages either with an editorial [*sic*], or have supplied missing letters in a bra[c]ket. Webb's original underlining has been retained, and not converted into italics. All ampersands are similarly left in their original form. I have decided not to standardise the use of quotation marks – he often uses single and double marks interchangeably within the same letter – but for reasons of clarification I have occasionally changed single marks to double. One editorial intervention I have made is to break up long passages of text into more digestible paragraphs, but usually by taking the clue from Webb himself who, without starting a new line, would often leave a bigger than normal space between the end of one sentence and the start of the next. His reason for not starting a fresh line was usually to save paper.

Webb's writing is usually perfectly legible, and there are relatively few irretrievably damaged portions to his letters. All suggested reconstructions are placed within square brackets. Where I have hazarded a reading of an illegible word or two, I place this within <angled brackets>, and where that passage is hard to read because it is one which Webb has deleted, I indicate it <~~thus~~>. Where a heavily deleted or illegible passage cannot be reconstructed, I record this as [*words illegible*].

Pre-printed letterhead addresses are shown in italics, whereas those written by hand appear as standard text. For reasons of space, addresses spread over more than one line are usually contracted, with original line breaks indicated with a vertical slash. I have similarly contracted closing valedictions. I have chosen not to standardise the different ways in which Webb dated his letters, but I have consistently placed the address before the date, even on the few occasions when he reverses this.

I am conscious that in an edition of this kind, repetition within the editorial notes is hard to avoid, and is sometimes desirable. How many times, for example, should one identify a name which may be relatively unfamiliar, or explain an allusion, especially for the reader who may not be reading chronologically but

PREFACE

dipping in and out of volumes? I have tried to minimise this by cross-referring in the endnotes to letters, and by trusting to the reader's judicious use of the Index. But occasional repetitions have proved to be unavoidable. Wherever possible I have endeavoured to contextualise a letter by incorporating within the editorial notes cross-references to the surviving letters of Webb's correspondents, using many published and unpublished extracts where such material survives and has been traced. I hope that this will also offer new insights into some of those correspondents whose names may be well-known but about whom relatively little has previously been published.

With just a few exceptions, I have avoided repeating citations or the use of 'ibid'. For each letter, any source is therefore identified within the endnotes only after the first passage of quoted material, and any subsequent quotations from the same source simply carry forward the initial citation.

Acknowledgements

For allowing me to include letters and other materials held within their collections, I am most grateful to the following: International Institute of Social History, Amsterdam; Local Studies, Bedford Central Library; Cadbury Research Library: Special Collections, University of Birmingham; British Library; Cheltenham Art Gallery and Museum; Courtauld Institute of Art; Emery Walker Trust; Fitzwilliam Museum, Cambridge; Houghton Library, Harvard University; Castle Howard (by permission of the Hon Simon Howard); Huntington Library, San Marino, California; National Archives, Kew; Red House, National Trust; Society for the Protection of Ancient Buildings, London; Harry Ransom Center, University of Texas at Austin; Victoria and Albert Museum, Archive of Art and Design and the National Art Library; West Sussex Record Office, Chichester (the Blunt papers by permission of John Lytton, fifth Earl of Lytton); William Morris Gallery, London Borough of Waltham Forest; William Morris Society and Museum, Hammersmith. In addition, I am grateful for information provided by The Crown Estate, by Trinity College Library, Cambridge and by Stratford Library Local Studies Collection, Warwickshire County Council.

I am especially indebted to Frances Cockerell for granting me permission to quote from the invaluable diaries and letters of Sydney Cockerell.

I am grateful to the following, who have assisted me in a wide range of ways, for their interest and support: Judith Bronkhurst, David Chambers, Jane Cohen, Heather G. Cole, Christine Conboy, Michael Drury, Helen Fisher, Anne George, Mary Haegert, Kirsty Hartsiotis, Kathy Haslam, Charles Hind, Lynn Hulse, Sue Hodson, Antony Hopkins, Roisin Inglesby, Carien Kremer, Karin Kyburz, Frances Lansley, Christopher Marsden, Amy Marquis, Jan Marsh, Claudia Marx, Anne Louise Mason, Jaimee McRoberts, William S. Peterson, Ines Pina, Chris Ridgway, Gayle Richardson, Nicholas Robinson, Robin Stannard, Virginia Surtees, Anne Thorne, Viem Tummers, Rick Watson, Nick Wilde and Chris Woodham.

A particular word of thanks is due to the unfailingly helpful staff of the Manuscripts and Rare Books and Music reading rooms of the British Library, as well as to the staff of the London Library.

I have been exceptionally well served by the Society for the Protection of Ancient Buildings, the organisation closest to Philip Webb's heart, and I am particularly grateful for the help extended by Matthew Slocombe and Maggie Goodall, who have been generous with their time and advice. Tessa Wild, National Trust curator for London and the South East, has kindly resolved queries relating to Red House and Standen. Helen Elletson, curator of the William Morris Society and Museum, readily gave me access to Emery Walker's house at 7 Hammersmith Terrace so that I might hunt down one or two fugitive letters, and she shared in my pleasure when I found them. She also supplied an image of Webb's 'Sniffing Lion' sketch for use as a frontispiece. I am especially indebted to my former colleague Penny Lyndon, now volunteer librarian of the William Morris Society and Museum. At an early stage of my research she put me in touch with several useful contacts, and made a number of helpful suggestions.

I am particularly grateful to Mark Pollard, commissioning editor for Pickering and Chatto, for his faith in this project, and to Eleanor Hooker who helped to promote it. I have since been served well by the helpful team at Routledge, to whom the project transferred at a late stage.

Frank Sharp's compendious knowledge of the William Morris circle has meant that he has been able to provide almost instant answers to what I thought were arcane queries, and he has enabled me to plug several gaps in my editorial notes. I am grateful for his generosity. Godfrey Rubens kindly shared his expertise on W.R. Lethaby with me, lent me materials, and also allowed me to use some letters in his possession.

Chief amongst recent commentators on Webb's professional work is Sheila Kirk, whose authoritative *Philip Webb. Pioneer of Arts & Crafts Architecture*, published in 2005, is an exceptionally valuable and superbly illustrated study of his buildings. It will be evident to readers of this edition just how much I have relied upon her understanding and clear accounts of Webb's building techniques. Indeed, Webb's letters – particularly those pertaining to his buildings – are best read with her book to hand.

I am greatly indebted to Chris Rycroft, who has been most generous with his time and read virtually all of my transcriptions and editorial notes, offering many helpful suggestions. It has resulted in my reconsidering and refining a number of my assertions. Any errors and misconceptions which remain are of course my own, but without his involvement there would have been rather more.

To Peter Burman, whose sympathetic appreciation of the work of Philip Webb and his contemporaries is second to none, I owe several unpayable debts. He has generously shared with me his expert knowledge, and loaned me invaluable material given to him by the late John Brandon-Jones, including Webb's office letter-books. He also made available to me his own transcriptions of Webb's letters to George and Rosalind Howard, and these form the basis of my selections from the Castle Howard material, although the editorial notes are mine. I have much

PREFACE

enjoyed our long discussions and email exchanges about Webb, whose world Peter understands so well.

Peter Collister has lived with this project since the beginning. Even whilst engaged in his own major editorial projects relating to Henry James, he has been able to offer suggestions on matters of style and detail, and I am grateful for his continuing support.

Note

1 Sydney Cockerell to W.R. Lethaby, 2 August 1915, *BL Add 52731* ff. 117–8.

ABBREVIATIONS AND CUE TITLES

Printed sources

CAGM   *Originality and Initiative. The Arts and Crafts archives at Cheltenham*, edited by Mary Greensted and Sophia Wilson (Cheltenham: Cheltenham Art Gallery and Museum, in association with Lund Humphries, 2003).

CDGR   *The Correspondence of Dante Gabriel Rossetti*, 9 volumes, edited by William E. Fredeman (Woodbridge: D. S. Brewer, 2002–10).

CLJM   *The Collected Letters of Jane Morris,* edited by Frank C. Sharp and Jan Marsh (Woodbridge: The Boydell Press, 2012).

CLWM   *The Collected Letters of William Morris*, 4 volumes, edited by Norman Kelvin (Princeton: Princeton University Press, 1984–96).

Dakers   Caroline Dakers, *Clouds. The Biography of a Country House* (New Haven and London: Yale University Press, 1993).

DNB   *Dictionary of National Biography* (Oxford University Press: online resource consulted).

Drury   Michael Drury, *Wandering Architects* (Stamford: Shaun Tyas, 2000).

Elliott   David B. Elliott, *Charles Fairfax Murray. The Unknown Pre-Raphaelite* (Lewes: The Book Guild, 2000).

Gaimster   Amy Gaimster, *George Jack 1855–1931. Architect and Designer-Craftsman* (Waltham Forest: William Morris Gallery, 2006).

Greensted   Mary Greensted, *The Arts and Crafts Movement in the Cotswolds* (Stroud: Alan Sutton, 1993).

JRIBA   *Journal of the Royal Institute of British Architects*

JWMS   *Journal of William Morris Studies*

Kirk   Sheila Kirk, *Philip Webb. Pioneer of Arts & Crafts Architecture* (Chichester: Wiley-Academy, 2005).

LeMire   Eugene D. LeMire, *A Bibliography of William Morris* (London: Oak Knoll Press, 2006).

Lethaby   W.R. Lethaby, *Philip Webb and his Work* (London: Oxford University Press, 1935).

LTF   William Hale White, *Letters to Three Friends* (London: Humphrey Milford, 1924).

LPW   John Brandon-Jones, 'Letters of Philip Webb and his Contemporaries', *Architectural History*, VIII, 1964, pp. 52–72.

LTF   William Hale White, *Letters to Three Friends*, edited Dorothy Vernon White (London: Humphrey Milford, Oxford University Press, 1924). This volume contains a selection of Hale White's letters, and some extracts from letters, to PSW.

MacCarthy, LPR   Fiona MacCarthy, *The Last Pre-Raphaelite. Edward Burne-Jones and the Victorian Imagination* (London: Faber and Faber, 2011).

MacCarthy, WMLT   Fiona MacCarthy, *William Morris. A Life for Our Time* (London: Faber and Faber, 1994).

Mackail   John William Mackail, *The Life of William Morris*, 2 volumes (London: Longmans, Green & Co, 1899).

Miele   *From William Morris: Building Conservation and the Arts and Crafts Cult of Authenticity 1877–1939*, edited Chris Miele (New Haven & London: Yale University Press, 2005).

NBS   John Brandon-Jones, 'Notes on the Building of Smeaton Manor', *Architectural History*, I, 1958, pp. 31–58

OED   *The Oxford English Dictionary*

Penn   Arthur Penn, *Brampton Church and its Windows* (printed by Howe of Brampton Ltd, 1993).

Peterson   William S. Peterson, *A Bibliography of the Kelmscott Press* (Oxford: Clarendon Press, 1984).

Surtees   Virginia Surtees, *The Artist and the Autocrat. George and Rosalind Howard, Earl and Countess of Carlisle* (Salisbury: Michael Russell, 1988).

White   Dorothy Vernon White, *The Groombridge Diary* (London: Oxford University Press, 1924).

Note: All textual references to Shakespeare within endnotes employ *The Riverside Shakespeare*, 2nd edition (Boston and New York: Houghton Mifflin, 1997).

Sources for manuscript material

Amsterdam   International Institute of Social History, Amsterdam

BCL   Local Studies, Bedford Central Library ('Mark Rutherford' collection)

Birmingham   Cadbury Research Library: Special Collections University of Birmingham

BL   British Library, London

CD   The year diaries of Sydney Carlyle Cockerell, at the British Library (Add MSS 52623–52702)

Cheltenham   Art Gallery and Museum, Cheltenham

ABBREVIATIONS AND CUE TITLES

Courtauld	Library of the Courtauld Institute, London (two boxes of PSW-related materials; most of his letters to GBO are in the form of old photostats, probably produced no later than the 1930s)
EWT	Emery Walker Trust, London
Fitzwilliam	Fitzwilliam Museum, Cambridge
Houghton	Houghton Library, Harvard University, Cambridge, Mass.
Howard	Castle Howard, Yorkshire; PSW's letters to George and Rosalind Howard, in transcriptions made available by Peter Burman
Huntington	Huntington Library, San Marino, California
LB-1; LB-2	Letter-book 1; Letter-book 2. PSW's office drafts/copies for 1874–88. Private collection
LPW	(See printed sources)
NA	The National Archives, Kew
NBS	(See printed sources)
Red House	Red House, National Trust
SPAB	Archive of the Society for the Protection of Ancient Buildings, London; individual case files recorded where appropriate
SPAB W-W	Volume of letters from PSW to William Weir at the SPAB
Texas	Harry Ransom Center, University of Texas at Austin
V&A, AAD	Philip Webb papers (formerly part of the Brandon-Jones collection) in the V&A, Archive of Art and Design (ref. AAD/2014/5), London
V&A, NAL	V&A, National Art Library, London
WMG	William Morris Gallery, London Borough of Waltham Forest
WSRO	West Sussex Record Office, Chichester

Main correspondents

CF	Charles Joseph Faulkner
CFM	Charles Fairfax Murray
DGR	Dante Gabriel Rossetti
DJB	Detmar Jellings Blow
EBJ	Edward Burne-Jones
EW	Emery Walker
GBJ	Georgiana Burne-Jones
GBO	Giacomo Boni
GH	George Howard
GPB	George Price Boyce
GWJ	George Washington Jack
GW	George Wardle
HTT	Hugh Thackeray Turner
JEM	Jenny Morris
JM	Jane Morris
JR	John Ruskin

ABBREVIATIONS AND CUE TITLES

JWM	John William Mackail
KF	Kate Faulkner
MM	May Morris
PSW	Philip Speakman Webb
PWY	Percy Wyndham
SCC	Sydney Carlyle Cockerell
WHW	William Hale White
WM	William Morris
WRL	William Richard Lethaby
WSB	Wilfrid Scawen Blunt
WW	William Weir

Organisations

MMF & Co	Morris, Marshall, Faulkner & Co
RIBA	Royal Institute of British Architects
SPAB	The Society for the Protection of Ancient Buildings

INTRODUCTION

It is perhaps curious that none of Philip Webb's extant letters so far recovered date from his earliest years, and indeed that nothing survives until after he had completed the construction of his first major architectural project, Red House. Nor, with the exception of a congratulatory letter from his mother on his twenty-first birthday, did he keep any of the family correspondence that certainly would have passed between parents and siblings and which might have offered us unfiltered access to the events of his childhood and early adult life. What we know of those years is derived instead from what he chose to recall for friends in later life, unconnected pieces of information which they in turn refracted. But that Webb afforded a special status to the solitary survival from amongst his mother's letters is suggested by his careful annotation on its reverse – 'Mater Jany 1852' – an aide memoire to indicate that this one, at least, was to be kept until the end.

Addressing him by the French spelling of his name with which he had been christened, Elizabeth Webb is affectionate but also somewhat formal and a little awkward, suggesting a woman rather shy of her sons as they began to make their own way in the world. Her husband, Charles Webb, a family doctor with a practice in Oxford, had died four years earlier when Philip was seventeen, and the black edges to her sheet of paper present a conventional image of mid-Victorian mourning whilst also emphasising the loneliness of widowhood and its obvious financial constraints when it came to assisting the careers of her children.

January 11th 1852

My dear Phillippe

Tomorrow being the anniversary of your Birthday as well as being the Most important one you having attained your 21st year, Aunt Sarah with me my dear Boy offer you our best wishes on the occasion, for your Health, & happiness as well as success in all your undertakings in your Profession. May you be fortunate, put your trust in the Almighty my dear Boy & he will give you patience & perseverance which in the end will bring you I trust, & believe to prosperity.

    Imagine our disappointment that you are not at home with Harry, did you not think him looking very thin & ill? did he tell you he had a bad

INTRODUCTION

knee? I much fear he is very out of health but he would not hear of it. I want much to know how long he staid with you also if anything was said to him by Mr & Mrs Billing[;] when you write give all particulars[;] everything here is going on as you left it. Yesterday was a very sharp frost today windy, wet & mild. I am sorry to say Harry tells me he cannot aprise me as regards Frank which has much disappointed me so that I must again exercise my patience again[.] wishing you many happy returns of the day believe us to Remain with true affection my dear Boy & our sincere well wishes

Mother & Aunt Sarah[1]

Webb had already completed three years of his architectural apprenticeship under John Billing in Reading by the time he was 21, and was committed to his chosen career path. The virtues of 'patience and perseverance' which Elizabeth Webb wished for her son found a resonance in him – 'Well did my mother preach to me, that work kept people out of trouble & mischief' (*Letter 32*) – even if he did not share her confident trust in the reality of a personal God. He was the second of four brothers, all of whom (like their sisters) were given their mother's maiden name, Speakman, for their own middle names. The eldest, Henry (Harry) became a doctor, training at St Bartholomew's Hospital in London, whilst Frank became a successful brewer – Philip later designed at least one label for his beer bottles, and a house for Harry, in Welwyn, Hertfordshire. The fourth brother, not mentioned in this letter, was Perceval (Percy), who entered the church: in the 1890s he would keep the Society for the Protection of Ancient Buildings apprised of unwelcome proposals for restorations at Chichester Cathedral, where he became a Canon.

A childhood spent in Oxford profoundly shaped the sensibilities of the intelligent, observant boy born at 1 Beaumont Street on 12 January 1831. When he was aged about three, the family moved to a large house in St Giles's, formerly owned by the Dukes of Marlborough, not far from St John's College. We learn from his first biographer and devoted admirer, William Richard Lethaby, who had privileged access to all the papers which passed to Emery Walker as executor in 1915, that Webb greatly admired the work of his paternal grandfather, the Birmingham-born medallist, Thomas Webb, who was known for the accuracy and technical adroitness of his portraits. Something of the grandfather's artistry was inherited by Webb's doctor father, who drew animals and passed that interest in turn to his own son, whose later sketches are exceptionally well-observed. Lethaby remembered being told that 'To draw animals you must sympathize with them; you must know what it feels like to be an animal'.[2] The boy would accompany his father on some of his visits to patients, getting to know Oxford's streets and buildings, storing away his direct experience of the lives of its residents to be retrieved in moments of delicious reminiscence and shared 60 years later with Jane Morris, whose recollections of an Oxford childhood were not so fond as his own. He recalled Holywell Street, where she had been brought up. 'My father had two or three regular patients there, and when I was a little modest boy I used sometimes to go to the house of one of them & spend the day, but that was on the north side of the street, with the garden down to the pig-styed [*sic*] path-way leading between garden palings direct – in a winding way – to Holywell Church. I loved that pig and apple tainted air, as children do in the making of mud-pies.' (*Letter 606*) The way in which memories could be triggered by chance associations intrigued him, and Lethaby remembered being told that they 'seemed to be stimulated by something in the nature of vibrations'.[3] The demolition and unsympathetic restorations of Oxford's historic buildings (not least among them the work on the spire of St Mary the Virgin) was always a cause for distress, but his learning in 1874 of the clearing away of his own past had an almost tragic poignancy. 'The Oxford houses are sold, and the Webbs & Speakmans swept away and the town purified. Poor old town, poor old memories.' (*Letter 68*)

'Being born & bred there my first perception of anything was of the beauty and seriousness of the buildings – that was my earliest and unconscious "study of architecture" – that good breeding – at all events has never left me. I may say, the manners of the Oxford buildings were the making of me.' (*Letter 614*) His powers of recollection even encompassed the act of imagining himself as a child still haunting the old streets, an image prompted by Giacomo Boni's first visit to Oxford in 1889. 'If you saw a little & wonderstruck boy in Oxford trotting along the pavements of the streets there, it might have been the ghost of my youth, for I was born in that <u>seat</u> of learning, but not in its <u>head</u>.' (*Letter 353*) This making a distinction between being a native of the town, rather than having been an undergraduate there, is telling, for Webb was acutely conscious of his lack of a formal university education. In his mind, if in no-one else's, it set him somewhat apart from the close friendships he formed in the later 1850s, principally with William Morris, Edward Burne-Jones and Charles Faulkner, all Oxford men in a way that he was not. He comes close to confessing this sense of inadequacy in a letter to Rossetti in 1866. 'Ever since fate was kind enough to make me acquainted with Topsy [*i.e. Morris*] & through him with Ned [Burne-Jones], [Madox] Brown & yourself I have always thought that to allow of my being considered as one of such a company, there must be something about my mental constitution wh' excused the seeming disparity. To a certain extent I have thought the allowance to be this, that I had the capacity of understanding my men, if I could not compete with them.' (*Letter 5*) He admired and envied those who were able to speak out in public without apparent self-doubts, for it was something other than natural reticence which inhibited him.

On completing his articles, Webb stayed with Billing for a further two years before moving to the Wolverhampton practice of Bidlake and Lovett in April 1854, carrying with him a reference which spoke warmly of his 'assiduity and perseverance' and the proficiency of his drawing and design skills 'particularly in the several Gothic styles',[4] but within four weeks he knew that he could not endure living and working in such close proximity to the symbols of modern industrialisation and deprivation. He was offered instead the happy chance of a move back to his hometown, and in May 1854 joined the office of George Edmund Street, the Oxford diocesan architect, whose chief assistant he became and within a year saw his annual salary doubled to £100.[5] He remembered with affection the comradely spirit of the office, and would always remain grateful to Street, even after he drew away from the older man's quasi-medievalism. 'He was everything that was honourable, and industrious beyond words, a very able architect according to his lights.'[6] But whilst the years with Street ensured his acquisition of a surefooted professional confidence, enabling his move into independent practice, he was shaped even more profoundly by the cementing of a friendship that was to be the most important of his life. After completing his degree at Exeter College, Oxford, William Morris joined Street's office in January 1856 as an articled pupil, having told his mother that Street was 'a good architect, as things go now, and has a great deal of business, and always goes for an honourable man; I should learn what I want of him if of anybody.'[7]

Morris's restless intelligence and active interest in both visual and literary culture made him seem like a new kind of creature altogether, and Webb later told Lethaby that he remembered perfectly first meeting this 'slim boy like a wonderful bird just out of his shell'.[8] By the summer of 1856, Street moved his practice to London, and Webb and Morris went with him, but already Morris was thinking of moving on. Soon afterwards, influenced by his new friend Dante Gabriel Rossetti, he gave up architecture to try his hand at painting. But the friendship established with Webb was never broken, and their very different personalities seem to have created a symbiotic relationship essential to both men. A trip they made to northern France together in the summer of 1858 to see medieval cathedrals – one of only three foreign visits Webb ever made – was a seminal experience which fed his imagination thereafter. Thirty years after their first meeting, he described how the experience of knowing Morris had challenged his own reticence, recognising that he took sustenance from the other man's vitality.

> I can always read Morris, partly, I think, because he is most free of modern poets from thinness of thought in verse, and partly because he enjoys doing his verse, as he does in doing a piece of dyeing, or hand weaving – and all just like a child. His very egotism is amusing and childlike. Again, you see, I am a poor non educated ill furnished bundle of strange fancies and ideas. Well, Morris understands me, and <u>never</u> praises what I do, so that I have no call with him to pull out my too ready scepticism. Now, don't laugh, I am most surely of a melancholy temperament, and I have found for more than 30 years it has been good corrective to rub shoulders with Morris's hearty love-of-lifedness. (*Letter 324*)

And in a real sense, Morris framed Webb's own independent architectural career. Red House, near Bexleyheath in Kent, Webb's first major project after leaving Street's office in May 1859, was designed and built for Morris and his wife, whilst the two simple workers' cottages at Kelmscott commissioned by Jane in memory of her husband were not finally completed until 1903, more than

INTRODUCTION

two years after Webb's retirement to Sussex. 'Almost the very first building I set up was for you, and the very last, if I can so make it, will also be for you.' (*Letter 666*) His affection for Morris extended to the whole family, and continued almost as a duty of care to Jane and the children after Morris's death.

After Red House was completed in 1860, the happy cooperative endeavour of working on its internal decorations, which drew in Rossetti, Burne-Jones, Charles Faulkner and other friends, seemed to lead naturally to the formal establishing of Morris, Marshall, Faulkner & Co, the first incarnation of what later became 'Morris and Co', or the Firm, in which Webb's own contribution as a designer during the early years was always fundamental. But the most fruitful and dynamic aspect of the special relationship between Morris and Webb emerges through their founding of the Society for the Protection of Ancient Buildings (the SPAB), which they affectionately called 'Antiscrape'. They both brought to this enterprise a belief in conservation through repair, and a fierce opposition to restoration and sham copying, attitudes born of their deep love of old buildings, and their sympathy for Ruskin's vision, who had first raised the banner for such a cause. It was a matter of fortuitous chance, but one which proved essential to the success of the new society, that they brought together a set of complementary skills. When the SPAB began its work in 1877, Morris was already a public figure, a prolific writer and, increasingly, a voice shaping the direction of interior design in middle-class homes. It was inevitable and indeed right that his energy and willingness to promote ideas effectively would make his the prominent public voice of the SPAB, even if the hard graft of its casework was shared between a few of its more active committee members. Of course, Morris also had real architectural understanding, more than that of an informed amateur, and readily engaged with controversy.

What Webb brought to the table was no less essential to the success of the enterprise. As a practising architect, he spoke with a palpable and precise authority derived from experience, and until he retired at the end of 1900 it was his meticulous analysis which found practical working solutions to many of the cases which passed before the committee. For nearly 25 years he remained the undisputed first amongst equals of the Society's working architects. The evidence for this is the number of letters he drafted to be sent to churchwardens, vicars and cathedral chapters, as well as to newspapers and secular officials, although these always went out signed by the secretary. We cannot now know quite how many of these were authored by Webb, although a good many survive in his hand in the SPAB files.

As the years passed, and as Morris's growing commitment to the socialist cause loaded more pressures upon him, not least as a public speaker, it was inevitable that he was able to give less time to the SPAB. Webb would assume an even greater importance at the heart of the Society, although he began to fear for its long-term survival as the exponential growth in casework was being handled by so few of its committee members. The confidence placed by the SPAB in Webb's exceptional expertise and professional sureness-of-touch, and indeed the affectionate respect extended to him by his colleagues, may be measured by the fact that, even after his retirement, he continued to be asked to advise on specific repair projects. The SPAB has survived as one of the lasting testimonies to Morris's inspirational far-sightedness, but it would have struggled without the tireless commitment which Webb devoted to it, work which he quite possibly felt was of more real value than any one of his own building designs. Without Morris, the SPAB would never have been formed, but without Webb, it might not have endured.

The influence of Morris's political sympathies upon Webb are more difficult to disentangle. The journey into socialism appears to have been a shared one, with Morris as leader and Webb as a committed fellow-traveller, but there is enough evidence in the letters to suggest that Webb had always been a socialist in his beliefs, but perhaps one whose instincts were to work at a modest level, helping his fellows more practically and immediately, rather than someone who had high expectations of success through revolutionary struggle. His belief in an elected democracy, however flawed, was something he affirmed towards the end of his life.

> To me, and in spite of the detested contest in declamation, either by lies or honest speech, I prefer – in the long run – this rule by parliament of tongues, & seeming waste of words, to the rule of blood & thunder. (*Letter 1076*)

That said, his personal notes survive to show that on two occasions he stood in for the absent Morris, leading off discussions at the Bloomsbury branch of the Socialist League in September 1886 and at the committee of the Hammersmith Socialist Society in August 1891. Webb's loyalty and simple decency is why Morris described his friend as 'the best man he ever knew', conscious also of the straightforward wisdom which allowed him to steer others towards correct decisions in their own lives. An absence of personal self-aggrandisement, coupled with an unwavering commitment to principles of honest dealing and modest living, meant that Webb was never to be wealthy. Indeed, throughout his professional life his means were slender, though he would give money to friends and causes in which he believed, often at times when he could not easily spare it. His elder brother recognised this quality, confessing that 'I consider him Quixotic in the extreme. He likes to pay double fee for all that is done for him, & will only take half its value for work he does for others.' (*Letter 1033, note 2*)

That no letters survive from his earliest years might be read as a wish to be judged by what he achieved, rather than by who he was. And yet, Webb never represented any of his buildings as being anything more than honest and workmanlike, even saying once to his assistant, George Jack, that 'I was never satisfied with any one building of my contriving' (*Letter 971*). He was almost pathologically reticent and, unlike most significant Victorian architects, he resolutely refused to write about his own work, or indeed to make any public utterance about any aspect of his profession. He carefully avoided joining any professional associations, except for one, the important if somewhat eccentrically named Sanitary Institute of Great

INTRODUCTION

Britain. He turned down invitations to formal dinners as a matter of course and generally avoided anything which might loosely be termed 'society'. This was maintained until the end of his life. In 1912, he refused the offer of the Royal Gold Medal of the Royal Institute of British Architects – as had Ruskin, and as would Lethaby – having avoided membership throughout his working career.

Despite this rather ascetic modesty, he was no recluse. He had a following of friends whose admiration bordered on devotion, and invariably was one of the small company of active members of the SPAB who would repair after the weekly Thursday committee meetings to Gatti's restaurant in the Strand, where the gossip and jokes ran freely. If a man is defined in large part by his friendships, this seems especially true of Webb. For it is in the surviving resource of letters retained by his friends that we discover his charm, humour, affection and rich imaginative life, enabling a more nuanced view of his mercurial personality to emerge. At the same time, we are often offered revealing insights into the lives of those other correspondents, several of whom though important are not currently well-represented in published documents. Fortunately, letters also survive to clients, builders and other contractors, so that for some projects (such as the Palace Green town house he built for George Howard in Kensington, or 'Clouds' at East Knoyle for Percy Wyndham, or the textbook repair of the medieval tower at East Knoyle's parish church, or indeed for his new church building at Brampton in Cumbria) an enhanced understanding of his professional life is made possible, although an even clearer view of his working-methods emerges in those letters which he wrote to his long-term assistant George Jack and his former assistant William Weir. The current volumes draw in full measure from the range of these sources.

Few of Webb's letters have previously been published, but his privileged situation within the William Morris circle would alone justify this new project. At his death in April 1915 his surviving papers passed to his executor, Emery Walker, who was one of Morris's trusted intimates, and quite as reticent as Webb himself. With the help of Sydney Cockerell – Morris's former secretary and subsequently a remarkably successful Director of the Fitzwilliam Museum – Walker arranged the removal of the contents of Webb's retirement cottage in Worth, Sussex, to his own house at 7 Hammersmith Terrace, just a few hundred yards upriver from Kelmscott House, Morris's final London home on the Thames at Hammersmith. Amongst the letters were those Webb had received in later years from correspondents such as Walker himself, Cockerell, W.R. Lethaby, George Jack, George Wardle and Giacomo Boni, but Webb seems to have destroyed most of the incoming letters from earlier years. Thus there is next to nothing from his close friend and former client, the water-colourist George Price Boyce, or from Jane, Jenny and May Morris. Wardle had died in 1910, so his letters were retained by Walker, as were those from Boni, and in due course both collections were given to the Courtauld Institute. The other letters were returned to their senders.

When Webb died, his own surviving letters, naturally, tended still to be with their original recipients, but in due course several important sets found their way into public collections. Sydney Cockerell was responsible for ensuring that

INTRODUCTION

a number of major holdings were secured in this way. As an instinctive but discriminating collector himself, Cockerell kept everything that he ever received from Webb, and arranged for three bound volumes of these letters to be deposited in the library of the Victoria and Albert Museum (though he had first contemplated giving them to the Courtauld), as well as a small group to Rossetti and Warington Taylor, and several important letters to Kate Faulkner, written from Italy during the winter of 1884–5. Also deposited at the V&A are the surviving letters from Webb to Morris, and Cockerell's precise prefatory note to the volume characteristically contextualises the circumstances of their survival.

> William Morris died on Oct 3 1896. He was not in the habit of keeping letters and this book contains only a small number of those which he received from Philip Webb which, like those received from other friends, were too often used as pipe lights. After his death they were collected in order that they might be returned to the writer, who admitted that he would immediately burn them, and at my request gave me leave on Nov 5 1896 to keep them; which I thankfully did as a memorial of a friendship of forty years between two of the noblest men of our day.
> (*V&A, NAL MSC/1958/687*)

Webb's letters to Boyce, given to Cockerell by Boyce's widow, as well as letters to the wife of another of Webb's clients, Elizabeth Wickham Flower, were presented to the British Library (formerly the British Museum). Cockerell's own letters to Webb were divided between the V&A and the British Library, the latter institution also receiving s significant part of the large collection of picture postcards of ancient buildings which in later years he sent almost daily (and sometimes several in a day) to Webb. Amongst the many volumes which form the large collection of Morris papers, the British Library also holds Webb's surviving letters to Jane Morris and those to her daughters. Amongst the letters of William Hale White ('Mark Rutherford') at Bedford Central Library are those from Webb, whilst Charles Fairfax Murray gave his to the Fitzwilliam Museum. The Castle Howard archives contain Webb's correspondence to George and Rosalind Howard, whom he first knew as part of the Morris circle when Howard's own real ambition was to be a painter, long before he inherited the responsibilities and expectations placed upon him as ninth Earl of Carlisle. In the archives of the SPAB there survives an important group of letters to his former assistant, William Weir, most of them dealing with repair projects which Weir undertook for the Society and upon which Webb's advice had been sought, whilst at West Sussex Record Office are letters to the landlord of his retirement years, the poet and society philanderer, Wilfrid Scawen Blunt, who counted Jane Morris amongst his successes.

Nor should the charming set of letters written during his retirement to his housekeeper be overlooked, for they show Webb's skill in adjusting his register to the expectations and experiences of any intended recipient, without ever being patronising. This might suggest that putting pen to paper came easily to him, but

INTRODUCTION

if so it challenges his own claims that letter-writing was never anything other than a difficult and at times tortured process. Indeed, it was normal for him to make a draft, and sometimes more than one, before despatching a final version, the draft often being retained as his record, this being his practice not just for business correspondence but occasionally also when writing to friends. As a result, there is far more material to draw upon than if we had to rely only upon the survival of letters in the hands of his correspondents. His collection of drafts was amongst the papers which Walker and Cockerell transferred from Sussex to Hammersmith in 1915, and seems to have stayed in Walker's house until after his own death in 1933.

All of the papers that went to Hammersmith were made available to W.R. Lethaby when he was working on the series of essays which first appeared in *The Builder* during 1925, and were subsequently republished in 1935 as *Philip Webb and his Work*, providing us with the first authoritative biography. Friends had made other letters available, but there was much which Lethaby did not see, or chose not to use. It is frustrating that some letters from which he did quote (including a few of his own from Webb) have not since been traced – at least, not yet – but it is quite possible that they were destroyed by his sister-in-law after his death. The flame of interest in Webb studies was kept alive after the deaths of those who knew him – most importantly Lethaby, Walker, Jack and Cockerell – by younger champions, first amongst them being the architect, John Brandon-Jones. When he published a few of the letters in *Architectural History* in 1964, Brandon-Jones explained how 'on the death of Emery Walker, his daughter, Dorothy, inherited the Webb papers and passed them on to the present writer'.[9] It formed the basis of a superb personal collection, to which in due course Brandon-Jones added Webb's letters to and from George Washington Jack, given to him by Jack's twin daughters. Since his death, the bulk of this collection has been deposited in the Archive of Art and Design at the V&A, and provides the source for many of the materials within the present edition, including letters to Walker and his wife, those which survive to Lethaby and his wife, to Detmar Blow, Alfred Powell and to a wide range of other individuals, as well as letters relating to particular building projects, including St Martin's church at Brampton, 'Clouds' and the restoration of the church tower at East Knoyle.

Particularly interesting survivals from the Brandon-Jones collection are two volumes covering the years 1874–88, which probably formed part of what Dorothy Walker passed on to him. These contain Webb's drafts (rather than copies) of letters which he sent to clients, and which formed the office record. The two office books are probably a chance survival, for they are in no sense a comprehensive record of his business correspondence even for those years, and there was no particular reason for Webb having chosen to spare these whilst destroying so much else, probably on removing from London to Sussex. They feature just a few of his projects in progress, whilst others are not even mentioned, and it seems reasonable to suppose that there were once equivalent volumes which dealt with those other buildings. Nor should it be supposed that his good office habit of recording

INTRODUCTION

all of his business transactions only operated during these years: doubtless, it was followed throughout his career. The fortunate recovery of these two volumes only serves to indicate the richness of what has been lost. They contain drafts of letters not just to his clients, but also to builders, clerks of works, and to other contractors, making them a fascinating insight into the working practices of a busy nineteenth-century architect.

All of the content selected from the two office books for inclusion in the current edition falls entirely within the year boundaries of this first volume, which ends in 1887, when Webb was aged 56. Much of his defining architectural work was already behind him by then, whilst some of his key friendships with men of the next generation were still in their early stages, or yet to be established. Indeed, some of the very best of his letters lie ahead. These earlier pages are underpinned throughout by the relationship which profoundly shaped the contours of his working life, and which continued until William Morris's death in 1896. Webb would later tell Morris's younger daughter that 'his brotherly love has left a mark on me which has clung as if I were branded like a sheep's back with W.M – an assertion of "property" . . . he having run me down in the chase of his early life. There was something out of the "common" in that.' (*Letter 592*). Morris had married Jane Burden in 1859, and after their daughters were born the unmarried Webb had extended his affection to encompass them all, something which would take on a particular poignancy after Morris's death, when Webb reached out to the survivors. Several other close friends during these years were acquired through a mutual friendship with Morris – including Charles Faulkner and his sister Kate (had Webb ever felt inclined towards marriage, Kate would surely have been in his mind as a possible partner), as well as Rossetti and Edward and Georgiana Burne-Jones. The strength of these affections show up clearly enough, even if there are few surviving letters to Rossetti and apparently none at all to the Burne-Joneses. George Howard, George Price Boyce and Percy Wyndham all feature importantly as friends who were also clients (or in Wyndham's case a client first, who became a friend) and to the wives of each Webb also extended his friendship, though there is always the sense that women are to be treated with a certain caution.

Although Webb was able stubbornly to defend his work when it seemed necessary – and did so during the earlier part of his career when the office of the Commissioner of Woods and Forests objected to his plans for George Howard's house at Palace Green – his instinct was to refrain from controversy and public comment, however strongly-held his private views might be. When invited to supply some notes on his principal buildings to assist in a book on the English Gothic revival, he politely but firmly refused to break his rule 'not myself to make unnecessarily public any work which I've designed or completed' (*Letter 34*), and although he was persuaded by Burne-Jones to provide quite detailed information when John Mackail's *Life of William Morris* was in preparation, he was reluctant to be publicly associated with it. 'I hope you will be able to do with as little mention of my name as may be – and if it were nil, I should be the more content.' (*Letter 614*) It seems almost wilfully obtuse. But through the confidences of his

INTRODUCTION

letter-writing the complex and elusive character of this fiercely loyal and abundantly affectionate man is allowed to reveal itself. We are permitted to see how such uncompromising integrity lived itself out, but it is difficult to escape the conclusion that so consistent a clinging to simple ideals was bought at the high price of a sometimes heroic loneliness.

Notes

1 *V&A, NAL MSL/1958/688/5*
2 *Lethaby*, p. 3.
3 Ibid, p. 5.
4 John Billing, quoted in *Lethaby*, p. 9.
5 *Kirk*, p. 13.
6 *Lethaby*, p. 17.
7 WM to Emma Morris, 11 November 1855, *CLWM*, I.
8 *Lethaby*, p. 15.
9 *LPW*, p. 52.

LETTERS 1864–1887

1 • To William Morris, 18 November 1864

Transcription from Marsh[1]

1, Raymond Buildings, Gray's Inn, | London,
Nov. 18 *1864*

My dear Morris.

I saw Brown[2] the other day upon his return from Red house, & Ned read Janie's letter to me this afternoon, so I just know something of you.[3] I can only hope that you are not in great pain, and that you manage to keep up your spirits.

I must say that Ned's case has been a striking example of things all coming round after a depth of trouble – and things are never quite so bad as they look.[4]

Charlie Faulkner comes up to town again tomorrow,[5] so Campfield[6] and I manage with him to keep things going pretty smoothly at the shop, and it will do some of your brutes of customers good to wait a bit. Some of the Cambridge glass goes off tonight which has stopped Bodley's mouth.[7]

I've set them going at S. Philips Bethnal Green with a pattern for the roof ^{of chancel} and I am now going to give them a wall & dado patterns for the same.[8]

I am rather pushed in a corner just now with work as I was away in Norfolk for 2 days & a night.

Best love to you both | Yours ever | Philip Webb.

Red House

---

1 During a programme of repairs and renewals overseen by the National Trust in 2006, this letter was discovered beneath the floor of one of the bedrooms of Red House, Bexleyheath. Designed by PSW for William Morris (WM, 1834–96) in 1858–60, Red House now attracts many visitors principally for its associations with WM, but is important in its own right as PSW's first independent architectural project. My text and notes are here informed by Jan Marsh's transcription in 'Red House: Past and Future', in Philippa Bennett and Rosie Miles (eds), *William Morris in the Twenty-First Century*, Oxford: Peter Lang, 2010 (pp. 65–6). Dr Marsh also kindly shared digital images of this letter with me.

2 The painter and designer, Ford Madox Brown (1821–93), was one of the original seven partners in Morris, Marshall, Faulkner & Co ('the Firm', referred to here as MMF & Co).
3 Ned is WM's Oxford friend, the painter, Edward Burne-Jones (EBJ, 1813–98). WM married Jane Burden (JM, 1839–1914) in April 1859.
4 Three days after the date of this letter came the death of the infant son of EBJ and Georgiana (Georgie) Burne-Jones (née Macdonald, 1840–1920, hereafter GBJ). She had herself been dangerously ill with scarlet fever since the birth.
5 See below, Letter 3.
6 George Campfield was a glass painter and foreman of MMF & Co at its Red Lion Square premises, where its shop was based.
7 The English Gothic revival architect, George Frederick Bodley (1827–1907), commissioned decorative work and stained glass from MMF & Co for a number of his newly-built churches, including the East window of All Saints', Jesus Lane, Cambridge.
8 'Saint Philip's, Bethnal Green, one of twelve new churches built in the poorest parish of London's overcrowded East End, opened in 1842 to a Romanesque design by T.L. Walker. . . . Decorative work by [MMF & Co] for the interior of the church has not previously been documented, and Webb's patterns – probably stencilled – for the chancel ceiling, walls and dado are not recorded.' Marsh, p. 66, note 30.

2 • To George Price Boyce, 11 April 1865

1, Raymond Buildings, Gray's Inn, | *London,*
April 11 *1865*

Dear Boyce

I quite forgot on Saturday when I half accepted your invitation for Wednesday that I had a 3 weeks engagement to be at G: Rossetti's on that evening.[1]

I am very sorry that this will hinder me from being introduced to Wolff[2] – for whose work I have a great admiration.

On my next passing Chatham Place I shall look in with the hopes of see[ing] you and yours.[3]

Yours very truly | Philip Webb

BL Add 45354, f. 1

---

1 Dante Gabriel Rossetti (DGR, 1828–82), poet, painter and founder-member of the Pre-Raphaelite Brotherhood. He was also a founding shareholder of MMF & Co.
2 Probably Joseph Wolf (1820–99), the German-born wildlife artist and illustrator, regarded by many – Sir Edwin Landseer (1802–73) amongst them – as the finest animal painter of his generation.
3 Late in 1862, DGR having moved to 16 Cheyne Walk ('Tudor House'), the watercolour painter George Price Boyce (GPB, 1826–97) took over his former studio at 14 Chatham Place. GPB had formerly shared chambers at 15 Buckingham Street with the architect, William Burges (1827–81). From Chatham Place he would transfer to West House, in Glebe Place, Chelsea, built for him by PSW (1868–70). See *Kirk*, pp. 75–6 and 297.

3 • To Charles Faulkner, 27 May 1865

1, Raymond Buildings, Gray's Inn, | London,
May 27 *1865*

My dear Charlie.[1]

I have waited 'till now to answer because I could only see Top last night.[2] – He does not take to the idea but rather makes up his mind to a more extended affair on the <u>lower</u> river sometime in season.

I think I could safely say I could run down to Faringdon for the 22nd or 23rd of June, but I am sure I could not get away before.[3] – Should we go let us hope all natures stock of West wind won't be blown out, for then we might enjoy A. West Wind. B. Burgundy bottle. C. bow ripple. [*PSW sketches a boat under sail, to which these labels refer*]

Yours very surely | Philip Webb

C.J. Faulkner Esq

Texas

---

1 The mathematician Charles Joseph Faulkner (CF, 1833–92) was a contemporary of both William Morris (WM, 1834–96) and the painter Edward Burne-Jones (EBJ, 1833–98) at Oxford, where he subsequently became a fellow of University College. He trained as a civil engineer, became a founding shareholder of MMF & Co in 1861, and was its first financial manager. These ties were loosened when he returned to Oxford in 1864, but he continued as a shareholder until the firm's reorganization as Morris & Co in 1875 and with WM and PSW would be a committed member of the early socialist movement. A stroke in 1888 left him speechless and housebound. PSW would visit daily to sit with his friend, thus easing the pressures on Kate Faulkner (KF, 1841–98), her brother's nurse in the house they shared in 35 Queen Square, Bloomsbury. See also Vol. II, Letter 587.
2 'Topsy' (or 'Top') was WM's nickname amongst his closest friends, supplied by 'Ned' (EBJ) as 'an in-joke referring to his mop of hair'. *MacCarthy, WMLT*, p. 74. The fictional Topsy was the slave girl in Harriet Beecher Stowe's influential *Uncle Tom's Cabin* (1852).
3 The Oxfordshire market town of Faringdon, in the Vale of the White Horse, lies about 3 miles to the south of the River Thames and WM's future country house, Kelmscott Manor. The River Ock, south of Faringdon, is a tributary of the Thames, joining it at Abingdon, and is probably what PSW means by the 'lower' river.

4 • To John Ruskin, 17 October 1865

Unsigned draft; incomplete?

1 R.B. G.I Oct. 17. 1865

Dear Mr Ruskin.[1]

A gentleman of the name of F Warburton Stent – an Arch[l] & Surveyor[2] – wrote to me & also called, to explain a plan for forwarding the building of middle class houses of a sound & seemly character.

Mʳ Stent told me that he had laid the plan before you, and that you desired to have my opinion upon the subject.³

I told Mʳ Stent that I thought it mig^ht be possible to find tenants for houses, where the best part of the cost was put into the substance and conveniences of the building instead of into the tricking out, but that in my practice I had not found it so – that the main body of ^the people never really accounted for their ills of housing – & would probably refer a bad smell from the drains to ^the bad taste of the Architect.

Still I have seen many things for wh' I myself have not thought it reasonable ~~of~~ ^to make effort wh' have been carried through by abundant energy to a fair end.

Another main difficulty I think would be that it would be impossible to give an equivalent to the people in sound work for the bad ornament wh' has had its value in their eyes – in the same way that a badly painted scene at a play is accounted for and accepted.

Even the entire class of designers who are determined to solve the problem, & give solid practical decoration – by jutting a brick out here & blocking another in there – have scarcely such contented tenants as the more wise and fashionable builders.

It is found also ^now by the mercantile classes that they can build houses for one purpose, wh' by management can be used for another, and pay ¹² ᵒʳ 15 p ct interest – 6, 7 ᵒʳ 8 ~~or 9~~ per ct would be the utmost that could be got I fancy from the class of house in question, if the purpose were honestly kept in view – it is scarcely likely that there wd be rush of capitalists, for such a ^proposed return for their money.⁴

Texas

---

1 Indisputably the most celebrated art critic of the nineteenth century, John Ruskin (JR, 1819–1900) was also a social commentator of great importance. His writing and thinking profoundly influenced both PSW and WM, not least in the principles underpinning their founding of the Society for the Protection of Ancient Buildings in 1877.

2 The London-based Frederick Warburton Stent (fl. 1846–94), architect (with Augustus Laver), of the Parliament Buildings in Ottawa (1865).

3 A month earlier, the *Daily Telegraph* had published a series of letters from JR about domestic servants, in the last of which he commented on the poor quality of suburban house-building. 'Round every railroad station, out of the once quiet fields, there bursts up first a blotch of brick-fields, and then of ghastly houses, washed over with slime into miserable fineries of cornice and portico. A gentleman would hew for himself a log hut, and thresh for himself a straw bed, before he would live in such; but the builders count safely on tenants' (18 September 1865). It is surely more than mere coincidence that on the same day that PSW was writing to JR, the *Daily Telegraph* published another JR letter (dated 16 October) headed 'Modern Houses', itself prompted by a correspondence to which he would direct PSW's attention (see note 4). JR was responding to 'W.H.W.', whose letter had appeared in the paper the day before, seeking JR's advice for effecting an improvement in modest, middleclass housing. This was the author and civil servant William Hale White, 'Mark Rutherford' (WHW, 1831–1913), for whom PSW would design 19 Park Hill, Carshalton, Surrey (1867–8). They became close friends, JR bringing the two together. 'I am happy to be able to tell you of an

architect, Mr. Philip Webb . . . who will give you perfectly sound and noble work for absolutely just price.' JR to WHW, 27 October 1967. See *White*, p. 41.
4 JR's reply is somewhat equivocal.

'Sincere thanks for your letter. I have no hope in such business myself – but do not choose to discourage others, and it seems to me at least conceivable that a company might be founded for useful & permanent building – and drag on a miserable, but a very honourable and useful existence. Did you see the letters in the Daily Telegraph yesterday and Tuesday or Monday, on this subject.

I expect further communications on the matter, and will write to you again.' JR to PSW, 19 October 1865, *Texas*.

5 • To Dante Gabriel Rossetti, 21 May 1866

Unsigned draft, annotated by SCC '?21 May 1866'

1, Raymond Buildings, Gray's Inn, | *London,*

My dear Gabriel.

I am so much obliged by your kind letter,[1] that I think it worth while to run the risk of boring you to explain, that, what you said in it has been carefully read & more carefully considered – let me start by saying that I quite agree with your argument in the abstract, but I cannot think that you would have ~~considered~~ thought it necessary of application if you had known more of the person to whom it was applied.[2]

Ever since fate was kind enough to make me acquainted with Topsy & through him with Ned, [Madox] Brown & yourself I have always ~~considered~~ thought that to allow of my being considered as one of such a company, there must be something about ~~such a~~ my mental constitution ~~as mine~~ wh' ~~w^d~~ excused the seeming disparity.

To a certain extent I have ~~considered~~ thought the allowance to be this, that ~~I knew~~ I had the capacity of understanding my men, if I could not compete with them.

I am certain that I never made a mistake in judging of either of you – and I am also certain that I know of some men whose work at first sight w^d seem to lead to the belief that they were deserving of greater attention, but an experience of their ways of thought ~~lead~~ to a certain knowledge of their real incapacity.

Mere flattery would not blind me to defect, for instance [Warington] Taylor was treated by me for a long time in a less kind way than was ^his right on acc^t of his sweeping praise & blame – and to a certain extent it was you who gave the casting vote to my mind for accepting him as very genuine in his way.[3]

I am quite sure Gabriel that you will agree with me that the present time is not an artistic one, and that any one who wishes to follow ~~it~~ ^art with advantage to the world at large and with hope of competing with ~~that~~ ^art gone before must be very severe on the liability of disturbance from collateral causes, such as payment, popularity, position &c. None of these are of necessity ruinous to art, but they do often ruin the workman.

In fine Gabriel if I was not so gauche a companion you would know me to be very large-minded with regard to all ability and exceedingly thoughtful of the unhappiness of those who do not possess it, careful not to give them offence – but in reality irritated beyond measure by presumptuous ignorance & wrongdoing.

Please read this in a good temper & burn it before you are in a bad one & believe me, | Yours very truly

V&A, NAL MSL/1958/691/11

---

1 'Thanks for your good letter most sincerely. I considered you grossly abusive but not in the least unfriendly, which was all right and as it should be between members of a firm headed by Topsy & sentinelled by Taylor.' DGR to PSW, 20 May 1866, *CDGR*, III.
2 Of MMF & Co DGR had written that 'I do not see that our views are best fostered by notorious over-exclusiveness, nor that a gifted and enthusiastic artist who is outside of our circle [*SCC annotation:* '?Whistler'] need be described or thought of as a "blackguard" because we do not exactly agree with his aims or their result, nor even because he does not exactly agree with ours. There are such things as Art-criminals; but, such an one, if intellect and devotion to Art are worth anything, cannot be reckoned among them, whatever his style.'
3 George Warington Taylor (1835–70) was appointed manager of MMF & Co in 1865, a position which he held until his death five years later. His endeavours to place the firm on a sound footing met with some success, although this was predicated on the kind of business discipline to which some of the partners were not likely to be sympathetic. A case has been made for Taylor's role being less crucial than is sometimes claimed, and that WM's own grasp of business competence was already well developed by this time. Jon Press and Charles Harvey, 'William Morris, Warington Taylor and the Firm, 1865–1875', *JWMS*, VII (Autumn 1986), pp. 41–4.

6 • To Charles Gore, 22 August 1867

1, Raymond Buildings, Gray's Inn, | *London,*
Aug 22 *1867*

Sir:[1]

On the behalf of Mr George Howard, I left the plans of the proposed house in Palace gardens at 1 Whitehall Place today, and I explained the peculiarities of arrangement to the Clerk.[2]

I also saw Mr Pennethorne's clerk and arranged that tracings of the plans sh^d be sent to Mr Pennethorne on Wednesday evening for his approval.[3]

As the building season is far advanced, both Mr Howard & myself w^d be much obliged by any assistance of expedition that you could give us in the matter of official assent to the plans.

Should personal explanation be required I will attend in Whitehall, at your request.

I am Sir: | Yours faithfully | Philip Webb: | Arch^t

The Hon C: H: Gore.

NA CRES 35/21217

1 The Hon. Charles Alexander Gore (1811–97) was Commissioner of Woods and Forests, the government office in Whitehall Place which oversaw the public and commercial interests of the Crown Estate. Approval for any building on Crown property therefore came within his authority.
2 For George Howard, see next letter. In March 1867, he had 'purchased the lease of the old grace-and-favour residence at No. 1 Palace Green for £1,600. This lease, which was for eight years from 1863, contained a provision that the old house had to be demolished and a new one built at a cost of at least £3,500.' *Survey of London*, General Editor: F.H.W. Sheppard, XXXVII, *Northern Kensington* (London: The Athlone Press, 1973), p. 185.
3 The neo-classical architect James Pennethorne (1801–71) trained under John Nash and learned drawing from Pugin. Most of his professional work involved government contracts, and he exercised significant influence from 1839 when he was appointed Architect and Surveyor to the Commissioners for Woods and Forests. His advice and recommendations would be sought for building proposals on the Crown Estate. Pennethorne received a knighthood after he retired in 1870.

7 • To George Howard, 7 September 1867

1, Raymond Buildings, Gray's Inn, | *London,*
Sep 7 *1867*

Dear Mr Howard.[1]

After quite unavoidable delay I have this day got tenders for the house in Palace Gardens Kensington. The amounts are tolerably satisfactory – but not quite. They are for total works & everything for use except papering – £6,664.0.0. For hot water supply to all floors with kitchen cooking apparatus grates &c and the Lift from basement to all floors up to 2nd floor £272.0.0.

The total sum will be £6,936.0.0. and is within the boundary which at your request I feel myself bound to keep, viz £7,000 but I cannot allow you to suppose that in a work of this size no unforeseen or accidental costs will have to be met – at least £300 ought therefore to be allowed for this and £50 for a temporary clerk of works which brings the total to £7,286.

At your desire upon hearing from you I will go over the quantities and reduce where possible to the amount of £286.

I am afraid that we are likely to suffer further delay on account of Mr Gore or Mr Pennethorne, for one or both of them (I cannot tell which) object to the character of the elevations.[2] Now this I do not think we were led to expect, more especially as I have taken particular pains to avoid anythink [*sic*] like obtrusive or erratic design, and I think you know enough of my work to be able to say that it is not likely to err on the side of ostentation. In a letter which, at the request of his Clerk, I sent to Mr Pennethorne who is abroad, I explained the motives of the design and how I had endeavoured to keep the artistic impression of the Palace neighbourhood always in mind subject always to the necessity of a modern difference.

If you could bring any friendly pressure to bear on Mr Gore it would perhaps be advisable to use it, so as to avoid delay as much as possible.³

[Yours very truly | Philip Webb:]

Howard

---

1 George James Howard (GH, 1843–1911), who in 1889 succeeded his uncle as ninth earl of Carlisle, inheriting substantial family estates in Cumberland (Naworth Castle), Northumberland and Yorkshire (Castle Howard), was a regular member of the WM circle in these earlier years. He was a capable landscape painter, and a close friend of EBJ. After his marriage to Rosalind Stanley (1845–1921), daughter of Lord Stanley of Alderley, GH commissioned PSW to build 1 Palace Green, Kensington (1867–70), which was subsequently decorated throughout by MMF & Co. See *Kirk*, pp. 71–4 and 297. PSW also undertook projects for GH's northern estates.

2 Evidently, PSW had heard word that the plans were being challenged. Pennethorne (who was on holiday in Switzerland) had written to Gore with his initial reactions, setting the tone for an increasingly personal dispute between two architects of fundamentally different outlooks, and which has been aptly described as epitomising 'the passing of an age'. See Geoffrey Tyack, *Sir James Pennethorne and the Making of Victorian London* (Cambridge: University Press, 1992), p. 305.

'I have looked at the plans & elevations proposed by Mʳ Webb for Mr Howard's House at Kensington but am very unwilling to report officially upon them until you have had an opportunity to consider them.

The plans could not be reported on because only two floors are shewn – and though the arrangements are more for Mʳ Howard than for the Office I may observe that the Dining Room is small – and the Stable yard so narrow I doubt if a carriage could be turned in it: and it might be more convenient and less objectionable to Mʳ Huth if the Stables were turned to the North end.

The Elevations as drawn are almost unintelligible, but I am quite certain that the House if built according to them would be <u>far inferior</u> to any one on the Estate – it would look most commonplace – and in my opinion be perfectly hideous – it is probably intended for dutch or german but is unsuitable for London. The plain wall of the Stables and the Terrace above them would both be objected to by Mʳ Huth.' Pennethorne to Gore, 31 August 1867, *NA CRES 35/21217*. Henry Huth (1815–78) and his wife, Augusta Westenholz, would be the Howards' immediate neighbours, having bought 2 Palace Green, the house built for William Makepeace Thackeray, after the novelist's death in 1863.

3 'I have this morning heard from Mr Webb that there is some delay in sanctioning the plans for our house in Kensington Palace gardens; I can not understand the reason for this as the design is extremely simple and purposely designed to harmonise with the palace opposite; I thought that the only stipulation that the Crown made, was that the house should be well and substantially built and over the value of £3000; now the building of this will cost £6000 and Mr Webb's building is known to be exceptionally solid and good. If I had not understood that I was free to have a different design from that of the neighbouring houses (since it will be a detached house) I should not have bought the ground.

The house will look most unobtrusive, it's only peculiarity being that it will be built of red brick & with a gable roof.' GH to Gore, 8 September 1867, *NA CRES 35/21217*. GH's father, the MP for East Cumberland, Charles Howard (1814–79), also wrote to Gore a few days later, concerned that approval was still awaited, but Gore defended his adviser for not yet having provided an official report on them. 'If Mʳ Webb had sent these plans before everybody was scattered about, Mʳ Pennethorne's report would come to me sooner, but it seems to me not quite reasonable that because Mʳ Webb takes several months to prepare plans, Mʳ Pennethorne is to be considered as obstructive, if his Report upon them is not made in as many days. Mʳ Pennethorne's duty with reference to plans for buildings proposed to be built on Crown Property is a very responsible one. He has to regard the effect upon the Crown Estate, the effect upon the Crown Lessees adjoining and in the case of the Kensington Garden Estate, the effect upon the Palace itself.' Gore to Charles Howard, 12 September 1867, *NA CRES 35/21217*.

8 • To Dante Gabriel Rossetti, 24 September 1867

1, Raymond Buildings, Gray's Inn, | *London,*
Sep 24 *1867*

My dear Gabriel.

I fully understand the evils of your situation & will do all I can to help you out of them.

I am sorry to say that I am out of town on Sunday and have business engagements on Thursday but if tomorrow (Wednesday) or Saturday – both days before 3. oclock ^{or at any time on Friday} would suit you I could come up to Chelsea, & talk the matter over? As you have a good memory anything instructive wh' I may say you can report to Brown.

Unless under some extraordinary private arrangement, you would have to pay the builder in instalments. Say of half the amount, during the progress of the work, & the balance, 3 months after completion – and as for my energies in the business, they will be more likely ^{to be} employed in keeping him ^(the builder) from cheating you than you from making him a fool.

I have not been into your stable at all.[1] Let me know what you can do in the way of appointment.

Yours ever | Philip Webb:

Texas

---

1 For renovations done for DGR at 16 Cheyne Walk, including to the stable, see below, Letter 44, note 1.

9 • To H. Perkins, 3 October 1867 [*possibly W Perkins?*]

1, Raymond Buildings, Gray's Inn, | *London,*
Oct 3 *1867*

Dear Sir:[1]

Since your call upon me this morning, I have carefully considered the matter of your proposition that the works of Mr Howard's house in Palace Gardens should be begun at once – leaving the questions, of "mere details" to be settled between the "Woods & Forests" and my client & myself at some later time.[2]

I'm very sorry that I cannot assent to this, for it would seriously compromise my client's interests, as I think I explained to you this morning, that the very reasons which induced my client to purchase the lease of site, would make it very unwise on his part to enter into an agreement, which – quite possibly – would negative his purposes.

I am Sir, Yours truly | Philip Webb:

H: Perkins Esq:

NA CRES 35/21217

---

1 Perkins was presumably an official within the Commissioners of Woods and Forests, who on Charles Gore's instruction had seen PSW in James Pennethorne's absence abroad. See above, Letter 7, note 2.

2 On 12 October, Pennethorne sent an internal memorandum to Gore, summing up his objections to PSW's plans for 1 Palace Green:

'In my opinion M[r] Huth might not have any legal or equitable right to object to the house if so built; but as, according to my judgment, the enjoyment of his house would be lessened by the erection of so unsightly an Elevation near it is important that his interests should be borne in mind.

So far as I understand the drawings there would be scarcely any stone visible in the fronts of the house, the whole of the surfaces would be masses of red brickwork without relief from stone or from any important strings or cornices and I fear that such a house with its high roof and gable towards the Road (the drawing for which I do not understand) would be far inferior in appearance to other houses upon the Estate; would be objected to generally by the Crown Lessees, and may hereafter become a difficulty in the event of large additions being made to Kensington Palace.'
NA CRES 35/21217.

10 • To James Pennethorne, 18 October 1867

1 Raymond Buildings | Gray's Inn London.
Oct 18th 1867

Dear M[r] Pennethorne

I beg to acknowledge the receipt of your letter of the 16th and to express my regret that you are still suffering from your severe attack of illness.[1]

If you had not so fully expressed yourself with regard to the design for M[r] George Howard's house in Palace Gardens, I would have at once come to Worcester Park with the hope of hastening the settlement of the business,[2] so as to save M[r] Howard from any further serious loss of time.

It is not customary for an Architect to be forced to explain to a gentleman of the same profession, what he may consider to be the merits of his own work, and I would have gladly refused the office at once, did I not hope to assist my client by the apology.

M[r] Howard has been allowed to purchase the site in question, without so much as a hint that the disgracefully heterogeneous forms and colours of the greater number of houses in Palace Gardens, would have to be followed in one form or another in new and more carefully considered work; or that the various crude ideas of the uninformed inhabitants of the district would have to be considered by an architect who was desirous of attending to the really artistic character of the neighbourhood.

As an Architect who has given much and careful attention to the subject of house building in London, I must decidedly disagree with you, that the proper proportioned window opening which I have used, fitted with well-divided sashes, is an "unattractive" form; – Sir C: Wren, Sir J: Vanburgh, H: Hawksmoor, T: Ripley and many other Architects of acknowledged artistic power, who constantly used the form; and from hundreds of examples in London now existing – visibly with great simplicity & breadth of effect – support me in my opinion; and I am perfectly satisfied that for most purposes of modern convenience whether of light, ventilation, internal fittings or facility of construction, there is no form of window so suitable for English town architecture.

I must also beg to differ from your opinion that the materials used would not give the proper relief. A well chosen full coloured red brick, with pure bright red gauged brick mouldings, arches, string courses, cornices &c with the addition of white Portland stone, whiter sash-frames, lead, and grey slates, are in my opinion the very best and most harmoniously coloured materials to be used in London, & more specially in a neighbourhood so happily full of green foliage; and again, the many existing examples of work of this kind done by the above mentioned Architects, and remaining to us with a perfectly delightful effect through years of accumulated soot and dirt, give me most faithful support, even if modern carelessness and ignorance of this subject did not daily testify to the soundness of my opinion.

In conclusion, I must express my great surprise that you should consider it worth your while to hinder the erection of a building, which – whatever may be its demerits – possesses some character and originality, tempered most certainly with reverential attention to the works of acknowledged masters of the art of Architecture, and as certainly framed with the wish to avoid ^{adding} another insult to this irreparably injured neighbourhood.

A copy of your letter shall be sent to Mr Howard, and I will not in any way advise him to hinder his most necessary business, by persisting in requiring the assistance of an Architect whose work seems to be so likely to cause delay.[3]

Believe me to be | Yours very faithfully | Philip Webb:
James Pennethorne Esq

NA CRES 35/21217

---

[1] 'Mr Gore has returned to me your Drawings for Mr Howard's House at Kensington, with a request that I would see you upon the subject.
I regret to say that I am forbidden by my medical advisers to go to London for some time hence; but should you think it necessary to come here I shall be most happy to see you at any time.
I believe you are aware I have expressed to Mr Gore a very strong opinion that the exterior of the house if built according to the design submitted would not be suitable to the locality – it would not

assimilate with others built of late years on the Estate; it would probably be very dissimilar to any buildings hereafter erected should Kensington Palace be enlarged, and, above all, it would I fear be objected to by Mʳ Huth, and the other Crown tenants of Houses on the Estate.

My objections to the Design are perhaps, not so much to the style (though that I think unsuitable) as to the fact of the whole house being a mass of red without relief of any kind; the windows small & the forms not attractive; - the gable also of the roof towards the road would not I think produce a good effect.' Pennethorne to PSW, 16 October 1867, *NA CRES 35/21217.*

2 Pennethorne lived at Worcester Park House, Long Ditton, in Malden, Surrey.

3 On receipt of this letter, Pennethorne wrote to Gore. 'Considering the tone and purport of Mʳ Webb's letter it appears to me hopeless to expect any good result from an interview, or from communications between us; and it only occurs to me to propose to you to follow one of two courses – viz:- First – To submit the drawings with the letters of Mʳ Webb and myself to some impartial professional Man of high standing, and to be guided by his opinion – such a course has been pursued on former occasions: - the only one that at present occurs to me is the Convent in Osnaburgh Street the drawings for which (prepared by Mʳ Butterfield) I objected to; though, on the advice of Mʳ Hardwick, they were approved by the Board. Mʳ Burn, Mʳ Donaldson, Mʳ Salvin or Mʳ T. Wyatt are names I would suggest for your consideration. The second course would be for you to act entirely upon your own judgment after having requested Mʳ Huth to look at the drawings with reference to his own interests'. 23 October 1867, *NA CRES 35/21217.*

11 • To George Howard, 22 October 1867

1, Raymond Buildings, Gray's Inn, | *London,*
Oct 22 *1867*

Dear Mr Howard.

In answer to your letter of the 20ᵗʰ – I would advise you not to consider the matter of the Palace Gardens site a hopeless affair.

It was absolutely necessary for political purposes that I should write Mr Pennethorne that most heartrendingly affecting letter of which I sent you a copy; and it would not have been quite reasonable in me to have settled upon a design for a client, if I did not think it at the time worth fighting for: – I also considered, and now consider, that I have reason on my side.

It would be wise I think to take it for granted that we shall not be able to begin building until next Spring, and that we shall thus have the winter in which to be able to make up our minds as to what we can modify, and what stand by in the design; and by a little patient pertinacity make our opponents as tired of us, as we are of them.[1]

I am not at all afraid of making alterations in the design, which may not injure the fundamental principles – and I have already made another drawing for the large window in the studio, the former design of which was so emphatically condemned.[2]

I shall be at home on Monday next at 11 oc & ready to talk over, & explain anything, which you may require to know.

[Yours very truly | Philip Webb:]

Howard

1864–1887

1 Minded to follow Pennethorne's suggestion to consult another architect (see previous letter, note 3), Gore wrote to GH on 25 October to say that he was 'willing to submit the Drawings with the Correspondence that has passed upon the subject to Mr Burn or Mr Salvin', whereupon GH requested that a second architect, to be proposed by himself ('either Mr Street, Mr Bodley or Mr Butterfield') should also be consulted, as 'I believe that it is usual in any case of arbitration for each party to name its professional referee and this course seems to me the more necessary in the present case, as professional differences of opinion on the most fundamental subjects are known to be so strong'. GH to Gore, 29 October 1867, *NA CRES 35/21217*. Gore acted quickly to clarify the position. 'I have no desire to refer the question to another Architect. There is no question of Arbitration. Plans of Buildings upon the Property of the Crown in London must be approved by me, and it was solely with a friendly view & to shew you I was not an obstructive, that, contrary to practice, I expressed a readiness to consult either Mr Burns or Mr Salvin, as impartial and competent judges, upon the disputed question'. Gore to GH, 31 October 1867, *NA CRES 35/21217*.

2 Gore evidently felt that matters could be resolved, if only PSW were prepared to be more forthcoming and amenable to compromise. 'Mr Webb had better go and see Mr Pennethorne and take with him the amended Plan of your intended House, and give such explanations as may be necessary to make it intelligible. I shall be very glad if the altered Plan and Mr Webb's explanation succeed in removing Mr Pennethorne's reasonable objections. Mr Pennethorne in his letter to Mr Webb suggested an interview, which Mr Webb in his answer declined, in terms which your own observation will best know how to characterize.' Gore to GH, 31 October 1867. Accompanied by GH, PSW did meet Pennethorne on 11 November, and showed the new window design in the east elevation, but refused to make other changes:

'Mr Webb maintained that his designs are perfect, and such as would have been proposed by Sir Christopher Wren or Inigo Jones if they had lived at the present day: and he thought the objections I had stated arose from my inability to appreciate them. Mr Howard approves of Mr Webb's design and wishes to have the house built accordingly because it would be entirely of red brick; and he considers that before he purchased the lease he had obtained your verbal consent to use that material. I explained to Mr Howard that the term "Red Brick House" did not imply commonplace forms built entirely of brick, and without any relief, but rather such buildings as the Admiralty or Marlborough House should he prefer that style: or Hampton Court Palace and many other country houses should he prefer a style of the time of Henry the 8th, Elizabeth or James 1st.' Pennethorne to Gore, 18 November 1867, *NA CRES 35/21217*. Gore now informed GH that he would submit the plans and correspondence to Anthony Salvin (1799–1881), 'whose eminence as an Architect will be a justification to me to abide by his opinion upon the subject in dispute'. 19 November 1867, *NA CRES 35/12127*. Salvin asked that he might consider the case jointly with Thomas Henry Wyatt (1807–80), but any sense of independence in their brief report is flawed by its close dependence upon Pennethorne's initial criticisms.

'It will probably be sufficient, as a guide to you in dealing with this question, if we state our belief that in their present state the Elevations could not be considered pleasing in composition, or satisfactory in their relation to the locality, & to the other Buildings on the Crown Estate.

We agree with Mr Pennethorne in thinking that "they would be objected to generally by the Crown Lessees" that "the design submitted is not suited to the locality; it would not assimilate with others built of late years on the Estate; it would probably be very dissimilar to any Buildings hereafter erected there (whether Kensington Palace be enlarged or not)" and we are prepared to share Mr Pennethorne's responsibility in advising you not to approve this Design.' Salvin and Wyatt to Gore, 9 December 1867, *NA CRES 35/12127*. Gore sent the report to GH, and turned down PSW designs. GH's response was to ask for clarity as to the reasons for refusal. 'I could then ask Mr Webb to consider the possibility of designing a house subject to the given conditions. I can only regret that those conditions were not stated to me before the purchasing of the land; I then stated my intention to you of building a red brick house designed by Mr Webb different in character from the ordinary model of London builders houses.' GH to Gore, 16 December 1867, *NA CRES 35/12127*. See below, Letter 13.

12 • To George Price Boyce, 20 December 1867

Annotated: 'rec^d Decr 20 67.'[1]

1, Raymond Buildings, Gray's Inn, | *London,*
Friday

My dear Boyce

I knocked at your door with the hope of being able to give you half an hour's chat, good for convalescence as Wells[2] had just then said by letter that you were getting better after a severe touch of illness – but did not say that you were not at Chatham Place.[3]

I shall hope soon to see you at work again or hear that you are gone into the country to make hay where there is a possibility of sunshine.

In spite of an exhibition I enjoyed your pictures at the W: C^o:[4] – Was it not a "Bradley" who did some teams of horses (or oxen) last year that were interesting?[5]

If it was the same man he has not done so well this.

I am trying to screw up my courage to go & hear the great "Chorale" at Sidenham [*sic*] tomorrow.[6] I do not know whether you know it well enough to hum it to your toes in bed.

Let me know that you are better. | Yours very truly | Philip Webb:

BL Add 45354, ff. 3-4

---

1 GPB often recorded the date of a letter's receipt.
2 The portrait painter, Henry Tanworth Wells (1828–1903) married GPB's sister, Joanna Mary Boyce (1831–61), in 1857. She had herself been a painter. Wells was a staunch defender of the Royal Academy and its traditions, and would act as Sir Frederic Leighton's occasional deputy as President during 1895.
3 See above, Letter 3, note 2.
4 The sixth winter exhibition of the Old Water-Colour Society had opened at the end of November, *The Times* (28 November) noting several works by GPB: 'his small drawing of "Hay-carting at Arisaig", his autumn study in Wotton-woods [*Tate Gallery, London*], his moonlight view of San Giorgio, Venice, and his "Deserted Colliery, near Durham", all show that characteristic quality of sweet and solemn calm and fine sensibility to the harmonies of subdued colour which give this painter a place high and apart, in spite of his systematic indifference to grace of line, amounting almost to defiance of the accepted practice of composition.'
5 *The Times* reviewer concluded with praise for two pastel drawings by Basil Bradley (1842–1904), 'one of the most recently elected associates of the Society.'
6 On 21 December, Beethoven's ninth Symphony (the 'Choral') was given at Crystal Palace, Sydenham, under its musical director, August Manns (1825–1907).

13 • To George Howard, 17 January 1868

1 Raymond Buildings Gray's Inn | London
Jan.y 17. 1868

Dear Mr Howard

I beg to acknowledge the receipt of your note, enclosing a letter from M.r Gore to you, with a copy of Mess.rs Salvin & Wyatt's second report on my design for your house.[1]

The following are the only remarks I can make on this most unjustifiable obstruction.

I do not see why Mess.rs Salvin & Wyatt should wrest your remark, of the site being overlooked, to a complaint on your part, that light was difficult to be obtained.

Mess.rs Salvin & Wyatt commence with saying that "we find it difficult to define portions which appear to us objectionable, when the whole composition has in our eyes little to recommend it" and finish with "we have however, the satisfaction of knowing that M.r Webb may without any interference with his general plan, and with little if any addition to the contemplated expenditure, meet the objections we have raised"[;] this, with a former regret that it was possibly on the "score of economy" that some of what was objectionable in their eyes, existed in the design, is to say the least, a strange effort of criticism.

That the ordinary mercantile Architect does design his elevations without reference to the plan, to escape labour, & please the ignorant, can be no excuse to a man who takes an artistic interest in his work.

That Mess.rs Salvin & Wyatt are "unable to discover what actual style or period of Architecture" I have used, I take to be a sincere compliment, as the greater number of existing houses in Palace Gardens have their origin fairly written on their faces, though it is a question whether their fathers would be pleased with the likeness.

I distinctly deny that the parapet to the bay window on East elevation, is fantastic in the sense used by Mess.rs Salvin & Wyatt. That it has some fancy or fantasy of design about it I will allow, and that in that position a most delightful effect has been gained in all ages by an extra allowance of imagination I can prove; and in fact, throughout the elevations the simple forms of decoration suited to the material, are all legitimately derived from admired examples, subject to the necessary adaptation to make them mine, & fit for the time & place.

I would willingly – to help you out of the trap, in which you have been most unreasonably caught – re-design the whole of the house, were I not certain, that if the new design possessed any character & proper simplicity it would be again objected to by Mess⁻ˢ Pennethorne[,] Salvin & Wyatt – but, if M⁻ʳ Pennethorne will consider his objections sufficiently attended to, and that I have bowed low enough to his superior knowledge of the art: First, by redesigning the chimnies [*sic*] above the parapet (2) by broadening the pilasters of the parapet to 14" instead of 9" (3) by putting stone moulded sills to the windows instead of brick & tile, (4) by ~~arranging~~ carrying round the East and North elevations, at the level of base of drawing room bay & balcony, a stone moulded string (5) by adding broad pilasters to East wall of stables (6) and by redesigning the Entrance Porch with more ornamental stonework – I will so do at your request.[2]

      Believe me Dear Sir: | Yours very faithfully | Philip Webb:
George Howard, Esq⁻ʳᵉ

NA CRES 35/3106

1 GH having asked for more details as to the rejection of PSW's designs of 1 Palace Green (see above Letter 11, note 2), Gore asked Pennethorne to consult further with Salvin and Wyatt and seek amplification. They met on 3 January 1868, and submitted a report, the substance of which Gore communicated to GH ten days later.
'With regard to a remark in one of the letters that "the peculiarities of the ground are so great rights of light &c interfering in all directions that much of the peculiarity of the design may be attributable to the necessities of the situation" we feel that it would be very difficult to find a site in London in which fewer difficulties on the score of light or level actually exist, Light being really obtainable on all 4 sides. . . .
Dealing with the Elevations, we find it difficult to detail portions which appear to us objectionable when the whole composition has in our eyes so little to recommend it. We are unable to discern what actual style or period of Architecture M⁻ʳ Webb has sought to adopt. We think the combination of Square, Circular & Segmental forms for the windows & pointed arches for doors & recesses unusual & objectionable. The upper portion of the Bay window on East front appears fantastic, unpleasing, and unnecessary. The window of Drawing room on North front in which the principal attempt of Ornament has been centred, presents to us a most unfortunate & unpleasing combination of forms. We think the recess in North Elevation might be made a very pleasing & effective feature, but as treated, with the 2 Circular windows & pointed arch over the recess, we feel it to be much the reverse.
We think the Pilasters on upper storey & on the Chimney Stacks, rising from a projecting string course are not satisfactory. They are thin & poor. The very long one on the Chimney shaft in North Elevation we think especially so. We feel that the Chimnies, from the absence of sufficient base & from the poverty of their upper members, have a very meagre effect.
We think the large surface of unbroken wall on East Elevation, most <u>unpleasing</u> & unnecessary. We regret the necessity (if on the score of economy such exists) of so large a mass of Brickwork without any relief of color or stonework on its surface, but for the Window Sills <u>at least</u> we hold stone to be essential.
It is to us a matter of regret to have to express opinions so adverse to this Design, but as you have sought our candid opinion we have no alternative. We have however the satisfaction of knowing that M⁻ʳ Webb may without any interference with his general Plan & with little, if any addition to the contemplated expenditure, meet the objections we have raised.' Salvin and Wyatt to Gore, 3 January 1868, *NA CRES 35/3106.*
2 'I beg to enclose M⁻ʳ Webb's letter to me in answer to the report of Mess Salvin and Wyatt; the general objections of those gentlemen to the whole appearance and style of the design are so strongly

expressed that I fear any new design by Mr Webb would be equally objectionable to them; but you will see that Mr Webb proposes to introduce six important alterations in those parts of the design which do not affect the proportion or construction of the house.' GH to Gore, 18 January 1868, *NA CRES 35/3106*. 'If Mr Webb would have the goodness to submit to you fresh drawings for the three Elevations I could give an opinion upon them, and could if necessary consult Messrs Salvin & Wyatt – and it is to be hoped that he will see the prudence and propriety of doing so – for upon verbal description only I could not recommend you to approve of any design.' Pennethorne to Gore, 21 January 1868, *NA CRES 35/3106*.

14 • To George Howard, 18 February 1868

1 Raymond Buildings Gray's Inn | London.
Feby 18 1868

Dear Mr Howard

The new Elevations to your house are now ready to be sent into Mr Gore.[1]

I have spared no pains in endeavouring to remove from the designs anything which would be likely to incur Mr Pennethorne's disapproval, and also in adding such features as would make the building more attractive to him and the general public. I have been aided in this matter by the advice of an Architect of great reputation with whom I was not before personally acquainted.

On the East Elevation, I have raised and broadened the porch, and added a considerable amount of carved decoration.

To the bay window an attached shaft cap & base has been put to support the bracket, the parapet altered and finished with pierced panels, instead of the engrailed outline as before.

To the Studio the window has been redesigned & set in a more ornamental gable of diapered brick & stone.

On the North Elevation – the recess against back stairs has been fitted with couplet windows & pilasters running up to support the springing of vault & the vault is now thrown over the recess from the staircase wall to the back of front wall – i.e. from the South to the North, instead of from East to West as before.

The buttress pilaster to chimney has been stopped at the gable, & narrow double pilasters substituted from the parapet coping upwards – the exposed portion of this gable has also been disposed as that on the East Elevation.

The Drawing room window looking north has been modified and a considerable amount of ornamentation added.

A broad band of stone, in combination with moulded sills & large string course and a massive stone moulded plinth have been run round both sides of the house, and bracketed stone moulded sills have been substituted for brick & tile to the bedroom windows.

The chimney caps have been finished with stone moulded strings & gabled hoods.

In fine both the Elevations have been much enriched, and I have taken particular care to tint the different materials in such a way that no mistake can be made as to their variety.[2]

You will of course not be surprised to learn that the above alterations & additions will cost a very considerable sum over and above the 7,000£ of the lowest tender, though I can assure you that I have tried to keep the cost as low as possible, but unless external decoration is of the ordinary stupid pretentious kind, it costs a good deal of money.[3]

If you will kindly send your letter to me I will forward it with the drawings to M[r] Gore at once.

Believe me Dear M[r] Howard | Yours very faithfully | Philip Webb:

George Howard Esq[re]

NA CRES 35/3106

---

1 'I beg to enclose a letter of M[r] Webbs together with fresh elevations for my proposed house at Kensington. I hope that these new designs will be approved of by M[r] Pennethorne as the proposed alterations will add considerably to the former estimated expense of my house.' GH to Gore, 14 February 1868, *NA CRES 35/3106*.

2 'The drawings now under consideration do not shew any radical change of deign but only a few extra embellishments, and as it is now clear nothing will ever convert the original into a good design, it appears to me necessary either to require M[r] Howard to abandon it altogether, or to permit him to proceed to build according to these new drawings, and this latter alternative under the circumstances I would submit to you as to be preferred – because M[r] Howard has already been greatly delayed and annoyed (though by fault of his own Architect), - the building as regards expenditure will meet the requirements of the Agreement – and (except that you refrain from using stringently your compulsory powers) you will have done all within your means to secure the building of a respectable House.

... [T]hough I have proposed to you to approve it, I would, if you should be pleased to act on this suggestion, submit to your consideration the propriety of requiring still further improvement in two of the details. First, I think the rubbed arches over all the windows should be made double the width they are shown by the drawings, and secondly that the main cornice which runs along above the heads of the Chamber windows should be of stone at least 18" in depth, and with a projection of about 18". Pennethorne to Gore, 27 February 1868, *NA CRES 35/3106*.

3 'The alterations from M[r] Webb's original design as proposed by these amended Elevations are enumerated in his letter, and it does not appear to me necessary to remark on them seriatum – but, with reference to his statement that "the alterations and additions will cost a very considerable sum over and above the £7000 of the lowest tender", I would observe that the additional cost occasioned by these changes ought not to be considerable; and that although the total cost to be incurred by M[r] Howard will be equal to his Agreement, the decoration work of the exterior will be much less than usual for the class of House.' Pennethorne to Gore, 27 February 1868.

15 • To George Howard, 3 March 1868

1, Raymond Buildings, Gray's Inn, | *London,*
Mar 3 *1868*

Dear Mr Howard.

I am sorry that I could not send you the following information before; but I have been much pressed with work the last few days.

With regard to 1st requirement of Mr Gore's letter of the 27th of February.[1]

"Mr Webb will not object to modify the arches of windows as there required – that is – to double the thickness of those arches which on the last submitted elevations only show to be one course.

"Mr Webb is much surprised at the second requirement, which is that 'the main cornice which runs above the heads of the chamber windows is to be of stone at least 18 inches in depth and with a projection of about 18 inches.'

"Mr Webb cannot conceive it possible that the elevations should have been carefully examined; or such an incongruous detail would not have been specified.

"The chief feature in the design is the gauged brick band or string course in combination with the pilasters of parapet – & Mr Webb has been most careful in the altered elevations not to impair or destroy this most necessary feature, or damage the surface of colour, which the material would give; and he is satisfied that, no person desirous of injuring the design and bringing ridicule upon the architect, could have hit upon a more successful idea than that of substituting the stone cornice specified.

"Mr Webb therefore declines to accede to the above requirement on the grounds that no Architect who is worthy of the name, will allow his work to be mutilated by irresponsible hands; & he is decidedly of opinion, that the arbitrary rule of another professional man in such a matter of detail – even if he should happen to be a man of genius – would not tend to improve the work of any architect who has taken pains to make his design a consistent whole."[2]

Perhaps you might follow up here with your surprise &ct & about the concessions made by you in regard to cost & by me in design, being entitled to more respect, and that the risk of the exposure of a great scandal with so palpably gross an assertion of right & the probable withdrawal of Mr Webb from the unequal contest, with certainty of intense annoyance, great delay, & loss of money as a consequence would be scarcely repaid by the pleasure another architect would have in seeing his own handiwork on the design.[3]

Please do not hesitate to cut I hope & alter in any way that you may fancy and believe me

[Yours very truly | Philip Webb:]

Howard

---

1 See previous letter, note 2.
2 'To the second requirement . . . [Mr Webb] is altogether unable to accede, as it would completely destroy the effect of the elevation in his eyes. . . . I can only say that I agree entirely in Mr Webb's objections, and was of the same opinion before I heard his strong objections. If you insist upon this condition the whole process will certainly have to be given up as the introduction of the stone cornice into the present designs is impossible. I hope however that you may give your consent to the plans without this concession, as Mr Webb has spared no pains in altering his original plans and in modifying them very considerably to secure their adoption, while I shall have to make considerable

sacrifices in money to meet the increased cost which the alterations necessitate.' GH to Gore, 6 March 1868, *NA CRES 35/3106*. Upon Pennethorne's further advice, that 'Mr Webb appears to forget that having regard to the Agreement he is not in a position to <u>accede</u> to anything, but that you have the power to compel compliance with the conditions named' (Pennethorne to Gore, 18 March 1868, *NA CRES 35/3106*), Gore wrote again to GH, reaffirming that his agreement was conditional upon the need for a stone cornice.

3 GH responded to Gore by stating that PSW was 'unable on this condition to continue the undertaking', and complained that although the eight objections raised in the report made by Salvin and Wyatt had been met, approval was still being withheld, due to the 'prejudice' of Pennethorne. '[I]nstead of obtaining your assent we were met by a fresh demand which we consider entirely inadmissible. I must say that such a course as this seems to have been dictated rather by professional animosity than by a spirt of just and impartial criticism.' GH to Gore, 22 March 1868, *NA CRES 35/3106*. He sought William Butterfield's assistance, although in the circumstances it was an approach unlikely to succeed. 'Since I wrote to you yesterday, I have ascertained that M‍ʳ Butterfield will not undertake to design any plans for my house at Kensington Palace Gardens; he refused for two reasons. First, because he considers that Mr Webb (who is no personal friend of his) has had a great injustice done to him, and is therefore unwilling to take his place. Secondly, because he is unwilling to place his work under the control of M‍ʳ Pennethorne's taste after seeing the way in which it has been exercised. You will observe I am thus placed in a position of peculiar hardship, as I am unable to obtain your consent to the plans which have been made – modified as they are according to the suggestions of your advisers, and in consequence of this refusal of yours and of the treatment of Mr Webb, I am unable to secure the assistance of an excellent architect for the designing of new ones.' GH to Gore, 23 March 1868, *NA CRES 35/3106*.

16 • To Thomas Henry Wyatt, 28 March 1868

1, Raymond Buildings, Gray's Inn, | *London,*
March 28 *1868*

Sir:

(M‍ʳ Howard's House Ken‍ⁿ Pal Gardens)

I beg to acknowledge the receipt of your letter of this morning.[1]

I shall be very willing to meet you with the hope of bringing (what you reasonably call) "this most disagreeable matter" to a conclusion.[2]

I will come with the drawings to G‍ᵗ Russell S‍ᵗ on Monday at 11.45.[3]

Yours truly | Philip Webb:

T:H: Wyatt Esq

NA CRES 35/3106

---

1 In a final effort to resolve the disagreement, and responding to GH's heartfelt sense of injustice (see previous letter, note 3), Gore once more asked Salvin and Wyatt to advise on the remaining matter of the stone cornice.

2 'M‍ʳ Salvin will not be in town for some time & in the hope of aiding to bring this disagreeable matter to a practical, if not satisfactory conclusion, I will waive my own feelings & propose an interview. . . . As however I believe that the only difficult <u>now</u> existing may be met

[by] a few minutes conversation, I am ready to make the attempt.' Wyatt to PSW, 28 March 1868, *Howard.*

3 Thanks more to Wyatt's pragmatism than to PSW's willingness to compromise further, the two men met on 30 March and finally reached agreement over the revised designs for 1 Palace Green:
'I gather from the correspondence which was sent from your office that the only point now at issue is the material of the cornice. In asking for stone, I conclude that Mr Pennethorne's principal object was to ensure greater solidity of construction & perfect protection from injury to the upper part of this projecting feature; & though as a matter of color & taste he would probably prefer a rich colored stone to the monotony of the red brick (a feeling which is shared by Mr Salvin & myself) yet as both Mr Howard & Mr Webb are particularly anxious to retain the Brick Cornice, & as there is abundant authority for this material in cornices, I venture to advise that you should sanction such a cornice merely stipulating that Mr Pennethorne should be satisfied as to the solidity & safety of its construction prior to the Lease being granted.
Mr Webb would then have to bear (as the Architect always should) the whole responsibility on the score of taste and propriety.
I enclose a Section shewing the description of Cornice Mr Webb proposes to erect. He will adopt any suggestions which may be thought necessary to ensure strength and safety in its construction, & the whole of the Cornice & the wall above will be executed in cement.
I trust that your concession will relieve you from further correspondence & misunderstanding on this very troublesome matter.' Wyatt to Gore, 31 1868, *NA CCRES 35/3106*. With a resolution achieved, the builders moved on site on 8 June, the contract having been awarded to Richard Ashby & Sons. The existing grace and favour house had first to be demolished. 'The poor old house was very rotten – but I have saved such things as would be possible to reuse as memorials.' PSW to GH, July 1868, *Howard.*

17 • To George Warington Taylor, 27 July 1868

Draft?

July 27, 1868

Dear T.

I am delighted to hear that you had a nice interview with Gabriel – he is – if he chooses – very straightforward and his intellect is very keen and I take it for granted you were sure of what he was saying at the time, from the character of your letter to me.[1]

With regard to your reversionary interest in the property I can speak less comfortably.[2] I think you know pretty well my ideas on the subject, viz. ^{that} the attempt to guide by trustee or will the channel into wh' it shall finally flow is a fal[l]acy and I have the strongest dislike to preaching one doctrine & practicing the opposite. I would say appoint your solicitor in the will to see to the carrying out of it and then let the matter rest – but I am sure that there ^{are} many men who would consider this absurd – Gabriel perhaps among the number – therefore I shall not be at all surprised at your not considering my opinion worth much. And I myself have a sufficiently low estimate of its value – but that would be no reason for my going against my settled convictions however poor they may be.

By this preamble you will I suspect make ready to be offended at my refusing to be a trustee as you propose, and I can only hope that you may make an exception to treating me with the contempt which is sure to find me out at the tail end of a friendship. I can only say that I am not quite light hearted at thus refusing your request

       If possible – Believe me | yours ever | Philip Webb.

V&A, NAL MSL/1958/691/79

---

1 'What a splendid woman she has been to me all through. What might she not have done – & with right too – never was there a woman so damnably ill-treated as she was by me. . . . Gabriel has told me rightly what I was – he has hit me so hard. How rightly he summed me up. He never was so splendid as on Friday when he told me what he thought of it all, & what a damned scoundrel I was. And now after all this she takes me back again.' Warington Taylor to PSW, 26 July 1868, *V&A, NAL MSL/1958/691/77.*
2 'Once more I appeal to you. Will you be a trustee – & I wish to ask also William Rossetti as a man of truth & also my solicitors Cookson & Wainwright. If I had really ever given any thought to the matter I should have seen the idiotcy [*sic*] of leaving a lovely woman sole trustee to her own property throwing her open to every designing villain in the world. Therefore now this must if possible be changed & may I once more ask you to take the work. You know why I trust in you but you always forbid me having confidence in you!' SCC later commented of Warington Taylor's marriage that 'This truly remarkable man married a girl out of an eel pie shop in Bristol. He was devoted to her & much tragedy resulted therefrom'. SCC to WRL, 2 August 1915 *BL Add* 52731, f. 117.

18 • To Charles Augustus Howell, 17 October 1868

1, Raymond Buildings, Gray's Inn, | *London,*
Oct 17 *1868*

My dear Howell[1]

It would be very nice to get some tiles done in a genuine way by others than the British workman[2] but as it would be difficult to arrange matters by letter would it not be better for us to meet & talk over the matter. – 'tis true we should have to undergo the horror of seeing you but perhaps you could put up with this for once?

 The bestial drawings belong to Top, but I don't mean to let him have them except for use by the firm, as they are not fit for anything ᵉˡˢᵉ than rude decorative purposes.[3] The question seems to us to be, for first to get specimens of work from manufacturers and then order so many for the shop, giving you some for your trouble – if this would not add to it. But more of this if you choose to undergo the pain of a personal interview.

               Yours ever | Philip Webb:

C: A: Howell Esq

Texas

1 Charles Augustus Howell (1840–90) was a complex and elusive personality, whose career is summed up in his *DNB* entry as being that of 'agent and rogue'. Born in Portugal of English and Portuguese parents, his recounting of the story of his early life may have been imagined, at least in some of the livelier details. After his arrival in England a winning personal charm allowed him to build useful contacts, and he was soon moving in influential art circles, having, as Whistler put it, 'the gift of intimacy'. JR, DGR, EBJ, Swinburne and Whistler all placed their confidence in him, which sometimes they had cause to regret. He often used this trust to his own advantage, for he combined an exceptional artistic eye with rather shady business practices, acting as an intermediary for unwitting artists or simply on his own behalf.

2 'I am in communication with the Lisbon people, and they are ready to try their best with the tiles. Can I have your beautiful designs the Crow, Cock & Hare? Should you like to design any flower tiles for yourself, ie for your grates, you can do so, and I will get them made for you.' Howell to PSW, 15 October 1868, *V&A, AAD*. PSW's Delft-style blue and white designs of a Hare, Raven and Cockerel, were sold from 1869 and 1870 by MMF & Co. See the colour illustrations of the Hare and Cock, 'for decoration by a Dutch tilery ... thought to have been prototypes, possibly painted by Webb, and kept by the Firm until after 1934', in Richard and Hilary Myers, *William Morris Tiles. The Tile Designs of Morris and his Fellow-Workers* (Shepton Beauchamp: Richard Dennis, 1996), p. 55. See also *Kirk*, p. 39. This exchange between Howell and PSW places the prototype drawings a full year before PSW recorded the tiles in his account book (see Myers, p. 135).

3 It was in character for Howell to seek to make himself indispensable, ever alert to an advantageous business opportunity. 'Regarding your three designs (the crow, hare &c) I should like to know exactly how the matter stands, if they belong to you or to the shop. I should like to have the drawings for myself, but not the copyright, and therefore would like to know distinctly whom the tiles belong to when ready and paid for by me. Will they be yours and sold by the shop for you. Will they belong to the shop (who will pay me their cost and sell them for what they like) or what?'

19 • To Jenny and May Morris, 31 October 1868

Postmark LONDON. W.C. OC 31 68 *Address* Miss Jane & Miss Mary Morris: | 26 Queen Square: | Bloomsbury.

1, Raymond Buildings, Gray's Inn, | *London,*
Saturday

My dear Jenny & May[1]

Though I have a great dislike to eating and drinking, and can't bear to do either at your house, I cannot resist your polite invitation to dinner tomorrow.

I will come to you at half past one, and will so carefully hide my disgust, that you shall not be able to see from my appearance that I am anything but happy & contented.

Your affectionate | Old Webb:

BL Add 45342, f. 2

---

1 Jenny (JEM, 1861–1935) and May Morris (MM 1862–1938) were aged 7 and 6 respectively when PSW wrote this letter.

20 • To Elizabeth Burden, probably 1868

1, Raymond Buildings, Gray's Inn, | London,
Tuesday 18 [[pre-printed year, not day]]

Dear Miss Burden[1]

I send you designs for two altar cloths wh' I hope you will like. I have told Morris what I wish Wardle to do, in drawing them out for you[2] – that is, to make them pretty drawings for you to shew.

I will do two more of a simpler kind, if you like these

Yours very truly | Philip Webb:

Please to make any suggestions.

Huntington MOR 578

---

1 Elizabeth (Bessie) Burden (b. 1842), youngest sister of JM, and like her a skilled needlewoman who executed many projects for MMF & Co. 'In the 1860s [Jane and Elizabeth] began to work embroideries to designs by Morris and Webb.... A frontal embroidered by Elizabeth in 1868, to a design by Webb, is one of only two extant pieces to represent this decade [in the history of MMF & Co embroidery].' The surviving frontal is the 'Lamb and Flag' design at Llandaff Cathedral. See Mary Schoeser, *The Watts Book of Embroidery. English Church Embroidery 1833–1953* (London: Watts & Co., 1998), p. 79; see also Schoeser, p. 80 for an illustration of the Llandaff Cathedral frontal. See also Lynn Hulse, 'Elizabeth Burden and the Royal School of Needlework', *JWMS*, XXI (Winter 2014), pp. 22–34.
2 For George Young Wardle, see below, Letter 25, note 8.

21 • To Jane Morris, ?about January 1869

Annotated 'Watermark 1868 | ?Jan. 1869'

1, Raymond Buildings, Gray's Inn, | London,
Wednesday

My dear janie[1]

I take it as very kind of you, that the nice comforter you have sent me, is not knitted in the form of a rope.

This piece of soft work done by your hands shall be to me as a promise that you are not going to withdraw from me, what has hitherto been unfailing kindness on your part.

Good luck to you at Hastings – I sincerely hope that the air will do you much good.

Believe me to be | Yours very aff.y | Philip Webb:

BL Add 45342, ff. 3-4

---

1 In these early letters to JM (and occasionally to JEM), PSW sometimes uses the lower-case 'j'.

1864–1887

22 • To George Howard, 2 January 1869

1, Raymond Buildings, Gray's Inn, | *London,*
2 January *1869*

Dear Mr Howard

Thank you very much for your new year's wish, that I may have better clients for the future. For myself, I've never grumbled at the race. They have treated me quite more than fairly and allowed me to live without many reproaches.[1]

For a return, I wish you a better house than you will get, and the same full of friends that you may forget your disappointment.

I have told Morris about the chairs in which matter I quite agree with you.

The building is progressing satisfactorily, as there is plenty of small work to occupy the time of doubtful weather.

I think that when you come back, a couple of pounds spread over 4 payments will be more likely [to] reach all hands, than if made in two.

With kind regards to Mrs Howard | [Yours very truly | Philip Webb:]

Howard

---

1 But he might have felt rather differently a few months later. See below, Letter 32, note 2.

23 • To James Pennethorne, 31 May 1869

1, Raymond Buildings, Gray's Inn, | *London,*
May 31 *1869*

Dear Sir

Mr Howard's House | Palace Green

The carcase of the house is now completed and I shall be obliged by your sending me a certificate to that effect, as I believe that Mr Howard's solicitor requires the same before completing certain forms.

Yours truly | Philip Webb:

James Pennethorne Esqre

NA CRES 35/3106

24 • To George Price Boyce, 12 July 1869

1, Raymond Buildings, Gray's Inn, | *London,*
July 12 *1869*

Dear Boyce

I was at Chelsea to-day[1] – the roof was all but on, and they will begin tiling shortly.

25

'Tis quite possible that we may be able to change the sewer manhole, from where it is to a less objectionable position & as soon as we apply to open into the sewer, I will try what can be done with the "board".[2]

I've nothing whatever to say against the red colour you propose and should be glad if you w[d] try in watercolours to get a tone you would like.

The use of your Bramah locks is specified.[3]

Here we have summer weather 80° in the shade.

I hope you are picking up health, and are making yourself good company. Here except for the hope that the "Commons" will sit upon the "Lords"[4] we are dull enough.

Yours very truly | Philip Webb:

BL Add 45354, ff. 13-14

---

1 West House, Glebe Place, Chelsea. See *Kirk*, pp. 75–6 and 297.
2 Under the provisions of the Public Health Act (1848), local Boards of Health were given extensive powers over sanitation.
3 The founder-designer of the Bramah lock company, Joseph Bramah (1748–1814), patented his first design in 1787.
4 The Irish Church Act, or Disestablishment Act, was an important plank in Gladstone's support for Irish Home Rule. The state (Protestant) church had the loyalty of perhaps only a ninth of the Irish population, which formed a natural Catholic majority. Despite fierce opposition from the House of Lords, the legislation passed rapidly through parliament. '[T]he bill was introduced in the House of Commons on 1 March 1869 and received the royal assent on 26 July. The Irish Church ceased to be established by law on 1 January 1871.' Alan Megahey, 'Gladstone, church and state', in D. George Boyce and Alan O'Day (eds), *Gladstone and Ireland. Politics, Religion and Nationality in the Victorian Age* (Basingstoke: Palgrave Macmillan, 2010), p. 56.

25 • To William and Jane Morris, 23 July 1869

Gray's Inn
Friday July 23.

My dear Janey & Top[1]

I got your kindest of letters this morning,[2] and was a king for the time being, when you went away nearly my all was gone. Ned & Georgie & Gabriel are part of the family but we look at each other in a kind of rage that the rest are not by – I make solemn vows that if I see you again I will be better, kinder and less selfish, but shall please myself just now by thinking that you would not like me so well if I changed.

I was at Fulham on Tuesday,[3] but had the edge of my nervousness taken off by old Müller[4] who dined there before going to Italy. We tried to talk of anything but you but burnt our wings in that flame occasionally. Of course I sat right & then left, expecting Ned to say, "Webb, why are you such a bloody fool?" but he was good-natured & didn't. For God's sake dear Janey use your English privilege and keep on saying "demain" instead of giving up and I shall see you tomorrow better than yesterday.

I see the effect of going into society (Brown's!!!) by a note in the Spectator that the great Stephens has said that Mr Morris is going to publish another portion of the E.P: in November.[5] I hope it will be good, Top, and free from spite. You never go a journey but you find the world – however shocking in the change – all of a piece warp & woof very much alike & you'll tell of your neighbour there, what will amuse the thief here. As for newspapers it is this. The Lords have "caved in," the bill is to pass[6] – trimmers are to be considered excellent,[7] and the world a marvel of beauty.

Wardle[8] carried me yesterday to Beddington – – Oh what magnificence – what disporting – English Oak 'in excelsis'.[9] I hope the whistleing [sic] from that bird cage will be pure Handel.

Now my dear Top & Janey I ought to wind up with something unkind, for you to recognise me – but Ive always said that people misunderstood me. Try for this once to believe that I am your most affectionate

Phil Webb:

BL Add 45342, ff. 7-8

---

1. It is not certain when the affair between DGR and JM began, but it was almost certainly under way by the time that WM took her to Bad Ems in July 1869, where they spent two months so that Jane might take the waters. Her symptoms may have been as much nervous as physical, but it is possible that the Bad Ems treatment was for a gynaecological condition. Although her 'ill health continued intermittently for much of her life ... there is no evidence that she ever suffered from a serious organic disease'. *MacCarthy, WMLT*, p. 201.
2. WM and JM wrote to PSW from Ghent on 22 July, *CLWM*, I.
3. EBJ and GBJ moved from Kensington Square to The Grange, North End, Fulham at the end of 1867. It remained their London house and studio until the painter's death.
4. Friedrich Max Müller (1823–1900) was a German-born Sanskrit scholar and a specialist in the anthropological disciplines. He lived in England from 1846, was appointed Professor of Modern European Languages at Oxford in 1851, and took British nationality in 1855. His six-volume translation of the *Rig Veda* was published by OUP (1849–74).
5. PSW means *The Athenæum*, not *The Spectator*. Its art editor from 1851 to 1901 was Frederic George Stephens (1828–1907), who, with (unrealised) hopes of becoming a painter had joined the Pre-Raphaelite Brotherhood in 1848. He was a model in several paintings, including *Jesus Washing Peter's Feet* (1852–6) by Ford Madox Brown, the friend whom PSW asserts to be the source of the information published in the 'Literary Gossip' column of *The Athenæum* on 17 July 1869. 'We hear that Mr. William Morris has determined on publishing a further portion of his poem, "The Earthly Paradise," in November, instead of delaying it till the whole of the work is completed. The volume to be published in November will comprise the tales for Autumn; and we understand that the final volume of tales for Winter will follow in May next.' PSW's own set of the six-volume edition of *The Earthly Paradise* (London: F.S. Ellis, 1868–70), of which only 25 copies were printed (presentation copies from WM), is in the Emery Walker Library. See *CAGM*, p. 141.
6. See previous letter, note 4.
7. Trimmer: 'One who trims between opposing parties in politics, etc; hence, one who inclines to each of opposite sides as interest dictates.' (*OED*).

8 The artist George Young Wardle (GW, 1836–1910) became the highly skilled general manager of MMF & Co on the death of Warington Taylor, a position he then filled for twenty years. A good number of his letters to PSW survive (mostly at the library of the Courtauld Institute), but scarcely any from PSW to him. His drawings of historic buildings were highly regarded by both PSW and WM.
9 The Tudor Great Hall of Beddington Park, Sutton, the former manor house of the Carew family, has a fine hammer-beam roof of four bays.

26 • To William and Jane Morris, 31 July 1869

1 Raymond Buildings Gray's Inn
Saturday July 31

My very dear Top & Janey

I was delighted to hear yesterday that you had got to Ems all safe and in better condition than you could have expected. I hope you will not be astonished when I say that we feel mutilated, a great member gone – and none of our work or pleasure quite coming comfortable to us. I'm sure you won't be surprised when I say that we seldom mention you, as we thus avoid a difficulty wh' can't be got over better, than by silence – how can I tell you anything wh' you have not guessed before?

Gabriel invited us to a tent dinner last Monday and tried to make us cheerful by getting Val[1] & Howell to "carry us off" – the latter didn't come but Val work[ed] admirably; a grunt set him going and a roar approved him. Gabriel was very kind, and received the points of his friends' tempers in the side of his own.

Ned & Georgie are quite as well as can be expected. I bore them on Tuesdays, but they kindly put up with it, & I was there yesterday to help with Burton[2] & Crom Price.[3] Crom, I think, betters instead of worsens, as is not usual with absentees. I can only see a difference in his lobs, by their coming slower than they used to do.

Taylor is very anxious to run a tilt at Howell with a Sheriff's officer, but I am just going to write to him to stop any hasty burst of that kind – as I don't think we have any right to expect Howell to change his manners and customs – for us, particularly. We knew what he was before allowing him to draw on us.[4] I say Top, dont have this letter in your pocket, and drop it in his garden.

Ellis[5] has very politely made me a present of "Speed", see what comes of being allied to poets but he also good natured like, sold me at what he gave for it, that large 4 vols of serpents bugs & beetles – (wh' I daresay you know) – for me to give to the 2 Neds,[6] for Phil is a "chip" indeed.[7]

We thought last night of collecting a hundred pounds to send out to you, for you to make a proper appearance at the green cloth table,[8] if one is allowed at Ems. Janey might make "eyes" at the people & break the bank. Sing out in your next letter, at my broad-wheel'd waggon wit if it is unbearable. We are here 72° in the shade today, & it has been much the same for some time. If you are hotter I hope you bear it with some ease, and this puts me in mind of drink – what do you drink? – Janey, of course, water, sandwich fashion with every act of her life, but intermittently, you must both try something stronger, what is it?

I am a Father to the shop,[9] and go in there as a fine protecting spirit making a touch here & speech there to vindicate my character, 'tis slightly a "do" but as they don't laugh in my hearing, what does it matter. If I could hear both yours I would forgive it, if it were against me.

Your affectionate | Phil Webb:

BL Add 45342, ff. 9-10

---

1 The personable Valentine Cameron Prinsep (1838–1904), son of Henry Thoby Prinsep and Sara Monckton Pattle (patrons of the society portraitist, George Frederic Watts), was amongst the group of painters who assisted DGR in decorating the Oxford Union debating hall in 1857.
2 The Irish-born watercolour painter, Frederic Burton (1816–1900), became director of the National Gallery in 1874, and received a knighthood in 1884. He supported EBJ's 1864 election as an associate member of the Old Watercolour Society.
3 Once schoolboys together in Birmingham, EBJ and Cormell ('Crom') Price (d. 1910) remained life-long friends. Price is best-known as the first headmaster of the United Services College at Westward Ho! in Devon in 1874, where he oversaw the education of the young Rudyard Kipling (a nephew of GBJ). He encouraged the young writer, who portrayed 'Uncle Crom' affectionately as the headmaster in *Stalky & Co* (1899). Late in life, Price married his housekeeper (he was 60, she 32), and they named their son Edward William, after EBJ and WM.
4 WM and PSW were less easily taken in by Charles Augustus Howell than some in their circle (see above, Letter 18, note 1). Although WM had been a witness at Howell's marriage, 'he became disenchanted, perhaps at the point at which Howell had invoked Morris's authority to trick Warington Taylor into letting him have wallpapers at a special discount price.' MacCarthy, *WMLT*, p. 218.
5 WM's friend and publisher, Frederick Startridge Ellis (1830–1901), was an author and dealer in antiquarian books and manuscripts. Later, with JM and Sydney Carlyle Cockerell (SCC, 1867–1962), he was one of WM's executors.
6 PSW seems to be referring to two different books. 'Speed' may be John George Speed, *The Borderer's Leap, and other Poems* (London: E. Stock, 1869); the four-volume collection has not been identified.
7 Philip (1861–1926), the elder of the two surviving Burne-Jones children, was aged seven.
8 The gambling table.
9 In 1865, the Morrises gave up Red House and moved to 26 Queen Square, living above the office and showroom of MMF & Co.

27 • To William and Jane Morris, 3 August 1869

1 Raymond Buildings Gray's Inn
Tuesday. Aug 3.

Thank you very much dear Top & Janey for your letter of Saturday – got last night. That you are there, is something – that you are not worse is more – let me see if I've virtue enough to allow me to preach – no I haven't – therefore I won't. I like your soberness of style in your letter dear Top. It is as if God were laying on the stripes and you changed your tone from "damn" to "whee! Whaa! 'tis all my fault". There is no doubt, Janey in the corner on the sofa, is thinking of the "provincial" people she has left behind.

I will open your letters, keep your secrets, & send only those wh' require your own attention and tie the rest up in a bundle for future amusement.[1] I'll make inquisition about the cruets you mention and do what I can – the soup plates I'll take when I can get them, as a "retainer" from you both & what is more, will make an effort to deserve 'em.[2] You know that it has been said, that repentance is the only chance for a chap.

Dear old Taylor has written to me to say that he will be quiet, but speaks feelingly as a father to our finances. I think from his letter that he must be a shade more in spirits. I've heard of Bodley that there is great doubt as to whether he will ever use his leg again – crutches being thought of.[3]

Like Gabriel's parrot[4] I find myself going, with a "humm – whoo!! whoo!! whoo!!" for I miss the sound of poetry – you'll test our eyelids when you come back. If Acontius has laid Cydippe on her back I hope he hasn't, you.[5]

I hope you got a letter of mine ~~from~~ at Poste Restante Cologne – and one wh' was addressed from here last Saturday – Poste Restante Ems 'Nassau' – they would have been dry chips, but they would put you in mind of the fellow you keep alive by your letters.

Day's poor Mother came looking after her son yesterday & Wardle & I did what we could – and it now remains for Day himself to have a try.[6]

The Lord Chamberlain was a little to[o] late in clothing the legs of the Drury Lane beauties.[7] Janey ought to pick me up a tune from brass bands at 90°. You'll be able to absorb the music of the future along with the water – and I shall scarcely be able to say Mozart – before you batter my brains out with Wagner. However they are not gone yet for I still think of you both.

Phil Webb

BL Add 45342, ff. 13-14

---

1 '[W]ill it give you too much to do to open any letters for me; if there were any secrets between (as there are not) you would hardly come across them'. WM to PSW, 31 July 1869, *CLWM*, I.

2 '[W]ill you ask Wardle to send round and ask Lucy Brown if the soup-plates and delft cruets came safe to hand – the soup-plates are for you if you care for them – the cruet bottles have had tops to them – I think: Could you get Barkentyne to fashion these again; if you think it a fitting end to them – if not silver mounted corks would do I suppose though not so well – I bought them and the plates in Ghent on Georgie's birthday and meant them . . . for her – will you give them to her with my love when what is necessary is done'. See next letter, note 3.

3 For Bodley, see above, Letter 1, note 7. He was left very lame after an illness during 1868–9.

4 At Cheyne Walk, DGR indulged his fascination with animals and birds by maintaining a small but exotic menagerie in the garden. William Rossetti would recall that, during the years after 1863, his brother's collection included such esoteric specimens as armadillos, kangaroos, a racoon, a deer, several varieties of non-native owls, an African grey parrot (the talker noted by PSW), chameleons and salamanders, as well as more standard pets – dogs, mice, rabbits and the like. One of the most

charming of DGR's sketches is a self-portrait of him weeping over the upturned body of his pet wombat. See Jan Marsh, *Dante Gabriel Rossetti. Painter and Poet,* London: Weidenfeld & Nicolson, 1999, p. 267 (the drawing is reproduced between pp. 242 and 243).

5 While he was away, WM worked on 'Acontius and Cydippe' for the forthcoming third volume of *The Earthly Paradise.*

6 Unidentified, but Day may have been an employee of MMF & Co.

7 Allusion not identified.

28 • To William and Jane Morris, 10 August 1869

1 Raymond Buildings | Gray's Inn.
Aug. 10.

My dear Topsy & Janey.

This is the first letter for you that I have got.[1] The first glance without further reading shewd me – that it was poet's work, and must be delivered at once or the world would "smoke for it". I read the prospectus and grinned a broad, & cheerful grin – and you may thank both your stars that during your absence, there is any grin on my face. Ned don't help me to grin, Georgie don't either and I don't help them neither but we've made up our minds to do nothing else than grin during the remainder of our term.

Instead of a quick hob a knob at Fulham we meet tonight at cheerful Poynter's.[2] The scoundrel Barkentin is engaged upon the cruets to be done in ab[t] 3 weeks, cap to be this [*sketch of top of jug, with* 'German silver' *indicated*] without any rim to the top edge of jug. The cruets are very pretty – I've not got my soup plates yet.[3]

Ellis rec[d] me with a guffaw the other day upon the subject of the length of <u>nets</u> hung on the banks of upper Thames wh' we did not take proper note of – the length of bottle & countenance being our fist.

I hope your harvest is better than ours. We have a wet one, though the weather is often pleasant enough though cool – now, 4. Oc in the afternoon & 62°. Ask Janey to put a female scratch at the end of your next letter, just to keep [me] in mind of her fingers ends. My cheer is the usual and D[d] – B[d]. The buildings clients and architect, all, ought to be drinking the waters, at a depth of 20 feet, with a fireproof safe hung to their necks, to sink & save 'em.

Ned rather talks of going to have a day or two in Crom's Folly[4] – but is waiting to know if the coast is clear enough. Boyce, M[c]Donald[5] & an actor named Belford have aired the place just now – but there are sweetening gales in those parts.

My most affectionate love to you both. | Phil Webb.

BL Add 45342, ff. 11-12

---

1 The letter (now lost) which PSW forwarded was from Edward Nicholson, an undergraduate at Trinity College, Oxford. WM responded on 12 August (*CLWM*, I), but Nicholson's plans for an undergraduate magazine came to nothing.

2 The painter Edward John Poynter (1836–1919) married GBJ's sister, Agnes Macdonald (1843–1906), in 1866. He was appointed director of the National Gallery in 1894, succeeded John Everett Millais (1829–96) as president of the Royal Academy in 1896, and became a baronet in 1902.
3 See previous letter, note 2. Barkentin & Krall, 'Goldsmiths and workers in all metals', had premises at 289–291 Regent Street. The co-founder, Jes Barkentin (c. 1815–83), was a Danish-born silversmith.
4 Between 1866 and 1874, Crom Price rented The Tower, a 65-foot high folly on Broadway Beacon in Worcestershire, dating from 1800, where friends visited frequently. EBJ signed the visitors' book for the first time on 22 August 1869. See Lorraine Price, 'Cormell Price Esq., The Tower, Broadway', *JWMS*, V, (Winter 1983–4), pp. 30–9.
5 Probably GBJ's brother, Frederic Macdonald, a Methodist preacher regarded by Rudyard Kipling, his nephew, as 'the wit of our family'. *MacCarthy, LPR*, p. 394.

29 • To William and Jane Morris, 17 August 1869

1 Raymond Buildings Gray's Inn
August 17. 1869.

My dear Top & Janey:

Thank you very much for your two last letters. When reading them I burn to answer, but before I've sighed over the recollection of their contents business & idleness come in & stop one. As it is well as you say to get over the root of evil at once, I say that I was pleased that you depended on me in the matter, and as I thought it would save us all trouble, I cashed a cheque of my own at Praeds' and they sent me to Coutts's for the enclosed letters of credit for 60£ wh' I hope you will get all safe & that the form will be convenient.[1] You & Janey will give me great pleasure if you will take them as a little present from me, and as expressing only a bare outside of my affection for you both.

As I was returning from Coutts's I turned in to wet my whistle with a glass of "cocks eye" and stumbled with dew dropping mouth, on Gabriels familiar – Dunn[2] – who told me that <u>he</u> came <u>there</u> to cheer himself after packing off Gabriel to Scotland. Dunn said, Gabriel was pretty cheery as no doubt Dunn would be in time, if he cocked his eye sufficiently.

Since you hint at amusing contents of the Oxford poet's letter I wish I had read it. Keep it in mind to amuse on return.[3] I'm glad the <u>work</u> proceeds.[4] 'Tis the best cure for weariness. I'd turn-to ^{with a will} on mine if I could do it, when I did turn-to. I say Top, don't sit down on wet green banks. I've the Rheumatism in my shoulder now from a soft wet draught at the back of my neck, taken carelessly. But the adders will keep you out of that mischief. O Lord! How frightened I should have been.[5] I'm pretty kind to beasts as a rule, but the serpent tribe – all except the innocent worm – put me in a mortal terror & therefore make me cruel.

Ned or Georgie will no doubt write to you that the former is gone to Crom's Tower.

Out with you Janey. If you'll make your first presentiment come true, I'll insure that the second shan't.[6]

I've finished my Clarissa – 'tis, after all is said – a very fine, notable book,[7] and I can't for the life of me call it prolix, if once it has the character of merit at all, as its accuracy is its chief merit. I do not envy the jackass who could set himself ~~down~~ to reduce it.

Taylor came down upon me on Friday and stayed talking for 2 hours or more – he spoke very nicely about you, put all upon his affection, wh' I believe to be true.[8]

I've to write 2 or 3 more letters before post therefore break off – not before wanted, you'll say.

Your affectionate | Phil Webb:

BL Add 45342, ff. 15-16

---

1 'The root of all evil, is, if not *the* root yet one of the roots of this letter, lets get done with that first. I want to make myself safe from being kept in pawn, and set to hard labour at Ems (say sweeping up horse-dung, an office religiously observed here,) I want £60 somehow; I suppose Wardle will be able to let you have it; if not would it strain your resources to be so kind as lend it me'. WM to PSW, 15 August 1869, *CLWM*, I.

2 The painter, Henry Treffry Dunn (1838–99), was DGR's studio assistant until they quarrelled in 1880. His unpaid salary was settled only after DGR's death.

3 'Ah hah! the letter you sent me wasn't sent on for nothing. Janey got a pain in her back from laughing at it; I hope you read it right through.' WM refers to the letter from Edward Nicholson (see previous letter, note 1).

4 'I also brought Paris' Death to an end roughly; again I'm not very sanguine about the merit of it; but I shall get through the work I set myself to do here in some way, and have a month to turn over the first of the tales before I go to press when I come home.' WM to PSW, 15 August 1869. 'The Death of Paris' appears in the third volume of *The Earthly Paradise*.

5 '[T]he adders are lively too in this wet warm valley: yesterday morning I heard a rustle in the dry leaves behind me and out crept one as long as my umbrella. . . . I kept feeling the legs of my trousers all the way home after that, and feel a little shy of sitting down on green banks now; however they are always wet.'

6 JM added a note to the letter of 15 August. 'I have a sort of presentiment (though of course you don't believe in such things) that I may make a rapid turn – and feel myself well all of a sudden – and then I have another presentiment that should this change come – all those I now call my Friends would also change – and would not be able to stand me.'

7 *Clarissa* (1748), Samuel Richardson's long epistolary novel tells the story of its tragic heroine, Clarissa Harlowe. 'What a glutton at reading you must be to get through C.H in such a short time; I have done but little more than half of it, though certainly I never found it a tiresome or dull book nor, if one takes it on its own grounds, even prolix.' WM to PSW, 20 August 1869, *CLWM*, I.

8 'What news of Taylor again?' WM to PSW 9 August 1869, *CLWM*, I.

30 • To William and Jane Morris, 24 August 1869

1 R: B: G: I. London
Aug 24. 1869.

Dear Top & Janey

Let me begin by saying, bother to all matters wherein "tin"[1] is concerned. It is a pitch which can't be touched without defiling. Gold is never sweated half so much as it drains us of nerves-water, and I'm sorry I should have made your flesh creep.[2]

With regard to Taylor you need not be afraid that I shall give his dicta more than their due value.³

I hear that Ned came back yesterday and as this is Tuesday I go up to look at him this evening. I'm rather tired of standing on one leg – my own peculiar – in London, a second at Ems – and the third in Crom's tower, and shall be glad when they are drawn together again within reasonable compass. The devil will be in it, if one quarrels with ones limbs even if they be the devil's own.

I've two little bills for you when you come back and they are the only love letters of yours come to hand, since the Oxford genius's.

Wardle was here this morning, report satisfactory – he was at Cambridge yesterday. Young Scott seems to be dancing a professional hornpipe at Peterhouse to which he wants us to pipe.⁴ I'm going to talk to Ned about it to night to see what can be arranged. Shall be cautious.

Was at Ken︐ Mus︐ on Saturday – thought the room interesting & pretty – somewhat comic in character but happily not much galvanized.⁵

I like your telling of the landscape at Ems. It might have been ᵘᵍˡʸ b̶a̶d̶ ᵗʰⁱˢ ʷᵒʳᵈ ᵗᵒᵒ ˡⁱᵏᵉ ᵃ ʷᵒʳˢᵉ ʲᵒᵏᵉ & that you wᵈ have had to take exercise with shut eyes. You'll surely make use of it for future seasoning to your trifles of 20,000 lines? I hope Gabriels parrot has a better memory than I have, for I've nearly forgotten the sound of verse – wh' ⁽ˢᵃⁱᵈ ᵛᵉʳˢᵉ⁾ luck has made a kind of brine or pickle to my mind to keep it from stinking.

Brown looked in 2 or 3 nights since, smoked & drank and talked most amiably – and went with the nicest steps, over the sore points of my vanity. There must have ᵇᵉᵉⁿ 'ozone' or something in the air in large quantities – he even volunteered to allow of the Brumagem⁶ ᴮʳᵒᵐʷⁱᶜᵏʰᵃᵐ door-knocker character of <"Teb"> in mind & body.⁷

My rheumatism, hangs about my shoulders in harmless fashion still – bless my soul – I said just now that I'd forgotten the sound of verse. The truth is, Janey I believe <u>I'm</u> a poet also. If this don't make you both laugh nothing I can write will. Therefore do laugh.

Yʳ affeᵗᵉ | Phil Webb.

BL Add 45342, ff. 17-18

---

1 Money: the term was much used by DGR.
2 WM had received the notes of credit which PSW had enclosed with his letter of 17 August 1869, but refused to accept them as a gift. 'I think the money will be much more equally divided by your keeping it, than by your casting it on the dry and thirsty ground of a ne'er-do-well – the best of thanks all the same for the offer, and for the trouble of getting & sending the money.' WM to PSW, 20 August 1869, *CLWM*, I.
3 'Taylor is better then, I hope? I hope he don't think I am seriously vexed at any thing he has said, or otherwise than very much obliged by his friendliness: I think I understand the whole matter

perfectly well; and know there is a great deal of reason in what he says, though he is not at present quite master of the details.'
4 George Gilbert Scott Jr (1839–97) was the eldest son of Sir George Gilbert Scott, and like him an architect. He was responsible for the restoration works at Peterhouse, Cambridge (1866–70), for which MMF & Co designed the stained glass windows and decorative tiles in College Hall and the Combination Room (1868–74).
5 MMF & Co's first important secular commission came from the South Kensington Museum in 1866, for the decoration of the Green Dining Room. PSW planned and supervised the project, the frieze being his design 'modelled in relief with a dog chasing a hare, based on a sculpture he had seen on the font in the cathedral of Newcastle upon Tyne'. *Kirk*, p. 46.
6 PSW seems here to use the term in both of its meanings, suggesting something cheap or counterfeit, and also alluding to Birmingham.
7 Allusion not identified.

31 • To George Howard, 26 August 1869

1, Raymond Buildings, Gray's Inn, | *London,*
Aug 26 *1869*

Dear Mr Howard.

I take it from Mrs Howard's letter to me of the 17th that you are now in London, therefore I send this to Park St.[1]

I have to go out of town tomorrow (Friday) but shall hope to be back the same night, but at all events not later than Saturday morning.

Mr Taylor, the foreman at Palace Green, was here this morning and I told him that you would most likely be here – and would be looking in at the house. I wished him to settle with you in which room you would prefer having the Dutch tiles fixed.

If you think they would be a too shocking "lark" in the drawing room, they – or part of them – could be used in the dining room or Library fireplaces – in the last – perhaps – only.

I hope you will find the house as comfortable as you expected. Please to name to Taylor any alterations or additions you would like made. The work up to the present time has been admirably done.

Please to let me know if you would like to see me, and if <u>here</u> or elsewhere and I will arrange.

[Yours very truly | Philip Webb:]

Howard

---

1 GH's maternal grandparents were the late James Parke, Baron Wensleydale (1782–1868) and Celia Arabella Francis, Lady Wensleydale (d. 1879), whom he married in 1817. Their London house was 122 Park Street, Grosvenor Square.

32 • To George Howard, 7 September 1869

1, Raymond Buildings, Gray's Inn, | *London,*
Sep 7 *1869*

Dear Mr Howard.

I will go to the house one day this week and see what can be arranged for your sending furniture to be stowed away – at present I fancy that the lady's maids rooms would be drier and more out of the way than any other – but a watchman would have to be provided as soon as you put anything into the house which is not the contractors – this, however, could be done without difficulty – & fires could be kept up by the watchman.

I quiver with fear when I think of the risk I have run of meeting, such tremendous celebrities at Naworth. Well did my mother preach to me, that work kept people out of trouble & mischief – only fancy my concentrated ignorance "cheek by jowl", with that compendium of knowledge "Browning", & in a country house too![1] But seriously, I am sorry to be obliged to say no, to such kind reiterations of hospitality.

It is most probable that the Cortachy work will keep me here, until I am obliged to go there.[2] With kind regards to Mrs Howard.

[Yours very truly | Philip Webb:]

Howard

---

1 During September, the guests at Naworth Castle included the poet Robert Browning (1812–89) and his friend the American sculptor and writer, William Wetmore Story (1819–95), his wife, Emelyn, and their daughter, Edith, later Edith Peruzzi (1844–1907). See *Surtees*, pp. 77–9.

2 In 1868, PSW was asked by David Ogilvy, tenth Earl of Airlie (1826–81), who married Rosalind Howard's sister, Henrietta Blanche Stanley (1830–1921), 'to consider the feasibility of building a new country house on the site of the old family seat, Airlie Castle [near Kirriemuir, Angus, in Scotland], destroyed by the Campbells in 1640, and an alternative one of improving and enlarging its substitute Cortachy [Castle] – an ancient rectangular tower to which a wing, stair tower, and porch, all in the Castellated Gothic style, had been added in the early nineteenth century.... He produced designs for both schemes between 1868 and 1869, after warning Airlie that the costs would inevitably be high.' *Kirk*, p. 182. PSW estimated £50,000 for the first scheme, and £36,000 for the second: only then did Airlie reveal that his budget could not exceed £25,000. Having been asked to make reductions, PSW had to insist that Cortachy could not be enlarged within that smaller figure, although a separate scheme for repairing a turret and enlarging the library was completed. Airlie did not proceed further, and paid PSW £600 for the designs and work which had already been undertaken. 'Lady Airlie was pleased with the library but she added to Webb's distress, after his second scheme for enlarging Cortachy – over which she had enthused – had had to be abandoned, by putting it about that she disliked it.' (ibid). As Kirk remarks, this experience led PSW to treat his clients with much greater caution, requiring that they should agree to his terms of business before he accepted their commissions.

33 • To William Butterfield, 27 November 1869

Draft/copy

1 R: B: G: I:
Nov. 27 1869

Dear Mr Butterfield

I was at Oxford yesterday for the first time since I got the permission to look over your college[1] – Mr Braithwait was very polite & took pains to shew me the works.

You were quite wrong in supposing that I should not like the buildings. I like them very much indeed. I admire the general arrangement, the planning, the proportions and details.

If my own work bears no resemblance to yours it is because I could not do good work like yours and therefore I do not try, but I am quite capable of observing with huge pleasure a successful effort of a contemporary – (please excuse the impudence of this last remark)

I take it that on looking round the neighbourhood of the college you saw that there was an activity of life in building w^h though you might not relish the out come – it would be wise in you not to ignore, & thus came your idea of planting a vigorous red brick work in Grey Oxford. I wish that Kebles own work had been as vigorous.

The skill you have shewn w^h I wish most to praise, is that of having managed to put together the requisite little boxes of rooms and yet that your building should not look small – and this without the advantage of the larger parts, such as Library, Hall & Chapel. I think you are quite right in your large Quadrangle and in pushing the East front close to the trees – both bold ideas.

I cannot forgive you for using cold blue slates, this colour is a real drawback. You will most likely say that you had no money for grey Westmoreland slates, and I shall say in answer, 'tis a great pity that you hadn't.[2] The contrivances of Scouts rooms, cisterns, lifts, stairs, sliding "Oaks", paving &c were interesting and I thought quite good.

If in these days of dolour the mocking of a new peel of bells could be allowed – I should rejoice that you should have a hand in keeping up the tunefulness of Oxford and of adding yet another tower to the view from Hinksey.[3]

Believe me to be | Yours very truly | Philip Webb:

P.S. I tremble for the filling up of a yawning gap on the South side of Lower High S^t.

LPW

1 An enthusiast of the Gothic Revival, William Butterfield (1814–1900) was the architect of Keble College (1868–70), named after John Keble of the Oxford High Church movement.
2 'I of course feel with you about the blue slates . . . .A low tender helped me much, but the Committee was bent on economy and was composed of persons who did not I imagine care for the question of colour in slates, and I had not the courage, with further works in prospect for wh. I knew there was not enough money, to ask them for any extras of an artistic kind.' Butterfield to PSW, 11 December 1869, *LPW*. PSW was not alone in expressing reservations about the chosen materials. In 1872, Charles Eastlake felt that 'the horizontal bands of stone, of black brick, and of white brick, oppose each other so crudely that . . . one can see nothing but stripes.' *A History of the Gothic Revival*, p. 262. For details of this book, see next letter.
3 Hinksey Hill, two miles south of the centre of Oxford, affords a fine view of the college spires.

34 • To Charles Eastlake, 14 March 1870

1, Raymond Buildings, Gray's Inn, | *London,*
March 14 *1870*

Dear Sir,[1]

I should have much pleasure in complying with your request[2] did it not break a rule which I've had some satisfaction in keeping, up to the present time – viz – not myself to make unnecessarily public any work which I've designed or completed.

I should have been less able to have refused your polite proposal, if my work could have properly come under the category of the "Gothic Revival in England"

Yours truly | Philip Webb

LPW

1 The architect and furniture designer, Charles Locke Eastlake (1836–1906), was appointed director of the National Gallery in 1878. He was researching for *A History of the Gothic Revival: an attempt to show how the taste for mediæval architecture which lingered in England during the two last centuries has since been encouraged and developed* (London: Longmans, Green, and Co., 1872).
2 'I am very anxious to obtain authentic information regarding the most notable buildings of a mediaeval character which have been erected during the present century. May I venture to hope that you will kindly assist me in this endeavour by supplying me with a few brief notes on the principal works which have been executed from your design?' Eastlake to PSW, 10 March 1870, *LPW*.

35 • To Fanny Warington Taylor, 19 July 1870

1, Raymond Buildings, Gray's Inn, | *London,*
July 18 *1870*

Dear Mrs Taylor[1]

I enclose you the memorandum of acc^ts and I think you will find it correct.

You will see that Morris & Co have paid me the balance of acc^t as I told you I should arrange with them to do – that is to pay to Warington Taylor an extra quarter's salary. The balance paid by Morris & Co is £63.7.9 wh' leaves a balance due to me from you of £26.11.3 – but I should much prefer that you should consider me ^{as} paid, and allow me to bear this small cost in memory of my poor friend.

I am sorry to hear that you are unwell – ~~though~~ this continued beautiful weather is trying to many people, & may acc^t for it.

Believe me to be | Yours very truly | Philip Webb:

Account rendered by Mr Webb, of payments made & received by him for Mrs Warington Taylor, with accompanying vouchers.

[*Here PSW lists various funeral expenses and payments to Mrs Warington Taylor, paid by him*]

	£89.19. 0
Rec^d of Morris & Co the balance of acc^t with Warington Taylor	63. 7. 9
	£26.11. 3

V&A, NAL MSL/1958/691/108-9

---

1 Widow of George Warington Taylor. It is evident from this letter that, despite his reluctance to act as a trustee (see above, Letter 17), after Taylor's death PSW responded extremely generously on his behalf.

36 • To George Howard, 17 August 1870

1, Raymond Buildings, Gray's Inn, | London,
Aug 17 1870

Dear Mr Howard.

Thank you very much for the grouse, though I prefer the letter very much to the birds. The letter certainly mixed up friendliness & business – the business I will attend to, but how can I make a return for the sacrifice of the delights & laziness at Naworth in writing to so fearful an old fogy? This letter can be no return for I am bound to write it.

My "Imperial hero" has fallen, & I fancy not all the imperial horses & men can set him up again.[1] I hope you are prouder of France, than I am of the "lost one"! I still think, that till now, France has been well served by Napoleon. The French must look out for some other dictator, for they evidently have no head to manage their own affairs themselves.

I am very glad that you liked "our Mr Morris" – if stroked the right way, the beast is tame enough for practical purposes.[2]

Thank you again for your inquiries at to my well doing. London is not so bad a place when empty, the 3 millions run on pretty comfortably, and if they are hot, they take their handkerchieves [*sic*] and wipe their faces, and go on again, with the delightful expectation, of town once more being full, when serene happiness will take the place of dull care[3] – but apart from joking, I am glad that you don't look with much horror on the time of your return. You will no doubt laugh, when such a being as myself, says that he has a pleasing recollection but I distinctly remember the few days spent at Naworth as delightful & most enjoyably lazy.

I will look after the organ, and the organ hole, at once.[4]

[Yours very truly | Philip Webb:]

Howard

---

1 Napoleon III (Louis-Napoléon Bonaparte, 1808–73, Emperor of the Second Empire), had suffered French defeats against the Prussians. The 'imperial horses & men' is an allusion to the children's nursery rhyme, 'Humpty Dumpty': 'All the kings' horses and all the king's men / Couldn't put Humpty together again.' For PSW's later, modified view of Napoleon III, see Vol. II, Letter 351, note 3.
2 WM had holidayed at Naworth with JEM and MM, his daughters striking Rosalind Howard as 'the cleverest little things I ever knew'. WM read to the Howards from *The Earthly Paradise* 'most beautifully'. See *Surtees*, p. 87.
3 'Begone, dull care! / I prithee begone from me' (*Anon: traditional*).
4 See below, Letter 46, note 5.

37 • To George Price Boyce, perhaps December 1870

Annotated 'Dec 70?'

1, Raymond Buildings, Gray's Inn, | London,
Tuesday 1. Oclock

My dear Boyce

I am altogether in the dark as to what you mean, all except the thoughtful kindness wh' made you send me the note just rec[d].

We may be able this even[g] to have a few words in a corner, wh' may do away with any awkward feeling wh' may have arisen from any carelessness of speech either on my part or yours – if there is evil about in the air, it was probably brewed by me; for I find that when I get out in the evening, (sometimes) with kindly disposed friends, my natural melancholy departs, and I am merry & thoughtless enough, or more than enough, to create disagreeable mistakes by the dozen.

Please to believe me that I should deeply regret that even a careless word of mine should give you pain, much more that I should say or do anything of malice or forethought wh' should hurt – but this latter is I hope impossible.

Thank you again for your note.

Yours very truly | Philip Webb:

Good God! To think that while that heaven sent music was going on, any other than heaven sent thoughts should be in our hearts.

BL Add 45354, ff. 30-1

1864–1887

38 • To Alexander Ionides, 26 December 1870

Draft/copy

G[ray's]. I[nn]. Decr 26. 1870

Dear Aleco Ionides.[1]

I shall have much pleasure in doing what I can for you at Walton.[2] The only difficulty, at present is that I am barely my own master, as this weather keeps me close ᵃᵗ home – however I am daily hoping to get about.

I enclose a letter for Ashby & Sons (your brother's builders) wh' you can either post or take to their office – wh' is close to you in the City, and make your own appointment. Friday would be the safest day for me.

I had better tell you ~~at once~~ that it will cost very considerably more if Ashby's ~~did~~ ᵈᵒ the work,[3] than if some local builder (say a Kingston ~~bui~~ man) ~~did the work~~ undertook it – tho' Ashby's would, of course do it much better.

Believe me to be | Yours very truly | Philip Webb:

V&A, AAD

---

1 Alexander (Aleco) Ionides (1840–98), son of Alexander Constantine Ionides (1810–90), the businessman and art collector for whom PSW made substantial alterations to the interior of 1 Holland Park, Kensington in 1879–83 and later.
2 Ionides wrote from Southend about a cottage at Walton on Thames, 'which if you will kindly lend me your assistance, I believe will realize all the wishes I had. I have only seen it once & then hastily, but I think that with very little work it would become one of the prettiest little places I have seen'. Ionides to PSW, 25 December 1870, *V&A, AAD*.
3 The builder, Richard Ashby & Sons of Bishopsgate, had undertaken a rear extension designed by PSW for Aleco Ionides's brother, Constantine, at 8 Holland Villas Road, Kensington (1870). See *Kirk*, p. 298. Ashby was also the builder for 1 Palace Green, Kensington.

39 • To Robert Chamberlain, 20 February 1871

1, Raymond Buildings, Gray's Inn, | *London,*
Febr. 20 *1*871

Dear Chamberlain,[1]

I have put off answering your letter with the hope of finding something to tell you of in the way of help, but I can think of none. Your advance on Butterfield was unfortunate. I think only that. But it seems to me that you had better try him again, by letter, and you may say that I have promised you to call & see him if he would like it & tell him what I think of you. This I shall be pleased to do. I would write to him openly saying that it is absolutely necessary for you to get regular work – and that harder work & less well paid under an architect whom you respect, would be preferable to easy work in most offices.[2]

Thank you for openly explaining your circumstances to me.[3] I can manage to let you have 20£ to help you pay off your debts, (the worst item of your trouble) on the only terms on w[h] I lend money, viz. to pay again if you can, but if you can't not to trouble about it.

If your Father can afford to let you have the allowance, I do not see why, so long as you really need it, you should not take it, for of course you would be only too glad to do <u>without</u> taking it.[4]

If you like you may say to Butterfield that you have asked my advice & that I recommended you to apply to him again. I suspect his work would be irksome – but if it is, straightforward & honest habit will soon make it less tedious but behind all is the devil of "impecuniosity" w[h] should be met in as manly a way as possible.

Yours v[y] truly | P.W.

LPW

---

1 Not identified.

2 Chamberlain had written of his failure to obtain an architectural clerk's position with William Butterfield. 'The fact is I <u>must</u> get work in some office without any more delay. If it cannot be in one I like; temporary employment would be most pleasant while I was looking for some other. Can you do anything with anyone you know to help me? Terms (I think) not less than £2:10: a week, tho' I would take £2. from Butterfield – or less, if he would at any rate be civil till I <u>was</u> his clerk. . . . I took no introduction & probably began in a rather shoppy way. . . . I said I'd called to ask if he would be so good as to remember me when he should be in want of a clerk – if I was likely to suit him. He turned sharp round on me with "So good as to <u>remember</u> you Sir! Why should I do that? when I know nothing of you." . . . [I]t ended by his saying he had others in view when he wanted assistance.' Chamberlain to PSW, 11 February 1871, *LPW*.

3 '[L]et me add that my Father allows me £75 or if necessary £100 a year, indicating at the same that I ought to be independent. Also that I owe about £75: a good part of which I ought to pay off this year.'

4 'I made up my mind to take your advice when I asked it, and will do as you say. . . . For your offer of help . . . I shall always thank you most heartily, but at present, if I get work I think my debts are well in hand.' 23 February 1871, *LPW*.

40 • To George Howard, 20 February 1871

1, Raymond Buildings, Gray's Inn, | *London,*
Feb 20 *1871*

Dear Mr Howard.

I will get the new stalls put in hand as soon as possible[1] – some care will be required to secure good ventilation &c.

We just missed each other the last time I was at Palace Green, for I think I saw you riding home after I left.

I have a greater repugnance than ever to having my portrait painted and not even my vanity – which you have shocked by the request – will make me sit – and besides it is too late.² What little shew of nobleness my face may have had in youth, is quite gone now, through my own bad temper & the worse temper of the Metropolitan Board of Works, evil living, & bad company, & old age (premature).

I will look in upon you on the first opportunity.

[Yours very truly | Philip Webb:]

Howard

---

1 For stabling at 1 Palace Green, presumably, and perhaps not unconnected with Rosalind Howard's new horse. 'I shall hope to like the look of him, and to believe that he will be safe for you – if he be tame – his 5 years only will be an advantage but perhaps I am writing to a horsewoman superior to effects of temper in a horse. I've only seen you riding the Eastern beast with long ears.' PSW to Rosalind Howard, 18 October 1870, *Howard*.
2 GH's fine sketch of PSW in profile, dating from the 1870s and reproduced as the Frontispiece to the present volume may well have been done surreptitiously.

41 • To George Price Boyce, 14 April 1871

1, Raymond Buildings, Gray's Inn, | *London,*
April 14 *1871*

Dear Boyce.

You cannot but have eased your sense of obligation to me by writing your kind letter, because you must have known, that kindness is the thing above all others wh' repays – in fact is the only thing which can repay me for any effort I make for another. Now let me relieve you still more by quite honestly explaining myself.

When you asked me to do your house for you, I was uncomfortable, as I always am at doing work for a personal friend, and I would not have done it at all, if I had seen a graceful way out of it – however as that could not be, I did the work as well as I could – not so well as it should have been done, and I believe could have been done by someone else – and it has only been your delicate kindness which has kept ᵐᵉ from feeling even deeper disappointment than I do.

Now please to try & get rid of any sense of obligation to me. You are under none rightly, none whatever – you gave me no more trouble than was absolutely necessary, and less than I expected you would, and you express a contentment, more than I usually get from my clients.

I will send you the original, signed sheet of plans with pleasure, for you to keep – and if you ever return architect¹ you may copy it put one of your own windows in it à la Pecksniff,² and spoil it & build it 20 times over without admonition from me.

I thank you for being quite sure that I could not have been content with any more than my legal payment. For the generosity of your offer to send me a memorial of your good nature, I can only thank you, and bear the thoughtful kindness in mind – really never forget it. For the "Rossettis" I cannot receive one,³ and for any work of yours I shall look forward to give you a commission, when I have the money, to do me something – that may strike me – in the way wh' only you can do. Please let the matter remain like this, and believe this letter to be faithfully honest.

I think I shall try to hear "Israel in Egypt" on Wednesday next at S[t] James' Hall. Would you care to victual with me there & go?⁴

Yours very truly | Philip Webb:

BL Add 45354, ff. 34-5

---

1 GPB trained as an architect before devoting himself to painting.
2 Dickens's creation, the sanctimonious and hypocritical architect Mr Pecksniff, takes on Martin Chuzzlewit as an architectural apprentice, and sets him as an exercise the task of preparing plans for some 'proposals for a grammar school'. Martin produces a skilful design, which Pecksniff later passes off as his own more, merely adding four windows which manage to destroy its proportions. *Martin Chuzzlewit* (chs 6 and 35).
3 GPB would give him DGR's *The Meeting of Dante and Beatrice in Paradise* in 1885. See below, Letter 267.
4 St James's Hall opened in 1858, and had frontages on Piccadilly and Regent Street. There were two restaurants. Handel's oratorio *Israel in Egypt*, performed on 19 April, was advertised as one in a series of 'Oratorio Concerts', and involved 350 choral and orchestral performers.

42 • To William Reid, 20 April 1871

1, Raymond Buildings, Gray's Inn, | *London,*
April ~~19~~ ²⁰ *18*71

Dear Sir

Arisaig House¹

The spring of drinking water at Arisaig House has been analysed, and it has been found that sewage or other poisonous matter finds or has found its way into the current w[ater] cistern.

Lord Abinger² – one of the trustees to the late M[r] Astley – has directed me to advise and obtain an estimate for providing a supply of drinking water ⁱⁿᵗᵒ ᵗʰᵉ ʰᵒᵘˢᵉ wh' shall certainly be free from contamination.

I think the best way would be for you to send to Arisaig some competent man who ~~will~~ ᶜᵒᵘˡᵈ look into the matter carefully, and who ~~will~~ ʷᵒᵘˡᵈ be able to advise as to the most economical and effectual way of supplying the water, either from ~~catching~~ ᵗᵒᵘᶜʰⁱⁿᵍ the spring at a higher level or from taking water from somewhere else.

I have a feeling that it would be best to hit the present spring somewhat higher up, as I know the spring to be a constant one. Upon your mans returns I should be glad if you would send me an estimate for laying on the fresh water in enamelled iron pipes to the basement – and for cutting off the present supply, or rather for securing that no more water shall be taken from it.

[*sketch plan*] The ^present^ spring supply ~~now~~ is taken at A in the basement of house. I think now it should be taken at B outside the Kitchen yard and carried to the basement ~~as~~ in iron pipes as above.

I shall be glad to hear from you on the subject.

Yours truly | Philip Webb.

Mr Wm Reid.

V&A, AAD

---

1 William Reid was the plumber engaged when PSW built Arisaig House (1863–6), in Arisaig, Inverness-shire, together with its adjacent stables and farm buildings. The house was commissioned by the colliery owner Francis Astley (1825–68), once a member (like PSW) of the defunct Hogarth Club. See *Kirk*, pp. 104–11 and 296, and also below, PSW to WW, 4 October 1901, note 8.
2 William Scarlett, third Baron Abinger (1826–92).

43 • To Jane Morris, June–July 1871

Annotated 'Watermark 1870.'

1, Raymond Buildings, Gray's Inn, | *London,*
Saturday

Dear Janey.

I thank you very much for your pleasant letter. I had not forgotten that you were gone from these parts, though my not having written or sent the design for [the] cushion, might have made you think that I had – but I am a poor letter writer, and also a lazy man with much to do.

Your description of Kelmscott with landscape on one side of the river at least, is quite true it is naked & plain, but with all that I still think it has a great deal of character, at least it has that look to me, and the river makes up for the want of variety.

I have almost forgotten Lechlade church but I remember going up the steeple on to the parapet, and making out that it was built late in the 14th century, and that it was very pretty.[1]

I looked in W. Rossetti's life of Shelley and the following is there said – "At the end of August, (1815) Shelley, with Mary[,] Peacock,[2] & Charles Clairmont,[3] went in a wherry towards the source of the Thames beyond Lechlade in Gloucestershire. The beautiful 'Lines in Lechlade Churchyard' were the result."[4]

I almost quite agree with you about the effect on one's mind, wh' Goethe's works have, namely that of a theatrical unreality, but then after the outward effect is gone, there remains a huge reality behind; not often a pleasant one, seldom in fact a pleasant one, but nevertheless fearfully true and therefore enchaining. I do not think I am ever happy when reading Goethe.[5]

I am most glad that you are stronger, so as to be able to get about.[6] If you could manage to get your handyman Comely[7] to hire a tax cart[8] and drive you over to Uffington you and Jenny & May could crawl up to the White horse hill and enjoy a delightful look round.[9]

I send you by book post the design for the cushion wh' I hope you will like.[10] I have coloured in the pattern over my first drawing, how I think it would look well to be worked – but you need not let the colours bind you.

Love to Jenny & May and affectionate regards to you | from | Philip Webb:

BL Add 45342, ff. 21-2

---

1 'I have been to Lechlade, I want to ask you about the church there. Is the spire as old as the church itself, and do you happen to remember if Shelley was living in the town at the time he wrote his poem in the churchyard.' JM to PSW, June-early July 1871, *CLJM*. She was writing on the occasion of her first visit to Kelmscott Manor.
2 The satirical novelist, Thomas Love Peacock (1785–1866), author of *Headlong Hall* and *Nightmare Abbey*, was one of the closest friends of Percy Bysshe Shelley (1792–1822).
3 Charles Gaulis Clairmont (1795–1850), Mary Shelley's stepbrother.
4 William Rossetti, *Memoir of Shelley* (London: 1870), pp. lxxx–lxxxi. The text from which PSW quotes reads: 'At the end of August, Shelley, with Mary (always called Mrs Shelley), Peacock and Charles Clairmont *etc*'; PSW omitted the words in parentheses, and the comma which followed them, leading the editors of JM's letters mistakenly to suppose that PSW was referring to Mary Peacock, not born until 1820. *CLJM*, p. 46, note 2. A civil servant in the Excise Office until his retirement in 1894, William Rossetti (1829–1919), younger brother and future biographer of Dante Gabriel Rossetti was also a prolific art critic and editor. He was secretary to the Pre-Raphaelite Brotherhood, editing its short-lived magazine, *The Germ* (1850).
5 'I have nearly finished "Elective Affinities." I think with all due respect to Goethe it is a most unsatisfactory book. What! is nothing real? Must everything that is delightful change and leave nothing behind? I can't believe it; one begins by liking his characters very much, then they change, and one can no longer look upon them as real people.' JM to PSW, ibid. She was reading J. A. Froude's English translation of Johann Wolfgang von Goethe's *Elective Affinities* (London: Henry G. Bohn, 1854).
6 'I am already so much better that you would scarcely recognise me. I have actually got some suspicion of red in my face – am feeling quite a different creature, I get down to breakfast comfortably with Jenny and May at half past eight.' JM to PSW, ibid.
7 Philip Comely was the caretaker and his wife the housekeeper of Kelmscott Manor.
8 Two-wheeled horse-drawn cart, subject to a tax.
9 The White Horse on the chalk hillside at Uffington in Oxfordshire, dating from the Bronze Age, was a favourite haunt for both WM and PSW, and the place where SCC and W.R. Lethaby (WRL) would scatter PSW's ashes on 10 July 1915.
10 'I shall never dare ask you for any design again. I had not expected anything half so elaborate or beautiful, thank you very much for it. I shall work it carefully in fine wool on blue serge I think, taking care to get different shades of blue for the flowers.' JM to PSW, 25 July 1871, *CLJM*.

1864–1887

44 • To Dante Gabriel Rossetti, 29 July 1871

1, Raymond Buildings, Gray's Inn, | London,
July 29 *18*71

Dear Gabriel

I send by ~~book~~ ^pattern^ post the patterns of paints. The green, is said by the painter who made it, to be an exact match of the lighter parts of that in your dining room, the white~~s~~ & reds are such as I should use with alterations for different circumstances.

The little frame which Dunn shewed me could have an eighth of an inch cut away all round the sight opening with but little injury to the frame this would give you a quarter of an inch more in width & height. For the little pillars I would replace those wh' seem to have belonged to it, and look fairly well.

I was at No 16 yesterday and ^found^ no Brass at work. I met him in the street on Tuesday & he promised to begin on Wednesday morning last. I think you had better send him an eloquent letter, to dim the lustre of his countenance.[1]

There is an old fellow at N° 4[2] who keeps snakes by the hundred, from Lillebut [*sic*] size to ^that of^ him who could crush an elephant. One of the snakes four feet long (so tis said) got into the garden of no 6, and gave the workman a dinnertime's hunting, but without result. Who can ever ^again^ unbutton with ~~ease~~ ^comfort^ in any garden within 2 miles of the house? The price of broken bottles for topping the walls of the neighbourhood is going up.

Yours | Philip Webb.

Texas

---

1 Lot Brass, a builder, was engaged by DGR to undertake minor repairs at 16 Cheyne Walk, under PSW's supervision. 'I have taken your advice, & written strongly to Mr. Lot Brass, who must be more brazen than his namesake Samson if he is not shamed into action by my objurgations.' DGR to PSW (written from Kelmscott Manor), 31 July 1871, *CDGR*, V.
2 4 Cheyne Walk was formerly the home of the artist Daniel Maclise (1806–70), and was where George Eliot spent her last weeks in 1880, but in 1871 it appears to have been occupied by the antiquarian William Sandys Wright Vaux (1818–85), a fellow of the Royal Society. If his various interests included keeping snakes, it is not recorded.

45 • To Heynes Hardwicke, 14 August 1871

Draft

1, Raymond Buildings, Gray's Inn, | London,
Aug 14 *18*71

My dear Hardwicke[1],

~~Your~~ ^To get a^ letter ^from you^ was a bigger surprise than if anyone had gratuitously given me a hundred pounds, & was a pleasanter gift. I cannot ~~help you~~ ^accept your proposition^

47

though, mores the pity, as you have troubled so kindly to write to me – but I'll try to explain.²

My business ~~(of wh' I have as much as I can do)~~ ⁽ʷⁱᵗʰ ʷʰ' ᴵ ᵃᵐ ᶠᵃⁱʳˡʸ ᵉⁿᵒᵘᵍʰ ˢᵘᵖᵖˡⁱᵉᵈ ᵃᵗ ᵗʰᵉ ᵖʳᵉˢᵉⁿᵗ ᵗⁱᵐᵉ⁾ consists chiefly in trying to put up buildings in this country wh' shall be free from art vulgarity – no easy matter this – & with all ᵐʸ care I do not succeed too well; but I have only succeeded as well as I have, by strictly avoiding the attempt ~~by 1ˢᵗ to give people generally what they want 2ⁿᵈ~~ of ᵗʳʸⁱⁿᵍ ᵗᵒ satisfy~~ing~~ the wants of the great majority of people in the way of architecture. There are some few people who think it worth ᵗʰᵉⁱʳ while ~~putting~~ ᵗᵒ ᵖᵘᵗ up with my fancies on account of something wh' pleases them, after all, in my work – but this is quite apart from the fashion of the day or commercial advantage.

Now a place like Bournemouth depends much on the fashionable character & commercial value of its buildings, & to wh' everything else must be subordinated in the art of building – whereas, the art of building as a fine art, must just reverse this order of things.

Supposing that I was so unwise as to go contrary to my ~~ideas~~ ˢᵉᵗᵗˡᵉᵈ ᵛⁱᵉʷˢ, & ~~undertake to~~ attempt to assist your friend, I should be doing him an injustice, for I could not do so well for him, as even an inferior man, who was experienced in the ways of the place ~~and~~ ᵒʳ ⁱⁿ the manners & customs of such places generally.

Please take it kindly that I am thus open with you, ~~as~~ I ~~thank~~ take it as very kind ᵒᶠ ʸᵒᵘ that you should have thought of me at all.

With kindest remembrances to Mʳˢ Hardwicke. Believe me to be your sincere old friend.

Philip Webb:

V&A, AAD

---

1 Heynes Roger Hardwicke (1815–1901), medical officer of health. He lived at Saxlingham Nethergate, Norwich.
2 Hardwicke had written about a potential new project in Bournemouth. 'Building is going on rapidly at B. Mr Durrant tells me he is now about to dispose of land in the very centre of the Town for public buildings &c. I mentioned your name again & he said I was at liberty to tell you that Crick was no longer his man and that there is a splendid opening for a clever fellow as Architect at B. If you entertain the least idea of doing anything there & wᵈ like to come down here I will introduce you to him.' Hardwicke to PSW, 11 August 1871, *V&A, AAD*.

46 • To Rosalind Howard, 30 September 1871

1, Raymond Buildings, Gray's Inn, | London,
Sep 30 *1871*

Dear Mrs Howard.

You will remember an old proverb "Tis an ill wind" &c, now an ill wind has blown Ned & Georgie away and cleared London of other good folk, but it has blown me a letter from you, to make amends. The letter has somewhat of a semblance of saying, "Well, if the best are away, I must put up with the inferior" however as proverbs are afloat, I may say, "tis rude/unwise/stupid to look a gift horse in the mouth".[1]

Ned went off alone to Italy about a fortnight ago, much wanting a change.[2] Georgie went to her sister in Worcestershire,[3] when they will be back, the fates and the purses provided, only know.

Morris is returned from Iceland after a most successful journey; he is in London, having just come back from Kelmscott.[4]

If to dinner at Palace Green be quite quiet, I will come to you with pleasure on Tuesday, but if not I would prefer to call on you & see how you all are.

Would it not be well to let Mr Ferguson (the architect) make arrangements with Mr Lewis for the organ.[5] The architect should know what it best, though sometimes (I speak from experience) they have to make believe that they do.

With kind regards to George and Sir Charles Howard[6] | [Yours very truly Philip Webb:]

Howard

---

1 In Rosalind Howard, PSW had his first experience of 'a client's wife who took as keen an interest in every aspect of the new building [1 Palace Green] as her husband. He stood up with spirit to [her] domineering manner but consulted her about interior details and fulfilled her requests whenever he considered them wise. They soon became good friends.' *Kirk*, p. 73.
2 Out of sorts and depressed, EBJ arrived in Turin on 21 September, spending about three weeks travelling in Italy. He had decided to leave England at short notice, with a minimum of fuss, though GBJ was upset. She wrote to Rosalind that 'I can write of nothing else, and disappointment is an unlovely theme'. *MacCarthy, LPR*, p. 224.
3 GBJ's youngest sister, Louisa, married to Alfred Baldwin. See below, Letter 54.
4 For WM's Icelandic journeys, see below, Letter 57, note 4.
5 For the Carlisle architect, Charles John Ferguson, who would succeed PSW as architect to Naworth Castle, see below, Letter 104. The Howards may have been planning to transfer an organ from Naworth to 1 Palace Green: 'I took the measurements of the organ-case opening the other day'. PSW to GH, 14 August 1871, *Howard*.
6 GH's father. See above, Letter 7, note 3.

47 • To George Price Boyce, ?autumn 1871

Annotated 'Autumn 1871?'

1, Raymond Buildings, Gray's Inn, | *London,*
Saturday

Dear Boyce

Thank you for your letter. I thought you had buried yourself and were rejoicing at your success. I'm half inclined to fancy that if I should take you at your word and appear in Ludlow Street, next week, you would mutter "damn the fellow, can't he take a civil letter as if it was meant, & stop away" but as I have great pleasure in paying people out for professing to take an interest in me when they really do not, you had better look out, and bolt if wise.

I've a case in point – some stranger to me wrote some time back, for a design of mine for some buildings, after considerable care of thought, I send them. I hear this morning that he is much obliged, but that some of the design he does not like, and the rest is unsuitable. So I shall send him in (with great glee) the highest possible charge I rightly can – but all this is not apropos of your politeness for I believe if I can come down, you will be very glad to see me.

If I should come (this week) it will be somewhere ab^t Tuesday or Wednesday but you need in no way put yourself out, for the "Feathers" will no doubt hold me beautifully.[1]

Thanks for the photograph – as Carlyle w^d say, the coach maker should be "more particularly damned".[2]

For myself I have been working slowly and unsteadily, and as you see from the foregoing, to little purpose. I've been much pleased to see Beresford Hope[3] & Ld Elcho[4] sit upon themselves and Ayrton on the top of that, flat.[5] – And the "Lords" too, but I'm afraid your fingers are already in your ears or eyes.

I'll look after Boyd – I gave him orders to prepare a stove in the rough, some time since, but I've not done my part of it.

Music, I've had none – not even the blackbird in my neighbours window, for he has left off singing, and is having his throat relined, for it must have been worn as thin as a wafer. There, I'll have done with this rubbish, and will bend my mind to think of hoping to leave, for 2 or 3 days, this earthly paradise in Middlesex.

Yours | Philip Webb:

BL Add 45354, ff. 38-9

---

1 Featuring a striking seventeenth-century timber façade with motifs of ostrich feathers, Ludlow's most famous building was built in 1619 as a private house. It has long served as an inn, and was named 'The Feathers' in 1863.

2 A precise source has not been traced, although in a letter to his wife (1 October 1852), the historian Thomas Carlyle (1795–1881) picks up some of her words: 'Driven out of the house again, and sleeping solitary in a little lodging! I declare it makes me quite sad to think of it; and --, if – is the fundamental cause of it, deserves to be, as you say, "particularly damned".' Cited in James Anthony Froude, *Thomas Carlyle: A History of his Life in London, 1834–1881* (London: Longmans & Co, 1884), p. 117.

3 Alexander James Beresford Hope (1820–87) was a politician, journalist and influential proselytiser for Gothic revivalist architecture. He was President of the RIBA in 1865–7.

4 Francis Wemyss-Charteris-Douglas (1818–1914), styled Lord Elcho from 1853, and from 1883 eighth Earl of Wemyss and sixth Earl of March, was at this time Conservative MP for East Lothian.

5 Acton Smee Ayrton (1816–86), Liberal MP for Tower Hamlets, was First Commissioner of Works, in which government position he demanded that major public spending should be constrained wherever possible, but also was sure-footed in advancing his pet projects. On 14 August 1871, the *Pall Mall Gazette* carried the report of a House of Commons debate and Beresford Hope's failed attempt to move a resolution critical of Ayrton's approval of a new road in St James's Park, which Beresford

Hope called an 'inconceivable act of subordination. . . . Mr. Ayrton replied that . . . there was, perhaps, nothing more remarkable than the mistakes which men fell into when they were carried away by feelings of personal hostility, increased by a sense of humiliation and defeat'. Lord Elcho entered the fray the next day, commenting on Ayrton's incivility. 'Regarded from an artistic point of view, his appointment to the post of First Commissioner of Works was most incongruous and astounding.' Ayrton deftly brushed Elcho aside. 'For his own part, he did not profess in a loud tone to have a profound knowledge of every question relating to art. . . . and he would therefore confine himself to the assertion that he perhaps knew as much of these subjects as the noble lord did. (Much laughter)'. *Pall Mall Gazette*, 15 August 1871.

48 • To Charles Augustus Howell, 9 November 1871

Draft

1 R.B. G. I.
Nov[r] 9. 1871

Dear Howell

In answer to your letter rec[d] ~~this afternoon~~ yesterday ~~I will~~ I should be glad enough to lend assistance ~~to~~ [in] settling ~~matters~~ between you and Mess[rs] Dunn – for ~~they the matter~~ certainly should be settled, but I will not attempt to do so, unless you will allow me to produce to Mess[rs] Dunn all the memoranda you enclosed with your letter to me, and also ~~your letter~~ so much of your letter [to me] as relates to [your] dealings with them.[1]

I should think the torrent of virtue poured on you by the "Vox populi" whether worldly or spiritual, need not disturb your serenity, seeing that the article of virtue in any form, [(according to wise-heads)] is a useful one to be assumed even if we have it not.

For myself, with regard to you – ~~I say one~~ I have said ~~very~~ ~~little~~ in public [next to nothing], ~~& in private~~ & to myself but little more. Except that [I thought that] you did not know when you were well off, or if you did know, did not care.[2]

The habits of my life and its surroundings would make it impossible for me to get on well ~~with~~ in your society – ~~and~~ I have always held it best, to live in quiet good nature with as many as possible and to do that ~~one must have no reason to~~ [one has to live apart from a good many in order to] avoid ~~a~~ [stupid] failure.

I am yours faithfully | Philip Webb.

C: A: Howell Esq

V&A, AAD

---

1 Howell was in dispute with the builders, Samuel and Samuel Dunn, of Brewer Street, Golden Square, who were pursuing him for unpaid money, and as PSW employed the firm for some of his own work (they were currently completing repairs under his direction to the church of St Dunstan, Hunsdon in Hertfordshire), Howell sought his advice. The fault and prevarication probably lay all on Howell's side, despite his pleas for sympathy. 'I find myself accused of crimes I never committed, some of them being really old stories of the time of Queen Anne, and the Georges, quite spoiled

by being badly dressed in shoddy, and thrown on my poor shoulders.' Howell to PSW, 5 November 1871, *V&A, AAD.*

2 'What Mess[rs] Dunn may have said to astonish you I do not know, the only – to me – astonishing thing in the affair is the bill itself, and the letter which I enclose. On the other hand let me say that I am heartily sorry if the fact of my having been unable to meet this bill at the time it was sent in has caused you the least annoyance. Believe me or not, I would do very much to please you, and suffer much to save you pain.'

49 • To Charles Fairfax Murray, 26 November 1871

Annotated 'Nov 26/71'

1 Raymond Buildings | Gray's Inn.
Sunday.

Dear Murray[1]

I went in to Ellis's yesterday to ask him to come to me on Wednesday evening at 7. oc. to victuals and meet you & Morris – but he told me that he thought you might be obliged to say no. I hope you can get into a cab at your door and out at mine, and I will pack you off again in the same way at good time. Try & come if you think it right, as I should like to see you go before you go to "happy land".[2] I fancy that by shutting the sash down of a Hansom you need not fear – and as you must be proof against all other diseases, perhaps a closed cab would be as good as your own room, and your company would soften our manners.

I am indeed sorry that fate is pegging at you so, but, somehow envy you your way to Italy.[3]

Come if you possibly can to yours, | Philip Webb:

Fitzwilliam 3

---

1 Early in his career, the painter, art connoisseur and collector, Charles Fairfax Murray (CFM, 1849–1919), undertook copying work of various kinds for DGR, EBJ, JR and WM. His personal life was complicated, for as well as marrying an Italian girl in 1875, with whom he had six children, he also raised a family in London with Blanche Richmond (d. 1952). He continued to visit his Italian family in Florence, whilst also maintaining a house in London. His complex domestic arrangements came to light after his death, when his legitimate Italian children disputed the will, and SCC spent considerable time advising his English son, Arthur. CFM was generous in gifting paintings and manuscripts from his collection to the Fitzwilliam Museum during SCC's early years as Director.

2 Italy.

3 During this first Italian trip of several months, CFM began the close studies which resulted in his detailed technical understanding of Italian paintings, based on 'painstaking examination of hundreds of works of the great masters allied to an extraordinary visual memory'. *Elliott*, p. 36. JR wrote 'with somewhat mortified respect of my friend . . . as knowing more in many ways of Italian pictures than I do myself . . . [E]very picture he buys for you is a good one'. *Fors Clavigera*, letter 79, in E.T. Cook and Alexander Wedderburn, *The Works of John Ruskin*, XXIX (London: George Allen, 1907), p. 155, note 3. JR described him as 'a heaven-born copyist'. *Elliott*, p. 43. In 1885 PSW commissioned from CFM a copy of Carpaccio's *St George and the Dragon* at the Scuola di San Giorgio degli Schiavoni, in Venice. See below, Letter 253.

50 • To George Price Boyce, 22 August 1872

1, Raymond Buildings, Gray's Inn, | *London,*
Aug 22. 1872

Dear Boyce

I have to go to Shrewsbury on the 27th (Tuesday next) and ~~that~~ on my way back I could look in on you – but, it also occurs to me that possibly you might like to join me on Wednesday morning at Shrewsbury and that we might take a cart and go & look at Wroxeter (is not that the Great Roman Station?)[1] then to Buildwas Abbey & back by Wenlock Abbey[2] & Acton Burnell[3] to Dorrington on the Shrewsbury & Ludlow line.[4]

The round would give an embarrassment of riches, but the wealth would not injure us, I hope.

Possibly you have seen all these, or probably your work ties you to Ludlow, & you could not give the day – in either case do not hesitate to say that it would be inconvenient.

You could leave Ludlow by the 10.14 am train for Shrewsbury & hear of me at the "Raven" on Wednesday morning ab^t 11.30.[5] We could spend ½ an hour in looking at Shrewsbury & then journey away as above.

Let me hear, but in no case inconvenience yourself. | Yours | Philip Webb:

BL Add 45354, ff. 45-6

---

1 The village of Wroxeter in Shropshire, on the River Severn, is the site of Viroconium Cornoviorum, the fourth largest Roman city in England. Excavations had begun in February 1859, and Charles Dickens was an early visitor.
2 Buildwas Abbey, a ruined twelfth-century Cistercian abbey, is situated on the Severn not far from the ruins of Wenlock Priory, a Norman foundation of Cluniac monks. See also below, Letter 85.
3 Near the Shropshire village of Acton Burnell are the ruins of Acton Burnell castle, a thirteenth-century fortified manor house.
4 Opened in 1852 on the Shrewsbury and Hereford Railway, Dorrington station closed in 1965.
5 The Raven Hotel in Castle Street, Shrewsbury, was demolished in 1960.

51 • To Jane Morris, 7 September 1872

1, Raymond Buildings, Gray's Inn, | *London,*
Sep 7. 1872

Dear janey

I was very glad to have your letter, because it was written without my asking for it – and I very much wish to have your confidence in my sympathy (if you think it would be worth anything).[1] By "sympathy" I do not mean to express anything more than a wish that you – an old friend – should find a comfort in liking me, and being liked by me and that no real untruth sh^d pass between us, and as little mistake in expression as possible.

Of course I know the strength of resource in despair, well enough – that is, the willingly cutting oneself off from the help of any one, so as to avoid the risk of being deserted by them – but, "nothing venture", you know – well, one must venture in friendship, for such a thing to be possible; and, assured friendship is very beautiful, and at times deeply soothing in the mere belief in it.

I send 3 books, not at all knowing whether you have read all or any of them. I've not seen Topsy to ask him.

Very much should I like to come to Kelmscott again, and will try to do so, if you stay much longer. The last visit, on arriving, did give my soul a twist, wh' I hope my face did not express, as it was quite unavoidable (i.e. the unfortunate circumstance). Like a fool I stayed in my damp shoes at Kelmscott, and have had a return of Bronchitis, slightly, wh' still hangs about me. I spent a day & a half free from business in Shropshire last week, and rather enjoyed going to the Roman station Uriconium, [sic] (Wroxeter) – Buildwas, Much Wenlock and Acton Burnell – all very interesting places, specially the Roman one, for, I cannot resist (& don't try) the effect of looking on these strange visible expressions of long past life.

To see twenty miles of Roman ruins in Italy would be trifling, but as many yards of the same in this northern place, is entrancing.

Yours affectionately | Philip Webb:

BL Add 45342, ff. 23-4

1 Although the letter has not survived which prompted this notably sensitive response (and also the letter following), JM's turning to PSW at this time was prompted by DGR's mental collapse and probable suicide attempt in June 1872. 'Many friends blamed his infatuation with [her] for this.' *CLJM*, p. 49, note 2. It is touching to see PSW's refusal to rush to judgment. He wanted Jane restored to health and happiness no less than he wished for the peace of mind of her husband, his closest and oldest friend, though it is hard to see how both outcomes were equally achievable.

52 • To Jane Morris, 12 September 1872

1, Raymond Buildings, Gray's Inn, | London,
Sep 12. 1872

Dear janey.

Thank you for your letter, wh' is simple & straightforward, to my minds content. I do not think I misunderstood your former letter, for I had no idea that you would think it worthwhile to tell me a lie, any more than I would really lie to you. There is something in human nature, pure & simple, wh' touches me closely, and when I see any one clinging to the natural parts of life, I feel much inclined to become one of their friends. This is not often, as you know. So many things come between a human being & simplicity, and so few can resist the inter attraction.

I have always taken a great interest in you, and none the less that time has tossed all ^of us^ about, and made us play other parts than we set out upon. I see that you play yours, well & truly under the changes, and I feel deeply sympathetic on that account – for, my ~~old~~ own tumbles are not so absorbing that I cannot attend to the tumbles of those who are wrapt about, with the pains of life wh' are not ignoble.

Please believe that I, in no way wish to penetrate into sorrows wh' I can in no way relieve. I, from my own self, know the impossibility of two people bearing one's burden.

Yours affectionately | Philip Webb:

BL Add 45342, ff. 25-6

53 • To Rosalind Howard, 17 September 1872

1, Raymond Buildings, Gray's Inn, | London,
Sep 17 1872

Dear Mrs Howard.

Your letter gave me real pleasure, for though I can manage to steel myself against offers of friendship pretty well, any resuscitation of what has looked in passed times to be real good nature, always overpowers me – is irresistible – and so, your kind letter coming after such persistent silence & in itself seeming to be so full of spontaneous good nature, beat down my natural defence, and has laid me open to the possibility of finding one of these days that I have been mistaken. This is pride, mere pride, is it not? but then one has a right to one's pride, as much as to the shape of one's nose and no amount of education will get rid of the latter, without destruction.

I rejoice that you acknowledge that you are a "hum bug" for a portion of your time, for the mere acknowledgment shows that it oppresses you to be it. In fact I think you do better, and look better, when you are quite honest – i.e. it "becomes you".

Your notice of the effect of your scepticism interested me very much; but what I should like to know, is, if you ever believed? Also, do you not think it quite as difficult to be sure of what you disbelieve, as to what you believe? I think you might perhaps have answered your friend the organist by saying that you were not certain of your disbelief and therefore did not attempt to help others into the same difficulty.

I am afraid you will have some difficulty in teaching your boy that injuring live things is not beautiful; I believe that the love of injuring is deeply ingrained in humanity, and that all interference will be mere education, to be washed away with change of fashion. In myself there is a strong natural bent that way, and, perhaps only the advocacy of such an advocate of sporting as Anthony Trollope makes me look upon it with disgust, & keep it down.[1] This education however is self education & therefore the best of that matter. Let me return you your quotation "Lord what fools these mortals be".[2]

I met Colvin the other evening & he told me he had been with you & had had wet weather.[3] I am sorry for you, tho' I think you wise to brave it and make up your mind to enjoy even the bad weather. The heavy grey clouds & driving wind must be very fine on your lovely hills for, lovely they are, though so far north, and if it were not for my habit of making & keeping to "shallow excuses" I would come and look upon them (the hills) with you.

Your own self-addressed birds came this morning and at same time a letter from George, to say that they were all right &c. Thank you very much for them, though your letter was the more delightful. You <u>must</u> have enjoyed your laugh (I even did myself) at my writing to remind and then to send me a present.[4]

Please to forgive the rudeness of this scrawl, & write me a lecture (for education's sake) when you have time and inclination.

[Yours very truly | Philip Webb:]

Howard

---

1 Trollope contrived to include extended fox-hunting scenes in many of his novels, even when incidental to the plot.
2 Puck, in *A Midsummer-Night's Dream*, III.ii.115.
3 The fine arts critic, Sidney Colvin (1845–1927), like GH a graduate of Trinity College, Cambridge. Through his close admiration of the work of EBJ, he was drawn into that circle of friendships, which also included DGR, WM and Robert Browning. Colvin was appointed Director of the Fitzwilliam Museum in 1876, and Keeper of the Department of Prints and Drawings at the British Museum in 1884. He was an occasional guest at Naworth Castle.
4 'Some time since, 3 brace of grouse were sent to me from the north, and I wrote and thanked a friend of mine for them; this was a bad shot of mine for he had not sent them to me, but he took my letter as a reminder & sent me some birds later on; since then, another friend has sent me birds and now I think all have sent who usually do send; so that I may safely label you with the first gift of 3 brace; you ought to be ashamed of yourself for not letting me know that you were doing the kind turn, so that I might have avoided one blunder in my life.' PSW to GH, 13 September 1872, *Howard*.

54 • To Louisa Baldwin, 15 December 1872

1, Raymond Buildings, Gray's Inn, | *London,*
Dec.[r] 15. 1872

Dear Louie.[1]

I am not sure that it is pleasant to be quite forgotten ^{even} by ones enemies, but I am quite sure that it is very delightful to be remembered by ones friends.

Thank you & Baldwin, very much for your kind invitation.[2] I cannot come to you just now but I intend to come when it is possible for me to do so.

For many years I have gone to my mother at Oxford at X[t]mas time, and should do so this year is she were in better health; but, she has taken to her bed and I think will never be able to leave it – however, as she is over 80 years of age this is not wonderful. When this X'mas engagement is broken through, I think I shall please myself by never making another, as I so much prefer, seeing my friends when I can, even at a moment's notice, ~~than~~ to looking forward to the pleasure, wh' ~~is so often~~ ^{may end in} disappointment.

I have often to go northward and north westward on business, and if it would not be unpleasant to you & Baldwin I sh^d be glad on one of my journeys to turn out of my way, & stay a day with you, after giving you due notice of my coming? I say, a day, but I sh^d like to stay a week, though this, as time has gone for years with me, seems quite impossible.

The last time I saw Georgie, she was looking very well. Agnes I have not had the pleasure of seeing for a long time.

With kind regards to Baldwin | Believe me to be | Yours very truly Philip Webb.

V&A, AAD

---

1 Louisa Macdonald (1845–1925) was the youngest of the four celebrated Macdonald sisters: her eldest sister, Alice, was mother of Rudyard Kipling; the second eldest was Georgiana (Georgie), who married EBJ; Agnes, who was closest in age to Louisa, married the painter Edward Poynter who became Director of the National Gallery in 1894. In 1866 Louisa married the Stourport industrialist Alfred Baldwin (1841–1908). Their only child, the future Conservative Prime Minister Stanley Baldwin (1867–1947), succeeded his father as MP for Bewdley in Worcestershire in 1908. PSW probably came to know the Baldwins through his friendship with GBJ.
2 Louisa wrote to PSW on 12 December, from Wildern House, Stourport, inviting him for Christmas Day, 'or failing that between then and New Year's day'. *V&A, AAD.*

55 • To Charles Fairfax Murray, 18 March 1873

1, Raymond Buildings, Gray's Inn | London,
Mar. 18. '73

Dear Murray

You brought me last evening the most graceful as well as the most delightful present you could have made me – namely, the portrait of my life's friend.[1] In sending you 10£ I only wish to recognise the value of ~~the~~ ^{your} gift in a way that cannot intend that such a gift should even appear to be repaid, only that my present shall cost me some thing, to shew my gladness. The mere money will defray (perhaps) the cost of the antiquarian's print but cannot in any way represent the value of the gift.

Yours, in the flesh you have kindly laboured to represent, | Philip Webb:

Fitzwilliam 4

1 CFM's fine watercolour portrait (Tate Gallery, London) is one of the very few known images of PSW, and therefore much reproduced. None of the few surviving photographs of PSW are formal poses, and were usually taken without his knowledge, most of them late in his life. It is therefore surprising that he should ever have agreed to this portrait, but despite himself seemed pleased with the outcome.

56 • To Charles Faulkner, 26 May 1873

Draft/copy

1. R.B. G.I.
May 26 '73

My dear Faulkner,

Thank you for your very kind letter of Saturday.[1]

I cannot but admire your boldness, your quite wonderful courage. Supposing it possible I could agree to undertake the work in question, if it were offered to me, and that I succeeded in building it. Your life in Oxford would be simply unbearable for ever afterwards, and I do not know if you could quite escape obloquy if you spent the rest of your natural life in Wagga Wagga.[2]

In the second place therefore know my deep aversion to having any hand in turning exceptional Oxford into a place of ordinary architectural expression – well, my mind is in no way changed, since I said to you that I never w^d help in that way.

There is great improbability that any committee w^d think of allowing me to try my hand at a design, and even if it did and I was so far lucky as to moderately satisfy myself, I am quite sure that I should never satisfy anyone else, except perhaps, Morris.

There is only one architect living who I think could do something w^h w^d not seriously hurt Oxford and who w^d be capable of carrying with him some opinion more extensive than that of himself and one dis-honourable friend (this friend will be here in half an hour & I'll tell him what I've said) and that is Butterfield.

So, accept my very sincere thanks and forgive any seeming rudeness | from yours ever | Philip Webb:

LPW

1 'Yesterday convocation was called on to approve of designs for new Examination Schools prepared by John O. Scott (a son of GGS) but convocation by a large majority rejected and sat upon the designs, & this I think they deserved. . . . I hope that opinion may now prevail that it will be better to appoint a committee to select an architect . . . [without the university] reserving to itself any right of subsequent approval or rejection. If such a committee were appointed and were to crawl up the steps of No 1 Raymond Buildings on their knees, would you kick them out or would you consent to entertain the idea of making designs for these examination schools? I know you dislike Oxford

being pulled about and still more of having anything yourself to do with the matter. But this is a case of necessity. We must have a building and it does seem as if we might as well have a decent one while we are about it.' CF to PSW, 24 May 1873, *LPW.* For the Examination Schools, see also below, Letter 169.

2 Now the largest inland city in New South Wales, Australia, Wagga Wagga grew rapidly between 1850–70 from a small village to the size of a modest town. PSW's point here is to suggest a location almost inconceivably removed from CF's Oxford.

57 • To Charles Fairfax Murray, 6–17 July 1873

1 Raymond Buildings Gray's Inn.
July 6. '73

Dear Murray

From one of your own natural instincts you will have allowed exactly for the cause of my not writing – idleness to wit. I was very glad to have both your letters – the first of date May 7 – & the second of June 1. I cannot but think that a blessing has been laid on your black-haired head, and that often you must shake it with intense satisfaction, that the fates laid it, for once, in such a bed of clover.[1] I assure you that the evil sights, smells, and associations of London, have in no way changed for the better – so that you may comfort yourself during any time of depression with the certainty of your better surroundings.

When you had last the tingling of vexation, at your hindrances in getting to see what you had to see at Rome, you must have had great satisfaction also, that for once, railways had been made for one useful purpose – that you had been able to use them for it in particular. Your liking or disliking the Sistine ceiling pictures w^d have all depended on your way of having thought of them. I sh^d not easily forgive myself if they disappointed me at first sight. The quantity of saffron colour in them, of wh' you speak, does not surprise me – and the white being a pale blue one also seems to me to follow naturally. Would it not be possible to make a tracing of one of the photographs and try and fill in the colour of one of them it would not take long in that way, and it would interest me immensely?[2]

July 17 – 4 pm. There, you see when this letter was begun & you see the new ending – unless I send it off in 10 min time, you will <u>never</u> hear from me.

In case <u>no one</u> has written to you I will just say, that Mr Jones is much better, I suspect the over stimulant of wonderful Italy is just subsiding, for I've heard him calling for more of that liquor.[3] Mr Morris is I suspect at this moment leaving the embraces of the chaste "Diana" & preparing to pickle his bottom on the Iceland poneys.[4] [*sic*] Mr Rossetti is I believe flourishing.[5] For myself – well! here I am! With my bottom thoroughly pickled by my usual chair, or, if it is not, it will be, by continued use for at least 12 months to come – I've expended a pound or two more on some photographs of MAB[6] over which I dream, and try to believe that there is "such such person" or has been.

I think of you often, and always with that kind of pleasure, wh' you know human nature will take, in seeing unworthy persons receiving the rewards of merit wh' properly belong to the sigher. Dear Murray, write to me if it is no trouble, and only expect an answer from me when it is no trouble to me to write.

May the shadow of your hair never be less, | Yours sincerely | Philip Webb:

Phil & Margaret [Burne-Jones] & Jenny & May all flourish, so also flourishes the birch rod.

Fitzwilliam 7

---

1   He means CFM's being in Italy.
2   In January 1885, PSW would eventually see the Michelangelo Sistine frescos for himself. Meanwhile, he relied on photographs and the reports of others for his impression of the impact of these works.
3   Towards the end of his protracted affair with Maria Zambaco, EBJ left for the last of his visits to Italy, in April 1873. His companion for the first few days was WM, on this his first Italian journey, but on 13 April WM started his return trip from Florence. EBJ continued to Siena (where he met CFM, himself on his way to Rome to make Botticelli copies for JR) before travelling to Ravenna, where he developed a fever. 'Returning homewards at Bologna, he collapsed for several days, delirious, having to abandon his plans for Umbria.' *MacCarthy, LPR*, p. 249.
4   WM and CF made two trips to Iceland, the first in 1871 in the company of the Icelandic scholar Eiríkr Magnússon. They embarked on this second expedition in early July 1873, transported once again on the Danish mail boat, *Diana*. PSW's thought of WM on horseback was perhaps prompted by EBJ's sketch inspired by the previous trip, reproduced in *MacCarthy, WMLT*, p. 294.
5   DGR was living at Kelmscott Manor at the time, and had recovered much of his strength since his collapse of just a year earlier (see above, Letter 51, note 1). During these years he painted JM many times.
6   Michelangelo Buonarroti (1475–1564). The earlier mention in this letter is evidence enough to reveal the reverence in which PSW held the work (particularly the sculptures) of Michelangelo. Amongst other masters whose portraits he admired for the same truthfulness, and flawless technique, are Durer and Holbein. His annotated copy of C. Heath Wilson, *Life and Works of Michelangelo Buonarroti* (London: John Murray, 1874) is in the Emery Walker Library. See *CAGM*, p. 147.

58 • To George Howard, 25 July 1873

1, Raymond Buildings, Gray's Inn, | *London,*
July 25 1873

My dear Howard.

After struggling with Ashby's I have brought their estimate for the new south addition to Palace Green House down to 1066£.[1] I've no doubt that by putting the work out to tender we could get it done for 100£ less, but it is a question if Ashby's and Taylor's proved care would not be worth the other hundred pounds.[2]

Will you let me know, as soon as possible, if I shall proceed with the work as it is, or reduce the design?

Yours very truly | Philip Webb:

Howard

1 Ashby Brothers (formerly Richard Ashby & Sons) had been the original builders for 1 Palace Green. They now undertook to add a schoolroom and bedroom to the third floor. See *Kirk*, p. 296. 'Mr Cates – the Archt to the Crown lands – since the death of Mr Pennethorne – was pleased to say that he thought the addition to the house was a great improvement and that he would forward its carrying out as much as possible'. PSW to GH, 4 July 1873, *Howard*.
2 Taylor was the works' foreman for Ashby Brothers.

59 • To Frances Hohenthal, 29 July 1873

Postmark LONDON. W.C. JY 29 73 *Address* Frances Hohenthal | Hamilton | Canada.

1, Raymond Buildings, Gray's Inn, | *London,*
July 29. 1873

Dear Frances Hohenthal[1]

I was very glad indeed to have your letter, telling me of your safe arrival in Canada & Niagara, and of your having met with an employer. Now, there looks to be a good chance for you to do well. You are free from the impediments to right progress wh' met you at each step in England, and you can depend upon your own honourable labour to carry you through life, without unreasonable drawback.

I have been very busy ever since you left, or I sh^d have answered your letter before. My business gives me many letters to write, wh' has caused me to put off writing this for so long.

London has not changed since you left – it is still a very dirty overcrowded place, and it makes me very often wish to be – where you are – that is, with more fresh air about me.

Keep up your courage – behave honourably – (that you can always do) and you will live to be happy on your own exertions.

Yours very truly | Philip Webb:

LB-1, loose insertion

1 Although the identity of this correspondent is uncertain, and her relationship with PSW unclear, it is evident that this was someone whom he had done his best to assist and presumably encouraged in her decision to emigrate. He had also provided her with a reference.

60 • To George Howard, 4 August 1873

1, Raymond Buildings, Gray's Inn, | *London,*
Aug 4 1873

My dear Howard.

Ashby's will begin as soon as possible.[1] I was only able to settle with them today as I had not included the parquet &c &c in the 1066£ and have had to cut and carve a little to get it to fit – however now we are straight & I will urge on as fast as possible. Ashby's will sign the accurate bills of quantities and for their own sakes will hurry to get covered in before the autumn wet & frost comes on them.

I have not put in the carving for at the present moment I don't see my way to its being done properly.

I am surprised at your suggesting a journey to Cumberland when I must be on the ground to push the Palace Green affair forward.

Also, you know my sentiments as to taking the appropriate morsels out of the mouths of local men. The Cumberland men must be of different mould (& no doubt are very different indeed) to Scotch men or the whole county would have howled at the thought of a London architect having so much as been inside Naworth.[2] Please take care – both of Naworth & Lanercost – there was a good article in the Athenæum on Saturday on the subject of historical monuments which have nearly ceased to remain with us.[3]

The stable door however is I believe reduced to one broken hinge and half a bolt.

Yours | Philip Webb:

Howard

---

1 See above, Letter 58, note 1.
2 Between 1873 and 1879, PSW undertook a number of works for GH at Naworth Castle, including converting the Moat House into a studio for GH, creating an additional room in the Morpeth Tower, and designing staircases, fireplaces, bookcases and other library fittings. See *Kirk*, p. 299.
3 On 2 August, *The Athenæum* carried an anonymous article headed 'Exeter Cathedral' (pp. 152–3), which used the then current restoration work of Sir Gilbert Scott to bemoan such practices, anticipating by a full four years the underpinning philosophy of the Society for the Protection of Ancient Buildings, founded by WM and PSW. 'We prefer to speak of the "renovation" of Exeter Cathedral, rather than describe the works we carefully examined the other day as "restorations," which they are not, in the opprobrious sense of that term, at least. . . . Whether it is desirable to turn an old cathedral into a new one, is a question upon which we need not give our opinion. There is now no first-class cathedral left to be meddled with, and Westminster Abbey is the sole work of the kind which remains substantially unrenovated. We do sincerely trust that the Abbey Chapter will control the iconoclastic zeal of their Dean, and that the church may be allowed to remain as it is, if only that we may have a specimen of what churches were before the avatar of Sir G. Scott.' p. 152.

61 • To George Howard, 27 August 1873

1, Raymond Buildings, Gray's Inn, | *London,*
Aug 27 1873

My dear Howard.

I should be very sorry to vex you. Would indeed sacrifice some of my own most valuable moral satisfaction to avoid doing so, provided, that I find your wish to have me as a coadjutor is not more vicious than wishing to join me with you to rob the Bank of England of 100,000£; prove that, & I'll make some effort.

You will know that it would be utterly impossible for me properly to advise you upon the Brampton work, without my looking into the affair on the ground.[1] Well I cannot come just now at all events for I am kept close by two or three things which have to be roofed in before the end of December. Would it be possible & well for us to journey to Brampton in the winter, and look into affairs there, in the calm of blood, caused by the thermometer being at 32 degrees? I dare say that I can arrange this, and it might not be inconvenient to you.

I will not forget the vane, but shall probably raise difficulties about the carving at Palace Green.

We could surely find a place for the small terracotta, easily, in the new study.

I've been obliged to arrange for scaffolding to be bracketed out from our ground, as the tenants in the court, whether of their own will or by superior advice, refuse to allow scaffolding to be used on their ground.[2] This will cost us 10£ but we should have had to pay more than that in bribes the other way.

I'm sorry you have had bad weather – hope it will give over for a fortnight at least before you leave. London is dull, but we bear up under the loss of beauty & fashion.

With kind regards to Mrs Howard & your father. | Yours | Philip Webb:

Howard

---

1 As the patron of the existing parish church at Brampton, which was 'of poor quality, badly in need of repair, and had no free pews for the poorer townsfolk' (*Kirk*, p. 261), GH was keen to replace it with a wholly new building on the same site. See below, Letter 75, note 3.
2 This relates to the additional works carried out at 1 Palace Green in 1873–4. See above, Letter 58, note 1.

62 • To Charles Fairfax Murray, 3 October 1873

1, Raymond Buildings, Gray's Inn | London,
Oct 3. '73

Dear Murray.

Thank you very much for your letter – and also for the photographs, or, as they might better be called the invisible pictures.[1] By the aid of strong magnifying glass I can make out that it must be beautiful at Siena. Your description is a great help. 'The invisible part on the left is so & so, that in the middle such & such the jet black of the right hand is very delightful'. The architecture is evidently good as also the round crested horses. Italian horses are always well done. They must have been a good breed of horse. Your pleasant description of the colouring of the MA Holy family is a great help to me over & above my own power of divination.[2]

It rather enrages me, however, that I cannot see it with the eyes that water in my own head. What a blessing it is that pictures & music don't want translating. If you were to buy a live Italian he would have to be translated before ^being^ of any use to an Englishman.

I've lately got some Philpotti photographs of ivory carvings,[3] very much more interesting & valuable than I expected – of Byzantine & pre-Byzantine date & with mediævae many of the designs quite wonderful & some of the execution wonderful to a degree.

I take it that you have heard from Morris, who has come back very like a Scandinavian skipper, as brown as a berry – & much less portly, on acc^t^ of hard fare & laborious journeys – if he writes he will tell you of his doings, no doubt.

I am glad to find you are so industrious, it confirms what I have often felt that this damp oppressive climate is a serious breaker of good resolutions. The fine climate of Italy making you feel inclined to work as long as light & your back hold out, confirms me in my opinion. The little awkwardness of your desiring to do the work you ought not to do, will also give way under the better climate, no doubt. Heaven help you in your strife. For myself, my work goes a little awkwardly, but I try to frighten it by making faces at it. I sometimes succeed in frightening it to death, wh' keeps it from killing me. You will be pleased to hear that they are diligently searching for coal in the remaining pleasant places of England & sometimes finding it. In another 20 or 30 years most of the country will be more or less of a cinder heap, at that time America will have gained the iron trade so that we can then enjoy our wealth & witness the ruin – perhaps, for ^a^ great treat, now & then, going over to American to see Canterbury Cathedral, wh' they will have there under a glass case – no doubt. If this something bitter spirit of mine does not "inspire" you & make you "speak like an oracle" tell me in a long letter what will.

Yours very truly | Philip Webb:

Fitzwilliam 10

---

1 Throughout his professional life, and on into his retirement, PSW placed great value on the detailed evidence to be gleaned from photographs about historic buildings or works of art, and he was always grateful to receive them from friends. The development of the commercial picture postcard was a godsend in this respect, but he was equally pleased to receive the traveller's own snapshots.
2 The circular panel painting of the Holy Family by Michelangelo (c. 1506–7; Uffizi Gallery, Florence) was commissioned by the businessman Agnolo Doni at the time of his marriage.
3 John Brampton Philpot (1812–78), a British photographer resident in Florence. His photographs of art works included a series of 265 images of fictile ivory (now in the Hungarian National Museum, Budapest).

63 • To William Morris, December 1873[1]

Draft

1. R.B. G.I.
Dcr. '73

My dear Morris,

Some time I ago I wrote to Wardle upon what I considered was necessary for the good of the Firm under its present circumstances, namely, to have an accurate account made of its value and financial state by some perfectly unconcerned and professional accountant, & he agreed with me (at least such is my recollection) that it would be well to do so. Since then I have further considered the matter, and am more sure that I was then right as to what would be for the good of the Firm, as well as I am now, for myself. For, I know that the "concern" is active, and therefore very considerably involved in a mercantile way, but, I also know that I, personally, have no control over the business; though I am personally interested in its prosperity, and sh^d be involved in its adversity. In either case the result would be unjust. ~~Now, this is not a reasonable state of affairs; and, although I am dealing with artists, perhaps it would be as well to try and amend it~~. I have therefore concluded to withdraw from the Firm as a mercantile partnership – though proposing to keep to the friendly and artistic conjunction, so long as I can be of any use to it. I must ask you – whose daily work it is to interest yourself in the matter – not to fancy that I am suspicious of the Firm's stability, but to understand only that my work will not let me be as certain of the "Queen Square" affairs as I am of those w^h keep me alive every day. Also let me say, that I am glad of the business activity shewn, (though as before explained I cannot involve myself in it) because I am sure of the usefulness of the Firm's labours, as well as the harmlessness of them, in comparison with the monstrous rubbish usually turned out under the name of fine art ~~w^h makes such sober work as yours (apart from drunken poetry) most agreeably honourable~~.

Yours very affectionately, | Philip Webb.

P.S. You can use all, or any part, of the above, in letting the other members know that I wish to put myself on a new standing with the business.

Also, I sh^d propose that in the Christmas account, the value of each of the members shares should be named, and that any portion belonging to me sh^d remain in the business as long as it is required, at the rate – say – of the English Funds – 3 per cent.

LPW

1 This is an important letter in the history of Morris, Marshall, Faulkner & Co, for it was almost certainly written with the intention of assisting WM in his subsequent decision to re-organise the firm so as to take sole control, against much opposition from three of the partners (Madox Brown, DGR and Marshall). It may even have initiated the momentum for change. It is a skilfully constructed document, for although PSW may seem to be protecting his own interests, it can be argued that his real motive was entirely selfless. Ever since the initial equal investments from the original partners at the firm's founding, subsequent capital injections had come from WM, and although he was the sole partner taking a regular salary, he was also the only one who was 'full-time', and much of the risk fell on his shoulders. By seeking to initiate a debate between the partners (the postscript suggesting that his ideas might be circulated was probably no afterthought, but the whole point of the letter), PSW probably hoped that the ensuing discussions would be amicable and reasonable, and might lead to the kind of outcome which WM eventually achieved in March 1875, the dissolution of the partnership and the re-branding of the business as Morris & Co., under his sole ownership. WM agreed a settlement of £1000 to each of Brown, DGR and Marshall, but EBJ, CF and PSW all waived this payment. It is entirely characteristic that PSW should additionally refuse to take the £640 of fees due to him for work done over the years for the firm, and should continue to recommend Morris & Co. whenever possible to his own clients. For the protracted negotiations which led to the establishment of Morris & Co., see *MacCarthy, WMLT* pp. 341–7 and Charles Harvey and Jon Press, *William Morris. Design and Enterprise in Victorian Britain* (Manchester: Manchester University Press, 1991), ch 3.

64 • To Elizabeth Burden, 4 April 1874

1, Raymond Buildings, Gray's Inn, | London,
April 4. '74

Dear Miss Burden

Thank you very much for your letter, I shall be very pleased to become a subscriber or double subscriber as you may feel the want.[1] Mind, I take it on <u>your</u> responsibility, if a church & state ware sh^d happen, not on mine

With kind regards | Yours very truly | Philip Webb.

Huntington MOR 579

1 Bessie Burden taught students for the School of Art Needlework (later the Royal School of Needlework) from 1872, and also took on private pupils before endeavouring 'to set up her own teaching establishment. On 13 April [1874], she received a letter from Rossetti . . . offering to be a "large Donor to your School".' Lynn Hulse, 'Elizabeth Burden and the Royal School of Needlework', p. 33 note 16.

65 • To George Price Boyce, 16 May 1874

1, Raymond Buildings, Gray's Inn, | London,
May 16. '74

Dear Boyce

I've written to my "sawbones" brother to ask him to look in upon you on his next visit to London.[1] If you feel able, & inclined you sh^d go down to Welwyn & have

lunch with him. It is a pleasant place & the fresh air w^d probably do you good. Journey under an hour, and cab at Welwyn Station – address
"H: S: Webb Esqr
Welwyn | Herts."

There are many old fashioned plants in the garden wh' has a gravel bottom & poor soil. Trains, Kings Cross to Welwyn Station, wh' is the next below ~~Welwyn~~ Hatfield.

My brother is a careful & patient surgeon, knowing the exceeding value of both.

Yours very truly | Philip Webb:

My brother is a Bartholomew's man & keeps up his connection, & knows of new hospital treatments &c & knows Paget very well.[2]

BL Add 45354, ff. 58-9

---

1 PSW's elder brother, Henry (Harry) Speakman Webb (1827/8–1911) was a general practitioner in Welwyn, Hertfordshire. Their younger sister, Caroline (d. 1909), lived with him, and after her death another sister, Sarah (?1826–1922), moved in, by which time he had retired to Winchester. All three, like PSW himself, never married. PSW often spent Sundays with Harry and Caroline, and would design and build New Place (with surgery) in Welwyn (1877–80). See *Kirk*, pp. 224–6 and 300.
2 St Bartholomew's Hospital (Barts) in Smithfield, in the city of London, was founded in 1123. The surgeon, Sir James Paget (1814–99), had a long association with Barts, having trained there before returning to teach, serving as curator of the museum and as warden of the medical school. Paget was celebrated for his surgical and pathological work, and for new procedures in treating a range of diseases.

66 • To Lady Fitzhardinge, 7 July 1874

Draft/copy

[1, Raymond Buildings ...]
July 7. '74.

To Lady Fitzhardinge.
Cranford house | Hounslow.

Dear Lady Fitzhardinge[1]

I have obtained an estimate from Morris & Co of Queen Square[2] for reglazing the Hall windows of Berkeley Castle from my design, with reinsertion of the existing shields of arms. I propose to glaze the lower portion of each light with a flowered quarry and coloured border, and the upper portion, in wh' the shields are set, with a flowing grisaille[3] border. Each window, composed of two under and two upper lights w^d cost between 18 & 20 pounds, and as there are 4 windows, this w^d amount to about 80£. There w^d in addition be the usual charge for carriage & fixing.

Yours very truly, | Philip Webb:

LB-1, p. 1

1 Georgina Holme-Sumner (d. 1897) married Francis Fitzhardinge Berkeley (1826–96) in 1857. On the death of his father in 1867, Berkeley became the second Baron Fitzhardinge. The family seat was Berkeley Castle, in Gloucestershire, where between 1874–7 PSW oversaw various alterations, decorations and glazing work, the latter involving MMF & Co. See *Kirk*, pp. 183–4 and 299.
2 PSW here uses the Morris & Co. designation about eight months before the official demise of MMF & Co, though perhaps as a convenient shorthand rather than in deliberate anticipation of the future changed status of the firm. See above, Letter 63, note 1.
3 Grisaille: 'Decorative painting in grey monotone to represent objects in relief' (*OED*).

67 • To George Frederic Watts, 8 July 1874

Draft/copy

[1, Raymond Buildings . . .]
July 8. '74.

To G: F: Watts Esq[r]
Little Holland House | Kensington
Dear Watts.[1]

In answer to your letter just rec[d]. It is with real distress that I find come true, what I could not but have anticipated. The encouragement offered to the interested people in the Isle of Wight to gratify their angry disappointment at the employment by me of a London builder ^on your house^ has told.[2]

When I paid my lawyer for his advice in the ^disgraceful^ matter of Saunders & Waterfield[3] I resolved not to further trouble myself where great care and anxiety had been of no avail, and my professional reputation had gained no consideration for my opinion.

I will send for Tyerman, and as carefully as possible put the matter before ^him^ to see if there is any probability of his considering himself responsible, since (as I heard from Tyerman) other workmen than those employed by him have been engaged upon the house, and wh' report is confirmed by your letter ^& enclosure^ of today.

There is still a balance of 30 or 40£ due to Tyerman under my direction and I will do the best I can, though I am not at all hopeful. ~~The rest~~ ^Each day^ of this week I am engaged and I have to go into Yorkshire next week,[4] so that I cannot possibly go to Freshwater 'till the week after next.

Yours faithfully, | Philip Webb.

LB-1, pp. 1-2

---

1 The painter, George Frederic Watts (1817–1904).
2 The difficulties which arose in connection with the building works for The Briary, the studio-house PSW designed for Watts at Freshwater, on the Isle of Wight (1872–4), made this an unhappy commission. In order to reduce the costs for Watts, PSW turned to the London builder, John Tyerman, whom he had previously employed to build houses for GPB and the painter, John Roddam Spencer

Stanhope (for whom see below, Letter 96, note 6), and risked doing without a clerk of works. A disgruntled Isle of Wight builder chose to make trouble and criticised the work as inadequate: 'after examining it, Webb found that this was not the case, and the accusation was withdrawn. Unfortunately, Watts took up residence before the house was finished and, finding the house damp, he wrote angrily to Webb impugning his professional integrity, got the local builder to investigate the problem, and brought in local tradesmen.' *Kirk*, p. 274.
3 The dispute resulted from PSW's work being challenged.
4 He was overseeing work on his house for Isaac Lowthian Bell. See below, Letter 73, note 5.

68 • To Jane Morris, 13 July 1874

1, Raymond Buildings, Gray's Inn, | *London,*
July 13. '74

Dear janey

Thank you for your affectionate letter. I'm afraid I shall not see you before I go.

I've no recollection of Morris having mentioned your wish for me to come up, but then I know that my memory is worse than his, & therefore he may have done so. I have been very busy, partly unavoidably, & partly through a bad way I have of letting work get into a knot. 'Tis in that state now, & I'm untying it.

I go into Yorkshire tomorrow morning, & shall not be back 'till Thursday or Friday night. It pleased me to think of your going to the Flemish towns, a van Eyking. How the childrens eyes will round in their heads.[1]

I am glad that you liked the Goethë conversations. The old boy found out his own proper Boswell, did he not? Johnson managed his, with verbal bangs & buffets – Goethë with the most delicate flattery.[2]

Oh the wonders for the 2 girls & the boy.[3] You and me never had such wonders.

The Oxford houses are sold, and the Webbs' & Speakmans' swept away[4] – and the town purified.

Poor old town, poor old memories. I commission you to drink a bottle of wine for both of us, for forgetfulness sake.[5]

Yours faithfully | Philip Webb:

BL Add 45342, ff. 31-2

---

1 WM took JM, their daughters, and the Burne-Jones children on a trip to Belgium in July, from Calais travelling to Tournai, Ghent and Bruges. Jan van Eyck (c 1395–1441) was one of the most significant Flemish painters of the fifteenth century, and is known to have worked in The Hague and Bruges.
2 Much of Goethe's biographical history depends upon the published work of Johann Peter Eckermann (1792–1854). *Conversations of Goethe with Eckermann and Soret* first appeared in English in a translation by John Oxenford (London: Henry G. Bohn, 1846). James Boswell's *The Life of Samuel Johnson* was first published in 1791.
3 Philip Burne-Jones.
4 The end of the Webb family home in St Giles', Oxford.
5 It was a regular theme of PSW's that he and JM had a special link through their Oxford childhoods.

69 • To George Frederic Watts, 17 July 1874

Draft/copy

[1, Raymond Buildings . . .]
July 17. '74

To G: F: Watts Esquire
Little Holland House | Kensington

Dear Watts.

Upon finding it impossible for myself to visit Freshwater at once, I considered it w^d be best to employ another Arch^t (whose professional character w^d be ~~above dispute~~ $^{beyond\ suspicion}$, and who might be considered unprejudiced –) to visit the works and examine them, in the presence of Tyerman $^{the\ builder\ employed\ by\ me}$, and the several tradesmen who had been called in without my consent or approval to report upon Tyerman's work.

I enclose a copy of the report of Mr Vinall[1] – the Architect I employed – and wh' ^{report} I consider to be a careful and dependable one. It will be seen by the report that Mr Tyerman expressed to Mr Vinall his willingness ~~even now~~ to do $^{-\ even\ now\ -}$ all that was required of him to remedy defects. I beg to say for myself, that Tyerman has never hitherto objected to do any work to the house that I expressed a wish sh^d be done.

I propose, now, ~~to request~~ that Tyerman ~~shall~~ ^{should} receive ~~the~~ instructions ~~of~~ from Mr Vinall, and carry out the necessary repairs under his direction, before ~~any further~~ the balance or balances due $^{from\ you}$ to Tyerman are paid to him.

I shall be obliged if you will let me know at what time it w^d be convenient to you for Mr Vinall to direct Tyerman to begin the repairs. As soon as these repairs are completed I must beg you to release me from any further interference in a matter wh' has been so ~~little~~ $^{far\ from}$ satisfactory to me.[2]

Yours faithfully, | Philip Webb.

LB-1, pp. 3-4

---

1 Charles George Vinall, of Goodman and Vinall in Buckingham Street, the Strand, from whose architectural practice GWJ would join PSW's office, in early 1882. Vinall would serve as an Honorary Secretary for the SPAB (1880–89), and a regular committee member, reporting on particular cases.
2 Vinall oversaw the completion of the project. Finding the whole affair distasteful, PSW refused to accept any fee from Watts. Remarkably, their relationship was not permanently soured. See *Kirk*, p. 77.

70 • To William Tatham, 25 July 1874

Draft/copy

[1, Raymond Buildings . . .]
July 25. '74

To W: Tatham Esq[r]
118 Pall Mall | S.W.[1]

Dear Sir:

I beg to acknowledge the rec[t] of ^and to thank you for^ your letter of the 23rd ^inst^ and to say in answer, that it will be impossible for me to enter upon any fresh work for some time to come on acc[t] of present engagements. Also, to avoid any possible^ity of^ misunderstanding I will ~~tell you~~ ^say^, that for some time past, I have decided not to undertake ~~work~~ ^to build^ for any one who is not conversant with my work, and able to judge of what would be the finished effect of ~~what~~ ^that wh'^ I should ~~propose~~ ^agree^ to carry out.

Yours truly, | Philip Webb.

LB-1, p. 6

---

1 William Tatham (1834–76), wine merchant.

71 • To Reverend Oswald Sharp, 4 August 1874

Draft/copy

[1, Raymond Buildings . . .]
Aug 4. '74

To Rev[d] Oswald Sharp.
Martyrs Mem[l] Ch. | S[t] John's S[t] R[d] E.C.[1]

Dear Sir:

I awaited your answer to my letter of Saturday ^last^ & deferred writing again, thinking it possible that you might not have rec[d] ~~my letter~~ ^it in proper time^.

In your letter of Saturday you presuppose that it is my wish to keep Alice Burbridge away from her duty. The suggestion is completely erroneous, and I must beg to refer you to my letter ~~of~~ ^to you^ at the time when Alice's mother's life was in such a critical state, that it was absolutely necessary that her daughter sh[d] attend upon her personally.[2] I rec^d no answer from you to ~~this~~^at letter though in it I proposed to become responsible for ~~any~~ ^the cost of providing a ~~monitor~~ substitute for Alice during her ^enforced absence from school.

If from your continued silence I sh^d be obliged to consider the necessity of applying to the ^committee of Privy Council for assistance, I must beg you to remember that I ^shd only do so, because you deny me the usual business attention to my appeal to you ^as manager of ^the School to which Alice Burbridge is attached.

Y^rs truly | Ph. Webb.

LB-1, pp. 7-8

---

1 The Reverend B. Oswald Sharp was the first vicar of the new church of St Peter's, Clerkenwell, also known as the Smithfield Martyrs Mission Church, consecrated in 1871. The building stood on the site of the former town house of the Marquesses of Northampton, used as a school until its demolition in 1869. The church suffered severe bomb damage in 1940, and was demolished in 1957.
2 'A quarter's salary is due to-day for Alice Burbridge's services: but as she has rendered scarcely any service of late & you still propose to keep her away, it is fair to the Managers to ask if you are prepared on her behalf to make some arrangement on this score.' Sharp to PSW, 1 August 1874, *Cheltenham* 1991.1016.665.i. The history of PSW's philanthropic interest in Alice Burbridge is unknown. She was employed as a pupil-teacher at the parish school attached to the Martyrs Church, based at 12 St John Street Road, but the critical illness of her mother kept her away from work. Earlier in the year, PSW had written to explain this: 'The comfort of her daughter's attention is so great, that I sh^d be much obliged if you could arrange that Alice's place at the school sh^d be filled by a substitute, 'till such time as death or increased strength relieved Alice of the sad necessity of breaking in upon her work. If the providing a substitute sh^d cause the school an additional expense, I shall be glad to be responsible for the same.' PSW to Sharp, [1874], *Cheltenham 1991.1016.665.h*.

72 • To the Managers of the Martyrs Memorial Church Schools, 5 August 1874

Draft/copy

[1, Raymond Buildings . . .]
Aug 5. '74.

To the Managers of the "Martyrs' Mem^l" Ch' schools.
St John's St R^d E.C.

Gentlemen.

Having been enabled to see The Revd Mr Sharp – one of the managers of your School – I explained to him that it was the wish of Alice Burbridge's mother, expressed to me just before she died, that her daughter should be transferred from your school to one in the country, more particularly on acc^t of her health.

I beg therefore to ~~give~~ ^send you this as a formal notice that ^it is necessary that Alice Burbridge sh^d leave your school at the end of 3 months from this time. I sh^d ~~also~~

be obliged, if I ˢʰᵈ succeed in shortly finding a proper school in wh' to place Alice Burbridge, that you will ᵃʳʳᵃⁿᵍᵉ ᵗᵒ let her leave ~~you~~ – if necessary – before the whole time of 3 months has expired.[1]

         I am Gentⁿ Yours faithfully, | Philip Webb.

LB-1, p. 8

---

[1] 'I beg, in the name of the Managers to accept your 3 months notice for Alice Burbridge, from Aug 5. If you get a School before that time & they can obtain a candidate in her place, they will release her as you wish.' Sharp to PSW, 10 September 1874, *Cheltenham* 1991.1016.665.e. PSW found an equivalent position for Alice Burbridge as a pupil-teacher at a parish school in Datchworth, Hertfordshire, but two years later was writing to the vicar there, fearing that she might be wanting to join her stepsister in Russia. 'I think, if Alice goes to her sister to live with her, it will be one of the worst things that could happen to the girl. However, I have no power to hinder it, personally; and I could only hope that some aid might have been given, if it had been this wish as well as in the power of Rector or Church (or School) wardens, ~~to~~ ᵇʸ keepⁱⁿᵍ her to her signed indentures 'till they were completed.' PSW to Reverend John Wardale, 3 August 1876, *LB-1*, p. 44.

73 • To George Price Boyce, 1 September 1874

1, Raymond Buildings, Gray's Inn, | *London,*
              Sep 1. '74

Dear Boyce

I have your double dampy [*sic*] letter, and therefore let me begin at once by damning you, for no force of words can lower your tone; let us hope they may brace you with echoes of many damns from the ring of the one "damning" against Dartmouth rocks. I see, that if <u>you</u> are not worth coming for to see, the old church is. I beg you to preach at the parson on each Sunday & Saints day, that he may not blast his church by restoration. Tell him what evil minded persons all Church restorers are, and that you have it from the highest authority, that if he does not keep the Scotts' & Streets' & Burgesses'[1] out of the church he – the parson – will never see Heaven or, if he does he will not be able to appreciate it, & it will be Hell to him.

 If you shᵈ go to church please make one or two notes of the details of arches ᶜᵃᵖⁱᵗᵃˡˢ &c, wh' I see are peculiarly Devonshire – the parson will think you are taking down the heads of his sermon, & he will fire up with disestablished force. I ha~~ve~~ᵈ a book with the pulpit in it, but someone has stolen the book from me. Altogether, I fancy the screenwork & pulpit &c must be very beautiful.[2]

 It looks to me that it may be very well for you to be at the warm end of England, even if it is not bracing now, for you will be able to stop on late into the Autumn. You probably want 3 or 4 months of real change. I shall not see my brother for a fortnight, unless he looks in upon me, but I will give him your message when I do see him.

There is not any probability that I shall come down and see you as I'm fairly tied by the leg – worse luck for me, better for you, if it is not unkind to say so, & I don't mean it as such – but, I'm losing that natural sweetness of temper, a characteristic of me wh' you can't have forgotten.

As ill luck w[d] have it I've made a deadly enemy of Wells,[3] by building stables at Bowman's in front of a telescopic view of his ([Wells]). I'm very sorry to have done it, but nothing will make him believe that is not malice on my part.[4] How shall I ever get to be an RA now, good God! What ill luck.

I go to Rounton again next week for a day I believe,[5] & am only anxious to avoid beautiful Doncaster with your bloody aristocracy & their brutal sports.[6] I suppose you are setting-to at a large picture, one that will torture you well, & keep you from troubling about any other evil on Earth. Hope you've got pleasant rooms, & feeling Landlady, and many bottles of good wine; O Lord how lazy I could be, & what a lot of wine I could drink.

Yours with a pinch for remembrance, | P Webb.

BL Add 45354, ff. 62-3

---

1 For William Burges, see below, Letter 76, note 2.
2 Mention of the roodscreen makes it clear that PSW refers to the fourteenth-century church of St Saviour's, Dartmouth, in Devon.
3 See above, Letter 12, note 2.
4 PSW had built Joldwynds, at Holmbury St Mary, Surrey (1870–5), for the eye surgeon William Bowman (1816–92), created first baronet in 1884. Bowman was consulted by DGR on his eye disorders, and also became PSW's oculist.
5 PSW was currently engaged in overseeing the construction of Rounton Grange at East Rounton, in the North Riding of Yorkshire, the house he had designed for the iron and steel manufacturer, Isaac Lowthian Bell (1816–1904). 'The interior, which was comfortable rather than grand or luxurious, [would be] furnished and decorated almost entirely with Morris & Co. products, many of them designed by Webb'. *Kirk*, p. 123.
6 The annual St Leger horserace was run at Doncaster on 16 September.

74 • To Lord Sackville Cecil, 11 September 1874

Draft/copy

[1, Raymond Buildings . . .]
Sep 11. '74.

To The Lord Sackville Cecil.
Great Eastern Rail:[y] Bishopsgate
My Lord.[1]

I beg to acknowledge the receipt of your letter of the 9th ins[t] enclosing [a] cheque for £218.1.8 wh' I return.

If your Lordship will refer to my letter to you of the 16th of April last, you will see that I declined to accept ~~no~~ ^{any} remuneration whatever for my work in respect of your house at Hayes.[2]

I told Messrs Goodman & Vinall that I sh^d not object to their charging the whole 5 per cent for their ~~works~~, as I considered, & still consider that they would barely be remunerated – even by the full amount – for their labours in the matter.

Yours faithfully. | Philip Webb.

LB-1, p. 9

---

1 Lord Sackville Arthur Cecil (1847–98), for whom PSW designed Oast House, Hayes Common in Kent (1872–3). He was a younger half-brother of the third Marquess of Salisbury, the future Prime Minister.

2 As in the case of The Briary, PSW's house for Watts (see above, Letter 67), here is evidence of the upset which followed a client's interference in the building work, with the result that (as before) PSW refused his fee. 'Cecil might have been expecting to get on well with Webb, with whom he had in common a capacity for conscientious work and sympathy for those in difficulty. However, during construction in 1873, a problem arose, probably as a result of Cecil attempting to direct the building work himself, which certainly Webb would have taken as an insult to his experience and skill. Charles Vinall took over the supervising of construction.' *Kirk*, pp. 217–8.

75 • To George Howard, 29 September 1874

1, Raymond Buildings, Gray's Inn, | *London,*
Sep 29 1874

Dear Howard.

In answer to your letter of the 24th. It does not at all surprise me that your working estimate for the Brampton houses should be as much as £2,990, as on referring to my papers, I find that I estimated the work at £3,350.[1] You must bear in mind that practically there would be 9 houses, namely the Carpenter's or archway house, 6 intermediate houses, and we must count the lodging house as two, for it has that capacity. There is no doubt that the size of the houses could be reduced, but the plans would have to be re-drawn, so as to reduce everything in proper proportion. You must know that I always considered that they were to be larger & in every way somewhat superior as <u>town</u> houses, to the cottages you ordinarily build in the fields. Therefore if Warwick[2] puts down £250 as the price of a country cottage, I do not think that £332 or thereabouts would be unreasonable for the town houses. Don't you think you could get an average of 25£ a year for each house?

Mind you, there would be no <u>difficulty</u> in reducing the size of the houses and still keeping the character of them.

As to the Church – when I looked at the present church and its site in Brampton, I made up my mind as to the character of the church for a new one to suit that site, which is a good one for a town church.³ So that if you would let Warwick make me a plan of the ground with a section from north to south giving the fall of the ground and position of the present building I would make a plan of new church in sufficient manner to let me make an estimate of the cost which would enable you to set to begging with some certainty as to how much you would want to collect. I would do this at once on your sending me the plan of the ground – and section [*small sketch of existing church and churchyard*]. The section, if I recollect rightly is something like this sketch.

Our branch of the family of the Smiths has been very remiss.⁴ I've no doubt in my own mind that they have only just now begun upon the clock. A workman came here this morning and promised that the clock & dial should be ready in 15 or 16 days from this time. Warwick has the address of Smith, and you can thunder at them as soon and as often as you please.

I saw Ned on Friday last and I thought him pretty bright, but perhaps this came of the reflection from some new Botticelli photographs which he was shewing me.⁵ However, I did think that he was looking pretty well. I hope that Rosalind is stronger than she was.⁶ Please to put my kind remembrances to her in as pretty a form as possible. I don't believe so much in your "beastly" weather as you are too far from London or any of the "black countries" – wind & wet are as nothing in comparison with the clouds of prosperity. I cannot come and see you now, or I would do so, as I encourage a feeling that you would not ask me to come unless you wished to see me.

Yours very truly | Philip Webb:

Morris is laid up with a strong touch of rheumatism first in one foot & then in the other.⁷ P:W:

I was at Palace Green last Thursday. I think they must have nearly if not quite done the work they had to do there. I was obliged to give orders for them to paint the iron trellis over the stable wall as it was rusting through. Indeed outside painting should be done generally as soon as it can be arranged. PW.

Howard

---

1 GH was wanting to erect a terrace of workers' houses in Brampton, close to the Naworth Castle estate (see also below, Letter 77). PSW drew up three different schemes between 1874 and 1876, but they were never executed. See *Kirk*, p. 299.
2 Thomas Warwick was GH's clerk of works for the Naworth estate.
3 The appointment of a new incumbent to the parish church of Brampton, the Reverend Henry Whitehead (1825–96), made GH's wish to replace the dilapidated existing church more likely of success. See also above, Letter 61, note 1, and for Whitehead, below, Letter 214.
4 The London clock-making firm, John Smith of Clerkenwell, founded in 1780, had been engaged to make a clock for Naworth Castle – and is not to be confused with the unrelated but equally prestigious firm of clock-makers, Smiths of Derby.
5 EBJ had visited Naworth during the summer, and was joined there by WM. 'They had been given for their use a room in one of the towers, once the old library, and not touched since Tudor times.

Twenty tourists were ushered in one day: Rosalind thought that "two lions in the old room ought to enhance its interest".' *Surtees*, p. 101. For EBJ's admiration of Botticelli ('no one is like him and never will be again'), see *MacCarthy, LPR*, p. 101.
6 Rosalind Howard's elder sister, Kate, Viscountess Amberley (1844–74), had died in June, having caught diphtheria from her daughter.
7 Probably gout, to which WM was prone.

76 • To George Gilbert Scott junior, 6 October 1874

Draft/copy

[1. Raymond Buildings . . .]
Oct 6 '74.

To G: G: Scott Junr
7 Duke St. Portland Place W:
Dear Mr Scott.

In answer to your letter of yesterday. The $^{\text{firm of}}$ London builders who have done most work for me is that of ~~the firm~~ R Ashby & Sons of 24 Bishopsgate without, and I have always found them ~~both~~ willing, ~~&~~ capable and responsible men of business, and doing good sound work.[1] They have never built a church for me, but I hear that they have built one for Mr Burges.[2]

With regard to Washington Church, I sh^d be very glad to lend you any assistance.[3] Mr Lowthian Bell is abroad for 3 months, but I shall see his son, Hugh Bell, in a few days & I will mention the matter to him & urge him to use any influence he may have $^{\text{for you}}$.[4]

I shall be glad when the foundations of your church are getting in to go and look at them, as the new ground with its varieties is always useful.

Yours very truly | Philip Webb.

LB-1, pp. 11-12

---

1 PSW had used Richard Ashby and Sons for at least four of his London commissions by this time. See above, Letters 16 and 38.
2 The architect and designer, William Burges (1827–81), much of whose stained glass and other decorative work rivals that of Morris & Co. He was close to many in the broader Pre-Raphaelite circle. The Ashby firm would be the contractors for his own Tower House, in Melbury Road, Kensington (1875–7). The foundation stone for Scott's new church of St Agnes, Kennington Park, Lambeth, was laid in August 1874, but there was 'a succession of difficulties with different contractors. Dove Brothers were to have undertaken all the work but a dispute over prices confined their contribution to the foundations.' Gavin Stamp, *An Architect of Promise. George Gilbert Scott Junior and the Late Gothic Revival* (Donington: Shaun Tyas, 2002), p. 75.
3 Scott prepared designs in 1874 for a new chancel and tower at Holy Trinity, Washington, co Durham, but the plans did not proceed.

4 Although currently engaged on work for Lowthian Bell (see above, Letter 73, note 5) PSW had previously designed Red Barns at Coatham, Redcar (1868–70) for Bell's son, Thomas Hugh Bell (1844–1931), who succeeded his father as second baronet. The celebrated archaeologist and diplomat, Gertrude Margaret Lowthian Bell (1868–1926), was Hugh Bell's daughter.

77 • To George Howard, 15 October 1874

1, Raymond Buildings, Gray's Inn, | London,
Oct 15 1874

My dear Howard.

I do not think anything can equal your good nature towards me, except your folly towards yourself. Bundles of rods are you binding together with which to birch yourself. However, don't say that I did not try to open your eyes – when some years hence you have to stand in that "Public" at Brampton, & lay your hand on your heart, & speak of the help you have been to the town,[1] what'll you answer to the little fresh coloured farmer wife, who will sing out in Cumbrian treble 'how about that "shitten yellow coloured" architect who you saddled us with'? Oh sirs! where'll you be I should I like to know? By good luck I have to go to Rounton in the early part of next week, so that I can come on without much loss of time to myself, or expense to your committee.[2] I think that trains will serve for me to get to Naworth-gate by the train 7-oc there on Wednesday evening. I could spend Thursday in the several businesses, and get back to town by the 8.41 train from Naworth to Carlisle on Friday morning.

By these means I could be better judge of the amount of mischief you intend for the "moat house",[3] Brampton cottages &c &c, and display a dignified face before your church committee; the interspaces of time being filled up with Naworth ale. I went to Clerkenwell today, and taxed the Smiths with negligence; but they, with unblushing effrontery (which could only have come from their relationship to the Foreign Office) turned to memoranda to see if such a thing as an order had been given: however, it stands now that their man is to come to me on Saturday with such dimensions &c as will allow me to look into Warwick's part of the clock business.[4]

If you see "your committee" will you be so good as to say that I will attend to their request, and be at Brampton on Thursday 22nd.

You will understand this light letter of mine for what it is worth and believe, that beneath the lightness, there remains very real appreciation of your kindness, mixed with grave doubt as to the object on which you expend it.

With kind remembrances of Rosalind [Yours very truly | Philip Webb:]

Howard

---

1 PSW envisages GH canvassing in a future election campaign. Indeed, after his father's death in 1879 he was elected in his place as MP for East Cumberland.

2 For the Brampton church building committee, see below, Letter 80. PSW was remarkably prescient in foreseeing some of the local opposition which would surround the erection of his new church, something which he would put down to mean-spirited provincialism.
3 The room at Naworth which PSW converted into a studio for GH.
4 See above, Letter 75, note 4.

78 • To Rosalind Howard, 26 October 1874

1, Raymond Buildings, Gray's Inn, | London,
Oct 26 1874

My dear Mrs Howard.

Thank you very much for your admirable letter. A mere word or two saying that Howard was better of worse would not have satisfied me, for I was very anxious to know clearly something of his state – now, I can think reasonably of his attack.[1] I rejoice to hear that your sister is going to be with you so that you may more easily get some rest for yourself, for unless you are careful of your own health you will not be kind to anyone.

On the whole Dr Baylis's opinion seems to me to be a hopeful one, and the disappointment at George having to go away this winter, is as nothing compared to the confidence given at his pulling through, if care is taken. Indeed, I am very much relieved by your letter, and also impressed by your kindness in thinking it worthwhile to write it to me.

I found our friends all fairly well on my return but they were quite upset by my dolefulness. Fortunately, I had not to write it to them, for Morris and Burne-Jones were at Queen Square, where I saw them by 9 o'c on Friday night, and I was able to speak clearly of George's state; their expressions of affection were also very agreeable to me.

The ending of your letter is something of a relief to my mind, for, on finding George ill when I had looked forward to seeing him well, was a trial to my spirits, and made me rather savage I thought, and that again vexed me. If there was any apparent kindness in me, it was my real feeling shewing through, in spite of circumstances.

When George is well enough, I will write him word of how his Naworth affairs have been working in me, and that will help to drive away the bogies of weakness & weariness from him. Pleasant Naworth, I know of no country house, so free from the things which make them so really dismal, as yours; you will understand, then, why I do not wish to be an instrument of change in it.[2]

As you say nothing of the children I take it that they are getting on well.

I send your letter on to Georgie[3] at once.

[Yours very truly | Philip Webb:]

Howard

1 GH was suffering from 'pneumonia and severe bronchitis'. *Surtees*, p. 101.
2 See above, Letter 60, note 2.
3 GBJ.

79 • To Ford Madox Brown, probably 8 November 1874

Gray's Inn
Sunday

My dear Brown

I heard last night of the fatal end to the illness of your poor boy.[1]

    Please accept my sincere sympathy with you, in this great loss to you and your wife.

Believe me to be | Yours very truly | Philip Webb:

Huntington HM 45439

1 Oliver ('Nolly') Madox Brown (1855–74), son of Ford and Emma Madox Brown, was a gifted painter and writer. He died on 5 November from peritonitis and septicaemia, leaving his father bereft.

80 • To Thomas Forster, 17 November 1874

Draft/copy

[1, Raymond Buildings . . .]
Novr 17. '74

To Thos Forster Esqr
Brampton Cumb^d
Dear Sir.[1]

Brampton Parish Ch

I beg to acknowledge the rec^t of your letter of the 11th instant, conveying to me the directions of the Committee for me to proceed with the necessary plans for rebuilding Brampton ~~Parish~~ Church.[2]

    I will put the matter in hand in due course, keeping in mind the memorandum as to the cost ^{that it shd} not ~~to~~ exceed~~ing~~ £6,000.[3]

I am dear Sir | Yours very truly | Philip Webb:

LB-1, pp. 13-14

1 Thomas Forster, a local solicitor, was secretary of the Brampton church building committee.
2 PSW had attended a meeting of the committee on 22 October, and sent them a report a week or so later. 'As I have sent in to the Brampton people my reports as to the Church affair and as Howard will not be there, to see the babe he has so tenderly nursed, I send a copy to you to read to him if he is well enough to undergo it; if you are too anxious to be bothered by it, just put it in the fire.' PSW to Rosalind Howard, 4 November 1874, *Howard*.
3 'I think I am right in the way of taking the Brampton instruction.' PSW to GH, 21 November 1874, *Howard*.

81 • To Charles Fairfax Murray, 25 November 1874

1, Raymond Buildings, Gray's Inn | London,
November. 25. '74

My dear Murray

It was very good of you to send me those translations of the Ourchael Angelo letters.[1] They have stirred me to read Grimm again.[2] None of my enthusiasm about OA. is at all dimmed. He is a very good expression of the best kind of power of the Italian artists, because he has such a variety of their capacity almost unmixed with any other faults than his own. I would rather that you sh^d go through the letters in order, than pick out the plums. First, because it will induce you to translate them and secondly, because I don't know wh' are the plums. Also, I can stick them into my Grimm. I've lately read again George Eliot's "Romola" – it is, as you must know, all about Florence & Savonarola – but there is not a word about the said master.[3] This reading on my part came from a longing to read of Italian matters, as I could not see the places & remains of the people. Also, the thoughts of the places counteract the catarrh & rheumatic pains, which rack our northern noses and joints, in this November weather here. So you are at beloved Pisa again! Though, if you are warm, is a question, for, I heard from Florence the other day, saying that it was very cold there, and snow on all the hills.

I've nothing whatever to tell you, except that our Burnejones is doing pretty well, though nearly chained to his hearth. Mr Morris is at work on his Italian parchment and doing very pretty things on it[4] – but is "so so" in health. I am building houses for people who w^d prefer them other than I can do – this they find out when they are done. Poor them.[5] The newspapers are banging about the poor pope, "him not caring one straw".[6] Quaritch[7] is in despair since your departure as he sells no books, except a pounds worth to me in the shape of Plutarch's lives – but what is a pound? There, if this cheers you up, a very little will do so indeed. Again I thank you for the translation.

Yours very truly | Philip Webb.

Fitzwilliam 14

1 'Ourchael Angelo': a wordplay on Michelangelo. CFM presumably sent his own translations of letters from the recent *Le Lettere di Michelangelo Buonarroti* (Florence, 1875).
2 Herman Grimm, *Life of Michael Angelo*, translated by F.E. Bunnett, 2 volumes (London, 1865).
3 George Eliot's historical novel, *Romola*, first appeared in serial form in the *Cornhill Magazine* (1862–3).
4 On 18 February 1874, WM had written to CFM, seeking a supply ('100 skins') of Italian vellum, as he wished to try his hand at his own illuminated manuscripts. 'In March, he began a vellum manuscript of the *Odes* of Horace. At the same time, he planned to transcribe one of his own tales, "Cupid and Psyche," which was to include the pictures and designs made by Burne-Jones in 1869 for the original scheme of an illustrated *Earthly Paradise*.' *CLWM*, I, p. 214 note 2: see also WM to CFM, 9 and 26 March, 1874, 1 June 1874 and 11 March 1875, *CLWM*, I.
5 He means G.F. Watts and Lord Sackville Cecil.
6 W.E. Gladstone's article, 'Ritualism and Ritual', *The Contemporary Review*, XXIV (October 1874), pp. 663–81, prompted some discussion, initiated by *The Times* which, as well as publishing substantial extracts, commented in a leading article that 'we shall esteem that to be the safest error which keeps us at the greatest distance, we will not say from Popery, but from those doctrines and influences which have made Popery detestable' (28 September 1874). For Gladstone, sell letter following, note 3.
7 The second-hand and antiquarian specialist bookseller and publisher, Bernard Quaritch (1819–99) operated from a shop at 15 Piccadilly, although much of his business came from the postal distribution of his catalogues. '[A] voracious though discriminating collector' (*Elliott*, p. 166), over the years CFM would amass an important collection of rare printed books, pictures, manuscripts and autograph letters. PSW's comment suggests that his buying habits were already in place.

82 • To Rosalind Howard, 6 February 1875

1, Raymond Buildings, Gray's Inn, | *London,*
Feb 6 1875

My dear Mrs Howard.

If a kindness comes after some delay perhaps it is none the less sweet. Your good natured letters burst upon me with equal surprise and pleasure. I have delayed answering them till now, because I have had before me the risk I shall run of endangering the continuance of "that firmly established friendship" of which you, in your sweetest manner, have given the name.

Let me ask you in future not to use the word "snub" in connection with me and any one, much less you. If there is anything in me which has such a horrid appearance please believe that it is only my nervousness putting on armour. In fact I must be in mortal fear, but thinking it best to cry out "who's afraid?" Your absolutely & purely delightful description of the joys you could give me if I came to you in Italy were not dashed by my feeling that I would prefer to be with other people in that land, for I know of none with whom I should so well like to be with amongst those scenes and associations;[1] I am sure both of you would put up (with infinite kindness) with my dulness, my entranced spirit or witless wonder. So, when I tell you that I cannot come, you will know that I shall feel very much the loss of the opportunity of being with you, and in Italy. It is impossible that I should leave England now; death & destruction with all kinds of malignant influences would attend upon me. I am 3 deep at least with work promised, and 50 deep with work which people promise themselves of me. You will understand I am sure, and not wilfully disbelieve me.

I go to Yorkshire in next week, which will cost me four days, and having turned off my clerk of works there something more is added to my own work and annoyance.[2] All this means, you see, that I am afraid that you will be angry with me, and nip the friendship in its 8 years bud. Your cheering news of the good & promising health of you all is wonderful and makes me hopeful of your good temper and forbearance. When people are not well they are apt to be snappish. Don't let George be reckless if you can help it. They tell me, that at this time of the year the Italian towns you name are almost always fearfully cold, and that not before April should people go there who have not been living there regularly, excuse the Irishism.

It does not seem to me to matter one way or the other as to which man the leadership of the Liberals is given (Lord Hartington has it) for, with a few exceptions, they are a base lot.[3] Perhaps Lowe would have been the wisest choice, as he might have been able to frighten the small fry of the Conservatives – and, Oh, what a small-fry![4] Happy, thrice happy Gladstone, to be quit of them. Have you read the Newman pamphlet? If you have not, do so, for 'tis the sweetest of reading, and Gladstone may well study the style and exercise his faculties in answering it.[5]

I was at Northend last night and gave your letters to read as best conveying your "love" to them.[6] The weather here has turned out very cold and villainous foggy. Ned is I think quite as strong as could be expected. Morris has been really unwell but is very much better, having wisely studied to be so.[7] In answer to your kind expressions as to my health, I've got through the cold very well indeed, and shall do very well if you are not hard upon me. Is it of any use telling you to be careful of yourself? To the children please give my prettiest remembrance, and to you my most distinguished esteem and valorous efforts to continue

Yours very faithfully | Philip Webb:

Howard

---

1 For the Howards' invitation to PSW to join them in Italy, see next letter.
2 For his work on Rounton Grange for Isaac Lowthian Bell, see above, Letter 73, note 5. The clerk of works had initially been John Graham, 'who, having failed to give satisfaction, was replaced by W. Taylor in early 1875'. *Kirk*, p. 298.
3 The former Liberal Prime Minister, William Ewart Gladstone (1809–98), resigned as party leader in December 1874 after losing the general election earlier in the year. Spencer Compton Cavendish, Marquess of Hartington and later eighth Duke of Devonshire (1833–1908) became leader on 3 February 1875.
4 PSW believed that Robert Lowe, later Viscount Sherbrooke (1881–92), who had held the cabinet posts of Chancellor of the Exchequer and Home Secretary under Gladstone, would have been a stronger replacement.

5 Angered when his friend J.J. I. von Döllinger was excommunicated for opposing the doctrine of Papal infallibility, Gladstone attacked British Catholics for falling into line with the Vatican. His pamphlet *The Vatican Decrees in their Bearing on Civil Allegiance: a Political Expostulation*, published in November 1874, prompted responses from the English Catholic divines, Henry Manning and John Henry Newman (both of whom became Cardinals). Newman's *Letter to the Duke of Norfolk* appeared in January 1875, which in February was answered by Gladstone's *Vaticanism: an Answer to 'Reproofs and Replies'*.

6 Since 1867, EBJ and GBJ had lived in Fulham, at 'The Grange, Northend'. It was to be their London home until his death in 1898.

7 At the beginning of the year, WM had complained of 'cold & – liver' (to Aglaia Ionides Coronio, 1 January, *CLWM*, I) and of being 'so full of indigestion' (to Eiríkr Magnússon, 4 January, *CLWM*, I).

83 • To George Howard, 6 February 1875

1, Raymond Buildings, Gray's Inn, | *London,*
Feb 6 1875

My dear Howard.

I am like that one of them in the Bible story, who when invited to the feast said "I cannot come". I've not bought a horse or a house or married a wife, but still I cannot come & that is Gospel truth.[1] I fully enter into your enthusiasm about the little "estate", and, if you can lay hands on the money without going to Monaco for it, I don't see that you will be unwise to pour it out on pretty Italian soil.[2] 'Tis much better that you should do so than find a coal mine there. And now about the house, if you get the ground I would advise you to get hold of some small Italian architect who will make plans by your side, and you can send me memoranda of what you are about, and I can probably help you as well from here as there. I think I should try to keep the old house, unless it is very badly situated, and add on where you want and cut off what you don't; and have nothing architectooralooral about it[3] – whitewash of course, and window openings and doorways, thus: [*sketch*] and you can't go far wrong.

You will see by my letter to Rosalind, how I appreciate your anger at my refusing to listen to the voices of the charmers.[4] But, how can I? Here I have had Routledge and Colonel Thompson conning over the Church plans,[5] and at Mr Whitehead's urgent request to name a date, I have promised that they shall have the general plans by the end of this month.[6] Then, I have not touched the Estate cottages for Brampton, and other things in number that I don't like to think of, but must. I went to see the Naworth clock before it was sent off, & tried the bells. Smiths' write me word with their bill (they have kept to their estimate of 142£) that the clock is fixed, so that I hope it will "ting tang" on your arrival there in the summer.[7]

Now listen, please. Do take care not to run risks 'till you get fearfully and wonderfully strong. Don't be a wilful fool and try to have breakfast lunch & dinner of Italian delights all at once. If you get the house, please make little sketches of it from the S.W. & N.E. and East-North by South-West, and trace them for me as "consulting" architect – surely my years ought to allow me that dignity. If only you could see what I see at this moment (1:oc) out of my window – a cold white fog, with spiderswebs of tree boughs, and thermometer at 37 degrees – you would hug yourself with joy, and be good. I am sorrowful, and yet keep good. What it will be in Yorkshire next week heaven only knows, or the dormice & squirrels.

I will give your love to Morris but I will tell him not to go to you, for he ought not to go: write to him and ask him yourself if you want to do him an injury.[8] I've said nothing of your kindness in wishing me to come & help you & enjoy myself, but I feel it very much, more particularly as you are a man for whom I have built. I find it very general that so soon as I have walled a man in, he walls me out of his esteem. You have not done this, & therefore I want you to get hearty-strong, and live for ever, and when you die be sorry for it.

[Yours very faithfully | Philip Webb:]

Howard

---

1 'Then said he unto him, A certain man made a great supper, and bade many; / And sent his servant at supper time to say to them that were hidden, Come: for all things now are ready. / And they all with one consent began to make excuse. . . . / And another said, I have married a wife, and therefore I cannot come.' St Luke 14:16–8, 20.
2 'For some few weeks George was fired with the possibility of buying property at San Remo and rebuilding an old house on it.' *Surtees*, p. 105.
3 'Architectooralooral' – used to suggest something over-fancy in design – is coined by Joe Gargery, the blacksmith, in Dickens's *Great Expectations* (ch 27).
4 GH had urged PSW to come to Italy to advise and make designs for his San Remo venture.
5 The publisher George Routledge (1812–88), a Brampton man, was a committed member of the church building committee. 'He acted as agent in soliciting subscriptions from people in London with a Brampton connection.' *Penn*, p. 12. Thompson was presumably another member of the committee.
6 For the Reverend Henry Whitehead, see above, Letter 75, note 3.
7 See above, Letter 75, note 4.
8 See previous letter, note 7.

84 • To Sir Baldwyn Leighton, 15 March 1875

Draft/copy

[1, Raymond Buildings . . .]
Mar: 15. '75

To Sir Bal[d]wyn Leighton Bar[t]
2 Upper Berkeley St Portman Square

Dear Sir Bal[d]wyn[1]

I beg to acknowledge the receipt of your letter to me of the 13th.

You will possibly remember some of my strictures on those people called Architects who go about the country, and, under the pretence of "restoring" old the remains of ᵒˡᵈ buildings, end in destroying them. ~~and~~ If so, you will be able to advise your friend Mʳ Gaskell, that, if he wants to know how not to do anything, to such notable works as the mediæval buildings at Wenlock (wh' I went to see some two or three years ago) I could, perhaps, advise him as well as most architects.[2]

But, if the reverse is his intention he would only find me a hindrance instead of a help. My charge would be 6 guineas and travelling expenses if the visit did not occupy more than two days.

Thank you for your good-natured wish to have me to dinner at your house, but, though I do not altogether refuse to go out I do ~~so as little seldom~~ ʳᵉᶠᵘˢᵉ ᵃˢ ᵒᶠᵗᵉⁿ as possible.

With kind regards to Lady Leighton[3] | Believe me to be
Yours very truly P: W:

LB-1, pp. 17-18

---

1 Sir Baldwyn Leighton (1836–97), eighth baronet, became Conservative MP for South Shropshire in 1885, and positioned himself as a liberal.
2 The lawyer, Charles Milnes Gaskell (1842–1919), became Liberal MP for Morley in 1885. In 1873 he inherited Wenlock Priory, in Much Wenlock, Shropshire, from his father, James Milnes Gaskell, who having purchased the site in 1857 from his wife's cousin, Sir Watkins Williams-Wynn, set about restoring the Priory ruins and turning the Lodge into a family home. PSW's previous visit to the Priory ruins was in the company of GPB. See above, Letter 50.
3 The Hon Eleanor Leicester Warren (1841–1914), daughter of George Warren, second Baron de Tabley.

85 • To Thomas Forster, 23 March 1875

Draft/copy

[1, Raymond Buildings . . .]
Mar: 23. '75

To Thomas Forster Esqʳᵉ
Hon Secʸ to New Ch' Committee ᴮʳᵃᵐᵖᵗᵒⁿ
Dear Sir.

I beg to acknowledge the receipt of your letter of the 18ᵗʰ enclosing several questions put to me by your Committee, and wh' I will answer in the order given.[1]

1ˢᵗ It certainly would be possible to transpose the vestry, putting it on the South instead of the North side as shewn, but I wᵈ seriously recommend that this shᵈ not be done. The composition as it now stands is one of very careful consideration, and the position of the vestry has considerably regulated the disposition of parts of the whole of the North side – the displacement of one ~~side~~ part wᵈ affect the whole. Also, the vestry chimney as it stands is at the greatest distance from the highest or central roof & is best placed there with regard to ᵗʰᵉ South West wind.

Again the effect of the chimney (artistically) will help to balance the tower at the West end.

2nd The so called prayer desks are in reality mere extensions of the stalls Westward. The ~~western~~ desk [facing West] on each side is intended for a lettern[2] use, instead of a separate lettern – however these desks could be omitted and a lettern standing clear substituted.

3rd The exact position of the pulpit as shewn need not be insisted upon, but it w[d] not do to put it more eastward, as that would be into the stall space behind ~~them~~ [the stalls], but it might be moved more south, as then the sloping roof of south aisle would act as a sound board, but I have, myself, no fear but that all persons in the church w[d] be able to hear the preacher distinctly.

4th Answered in the 2nd place.

5th There are examples of double sedilia, but if the Committee w[d] prefer it, I see no reason why the seats sh[d] not be three instead of two as shewn.[3]

6th I w[d] put a credence table[4] & piscina[5] combined in the southern jamb of great east window.

7th The mullioned screen between nave and ringers loft is to be glazed.

8th The screens to chancel are to be of fair ashlar stone, and I think about 3 feet 6 in [high] from pavement on the chancel side. They will be higher by the height of the added steps on the aisle sides.

I am Dear Sir, Yours very truly | P: W:

LB-1, pp. 18-20

---

1 PSW had estimated that, by leaving the construction of the belfry tower to a later time, when more funds might become available, the building costs would be £6070.
2 Lectern (obsolete).
3 The sedilia (usually three in number) are the clergy seats normally on the south side of the choir, near the altar.
4 'A small side table or shelf to hold the Eucharistic elements before consecration' (*OED*).
5 'A perforated stone basin for carrying away the ablutions, generally placed in a niche on the south side of the altar' (*OED*).

86 • To Charles Fairfax Murray, 25 March 1875

1, Raymond Buildings, Gray's Inn | London,
Mar: 25. '75

Dear Murray

It was partly your own fault that I did not answer your last letter but one. If I'd written at once (a most improbable thing with me) it w[d] have been all right, but your saying you were shortly going to Rome & giving me no address [for] there made me seize the idle excuse & wait 'till I heard again. Now that I have your Pisa (in an aureole)[1] letter of the 13 of this mo: you see, I do write, tho' late as usual.

You see ^{also} the reason why M'Angelo is a lasting joy to me, is, that he never dropped the mediæval directness of expression and yet is free from archaic mannerism. In truth I fancy he had the power of giving the greatest amount of collected good in his work, though no doubt some of the earlier folk were purer and more direct in some one characteristic. With all of Raffaele's[2] wonderful facility & grace he did drop into sentimental sloppiness (forgive the slang) and gave smiles of uninteresting cleverness. Then you see again I'm a huge lover of frescoe painting over every other kind, well, I find the execution of the Sistine work incomparably the finest. I w^d give a good deal just to fly up to the ceiling and rub eyes over the surface before I die, or restorers have their own wicked will on it.

Perhaps one of these days you'll be able to get a photo: of the new-old Baptist statue. I don't much care whether it be the one or other master's work – Donatello being so splendid a master.[3] The fretful stupidity of most people in thinking of any particular part of the earth – where they happened to be born – as "home", makes them, I suppose, when they are in Italy to wish to get to New York or Paris or London again. Everybody goes to Italy who can, but they grumble at being away (for more than a few months at a time) from soot and ugliness. This is what I thought when I heard that you hoped to get back shortly: as for coming back to see friends, it is ridiculous for when you do see them you find all their bad qualities rampant – whereas when away from them you remember their good only. Also, in England at least, it is thought degrading to be prettily unfettered with wasteful encumbrances of living.

Painters even, ^{in England,} who cannot design a proper fold of drapery, look to keeping a carriage & pair, be knighted & dine with the Ld Mayor – damn them! So you have not yet done "<u>it</u>" and therefore Pisa is so.[4] When you <u>have</u> done it, I hope it won't be London [*sketch of smoking chimney stacks either side of 'London'*] and so – with you, with ^{pleasure} you must know, that I am very glad of your translations & take it as kind of you to do them.[5] I forgive all crowing as well as disgust on your part, & I look for more at your leisure.

There is nothing amusing going on here, people are so rich in England that they can't afford to be interesting and that blasted dillettantism is creeping over the nation more than ever before I fancy – so there is even less of hope for the next future. Mr Jones is doing good work, though I've not been able to see it by day time, and Mr Morris also is not idle & his work is also good.[6]

Our weather is pickleing, [*sic*] with fast wind, but the spring is well kept back by it; always a good thing for this climate.

Yours. | Ph Webb.

Please tell me how properly to address an Englishman (on envelope) who is living in Italy.

Fitzwilliam 15

1 Presumably CFM had highlighted his current location by placing 'Pisa' within a halo.
2 Raffaello Sanzio da Urbino (1483–1520), the Italian painter and architect whose name was purposefully chosen to lend significance to the intentions of the 'Pre-Raphaelite' Brotherhood.
3 The bronze statue by Donatello (Donato di Niccolò di Betto Bardi, c.1386–1466), of St John the Baptist (1457) is now in the Cappella di San Giovanni Battista of the Duomo at Siena, in which city the sculptor was resident between 1457–61.
4 He highlights 'Pisa' by encircling it, in imitation of CFM (see note 1).
5 CFM seems to have sent more of his translations of Michelangelo letter. See above, Letter 81.
6 The protracted arguments over the future of 'the Firm' had finally been resolved. 'On 31 March, an announcement was made that Morris, Marshall, Faulkner & Co. was formally dissolved and the business would continue under Morris's sole ownership, trading as Morris & Co.' *MacCarthy, WMLT*, p. 342. EBJ became sole designer for the company's stained glass.

87 • To George Howard, 9 April 1875

1, Raymond Buildings, Gray's Inn, | London,
April 9 1875

My dear Howard.

Your letter – at last but a very kindly long one. 'Tis true, being indolent, I did not so much care about the answers to questions, but I did want to know how you were both getting on. Of course I had heard of Mrs Howard's safety, but I wanted to know that you were both doing well.[1] If I look with "microscopic eye" in to your letter[2] I distinguish a tone of depression, which may only be the natural outcome of nature, and if so it cannot be helped, & we must take you as we find you.

The Italian Villa interests me very much.[3] I hope you are sure of the ground. Surely you might tell the owner, & he, the Pope, that your ancestors were good Catholics, and you yourselves are not much better; and that in your Castle in the north of England you have a Catholic Chapel – even Cardinal Manning would approve of such Catholic deceit:[4] also your most Catholic architect in England (<u>consulting</u> architect) is quite free from a "bloody-bones" spirit of desecration. Your ideas look pleasant enough on paper, as to what you hope to do in pulling down & putting up again, and if your architect is not a dunderhead he will be careful in knocking about the thick walls, brick vaulting &c. I hope you will keep to paved floors. They stop out bugs & beetles, and make a place quiet. How will the colonnaded balcony be covered?

The Brampton Committee are taking their own sweet time in making up their minds.[5] It will take to the middle of June at the least to get ready to start, and if much later than that, I should advise putting it off 'till next year. I do not mean to say that it is extraordinary, their not seeing the merits of the design as I do, for you know what even "cockeyed" children are to their mothers – well, a few dabs of the brush or architectooraloorool pencil,[6] are of more value in the tooralloorool eye, than many cockeyed children. The said chimney is part of the composition, the pulpit is a <u>moveable</u> feast, and eloquence could swell from any of the 4 corners of the church.

Now, about the cottages.[7] I redesigned them & sent the plan to Warwick, but he only took off two hundred pounds, when he should have taken 5 or 600 at the least from the whole block, so that when I went to DuCane he shook his head,[8] and I initiated him, & of my good nature promised to make a third plan which should come in a winner. This is not yet done, as you may guess, for, I am a little pressed with work, but it will be done in time. Also, I'm something malevolent at this time, and frown & bite my lip, & frown again. However, the sun of laughter will re-gild this countenance upon the return of the faithful. I will send the grates for the nurseries. Warwick has never sent me the memoranda of the moat house, but I will gird him to do so.

No Rome, poor you, I am sorry for you indeed I am for 'tis one of those disappointments which I should keenly feel myself; never mind, youth is on your side, and if steam holds good, you'll go a many times yet.[9] You people also are so greedy. It was not at all foolish my supposing you might be angry at my not coming at your call to San Remo, for I was vexed myself and could not expect you to be more reasonable.

Ashby's sent Heath to me the day before yesterday, to say that you had directed that the outside painting of Palace Green house should be done now. I've promised to go up on Monday and direct, and also meet Boyd, the engineer's man about some broken boiler which the frosts did for you. I passed the house yesterday on my way from Ned's, it looked solitary; some kind critic told me the work looked Italian, somewhat, and I forgave him. Good God! like me, he never can have been in Italy.

The Northend works looked very beautiful to me, and they are progressing finely, though not finished; however, much comes on at the head if little drops off at the tail, so the studios are full for our benefit.[10] I have the photographs of the Hampton Court Mantegna series, so that time is pleasant while I look at them and I do not care that Agnew & others have been paying between 2 & 300£ for D. Cox's landscapes when the Cox only got 30, 40 or 50£ for them.[11] My Mantegna's only cost 2 guineas the set.

It has been said that Mr Gladstone & the Prince of Wales, are the two orators who most aptly notice accidental circumstances during their speeches. I see that the latter used an unusual appearance of the sun with tremendous effect the other day.[12] There, that is all my scandal, and now I wish you well, with very kind regards to Mrs Howard and remembrance to the children.

Yours very truly | Philip Webb.

Howard

---

1 On 14 March, Rosalind had given birth to Oliver Howard (1875–1908) whilst in San Remo, following which GH fell ill with congestion of the lungs. His thoughts of building in San Remo were set aside. See above, Letter 83.

2 This may have been one of Ford Madox Brown's sayings. William Holman Hunt recalls Brown visiting his studio and in commenting on his work 'he cited certain artists as unappreciated whom

he championed earnestly and humorously in turns, meanwhile indulging in playful irony upon what he termed my "microscopic detail".' *Pre-Raphaelitism and the Pre-Raphaelite Brotherhood*, 2 vols (London: Macmillan & Co., 1905), I, pp. 126–7. PSW uses the coinage again in Vol. III, Letter 835 (see note 7).
3 See above, Letter 83, note 2.
4 For Manning, see above, Letter 82, note 5. He had been appointed Cardinal only a few days previously, on 29 March.
5 See above, Letter 85.
6 See above, Letter 85, note 3.
7 See above, Letter 74, note 1.
8 As clerk to the trustees of the Earl of Carlisle, Richard Du Cane was the formal contact in PSW's relations with the Naworth Estate. See below, Letter 112.
9 In fact, the Howards set out in January 1876 for a three-month visit to Rome.
10 Almost certainly this refers to the work which EBJ was doing for Morris & Co.'s extensive decoration work at 1 Palace Green, which continued through the 1870s and into the next decade. 'In designing the dining room . . . Webb had carefully provided a "very good space" flowing around the upper panelling, awaiting s sequence of murals by Burne-Jones [who] had already planned out the frieze and made preliminary watercolour designs when the canvases were ordered. It was an ambitious sequence, a cycle of twelve panels in the grand Italian manner of Pinturicchio, Perugino and Mantegna, painters that the Howards, like Burne-Jones, had admired on their travels in Italy. . . . The panels were begun in Burne-Jones's studio and gradually moved to Palace Green to be worked on *it situ*. But as so often with Burne-Jones's ambitious projects, progress was extremely slow.' *MacCarthy, LPR*, pp. 266–7.
11 On 8 April, the auctioneers Christie, Manson and Woods had sold the Quilter collection of British watercolours, with works by the landscape painter David Cox (1783–1859) selling very well. The buyers included the art dealer, William Agnew (1825–1910). *The Times* recorded (9 April) that one of Cox's drawings, *Green Lanes* (originally sold by the artist for £33), went under the hammer for £1,470, and that *The Hayfield*, sold by Cox in 1850 for 50 guineas, was the subject of spirited bidding between a Mr Addington and Agnew, the latter securing it for £2,950.
12 Although the precise allusion remains unclear, this probably refers to the visit on 7 April of the Prince and Princess of Wales to the Chatham dockyards for the launch of the ironclad ship, the Alexandra, named after the Princess. The weather earlier in the day had been torrentially wet, but the sun appeared for the launch. The Prince of Wales was Queen Victoria's son, Albert Edward (1841–1910), who as Edward VII succeeded her in 1901.

88 • To Lady Fitzhardinge, 18 May 1875

Draft/copy

[1, Raymond Buildings . . .]
May 18. 1875.

To the R[t] Hon The Lady Fitzhardinge
Berkeley Castle

Dear Lady Fitzhardinge.

In answer to yours of the 14th instant. I well recollect the window in question in the other drawing-room at Berkeley Castle and I will make a diagram for the Carpenters to work by, but I must first get from them, fuller dimensions & instructions as to the present frame of the window. In comparing your drawing with a tracing of the window already altered, I fancy it may be better to put only one mullion but this will depend upon the ~~diagrams~~ ᶜⁿᵒᵗᵉˢ⁾ I get from the foreman.

With regard to the Hall fireplace, I am very anxious to do this quite rightly. The fireplace itself does not belong to the date of the hall, and though I think it sufficiently good to be kept, the treatment of its decoration will have to depend upon the woodwork adjoining. I propose to decorate it ⁽ᵗʰᵉ ᶠⁱʳᵉᵖˡᵃᶜᵉ⁾ with gold on a dark ground and by this means soften those parts wh' are incongruous, but to do this properly, it w^d take more than two months and I must make some trials here first before sending a man down to do the work. Upon your request I will make these trials. Also, if you wish it, I could put in hand one of the lights of the hall windows as a specimen, but in that case the glass itself of the light w^d have to be sent to town.

I enclose mem^a for the Carpenter.

Yours very truly | P.W.

LB-1, pp. 22-3

89 • To Lieutenant-Colonel William James Gillum, 13 September 1875

Draft/copy

[1, Raymond Buildings . . .]
Sep 13. 1875.

To Lt Co^l Gillum
Ch. Hill H^{se} East Barnet

My dear Colonel[1]

In answer to your letter rec^d on Saturday ~~containing~~ ᵉⁿᶜˡᵒˢⁱⁿᵍ Mr Sydney Turner's objections to school building scheme. I must insist again that it is for the very purpose of <u>spreading</u> the warm fresh air that a gill stove is strongly recommended by me ⁽ᵃⁿᵈ ᵒᵗʰᵉʳˢ⁾ for large school areas, when simplicity & economy of heating is absolutely necessary. I have proved this in as many as three artists' studios where two open fireplaces were quite ineffectual. Let me explain again that a good gill stove allows of the introduction of an immense body of fresh air into the room (the first necessity for effective ventilation) and this abundant supply of fresh (external) air keeps the surface of the gills from overheating. After 4 or 5 days of use the smell of the iron ceases. Of course, rather than throw any hindrance in the way of your committee getting what they want at once, if Mr Turner still insists, I w^d put in two open fireplaces, for, at some future time a stove could be applied.

With regard to the windows I must still be firm, as it is absolutely necessary for the proper lighting & ventilation of the school that they sh^d be as high as they are shewn, for a diffused light – not a direct light – is what is required – the reflection from the ceiling ~~taking~~ ᵈᵒⁱⁿᵍ away with all shadows.

Will you be so good as to stop Bradley² proceeding with the part of the wall against wh' the stove was to be set, and at the middle of the south east end wall.

Yours very truly, | P.W.

P.S. Mʳˢ Gillum will explain to you what I have just told her as to the concrete.

LB-1, pp. 27-8

---

1 PSW had known the former army officer and philanthropist, Lieutenant-Colonel William James Gillum (1827–1910), since their days as fellow-members of the Hogarth Club (1858–61). Gillum provided PSW with one of his earliest commissions, the construction of a terrace of six craftsmen's houses, each with a shop and workshop, in Worship Street, Shoreditch (1861–3), and followed this by funding the erection of an innovative Boys' Farm School, in East Barnet, Hertfordshire (1867–8) to which PSW also made later modifications, including the conversion of the cow house into a new schoolroom (the subject of this letter), dining room and kitchen (1874–5). Gillum's own Church Hill House, also in East Barnet, was executed by PSW in 1868–70. See *Kirk*, pp. 112, 208–10, 296–7 and 326–7.

2 The builder William Bradley, of Cockfosters, who was undertaking the current work at the Boys' Farm School.

90 • To Jane Morris, 28 September 1875

Annotated 'Watermark 1873'

Kelmscott Lechlade
Tuesday Sep 28

My dearest Janey

Thank you for your note. I guessed the minute that I saw the pencil marks, that you were bodily very weak again.¹ I shall ask Morris – who is expected to eat some of a duck of Mʳ Hobbs's here this evenᵍ – who & what your new doctor is.² I hope he will try to help you.

Fortunately for me there was not a clear space in my rooms on wh' to put the sole of one of my feet, I was practically squeezed out of the house, and had not to make up my mind if I could stay or not.

I am most methodically trying to get stronger here, and no doubt another week will tell upon my weakness.

You wᵈ have laughed to see me yesterday afternoon striving toes nails & teeth to get the boat out of its shed & up the little canal. The stream ran & the wind blew & I was so weak, that it took me ten minutes to do it, to say nothing of being twice blown down the small stream south of the house.

I eat all the fish Philip [Comely] catches but they don't tax my powers much. I live in the Hall, or passage room, & sleep over, & have not seen even the skirt of a bogey.

Yʳˢ affectionately | Philip Webb:

BL Add 45342, ff. 29-30

1 The choice of pencil by the Victorians for letter-writing almost invariably indicates illness, and certainly a letter being written somewhere other than at a table or writing-desk with an ink stand.
2 R.B. Hobbs was a Kelmscott farmer, and the owner of Kelmscott Manor. According to MM, in later years, he became a successful stock breeder.

91 • To George Howard, 1 October 1875

Manor House, Kelmscott, by Lechlade
Oct 1 1875

My dear Howard.

I am here as you see & your letter reached me this morning. It is quite against my inclination that I find I must not come to you as you ask. For the last 4 or 5 months I have been gradually sinking into a state of great bodily weakness & general want of vitality. Indeed I had sunk into such a state of worthlessness, with regard to my work in particular, that I let out all the reef of my sails & drifted down here, which place Morris most kindly put at my service. Here I am trying to revive, with the hope at some time or other of getting at least strong enough not to be a nuisance to my friends and to get power enough to think it worth while fighting my enemies. Do you not see from this that it would be impossible for me to come as you ask? I shall probably stay here for another week or even two, as my chambers are being scrubbed & painted.

If I do anything for Naworth I should wish it to be the best of me and therefore I must see the site of new Agent's house.[1] Could not you & the authorities make notes of what you want and I could get to Naworth in November or December and make up my mind what should be done in the shape and make of the house.

As for the church. The bishop is very stupid in the matter & I suppose is incapable of understanding a design.[2] (1) I should wish not to do away with the outside or ringers' stair. (2) The tower would have to be completely redesigned to ring from the nave floor, & thereby the effect of the design would be quite changed of the whole church. (3) I should have no objection to putting 3 dormers instead of one. (4) The little south door (which would air the organ-chamber) can be omitted. I put it in by particular request.

Moat House.[3] I would put the new chimney (if there is to be one) in the opposing corner to the present one, & carry up the flue without cutting in any way into the old walls. Warwick could leave a hole in the roof, thus: [sketch] I would let him have a drawing for flue &c when I get back to town.

Will you write me just a cheering word saying that you are not angry with me for not thinking your works of more value than my own health, as certainly they are.

Yours very sincerely | Philip Webb:

Howard

1 PSW would design Four Gables, near Brampton, a house with stable for the agent to the Naworth Estate, John Grey. See *Kirk*, pp. 221–3 and 300.
2 The Right Reverend Harvey Goodwin (1818–91), Bishop of Carlisle, had written to GH on 20 November 1875. 'I ventured to make notes of all the points which struck me with regard to Mr. Webb's plans. Of course on questions of pure architecture I should not venture to criticize him; but there are certain points of a practical kind to which I dare say he will give a little further consideration at my suggestion, e.g. The importance of not giving the ringers an outside entrance; of not having a corner for seats as at the S.W. angle of the plan; and the necessity in this latitude of giving tolerably capacious windows to the south. I am much obliged to you for kindly submitting my remarks to Mr Webb, and I cannot doubt that we shall have an excellent church.'
3 See above, Letter 60, note 2.

92 • To George Howard, 7 October 1875

Manor House, Kelmscott by Lechlade
Oct 7 1875

My dear Howard.

It is particularly good of you to put your natural feelings in your pocket & write me so good natured a letter as your last. You are probably right as to my perversity, but the clear truth is that I am exceeding weak in body just now, and some persistence in not doing much work is necessary. I cannot get much strength as yet, but am determined to find myself all the better for the rest and fresh air shortly.

If you could go with me to Naworth it would be very agreeable & for the good of the businesses. I would try to make the particular date suit you.

I hope that you have some good Bordeaux at Castle Howard to smooth away all discomforts and statelinesses.

Morris came down here last night with Faulkner of University, for a day.[1] They brought me a good bottle of wine of which you are now having the next morning effect. They two are gone afishing, & I wish they may catch 'em. We caught an eel in a basket last night; he did look slippery as we took him out this morning. The river is in that condition, however, with puzzled anglers, and takes their vocabulary of damning. Hooks in breeches, worms in your eye, oars in your back, stretchers on your shins & the fish visibly saying 'bother your poverty stricken enducements'.

Yours very truly | Philip Webb:

Howard

1 CF was a fellow of University College, Oxford.

93 • To Lucy Faulkner Orrinsmith, 22 February 1876

Draft/copy

[1, Raymond Buildings . . .]
Feb: 22. 1876.

To Mrs Orrinsmith
Beckenham Kent.

My dear Lucy Orrinsmith.[1]

Thank you for believing that I shd have pleasure in being of any assistance to yourself or husband if it were in my power. Your question is perfectly clearly put.

To build a detached house of 10 rooms (or even a "semi-detached") with any careful arrangement of plan & proportion out of the ordinary run of suburban buildings, in a sound & workmanlike way, with the most simple of good materials at present prices, would, I am satisfied, cost you more than £1200. If quite detached the cost would be nearer 15 or 1600£ I believe. Therefore I cannot recommend you to incur the preliminary cost of finding out the truth of this in practice.

You will easily understand that any departure from the usual way of building in or near large towns, even if there is no more space covered in or materials used than in the usual house, costs more in labour from the mere departure from routine. If the house is not to be better planned & better built it is never worth while to go through the trouble & run the risks of building for oneself – added to which, an exceptional house is not so easily let or sold for its cost value as one of an ordinary type.

With very kind regards. | Believe me to be | Yours very truly | P: W:

LB-1, pp. 31-2

---

1 Lucy Orrinsmith (1839–1910), sister of Charles and Kate Faulkner, had undertaken work for MMF & Co in its early years, including tile-painting. In 1870 she married Harvey Edward Orrinsmith (d. 1904), a wood engraver, bookbinder, and a director of the bookbinding firm, James Burns & Sons. Lucy Orrinsmith published *The Drawing Room: its Decoration and Furniture* (London: Macmillan & Co., 1877), in the successful Art at Home Series. See Emma Ferry, "'The other Miss Faulkner': Lucy Orrinsmith and the 'Art at Home Series'", *JWMS*, XIX (Summer 2011), pp. 47–64.

94 • To Charles Fairfax Murray, 1 April 1876

1, Raymond Buildings, Gray's Inn | London,
Sat: April 1. '76

Bless you my Murray for sending those wonderfully sweet & strong Donatello's.[1] They are after my heart altogether. I wd that the other sides of the pulpits were also photographed that you might send them likewise. Your proposition of sending me what you yourself delight in will be sure to fit my ease, because you will be quite aware when you are getting any for yourself if you are doing wrong. I'd like the MA drawing of "Ganymede" as I have it not.[2]

M[r] Morris is in Staffordshire up to his thighs in dyes and "darning his eyes" & Staffordshire lies,[3] for the former are too few & the latter too many. I am but weak & poorly, & do what I will I cannot get off for Florence before Wednesday week.[4] The Calligraphy of your letter was wonderful to say nothing of being easy to read. You'd better write to M[r] Morris at once before this style has worn out & your third period begins. Should you come across any Raphael drawings free from vanity affectation simpering &c please send me some photo[s] as I have not any of the "wonderful boy".

This is asking you to do things with a vengeance, but I merely mean, when you are wasting your time in the shops you might salve your conscience by picking out good for me. My state is "flat stale & unprofitable"[5] & I can say no more but thank you again for the blessed Donatello's.

Yours very sincerely | Philip Webb.

Fitzwilliam 16

---

1 CFM had sent photographs of the two late bronze pulpits by Donatello in the basilica of San Lorenzo, Florence, probably left unfinished at his death and completed by others.
2 In 1532, Michelangelo presented his drawing of *The Rape of Ganymede* to the young Roman nobleman Tommaso Cavalieri (1509–87). The lost original was widely copied.
3 Between 1875–8, WM made frequent visits to Leek in Staffordshire, determined to master traditional dyeing techniques from the silk manufacturer Thomas Wardle, brother-in-law of GW, by then manager of Morris & Co. He persuaded Thomas Wardle 'to co-operate with him in large-scale experiments, using the dye vats at Wardle's Hencroft Works'. *MacCarthy, WMLT*, p. 348.
4 PSW probably had no serious plans for visiting Italy at this time: it is unlikely that his work commitments would have permitted it. But see his next letter to CFM (12 June 1876), in which he contemplates an autumn visit to Florence.
5 'How weary, stale, flat and unprofitable | Seem to me all the uses of this world!' *Hamlet*, I.ii.133–4.

95 • To W. A. Cardwell, 6 May 1876

Draft/copy

[1, Raymond Buildings]
May 6 1876.

To W: A: Cardwell Esq[re]
6 Spencer R[d] Eastbourne
My dear Sir.[1]

I have delayed answering your letter of ~~yesterday~~ the 4th 'till today so that some of the annoyed surprise with wh' I read the same sh[d] have time to subside.

I think many of the facts ~~have~~ of the case must have escaped your memory, or you ~~have~~ would hardly have expressed your irritation in the way you have.

I will endeavour to call back to your mind ^(several circumstances) since your letter to me of August 28. '75. In that letter you say, that you hope to be able to secure my assistance, and I perfectly remember having recommended you to go & see Mr Tomes's house at Caterham,[2] so that you might be fully aware of the kind of work I sh^d be able to do for you; this visit you made, so that I was assured in my further proceedings.

After my visit with you & Mr Wheatcroft to Eastbourne, when I exerted myself to advise you to the best of my ability as to selection of site, ^(materials &c,) I had an interview here with Mr Wheatcroft, and in a letter to him in answer to his opposition to Messrs Wallis fixing the prices for the materials & labour of the new house, I wrote the following – "That Mr Cardwell's arch^t sh^d let his surveyor prepare bills of quantities, and that Skinner should price & money them out, & that then they sh^d be subject to the approval of Mr Cardwell's arch^t & surveyor". By a letter to Mr Vinall of the 16th of March last you thus express yourself "I received the plans safely and we are ~~much~~ ^(very) pleased with them. I have shewn them to Skinner. I shall be glad to have a duplicate of his estimate & should also like to see the bill of quantities if it can be managed".

After ^(I had many &) repeated conferences with Mr Vinall in making changes, alterations and adaptations to perfect the plans to your particular wishes so far as they could be done, consistent with economy & the character of the design, Mr Vinall wrote as follows "I have seen Mr Webb who approves of all the alterations we made in the plans on Friday".

In a letter of Mr Vinall's to you 21st Dec^r '75, he says, "I send you with this a tracing of plans showing another arrangement for your house". To some of the propositions made to me by Mr Vinall at your suggestion, I told him (more than once) they ~~can~~ ^(could) not be allowed, as the house w^d already cost at least £1800.

The "sketches" you speak of, & for wh' if we had gone no farther, I sh^d have been quite willing to charge a nominal price, w^d have been the first plans I made, from wh' in the final drawings we have completely departed. In these final drawings, from wh' only could accurate quantities be taken, everything is laid down with precision, all the important parts being amplified in half inch scale detailed working drawings, from wh' if the estimates had turned out satisfactorily we could have made tracings & proceeded with the actual works instantly – and this care & forethought was to meet your urgent wish; for in a letter to Mr Vinall on the 22nd Feby 1876 you say "I am very glad to hear that you are getting on with the plans, for I am extremely anxious to get into the house before next winter.

I need scarcely say more, for you will probably have a copy of your letter to me of last Thursday, and you will see how ~~thoroughly~~ ^(completely) the changes, therein made, are here met. I think Sir, when you quietly reconsider the ~~matter~~ ^(subject), you will understand how thoroughly & carefully both Mr Vinall ^(& I) have worked in your matter, sparing ~~no~~ ^(neither) pains ~~&~~ ^(nor) cost on our parts, to prepare for you ^a house wh' sh^d be both pleasant & comfortable to you as well as ~~a~~ credit^(able) to ourselves. That the work did not proceed further was your own wish, or reductions could have been prepared on the existing data to meet the too high estimates caused by the high price of labour & materials.

In conclusion I beg to say, that neither I nor Mr Vinall can make any reduction in our charges, wh' are barely sufficient to cover the expenses of the work of ourselves & our assistants.

Yours truly | Philip Webb:

LB-1, pp. 35-8

---

1 W.A. Cardwell, son-in-law of the surgeon, Sir Benjamin Brodie, to whose Regency country house in Tadworth, Surrey, PSW made alterations in 1872–4, commissioned plans for a new house in Eastbourne. Cardwell's failure to pay the fees, once the project was abandoned, led PSW to go to law. 'I feel it w^d be useless for me to enter further into personal discussion with you. I will, therefore, put the matter into the hands of my solicitors' (PSW to Cardwell, 11 October 1876, *LB-1* p. 47). The action was unsuccessful. See *Kirk*, pp. 275 and 299.
2 PSW's house, Upwood Gorse at Caterham, Surrey (1868–9), for the dental surgeon, John Tomes (1815–95). See *Kirk*, p. 297.

96 • To Charles Fairfax Murray, 12 June 1876

1, Raymond Buildings, Gray's Inn | London,
June 12. '76

My dear Murray

Your photographs have all reached me – viz. The paradise of Orcagna & the Inferno (also I suppose by him)[1] the roll of Benozzo Gozzoli's wh' EBJ has rec^d [2] – the early Pièta of MA & two copies of the late one, all of wh' are admirable, &, to my wilfully bad taste, good in the extreme.[3] The Inferno you need not have been nervous ab^t as it suits me to a T – Also I've rec^d your two last letters, the first written 29th May, the last rec^d this morning. I w^d have answer^d the former before, but awaited your new address, not being willing to enrich the Italian dead-letter box.

The Inferno, it is marvellous, so much so that I can put up with its indistinctness. The late Pièta my MA madness can rejoice in likewise, as I see so little of giggling company, and RA^s never venture up my stairs. Glory be to God for my tiring staircase and inhospitable countenance. If any of the filthy <u>should</u> come, I'll shew them the early Pièta, the Ultramontane black whirligig of wh', will just suit them.

I send you by this post the comic annual you ask for,[4] it will make you grin, & overcome seasickness on your voyage home, & save you the trouble of going to the Academy where you w^d be picture sick.

Please bring me a photo' of Orcagna's tabernacle work of which you ~~speak~~ write.[5] I dined with Stanhope the other evening.[6] M^{rs} S told me that she had begun to slaughter chickens & the fatted calf, when she heard a shout of laughter from her husband & stayed her hand.[7] This was from your message on your last return from England. I'll talk to you when I see you about my return with ^you to Florence this autumn (you may laugh if you can) of wh' I am considering;[8] as, since the Q was made Emperess [*sic*],[9] Architecture has been on the decline, & fifty flunkies to a Lord, absolutely necessary. What the devil do you mean, in sending your address, by writing "(ultimo piano)"?[10] does it imply 'ring the bottom bell softly'? I'm going to re-create myself this evening by listening to Mozart's "Jupiter" symphony, of wh' there is no parallel.[11] I dont know much of the cost of Pieta photo^s, save, that Wallis got me a small Mantegna the other day, private handed, wh' cost I think 5 francs[12] – he considered that high, but I thought it worth £20,000, ie double the cost of the lost Gainsborough. I'll tell Boyce of your kind regards, and Crippa's[13] address. I don't know about war, but expect shortly to have to pay 5^s/- income tax, but as architecture will only bring me £50 a year shortly it won't matter – to me – & the P of W is not nervous I believe, or anxious as to his debts.[14] Please bring me any outlandish Photo^s you may fancy as good food for my corrupt imagination. Is there such a thing as a photo of the Pandolfini Palace at Florence ascribed to Raffaelle?[15] If there is will you bring it. Please accept my very sincere thanks for all the trouble you have taken in so kindly helping on my education. Also bring your little bill, for my pocket burns to pay it before the war comes on.

Yours very truly | Philip Webb:

Fitzwilliam 17

---

1 A number of problems surround the traditional attribution of works to the Florentine painter, sculptor and architect Andrea di Cione, called Orcagna (c. 1315/20–68). The frescoes of the Triumph of Death and the Last Judgement in the Campo Santo in Pisa, attributed to Orcagna by Vasari, are now ascribed to Francesco Traini (d. after 1347). Similarly, the frescoes of Paradise and the Last Judgment (1354–7) in the Strozzi Chapel of the basilica of Santa Maria Novella in Florence (where the retable is certainly his work) are mainly the work of his brother, Nardo di Cione (c. 1320–1365/6). PSW probably refers to these Florentine frescoes.

2 CFM had probably sent reproductions of the Gozzoli frescoes in the fifteenth-century Magi chapel of the Palazzo Medici Riccardi in Florence, works which PSW valued highly when he visited in 1884–5. See below, Letter 242. EBJ's interest in the work of the Florentine painter Benozzo Gozzoli (1420–97) was fired during his Italian visit in the autumn of 1871. In the Campo Santo in Pisa he saw Gozzoli's celebrated series of biblical scenes (irreparably damaged during World War II), and in San Gimignano examined the fresco cycle on the Life of St Augustine (1463–7) in the church of Sant'Agostino, as well as an Assumption and a Martyrdom of St Sebastian in the Palazzo Communale. See *MacCarthy, LPR*, pp. 227–9.

3 The 'early Pietà' is the sculpture completed in 1500 for the tomb of Cardinal Jean Villiers de La Grolais, in St Peter's, Rome. There are two candidates for 'the late one' – that in the Duomo in Florence, and the incomplete and radically reductive Rondanini Pietà in the Castello Sforzesco, Milan.

4 Irony, surely. It is likely that PSW was sending a catalogue of the Royal Academy Exhibition, which ran from May to August.

5 Orcagna's ornately Gothic tabernacle (1355–9) in Orsanmichele, Florence.

6 The painter, John Roddam Spencer Stanhope (1829–1908), a friend of CFM for whom PSW had designed a studio-house in Cobham, Surrey (1860–1), his first work after Red House. See *Kirk*, p. 296.

7 Elizabeth King married Stanhope in 1859.
8 See above, Letter 94, note 4. He did not visit Italy until the autumn of 1884.
9 Encouraged by her Conservative Prime Minister, Benjamin Disraeli, Queen Victoria assumed the title of Empress of India from 1 May 1876, but a Royal Titles Act had to pass through Parliament, and it received opposition from Liberals who objected to the aura of absolutism. The Queen's title formally changed from 1877.
10 The top floor (*It*).
11 He heard Mozart's 41st (and final) symphony in C major at the Royal Philharmonic Society Monday 'Pops' concert at St James's Hall, which also included Beethoven's fifth piano concerto in E flat major (the 'Emperor').
12 The painter and collector, Henry Wallis (1830–1916), became an authority in foreign ceramics, his researches being published in twenty volumes. He served as secretary for the committee formed for the preservation of St Mark's, Venice (1882–90), though PSW would come to doubt his commitment to protecting Italian buildings. He is best known for *Chatterton* (1856, Tate Britain), his early painting of the dead poet.
13 Identity uncertain.
14 See above, Letter 87, note 11.
15 Work started on Raphael's design for the Palazzo Pandolfini in Florence in about 1518.

97 • To George Milburn, 3 July 1876

Draft/copy

[1, Raymond Buildings . . .]
July 3. 1876.

To M[r] Geo' Milburn (carver &c)[1]
Gillygate York.

Sir.

Being in want of a good carver in the north capable of doing ~~good~~ work in sound sandstone of the Cleveland quarries, I applied to M[r] Robert Johnson Arch[t], of Newcastle on Tyne, and he recommended me to apply to you as a person likely to suit ~~me~~ for my kind of work. What I want done, is carving of a bold & simple character on the outside of the house.

If you think you w[d] care to undertake the work, and could do so at once, would you meet me at Rounton Grange on Monday the 17th of this month to consider the matter? The house on wh' the work is to be done is "The Grange – East Rounton by Northallerton". The station to book to, is "Welbury" on the North Eastern Railway, and the station is about 3 miles from the Grange – a porter w[d] direct you to the house.

Yours truly | Philip Webb. Architect.

LB-1, pp. 38-9

---

1 The sculptor and wood carver, George Walker Milburn (1844–1941) had an established York business by 1881. Several of his statues are to be seen around the city.

98 • To Lady Fitzhardinge, 25 July 1876

Draft/copy

[1, Raymond Buildings . . .]
July 25 '76

To The R{t} Hon' The Lady Fitzhardinge
Cranford House Hounslow.

Dear Lady Fitzhardinge

I went to Berkeley on Thursday last, and I was fortunate in having Mr Morris with me.

I examined the "Princes" room, and came to the conclusion that the safest colour to use with the tapestry there, w{d} be white, "flatted", of the same shade as that I used in your bedroom. After the Hoppner portrait is removed[1] (is it necessary to remove this picture?) Mr Morris suggested hanging over the fireplace any piece of handsome <u>old</u> silk or other embroidery – that is, needle work wh' w{d} be sure to go well with the existing tapestry.

I found the windows in the first drawing room, inserted under my direction, very simple & unostentatious & therefore satisfactory; I sh{d} have no objection to changing the large drawing-room windows in the same way, with a difference, on acct of their size.

I cannot agree ~~to your~~ with the proposition to remove the organ from the music room & place it in the chapel, for these reasons, that, it suits the room it is now in, and is out of character with the chapel, & w{d} too much encumber ~~the chapel~~ it.

With regard to the small window on the landing of the great oak staircase, I w{d} propose that the ^coloured glass in the lead of it be removed, as it is very harsh & discordant, and plain white glass inserted, instead, to match the lower part of the window. Mr Morris & I made up our minds as to what ~~to do~~ w{d} be best to be done with the rest of ^the glazing of the great hall windows on the court side, when it is decided to have ~~them~~ it changed. I told Mr Cooke[2] that when you ~~agreed~~ had settled that the work sh{d} be done he was to send up to London the whole of the four compartments of the window of wh' one quarter has been altered and I w{d} insert the shields of the upper ~~glass~~ parts in ~~a~~ proper ~~frames~~ borders and slightly alter that wh' has been done to bring the whole together.[3] I considered the change already made, a great relief to the hall. ~~With regard~~ As to the new oak seats, it seemed to me that the simplicity of the ends was more suitable than any addition that I could make & that they had better remain as they are.

The decorating of the fireplace is ~~slowly~~ advancing and will come out satisfactorily when finished, as Mr Morris's man has put on a very good ground colour, in a right manner. I have directed him to leave the work at the end of this week, and he shall return with an assistant when the Castle is empty again, wh' Mr Cooke told me it w{d} be in August & a part of September.

Will you allow me to urge upon you the great necessity there is for providing a large quantity of ^English oak to be cut to proper size & stored in a dry airy shed, so as to be ready for use when repairs must be done, as they will have to be before many years have passed. This oak sh{d} be cut from the park or procured elsewhere

~~at once~~ as soon as possible. Also, whenever it is found that any of the chimneys must be rebuilt a proper design sh^d be supplied and the right stone & way of building ~~sh^d~~ be employed, all as to wh' I carefully explained to Mr Cooke.

It was discomforting to find that the gas had already begun to discolour the walls & ceiling of the Great hall, but that is not the most serious evil – for, certain & more rapid decay will go on in the timbers of the roof, unless the gas is removed. Permit me to urge you to have it removed at once.

I must ask your pardon for writing so decidedly on these points, but, unless I did so, I sh^d not consider it w^d be of any use my visiting the Castle at all.

Believe me d^r Lady Fitzhardinge | Yours faithfully | Philip Webb:

LB-1, pp. 40-3

---

1 The portrait painter, John Hoppner (1758–1810) was elected RA in 1795. In the Catalogue Raisonné which forms the main part of William McKay and W. Roberts, *John Hoppner, R.A.* (London: P. & D. Colnaghi & Co., 1909), two Hoppner portraits at Berkeley Castle are described (pp. 22–3). One shows the fifth Earl of Berkeley, Frederick Augustus, with his son, William Fitzhardinge; the other, the Countess of Berkeley, the fifth Earl's wife (he being her second husband), born Mary Cole, of Wotton, Gloucestershire.

2 J.H. Cooke was the Castle's Estate Manager, and something of a local historian, producing a Handbook on the Castle in 1881. After returning to London, WM sent Cooke a copy of *The Earthly Paradise*. 'I enjoyed my visit to Berkeley exceedingly; I think the castle can scarcely be matched among all the famous houses of England for romantic interest, using that much abused word in its best sense.' WM to Cooke, 24 July 1876, *CLWM*, I.

3 '[E]xcept in the case of the Great Hall windows, there seems to be no evidence of Morris's having supplied any new stained or coloured glass. The shields of arms were eventually reset by Morris & Co., in quarries and borders, since an entry in the Catalogue of Designs, dated November 1884, for a window for Holmstead, Mossley Hill, Liverpool, mentions that the same quarry and border design was used as for Berkeley Castle.' A. Charles Sewter, *The Stained Glass of William Morris and his Circle – A Catalogue*, 2 vols (New Haven and London: Yale University Press, 1975), I, p. 15.

99 • To George Black, 21 August 1876

Draft/copy

Aug 21. 1876

To Mr George Black.
Builder Devonshire St Carlisle
Sir.

<u>Brampton Ch</u>

As the tenders for the above works (only 3 in number after advertising) were far too high, I am going to Cumberland to arrange matters for getting fresh tenders to begin the work next spring.[1]

As your tender was the lowest, perhaps you w^d like to meet me there, when you w^d be able to look into the matter more closely with me, and perhaps come to the conclusion to give a more reasonable price for the works required to be done, and so avoid the necessity, otherwise, of getting altogether fresh tenders.

I shall be at Naworth Castle on Thursday the 24th of this month, and if you sh[d] think it worthwhile I sh[d] be glad to see you there (at the Castle) at 11. oc on that morning. Please give me an answer by return of post.

Yours truly | Philip Webb. Arch[t]

LB-1, pp. 44-5

---

1 The tendering process at Brampton was rather laboured. PSW had initially approached eight local builders, of which only two seemed interested in the work. Even after inviting tenders by advertisement, George Black's was one of only three received. After a further invitation in October, the contract was awarded to Beaty Brothers, of Wetheral Quarry. See *Penn*, p. 17.

100 • To Percy Wyndham, 28 December 1876

Draft/copy

[1, Raymond Buildings . . .]
Dec[r] 28. '76

To The Hon' Percy Wyndham M.P.
Wilbury House Wilts

Dear Sir.[1]

I was sorry to find on going to Stanfords',[2] that neither the 6 in[ch] nor 25 in[ch] scale maps of your district were yet published, ~~as~~ either of these maps w[d] be of great use to you.

I directed Stanfords' to send you four sheets of the 1" scale geologically coloured map of the district round Knoyle. The packet was to be addressed, to remain at Grateley station until called for.

Since my visit with you & M[rs] Wyndham to Clouds estate, I have carefully considered the matter, both from your point of view & my own, with regard to my entering upon the business of building a house for you there, if you sh[d] wish me to do so.[3] I have no doubt that the site of the small existing house, keeping in mind the absolute necessity of preserving the fine yew trees, w[d] answer very well in all respects as the position for a new house, & in many ways I consider it to have exceptional advantages.

I have thought that the suggestions I made, & the expression I gave as to what I sh[d] consider would be the best way of meeting the circumstances of the case (apart from the rude way in wh' I am afraid they often were given) seemed to meet your wishes, & therefore I sh[d] be quite willing to undertake the designing & superintending of the works in question if you sh[d] wish me to do so, subject to the following conditions – viz – That all drawings, whether of works done or only proposed, sh[d] be my property – (This not to exclude my providing you with all the necessary plans &c for your future use after the work was done). That my payment sh^d be at the rate of 5 per cent ~~for~~ ^(on the cost of) all works done under my direction, & further payment of ~~all~~ travelling expenses for myself and assistants. That if plans in whole and in detail are prepared ^(by me) ready to be laid before contractors and the works sh^d not be carried out ~~by me~~, 2½ per cent on my estimated cost of the ~~same~~ ^(execution of the works) be paid to me. That if only preliminary ^(sketches and) plans be made ~~by me~~ 1¼ per cent on my estimated cost be paid me for the same.

I must ask you to excuse these particulars, as it has been found that such care & explanation ^(between client & Architect) before any work has been entered upon, tends very much to the avoidance of any dispute or awkwardness afterwards.[4]

I am Dear Sir yours truly | Philip Webb:

LB-1, pp. 50-2

---

1 The Hon. Percy Scawen Wyndham (PWY: 1835–1911), Conservative MP for West Cumberland, married Irish-born Madeline Campbell (1835–1920) in 1860. At the end of 1874, they became tenants of Wilbury Park House, near Salisbury, and in November 1876 bought the estate of Clouds, East Knoyle, with the intention of building a new house as their family seat. As friends of the George Howards, they had seen the results of PSW's work when in June 1872 they were dinner guests at 1 Palace Green, whereupon they settled that he should design their house in due course. Indeed, PSW had already undertaken minor work at their London home, 44 Belgrave Square. For a full account of the Wyndhams, and more particularly of PSW's design and construction of Clouds (1877–86), see *Dakers*. See also *Kirk*, pp. 132–42 and 300.
2 Edward Stanford (1827–1904) established his business as a map-seller and printer in 1853, with shop premises in Charing Cross and a printing works at Long Acre.
3 PSW stayed overnight with the Wyndhams at Wilbury House on 15 December, in order that they might visit the prospective site for Clouds. 'I will bring any drawings I have wh' w^d be likely to assist, though I shall hardly be able to shew you anything but working drawings.' PSW to PWY, 12 December 1876, *LB-1* p. 50.
4 PWY replied at once: 'I give my adherence to all your propositions, and think your method of doing business a very satisfactory one'. *Dakers*, p. 51.

101 • To Percy Wyndham, 30 December 1876

Draft/copy

[1, Raymond Buildings . . .]
Decr 30. 1876

To The Hon' Percy Wyndham M.P.
44 Belgrave Square.
Dear Sir.
I rec^d your letter of yesterday, this morning. I fully understand your caution with regard to the future water supply for Clouds, but I am persuaded that at the present state of proceedings, it w^d be sufficient for you to express dependence, on the vendors of the estate proving to you, that the reservation of the water from "Barnes

Hill springs" would not leave ~~the estate~~ ^you without an equally good supply from elsewhere on the estate.[1] I think it probable that Mr Rawlence will be able to shew this without difficulty,[2] and if so, ~~I am inclined to think~~ that the proposed new house w^d be better supplied than from the lower situation of the Barnes Hill springs.

I am inclined to think that it ~~might~~ ^may be advisable to have the opinion of a skilled engineer to aid in carrying the best water in the best way to the site, but I ~~think~~ ^believe it w^d be premature to have him on the ground 'till after the vendors had proved their words, or at least given good grounds for their assertion. It is very likely that Mr Rawlence will do this when he meets you on Saturday next. I also have been thinking of the water supply & have thought it possible that the windmill might be turned to account as ^(the motive power for) a pumping engine as the soil in the neighbourhood must be full of springs.

With regard to the latter part of your letter about the sizes of rooms, I am very glad that you are so carefully considering the subject, and I shall not ^be likely to obstruct, ^except on the score of cost. I sh^d ~~be inclined~~ ^like to have the chief rooms 20 feet wide, and this width, with <u>recessed</u> fireplaces ^(on the <u>sides</u> of the rooms,) w^d give the right amount of serving way.

Yours truly | Philip Webb.

LB-1, pp. 52-3

---

1 When PWY purchased the Clouds estate from Alfred Seymour, a distant relative, there was an existing four-bedroom house dating from the late eighteenth century, with adjoining stone cottage, and two further cottages. 'The old house would have to be demolished, though Webb made a careful note of parts that could be used again: oak floorboards, oak stairs, cast-iron grates and even "a good brass knocker on N door".' *Dakers*, p. 51.
2 James Rawlence, of the Salisbury firm of land agents and surveyors, Rawlence and Squarey.

102 • To Lord Fitzhardinge, 10 January 1877

Draft/copy

[1, Raymond Buildings . . .]
Jan 10. 1877

To the R^t Hon' The Lord Fitzhardinge
Berkeley Castle.
My Lord.

I enclose you my charge for work done by me for Berkeley Castle since my first visit in April 1874.

In letters wh' I have written to Lady Fitzhardinge, I have mentioned that considerable works w^d have to be done in coming years in repairs to the Castle, more particularly in timber & lead work to the roofs. Also, at my last visit I carefully examined the several ~~new~~ chimney stacks wh' have been ^rebuilt, & wh' have are not been at all satisfactory as to the stone used or as to the design. If other chimnies [*sic*] are rebuilt, I w^d advise the use of different material, different design & the flues to be lined with fire-clay pots.

I also spoke to Mr Cooke as to putting by oak timber for future use, & if necessary the cutting down as soon as possible of oak trees for the sake of such timber, or, when any oak timber is in the market from 5 to 7 years old, from time of felling, it w^d be well to purchase.

I am my Lord, yours faithfully, | Philip Webb:

LB-1, p. 55

103 • To Percy Wyndham, 16 January 1877

Draft/copy

[1, Raymond Buildings . . .]
Jan: 16. 1877.

To The Hon' Percy Wyndham M.P.
Wilbury House by Salisbury

My dear Sir.

I sent to Mr Grantham a note of the probable height of the cisterns in the proposed new house at Clouds,[1] but I shall not be able to decide as to the position & arrangements of the house until I have spent some hours in particular examination of the site and surroundings. No arrangement can be made as to the Laundry until I can send down to take the plan & measurements of the cottage, and this, of course, could not be done until the tenant had left.[2]

I have been carefully considering the plan of the new house, & I have concluded that it w^d not be necessary to make the hall or common room more than one story in height; this w^d make a very considerable saving in the cost of the building. And, as I sh^d propose to make the hall itself large enough to give 1760 cubic feet of air space to each of 10 persons using it at the same time, the room w^d be much more thoroughly warmed than if it the ceiling was raised 2 stories or even 1½ stories in height, but of this & other matters I sh^d like to consult with you & Mrs Wyndham personally.

Yours very truly | Ph Webb:

LB-1, pp. 56-7

---

1 'I went this morning to Mr Grantham, a Civil Engineer who has lately arranged the water supply to Lord Normanton's house at Somerley in Hampshire. . . . The arrangement I made, was that Mr Grantham sh^d go on to the groins especially to advise you as to such supply of water as w^d be suggested by Mr Rawlence, and also generally to look to the high ground of the Estate for a good supply, beyond what might be pointed out to him.' PSW to PWY, 2 January 1877, *LB-1*, p. 54.
2 The tenant of the cottage adjacent to the existing Clouds House was the former estate gardener.

104 • To Charles John Ferguson, 6 February 1877

Draft/copy

[1, Raymond Buildings . . .]
Feb 6. 1877.

To Chas Ferguson Esqre
50 English Street. Carlisle

My dear Sir.[1]

A M^r J: Morland – ~~Clerk of works~~ – applied to me some time since for the situation of Clerk of works to the new church at Brampton. I was not then in a position to advise the committee to accept his services. We are now ready for a Clerk of works, and I again applied to Morland, & he wrote to say that he had again engaged himself; however, I had a letter from him this morning saying he had reconsidered the matter & wished to work for me. Now, if he was engaged to you, I sh^d be very sorry to cause him to leave ^you without ~~your~~ looking to your convenience in the matter. Morland also referred me to your firm for his character as to fitness for the position in question.

Will you kindly let me know, if it w^d inconvenience you his coming to me; and if it did not do so, if you thought him honest, sober, ~~& fit~~ ^& a fit & capable person to look after the building of a church over a contractor.

I hope you will not be disagreeably surprised at my so soon using your most friendly offer of assistance.

Believe me yours ^very sincerely, | P.W.

LB-1, pp. 59-60

---

1 The Carlisle architect C.J. Ferguson (1840–1904) was at this time in partnership with John Cory. PSW's respect for Ferguson's work was such that in 1879 he recommended to GH that Ferguson should succeed him as architect to Naworth Castle. See *Kirk*, p. 183.

105 • To Thomas Forster, 10 February 1877

Draft/copy

[1, Raymond Buildings . . .]
Feb: 10. 1877

To Thos Forster Esqre
Brampton Cumber^d

Dear Sir

(Brampton Ch)

In answer to your letter of yesterday's date. The sum of £5678.6.3 only includes the cost of the works authorised by the Committee to be entered upon and the cost of preparing the necessary "quantities".

108

I sh^d be anxious if possible to avoid the use of gas in the church, as it is found in practice that gas does serious injury to public buildings. A few lamps or candles at the darkest season of the year w^d be all that w^d be necessary in a Country parish like Brampton.

Yours truly | Ph Webb:

P.S. I sh^d like to have the drawings &c back as soon as possible, as Messrs Beaty are writing pressing for working details.[1]

LB-1, pp. 62-3

---

1 Beaty Brothers had been awarded the building contract. See above, Letter 99, note 1.

106 • To George Howard, 15 February 1877

1, Raymond Buildings, Gray's Inn, | London,
Feb 15 1877

My dear Howard.

Glory be! I am indeed glad that Mrs Howard has pulled through so well. I was a little anxious, but her courage is great & her constitution good, & so we rejoice again.[1] Yes, I will come with pleasure some day next week; perhaps you will have some evening when you will be dull & alone. Then would be the time for me to bring you my dulness. Two dulnesses making one round jolly face.

Let the Bramptonians fight it out together, I have done my part, & be damned to them. They are not bad sort of fellows though, but to want to go to church & have gas to pray by, Good Lord! One dim lamp (a la Tooth) at the East end,[2] & beating of breasts on account of having quarter day in front of them, would be ample. However, they shall have gas like to Drury Lane theatre if they please. I am glad it was Beaty who praised the Architect, not Webb who praised Beaty.[3] I can't have given him a "Commission", my pet law suit wouldn't allow of that, & he didn't offer me one.

Our poet, "on the premises", has returned, all glorious with Tyrian dyes – he didn't show me his feet, but I saw his hands.[4] A stammering lover would want to know if he was be-be-blue all over.

Kindest remembrances to Mrs Howard. | Yours sincerely | Philip Webb:

Howard

---

1 Rosalind Howard had given birth to her seventh child, Geoffrey, on 12 February.
2 Arthur Tooth (1839–1931) was an Anglican clergyman whose fondness for ceremonial ritual led to accusations of Papist sympathies. Having been instructed to refrain from practices such as the use of incense and altar candles, in January 1877 he was taken into custody for contempt of court, and was regarded as a martyr by Anglo-Catholic opinion. PSW's reference to a 'dim lamp . . . at the

East end' denotes the discreet candle in (Anglo)-Catholic churches which marks the location of the Blessed Sacrament (the consecrated communion wafer).
3 See previous letter, note 1.
4 For WM's involvement with dyeing techniques, see above, Letter 94, note 3.

107 • To Major Arthur Godman, 22 February 1877

Draft/copy

[1, Raymond Buildings . . .]
Feb. 22. 1877.

To Major Arthur Godman
Smeaton by Northallerton

Dear Major Godman[1]

I enclose you proposed plan of stables, cow byre, kitchen garden &c, for your consideration. I believe that the stable & cow byre <u>without</u> garden walls, greenhouse & pig styes [*sic*] would cost, as [I] have shewn, as much as £3,000 – so I should be glad if you w^d consider the matter, & on the basis of this plan suggest any reductions you can.

You will see that I have indicated two small Cottages for groom & coachman & helps bedrooms – but I should like further information as to what you would like for this part of the system. The hay, straw & corn lofts w^d be over the north wing of stables & loose boxes. You will see that I have allowed room for 2 (large) carriages only, would you require more?

Yours very truly | Philip Webb:

LB-1, pp. 68-9

---

1 PSW designed Smeaton Manor with stables and farm buildings in Great Smeaton, North Riding (1876–9) for the army officer and horse-breeder, Major (later Colonel) Arthur Fitzpatrick Godman (1841–1940) and his wife Ada Phoebe Bell (1850–1900), a daughter of PSW's client, Lowthian Bell. See *Kirk*, pp. 126–31 and 300.

108 • To Thomas Forster, 22 February, 1877

Draft/copy

[1, Raymond Buildings . . .]
Feb: 22. 1877.

To Thos Forster Esqre
Brampton Cumberland

(Brampton Ch')

Dear Sir.

I have directed a Mr J: Morland, Clerk of Works, to call upon you. After considerable negociation[1] I have selected him as a fit person ~~to advise~~ for the Committee to appoint; first, on acc^t of his experience in <u>church work</u>, and secondly on acc^t of the recommendation I have rec^d from his late employers – Messrs Cory & Ferguson – as to his honesty & capability.

The salary he will require will be £3.0.0 a week, and the committee could not get a properly experienced man for less, if he had to spend his whole time on the works of the church, wh' it ~~will~~ would be quite necessary for the Clerk of works to do.

Messrs Cory & Ferguson have kindly facilitated the transfer of Morland's services.

Yours truly. | Philip Webb:

P:S: The Clerk of works sh^d be appointed by the time the contractor commences work on the site.

LB-1, p. 69

---

1 This spelling, common enough in the nineteenth century, was favoured by PSW.

109 • To George Price Boyce, 15 March 1877

1, Raymond Buildings, Gray's Inn, | *London,*
Mar: 15. '77

My dear Boyce

Thank you very much for your trouble about the idea Utopian, as to preservation of noble old buildings. All I could expect was, that of your good nature you w^d lay the matter before friend Norbones,[1] leaving it to him to write or not, as he might please or be able.

We shall, I think make an effort to start a Society, not, however, anticipating any great success.[2] Tewkesbury will certainly be destroyed, but there are still some fine buildings, like Selby,[3] Howden[4] & others wh' might be saved, if sufficiently loud screaming were set up. A steam fog-horn blowing night & day in Trafalgar square might do good – and when the blood-thirsty have fixed their blasting eyes on a new found remnant, the fiery cross sh^d be sent round.

I have to go to Cumberland on Monday, but shall hope to be back by Wednesday night at the latest, and therefore in time for the Philh^c on Thursday.[5]

My calculation is easy for your work, and I send you the charge.[6] It w^d have been much more pleasant for me to have done this work for you out of pure love; but, if my enemies won't pay, my friends must, or society be shocked by the death of an arch^t from starvation appearing in the radical papers.

Yours very truly | Philip Webb:

BL Add 45354, ff. 91-2

1 The Reverend Thomas W. Norwood (1829–1908), from 1878 vicar of Wrenbury, Nantwich, was a founder member of the SPAB, and became the local correspondent for casework in Cheshire.
2 In a letter in *The Athenaeum* on 5 March, WM deplored the imminent 'restoration' of Tewkesbury Abbey, asserting that it would be 'destroyed by Sir Gilbert Scott'. The letter concluded with a statement of intent. 'What I wish for, therefore, is that an association should be set on foot to keep a watch on old monuments, to protest against all "restoration" that means more than keeping out wind and weather, and by all means, literary and other, to awaken a feeling that our ancient buildings are not mere ecclesiastical toys, but sacred monuments of the nation's growth and hope.' This is the earliest reference to the imminent founding of the Society for the Protection of Ancient Buildings (hereafter, the SPAB). Its first meeting was at Queen Square on 22 March, and GPB was present.
3 The eleventh-century Selby Abbey, in the former North Riding of Yorkshire, which, in the words of its website, was 'overhauled and repaired' in the nineteenth century. http://www.selbyabbey.org.uk/selbyabbeyhistory.htm [accessed 10 July 2014].
4 The east end of Howden Minster, in the former East Riding of Yorkshire, fell into ruin after the Reformation, although the nave survives as the parish church of St Peter and St Paul.
5 The Philharmonic Society concert at St James's Hall on 22 March was a mixed programme of orchestral works by Beethoven, Wagner, Schumann and others. When the inaugural meeting of the SPAB was fixed for the same day, PSW and GPB gave up their concert plans.
6 In 1876 PSW added a dressing room to GPB's Chelsea house.

110 • To George Price Boyce, 17 March 1877

Annotated 'March 17. 1877'

1, Raymond Buildings, Gray's Inn, | *London,*
Friday night.

This will never do my dear Boyce. It w^d be justice wrong way upwards. I've a devil of a lot of weakness in good, & strength in evil, but that of taking in-justice kindly, when I know it, is neither a strength nor a weakness of mine. If I'd done the same work for an enemy, or say a lord, I sh^d have made the same charge – so as you are a friend & not a lord I can not charge you double for your sweetness. To shew you that I was just, I <u>did</u> think of not putting ^{in} the item of £1.13.0 for Clerk's travelling expenses, but thought it w^d be affectation not to do so, & there & then writ it down.

Please be as just yourself & be not falsely "ashamed". Tho' I don't take the cheque I take the kindness of the thought, and shall put it in the balance against the unkindness of having to go to law with another client of mine for my due.[1] I suspect my rude jokes about my delightful lawsuit, have in some way made you over-sensitive. You a great deal more than repay me, if the bit of work I've done for you is not a torture to you.

I was at Dannreuther's last night, and had Brahms & Chopin.[2] I'm looking now for the choral Fantasia on Thursday,[3] if I'm not killed by the Midland[4] or by a stone "out of the blue" for meddling in church building. An arch^t w^d die properly, if a der[r]ick gave way, & a good lump of red sandstone dropped on his ignorance box.

I see Norland's letter is not in the Athenæum.⁵ If damning & blasting w{d} only bring Tewkesbury church tower down on the assembled destroyers I sh{d} think the noble old building well "restored" to mother Earth, and w{d} damn away like Hell itself.

I'll tell Morris about your promised name. Wallis also is willing to join in – but our vandals, like our parliament foes, are in a "brutal majority".

Best remembrance to Mrs Boyce⁶ from your touched but "lean" | "P.W."

BL Add 45354, ff. 93-4

---

1 The reference is to his grievance against W.A. Cardwell. See above, Letter 95.
2 Having added a teaching studio/recital room (1874–7) to the Orme Square, Bayswater house of the German pianist Edward Dannreuther (1844–1905), PSW attended a number of the chamber music concerts held there. Dannreuther's wife, Chariclea Ionides, was the sister of another of PSW's clients, Alexander Ionides. See *Kirk*, p. 299.
3 See previous letter, note 5.
4 The Midland Railway ran trains from St Pancras to Leeds, connecting with routes to stations further north.
5 He means Thomas Norwood. Presumably, a letter from Norwood to *The Athenaeum* supporting that from WM of 5 March about Tewkesbury was not published. Instead, Sir Gilbert Scott was defended in the edition of 27 March, to which WM responded on 4 April.
6 GPB had married the French-born Augustine Aimée Caroline Soubeiran in August 1875. After his death, she gave his PSW letters to SCC, who later gifted them to the British Museum.

111 • To Robert C. Driver, 22 March 1877

Draft/copy

[1, Raymond Buildings . . .]
Mar: 22. 1877

To Robert C: Driver Esqre
4 White hall.¹

Dear Sir

Mr Prinsep's H{se}

I am really very much obliged to you for your temperate letter of yesterday, and I hope from it that you are quite willing to believe that it was ~~complete~~ simple inadvertence on my part that the right & proper notice & inspection of the plans were omitted to be laid before you before ~~commencing~~ the work was begun.

I can only acct for the omission by the pressure of the business, for Mr Prinsep, having gone to India, left me but too short time in wh' to carry out the work during his absence.² It is the more surprising that the necessary notice escaped my memory, as Mr Prinsep left me a cheque for the estate fee, before he left. My clerk brings with him the plans, & will explain what is proposed to be done, and on his return with them a tracing shall be made for you at once.

Please accept this expression of my regret that you sh^d have been put to the trouble of reminding me of my negligence.

Yours very truly | Philip Webb.

LB-1, pp. 72-3

---

1 Robert C. Driver was the buildings surveyor acting on behalf of the Metropolitan Board of Works.
2 In 1876–7 PSW made some enlargements to the studio-house which he had originally built in 1865 for Val Prinsep at 1 Holland Park Road, Kensington. See *Kirk*, p. 296. Prinsep had gone to India at the invitation of the viceroy, Lord Lytton, to witness the formal ceremonial in Delhi celebrating the Queen's new title as Empress of India, and to prepare a commensurately grand painting, 'The Imperial Assemblage at Delhi', 27 feet in length. See also above, Letter 96, note 9.

112 • To Richard Du Cane, 22 March 1877

Draft/copy

[1, Raymond Buildings . . .]
Mar: 22. 1877.

To. Richard DuCane Esqre
Gray's Inn Square.
My dear Sir.[1]

I visited the works for the new agents house at Naworth on Tuesday last, and I am sorry to be obliged to ~~state~~ say that the state in wh' I found them was not at all satisfactory to me.[2]

I considered that undue haste had been used, and work begun on the ground without any information having been given to me that ~~the work~~ any building had been ~~begun~~ done upon the ground at all was quite contrary to the requirements of the specification. ~~I found~~ The work over the main part of the ~~building~~ house had been brought up to the finished ground line, and levels arranged for without regard to the possibility of any necessary deviation from the plans if the foundation ~~had~~ did not prove satisfactory – but, beyond this, I found the bricks being used were on the whole inferior, ~~but~~ what was worse than this, was, that no care had been taken to sort the bricks and reject those, wh', even a hasty glance w^d have been sufficient to ~~prove~~ have shewn, sh^d not have been used even in a quite inferior class of building.

The result has been that the wet & succeeding frosts have ~~most~~ injuriously affected the work, & the workmen have thus been encouraged to consider that bad work would be allowed & passed from the beginning. Added to this, the damp proof course, wh' it was most important sh^d be laid in the very best ~~manner~~ way, has been put on the walls in a careless manner & without questions having been asked as to the composition of the material to be used. I cannot acquit Thos Warwick of having been ~~much~~ to blame in these proceedings,[3] as, when talking with the mason I found no reason for believing, that, if proper attention and direction had been exercised by the clerk of works, the ^builder w^d have been perfectly willing to do his work in the proper way and according to my instructions.

May I ask you to aid me, by insisting that no unsound bricks shall be brought on to the ground at all, and that Warwick shall be required to superintend the carrying out of this order. The bricks sh^d first be sorted at the kiln, and those brought on to the ground picked over again, & ~~those~~ ^any of them found to be inferior sh^d be then broken up at once and only used for concrete or levelling up of ground under floors. That the most irregular shaped bricks sh^d only be used in the solid parts of brick work, as without this regulation the bricklayer cannot keep his narrow walls true & level. Even with the best of the bricks, only, being used, there will none of them be found sufficiently even & good for facing work, so that those walls in wh' facing is shewn to be done in bricks will have to be thickened out to allow of stone facing being applied.

A question was raised by Mr Grey[4] as to the use of fireclay flue pipes throughout the work. Now, tho' I prefer a good brick flue, pargetted with cowdung mortar, to any other flue, still, under the circumstance that the bricks are uneven, and that the ^best bricklayer w^d be unable to make a ^quite sound flue with their use, I sh^d be inclined to advise the use of the fireclay pipes. If you sh^d decide upon this, the bricklayer sh^d give an estimate for the extra cost of supplying & using the pipes, after deducting the cost of the labour of shaping the flues in brick. Also, Warwick should be particular in watching ^that the pipes are procured of proper shape for bends & in the use of the pipes that hasty filling in, and unsound bond in the chimneys sh^d be avoided.

I am going to write to Warwick to give him ~~directions~~ ^instructions as to ^the manner of remedying, as far as possible, the defects of the work already executed. May I ~~also~~ request that you will give orders that no ^further building in mortar be proceeded with 'till all ~~danger~~ ^risk of frost is over.

Yours very truly | P.W.

LB-1, pp. 73–6

---

1 Richard Du Cane was clerk to the trustees of the Earl of Carlisle. See above, Letter 87, note 7.
2 Whilst working on St Martin's Church, Brampton, PSW also built Four Gables (near Brampton), a new house and stables for John Grey, the agent to the Naworth Estate (1876–9). See *Kirk*, pp. 221–3 and 300.
3 Thomas Warwick was clerk of works to the Naworth Estate, but his role in this project was not productive. Warwick had himself initially estimated a price for the house which PSW considered 'most extravagant', so 'competitive tenders for the separate trades were requested by advertisement', PSW having to insert clauses into the individual contracts 'that required all trades not to hinder one another and to submit daily records of work done, materials used, and all extras' (*Kirk*, p. 221). PSW wrote to Warwick on 24 March with very precise instructions about the future supervision of the work. 'No more mortar work should be done until all danger of frost is over, in the meantime, I should wish you to have all the worthless & frost bitten bricks cut out of the cellar walls and replaced with sound bricks. Also, I sh^d wish you to carefully examine the tar damp course and remove such parts as are defective and irregular and make good with fresh asphalt. The asphalt to

be made of equal parts of pitch tar & sand constantly stirred while boiling, the same to be laid over the walls on a perfectly even bed.' *LB-1*, pp. 76–7. The relationship of trust had been irreparably undermined, and Warwick was replaced by William Marshall in September.

4 Agent to the Naworth Estate, for whom the house was intended.

113 • To Percy Wyndham, 18 April 1877

Draft/copy

[1, Raymond Buildings . . .]
April 18. 1877.

To The Hon' Percy Wyndham M.P.
Wilbury Park Salisbury.

My dear Sir.

I delayed answering your letter of the 16th as I had hoped that the printer w^d have sent me some copies of the Old Buildings society statement.[1] As soon as they do come I will forward some ~~copies~~ to you.

The weather was fortunate for me on the 11th and I had a good time on my return to Clouds. I went on to the first hill to the north – that with the fine Scotch firs – and then on to the top of the taller one north of that – the hill covered with gorse. From both places I could better make out the possible disposition of the parts of the new house. I felt, when there that it would be well ~~if possible~~ to keep as many trees as possible on the east of the present house including the two walnut trees – and I made out that the east end of the new house could very well be swung round more towards the south.

I have had a letter from a M^r [John] Harding of Salisbury recommended by Rawlence & Squarey as a surveyor who would plot the ground. Mr Harding is quite willing to do so, and I have sent him instructions today. I return you the reports on water supply. I agree with Mr Grantham that the Green & Trodwell springs are the most promising for supply.

In conversation with Mrs Wyndham I gathered that she was not quite content with the groundplan scheme for the house; now, as it is very important that she sh^d be quite satisfied as to the objects to be gained I sh^d be glad if she w^d again closely consider the matter since my explanation. The point I've aimed at in the hall, is to get north and south light & view – in the dining room north view and east light – in the staircases to serve the more private & the more public rooms, and in the offices, to screen the east garden. Nothing I saw on my last visit made me wish for another kind of plan, but as I am not to live in the house and you & Mrs Wyndham will, I sh^d like to have your expression of opinion again before anything further is done.

If you sh^d happen to be in London shortly & could find time to call here, I w^d gladly enter upon these points with you & Mrs Wyndham.

Yours very truly | P: W:

LB-1, pp. 82-4

1 The inaugural manifesto of the SPAB. PSW circulated copies to those of his clients and acquaintances whom he thought would be sympathetic to the cause, hoping to recruit members. PWY became the local correspondent for the SPAB in Wiltshire, and played a vital role in the conservation efforts for East Knoyle church, in which PSW was the supervising architect. See Vol. II, Letter 410, and subsequent letters.

114 • To Thomas Forster, 24 April 1877

Draft/copy

[1, Raymond Buildings . . .]
April 24. 1877.

To Thos Forster Esqre
Brampton
Dear Sir.

(Brampton Ch. Coulthard mem[oria]^{l})[1]

I am much obliged to you for your communication rec^d this morning. I am, naturally, much interested in the proposal, as it will altogether depend on the character of the ^{stained} glass put into the window as to whether the Church will be injured in appearance $^{by\ it}$ or not.[2] Messrs Morris & Co $^{of\ 26\ Queen\ Square\ Bloomsbury,\ London}$ do all such work for me, and I do not know any other stained glass manufacturer ~~to~~ ^{on} whom I could depend for ^{such} work ^{being} in accordance with the design of the Church and of sufficient artistic excellence.

Yours truly | P: W:

LB-1, p. 84

1 The inscription in the most westerly window on the north side of the church, reads 'To the glory of God and in memory of Joseph Coulthard of Croft House Brampton the founder of Croft House School who died on the 18th day of October 1871 and was buried in Lanercost Abbey churchyard.' See Sewter, *The Stained Glass of William Morris and his Circle*, II, p. 29.
2 Morris and Co. would design and supply fourteen stained glass windows for St Martin's, Brampton. See below, Letters 127 and 136.

115 • To Charles Fairfax Murray, 26 April 1877

1, Raymond Buildings, Gray's Inn | London,
April 26. '77

My dear Murray.

I had your last letter of Wed: evening.[1] I do not think you will find any letter from me awaiting you at Florence. You hit the mark when you supposed I deferred writing as I expected a face to face argument. Mr Morris was here when your letter came, & I read it to him to kill 2 birds with one Stone of Venice. What does

Venetian Ruskin mean by his objurgations? (thank the stars, I do, for so fine a word).[2] Are not his friends as well as enemies always ducking their heads to avoid his broadcast missiles? Do they not raise them again when the malignant darts are past, & say, 'please forgive, & don't do so any more'? Do not I remember when "he took the mighty metal & kissed the brass of war"[3] against a modest God of mine, MA to wit, who was once felt to be a giant even by his enemies?[4] Am I and the likes of me always to forgive? No! Sometimes we'll not forgive no, not for any wheedling. I'm really glad of the proposed His: of Venice tho'[5] and hope he won't treat it as once did a high church parson with the "Pilgrim's Progress" viz, turn it into a High Church novel. It sh^d be real hist^y (the Venice one) and not transform^{ation} of good into bad, & bad into good to bias luckless, pudding headed English boyish & girlish people. There, that is my infantine lesson as to how to suck eggs.

In your letter of Feb: 22, you speak of the landscape photographs you sent me, of yours, to look at and enjoy. Have I not done so & delighted myself with "threshing floors . . . haystacks & even vin[e]yards"? And the gentle white oxen, how I w^d rejoice to rub their patient noses; how much more interesting they are than Punch's jokes – the horn of whose scantiness is raised in this miserable capital, alas! once a week. Yea, truly 80£ w^d be nearer my mark (or 8£) than 800£ for the pleasant house for sale in Siena. The water w^d be cheap & nice tho: while here it is dear & nasty – what a place of fountains Siena is – and gardens too, there is one garden, back-with an arcade, wh' I covet intensely.[6] I'd rather be a gardener in that place than live in Burlington House & call myself RA:[7]

WM is still deep in his blue vats, occasionally recreating himself in red & yellow.[8] He is doing admirable work, and is as gentle in his dabblings as one of Pliny's doves.[9] I'm very glad to hear of your industry, not carried on in an architectural sooted brick house on the Regent's canal but in a place on a Canaletto's canal (the spelling, right or wrong, to suit the alliteration, you see) – yon eye shot windows quite delightful. Happy Murray, master of the situation.

The shop in Oxford Street is for fine ladies to go to for their half yards of chintz & carpet & paper.[10] The malefactor[11] still sits in the Old house in Queen Square, originating pretty devices in the old den – books, I fancy will again populate the cases, but no feasting & upturning of glasses. By the way, is good wine to be had in Venice? suppose one drank water for 6 days, could one get a fine bottle of wine on the 7th, say for 5 francs? If so, I'll come – one of these days.

I've no news, except that we have started an anti-scraping society to stop blasting restoration of old buildings.[12] In fact, backing up Ruskin, in his protests, so far back as "The Stones of Venice". This new thing is all of a piece with the fulmination from Q Square, ab^t not putting new wine – I mean to say – new glass into old windows.[13] The wind is East, East by north north East here & again by East – drying up the watery humours of the last 9 months or so. 'Tis a fine country this of ours – pity 'tis so small – not in land but in the men's manners of it. Adieu, after this grumbling. Many thanks for your letters, and kindest remembrance to the Signora.[14]

Yours sincerely | Philip Webb:

Fitzwilliam 19

---

1 CFM was in Venice, copying parts of Carpaccio's series of large wall paintings in the Accademia, the Legend of St Ursula, for JR. A portrait of JR himself (now lost) was also under way. From June CFM would base himself in Florence, spending several weeks in London during the summer. See *Elliott*, pp. 79–80.
2 Relations between JR and CFM were not always easy. CFM 'liked to challenge Ruskin's interpretations, and pointed out the inconsistencies in the St Ursula cycle; hence Ruskin's comment that his help was "given much in the form of antagonism".' Robert Hewison, *Ruskin on Venice* (New Haven and London: Yale University Press, 2009), p. 348.
3 'But Hogni turned to the great-one who the Niblung trumpet bore, / And he took the mighty metal, and kissed the brass of war,' from 'Atli speaketh with the Niblungs', Book IV ('Gudrun') of WM, *The Story of Sigurd the Volsung and the Fall of the Niblungs* (London: Ellis and White, 1877), p. 359. PSW's presentation copy is in the Emery Walker Library. See *CAGM*, p. 142.
4 JR attacked the mannerism of Michelangelo in 'The relation between Michael Angelo and Tintoret', a lecture given at Oxford in June 1871 and published 1872. EBJ, to whom JR had read the lecture privately in 1871, was especially upset. 'He read it to me just after he had written it, and as I went home I wanted to drown myself in the Surrey Canal or get drunk in a tavern – it didn't seem worthwhile to strive any more if he could think or write it'. Georgiana Burne-Jones, *Memorials of Edward Burne-Jones* (London: Macmillan, 1904) II, p. 18.
5 JR was contemplating a revised edition of *The Stones of Venice*, and adding a fourth volume.
6 His comments are based on CFM's photographs of Siena and the countryside round about.
7 'I had rather be a doorkeeper in the house of my God, than to dwell in the tents of wickedness.' Psalms 84:10.
8 See above, Letter 94, note 3.
9 A Roman floor mosaic at Hadrian's Villa in Tivoli, depicting doves at a drinking bowl, is thought to be a copy of a Greek original at Pergamon, described by Pliny the Elder in his Natural History (c. 77 AD).
10 'In the spring of 1877 [WM's] position as a general household furnisher was strengthened when the Firm leased a shop at 264 (later 449) Oxford Street, on the corner of North Audley Street.... [A] shop so close to Morris's most fashionable competitors – Liberty's in Regent Street, Morant's in Bond Street – contributed enormously to the future expansion of the Firm.' MacCarthy, *WMLT*, p. 409.
11 WM.
12 In 1878–80, CFM was the corresponding secretary of the SPAB in Italy.
13 After the foundation of the SPAB, WM decided that Morris & Co. should no longer provide new stained glass for ancient buildings, and announcements appeared in papers such as the *Pall Mall Gazette*. It led to misunderstanding from potential clients, as GW recalled. 'In the minds of most people who took any interest at all in Mr Morris's work the raison d'être of "Morris glass" was its so called mediaevalism, & it was supposed nothing could be more suitable for an ancient building. The profound misconception which this opinion implied & the other hopeless mistake which assumed that Mʳ Morris's work was purposely "mediaeval", made it impossible that the circular could be understood.' 'Memorials of William Morris. Christmas 1897' (prepared for JWM as he worked on *Mackail*), BL Add 45350, f. 24.
14 CFM had married Angelica Colivicchi of Volterra in April 1875. Of their several children, two died in infancy.

116 • To Lord Fitzhardinge, 4 May 1877

Draft/copy

[1, Raymond Buildings...]
May 4. 1877.

To the R{sup|t} Hon' The Lord Fitzhardinge
Berkeley Castle Gloucester{sup|sh}

My Lord.

On Jan{sup|y} the 10{sup|th} {sup|of this year} I sent to you my charge for professional assistance begun in April 1874, & on March the 5{sup|th} {sup|last} I wrote to your Lordship to remind you of my charge having been sent in: also, {sup|in} requesting payment I said that it w{sup|d} be a convenience to me {sup|to receive it}. I have had no answer from your Lordship to either of these letters.

If this present letter is not acknowledged, I shall suppose that your Lordship is unwilling to pay me for my work, and shall not again press the matter upon your ~~Lordship's~~ attention.

I am my Lord, | Yours faithf{sup|ly} | P: W:

LB-1, pp. 89-90

117 • To Lady Fitzhardinge, 10 May 1877

Draft/copy

[1, Raymond Buildings...]
May 10. 1877.

To The R{sup|t} Hon' The Lady Fitzhardinge
Berkeley Castle Gloucestersh.

Dear Lady Fitzhardinge.

In answer to your letter to me of the 6{sup|th} instant, I was very glad to find that the touch of irony in my last letter to Lord Fitzhardinge was not really necessary. M{sup|r} Cooke has sent me the cheque this morning, & if any blame was due for the delay in answering my letters, he has taken it on himself.

With regard to the glazing of the Great Hall windows. When M{sup|r} Morris was with me at the Castle {sup|last year},¹ we came to the conclusion that {sup|the} piece of glazing done ~~under our direction~~ at his works, was not quite satisfactory in its place, and we noted then & have decided since, that the better plan would be to glaze the windows with plain white glass of good kind {sup|in small panes in lead}, and simply insert the shields in this glazing in the upper part of windows. This w{sup|d} not take long to do, & one or two windows could be done at a time, & at such times as you may be away from the castle. So that, if you sh{sup|d} decide upon having this done the glass (of, say 1 or 2 windows) could be taken out & sent to Mr Morris at 26 Queen Square Bloomsbury and could most likely be returned in a month afterwards.

Believe me, yours faithfully, | P: W:

P.S. As I think it possible that you will take an interest in the subject of protecting ancient buildings, I enclose a couple of copies of the statement of a Society to wh' I have lately become a member. It explains itself & so I need say no more.[2] P: W:

LB-1, pp. 91-2

---

1 See above, Letter 98.
2 Lady Fitzhardinge joined the SPAB, but her membership lapsed after 1883.

118 • To Thomas Forster, 10 May 1877

Draft/copy

[1, Raymond Buildings . . .]
May 10. 1877.

To Tho's Forster Esqre
Brampton Cumb^d
Dear Sir.

Brampton Ch'

In answer to your letter rec^d this morning enclosing copy of a letter from Mr Hough. I think it ~~quite~~ possible that some very slight diminution of light may occur to Mr Routledge's house, but as the Church is a public building for the good of the town, and as we could not have used the site for the new church without placing it as we have, Mr Routledge is not likely I sh^d think to object in any way when he knows the circumstances.[1] For, if the church had been built elsewhere that part of the site w^d have had to be let for building on, and cottages small shops or a forge or public house w^d really have injured Mr Routledge's property, whereas, the church will considerably enhance the value of it – and the loss of light, if any, will be so trifling that it is not worth consideration in any other way than I have mentioned above.

Yours truly | Ph' Webb:

LB-1, pp. 92-3

---

1 Thomas Routledge, who owned a house to the east of the church, had conveyed through his solicitor, Mr Hough, 'his apprehension that his lights may be interfered with by the building of the new church'. See *Penn*, p. 18.

119 • To Thomas Forster, 17 May 1877

Draft/copy

[1, Raymond Buildings . . .]
May 17. 1877.

To Thos Forster Esqre
Brampton Cumberland
Dear Sir.

(Brampton Ch')

In answer to your letter to me of the 15th instant. I am naturally surprised at the want of public spirit in Mr Routledge, the more so that he is making it to appear that a serious injury is being wd be done to his property whereas the difference will be merely nominal would be hardly appreciable between what has been designed and what we shd have to do to be strictly within our legal rights. The enclosed tracing will aid you in explaining to the Committee the facts of the case. This diagram gives the worst apparent form of the case, as right and left of this vestry gable (that is East & West) the church recedes.

All I can say farther is, that unless the Committee can convince Mr Routledge and he shd prove willing to withdraw his obstruction I must re-design the upper part of Vestry to bring it down within a line of 45° from the sills of Mr Routledge's ground floor windows.

I have seen Mr Geo Howard one of the members of the Committee & he agrees with me as to the tenor of this letter.

I cannot possibly come to Cumberland before the beginning of June as my engagements 'till then are close. The slight delay will not delay hinder Messrs Beaty as they can proceed with the other parts, and in the meantime, if I hear from you that Mr Routledge will not withdraw his opposition, I will design the then necessary alteration.[1]

Yours truly | Philip Webb:

LB-1, pp. 94-5

---

1 Routledge remained aggrieved, and in December 1878 claimed £150 in compensation, before finally settling for £50, as he 'wished to avoid unpleasantness and considering also the object of the buildings by which he is injured'. *Penn*, p. 18.

1864-1887

120 • To Percy Wyndham, 18 June 1877

Draft/copy

[1, Raymond Buildings . . .]
June 18. 1877.

To the Hon' Percy Wyndham M.P.
44 Belgrave Sq^{re} S.W.
My dear Sir.

(Clouds Ho:)

I only got home from Cumberland on Sat: morning, & was too much worn out to give proper answer to your letter wh' awaited my return to London. This morning Howell the brickmaker has been with me,[1] bringing specimens of the green sandstone. I am also very much pleased with the Cle[e]ve hill specimen,[2] and I sh^d be glad to have some talk with you, as to the best course for us to pursue with regard to it and the bricks.

I am rather pleased with the appearance & speech of Howell, & sh^d ~~be glad~~ like that he sh^d be employed, if on consideration we thought it wise to do so. I could make an appoint^t either to come & see you in this week or to be at home here.

Yours very truly | Philip Webb:

LB-1, pp. 96-7

---

1 John Howell, of the East Knoyle Brickyard.
2 'An Upper Greensand ridge runs from north-east to south-west across the middle of the parish [of East Knoyle] to include Cleeve hill'. *Victoria County History: Wiltshire*, vol. XI, 1980. http://www.british-history.ac.uk/report.aspx?compid=115485 [accessed 13 July 2014].

121 • To George Howard, 18 June 1877

1, Raymond Buildings, Gray's Inn, | *London,*
June 18 1877

My dear Howard.

The Routledge lawyer did not turn up 'till Forster & Routledge had to leave to return to Brampton.[1]

Hough's questions were chiefly as to the possibility of pulling down what we have done of the vestry & putting it elsewhere – 'anywhere, anywhere out of the way' – as

I fancy Routledge thinks that Whitehead will be shewing his backside to Mrs R: out of the vestry windows for 5 hours on end. I could hardly say to Hough that Whitehead would have something else for his rump to do, or that probably Mrs R: would not mind if he did – and so & so, the lawyer left, and the Architect came his way.

Thanks for the numbers of folios' octavos' quartos' & little fry. As for the window-bay and the "gazebo" – "O you chorus (in yourself) of indolent reviewers". I will do what I think right and as little badly as possible; but I will mind your objurgations no more than the braying of your peacock. This puts me in mind, wouldn't Whistler come & paint paycaucks all over the room?[2] It would enliven the Castle, <u>that</u> would, and cheer up the gardener, as you could then slaughter the real ones.

London is pestiferous, but I've smelled little of it, as I went down to Welwyn on Sunday[3] to sleep off my tired spirits. I've just sent round to DuCane, but he is out. French matters look horrid threatening in this morning's paper.[4] O how I do hope cutting & carving of carcasses will be staved off.

Best reminders of me to Mrs Howard and the children; Van Dank and the girls will smile prettily, perhaps; the other boys will be rolling down precipices & will not care.[5] Health & good cheer to all from your obliged & faithful servant,

Philip Webb:

Howard

---

1 See above, Letters 118 and 119. Routledge's solicitor was Hough.
2 The American-born painter, James McNeill Whistler (1834–1903), produced his masterpiece of Japanese-influenced interior decoration, the panelled room known as *Harmony in Blue and Gold: The Peacock Room*, in 1876–7, for the Liverpool industrialist and collector, Fredrick Richards Leyland (1832–92).
3 To visit his brother.
4 In May 1877, a constitutional crisis in France arose over the relative powers of the President and the government. The dismissal by the President, Marshall MacMahon (1808–93), of a moderate Royalist Prime Minister was followed by fresh elections in October 1877 and a resounding victory by Republicans.
5 There were seven Howard children in 1877, five boys and two girls.

122 • To Charles Milnes Gaskell, 6 July 1877

Draft/copy

[1, Raymond Buildings . . .]
July 6. 1877

To Chas Milnes Gaskell Esqre
Wenlock Abbey Shropshire[1]
My dear Sir.

In answer to your letter ~~to me~~ of the 3rd instant. It wd be impossible for me to give you an opinion of any value as to what shd be done to that portion of the Abbey buildings mentioned in your letter as being in an unsafe state, without I examined it carefully with a view to sustaining it without injury to its historical interest. Speaking personally, I sh^d be exceedingly anxious to avoid any rebuilding even if the alternative ~~were the necessity~~ of putting any amount of plain mechanical supports or ties had to be resorted to, in keeping it standing in its integrity. If you ~~are of opinion~~ ^think that it w^d be dangerous to leave it till I happened to be in the neighbourhood & could then examine it, I w^d at your request make an appointment to come to Wenlock as soon as possible to ~~examine~~ ^look at the building in question.

I am daily getting more convinced of the great value, from historical and artistic points of view, of the remains of ancient architecture of wh' Wenlock is so fine an example, that I have lately assisted to form and have joined a society to ~~assist~~ ^aid in the ~~work~~ ^preservation of such works – and I enclose you some papers ~~of the society~~ wh' will I am sure interest you in the cause, & I sh^d be obliged if you w^d use them in any way in your power likely to increase the numbers & weight of opinion brought to bear on the subject by the society.[2]

Yours very truly, | P.W.

LB-1, pp. 98-9

---

1 For Charles Milnes Gaskell and Wenlock Priory see above, Letter 84, note 2.
2 'Your good natured reference to the Society, as, "somewhat Quixotic", I take to mean, that, the generality of people with whom it would have to deal w^d be as witless as windmills, wh' w^d, no doubt be true – but I sh^d have no difficulty in explaining to you that the Society is much more reasonable than the destroyers in question.' PSW to Gaskell, 9 July 1877. *LB-1*, p. 100.

123 • To George Price Boyce, 15 September 1877

1, Raymond Buildings, Gray's Inn, | *London.*
Sep. 15. '77

My dear Boyce

"Wonder" is not in my nature, if it ever was, it has been dulled by over use. I don't even wonder at the ways of the ministry in France,[1] or at the degradation of "restoration".

I thought, on not hearing from you, that you had got work in your eye, & were taking precautions to be undisturbed, & wise you would be. Take grateful thanks for the valuable cartes de visite you so kindly sent me, all three of them are peculiarly interesting.[2] Please to try & find out anything you can about the "Saxon chapel" as they have some hints at the anti-scrape society of its being about, once more, to be tampered with.[3] The flying figure, must be of Greek origin – i.e Byzantine, and is <u>wonder</u>-ful, even to me, in its deep interest. The bridge too; surely you must find time to make a drawing of it (if not, a study or sketch) as, with its turn-pike house it is a sweet subject, to say nothing of object. I'm afraid

I shall not reach you this time, as I've been pressed with work, & have had to grind in Cumberland, where the weather was pelting.

I hope ~~however~~ to have a few days holiday with Morris at Kelmscott next week. I shall, however, pass your way on Thursday, having to go to Knoyle on business, & I hope Morris will go with me. I shall go by way of Swindon & Chippenham to Warminster, getting to the last place at 11.26 am. Thence to drive to Knoyle. Can't you join us on the way & give me your opinion as to the thing to be done on the site at Knoyle?[4] We shall get back again in the evening.

The lawsuit, manages it itself in quite comfortable indolent fashion, & I expect nothing of it, except, that it will come on for hearing when I've forgotten all about it, as, indeed, I have even now.[5]

The antiscrape meetings are regular & attended by the virtuous few – members increasing, also the cause of its existence.

I'm not going to drain your generosity about small photographs, so, please to get me any you can, as valuable as those you sent me, & I will pay with delight. With kind remembrance to your wife.

Believe me yours truly | Philip Webb.

I've not seen the Welwynites for 3 weeks but go there this evening.[6]

BL Add 45354, ff. 102-3

---

1 See above, Letter 121, note 4.
2 GPB had sent picture postcards of places or objects seen.
3 GPB was staying in Bradford-on-Avon, where the chapel of St Laurence probably dates from about 1000. Partly converted into a school and a cottage, it was purchased in 1871 at the instigation of the local vicar.
4 His plans for Clouds.
5 His unsuccessful attempt to obtain payment from W.A. Cardwell.
6 To his brother and sister at Welwyn.

124 • To John Hebb, 10 October 1877

Draft/copy

[1, Raymond Buildings . . .]
Octr 10. 1877.

To John Hebb Esqre
Met^n Board of Works.[1]

My dear Sir.

I beg to acknowledge the receipt of your letter of the 5th. After having given careful consideration to your proposition I have concluded not to depart from my habit of reserve in putting forward my own ideas of art matters[2] – tho' in the present case, if I possessed any clear aptitude for impressing an audience with what I considered the truth of the subject, I sh[d] have been strongly urged to ~~depart from~~ put aside my rule for once, as I am so deeply impressed with the ~~urgency of the~~ cause advocated by the society ~~in question~~ for the protection of Ancient Buildings, of wh' we are both members.

May I be allowed to suggest to the council of the Architectural Association thro' you[3] (if you yourself are still disinclined publicly to advocate the cause) that they sh[d] apply to some ~~Architect~~ gentleman whose name represents higher authority than mine, ~~in the profession,~~ to press upon the attention of the younger Architects, the matter that M[r] Stevenson has so boldly done before the society of the older members of the profession.[4] In looking thro' the list of ~~our~~ members of our Society, the following names seem to me to represent possible lecturers – M[r] Aitchison, Rev[d] Stopford Brooke, J: S: Hodgson A:R:A, Lord Houghton, ~~Rev[d] J: W: Norwood,~~ Rev[d] Mark Pattison, J: H: Pollen, Henry Wallis. I shall be glad to speak further with you on the subject at our next meeting.

Yours very truly | P: W:

LB-1, pp. 104-5

---

1 John Hebb (1832/3–1916) was Assistant Architect for the Metropolitan Board of Works from 1876, and eventually became an acting Superintendent Architect for the LCC. He was an active committee member of the SPAB.
2 PSW always turned down invitations to write or speak either about the profession of architecture, or his own work, and unlike many of his fellow practitioners scrupulously avoided becoming in any sense a public figure. Although this habit of extreme reticence was counterbalanced by the tireless energies with which he devoted himself to proselytizing for the SPAB, not even for this cause was he willing to set aside his aversion to personal appearances.
3 'The Architectural Association was founded in London in 1847 by a group of young articled pupils as a reaction against the prevailing conditions under which architectural training could be obtained ... [L]arge premiums were advanced to private architects in return for imparting an education and training.' From a lecture by Edward Bottoms (February 2010). http://www.aaschool.ac.uk/AALIFE/ LIBRARY/aahistory.php [accessed 14 July 2014].
4 The Glasgow-born architect John James Stevenson (1831–1908). He was a proponent of the Queen Anne revival style, and built for himself Red House on Bayswater Hill, after PSW's house for WM. He was a founder committee member of the SPAB and the author of *Architectural Restoration: its Principles and Practice* (London: W. Clowes & Sons, 1877).

125 • To George Price Boyce, 12–15 October 1877

1, Raymond Buildings, Gray's Inn, | *London.*
Oct 12. '77

My dear Boyce

I was glad of your letter & sorry to hear that you are not strong. Why will goodness of nature always be "shaky", & health & strength only ally itself with your Howells[1] Palmerstons[2] Popes & Pagans? True, I sh[d] have liked to see 20 pleasant places with you, but my trade is a taxing one (see, it has put an end to poor Raphael Brandon)[3] and I could do no more than carry out my plan of getting a few days freedom of air & nothing to do in the friendly arms of Kelmscott and the Thames.

Thank you much for the photographs of the barn & church.[4] I'm your debtor for them, and any more you may consider improving to your friend's mind. I was at the "anti scrape" last night; dull meeting, for Morris was in his die-vats at Leek, and Norwood basking in the luxuries of Crewe Hall.[5] I mentioned the Saxon Chapel, but things are deferred 'till you report in person.

I have secured you a "Burnt Njal";[6] when you have read it, perhaps twice through (I speak from personal experience) you will most likely become acclimatised to the tremendous northern imagination, and feel inclined to attack the later translations of the Morris-Magnùsson series & be ready to enter into the noble poem wh' Morris has given to the English,[7] founded on "The Great Epic of the North"

"So draw ye round & hearken, English Folk,
Unto the best tale pity ever wrought!
Of how from dark to dark bright Sigurd broke,
Of Brynhild's glorious soul with love distraught,
Of Gudrun's weary wandering unto naught,
Of utter love defeated utterly,
Of grief too strong to give Love time to die!"[8]

I beg your forgiveness for throwing this weighty stanza at your head.

I'm afraid I cannot help you in suggesting a sea-side place to answer your present purpose. Would Swanage be likely to suit? it is well sheltered from the N & has S E exposure. It is, as you most likely know, not far from Corfe castle, and is got at from Wareham station – however, I see on looking again at your letter that you may have left Bradford by this time – but I shall send this, as your (late?) landlady will most likely know where to forward it.

Monday. 15th. I've delayed sending this and shall now send it to West house to be forwarded.

With kind regards to Mrs Boyce, believe me
yours very truly | Philip Webb:

P:S: I go to Smeaton tomorrow to see what the rains ~~of~~ have left of 800,000 bricks.[9]

BL Add 45354, ff. 106-7

---

1 PSW clearly had no illusions about Charles Augustus Howell. See above, Letter 18.
2 Henry John Temple, third Viscount Palmerston (1784–1865). His long political career, during which he moved from Conservative to Liberal camps, including periods as Foreign Secretary and Prime Minister. He was known for his abrasive style, and for his womanising.
3 The architect, John Raphael Rodrigues Brandon (1817–77), had more success as a writer than as a practitioner, co-authoring with his brother several books on English ecclesiastical architecture,

including *Parish Churches* (1848). He took his own life a week before this letter, shooting himself in his chambers on 8 October.
4 These would have been of the tithe barn and Saxon chapel at Bradford-on-Avon. See above, Letter 123, note 3. The barn became the subject of a watercolour by GPB, now in the V&A. See Vol. II, Letter 482, note 3.
5 Crewe Hall, a Jacobean mansion in Cheshire, which Hungerford Crewe, third Baron Crewe (1812–94) inherited on his father's death in 1835.
6 George Webbe Dasent, *The Story of Burnt Njal, from the Icelandic of the Njals Saga* (Edinburgh: Edmonston and Douglas, 1861).
7 *Sigurd the Volsung*.
8 This is the last stanza of a six-stanza prologue by WM, which he placed before his and E. Magnússon's translations, published in 1870 as *Certain Songs from the Elder Edda, which Deal with the Story of the Volsungs*.
9 For Smeaton Manor see above, Letter 107, note 1.

126 • To William Marshall, 15 October 1877

Draft/copy

[1, Raymond Buildings . . .]
Oct 15. 1877.

To Mr Wm Marshall
Clerk of Works. Naworth.
Dear Sir

Agent's House[1]

I am indeed very much annoyed at the accident, if such a piece of carelessness on the builders part can be called an accident. If the ~~work~~ gable had been of twice the thickness it shd not have been left without proper support against even an ordinary wind.

I must direct you at once to survey every part of the work likely to have been in any way affected by the fall, make notes on the ground of even any appearance of injury, & where the work has only been shaken order it to be taken down at once & rebuilt. Have all the ruined stone work taken out of the ~~work~~ building, the materials cleaned & stacked and all injured cut stone work, even if only a corner is [k]nocked off, broken up so that it shall not be re-used.

Please to examine the chimney & see that it has not suffered in the falling of the gable against it. Will you be so good as to shew this letter to Mr Grey as well as to Mr Sproat and further report matters to me.[2]

Yours truly, | PW.

LB-1, p. 107

---

1 Marshall was Thomas Warwick's replacement as clerk of works on Four Gables. See above, Letter 112, note 3.
2 The stonemasons contracted for this project were Sproat Brothers of Talkin. See *Kirk*, p. 300.

127 • To Thomas Forster, 24 October 1877

Draft/copy

[1, Raymond Buildings . . .]
Octr 24 1877

To Thos Forster Esqre
Brampton Cumberland.
Dear Sir.

Brampton Ch'.

I have rec^d the enclosed from Messrs Morris & Co, it is an estimate for ~~the~~ glazing with stained glass the 3 windows of the north aisle of the nave.

When I last was at the church, I stated that it w^d be best to consider any part of the ornamental glazing of the windows, with $^{regard\ to}$ the whole; therefore, the accompanying note is arranged in accordance with that resolution. In the estimate you will find the 3 windows numbered, 2, 3 & 4 and these numbers refer to the windows so numbered on this sketch [*sketch, with 3 windows marked in north aisle*].[1]

From Messrs Morris's estimate you will see that the cost of these windows, framed according to my directions on a system appropriate to the character of the building, is at a lower rate than when I was talking with you on the subject I told you was probable, so that it has seemed to me as ~~prob~~ likely that your subscriptions w^d enable you to put in two of the windows and the third w^d be supplied by the gentleman who proposed to glaze one as a memorial to a member of his family.[2]

I have examined the designs for the figures and find them ~~very~~ noble pieces of work, & very satisfactory to me from an art point of view. The cost of packing & fixing w^d probably amount to 7 or 8£ each ^{window}, if fixed separately, if the whole 3 were fixed ~~together~~ $^{at\ one\ time}$ the cost w^d probably not be more than 18 to 20£.

I have rec^d a memorandum from Mr Beaty, saying that M$^{r\ Geo}$ Routledge proposes to give the porch entrance,[3] but before sending the detail drawings for execution, I sh^d be glad to receive a ~~more~~ formal order for the same.

Yours truly | P: W:

LB-1, pp. 108-9

---

1 Morris & Co. supplied fourteen windows in the church.
2 For the memorial window to William Carrick see below, Letter 136.
3 For George Routledge, see above, Letter 83, note 4.

1864–1887

128 • To William Shearburn, 30 October 1877

Draft/copy

[1, Raymond Buildings . . .]
October 30. 1877.

To Mr Wm Shearburn
Builder Dorking.[1]
Dear Sir.

Dr Dowson's H^{se}[2]

In answer to your letter of the 24th instant I can only say that I disagree with you entirely that Dr Dowson has evaded payment of any money due to you ^{for any work for wh' I have been his adviser}. Dr Dowson has invariably placed the matter wholly in my hands, telling me that he was perfectly willing to abide by my decision.

You yourself have fully recognised my professional right in this matter, for in a letter to me so far back as June 1873 you wrote "but should you think that any item ought not to be allowed please strike it out and send me a certificate for the balance". My answer has always been to you that before I could certify for the payment of any balance due to you, certain things necessary to be done to complete the works to my satisfaction as Architect sh^d be done. In a letter to you of my assistant Mr Basset of 10th of July 1873 this passage occurs.[3] "Mr Webb will feel obliged if you will get these things done that the account may be settled as soon as possible." Well, Sir, you have never done any of the things to the house wh' were necessary according to my decision as Architect, and Dr Dowson has been put to great inconvenience & discomfort in consequence, and as he is obliged to have workmen about the house at the present time I have advised him to let those workmen do at once what you have failed to do at my repeated request.

If, when the necessary things are done, there sh^d remain any balance due to you over and above the cost of executing them, I will see that it is forwarded to you, but as much of your work has proved itself to have ^{been} done in an inferior manner, more so than even I had supposed when I drew up the list of requirements in 1873, I have ~~but small hope~~ some fears that Dr Dowson will himself be put to further expense.

Please to believe that I have no animus in the matter, and that I sh^d have ~~only~~ been ^{only} too ~~pleased~~ ^{glad} if you had at once set the thing at rest by acting in the usual way as between Architect & builder.

Yours truly | P: W:

LB-1, pp. 109-11

1 William Shearburn (b. 1833) of South Street, Dorking, is described in various census returns as builder, surveyor and architect.
2 In 1867–73, PSW had overseen work on an existing house at 77 Park Street, Mayfair (including the addition of a dining room) for Dr E. Dowson.
3 'Basset was Webb's draughtsman for many years, his name appeared for the first time in Webb's accounts for 1869 and he remained in the office until 1884.' John Brandon-Jones, *NBS*, p. 33.

129 • To Jane, Jenny and May Morris, 5 December 1877

1, Raymond Buildings, Gray's Inn, | *London.*
Dec[r] 5. '77

My dear Janey & Jenny & May:

You will be sure that I was very glad when Father Morris read me a part of Jenny's first letter home, and also when he told me on Monday that he had again heard that you were all resting, or rested, and that you were looking about at the wonders of creation in your part of Italy.[1] I repeat, that I was very glad to hear of you, as I fancied that you might all have died on the journey, or have stopped in mid-France declaring that you would not budge a mile farther. And now I find that you have oranges & lemons, if not the bells of S[t] Clements.[2]

The other day a friend of Murray's called on me to shew some paintings of Italian country and towns, amongst them I eagerly looked at 2 or 3 of the sea-side hills you inhabit. Oh how pleased I was to see that the big mountains were close, or seemingly close down upon you – I had had it in my mind that you could see the tops of them by running a mile or two & putting on spectacles.

Last night I went to hear the dyer's lecture,[3] & he spoke of this (my) country as being a pretty peasant land, but with nothing strange or visibly wonderful in it, with just the tail of the sun seen on lucky days, & with small sea-begirt land inhabited by small wealth-begirt minds. I never quite knew before why I was so stupid; you, no doubt, had known this long before, & when you return I shall expect you hardly to speak to me, & that if you do you will get no answer. As to the lecture itself, you will be glad to know from unprejudiced me, that it was a great success, full of truths & knock-me-down blows, but also tender & beautiful, & withal hopeful to poor folk if not to Kings & Lords.

I thought that the working men there seemed pleased at being talked to in a way that recognised their being men, not children. For myself, I assure you I was deeply excited, water running out at my finger ends, & sometimes very nearly out of my eyes & down my patient nose, but a pinch of snuff stopped the latter and I was comforted. I hear that the wild Irisher did not take the house at Turnham Green after all, but that someone else is nibbling.[4] If you see the [George] Howards, father, mother & children many, please remember me to them. Also, I shall be glad when either of your girls or both will snatch a few minutes to tell me of your condition, & of the flavour of the Mediterranean mullets & the red & yellow wine.

Please all three of you accept the love of your faithful | Philip Webb:

BL Add 45342, ff. 39-40

---

1 Jane and her daughters had left for Oneglia, on the Italian Riviera, on 21 November. They were abroad for several months, staying at a house found for them by Rosalind Howard, and not far from the Howards' villa. WM joined them at the end of April 1878.
2 A reference to the opening lines of the traditional English nursery rhyme, whose subject is the bells of London city churches: 'Oranges and lemons, / Say the bells of St Clement's'.
3 This was WM's first formal public lecture – many more would follow – and he had been nervous about his ability to project his voice adequately, practicing beforehand on GW, and listening to advice (some of it facetious) from EBJ. 'The Decorative Arts, Their Relation to Modern Life and Progress', was delivered to the Trades Guild of Learning on 4 December at the Co-Operative Hall in Castle Street, 'a dismal hole near Oxford St: I am not sanguine as to its reception'. WM to JM, 3 December 1877, *CLWM*, I.
4 WM was endeavouring to find tenants for their Turnham Green house, now that his family was away. '[T]he Homan lot are off: I was firm about Sarah [the cook] & so they refused: not at all to my grief: I am now advertising the house at 3½ guineas including the cook's wages'. WM to JM, 29 November 1877, *CLWM*, I.

130 • To Jane, Jenny and May Morris, 25 December 1877

1, Raymond Buildings, Gray's Inn, | *London.*
Christmas day in the evening. 1877.

My dear mother and daughters.

I need hardly try to tell you with what pleasure I had your letters, written on the 12th & 13th of this month. In the first place they solved the riddle of your ~~having got~~ ^{getting} to Italy, & then, that you were settling down to the life of the new home for the time being.

It must have been troublesome to you to tell again & again of the "cardboard" house, of the terraces, of the unripe lemons, of the sun setting & rising, of the wrangling with custom house officers, & of this that & the other, but it was news to me, & very pleasant news too.

May is right (I suppose?) for she makes her sun to rise over the sea; Jenny is wrong (I suppose?) for she makes her sun to set over the sea; probably she has been reading Walter Scott's Antiquary, where he is pleased to do the same.[1] In such a wonderful country the sun should be accommodating, if only to put to the blush (in setting) the cantankerous openers of boxes at the station. This kind of chaff (the light part, or the husk, winnowed from grain) will put you very much in mind of me, & that is what I want to do by this poor letter. If folk did not shew their faults, how w^{d} they be known by their friends from perfect people? I sh^{d} be sorry that either of you sh^{d} pass me in the street without recognition.

The other day the word "chitta bob" came into the top part of my body, and I tried to think of the rest of the abracadabra chatter wh' was so amusing at Kelmscott, but alas, no wagging of poll w^d do it, and I was forced to remember visible signs – The fire, the draught board, the kittens, & mother Janey coiled up on the sofa – To say nothing of ladders in apple trees, starlings, shooting the foot bridge at the weir, feasts in the dining-room, & plum cake in tapestry chamber – Jenny poring over her book, & when disturbed saying "bosh" & May drawing & when criticised saying (internally) "bother the fellow". How much easier it is to remember a picture than a sentence!

The last few days, here, in Gray's Inn, have been clear, and the rooks a-many. They don't shew in foggy weather, no doubt they are off to the clear aired fields then – and they have amused me mightily, coming down to my scatterings in a flock, like so many Oxford Dons in Masters' gowns. They are precious greedy chaps these rooks. They will take 8 or 10 pieces of bread, one after the other, & as they can only eat, say 7, they go & bury the other & walk a-way with their hands behind their gown – when in comes a watchful other one, & digs it up, & if he is full goes & buries it in some other place, & the starlings & sparrows look on, as I look on Lords & Ladies. Now, my friends, this is a picture, I don't give you a verse to remember.

Phil Jones came to see me the other day; he is grown a monstrous fine gentleman, sweetness beaming from his mouth & light from his eyes – he looked very well, and as if the air of the Marlborough downs suits him.[2] He was cheery and kind, and I felt, beside him, like a musty old cheese, only fit to be toasted, wh' I hope you will do in the best wine you can lay hands on. I will drink your health in whiskey & water you may be sure.

We are all on the qui vive here – believing that Dizzy is going to do – well, the devil knows what?[3] If you sh^d hear of an architect being trampled to a pancake in the streets you will know who is gone, & rejoice or be sad as the case may be. I think of taking a public house at Gravesend or Portsmouth and hocussing[4] the soldiers so that they shall not go to fight the Russians. Apart from jesting, we are in a mighty to-do about the ways of rascals in high places. If the blunder comes, in a ferry we will be, of that you may be sure.

Father Morris's lecture was quite admirable, & altogether delightful. I am dunning Ellis for a copy wh' he is having printed, as I won't read that in the building paper.[5] O my children (older & younger) there are such drawings at the Bond St Gallery (I don't like writing the "Grosvenor" for it smells of beefstakes! [sic]).[6] Botticellis', Mantegnas, Leonardos', Durers', M. Angelos', such a sight of fine things – all of which I've only had an hours glimpse of. Odours of Italy & Flanders enjoyed thro' all the cooking below.[7] There is one little Albert Durer water colour, about as large as half a crown – a mill & water wheel, beautiful indeed to see. I speak of this because it is of the smallest – I've no skill to write of the more magnificent.[8]

This is about all I have seen, & I've heard no music. Hard at work I am, that is, hard for me. I'm designing a kitchen at this present time, & as I do it I think of the overtaxed cook who will have to go to bed, as I must, having so much to do. You will have heard of the father & me going to Kelmscott[9] – we had fine weather, and Annie [Allen] cooked our pike very well for us. We were on the water all the daylight, both days, & came home to victuals so comfortably. My stars! did we not quarrel over cribbage? Did we not sleep afterwards? Was the garden pretty with its remains of flowers? did Mouse[10] ruminate (no, that belongs to cows) under his many long winter red hairs? Philip Comely looked quite as well as I expected, but a little too clear eyed & thin skinned to please me – however, I think he may round the corner of the winter & pick up strength in the warmer spring. The kittens are grown to ^{be} fine cats, but not handsome – but they make up for want of good looks by being cleaner than anything less than their country tongues could make them. As usual they were one in the room & the other out.

If by accident you should see M^r & Mrs Howard, will you kindly give them my professional "duty" and also my respects to their sweet little children. You might perhaps hint that I am in doubt as to the honesty of the Whigs – but no – do not enter on politics, keep that to raddle the bones of your affectionate | P.W.

BL 45342, ff. 41-2

---

1 'The sun was now resting his huge disk upon the edge of the level ocean, and gilded the accumulation of towering clouds through which he had travelled the livelong day, and which now assembled on all sides, like misfortunes and disasters around a sinking empire and falling monarch.' Walter Scott, *The Antiquary* (1816), ch 7. This was a favourite book for PSW, as well as for WM.
2 Philip Burne-Jones boarded for four years from 1874 at Marlborough School. Fiona MacCarthy questions his parents' motive for choosing it, 'a particularly brutal boys' public school in those days, for a boy already highly strung and difficult'. *MacCarthy, LPR*, p. 259.
3 For some months, during the unfolding crisis of the 'Eastern Question', it seemed as if Britain, in its existing alliance with Turkey, might go to war with Russia which sought a sphere of influence in the old Ottoman Empire. But enlightened opinion had recently cooled towards the Turks, following the brutal suppression of a Bulgarian uprising, and about which Gladstone published a pamphlet highly critical of the foreign policy of Prime Minister, Benjamin Disraeli. Matters came to a head in the second half of 1877, when Disraeli seemed determined on conflict. After Russia declared war on Turkey in April 1877, WM and PSW became enthusiastic supporters of the Eastern Question Association, a liberal pressure group which argued that Britain should not fight.
4 'Hocus' was used as a verb in the nineteenth century: to trick, to confuse.
5 'The Decorative Arts' was published first in *The Architect*, XVIII (8 December 1877), pp. 308–12, and then as a pamphlet in 1878. Note PSW's avoidance of the professional magazine.
6 The Grosvenor Gallery in New Bond Street, founded by Sir Coutts Lindsay as an alternative venue to the Royal Academy, opened on 1 May 1877. In that first summer exhibition, eight canvases by EBJ were featured, and also James McNeill Whistler's 'Nocturne in Black and Gold: The Falling Rocket' (c. 1875, Detroit Institute of Art), made infamous by JR's attack. See below, Letter 132, note 6. The winter exhibition featured drawings rather than paintings, an eclectic selection, from Old Master drawings (including examples from the Royal collection) to more recent British work.
7 The first-floor galleries were situated directly above the ground floor dining room, and the basement restaurant and kitchen. See floor plans in Colleen Denney, *At the Temple of Art. The Grosvenor Gallery, 1877–1890* (London: Associated University Presses, 2000), pp. 20 and 23–4.

8 Cat. 709: 'Landscape with Mill-Wheel in the Foreground. Highly finished in water-colours. Lent by E. Cheney, Esq.' *The Grosvenor Catalogue Illustrated Catalogue. Winter Exhibition (1877–78)* (London: Libraire de L'Art and Chatto & Windus, 1877), p. 83. There were thirty Dürer drawings on show.

9 'On Tuesday I believe Mr. Webb & I are going down to Kelmscott for 2 or 3 days: the river has been much flooded Annie says but is going down a bit now.' WM to JEM, 7 December 1877, *CLWM*, I.

10 WM's pony.

131 • To George Price Boyce, 17 January 1878

1, Raymond Buildings, Gray's Inn, | London.
Thursday. Jan: 17. '78

My dear Boyce

I'm very sorry to hear that the pains, & perhaps the penalties are upon you. I can only hope that you do not pay for coming here the other night.

I got your note on returning from Exeter Hall last evening. I did not stay there longer than enough time to see that the meeting was to be a success, for my cold is none of the most kindly.

If you do not show yourself at the anti-scrape I'll apologise for you and ask them to await your better day.

Both, the meeting on the Dardanelles question, at Willis's rooms, and that at Exeter Hall went off better even than we had hoped;[1] people were hearty, & had surely made up their minds. I missed Morris's verses sung to the tune of the "Hardy Norseman"[2] played on the organ at the latter meeting, but the poet tells me that the congregation fell in with the idea capitally. The Daily News gives a more full acc^t than the Times – tho' even that trimmer was steadily tho' cautiously on our side.[3]

Kindest remembrance to Mrs Boyce, & please tell her that the taste of the fruit is quite up to the appearance. Thank you also for the last "carte".

Yours very truly | Philip Webb:

BL Add 45354, ff. 110-11

---

1 PSW and WM attended these two anti-war meetings on 16 January, in the afternoon at Willis's meeting rooms, St James's, and in the evening at Exeter Hall, in the Strand (organised by the Workmen's Neutrality Demonstration), where WM spoke.

2 WM had been asked to write new verses to fit the song melody, 'The hardy Norseman's home of yore'. The audience was rehearsed before the meeting started, and later in the meeting WM's words 'Wake, London Lads! the hour draws nigh . . . cast off the lie, and cast the Turk away!' were sung by all present. The trade unionist Henry Broadhurst recorded that 'the effect when the burning words were thundered forth by the vast assembly was electrifying'. See *MacCarthy, WMLT*, p. 384, for an account of this occasion.

3 *The Times* reported on both meetings. 'The meeting at Willis's Rooms yesterday afternoon was chiefly occupied with the discussion of one special point – the opening of the Dardanelles to the

ships of war of all nations. . . . [That at Exeter Hall] was made up from the working men of London, who were invited to be present in order to protest against England being dragged into a war. . . . This they did with one voice, and the concord between "the brains and muscles" of the country was thus once more ratified' (17 January).

132 • To Jane Morris, 30 January 1878

1, Raymond Buildings, Gray's Inn, | *London.*
Jan: 30. 1878

My dear Janey

Thank you a-many times for your letter. It has given me great pleasure I assure you. I was not going to be done out of my native obstinacy as to the truth of the latitudes & longitudes of your two infants, so I took to the map (I have bought a big one since you have gone to Italy) and I find that Jenny & May are right, and that you have the blessing of the sun from early morn to dewy eve.[1] Jenny & May will say, 'O, mother, we told you so, what a positive & ridiculous old mule that Webb is'. True my children; what is bred in the bone, &c. But I have the advantage of you, I cannot be proud of my accuracy – a pride of the most dangerous kind, of which I warn you both, perhaps all three. Alas, your kindly scheme for bringing me to Italy in the spring will remain a scheme. 'Twill be impossible; what with my work, and the hindrance of the double dyed D'Israeli, stick to my work closely for the next 2 or 3 years I must. Never mind, it won't so much matter, as you will tell me all about it when you return.

I smiled over your "Glaum eyed" horrors. Still, matters have been very stirring, and we all have (the reasonable ᵃᵐᵒⁿᵍˢᵗ ᵘˢ) real cause for joy, that at present a European war has been staved off. Morris & some others have done more than yeoman's service to the state. We are not quite out of the wood yet, but I think I see light on the other side. "Lord, what fools these mortals be".[2]

If we succeed in avoiding war I think I shall subscribe to have the Windsor looms make a portrait of the Queen as large ~~of~~ as the Norfolk Giantess at St Giles's fair.[3] Christopher Sykes must not be allowed to have all the fun to himself.[4] What do you think of this subject, 'Triumph of the Imperial Indian Cæsaress ~~of~~ ᵃᶠᵗᵉʳ the manner of Mantegna at Hampton Court,' designed by Val Prinsep.[5] Field Marshall HRH Prince of Wales, his jack boots in the foreground. Whistler & Fortnum & Mason on white Elephants as attendant sprites – followed by Sir Coutts Lindsay with frying-pans à la Grosvenor Gallery?[6] Howell and the Bendizzy as thimble-riggers, by kind permission of the Derby day, might be thrown in.[7]

I had a letter on Saturday from Annie Allen. She said that the dining room & kitchen ceilings had been whitened, and the window put in to the "green room". This last "a great improvement". She also said that Philip Comely gets weaker, for wh' I am very sorry, as I had hoped he w^d pull through – hope against reason. I shall see Morris tonight, & I must talk to him about writing to Mr Hobbs to clear away the blown-down elm, wh' he has not yet done.

THE LETTERS OF PHILIP WEBB VOLUME I

I saw Lady Stanley in Harley S^t the other night, as brisk as a four-year-old, of this I was glad, because as I think Rosalind is very much like what her mother must have been, I hope the former will hold on in life as well as the mother does.[8] Your picture of the cows being milked close to the house door knocker, and Rosalind as monitory priestess over-aweing the neighbourhood pleased me mightily.

I hope May works at her drawing manfully, and that Jenny basks in the sun shine, and will call this "bosh" as soon as she hears of it. I had a letter from Stanhope the other day, telling me of the joy he had in reading the Trade Guild lecture – and, what do you think? he asked me if I had read Mazzini's "Duty of Man" – !!!⁹ What will the world come to next? he called it a "noble bit of thought," as assuredly it is.

Oh, the lovely mountains, to be seen at times when you can take a short walk. Then you think of that little peasant land, the description of wh' we have in all our mouths just now; never before has England been written of so closely and well.

Morris had a reception at Horrington House last week, of wh' I was one guest & a man named Vinall, who works for the shop, another.[10] I believe it was chiefly to give Sarah the cook something to do – & she did it. I went into the kitchen as I came away, & found her reading (life of late Prince Consort no doubt) and Jack the cat, lying full length, belly towards fire, a perfect picture of ease & dignity. I missed the 3 affectionate women-kind, but looked forward to embracing you all there once again at last. 'Till then I beg you to hold me in kindest remembrance, forgetting all the evil, mindful only of the little parcels of good scattered at intervals, for the making of wh' ^whole, God only knows the reason.

Your affectionate | Philip Webb:

BL Add 45342, ff. 43-4

---

1 This was a familiar phrase, and probably derives from Milton's *Paradise Lost*: 'from morn / To noon he fell, from noon to dewy eve' (I, 742–3).
2 Puck, in *A Midsummer-Night's Dream*, III.ii.115.
3 Mary Hales Laske (?1811–41), known as the Norfolk Giantess, was more than seven feet in height. PSW might well have seen her in his childhood (JM would have been too young), at the annual September fair held in the thoroughfare of St Giles, Oxford.
4 Christopher Sykes (1831–98), Conservative MP for the East Riding of Yorkshire, was known as the Gull's Friend for sponsoring a bill in 1869 for the preservation of seabirds. He regularly entertained the Prince of Wales at his Berkeley Square house. PSW's remark is prompted by newspaper reports of a visit by Prince Leopold (1853–84), the Queen's fourth son, to the Windsor Tapestry Works on 18 January. 'The Prince remained at the works for about two hours, attentively examining the various tapestries in hand, among which were Mr. P.M. Ward's cartoons intended for the town mansion of Mr. Christopher Sykes M.P.' *The Belfast News-Letter*, 22 January 1878. WM had been particularly irritated by the establishment of the Windsor works in 1875 under the Queen's patronage, just when he was wanting Morris & Co. to move into tapestry making, and was convinced that Victoria was robbing him of customers. See *MacCarthy, WMLT*, pp. 406–7.

5 PSW's inclusion of Val Prinsep in his facetious remarks is prompted by 'The Imperial Assemblage at Delhi'. See above, Letter 111, note 2.
6 This mention of Whistler and Sir Coutts Lindsay possibly alludes to the furore caused when JR attacked Whistler's painting, 'Nocturne in Black and Gold: The Falling Rocket', shown at the inaugural Grosvenor Gallery exhibition. 'I have seen, and heard, much of Cockney impudence before now; but never expected to hear a coxcomb ask for two hundred guineas for flinging a pot of paint in the public's face' (*Flors Clavigera*, 1877). Whistler decided to sue, and much to his embarrassment, EBJ was called by JR as a witness for the defence. Interestingly, the offending Nocturne was bought by PWY. See *Dakers*, pp. 56–7.
7 A thimblerigger is a professional cheat. The swindling game of thimblerig invited bystanders to bet as to which of three thimbles covered a pea. In linking Charles Augustus Howell and Disraeli, PSW flatters neither.
8 Henrietta Maria Dillon-Lee (1807–95), married Edward John Stanley (1802–69) in 1826. He succeeded his father as second Baron Stanley of Alderley in 1850. Rosalind Howard was one of their daughters; another married Bertrand Russell. Lady Stanley was politically active, and a campaigner for women's education.
9 The politician Giuseppe Mazzini (1805–72) argued for Italian unification. *Doveri dell'uomo* was published in 1860, and in English as *The Duties of Man* (London: Henry S. King & Co., 1875).
10 The reception was at Turnham Green. Charles Vinall undertook occasional surveying work for Morris & Co.

133 • To Salisbury Baxendale, 4 February 1878

Draft/copy

[1, Raymond Buildings . . .]
Feb.ʸ 4. 1878.

To Salisbury Baxendale Esq.ʳᵉ
Bonningtons by Ware Herts.

My dear Baxendale.¹

I duly rec.ᵈ your letter, and have taken time, as the judges say, to consider the judgment. I shall leave the most imperative reason to the last.

In the first place, I have allowed myself to be involved in an amount of work wh' will keep me from making any fresh engagement for a long time to come, and I am steadily refusing to do fresh work even for old & valued clients like yourself.²

Secondly, I'm not over-strong in health, & must therefore draw the line somewhere, and lastly, if I were able & willing to enter on more work, I have put it out of my power, in the matter of altering old churches or other valuable relics of history or art, by becoming a member of a very valuable Society of wh' I enclose you the manifesto and list of members. I think you will readily understand the meaning and use of the society from the papers, and I shouldn't be surprised if you yourself asked ~~to be allowed~~ to become a member.

When I repaired your church,³ I did as little in the way of transforming it as I possibly could, but when it was done I was dissatisfied with the amount of change, and at once determined to be even more radically conservative in future. The society is a kind of buttress to me and helps me to ^meet^ entreaties of friends wh' otherwise I sh^d^ not have been able to do without greater discomfort.

Naturally there has been some opposition to the object of the society, but on the whole it has been supported more ably & fully than I had expected.

With very kind regards to Mrs Baxendale, whom I congratulate ^heartily^,

Believe me ^to be^ yours very truly | P: W:

LB-1, pp. 116-17

---

1 Salisbury Baxendale was born in or about 1827, and served as High Sheriff of Hertfordshire in 1883.
2 PSW built Bonningtons for Baxendale, an estate cottage near Hunsdon, Ware in Hertfordshire (c. 1866). See *Kirk*, p. 297.
3 St Dunstan's, Hunsdon (1870–2). See *Kirk*, p. 298.

134 • To Alexander Cassavetti, 23 February 1878

Draft/ copy

[1, Raymond Buildings . . .]
Feby 23. 1878.

To Alexander Cassavetti Esqre
Fairfield Lodge Kensington[1]

Dear Alexander Cassavetti

I was rather annoyed on reading your letter rec^d^ last night, not because it w^d^ seem as if it reflected on me, but rather that my explanations to you ~~must have been somewhat misleading~~ ^could not have been full enough or clear to you^, & if that is the case I am really very sorry. It is not at an uncommon thing, I assure you, for Arch^ts^ clients to be surprised when the final acc^ts^ come in, as 'till that time, they have, ^as a rule,^ hardly realized the amount of things wh' have been added to the contract, beyond those things (especially in an altered house) wh' could not have been foreseen.

Allow me to explain a little now, so that when I see you on Monday you may be in a better position to judge rightly of the case.

Messrs Ashby's tender for the ^works^ made on the quantities taken out by your surveyor, was £3689.16.0[,] to that, you will recollect, I added as a note that 7½ per cent sh^d^ be allowed in such work for unforeseen contingencies, that practically brought the amount to £3965.0.0. Well, I found on carrying out the works that even more than that sum was necessarily expended by me. Added to this, I made the staircases better than taken in the contract, to meet your particular wish with regard to this part.

Then follow the additions of bow window in bedroom over east drawing room, and the wide stone stairs out of new dining-room to garden &c. To these was added, what I confess has much worried me, namely the great cost of the engineer's drainage. As the work was proceeding I found the existing drainage in such a miserable and even dangerous state, that the amount allowed for this work was utterly insufficient. And beyond this, the fall to the street sewer was so slight, that in any case the whole of the drains must have been taken up.

In my anxiety to get ^{the} thing done quickly, and in the best way, I incurred the responsibility of putting the management of the drainage into the hands of an expert (Mr Field) who had been strongly recommended to me.[2] Tho' I did this, I by no means left it in his hands with^t spending a good deal of time in watching & approving his process, ~~and tho'~~ ^{but} Mr Field said he w^d not & even could not give me an estimate of the cost, & his assistant told me that the amount of work to be done was found greatly to exceed what he, an experienced man, had anticipated. Well, tho' the total cost of this work has much vexed me I cannot, looking at your interest in the matter, regret that I ordered the work to be done as I did.

I think you are slightly in error as to my having told you that the total cost of drainage & superintendence w^d be £500. I could hardly have said that, for Mr Field had never told me what his charge w^d be – but before he made those alterations to draining the front garden, his assistant had said that he thought Mr Bartholomew's work w^d to [*sic*] amount to £100 more than the £400 already paid. I beg to say that I do not consider Mr Field's ^{own} charge excessive, for the skill shewn in dealing with the matter and the trouble he took in carrying out his scheme – and I am satisfied that if you wished to sell the house, the plan wh' you hold shewing what has been done w^d greatly add to the value of the property.

With regard to Messrs Ashby's payments, the^y ~~"two months" refers to the balance of £124.0.7~~ might have asked ^{me} for a certificate ^{for} £600 further on acc^t some 4 or 5 months ago.

I shall be glad to talk over the matter with you on Monday, when I propose to call on you at 4. oc.

Yours very truly | Philip Webb.

LB-1, pp. 118-20

---

1 PSW made significant alterations to Fairfield Lodge in Addison Road, Kensington, first for Mrs Euphrosyne Cassavetti (in 1871–2), and later (in 1876–8) for her son, the solicitor Alexander Cassavetti (1854–1923).
2 The civil engineer, Rogers Field (1831–1900), was a long-standing member of the Sanitary Institute of Great Britain, and at his death left £5000 to the Institute, which established a gold medal in his name, awarded annually 'for an exhibit of outstanding merit from the point of view of hygiene'.

135 • To Major Arthur Godman, 27 February 1878

1, Raymond Buildings, Gray's Inn, | *London.*
February 27th 1878

Dear Major Godman.
In answer to your letters of Feb. 23 & 24.

I received Hardy's suggestions for reducing the cost of cottages.[1] I now wait 'till you find whether you can or cannot buy the property which would serve instead of the cottages, before letting Hardy know what in his suggestions I can agree to – of course I should be glad if you could get the property in question, so as to be able to do without the new buildings.

I am exercised in spirit about the drainage of your house. The levels Hardy has sent me are so little an improvement on those of the first proposition, that I have returned to that, but as I am in doubt as to the best way of dealing with the sewage under the conditions of deep digging, I have consulted an engineer expert, and I am now waiting his report upon the propositions I laid before him.[2] I think in all probability we shall stick to the first scheme with, perhaps modifications, but as it would be impossible to put this scheme in shape just at once, I think you should go on laying down the grass. In any case we shall not much upset that. At all events there would be no difficulty in sowing such parts as are disturbed, again.

I don't think you quite realise the amount of hay, straw and corn room in loft – you have 96 feet in length – 20 feet in width and 8 feet high – with easy access from wagon at outer end. It would add considerably to cost if you made loft space (with timbers to bear weight) over the remaining part of coach houses &c, with some trouble and expense to get access. It could be done, if you found you really wanted it.

I have made notes of smithy and calf pen.

Yours very truly, | Philip Webb.

NBS

---

1 The clerk of works at Smeaton Manor, John Hardy, was described by PSW as 'honest as the Yorkshire stone amongst which he grew up, and as full of grit; a most stoical and hard living man – always on the job, winter and summer, before the men.' See John Brandon-Jones, *NBS*, p. 36.
2 The expert would almost certainly have been Rogers Field. See above, Letter 134, note 2.

1864–1887

136 • To John Carrick, 16 March 1878

Draft/copy

[1, Raymond Buildings . . .]
Mar: 16 1878

To John Carrick Esqre
Brampton. Cumberland
Dear Sir.

(Brampton Ch')

I have delayed answering your letter ^of the 5th until I had seen Messrs Morris, & consulted with them in the matter of your window.[1] The practice of sending out designs of stained glass windows from wh' donors may select that wh' most pleases them, is only followed by the regular manufacturers of stained glass ^in the gross. It could not be done by artistic workmen, such as Messrs Morris, who have to pay very highly for their designs. Also, in fitting to windows appropriate glass, all the circumstances of the case must be taken into consideration – two of the most important being, the character of the architecture of the building in wh' the glass is to be placed, and the <u>system</u> on wh' all the windows ^of the building are proposed to be glazed. In the ~~two~~ designs sent for glazing 2 of the 3 windows on the North aisle of nave, Messrs Morris have closely followed my explanations as to what character of glass would best fit that position, & I beg to say that I was much pleased with the drawings forwarded wh' were ~~made~~ ^arranged from the full sized cartoons made by the artist.

It is quite possible that you w^d be better pleased with a design applicable to a window ~~or windows~~ in another position in the church. Messrs Morris say that they have cartoons wh' would do for the 3 light window on the south side of the south aisle of chancel arranged in this way, [*sketch*] namely 3 single figures in the upper part of the lights A and subject panels at the bottom of lights B. But this window would most likely cost more than the window on the north side, ~~of wh' the design has been sent.~~

The square windows in the South aisle of Nave and the West window (circular) of south aisle would require ~~original~~ artist's designs to be specially made for them, & therefore w^d relatively be more costly. If you sh^d decide upon abandoning the design sent to you for ^one of the north aisle windows Messrs Morris would have to charge you £2/10/0 for the use of the drawing, the drawing itself ^still being their property.

143

Allow me to say in conclusion that, as the designer of the Church, I am very anxious to have stained glass in its windows of the best character and fitted for the building, and I particularly wish to avoid the use of harsh crude designs and inharmonious colouring, the ugliness of wh' spoil most of the churches in wh' they are placed.

Yours very truly, | Ph Webb.

LB-1, pp. 123-5

---

1 John Carrick was the son of William Carrick, a solicitor in the partnership which acted for the Naworth estate and 'one of the leading laymen in the church building project.... He died before the completion of the church and his son decided to commemorate him by giving the second [Morris] window.' *Penn*, p. 56. The subject of this letter is the central window in the North aisle, depicting the Old Testament figures of Moses, Solomon, David and Elijah.

137 • To Percy Wyndham, 10 March 1878

Draft/copy

[1, Raymond Buildings . . .]
Mar: 19. 1878.

To The Hon Percy Wyndham M:P.

My dear Sir.

I rec^d your letter yesterday with its enclosures, wh' ^{matter} I return. My opinion after reading them, is, that you may pipe 'till you are black in the face, but you will not save that building which so much pleased us on Thursday. The list of subscribers is great enough to deface a whole county.[1]

I intended that my former "notes" sh^d read like the utterances of a sorrowful lay-man, and not like those of a jubilant Arch^t, however, your request is quite reasonable, and I send you a few more notes, wh' you ~~can~~ are perfectly welcome to use or adapt at your pleasure, or even not use at all. I agree with you that some protest sh^d be made, and as you have been applied to for aid in the destruction, you have a perfect right to point out the proved disastrous result, of such proceedings as are proposed in the circular. You will not succeed in this case, but some one or more of the subscribers may make note of your piteous appeal, ~~of~~ ^{and} not be so sure of the virtue of their action when the next case comes before them.

Clouds House. I must beg you not to be too sure as to when we shall be able to begin, for the amount of work before me is very great, tho' I have been refusing further work, elsewhere, so as to give me as much time for yours as possible. I must beg you also to remember that I shall have to add 20 or 25 percent to my estimate, if a first-rate London builder is employed. I told you that it w^d be to my interest (apart from any money gain to me) that a London builder sh^d be employed, but you may be quite certain that it will cost about that percentage more if we do not try some local man.

I sh^d be glad to know what you decide to do ab^t the venetian fireplaces, as, if you buy them, I shall have to arrange so as to rightly dispose of them.

Yours very truly, | P: W:

P:S: I w^d have West Knoyle Ch' photographed inside & out, there is a very good man at Trowbridge who w^d do it without mentioning your name.

LB-1, pp. 125-6

---

1 The thirteenth century church of St Mary the Virgin, West Knoyle, was restored (1876–8) by J. Mountford Allen of Crewkerne. Local subscriptions covered the cost of about £1,800.

138 • To Jane Morris, 6 July 1878

1, Raymond Buildings, Gray's Inn, | London.
Sat: July 6. '78

My dear Janey

You must have thought me very loutish last night when I accepted your kind present from Italy – & I quite excuse you if you did, for I was so, and indeed I always am when taking a present, more than under other circumstances of my life, wh' is saying a good deal. Daylight shewed me the lovely colour and surface of the wonderful stone, and I am very glad that you thought of being so kind to me. The "verde antico" is a fit reminder of our green old friendship.[1]

Yours very affectionately | Philip Webb:

BL Add 45342, f. 47

---

1 'Verde antico', popular since antiquity as a decorative facing stone.

139 • To George Price Boyce, 18 September 1878

1, Raymond Buildings, Gray's Inn, | London.
Sep 18. 78

My dear Boyce.

I was very glad to hear from you, the more so that your news was good news. I quite understood your long silence, for if I had been in your place & you in mine, you very likely w^d not have heard from me 'till the day before my coming home, when I sh^d have written for you to prepare me dinner on my arrival. You lay a fine trap for me in your mention of a good cuisine at the Golden Lion of Vèzelay [*sic*] – gently gliding away from the sorrowful subject of wine, to spare my pledged conscience.[1]

However, wine or no wine, that is not the question,[2] & my coming to you is out of all question. I've not seen Wallis for a month I sh<u>d</u> think, and then he had just returned <u>from</u> Paris. I fancy he goes to Italy this winter. Morris is at Kelmscott, & has been so off & on for a month or more. My own work sits on my shoulders like the old man of the sea,[3] & I can't dislodge him & break his head with a lump of green sandstone, as I sh<u>d</u> wish.

Your little photographic card of Vézelay, gives me a good idea of the situation, & with your story of it, I can hardly think of a more delightful place to work and recreate in. I take it that the place is out of the line of bustle of tourists or active trade, wh' must be a comfort.

I went to Batsford's yesterday, but he could find nothing in his ^{French} catalogues of Vézelay.[4] If I get to South Kensington [Museum], I'll look in the library there. Murray's note of it in his guide, is lean & hungry in the extreme.[5] The situation puts me in mind of an Italian town, but the look is not so white. I suppose the wine you get there is of the Burgundy type? as it is in that province, seemingly just on the edge of it. By the time you come back I shall have got through my wine-fast, & shall enjoy a talk on its merits, & I'll look you out a bottle of my best to refresh your memory. If you'll promise not to tell V: Hugo, I don't mind saying that France is a notable place and a lovely – & if not <u>the</u> navel of the world, it is only because the Earth has a good many navels – and nationalities must not be allowed to label themselves, or the Irish would be quite unbearable.

Please tell M<u>rs</u> Boyce that I've been reading a translation of George Sand's "Consuelo" and its sequel[6] – some parts of the book I thought delightful, but others, extravagant & absurd. Consuelo herself w<u>d</u> have been a beautiful character, if she had not been thrown in to impossible situations wh' fairly washed her off her pleasant legs.

I've seen nothing of Norwood, have intended writing to him to ask for a walk in company, but have not found time & opportunity. I fully appreciated your note of the Paris exhibition, and the state of its Art show. I think there is hardly a doubt that if the French w<u>d</u> (could?) take seriously to art, that in these times they w<u>d</u> stand the greatest chance of succeeding of any European people, but if the Italians prosper, it will be they I think, as w<u>d</u> be natural, who will lead the rest. The English have imagination tho' little aptitude, the French have an abundance of the latter but little of the former. The Italians have both, if they were set fairly going. The Germans are doubtful, yet a-while at all events, as they have hardly recovered from topping the musical tree with their Beethoven. I sh<u>d</u> be glad if when you come back to Paris if you could find out anything more of the bronze heads of M: A:[7] & if photographs could be got of them.

I'll bear your remembrance to Welwyn when I next go there. I've designed the house for them, & it is being worked out[8] – but we are late in the year to do much this side of Christmas.

With my kindest regards to M<u>rs</u> Boyce | Believe me
yours sincerely, Philip Webb:

BL Add 45354, ff. 128-9

---

1 It would seem that for health reasons, PSW had temporarily given up drinking wine (of which he was very fond).
2 'To be, or not to be, that is the question', *Hamlet*, III.i.55.
3 In the Arabic stories of Sinbad the Sailor, the Old Man of the Sea tricks a traveller into carrying him across water, but then refuses to release his grip from the victim's shoulders.
4 The bookseller and publisher, Bradley Thomas Batsford (1821–1904), had a shop in High Holborn from 1843.
5 The first of John Murray's series of Handbooks for Travellers appeared in 1836.
6 PSW may have read the 1847 English translation of George Sand's *Consuelo*; its sequel, *La comtesse de Rudolstadt* appeared as *The Countess of Rudolstadt* in 1851. The character of Consuelo is thought to have been based on the soprano Pauline Viardot.
7 Not identified, but presumably he means bronze copies of Michelangelo sculptures.
8 See above, Letter 65, note 1.

140 • To Jane Morris, 8 November 1878

1, Raymond Buildings, Gray's Inn, | London.
Nov: 8. '78

My dear Janey

It was bad of you to taunt me in that way about my dining out. If I were not as bad as you in the way of ungracious jibes I w<u>d</u> not forgive you, no, not for a long time – however you threw in the soother of Jenny's face and so I unpuckered mine & grinned forgiveness already.

I <u>am</u> very busy; not that I get through much work, for my lumbering brain causes me to do & undo over & over again what a better head than mine would do easily once & well.

At last I have ordered the bookcase to take the place of, & the books out of your cabinet; wh' will I hope shortly be on wheels to your new old house. The possession of the beautiful wooden box has always rather tortured my tearing rag of a conscience, and I shall be glad to think of it standing in its new and proper home.[1]

I saw Morris last night, and between the yells & mingled gabble of a full antiscrape meeting he told me that you had all safely fled from the little shed on the high road to "Kelmscott house"!![2] Lord my dear Janey what a magnificent title to the house at t'other end of the river. I must take care when I do come to dinner, not to go off to Paddington to the other of that name.[3] That I will come to dinner shortly you may be sure, and as soon as I can "after next week".

Perhaps I may hire a boat one of these moonlight nights at Temple stairs, & row up to you, and sound you a pretty tune off my bassoon. You'll know it is me by the sublimity of the air.

Give my fragrant unbearded kisses to the girls, thank Jenny prettily for her likeness, (wh' is a good one) and yourself | believe me sincerely yours Philip Webb:

BL Add 45342, ff. 48-9

---

1 A fine French cabinet which PSW had kept in his rooms in Raymond Buildings, as it had been too tall for the Turnham Green house.
2 At the beginning of April 1878, whilst his wife and daughters were in Italy (and after much consultation with JM by letter), WM decided to take the riverside house on Upper Mall in Hammersmith as their future London residence. Called 'The Retreat' by its former occupant, the writer George Macdonald (1824–1905), Morris renamed it Kelmscott House, after Kelmscott Manor. It would be the house in which he died. PSW had helped him to decide on its suitability in March, offering persuasive advice about possible flooding at high tide: 'Webb thought that this might be easily guarded against, as it does not come up through the drains (since the house drains into the main sewer not into the Thames)'. WM to JM, 18 March 1878, *CLWM*, I.
3 Trains to Lechlade, via Oxford, started from Paddington station on the Great Western Railway.

141 • To William Lawrance, 16 January 1879

Draft/copy

[1, Raymond Buildings . . .]
Jan 16. '79

To M[r] William Lawrence
Builder. Datchworth.

Dear Sir

(M[r] [H.S.] Webb's house)

I was much annoyed on finding that after all my trouble taken in this matter, you, to whom I had given preference before other builders, sh[d] have both delayed matters and had failed to give me an estimate which I could accept. I now return you the quantities repriced (in red ink) according to a more liberal scale than better works in several places which have been done for me, when prices ran higher than they do now.

If you will agree to do the work [according] to the new list [of prices] for the total sum of £2403.0.0 I will arrange with my brother on Monday next as to accepting it. Otherwise I shall have to put the work out to competition.[1] I shall be at my brother's ^{at Welwyn} on Monday morning the 20^{th at 9. oc} when I shall be obliged if you will call with the quantities.

Yours truly | P: W:

LB-1, pp. 142-3

---

1 The building contract for New Place, Harry Webb's house, was finally awarded to Lawrence.

142 • To Major Arthur Godman, 13 March 1879

1, Raymond Buildings, Gray's Inn, | London.
March 13th 1879

Dear Major Godman.

I am glad you had the doorway made from the yard to the cellar, otherwise my wish might have stayed you against your own particular inclination. Of course the internal wood covering to the stair will do as I shew in drawing <u>without</u> the doorway from the inside, or you might put the door and lock it – as you please.

Certainly, colour such rooms as you want to make quite neat, taking care to use no arsenic in the colour. Perhaps the best colour would be to match a full toned piece of parchment: or if you use more decided colours match some of these on Morris's papers. I sometimes have used white, coloured pinkish with a little <u>venetian</u> red, or white coloured with a little brown yellow ochre.

Wednesday the 2nd April would do very well for me to come to Smeaton, and I will do so unless I hear from you to the contrary.

<u>I</u> am heartily glad to learn that Mrs Godman is stronger.

With kind regards, believe me, | Yours very truly, | Philip Webb.

NBS

143 • To Percy Wyndham, 14 May 1879

Draft/copy

[1, Raymond Buildings . . .]
May 14. '79

To the Hon' Percy Wyndham M:P:
44 Belgrave Square
My dear Sir.

(Clouds H^{se})

I went to Geo' Smith's on Saturday, & saw Mr Mansfield their manager, and Mr Fletcher their estimating clerk, but ~~could~~ ^{failed to} get ~~no~~ ^a definite date for my receiving the estimate.¹ ~~M͞r Fletcher was to have called upon me yesterday, but failed to do so.~~

The ill-wind of the present state of the sandstone quarry has reached Smith's, thro' Howell,² but I ~~set~~ ᵐᵉᵗ this difficulty with regard to their estimate, by saying that as we had successfully opened the quarry, we would continue to open further so as to be sure of providing the stone we shall want. ~~I think it is likely that Smith's have sent Mr Cross, their master mason, to look at the quarry, & that this has delayed them.~~ I will send you further news as soon as I have it.

Mr Fletcher has just been here, & he said that he thought it likely that they wᵈ be able to let me have the estimate by Saturday evening.

I went to Chance's yesterday.³ The 4 Sansovino frames⁴ are not of that excellence wh' wᵈ make me say 'buy them' for fear of missing an opportunity wh' shᵈ not be lost. The console tables would not suit the house at all. Chance had a small carved Italian frame wh' I asked him to let you have the refusal of, if some one who was looking at it did not take it. I went on to Sinclairs,⁵ and found the De Witt pictures of no value, that is, according to my lights.

Yours very truly, | P: W:

LB-1, pp. 145-6

---

1 PSW was drawn towards the Pimlico firm of George Smith & Co., as he had reservations about employing a country builder for a job the size of Clouds. However, settling on a contractor would be a protracted and frustrating process. See further letters to Smith and PWY, below.
2 The East Knoyle brickmaker, John Howell.
3 The carver, gilder, and picture frame-maker, James Henry Chance (1810–1902), had premises in Fitzroy Square.
4 A style of picture frame 'richly carved with scrolls, masks and swags of fruit . . . [and] named after the Italian sculptor and architect Jacobo Sansovino (1486–1570), whose Venetian buildings were particularly influential on the decorative arts from about 1530'. http://collections.vam.ac.uk/item/O134792/frame-unknown/ [accessed 17 July 2014].
5 The auctioneers, Sinclair & Son, of 381 Kingsland Road, NE.

144 • To George Smith & Co., 19 June 1879

Draft/copy

[1, Raymond Buildings . . .]
June 19. 1879.

Messʳˢ George Smith & Co.
9 Commercial Road Pimlico
Dear Sirs.

(Clouds House)

I have considered, with Mr Wyndham, the ˢᵘᵇʲᵉᶜᵗ matter of your letter to me of the 16ᵗʰ ~~inst~~ ᵒᶠ ᴶᵘⁿᵉ, but before stating to you the result of our conference, I wᵈ make note of one or two passages in your letter.

You state that your Mr Mansfield retained a conviction that I considered your prices generally consistent for really good work. What I intended to convey to Mr Mansfield, was, that I found no individual items of the prices for ^the work particularly extravagant, but that on careful examination I found the prices over all the many items to be what I considered full high, & that these prices and the sums allowed for contingencies carriage &c and the charge for profit did account ^to me for my estimate for the work (wh' I still consider a fair one) being below yours, but that I did not consider you were not justified in using such prices, ^&c, as it was most likely that your usual clients were quite ready to pay such prices for your work.

As to your remark, ~~as~~ of the misleading character of any price per cubic foot over the whole of ~~the~~ a building, I should not differ with you when proper precaution and experience are not used in such estimating. When time, and careful consideration to place, materials, labour &c are applied, & where, from accurate knowledge of the character of the work to be done, and ~~with~~ ^when full and ~~accurate~~ ^particular delineation of the substance and detail is made before estimating, I believe that cubing the contents of a building is even a sound check upon the individual prices ~~of~~ ^put to a very large number of items ~~taken~~ on full quantities.

After consultation, Mr Wyndham has decided not to ~~countenance~~ ^begin building until he is satisfied that the total cost of the works to be done for him ^under my direction will not exceed £75,000; and though he would be sorry ~~to have~~ to agree to the work I have designed being cut down, as I have proposed, to the amount of £5,000, with the further deduction of £1,000 for stables, and £2412 from the sum I have allowed for extras & omissions, (£8412 in all) yet, if you found it to come within the bounds of safe calculation on your part to make a reduction on your ~~charge~~ prices, say to the extent of 12½ percent on the total amount of your estimate, he w^d feel greatly inclined to agree to ~~it~~ what he considers would be a mutilation of the design. On the other side I have put down a statement in figures explaining the above red[uctio]^ns.

Allow me to conclude ~~with~~ ^by thanking you for ~~the~~ ^your courtesy ~~with which you have attended~~ ^to myself, and for your patience in attending to my serious difficulties in this matter.

Yours truly, | P: W:

LB-1, pp. 149-50

145 • To George Smith & Co., 25 June 1879

Draft/copy

[1, Raymond Buildings . . .]
June 25. '79

To Messrs George Smith & Co.
9 Commercial Road Pimlico

Dear Sirs

(Clouds House)

I have seen Mr Wyndham, and very carefully explained to him the details of your proposition for reduction on certain items of your estimate, with the resulting offer on your part to ^do the works of the main block of the building for £50,000. Mr Wyndham expressed himself as being pleased that you had been willing to entertain the necessity of making some reduction, tho' the result, as you would have expected, could not make the question a practical one for him. I was directed by Mr Wyndham to inform you that he had resolved to defer building at Clouds altogether ~~at~~ ^for the present.

Will you be so good as to send me a memorandum of any expenses you may have been put to in sending to Knoyle and elsewhere for information before making your estimate, so that I may put the same before Mr Wyndham for payment.

I am, Dear Sirs, with many thanks for your attention to this matter, | Yours truly | P: W:

LB-1, pp. 151-2

146 • To George Price Boyce, 26 September 1879

1, Raymond Buildings, Gray's Inn, | *London.*
Sep 26. 79

My dear Boyce

I duly had your letter of the 22nd and was glad of it. The kind offer of "the good extra bedroom" is very tempting, but I must say "get behind me" to it. One might say that the <u>evil</u> of the world was only "blundering" written small, so I must stay at home to scotch as many of the embryo blunders as I possibly can.

If the swallows are gone they will come back again, & the martins are still with us for best joy. If you are out of tune with your work, don't believe but that a happier view of it will come back to you as the swallows. Don't think for a moment that I read your complaint as "whining"; I did no such thing; for I well know that but little ^good is to be done in art, as well as other things, without the doer ~~is~~ ^being often troubled by the thought of its imperfection. I wouldn't for anything offer you any false comfort, but I did think that your last work had some of your strongest quality in it, as well done as ever. What w^d be your greatest cause of depression, is that of your being disabled by weak health, and I sincerely hope you'll get over most of that.

I went to West H^o last evening, and your dark-haired maid very politely shewed me the tiles and put in paper the little basket. I found the tiles in better condition than your letter led me to expect. I think I can use comfortably 24 of them, (all that I sh^d want) but I must beg you not to let me have them if there is the slightest chance of your wanting to use them.[1] I shall not take them away 'till I've paid for them, as the Welwyn "sawbones" is like me for this, that he has a dislike to "sponging" upon even his best friends. My sister will, no doubt, write to you or Mrs Boyce about the pretty basket. I'll take it to her on Sat: I've heard nothing about the mending of the neckless [*sic*] clasp.

I've seen nothing of Wallis – he's in Italy surely! and if so, getting rid of his Roman Catholicism scare, we will hope. Murray has gone back at last. Thanks for asking about my bronchial affection (the "sawbones" laughs at that). I have a cold, wh' has I suppose for the last 9 months thickened the tubes of my ears, so that I have a singing and "hum-buzzing" in my head nearly constantly, but, no doubt, by time of swallows-return I shall have their music in my ears instead.

You would have laughed if you had seen my face the other day, on receiving a bit of engraving wh' I had tried to get done from my design. Mrs Wyndham had asked me to get for her a gold toy map-meter, and have said design done on it. Casella said 'let Marino do it':[2] well, the design for was a "Talbot" dog[3] on a wreath, with a background; and the engraver didn't dog it, but bitched it, so I've to cancel the gold case and get another; that is easily done, but where to find an engraver I do not know – do you? Did you ever get anything of that sort done by Strongitharme?[4] [*sic*].

Stanhope very kindly sent me a capital photograph of the back of an altar-piece at Arezzo by John Pisani[5] [*sic*] – such a noble piece of work, wh' you'll be glad to see.

We've had very broken weather, with a drenching rain on Tues: aft: and the whole of the night. Hope you are better off, as it has been brightly fine, tho' cold, here the last 2 days.

Best remembrance to Mrs Boyce & a kindly cheer
to you f^m | Yours sincerely Philip Webb:

BL Add 45354, ff. 138-9

---

1 These are likely to have been tiles left over from work to GPB's Chelsea house, PSW having added a dressing room in 1876. His intention was to use them in New House in Welwyn, which he was building for his brother.
2 Louis Pascal Casella (1812–97) was head of the London firm of scientific instrument makers, located in Holborn. They manufactured drawing and surveying instruments, meteorological apparatus, thermometers, and similar items. Louis Marino was one of his sons, who worked for the firm.
3 A white hound once used for hunting.
4 Founded by John Strongitharm (d. 1839), this firm of engravers was situated in Pall Mall.
5 The marble altar and reredos (c. 1286) in the cathedral at Arezzo is by the architect and sculptor, Giovanni Pisano (c. 1250–c. 1315).

147 • To George Price Boyce, 8 October 1879

1, Raymond Buildings, Gray's Inn, | *London.*
Oct. 8. 79

My dear Boyce.

I duly got your letter of the 28th Sep: I can't say that I liked the tone of it, and was afraid that your liver was not in a good state when you wrote it. I hope Mrs Herrick is a pretty good cook, & that you can get some of Gilbey's wine, at least, to drink with your dinner.[1] You'll not forget that you are got a little to the north, and that it is Oct: after the wettest of summers.

The weather, here, the last few days, has been much finer; tho' the sun has had to struggle thro' mists. You are on higher grown, [sic] & perhaps it is better with you.

I had last week to go and look at a fine Elizabethan house, with earlier parts attached, in Essex; my would-be client wanted at once to pull down the earlier parts, and all the lovely garden walls, & cut down the fruit trees. I persuaded and enforced, and jeered, & beseeched for 12 frightful hours; to what effect I don't know; but I strongly suspect to none whatever. If he wd only leave it 'till next summer, you might go and picture it, so as to have some memorandum of one of the glories of this land; before the loveliness of it departs and can be no more seen. 'Tis a place called Moynes House, on the north border of Essex, a few miles west of Long Melford.[2]

"New Place" is getting on but slowly, but I hope this weather will allow of the tiling being done before more heavy wet comes. I had some difficulty in making up my mind as to the size of the bowling green, but as it wd only be used in that way some 10 or 15 times in the year, I determined to not to [sic] use too much ground in it, so I have made it some 20 feet longer than yours, on wh' we have played some quite comfortable games, & think that will do well enough for Welwyn.

No, I've seen nothing of the Burlington F A club catalogue,[3] in truth I see little of such things 'till some good friend lugs me to them.

We have had no meeting yet at the "Anti-scrape", but I hear that there is a pretty kettle-of-fish between the Socy, Christian,[4] Street,[5] and Tom-fool Becket[6] on the Southwell question.[7] It seems that the society, in criticising Christian's report, incidentally noticed that Street proposed pulling down the 14 c stone rood screen.[8] He denies this, & sends his report to the Bishop to the building papers. I read this last night, and in it he <u>does</u> suggest as an alternative the pulling it down if no other way can be decided on (accepted) for making the ecclesiastical arrangement of the choir &c, "correct". So Street is at daggers drawn with us – never mind, the publicity will do all the good & more than we can do. I think it is either Mazzini or Mill who says, that publicity is the soul of freedom, and it is the tyranny of autocrats like Becket & the Church, who sit upon freedom.

When are you thinking of coming back? I suppose the weather will decide for you. Kindest remembrance to Mrs Boyce from

Yours sincerely | Philip Webb.

BL Add 45354, ff. 140-1

1 The Gilbey brothers, Henry, Walter and Alfred were wine-merchants, with business premises in Oxford Street from 1867.
2 Moyns (or Moynes) Park, in Steeple Bumpstead, Essex, a late sixteenth-century mansion built for Thomas Gent, which remained the family home until the end of the nineteenth century.
3 *Catalogue of Bronzes and Ivories of European origin, exhibited in 1879* (London: Burlington Fine Arts Club, 1879).
4 As part of his role as architect to the Ecclesiastical Commissioners, Ewan Christian (1814–95) was closely involved in a number of major restoration projects, including the long-term works on Southwell Minster, in Nottinghamshire.
5 George Edmund Street (1824–81), in whose practice PSW had worked from 1854 when Street was Oxford Diocesan architect.
6 Sir Edmund Beckett (1816–1905), fifth Baronet and, later, first Baron Grimthorpe, was already a target of the SPAB's wrath for his 'highhanded proceedings' (WM to James Bryce, 3 June 1879, *CLWM*, I) in relation to restoration work at St Alban's Abbey, where he interfered at will with the wishes of Sir Gilbert Scott. He quarrelled enthusiastically with the many who disagreed with him.
7 The SPAB first became concerned about alterations at Southwell Minster, either proposed or implemented, in April 1878, when on behalf of the committee WM wrote to the Ecclesiastical Commissioners objecting to specific proposed changes, including removal of the existing low-pitched roofs and flat ceilings and replacement with high-pitched roofs, and thereby the threat to 'the obliteration of the wooden lantern between the western towers'. WM to Ecclesiastical Commissioners, 17 April 1878, *CLWM*, I. An exchange of letters in *The Architect* followed.
8 '[The SPAB] understands Mr. Street also advised the removal of the fourteenth century screen', WM to Ecclesiastical Commissioners, 29 July 1878, *CLWM*, I.

148 • To Percy Wyndham, 20 November 1879

Draft/copy

[1, Raymond Buildings . . .]
Nov: 20. 1879.

To Hon' Percy Wyndham M:P:
Wilbury House, by Salisbury.
My dear Sir.

(Clouds H$^{\underline{se}}$)

I enclose tracings of the ground, first, & second floors of the new design for the house, and I should be obliged if you and M$^{\underline{rs}}$ Wyndham would carefully consider them, and note anything which is unsatisfactory to you. You will see that I have added oriel windows to the chief bed-rooms on the south front on the first floor, M$^{\underline{rs}}$ Wyndham suggesting the convenience of them, and as they ^{would} go very well with the ^{general} design, I ~~have added~~ $^{thought\ it\ would\ be\ well\ to\ put}$ them ^{in}. Also, I have provided large coal bunkers on the first & second floors, and on the first floor a box-room and on the second floor a box or lumber-room.

On the ground plan in the central hall I have indicated a pair of "settles" to the large fireplace on M$^{\underline{rs}}$ Wyndham's suggestion – they would be moveable, but in their places they would not interfere at all with the passage way. I hope to be able to get the House, offices, Stables &c built for £75,000.

I had not forgotten about the parquet flooring matter, but it was only at the end of last week that I was able to see the French manufacturer I spoke of to you. I found that I had been mis-informed as to his price. It is 1ˢ/9ᵈ the foot superficial[1] laid, all expenses. His address is Mons' R: Gueraut, 2 Orris Villas Glenthorne Road Hammersmith W: I rather think that Howard's price for carpet parquet is 1ˢ/3ᵈ the foot superficial of a plain kind. Gueraut's is rather thicker and better laid. Howard's address is Messʳˢ Howard & Sons, 25 Berners Street, Oxford Street,

Yours very truly, | P: W:

LB-1, pp. 158-9

---

1 Per square foot.

149 • To Major Arthur Godman, 8 December 1879

1, Raymond Buildings, Gray's Inn, | *London.*
December 8ᵗʰ 1879

Dear Major Godman.

I received your note this morning. It was, may be, the frost, or perhaps the influx of callers which kept me from sending you on Sunday the final accounts which I now do.

You will see that I have directed you to keep back the odd money in Mackenzie's bill[1] 'till I am further satisfied by them as to the item of the well; I have written to them about it. However, you can at once pay them the £2,100, after <u>checking</u> the item of £8,480, which is put down as the total they have yet received from you in instalments on my certificates. I find in my certificate book that the last certificate I gave you was on September 5ᵗʰ 1879 for £2,000.

I also send you Mʳ Goodman's the surveyor's account for measuring the work. This item is sometimes put into the contractor's bill of extras, but I prefer as a rule that the client should pay it direct to the surveyor.[2]

My own terrible account comes last, and I should be glad if you would look to see that I have made no error in the same.

If the amount of my charge should seem large to you, will you be so good as to turn over the drawings from the first to the last (I suppose Hardy has put them into your hands?) and then it will not look so monstrous.[3]

Please get Hardy to write down in your own book a memorandum as to what taps pipes &c should be looked to in case of frost &c.

In making my final bow, will you and Mʳˢ Godman accept my sincere thanks for your very kind and courteous bearing towards me during the whole time of my work in considering and building your house.

Believe me, | Yours very truly, | Philip Webb.

NBS

1 The Darlington building firm contracted for Smeaton Manor was J.W. & M. Mackenzie.
2 T.W. Goodman's account was for £135.7.9.
3 PSW's total account was for £668.15.0, of which £300 had been paid on 26 November 1878.

150 • To Major Arthur Godman, 10 December 1879

1, Raymond Buildings, Gray's Inn, | *London.*
December 10th 1879

My dear Godman.

I very willingly drop all formality in thanking you very sincerely for your quite kindly letter accompanying the cheque.

As for the indemnification for my work I consider the customary 5 per cent quite sufficient payment; but when, on the top of that, one gets a thoughtfully kind letter of thanks one almost feels over paid.

You may pay me for the cottage design when the cottages are built, and if that is deferred 'till your boy comes of age I may have to come down upon him, so please warn him not to get into debt at college, if he should be so lucky as to go there.[1]

Your house is certainly a cheap one, but then you must remember that it is a quite plain one throughout. I have set Mr Basset to work to scheme out the glazed screen for the upper (first floor) corridor; but it is rather awkward to fit rightly, and if it does not come better than he has it at this moment, we must put our two heads together over it tomorrow, and I'll send it directly it is done.

There were some tracings of details of the house which Mr Goodman's assistant brought back here with him. I directed him to forward them to Hardy, so that you might have the whole bundle of drawings together.

With very kind remembrance to your wife. Believe me, | Very truly yours | Philip Webb.

If at any time you should be in this lawful neighbourhood, I should be glad if you would look in upon me. | P.W.

NBS

1 The two additional cottages were never built. See *Kirk*, p. 300.

151 • To George Hector Croad[1], 27 February 1880

1, Raymond Buildings, Gray's Inn, | *London*
Feb: 27. 1880

Having heard from Miss Burden, of 22 Upper Woburn Place, that she is applying to the School Board of London for the office of Lady Examiner of Needlework to the Board, I have much pleasure in bearing testimony to her special fitness for such work.[2]

I have known Miss Burden for 20 years, and have had occasion to ask her advice and assistance for all kinds of needlework, from the most simple & rudimentary to the most particular and complicated, and I have been aided by her with the greatest readiness and precision.

I have personal knowledge that Miss Burden is an industrious, capable, and honourable woman.[3]

Philip Webb. | Architect.

To G: H: Croad Esq[re] |
Clerk of the Board.

Huntington MOR 583

---

1 G.H. Croad (1829–1902) was appointed secretary to the London School Board in 1870. For WM's equally supportive letter of recommendation, see WM to Croad, 28 February 1880, *CLWM*, I.
2 For Elizabeth Burden (sister of JM), see above, Letter 20.
3 As well as herself producing work for Morris & Co., she was involved in organising the work of the other embroidery workers.

152 • To George Price Boyce, 19 May 1880

1, Raymond Buildings, Gray's Inn, | *London.*
Wed: morn: May 19

My dear Boyce

On no acc[t] would I wish to stop you f[m] the Richter concert. Not going there myself, I'd quite forgotten the time of the concert.[1] Neither can I go to the Berlioz evening, as I have a cold & do not care to face the gas.[2]

Often on the Sat: evenings that I am at home, I go to the S: Ken: Museum to pick up information. As you suggest Friday or Sat: could you meet me there – say not later than 6. oc – and come back here with me for some tea at 8. oc, when we could look at the plans and talk of the house matter in question?

I have to go to Bowman's in Surrey[3] on Thursday, (tomorrow) and I think it likely I shall not be back in time to attend the Rest[n] meeting of the anti-scrape,[4] therefore I hope you will be able to get there.

There is a long letter in today's Times, from their Italian correspondent, on the Ravenna Baptistery. It w[d] be well if Wallis also came to the meeting at Buckingham S[t].[5]

I agree, of course, ab[t] the keeping open of the Nat: Gallery, and shall write to members as directed by Wallis.

Yours very truly | Philip Webb:

P:S: Don't put yourself out as to meeting me at S: Ken, but if you cared to go, I would meet you about the Trajan column at the time above named.

P: W:

BL Add 45354, ff. 148-9

1 The leading Hungarian conductor of his generation, Hans Richter (1843–1916), appeared in a series of nine concerts in May and June at St James's Hall, which included performances of the nine Beethoven symphonies. The concert on 20 May featured the second symphony, as well as music by Cherubini, Wagner and Brahms.
2 Charles Hallé (1819–95) brought his Manchester-based orchestra to St James's Hall, for performances of Berlioz's *The Damnation of Faust* on 21 and 22 May.
3 See above, Letter 73, note 4.
4 In an attempt to encourage greater participation in the work of the SPAB from more members, WM's proposal to establish two business committees was implemented in January 1879. A general committee considered matters of principle, whilst the restoration committee handled the casework, meetings being scheduled on alternate Thursdays. In practice, the same small nucleus of committed members turned up on a regular basis to both, so that within two years the general committee was disbanded. 'The reconstituted committee met from 17 November 1881, and as the decade progressed admission to this inner sanctum became increasingly harder.' Chris Miele, 'The first conservation militants: William Morris and the Society for the Protection of Ancient Buildings', in Michael Hunter (ed), *Preserving the Past. The Rise of Heritage in Modern Britain* (Stroud: Alan Sutton Publishing Ltd., 1996), p. 35. In view of the sensitivity with which the SPAB came to regard the concept of 'restoration', as being in opposition to that of 'repair', it seems curious that one of the two committees was given this name.
5 The Italian authorities were concerned about the condition of the Ravenna Baptistery itself, and of the destructive effects of damp upon its ancient mosaics. They wished to raise the building 'from the swamp into which it has sunk full three metres'. Henry Wallis had already alerted readers of *The Times* to the crisis, which had prompted its correspondent to visit the scene, and to suggest a visit from competent representatives of the SPAB, so that they might examine the state of the building whilst listening to the opinions of the Italian architects and engineers. Mindful of the local offence which had been caused by the previous SPAB campaign against the damaging restorations at St Mark's, Venice, when in the autumn of 1879 WM had led a very public criticism of Italian 'headlong rashness', *The Times* now offered wise advice. 'Would not this be better than calling for an "English protest" on a subject which it is evident thus far the English people are absolutely uninformed?' (19 May 1880).

153 • To Thomas Richardson, 11 June 1880

Draft/copy

[1, Raymond Buildings . . .]
June 11. 1880

To Mr Thos Richardson[1]
Draper &c Brampton Cumber^d.
Sir

I beg to acknowledge the receipt of your letter of the 9th ins^t. In answering it, I would begin by saying that with regard to the organ itself I merely assisted the parish in explaining to the organ builder the situation and surroundings of the position in wh' it was decided to place ~~the organ~~ it.[2]

With regard to damp, and the effect it has had on your organ, I would say that organs always suffer considerably on being placed in ~~a~~ new Church[e]s; and, considering the thickness and solidity of the walls of your church, it is quite certain that it will be several years before they are ~~thoroughly~~ ~~quite~~ dry.

I see no reason whatever to doubt of the building becoming in time thoroughly dry, for, happily, the foundations are on good dry sand and rock – but the ~~very particular~~ construction used to make the church a dry one would be apt to make its drying a matter of some time. For instance, the damp proof course applied to keep moisture from rising in the walls, also hinders the water used in their construction from uninterrupted descent into the ground, consequently the walls have to dry wholly from the surfaces. This drying also, no doubt, has been delayed more or less by the late wet seasons.

I took the precaution to have a specially designed raised floor made on wh' to place the organ, ~~partly~~ chiefly to allow the air to pass under the instrument and help to keep it dry, partly to raise it up, and partly to add to the power of its sound.

I would urge on the church-wardens ~~to~~ the necessity of taking particular care to air the building in every possible way. During all fine days from sun rising to sun setting the doors sh^d be kept ~~opened~~. The iron ventilating doors on the inside sills of windows sh^d always be kept open, as also the ventilating doors in the ceiling of the nave roof. Any expedient to create a draught in the church when it is not being used, and during fine weather, would tend more than anything else to dry the building permanently, and when the heating apparatus is used it sh^d be allowed to ~~burnt~~ slowly for ~~one or~~ two or three days together, rather than fiercely or strongly for one day. Periodically, ~~at stated times,~~ all rainwater heads, pipes, gutters and drains sh^d be examined by a responsible person, for removal of any stoppage from leaves, dirt, or bird-building. I noticed when I was last at Brampton that one of the down pipes at the East end of church had become stopped and the pipe had evidently been leaking for some time at one of the joints.

Any parts of the organ-case wh' are moveable or will open, sh^d be opened on bright airy days, particularly when the sun and air could pass through the door in the South wall adjoining the organ. Also where the organ case abuts against the walls it would be well to have a series of circular holes drilled up the styles, thus [*sketch*] about one inch in diameter, ~~also~~ and holes of like kind might be drilled in the organ floor next the walls.

I am, Sir, | Yours truly | Ph' W:

LB-1, pp 166-7

---

1 Richardson was one of the Brampton churchwardens.
2 In July 1878 PSW had visited a Kentish Town organ-builder, Robson, who was at work on the instrument to be installed at Brampton. In order to save money, the Brampton authorities had decided on a reconditioned instrument, which required much remedial work, costing rather more than had been expected. 'I think it probable that the Committee w^d stand a greater chance of getting the value of the money they have already advanced, by advancing another £50, than if they refused to do so.' PSW to Thomas Forster, 13 July 1878, *LB-1*, p. 129.

154 • To unnamed architect, after 16 August 1880

Drafted on behalf of SPAB

[20 Buckingham Street . . .]

Sir

~~The committee of this society having been told that the Church of Saint Nicholas New Romney, Kent, was about to be repaired or "Restored" wrote to the vicar of that parish, and asked him for information as to what was proposed to be done to the building, enclosing one of their papers, "Table 1. Unrestored Churches", with the request that he should fill up the form describing the character and parts of the church and the condition of the building. The Vicar thought fit to refuse to give the information,~~[1] ~~on which the Committee applied to the Churchwardens, but failed to get an answer from them.~~

~~As the Committee was aware of the importance and special value of this ancient building at New Romney, it decided to send some of its members to examine and report upon it, which was done.~~

~~Since then the Committee has been informed that the work of restoration had been placed in your hands.~~

In writing to you on the subject the Committee is hopeful that anything it says may be looked upon by you as the doing a duty to which all Englishmen are bound with regard to their ancient historical fabrics; this Society being the more bound to take this course, as it was especially founded, with the assistance of competent members, to inform the general public as much as possible of the risk, which ancient buildings ran of being tampered with, often on insufficient grounds, but more often with mistaken zeal.

The Committee believes that New Romney Church is a case to which its efforts may be more than usually effectively applied, as the building has, as yet, been practically untampered with for many years; whereas, in many cases, the Committee is only informed of what is about to be done to an old building after it is too late for it to notice the fact for any saving purpose.

The Committee would call your attention, first, to the beautiful building in its present state of dignified antiquity, then to its great size as a parish Church, and lastly to its wonderfully good preservation.

These things being so, the Committee would urge upon you, in simplicity and good faith, to use your utmost endeavours, as an Architect of reputation, to save this lovely building from the fate which usually attends such when its guardians have determined to enter upon the task of renovation.

The Committee feels that the building in your hands will have all the prompt attention and sagacious examination which its fabric will require for repair and support; but the Committee would also respectfully urge upon you to see that no absolutely unnecessary change be made in its aspect, and that you may resist the introduction of the usual modern incongruous details and mis-called embellishments, such as marble reredos, pavements, pretentious deal fittings, stained glass, petty brass ornaments &c. Also, that in such repairs as may be found necessary, no plastering or other work of past times be removed except such as may be rotten, and that no architectural parts which may have been removed from the building be reintroduced in imitation of the old work lost.

The Committee was somewhat disappointed that the work of pulling down and renewing was going on at the extreme North West end – when its members visited the church[2] – and it hopes that the pulling down was ~~only on account of the danger of falling? For those persons noticed the fallen aisle on the South side, which at some time had suffered rough usage, but which now only wanted plain repair and no renovation~~. due to causes which they did not discover in the corresponding aisle on the South side, which, though it has at some time suffered rough usage does not need more than plain repair to make it perfectly sound.

In commending this old building to your careful professional attention the Committee expresses a hope, that on any of its members revisiting the church, after the repairs are done, they may find little or no change in aspect from its present grave and satisfying simplicity.

This Society would feel obliged if during your researches you were able to verify the exact dates at which the different parts of the church were built, you would kindly communicate the same to it.

I am, Sir, | (on behalf of the Committee) | Yours faithfully
Newman Marks, Sec[y3]

SPAB, St Nicholas Church, New Romney file.

---

1 On 8 June 1880, the vicar, Richard Marshall South, wrote to the SPAB secretary. 'I did not reply to your first note because I am not inclined to supply the information you require for 3 reasons. 1. Your reasons for the existence of such a society are to my mind, in many points very absurd. 2. Your Committee includes the greatest <u>radicals</u> of the day. 3. Your questions strongly suggest impertinent inquisitiveness.'
2 PSW and GW visited the church on 16 August 1880 and PSW wrote up their report for the Committee (*SPAB* file).
3 Valediction and signature in the hand of T. Newman Marks, the SPAB secretary.

155 • To Reverend Theodore Henry Marsh, 29 September 1880

Drafted on behalf of SPAB

Sep 29. 1880

draft

<u>Society for the protection of Ancient Buildings</u>

Sir:[1]

The Committee of this society having received from M[r] Wardle, one of its members, a copy of a circular on the "Restoration of the Roof of Cawston Church

Norfolk" together with some further information given in a letter addressed by you to Mʳ Wardle on the ~~same~~ subject, dated Septʳ 23. 1880, feels that it may be possible for the society to aid you in your efforts to support and sustain the valuable building you have under your care. That the remains of ancient art in Cawston Church are worthy of all care and properly directed attention there can be no doubt even if the report of Mʳ Phipson the Architect and Diocesan Surveyor had not particularly drawn attention to its ~~intrinsic value~~ ᵈᵉˡⁱᶜᵃᵗᵉ ᵃʳᵗ⁻ᵐᵉᵃⁿⁱⁿᵍ, and present condition.² With regard to the word "Restoration", the Committee would ask you in any future steps you may take in the matter to ~~carefully~~ avoid ~~that~~ ⁱᵗˢ use, ~~of~~ as it cannot but be misleading and is often injuriously so. ~~An~~ ᴺᵒ old building any more than an old man can~~not~~ be restored, it may be protected, strengthened, and its inevitable decay deferred, but it cannot be renewed without hastening the destruction of what is ᵐᵒˢᵗ worth preserving.

Given that £4000 ᶜᵒᵘˡᵈ ᵇᵉ ᶜᵒˡˡᵉᶜᵗᵉᵈ, instead of the £400 you mention as possible to be got, not a pound of the money should be spent in trying to reproduce the lost art ~~forms~~ ʷᵒʳᵏ and ᵗʰᵉ inimitable dexterity of the original. The Committee would urge upon you that, in any works undertaken in future, close and definite instructions should be given and maintained that only repairs of simple and mechanical construction should be attempted for, from experience, the Committee is certain that even a large sum would be needed ~~to~~ ⁱⁿ ᵒⁿˡʸ undertaking the repairs which will be clearly demanded, year by year, in sustaining the fabric.

With regard to the valuable report of Mʳ Phipson, the Committee would wish to explain that ~~by~~ ⁱⁿ any remarks ~~the~~ it may make on the same it would ~~not~~ wish it ⁿᵒᵗ to be inferred that ᵃᵗ ᵗʰᵉ ᵖʳᵉˢᵉⁿᵗ ᵗⁱᵐᵉ ⁽ᴹʳ ᴾʰⁱᵖˢᵒⁿ'ˢ ʳᵉᵖᵒʳᵗ ʷᵃˢ ᵐᵃᵈᵉ ⁱⁿ ¹⁸⁷⁵⁾ the Architect would not agree to the principle~~s~~ on which they are dictated. The Committee will take the items of the report in order. In paragraph ~~4~~ 5, we would advise that the roof should not "be reframed and brought together with new tenons and pins" but that the separated parts should be tied or strapped with iron to keep them from spreading further, ~~and,~~ as it is always dangerous to unsettle the existing bearings of old work.

Paragraph 6. We quite think with the architect that the work should be undertaken "bay by bay", as the work could then be done more gently, and ᵇᵉ more easily protected from weather. ~~Also~~ Though we think, ~~that~~ ⁱⁿ the recladding, the boarding should not be "tongued" as that weakens the edges & stops the circulation of air. Also, we would advise that the new lead should be cast, of 8 lbs to the foot, instead of milled lead of 7 lbs. ᴾᵉʳʰᵃᵖˢ ᵗʰᵉ ᴬʳᶜʰⁱᵗᵉᶜᵗ ᵐⁱᵍʰᵗ ᶠⁱⁿᵈ ᵗʰᵃᵗ ᵃ ᵍᵒᵒᵈ ᵈᵉᵃˡ ᵒᶠ ᵗʰᵉ ᵒˡᵈ ˡᵉᵃᵈ ⁿᵉᵉᵈ ⁿᵒᵗ ᵇᵉ ʳᵉᵐᵒᵛᵉᵈ. Of course ~~the architect~~ ʰᵉ would see that all old lead sufficiently sound ~~should~~ be retained & not recast.

Paragraph 7. We would advise that the new "troughing & fall pipes" should be strong and good, but ~~not~~ plain, & of no particular design. Also, in the "beam filling" the circulation of air should not be stopped.

Paragraph 8. Any ~~parts~~ of the merely decorative parts of the coving & cornice should not be renewed.

Paragraph 9. It is here stated that, fortunately, portions of the ornamentation still remain. Now the Committee would strongly urge that all such ornamental work be strengthened and supported in the most careful way, but that no reproduction of lost ornamental parts be attempted at all. ~~Also, in~~ The Committee thinks that it might be <u>un</u>necessary to clean the colour or whitewash from the stone corbels,[3] but that if such cleaning be done, it should only be <u>washed</u> off, no sharp tool being used ~~or chemical product~~; and in case of any decorative painting being found under the whitewash, this cleaning sh^d be done with the utmost care to avoid ~~removing the decorative painting~~ ^{disturbing it}. The notes on this paragraph would ~~naturally,~~ cover ^{the greater part of} paragraph 13.

In conclusion, the committee would beg that no delay should occur at any time in keeping out wet ^{by instant repair} should any weak spot be found. ~~from time to time.~~ Also, though the foregoing remarks have only been made with regard to the nave roof of Cawston church, still they ~~would~~ ^{might} and should apply to ^{such} other parts of the building standing in need of ~~examination and~~ repair.

V&A, AAD

---

1 Theodore Henry Marsh (c. 1826–1905) was the rector of St Agnes, Cawston in Norfolk, from 1855 until his death.
2 Richard Makilwaine Phipson (1827–84) was architect and surveyor for the Norwich diocese and oversaw the restoration of many East Anglian churches. His 1875 report on the condition of the church emphasised its outstanding historic value, and urged that any work undertaken should be approached cautiously. The quality of the hammer-beam roof 'will vie in beauty with almost any roof of the kingdom', and Phipson insisted that 'it would be much better to leave the roof as it is than allow it to be meddled with by rough and inferior hands'. Cited in Susie Timms, *Within These Ancient Walls. Discovering St. Agnes' Church Cawston* (County Collegiate, 2013), pp. 379–80.
3 Corbel: a projection jutting out from the face of a wall, to support a superincumbent weight (*OED*).

156 • To Constance Astley, 14 October 1880

Draft/copy

[1, Raymond Buildings . . .]
Octr 14 1880.

To Miss Constance Astley[1]
Arisaig House, by Fort William N.B.

Dear Constance Astley

I beg to acknowledge the receipt of your letter of the 9th instant. I still have the plans by me of the Chapel which I designed for your father. No kind of estimate was made ^{of the cost} at the time – 1866 – as it was proposed, (~~and~~ indeed some part of the stonework was prepared) to build it without contract, the Clerk of works getting together the materials and directing the labour, in the same way that the stables & other works, separate from the house, were done.

On looking now at the plans, & for the purpose of this letter roughly measuring the contents of the building, I think the work would have been done for ~~under~~ ^less than^ £2,000 in 1866, with the workmen then about who had got accustomed to the kind of masonry, and when ^both^ materials and labour were ~~both~~ cheaper than they now are. I believe ~~it~~ ^the chapel as designed^ would cost considerably more than that ^sum^ to build now under wholly altered circumstances. I need scarcely say, that before I could usefully advise you and your sisters in this matter, it would be necessary for me to see you and consider the whole question carefully. I beg you to believe that it would give me great pleasure to be of assistance to you.

Of course I heard of the great calamity which had fallen upon you, but refrained from writing, as in such letters genuine sympathy is hard to express, & pain is more often given than kindness of heart shewn.[2]

Please accept yourself and give to ^your^ sister[3] my sincere regard & to Beatrice also[4] if she is with you, & | Believe me yours very truly | Ph': W:

LB-1, pp. 170-1

---

1 Constance Charlotte Astley (1851–1935), younger daughter of Francis Dukinfield Palmer Astley (1825–68), for whom PSW had built Arisaig House.
2 The Astley sisters thought of erecting the chapel originally designed for their father by PSW in 1866, but not carried out at that time, to the memory of their brother, Francis Dukinfield Astley (1853–80). Nothing further came of this idea, but see next letter.
3 Gertrude Susan Astley (1849–1920), the eldest of the Astley sisters.
4 Beatrice Emma Astley (1858–1923), the youngest sister.

157 • To Constance Astley, 26 October 1880

Draft/copy

[1, Raymond Buildings . . .]
Oct 26. 1880.

To Miss Constance Astley
Arisaig House, by Fort William N.B.

Dear Constance Astley

I duly rec^d your letter of the 20th instant.

With regard to your questions as to the memorial cross, I also should ~~be glad~~ ^wish^, whenever possible, to use local materials.[1] The only stone ^on the estate^, so far as my recollection serves, wh' would be capable of being cut to shape, is the Basalt which in many places is called whinstone,[2] generally so at Arisaig, I think. When building the house a good deal of this was used, our chief quarry being in "the Glen"; afterwards we worked for it where the dyke crops out somewhere near the mains. A man named Murdoch was, I think, the quarry man. Now, this stone would be very durable, but it is rather treacherous to work, sometimes giving way when the work on it is ~~not~~ ᵘⁿfinished, so that ᵛᵉʳʸ large stones of this material cannot be depended upon.

The porphyry we used in the small dining-room fireplace was got from a ~~small~~ ˢˡⁱᵍʰᵗ projection on the road to ᵃⁿᵈ ⁿᵒᵗ ᶠᵃʳ ᶠʳᵒᵐ the head keeper's lodge (Sunning's). It was got with little trouble, but only in quite small pieces. I have no doubt that larger stone could be got, but it is so very hard and costly to work (the London mason said it was harder than Italian Porphyry) that it would be unwise to attempt it, so that I think we should have to depend on the whinstone. Your proposition for the monument to be about 10 feet high would be rather against my inclination, but as to this I could better explain my meaning when I saw you.

Might I suggest that a temporary & small wooden cross be ~~placed~~ ᶠⁱˣᵉᵈ at the present resting place? This could remain till another place and another memorial are decided on, or a more permanent memorial could be substituted at some future time.

I feel that in such a matter I cannot satisfactorily advise you 'till we can talk it over together.

With kind remembrance to Gertrude. Believe me yours very truly | Ph': W:

LB-1, pp. 171-2

---

1 The Astley sisters had decided to erect this memorial to their brother (see previous letter, note 2).
2 'A name for various very hard dark-coloured rocks or stones, as greenstone, basalt, chert, or quartzose sandstone.' (*OED*).

158 • To Eustace James Anthony Balfour, 9 February 1881

1, Raymond Buildings, Gray's Inn, | London.
Feb: 9. 1881

Dear Mr Balfour[1]

I feel some discomfort in following a rule with you which has been kept by me for several years, namely, to avoid "dining-out" whenever possible: but, as I have found the rule a good one I must not depart from it, even in this case, when I have felt inclined to set it aside and have the pleasure of being introduced to your wife.[2]

I hope to see you at the meeting of the society tomorrow,[3] with a smile of good nature on your face at my self-denial.

Believe me sincerely yours | Philip Webb:

Huntington HM 35060

---

1 The Scottish architect, Eustace Balfour (1854–1911), practised in London. His house and office was in Addison Road, North Kensington. Balfour's uncle was Lord Salisbury, Prime Minster on three

occasions, and his elder brother, Arthur (1848–1930), succeeded their uncle as Conservative Prime Minister in 1902.
2 Lady Francis Campbell (b. 1858), a daughter of the eighth Duke of Argyll, married Balfour in 1879.
3 Balfour served as an Honorary Secretary for the SPAB (1880–90), and a member of its Foreign Committee.

159 • To May Morris, 7 March 1881

1, Raymond Buildings, Gray's Inn, | *London.*
Monday. Mar: 7. '81

My dear May

I thank you for sending me the ticket for the lecture, and now I find I cannot go to it – such is my misfortune.[1]

I shall now have either to beg the sight of the manuscript f^m your father or – if he be not then to[o] weary of the matter – ask him to read it once more to the audience of myself alone with him!

I return the ticket, as I fancy there will be need of it for someone else.

I was glad of your note as to your mother, tho' the word "fever" is rather alarming, but I suppose the word means something belonging to place & season, and that her being now better is reasonably re-assuring.

Have you seen the terrible news from Ischia – The earth gaping and swallowing as it used to swallow?[2]

With love to jenny believe me your affectionate | Philip Webb:

BL Add 45342, f. 55

---

1 WM lectured on 'The Prospects of Architecture in Civilisation' on 10 March, at the London Institution.
2 Newspapers carried reports of a major earthquake which hit the island of Ischia on 4 March. 'The shock took place at five minutes past one on Friday afternoon, the hour at which the village clock of Casamicciola remained standing. It lasted seven seconds, and was accompanied by a noise like subterranean thunder. Then came the crash of falling houses, mingling with the shouts of the victims. Many were killed instantaneously, mothers being found crushed with infants still clinging to their breasts.' *Daily News*, 7 March 1881. The aftershocks continued for some days.

160 • To Jane Morris, 16 March 1881

1, Raymond Buildings, Gray's Inn, | *London.*
Mar: 16. 1881

My dear Janey

Yesterday came there came to me a packet by post from the South, containing brilliant "sarcasms" of blue, red & yellow.[1]

Speech is silver, & your silence was parti-coloured golden!!

Alas! I said to myself, as I opened the parcel, these poor pretty flowers are gone, past recovery. Still, I thought, I would cut off the stalk-ends and put them in water, when, in an hour or so, they revived, and I now look at them in a state not so very far from that in wh' you gathered them, and so your pretty thought for me came well home, and was not beaten by the weary ferrovian[2] journey.

I am still unsatisfied. I would be glad of a word from you, if only to say how you are – my last note of you from Morris was that you were mending a little from your feverish attack.

Please take my hearty thanks for the lovely flowers, & believe me yours affectionately | Philip Webb:

BL Add 45342, f. 56

---

1 JM was spending the winter months in Bordighera at George and Rosalind Howard's villa, Villa Margherita. This was where Henry James first encountered her, and was struck by 'the strange, pale, livid, gaunt, silent, and yet in a manner graceful and picturesque, wife of the poet and papermaker', noting especially her 'wonderful aesthetic hair'. James to Fanny Kemble, 24 March 1881, Leon Edel (ed.), *Henry James Letters*, II (Cambridge, Mass: Harvard University Press, 1975), p. 352. After leaving Bordighera, JM visited Florence and Siena, meeting WM in Paris at the start of May.

2 In other words, transported by railway on iron tracks.

161 • To Percy Wyndham, 3 June 1881

Draft/copy

[1, Raymond Buildings . . .]
June 3. 1881.

To Hon' Percy Wyndham M: P:
44 Belgrave Square.
Dear Mr Wyndham.

I enclose you a copy of the memorandum of estimates and provisional sums for the building of the house at Clouds.

In my personal explanations of yesterday I think I stated as subjects for your consideration that I w^d advise, if the difference of £4,375 ~~and odd money~~ between the estimates and the sum you had agreed to spend (75,000£) was of importance to you, you sh^d throw over Smith's estimate, have the quantities lithographed & laid before 3 or 4 first class country contractors – but, if the extra sum required on Smith's estimating was not of sufficient importance, I w^d advise you to accept the tender, and begin work at once.

During ~~my~~ ^{our} conversation ~~with you~~, I think I heard a remark f'm you, that delay in building would not be an inconvenience to you? If this was so, I would say that there need be no hesitation on your part in following that course. Smith's estimate having exceeded the sum allowed by you, you could decide not to accept their tender, ~~paying them their charge for making estimates,~~ and you could delay building and take up the quantities for use at any other time. If you decided on this plan, you would have to pay Mr Goodman, the surveyor, half the cost of his quantities and pay him the balance when the building was begun. I also, should have to make a proportionate charge in the same way.

~~Yours truly~~
~~Ph: W:~~

It occurs to me also that if you sh^d decide to delay building, you might think it well not to risk building so large a house, and that you might prefer to have a new design on a smaller scale and, possibly, from another arch^t. In any case I sh^d wish to be no hindrance to you.

Believe me yours faithfully | Ph: W:

LB-1, pp. 175-6

162 • To Percy Wyndham, 10 June 1881

Draft/copy

[1, Raymond Buildings . . .]
June 10. 1881.

To Hon' Percy Wyndham M.P.
44 Belgrave Square. S.W.
Dear Mr Wyndham

(Clouds)

I rec^d your letter last evening. As it is very direct, full, and to the point on ~~the~~ important parts ~~connected with the present state of things~~ with regard to the building, I will give such information as I can ~~to~~ further to help you in coming to a reasonable decision.

If we at once accepted Smith's estimate, you would not be able to move into the new house before the summer of 1884. If we set ourselves to finding satisfactory country builders, getting tenders f^m them, and on approval beginning works, we should be $^{delayed\,for}$ 6 or 9 months ~~later~~, and perhaps should find that the country builder, however willing, would not be able to give up the house to you from some months beyond the three years required for building.

You are quite correct in supposing that if you got a satisfactory tender, and the estimates were some £10,000 below Smith's, the saving would be so considerable as to make it of much greater importance than the matter $^{of\,the}$ 3 or £4,000 difference between Smith's tender and the sum you have proposed to allow for building;

and Mrs Wyndham's contention that "she does not see why we sh^d give Smith so much more than the thing can be done for by another" has reason on its side; but neither point quite states the whole of the question, as the work done by Smith would have cost more in the doing than ^(that of) even the best country builder we sh^d ~~obtain~~ ^(get) – & for these reasons ^(among others). The timber ~~employed~~ ^(used) w^d have been more carefully selected, would have lain in stock for a longer time, and fin[1] there being larger quantities on hand the workmen w^d more certainly be supplied with the best for any particular purpose. Then, as to labour, Smith's w^d certainly give higher wages to their men, & from working in a large way would be able to keep their best men; ~~and~~ ^(also, they) would have over their several trades, better educated and proved foremen.

I will now take the mason's trade. One of my chief reasons for wishing, if possible, to hold to Smith's was, that in ~~using~~ the Tisbury and the local green sandstone, they had largely used both at Longford Castle,[2] and the former at Lady Westminster's house at Fonthill.[3] If, as I suppose we should, have Mr Cross as the foreman of masons, we sh^d ~~have~~ ^(be) at ~~great~~ advantage, as he knows a great deal about the Tisbury stone,[4] and is well aware of the custom of the quarrymen of sending out from the quarry the first stone to hand, without regard to its lasting character. I have no doubt that Cross's salary is as much as £300 a year, if not more.

Again, as to iron-work. There are to be a number of iron girders used in the house, and ~~the~~ familiarity in their use, hauling, and setting is of importance – and, practically, the same reason would run through all the trades, tho' not in an equal degree. I think we should hardly be able to keep Smith's to their present prices without accepting their tender before we sh^d be able to arrive at a conclusion as to country builders, but of this ^(and other points, such as seeking country builders &c) I w^d speak to you more particularly.

I will come to Belgrave Square tomorrow, (Saturday) at 2.0-c.

Yours very truly | Ph: W:

LB-1, pp. 177-9

---

1 Used in its obsolete form of 'lastly' (*fine*).
2 The historic seat of the Earls of Radnor, Longford Castle at Bodenham, south of Salisbury, on the Avon, had some architectural alterations and additions (1870–5) made under the direction of Anthony Salvin (1799–1881).
3 Fonthill House, Fonthill Gifford in Wiltshire, was built in 1846–52 for Richard Grosvenor, second Marquis of Westminster (1795–1869), by the Scottish architect, William Burn (1789–1870). Victoria bestowed the title of the Duke of Westminster upon Hugh Grosvenor, the third Marquis (1825–99).
4 PSW later refers to this as Chilmark stone (PSW to Albert Estcourt, 3 January 1882), a cream-coloured limestone of exceptional durability favoured in the south of England for building (and now prized in restoration work, such as at Salisbury Cathedral and the chapter house of Westminster Abbey).

1864–1887

163 • To Henry G. Smith, 21 July 1881

Draft/copy

[1, Raymond Buildings . . .]
July 21. 1881.

To. Henry G. Smith Esqre
Messrs G: Smith & Co | 9 Commercial Road Pimlico. S.W.
Dear Sir.

(Clouds House)

I saw Mr Wyndham yesterday. After he had read the letter you sent to me on the 14th ins^t, I explained to him the proposition you laid before me at our interview ^here on the 18th. I found Mr Wyndham wholly averse to your proposal for taking into partnership another firm in order to enable you to enter into the contract for building the house under my direction at Knoyle.[1]

Before deciding upon what should be done under the present circumstances, I agreed with Mr Wyndham that it would be ~~well~~ best that you sh^d send me a letter of introduction to the solicitors of the Executors of your late father's will, so that I might learn from them the cause and probable duration of the injunction against your entering into ^any contract after March 1880.

Yours truly | Ph: W:

LB-1, p. 186

---

1 By the end of June, PWY had resolved to give the building contract to George Smith & Co., which was certainly PSW's own preferred choice, but the death of the head of the firm now threw up a very real difficulty. Under the terms of George Smith's will the firm was constrained from taking on new projects, hence Henry Smith's proposal to link up with another building firm.

164 • To George Edmund Street, 27 July 1881

Draft/copy

[1, Raymond Buildings . . .]
July 27. 1881.

To G: E: Street Esqre
14 Cavendish Place. W.

My dear Street.[1]

Having ~~been disappointed~~ ^failed in getting a ^satisfactory tender from a London builder for a house I have to build in Wiltshire, I am now looking to get tenders from 4 or 5 first rate country builders. As I believe you have done a good deal of work in the W & S.W. of England I thought ~~perhaps~~ that you would ^perhaps^ be able to recommend some safe man or men from your own experience of their ^character,^ work & their command of capital.

The work in ^question^ would be of considerable size, to the ~~extent~~ ^value^ of over £50,000, and both mason's & joiner's work sh^d be of the best.

If you can help me in this matter I shall be much obliged, and if you will forgive my troubling you I shall also be grateful.

Yours very truly | Ph: W:

LB-1, p. 187

---

1 Street was, of course, PSW's former employer. See above, Letter 147, note 5.

165 • To Emma Oldham, 29 July 1881

Draft/copy

[1, Raymond Buildings . . .]
July 29. 1881.

To Mrs Oldham[1]
The Vicarage Clay Cross.

Dear Mrs Oldham

I needed no apology for your writing to me. Your cause was sufficient excuse, even if it had not been put before me by your brother William, my own perfectly good friend.

I shall have ~~great~~ pleasure in helping you to the best of my power, and in order to do that in the most direct way I have set down, on the other side, a list of questions which I should be glad if you would answer as accurately as you can. I think I am right in so understanding, that you want laid down on paper sufficient plans to allow of a rough estimate of the cost being made, so that with the plans and the estimate you ~~will~~ ^would^ be able to explain ^in your district^ what ^money^ would be necessary to ^be^ got in the way of subscriptions?[2]

Believe me, | Yours very truly | Ph: W:

1 Will it be possible to set the building ^on the ground^ East & West in its length?
2 On wh' side of the ch' would most of the ^people^ come for entrance?
3 What is ^the^ soil on wh' the ch' would stand – Clay? Gravel? Sand? ^Rock?^ &c
4 Would the ground slope at all on the site of the area of build^s and if so, ~~would~~ wh' way w^d it slope E-W &c?
5 Will it be necessary to calculate ^for^ any boundary fence?
6 Would a Vestry be wanted, and if so what w^d be the least size necessary?

7   Would any heating be required?
8   Would chairs or benches be preferred?
9   Would there be any seats ᵂᵃⁿᵗᵉᵈ in chancel for a choir, if so for how many?
10 Would a font be necessary?
11 Would the people be satisfied with paving through't the ch'?
12 Are not the houses, amongst which the ch' w^d be put, mostly built of brick?
13 Are pan-tiles at all used in the neighbourhood for roofing? Pan-tiles are of this shape [*sketch*]

LB-1, pp. 188-9

---

1 In 1850 WM's eldest sister Emma (b. 1829) married Joseph Oldham (d. 1896), her German tutor and a former curate at Walthamstow.
2 PSW drew up plans and estimates for this proposed Mission Church in Clay Cross, Derbyshire, but the work did not proceed. Presumably the funds were not forthcoming. See *Kirk*, p. 300.

166 • To Thomas D. Ridley, 30 July 1881

Draft/copy

[1, Raymond Buildings . . .]
July 30. 1881.

To Mr Thos: D: Ridley[1]
Post Office B^{gs} Middlesborough
My dear Sir

(T: Hugh Bell's H^{se})

I am very glad to find that you are able at once to push on the work, as I know of Mr Bell's anxiety to get the present small add^n to his house done as soon as possible. I enclose further details wh', I believe, will be quite clear to you. I think it will be as well to send you a larger detail of the south or end w^w of the new dressing room as the inside fittings lead &c are somewhat different to the other w^s. All the rest of the new work (and in case of any doubt of detail to other parts of joinery) you can follow the character of the existing work.

I shall send in a few days a plan of the new drainage. Also I shall hope in a few weeks to be able to meet you personally at the house.

Yours truly | Ph: W:

P.S. Will ʸᵒᵘ be so good as to direct your foreman to be very particular in setting out the work, and ⁱⁿ exactly following the drawings as far as possible.

LB-1, pp. 189-90

1 Thomas Davison Ridley was engaged to make additions to Red Barns, PSW's Redcar house built for Hugh Bell more than ten years previously (1868–70). See *Kirk*, pp. 297-8.

167 • To Henry G. Smith, 8 August 1881

Draft/copy

August 8. 1881.

To Henry G: Smith Esqre
Messrs George Smith & Co. 9 Commercial R^d S.W.
My dear Sir.

(Clouds House)

Acting on the information contained in your letter to me of the 14th of July last, and upon my report to him of the result of my interview with the solicitors to the executors of your late father's estate, Mr Wyndham has, after careful consideration with myself of all the facts of the case, including your proposition to take into partnership for this particular work another firm of builders, come to the conclusion & decision that, he will not proceed any farther with you with regard to entering into a contract for building his house under my direction at East Knoyle.

I cannot but express my regret that circumstances sh^d have so ruled that the work intrusted to my care by Mr Wyndham should not have had the advantage of being carried out by the firm of George Smith & Co.[1]

Believe me | Yours truly | Ph: W:

LB-1, p. 191

1 This was a hard letter to write. PSW evidently held the firm's professional record in high regard, but he had to recognise that the legal constraints set by George Smith's will was an unacceptable risk for his client.

168 • To George Price Boyce, 27 August 1881

Annotated 'Bywell Aug. 28. '81'

1, Raymond Buildings, Gray's Inn, | *London.*
Sat: Aug 27. 1881

My dear Boyce

I was hoping, that as we had bad weather in the south you might be in better luck in the north, but as your letter, rec^d this morning, tells of doleful wet I can but sigh with you by post. I have no doubt that whatever the weather will let you set-to upon will turn out a sufficiently good subject, and that if Miss Davison[1] is reasonably humane, you and Mrs Boyce may find some set-off against disappointed hopes.

I've had out the ordnance maps and found your whereabouts, and in spite of the weather-damped tone of your letter I felt inclined to come & see you with a gig umbrella or two in hand.² The glass is now rising, but 'tis not to be depended on, and the unhappy farmers must have broken theirs in their useless rage.

Thank you for sending me the note and the Building News of August 12.³ I had to "stump" in the West, last week,⁴ but only got 20 min: in Tewkesbury C^h a Ch' wh', in spite of the late Sir Scott and the present suckling, (Lord how they have scraped it!) is one of the most interesting in England. I had not seen it before, and could have spent 20 hours in it instead of 20 min: I had not time at Gloucester to get to the Cath^l: I did however, see Wells, and Glastonbury. Also I had to go to Blandford, and it is one of the prettiest of little towns, tho' the fire of 1700 & something burned most of the old work away.⁵ The present town is composed mostly of dignified brick houses with wood cornices &c painted white. 'Tis the situation wh' is so pleasant – over the meadows, with high down-shaped hills around, with old camps on the top of them – however, I had but time enough to look as I ran.

I did not see the article in the D News, but the soc^y has already dealt with Lefevre about the pulling down $^{\text{of the Westm}^r\text{ courts}}$, and when [Newman] Marks or his successor returns to business we must look in to this matter again.⁶ I see they have made Bradley of Univ: Coll: Oxford the new Dean of Westminster, and I must ask Faulkner what sort of a dean he will make, as Bradley was his "head".⁷

I had to go to Oxford too, last week, in my builder-hunting, and I looked at the scraping there, wh' has gone on rapidly since I saw the place some 4 years ago. I found no excuse for their wanting to widen Magd: bridge – and as they are now making the road over it for the tram-way, I hope they won't touch it after the row we have kicked up.

Mrs Boyce, I suspect, will be in high glee at Gambetta's rebuff.⁸ It seems to me, withal, that the rebuff itself is not a bad sign, as it shows that Paris itself is not inclined to run the risk of a dictator, and Gambetta has wits.

I take your apothecary's pot to Welwyn this evening, stuffed with the good messages from you and your wife. Morris was here last night, and he and I gloated over the lovely painting on it.

I hope that if either of you want anything sent to you in the wilds of Northumberland, you will remember that I shall have pleasure in seeing to its being done. That is a pretty photog: of old Hexham houses, but there is a row of villainous boys aslant on the plinth of the bay window, wh' is exactly like the demons of boys Bewick so well did⁹ – the boys look as like embodyed [sic] mischief as ill can be. Surely the state sh^d have no "close season" for the protection of those wild animals. There sh^d be boy-clubs as there used to be sparrow-clubs!

Please keep me aware of your movements, for tho' there is next to no chance of my getting to you, I shall like to know about you. With best remembrance to Mrs Boyce.

Believe me faithfully y^{rs} | Ph: W:

BL Add 45354, ff. 163-4

1 The Boyces' landlady in the village of Bywell, Northumberland.
2 A gig umbrella was of larger than usual size, to cover the passenger(s) in a one-horse carriage.
3 The issue of *The Building News* for 12 August included a report and some lithographic illustrations of the restoration work undertaken by Sir George Gilbert Scott and his younger son, John Oldrid Scott (1841–1913) at Tewkesbury Abbey (pp. 195–6 and 204).
4 He was on the hunt for possible builders to tender for Clouds. See next letter.
5 A fire on 4 June 1731 destroyed the greater part of the market town of Blandford, Dorset.
6 In view of PSW's next sentence it is conceivable that the reference is to a letter from the Duke of Westminster about a proposed memorial to Arthur Stanley (1815–81), the late Dean of Westminster, in the form of an appeal for funds to purchase a suitable site and build a new Westminster Nursing Home and Training School for Nurses (*Daily News*, 3 August 1881).
7 George Granville Bradley (1821–1903), Master of University College, Oxford since 1870, was Stanley's successor as Dean of Westminster.
8 A seminal influence upon modern French parliamentary government, Léon Gambetta (1831–82) became the French premier for just three months in November 1881. His attempt to re-establish the *scrutin de liste* system for the election of deputies, supported by the Assembly, had been rejected by the Senate in June.
9 The wood-engraver, Thomas Bewick (1753–1828). PSW would have admired both the subject-matter and the craftsmanship of Bewick's *History of British Birds* (1797–1804), including the many lively and often amusing vignettes which crowded every empty space. Perhaps he had in mind a drawing such as 'Boys and Ships', from the title page of the second volume, showing a group of five boys on a riverbank, sailing toy boats, with the smoking chimneys of an industrial town in the background.

169 • To Percy Wyndham, 27 August 1881

Draft/copy

[1, Raymond Buildings . . .]
August 27. 1881.

To Hon' Percy Wyndham M:P:
Wilbury House. Salisbury
Dear Mr Wyndham

(Clouds H^{se})

I wrote to you on the 12th instant, enclosing copies of letters &c and I ~~sent~~ ^{posted} the letter to Wilbury, but as I have not rec^d an answer I am not sure if the letter reached you.

Last week I went to Blandford – Frome – Gloucester – and Tewkesbury $^{to\ see}$ ^{builders} – and this week I have been to Oxford to see some work there (the new ^{University} Schools) done by one of the builders ~~to~~ ^{from} whom I am to get a tender for your work.[1] And next week I am going to Bristol to look into the circumstances of another builder I have had recommended to me.[2]

At the present time I have four builders' ^{names} on my list who have ~~accepted~~ ^{agreed} to give me tenders, and ~~from~~ ^{on} whom I think I can rely for satisfactory work. Mr Simmonds – Ld Wolverton's Clerk of works – called here ^{yesterday}, he having heard from Ld Wolverton as to the Clouds' work. I shall have to see, or write to

Mr Waterhouse, as to his qualifications. I shall be glad to know, if you have seen Ld Wolverton, and ~~if~~ ^{what} his report of Simmonds was.³

Yours faithfully | Ph: W:

LB-1, p. 194

---

1 Albert Estcourt, of Gloucester, would win the contract for building Clouds, PSW approving of what he saw of Estcourt's work for Thomas Graham Jackson (1835–1924), the architect of the Examination Schools at Oxford (1876–83). For the sometimes bitter University politics involved in the eventual selection of Jackson for this controversial project, see William Whyte, *Oxford Jackson. Architecture, Education, Status and Style 1853–1924* (Oxford: OUP, 2006), pp. 92–103. In 1873, CF had been unsuccessful in trying to persuade PSW to put himself forward as a candidate for the work (see above, Letter 56), but kept him in touch with the internal debate, having become a strong supporter of Jackson's candidacy (Whyte, pp. 96 and 98). For Jackson's later spat with the SPAB over restoration works to the spire of St Mary the Virgin, see Vol. II, Letter 441.
2 Recommended by George Edmund Street, perhaps. See above, Letter 164.
3 James Simmonds, who would be appointed clerk of works for the Clouds project, had held the equivalent position in 1874 during the building of the large mansion on the Iwerne Minster estate in Dorset, designed by Alfred Waterhouse (1830–1905) for the Liberal politician, George Glyn, second Baron Wolverton (1824–87).

170 • To Emma Oldham, 29 August 1881

Draft/copy

[1, Raymond Buildings . . .]
August 29. 1881.

To Mrs Oldham.
The Vicarage Claycross: Chesterf^d

Dear Mrs Oldham.

I send you ~~by this post~~ ^{herewith} the design for the new church, arranged in the way that I thought best with regard to economy and the getting "some degree of dignity" as expressed in your letter to me of July 26.¹

I have estimated that the building will cost, <u>including</u> the fittings as shewn – but <u>not</u> the harmonium or the heating <u>apparatus</u> – about one thousand and fifty pounds (£1,050). And as I suppose that the bricks would cost about £200 to buy and put on the ground, so that if these were given the cost of the church would then be about £850. Some reduction could be made if the East end of the church was made as plain as the nave.

Your brother William has seen the design and expressed his satisfaction with it, and I hope that you and Mr Oldham will find it answer to your want.

Believe me, | Y^{rs} very truly | Ph: W:

LB-1, pp. 195-6

1 See above, Letter 165.

171 • To Percy Wyndham, 30 August 1881

Draft/copy

[1, Raymond Buildings . . .]
August 30. 1881.

To Hon' Percy Wyndham M:P.
Wilbury House. Salisbury.

Dear Mr Wyndham.

(Clouds H^{se})

I rec^d your letter, with the enclosed cheque, this morning – for which I am obliged – & I enclose receipt.[1]

It is ~~quite~~ true that Smith should have let us know before he did of the restriction under wh' his business lay – but as I had by ~~way~~ word of mouth ^{& letter} told him that his reticence had caused us ^{great} inconvenience, I thought it better to avoid useless irritation on taking leave of him. This course ~~has proved~~ ^{was} itself right, I think, as his offer of Mr Cross's ~~assistance~~ ^{services} might, in case of difficulty with the Tisbury quarry, be worth accepting.

I have to go into Yorkshire tomorrow, and I mean to take Bristol on my return, so that I shall not be in London before Saturday night. I sh^d have been pleased to come to Wilbury as you kindly propose, but these & other engagements will hardly allow of that before you leave home. I thank you very much for your condolence on my journeyings, [*sic*] but they ~~are~~ ^{will be} of little matter, if by looking closely at first into the country builders' resources I may be able to avoid having to do with untrustworthy ^{or unsubstantial} contractors.

Y^{rs} very truly | Ph: W:

LB-1, pp. 196-7

1 'As, necessarily, there will be some further delay, and as my outlay on the several designs for the house has been considerable during the last four years, I shall be obliged if you can, conveniently, let me have a thousand pounds on account.' PSW to PWY, 12 August 1881, *LB-1*, p. 193.

172 • To George Price Boyce, 9 September 1881

1, Raymond Buildings, Gray's Inn, | London.
Sep: 9. 1881

My dear Boyce

You are indebted for <u>this</u> friendly discharge of ink, to a report brought under notice yesterday at our first meeting of the society after the recess. The report is this. That an archaeological society – I think it was, but of this I am not quite sure – has been advising Mr Fuller to "restore" some painting (decorative) which remains at Great Chaldfield [*sic*] House.[1] I promised the Comm^e that I would ask you to write to your friend, Mr Fisher,[2] to find from him if there is any truth in such an absurd proposal. I sh^d have liked to send you something more clearly defined, but amongst the crowd of business we had to attend to yesterday, I could only gather what I have written above. At all events it will do no mischief if you will kindly ask Mr Fisher the question.

Every now & then as it comes across me & I think of you at work out-o-doors, I long for fine weather both for you & the farmers. When it has rained hard, or been very cold I've hoped that you had comfortable lodging, good books, and honest food. I was not so very far off you last week, when I was at Redcar. I was there to look after a little addition I'm making to Hugh Bell's house,[3] and I would have come on to you in spite of the cheerless & very cold weather, if I had not been bound for Bristol at once, which place I took on my return home. I have to go to Exeter next week. In these journeyings I am searching for sound builders, and am rather tired of questioning them as to their ways & means.

It was Thursday morning that I was at Redcar & having done my business at Bristol, I went, with Wardle who good naturedly met me there, to Cirencester on Saturday, & f'm thence drove to the site of the Roman Villa at Chedworth, ab^t 8 miles off.[4] Both Cirencester & Chedworth repaid fully, & the weather was less unkind on that day.

Try & screw up your courage (or failing, ask Mrs Boyce) to tell me what & how you are doing. Grumble as you like, but throw in such encouragement as you may have found. At all events you are in the country, anxious to do what you can, and I hope you ^{both} get hungry and bear up against the cold and the country gentlemen, without Rheumatism & too much bad language.

I wonder if my sawbones brother wrote to acknowledge his beautiful Apothecary's pot! both brother & sister were mighty pleased with it.

With kindest remembrances to both of you,
believe me sincerely yours, Ph: W:

BL Add 45354, ff. 165-6

---

1 Great Chalfield Manor, in Wiltshire, is a fifteenth-century manor house built for Thomas Tropnell (c. 1405–88). It was bought by G.P. Fuller, M.P. (d. 1927) in 1878. PSW may have in mind the late medieval wall-painting, possibly of Tropnell himself, in the parlour (now the dining room).
2 Perhaps George Fisher, who lived at The Folly, in Winsley Road, Bradford-on-Avon. GPB may have made his acquaintance when staying in the town in 1877, and had been made aware of possible restorations at Great Chalfield Manor.
3 See above, Letter 166.
4 About twelve miles from Cheltenham, in Gloucestershire, the Roman villa at Chedworth was discovered in 1864. Excavation 'revealed a series of huge and impressively intact mosaic floors, two bath houses, a water shrine, and over a mile of Roman walls. By 1865 a museum had been built on site, along with cover buildings to protect the main mosaics, and the villa ruins were being displayed to the visiting public.' http://www.nationaltrust.org.uk/chedworth-roman-villa/history/article-1355824095951/ [accessed 22 July 2014].

173 • To Percy Wyndham, 20 October 1881

Draft/copy

[1, Raymond Buildings . . .]
Oct: 20. 1881.

To Hon' Percy Wyndham M:P:
Wilbury House by Salisbury
Dear Mr Wyndham

(Clouds H^{se})

I rec^d your letter of the 13th inst^t authorising me to treat with Estcourt the builder if I rec^d satisfactory answers f'm Mr Jackson & others.[1] I wrote to Mr Jackson on the 14th, and as I had not had an answer up to this morning I sent my clerk to his office, and he found that he was in France, but that my letter or a note of its contents had been sent to him. Mr Jackson's assistant told my clerk that they were very well pleased with Estcourt.

I also wrote to Mr Chapple, assistant to the late Mr Burges, the architect, and I enclose a copy of his answer.[2]

Mr Simmonds has been to me again ab^t the berth of Clerk of Works for Clouds, so I wrote to Mr Waterhouse, the architect of Lord Wolverton's house at Iwerne Minster, and I enclose a copy of his answer. This, with your information f'm Ld Wolverton himself would be ~~satis~~ certificate enough I think to allow of our engaging Simmonds as soon as the contract is signed. If you agree with me, will you me so good as to let me know, so that I may write to ~~tell~~ Simmonds $^{at\ once\ to\ say}$ that we shall want him for the work if we should accept the builder's tender now under consideration?

Mr Estcourt is anxious to begin at once, so as not [to] lose any fine weather we may get before the winter sets in. If Mr Jackson's answer should confirm Mr Chapple's ~~reply~~ ^{letter} (I have also heard well of Estcourt from Mr Ewan Christian's office)[3] ~~will you let me know if I~~ shall I enter on the business of preparing the contract for signature as soon as possible? Before beginning at Clouds, it would be well if I could meet you there as to setting out the ground on which the builder could place his plant & materials. Should you be able to meet me ~~there~~ $^{at\ Clouds}$ on one day in next week?

Y^{rs} truly | Ph' W.

LB-1, pp. 197-8

---

1 For Thomas Graham Jackson, see above, Letter 169, note 1.
2 Albert Estcourt had undertaken work for William Burges at Cardiff Castle (1872–5), and was also the builder for his Gothic folly of Castell Coch, from 1871.
3 See above, Letter 147, note 4.

174 • To James Simmonds, 27 October 1881

Draft/copy

[1, Raymond Buildings . . .]
Oct. 27. 1881.

To Mr James Simmonds, C of Works
East Street Blandford.
Sir.

(Clouds House. East Knoyle)

I duly recd your letter of the 24th of last month.

I believe that I have ^now^ a contractor who will under-take the building of the house at East Knoyle for the Hon' Percy Wyndham M:P. and as I have spoken to Mr Wyndham on the subject, and had an answer from Mr Waterhouse with regard to inquiries I made of him I should be glad to know if you are still dis-engaged and would wish to undertake the office of Clerk of the Works under my direction to superintend the execution of the above-named works?

The salary you ask ^(four guineas a week)^ is, I consider, a high one for work which will extend over a space ^of time^ of between two & three years, but I shall not consider it too high if from <experience of your> ^the^ ability, energy, and honourable trustworthiness which I shall expect from you be confirmed by experience.[1] The work in question is an important one, and constant attention with aptitude, and judgment, will be necessary ^in you^ for the satisfactory carrying out of my intentions and the Contractor's responsibility.

'Till the contract is signed I am not sure that I shall require your assistance, but as it is probable that the signature may take place in next week, I should ~~then~~ ^shortly afterwards^ want you to enter upon the engagement. It would be necessary for you to give me a month's notice before requiring to give up your situation, and I should ~~have to~~ give you the same amount of notice before wishing to end the engagement between us. Also, I should require you to find an ^efficient^ substitute at your own expense ^but paid by me^ should illness, ~~tempora~~ for a time, disable you. I suppose that it would be ~~suff~~ satisfactory to you if you were paid your salary at the end of each month?

In case you sh{d} think it worthwhile to go to Knoyle to look at the ground and see about lodging, Mr Russell of Knoyle – Mr Wyndham's ~~agent~~ ^bailiff^ – would be able to ^shew you the site & in other ways^ assist you.

Yours truly | Ph. W: Arch{t}

LB-1, pp. 201-2

---

1 As the work on Clouds neared completion, PSW reflected that Simmonds had not been 'worth his salt'. See below, Letter 255.

175 • To Thomas Hugh Bell, 10 November 1881

Draft/copy

[1, Raymond Buildings . . .]
Novr 10. 1881.

To T. Hugh Bell Esqre
Red Barns Coatham. Redcar

Dear Hugh Bell.

(Middlesboro' Offices)

I enclose of tracing of [*sic*] the proposed offices for Bell Brothers.[1]

In planning the same I have carefully considered both the amount of accommodation, ~~given~~ set forth in your paper sent to me, and the disposition of the different rooms. I hardly consider ~~that~~ these plans to be likely to be of more use than to shew the amount of space taken up by such and such rooms, especially with regard to gaining as much light as possible under the circumstances. It is for this reason that I have ^tried^ to ~~try and~~ get as much sun as possible into the heart of the block from the south, by direct ~~south~~ light from the south wall in Brunswick S^t, and the glass roof running ^from^ South ~~and~~ ^to^ North.

On the North front, in Zetland Road, I should propose to put ~~3~~ [2] large bow-windows on the ground floor, and 3 on the first floor, on which ~~floor~~ ^latter^, I agree with you, it would be best to place the offices of Bell Bro^s.

On the ground floor I have thought it ~~best~~ ^well^, for instant communication ^& best light^ to put the entrance in the middle. Also, I have made a quite private entrance from Brunswick Street, to serve ~~also~~ as entrance to the basement either from the hall, or from this ~~subordinate entrance~~ ^street^.

As I wish~~ed~~ to get direct south light <u>over</u> the lavatory ^into the hall^ I do not propose to carry up the <u>lavatory part</u> beyond the necessary ground floor height. Over this part therefore could be a kind of gallery communication ~~and~~ between the east & west wings, but I hardly see to what purpose for general use. Would it not be well, in considering the basement accommodation, to put another set of watercloset & lavatory ^directly^ under those on the ground floor? If you wished a strong room, this also must be in the basement.

The second floor plan is only an indication of what might be made there. At all events I have put the Bell Bros' Boardroom and a book & paper room ^there,^ and noted the place where an occasional Board or other rooms might be made. The other parts the plans will sufficiently explain.

Will you be so good, when your firm has examined the plans, to answer the following questions. 1°. Is any communication wanted up & down by means of paper lifts? 2°. Are speaking tubes wanted ^and any bells^? 3. Is any safe required? 4. Any door of communication between ~~the~~ ^your^ general and Private office? (I have shewn one) 5. Should any or all of the floors be fire proofed? 6. Mark the rooms which should have fire places.

If you & your people should generally approve of the plans, would it not be as well, at once, to shew them to the Borough Surveyor? If you took a piece of tracing paper, and slightly indicated the walls of ground floor you might generally shew what conveniences should be supplied in the basement. Perhaps a caretaker's room might be put here?

LB-1, pp. 207-9

---

1 PSW undertook the design of offices for the iron-founders, Bell Brothers, in Zetland Road, Middlesbrough (1881–3), with construction occurring in 1889–91. See *Kirk*, pp. 239–42 and 300.

176 • To George Howard, 12 November 1881

Draft/copy

[1, Raymond Buildings . . .]
Nov: 12 1881

To George Howard Esq[re] MP:
My dear Howard.
Castle Howard, by York.

(1 Pal: Green Ken[n])[1]

Your letter of the 9th was rather startling. The amount of work to be done, as stated in your letter, would take at least 4 months in doing! Parliament will probably meet in the beginning of Feb[y]. I fancy that Morris & Co were not so much afraid of the injuries to workmen act,[2] as that if, while they were at work, some of the drawing-room ceiling came down, they would have to replace it. The winter time is a bad one for doing plaster work, but it [the ceiling] could be done [in the winter.][3]

As to the drainage, I have for some time associated myself with Rogers Field [Civil Engineer],[4] who with Corfield,[5] Richardson[6] and others are the chief lights of the Sanitary Institute of Great Britain & of which mighty nursery I am a sucking infant [up] in arms.[7] I would propose to arrange a scheme for the Palace Green house with Rogers Field and get it done [the work done] as soon as might be. The paving of yards &c would go on [in proper course] after the drainage was done.

It seems to me that there would be some risk in connecting your house with the "white house" without the Woods & Forests knowing.[8] At all events we should have to get the permission of the district surveyor, but if I remember rightly he is a decent body and would not [be] purposely vexatious. After the warning as to time [&c.] given above, please let me have your directions.

I am exceedingly sorry to learn that M[rs] Howard is not in her usual good health, & I should be glad if you would say so to her from me with kindest remembrance.

Believe me yours sincerely | Ph: W.

LB-1, pp. 209-10

1 Between about 1881 and 1896, PSW undertook various alterations to the Howards' house at 1 Palace Green, Kensington, including improvements to the drainage. See *Kirk*, p. 297.
2 The Employers' Liability Act (1880) gave some protection to workers sustaining injury at work, when the accident was a result of the negligence of a manager or supervisor.
3 Replastering and redecoration of the drawing room ceiling was done.
4 See above, Letter 134, note 2.
5 William Henry Corfield (1843–1903), appointed Professor of Hygiene and Public Health, University College, London, in 1869. He became Vice-President of the Sanitary Institute.
6 The physician, Sir Benjamin Ward Richardson (1828–96), was a pioneer in the fields of public health and sanitation. His address to the Social Science Association in 1875 'described a health utopia, a city of spotless cleanliness and hygiene; this was later published as *Hygiea, a City of Health* (1876)'. *DNB*.
7 PSW was elected to membership of the Sanitary Institute of Great Britain in May 1881.
8 Howard had it in mind to acquire this property, behind 1 Palace Green (see below, Letter 182). The trouble which PSW had encountered when his original designs for Palace Green were considered by James Pennethorne still rankled.

177 • To George Price Boyce, 28 November 1881

1, Raymond Buildings, Gray's Inn, | *London.*
Monday. Novr 28. 1881

My dear Boyce

Thank you for your letter. I will come with pleasure on Thursday not later than 6.30. Please do not, on my account, add to your usual bill-of-fare.

I had heard from Morris that the quantity of business in front had stopped the production of your information as to North-Allerton Ch'.

I may have to see Neave shortly and I should hear as to the quality of his old dutch tiles.[1] I might have good use for them, but I daily find from clients that they are not of my way of thinking in art matters, so that I am careful of risking my own money 'till I am assured as to what they really <u>do</u> want. I am, nevertheless, obliged to you for your note of this matter.

I believe that Keith Johnston's Atlas[2] is a better one than Black's (not, I think, "Blackies"). I have, myself, an old edition of the Black's & have always found it a poor one.[3] My brother has a <u>small</u> edition of Keith Johnston's wh' I got for him a long time ago, and I have found it good – however the <u>large</u> size is the one to buy. If you got one (Stanford's is the place) you might get them to bind a copy in a less abominable way than they do – (with a sceptre crown crozier, & whatnot of other nonsense ^{on the cover}_)

If I knew only a smattering of German I should, personally, prefer a German Atlas. 'Tis Spruner, I think, who has done a first rate historical atlas,[4] and probably at Williams & Norgate's[5] you could learn what is to be had, and see samples before making up your mind – be sure & have the latest edition.

Yours sincerely, and also to Mrs Boyce. | Philip Webb:

BL Add 45354, ff. 171-2

1 Neave was the builder/decorator who would be employed in the remedial works to 1 Palace Green. See below, Letter 182.
2 High-quality atlases were produced by the firm of Edinburgh cartographers, founded by Alexander Keith Johnston (1804–71) and his brother William, and continued by family members, including the younger Alexander Keith Johnston (1844–79). Of the several contenders, their *National Atlas of Historical, Commercial and Political Geography* (1849) may be what PSW had in mind.
3 Like Johnston, A. & C. Black was also an Edinburgh-based firm, founded by the politician and publisher Adam Black (1784–1874). *Black's General Atlas* first appeared in 1840.
4 Karl von Spruner, whose *Historisch Geographischer Hand-Atlas zur Geschichte der Staaten Europas von Anfang des Mittel-Alters* first appeared in 1846.
5 Publishers specialising in foreign scientific material, with premises in Henrietta Street, Covent Garden.

178 • To Albert Estcourt, 3 January 1882

Draft/copy

[1, Raymond Buildings . . .]
Jan: 3. 1882.

To Mr Albert Estcourt
Builder &c. 1 Barton St Gloucester.

Dear Sir.

(Clouds House)

In answer to your letter of Decr 28. I am trying to arrange to go to Knoyle next week (probably Wed^y the 11th) and I should like to know if you think that time would be a good one for me to see to the digging of foundations, surface drainage &c. Also as to the working of a specimen or two of the Chilmark stone?¹ If this would be too early for you I w^d defer my visit for another week.

It w^d be impossible to have any of the permanent drainage now laid, neither do I approve of drains being laid till the buildings have settled. I will certainly attend to carpenters & joiners details as soon as possible, and I am glad that you remind me of those you would wish to have first. As to the solid door & window frames for stables, it is better that they should be built in, but as you will be using these buildings when they are covered-in, we sh^d have to consider as to t̶h̶e̶i̶r̶ the protection $^{\text{of the frames &c}}$ from injury.

Yours truly | Ph: W:

LB-1, pp. 220-1

1 See above, Letter 162, note 4.

179 • To Nathaniel Ramsay and Son, 5 January 1882

Draft/copy

[1, Raymond Buildings . . .]
Jan: 5. 1882.

To Messrs Nathaniel Ramsay & Son
31 St Vincent Place Glasgow.

Dear Sirs.

(Arisaig House)[1]

I duly recd your report, and letter of Decr 31. Your report seems to me to be perfectly satisfactory in its character, tho' most likely more work would have to be done than is there indicated – however the "notes" you speak of would be incorporated in the specification you would prepare for the use of the Clerk of the works.

I can quite understand that it would be impossible to get a contract for the whole of the works to be done, and therefore we shd have to depend much on the judgment and honesty of the Clerk of works. Now, I could find a Clerk of works ~~here~~ for this short-time business, but I shd doubt whether an Englishman would be able, unless he had ~~Scotch~~ experience in Scotland, to understand local peculiarities and ways of work, materials &c. 'Tis true I had an English Clerk of works when the house was built,[2] but then I was often at the place myself for 8 or 10 days at a time. Do you think you could find a Glasgow or Edinburgh Clerk of works, with a good reputation, to undertake the business under your direction and occasional supervision, and my instruction and drawings?

I can see by your plan of the drainage, and from my recollection that the system there shewn is not far out, and I should have no difficulty in making the necessary improvements, with further information from the Clerk of works. The T nails for securing the slating would be a very good plan, but much would depend on the nails themselves, they should be light, strong, and the nail end ~~should be~~ long, and not too much tapered [*sketch*] and should be galvanized.

With regard to plumber's work, this is most important in such a climate as the West of Scotland. The extreme purity and softness of the rain water acts chemically on the lead. For some time I have had considerable doubts as to the use of "milled" lead in exposed positions, and I find other architects who agree with me, and in some places "cast" lead is being again used. Mr Wm Reid of 117 West George St Glasgow did the plumber's work at Arisaig House,[3] and at several times since he has worked for the estate, and as I have never found him other than a fair tradesman, & as he knows the place and the work, I think it would be well that he shd be employed on the repairs if he would give you reasonable prices? Will you see him, and ask him if he could make or ~~prepare~~ procure cast lead for the outside work, say at 8–10 or 12 lbs weight to the superficial foot? As to the mason, I think that Mr Routledge the bailiff spoke well of a local man who had done work, recently at the house & fairly well. Of course all the tradesmen should work under a schedule of prices for labour and materials.

All new hot and cold water supply pipes ^(except the closets & other such uses) should be "tin-lined" copper. With regard to the heating apparatus, I think you should consider as to a Glasgow man undertaking ^{the repair of} this.

Miss Astley most likely mentioned to you when she would wish the repairs begun and ended. I should propose that you should undertake the direction of the work, and if you sh^d agree to this I should be glad if you would send me a memorandum stating in what way ^{& in what proportion} you^r ~~want & expect to be paid~~ ^{charge would be made}?

I am obliged by your prompt attention to this matter. | Yours truly | Ph: W:

LB-1, pp. 221-3

---

1 Having been consulted by Gertrude Astley about necessary remedial works at Arisaig, PSW advised a full survey so that a timetable of priorities might be drawn up. This was undertaken by Nathaniel Ramsay, surveyor for the original works in 1863.
2 John Smith.
3 See above, Letter 42.

180 • To George Price Boyce, 11 January 1882

1, Raymond Buildings, Gray's Inn, | London.
Jany 11. 1882

My dear Boyce

I rec^d your postcard this morn^g. Was very pleased to think of Mrs Boyce and you frolicing [*sic*] in this fine weather. On the other side I note down such things as I have found in the books to remain (do they <u>now</u> remain?) in Coventry. I have only a dim recollection of the place, which I last saw in 1851! The Churches have, I fancy, all gone the way of the restorers – as some of the restorers are going the way of the Churches!

We have a note at the Antiscrape as to the Cross, and I think one of the local correspondents has been asked to go and see about it. It would be very well if you would note down for the society its present state, and how <u>little</u> should be done to keep it in repair – noting, also, how "restoration" would ruin what remains of value.[1]

If you could suggest any site in the City where the present restless folk could put up their proposed memorial, to their own glorification, instead of ruining an old & valuable object, please do so. So far as I can make out from Parker, the buildings of St Mary's Guild, with some furniture glass &c must be inviting – if they <u>now</u> remain.[2] Ford's hospital, especially, you will note.[3]

Parker puts Coventry along with Shrewsbury for remains of old houses – timber chiefly.

Yours sincerely | Philip Webb:

Notes.

Remains of Hall & other buildings. "St Mary's Guild" middle of 15th cent^y (finished 1414 (?)) – very valuable

---

Several "Decorated" window heads (timber) built into the walls of an Inn

---

Quantity of houses, or parts of houses; one in "West Orchard S^t" - temp: Rich^d 2^4

Fords Hospital – 1529

Bablake or Bonds Hospital – 1506

"Free School", was a Chapel of 14 cent: said to have belonged to St John's Hospital

---

White friars monastery in the suburbs "now workhouse" – (?)

BL Add 45354, ff. 173-4

---

1 The first stone of the Tudor market cross in Coventry was laid in 1541–2, a replacement for the two former crosses which had stood on the site. It underwent various repairs during the seventeenth and eighteenth centuries, and in 1880 was threatened with comprehensive restoration 'at the junction of Broadgate and Cross Cheaping . . . [A] committee has been formed to further the same, and we trust the object may be successfully accomplished'. T.W. Whitley, *The Coventry Cross* (Warwick, 1880), p. 18. Thomas Wardle was asked to check on the condition of the cross on behalf of the SPAB committee, and confirmed that the original no longer existed. 'I have not heard of more than a wish to erect a new one on the site of the old one which was where the Cab stand now is opposite the Castle Hotel. . . . [R]estoration would now I think be impossible if attempted.' Thomas Wardle to SPAB secretary, 8 January 1882, *SPAB, Coventry Cross file*.
2 The fourteenth-century St Mary's Guildhall, much altered in the early fifteenth century. 'This is probably the most perfect house of the period that we have remaining in England, and may be said to be quite complete, though somewhat spoiled, first by neglect, and then by modern improvements. . . . [The hall has] a long flat window of several lights at the upper end, which has the original painted glass, and under it hangs the original tapestry.' John Henry Parker, *Some Account of Domestic Architecture in England, from Richard II to Henry VIII*, 2 vols (Oxford: John Henry and James Parker, 1859), II, p. 239. PSW's notes at the end of the letter are gleaned from Parker.
3 William Ford, a Coventry businessman, established this almshouse in Greyfriars Lane to provide accommodation for five elderly men and one woman, a tradition of caring which by the mid nineteenth century was housing 40 women. Parker described it as 'a remarkably perfect timberhouse of the time of Henry VIII, with bargeboards and buttresses, and panelling, and windowheads, all of carved oak, in a very perfect state' (p. 240). The building suffered from bombing in 1940.
4 'The city of Coventry abounds with timber-houses, many of which have very good Gothic windows, most of . . . the fifteenth and sixteenth centuries, but one in the West Orchard is believed . . . to be of the fourteenth, and the forms of the tracery would agree very well with the time of Richard II.' Parker, I, p. 127.

1864–1887

181 • To James Simmonds, 14 January 1882

Draft/copy

[1, Raymond Buildings . . .]
Jan: 14. 1882

To Mr James Simmonds. Clerk of Works
Clouds House – East Knoyle. Salisbury

Dear Sir.

(Clouds H^{se})

I rec^d your mem^m of position [of] walnut tree this morning. Having considered matters carefully since my visit to Clouds I have concluded that things generally are in a satisfactory state of progress, and that Mr Estcourt and Mr Hibbins[1] seem ~~perfectly willing~~ anxious and able to make ~~a~~ good work of the buildings – but the ~~present~~ manner of ~~working~~ ^{tooling} the faced and moulded Chilmark stone is not as yet satisfactory – however from the appearance of the last piece of stone worked for me to see before I left I have no doubt that the kind of work to be done will be arrived at in a very short time.

Will you be so good so far as possible to see that the masons – 'till they get their hands in, only do plain work, or work which only includes the more simple mouldings, as, the moulded work yet done would ^{not}, if continued in that manner, ~~not~~ be useable. ^{In working all mouldings, sharp tools and a light mallet will be necessary.}

I must beg you also to see that no <u>dirty</u> materials be used in making the concrete, the gravel must be washed. Also the size of the ^{larger} lumps must be reduced. It would be well also to wash, and use with the larger gravel & broken bricks, some of the sifted gravel.

Please to find from Mr Russell[2] if Mr Estcourt buys the gravel for the concrete from Mr Wyndham? I should wish you to see that the men facing the green sandstone face a large quantity as <u>bond stones to tail into the walls</u>.

As I am not sure if you have yet removed f'm Mr Russell's I direct this letter there.

Yours truly | Ph: W:

LB-1, pp. 225-6

---

1 Estcourt's foreman.
2 PWY's bailiff, with whom Simmonds was lodging.

182 • To George Howard, 16 January 1882

Draft/copy

[1, Raymond Buildings . . .]
Jan: 16. 1882.

Castle Howard. by York.

My dear Howard.

(1 Pal: Green)

I went to Pal: Green on Friday and met Neave there who had set up some trestles for me to examine the ceiling in the drawing-room. I could not see that there would be danger of its falling, at all events at present, ^{neither did Neave,} so I directed ~~Neave~~ ^{him} first to use slips of paper to take the salting out of the pattern, then to trace one of each of the patterns of panels &c – after which, that the ceiling should be washed, stopped, and covered with strong paper, then painted in thin oils and afterwards distempered white. Neave thought of covering up the walls with sheets, leaving the pictures hanging, but I was afraid of risking damage to these valuable works, and directed their removal. They begin today. There was an awkwardness ~~of~~ ⁱⁿ finding other whitewashing people in the house!

Afterwards I went with Neave into the "white house" & found the shell a good substantial building.[1] The tenants, of wh' there are a crowd, looked on us as agents of a bloody landlord; and if any of them are Irish you may expect to have to billet a bullet.

I will now consider what sort of letter I shall write to you for the benefit of the "woods & forests". ^{I also directed as to repairing the yards paving temporarily.}

Hugh Bell was here the other day & told me of the doings at your North Riding contest. I sh^d be particularly glad if you got in Rowlandson whether he can open his mouth or not.[2]

Y^{rs} very truly | Ph: W:

LB-1, pp. 226-7

---

1 This was the building to the rear of 1 Palace Green, which Howard was considering purchasing. See Caroline Dakers, *The Holland Park Circle* (New Haven and London: Yale University Press, 1999), p. 104.
2 Following the death of the sitting MP, a by-election had been called for the North Riding parliamentary seat. The Liberal candidate, Samuel Rowlandson, a local tenant farmer from Newton Morrell, lost by 386 votes to the Conservative.

183 • To G. Sedger, 14 February 1882

Draft/copy

[1, Raymond Buildings. . . .]

Feby 14. 1882.

To G: Sedger Esqre
26 Great James St Bedford Row.

Sir.

I am sorry that you sh^d have had the trouble of calling here when I was not at home. I did not return yesterday 'till 12. oc.

I am looking out for a junior assistant, and if you thought that your brother, who is in want of work, would be likely to be willing and able to do the work I have to be done I sh^d be glad to see you on the matter. I want a young man who has already ~~obtained gained~~ ^{laid} the ~~information~~ foundation of his knowledge of the building arts in a practical way in a good business-like office, and would be anxious to extend his knowledge and give $^{the\ use\ of}$ his head and hands $^{-\ in\ an\ energetic\ way\ -}$ to ~~nothing but~~ the practical work which goes on in my office. The aptitude that I most require is that of a person who had a natural turn for construction, and would set himself to master the difficulties which ~~would~~ occur in adapting construction to art matters in various kinds of buildings. ~~In~~ A young man of fair education so inclined, and with ^{a} determination to make the ~~work~~ ^{business} he would be engaged on, his own $^{as\ it\ were}$, for the purpose of carrying on my ~~business~~ ^{intentions} ~~he~~ would, I believe, find interesting and instructive work here. He would have to work on my designs, $^{add\ to\ them\ \&}$ complete them, and then trace and make ~~them~~ the drawings perfect for the builders.

I am Sir, | Yours truly | Ph: W:

I shall be at home for the next two days between 10 & 12. am.

LB-1, pp. 232-3

184 • To G. Sedger, 20 March 1882

Draft/copy

[1, Raymond Buildings . . .]
March 20. 1882

To G: Sedger Esqre
26. Great James St B^d Row.

Dear Sir

Your brother, Thomas Sedger, having been in my office for a month – ~~I have been able~~ a sufficient time for him to get over ~~any~~ ^{the} nervousness accompanying a young man's entry on work in a strange place – I have ^{been} able to come to a conclusion as to his position in the knowledge of his profession, and ^{as} to whether he was sufficiently advanced to do the work which I sh^d have to expect of him.

I am sorry to say that he is not yet sufficiently forward to be able to assist me in the work to be done here. I am the more sorry that this is the case, as he seems to ^{be} a quiet and industrious fellow, and ~~if~~ a young man for whom I should have felt a pleasure in helping in every way in my power. I spoke to him on Saturday, and strongly advised him not to give up his exertions, but to try and get in to an office where there was plenty of work to do of a kind within the reach of his attainments.

I sincerely regret that his coming here has not been so successful as I had hoped, but I beg to thank you for the trouble you have taken in this matter.

Believe me | Y^{rs} truly | Ph. W.

LB-1, pp. 237-8

185 • To George Price Boyce, 18 April 1882

1, Raymond Buildings, Gray's Inn, | London.
Tuesday night April 18.

My dear Boyce

You may remember that I spoke to you of a Mr Jack (assistant to Mr Vinall, & now helping me in my work)[1] who would like to see any of your pictures which you may have by you, and your collection of works by both old and new masters. I have told Mr Jack that you, with your usual good nature, would be good enough to let him see these works, and he is looking forward to that pleasure when it may be convenient to you to do so.

Mr Jack has the Saturdays for himself, and would come to Chelsea next Saturday or any other Sat: more suitable.

I would mention that this good fellow is extremely shy, almost nervously so, and I the more move in the matter myself as, otherwise, he probably would not; and yet it would be good for him to see such good work, as he has a turn for art <u>though</u> he is modest.

Would you be so good as to let me know what Saturday would be least inconvenient to you for him to come to West house, and the best time for him to come in the day.

Yours very truly | Philip Webb:

BL Add 45354, ff. 177-8

---

1 John Brandon-Jones believed that George Washington Jack (GWJ, 1855–1931) 'joined Webb's staff in 1879' (*NBS*, p. 33), but this letter appears to suggest that he started working for PSW in 1882, perhaps replacing the unsuitable Thomas Sedger (see previous letter). For Vinall see above, Letter 69, note 1.

186 • To Constance Astley, 26 April 1882

Draft/copy

[1, Raymond Buildings . . .]
April 26. 1882.

To Miss Astley
33 Princes Gardens S.W.

Dear Miss Astley

I send you a tracing of the design for the memorial.[1] Having tried the matter in various ways, and carefully considered the circumstances, I concluded that it would be best to make the cross as different as possible to a, so called, Runic cross or a village cross; also to mark it as much as ~~possible~~ ^(might be) (considering its height) as a private memorial. To do this, I have placed the inscription close under the cross part itself, which will ^(more than anything else) mark the stone as a personal monument, and make a good position – out of the way of injury – for the inscription tablet. This tablet I would propose to have cast in bronze with the inscription on it in raised characters.

I think ~~that~~ you said that possibly you might note, in addition to the inscription to your brother, that the bodies of your Father & mother lay elsewhere. If you ~~thought~~ ^(now think) of this plan, I would make both sides of the memorial the same, instead of different, as shewn on the tracing, and this would give another panel for inscription.

I was obliged to make the stonework solid and simple, considering the character of the whinstone. I sh^d propose, if there is a chance of getting it, to cut the whole of cross & stem in one block of stone – ^(if this is not possible, to make it 2 or 3 stones.) It is intended to surround the plot of earth with a plain curb of whinstone 12 inches high.

Yours very truly | Ph: W:

LB-1, pp. 240-1

---

1 See above, Letter 157, note 1.

187 • To Albert Estcourt, 6 May 1882

Draft/copy

[1, Raymond Buildings . . .]
May 6. 1882.

To M^r A: Estcourt
Builder 1 Barton St Gloucester.
Dear Sir.

(Clouds House)

I have considered the matter of the kind of lime for use above the datum line[1] of the main building of house, and have decided that Lias lime in the lump shall be used.[2] It will be necessary therefore that <u>all</u> the mortar should be ground in the mill. As the mortar with our rather too fine sand would be much improved by grinding with it all broken bricks and stone chippings, I should wish you to direct that this waste should be collected periodically and used for this purpose. Will you also give strict orders to Hibbins that he should see that the sand is screened from all fibrous and other vegitable [*sic*] matter.

I will speak to Simmonds & Hibbins about ~~setting~~ ^{turning of} the vaulting as the work proceeds. I am providing the details mentioned in your letter of the 3rd May.

Yours truly | Ph: W:

LB-1, p. 242

---

1 A line serving as a reference for the measurement of other quantities.
2 Lias is a blue limestone rock occurring in the southwest, used in lime mortar.

188 • To Bella Duffy, 12 May 1882

Draft

1 R B: G. Inn, London. May 12. 1882

Madam.

I must ask your kind consideration for my seeming delay in answering your valuable letter ~~to me~~, dated April the 25th.[1] On receiving it, and also one from Mr Stanhope, I laid the matter before a^{n ordinary} committee ~~meeting~~ of the ^{English} Society for the Protⁿ of Ancient Buildings and it was decided to call ~~together~~ a meeting of the Foreign Committee of the Society to consider ~~the matter~~ ^{it} under the light of your letter. This Committee has met, and I believe ~~it~~ will send a report of the result of its consideration directly to you. As I have not ^{had} the advantage of ~~having visited~~ ^{seeing} Italy I was not a member of this Committee, but as most of its members are familiar with the buildings of great importance in several of the larger cities ~~of Italy~~ I was well satisfied in handing over to them the information you had been good enough to impart to the Society through me.

Personally, I feel that but little serviceable resistance can be made to individual works ^{already} entered upon by the ^{Florentines or other} Italians ~~themselves~~; ~~though~~ ^{but} I believe that no nation is quite free from a ^{reasonable} susceptibility to the notice taken of it by honourable and hearty foreigners, and as this English Society was organised and is most strongly supported by educated artists ^{practical architects} and able historical students, who have no other thought ^{in the matter} than the welfare of the infinitely valuable ancient monuments of the world, and is absolutely free from any mercenary bias, I am in hope that this spirit will in time be appreciated by the Italians and other nations, and that all suspicion of motives will die out as the increase of communion between nations does away with ~~that~~ ^{the} fear which ~~comes~~ ^{is bred} of ignorance.[2] I should be glad if ~~you~~ in your intercourse with cultivated Italians ^{you} could impress upon them that we in England would be sincerely glad if they would ^{familiarise themselves with} our monuments, and ~~they would~~ help us with forcible expression from their side when the intelligent English are hard-pressed ^{while striving} to save what ~~little~~ remains unfalsified in their own land. You may be sure that it is the minority in England which is active in saving, and I feel satisfied that there is a minority in Italy who only want banding together to make a society of its own which ~~will~~ would do more to save ^{its inestimable antiquities} than any outside elements ^{would}, though it ~~would~~ ^{might} be helped by foreign sympathy.

Believe me Madam | with much respect | Yours sincerely | Ph W.

All' Illustr^{ma} Signorina | Signorina Bella Duffy
Via Santo Spirito. 6 | Firenze. | <u>Italy.</u>

Courtauld 4a-b

---

1 The Irish writer Bella Duffy (d. 1926), a friend of Vernon Lee and a long-term resident of Florence, had written initially to John Roddam Spencer Stanhope (for whom see above, Letter 96, note 6) on 10 April, concerned about the dangers of likely future restoration work in Florence. She wanted the SPAB to become publicly involved, but doubted whether many Italian papers would be prepared to print the SPAB manifesto. 'I know of two & perhaps three that would publish it & without comment: but the remainder (and unfortunately those most influential in artistic matters) w^d probably only publish it in order to make it the text of a semi-comic & wholly resentful diatribe against the English.' Instead, she urged that a specially-composed pamphlet 'to be written very strongly' should be targeted at an Italian public, 'announced in the <u>Gazzetta d'Italia</u> & stuck up in the shop-windows'. Bella Duffy to Stanhope, 10 April 1882, *Courtauld* 3a-f. Through Stanhope, PSW sought more detailed information from Miss Duffy about the threatened buildings.

2 More than a year earlier, following rumours of planned restoration work on the Loggia del Bigallo, WM had written to the Prefect of Florence urging restraint, fearing 'that the threatened restoration aims at reproducing ancient features now lost or injured', and citing the instance of 'the disastrous so-called restoration of that loveliest of Churches, S. Miniato'. 26 January 1881, *CLWM*, II. Perhaps surprisingly, the response was encouraging, and Stanhope had the case in mind when writing to PSW. '[T]he careful way in which the Bigallo had been treated might be partly owing to an "awakened conscience" thro the efforts of the society.' 26 April 1882, *Courtauld* 2a-e.

189 • To John Howell, 25 May 1882

Draft/copy

[1, Raymond Buildings . . .]
May 25. 1882.

To Mr John Howell
East Knoyle Brick Yard. Salisbury

Dear Sir.

(Clouds H^{se})

I was much disappointed at not meeting you at the new house yesterday, as I learned f^m Mr Simmonds that you knew I was to be there on that day.

The sample of handmade facing bricks shewn to me by Mr Simmonds ~~were~~ was not at all satisfactory, and as the progress of the works will be seriously hindered if ~~in~~ ^{from} your next kiln a brick more nearly approaching what is wanted is ^{not} produced I sh^d have wished to consider with you what sh^d be done.

Mr Wyndham has often urged upon me his wish that the facing bricks should be of the character required, and as I have as often told him that you had assured me ~~that~~ you could produce bricks of the colour and quality wanted, he will be much disappointed if it sh^d be necessary ^for me^ to apply to other brickyards for the right quality of bricks.

I have directed Mr Simmonds to forward me a sample of ~~the~~ your next kiln's burning ~~which~~ ^as soon as possible &^ I hope ^they^ will be more to the purpose than the last.

Yours truly | Ph: W:

LB-1, pp. 243-4

190 • To Canon William Greenwell, 6 July 1882

Drafted on behalf of SPAB

The Society for the Protection of Ancient Buildings
[*pencil date*] July 6. 1882

To the Revd Canon Greenwell[1]

Sir

The notice in the "Durham Country Advertiser," of May the 19th last, of the meeting of the Durham & Northumberland Archæological Society ^held^ at Durham when you, as President, delivered an address on "Church Restoration", having been brought ~~before a meeting of the~~ ^under the notice of a^ Committee of our Society, it was resolved, that a letter should be written to you ~~to~~ express^ing^ the satisfaction which the Committee felt at so ~~outspoken~~ ^decided^ and otherwise satisfactory a declaration of opinion as to the evils attendant on church Restoration, from a Gentleman so likely to command the attention and respect of his audience.[2] It was also resolved ~~at~~ ^by^ the committee to ask you to consider a proposition then made that your address should be published by our Society for distribution in the usual way with other writings ~~of the society~~ in aid of the movement for protecting old buildings.

~~In~~ A letter of yours, ^to the editor of the Durham paper^ of June the 13th, which corrected a very palpable reporter's misunderstanding of one of ~~your~~ ^the^ arguments in your address, ^has^ confirmed the Committee in thinking that several other passages ^in the address^ had suffered in like manner, and it was decided that you should be asked – in case you agreed to the proposition of the Committee – to explain or ~~correct~~ ^alter other passages,^ before the address was published by the Society.

It is quite evident from the admirable tone of your address that you are a member of the Society for the Protection of An^t B^gs not only in name; and the Committee ~~therefore~~ feels that any remarks it may make on passages in your address will be received by you in a sympathetic spirit. ~~and It is also probable some of the passages marked by the Committee have,~~ ^from^ ~~self evidence, not been intended by you as they are set forth in the County newspaper.~~

1864–1887

You are represented as saying that "Restoration was a very valuable word because true restoration was a very valuable thing".³ The Committee ~~of our Society is constantly finding~~ from ~~their~~ experience would urge upon you that in 9 cases out of 10 "Restoration" is a ~~very~~ mischievous word, and ~~it also~~ the Com: can find no proper use for it, as it means simply an impossible thing: one can restore five shillings because another 5^s/- represents exactly the same value, but it is impossible to restore the lost art of one generation of people by the ~~new art~~ merely imitative art of another. The Com: therefore thinks that ~~you will~~ on re-consideration you would agree with it that the ~~use of the~~ word "restoration" had better not be used by ~~thoughtful~~ responsible people with regard to the maintenance of A[ncien]t B^{gs}.

In speaking of the necessity there will be at times to enlarge churches, you are reported as saying that "this was not a difficult matter". ~~Now~~ The Committee feels that this can hardly have ~~been the~~ expressed your intention ~~of your expression~~, for, the task of enlarging a venerable building must always be, to a sensitive architect, one of the most perplexing of ~~necessities~~ works. ~~Indeed,~~ Committees of our Society have from time to time expressed the opinion that no ancient church should be enlarged or otherwise dealt with in its structure & detail on the representation of the triple opinion of even the most experienced architect or ~~antiquarian~~ archæologist. Indeed this Committee is convinced that, ~~only~~ in cases where churches have been mutilated and ruined in some one or other part ~~of it, that~~, at that place only can an addition ~~can~~ be made without irreparable destruction of the evidences of art & history, and the loveliness of age & appreciation.

There are, unfortunately, many opportunities in this way for enlarging churches, but this Committee feels that a consultation, even in such cases, of several trained & unbiased minds should be insisted upon before ~~the~~ a plan was ~~settled upon~~ ~~decided carried out~~ accepted. ~~In speaking~~ On the subject of decoration the Committee would suggest that you add – where you speak so forcibly of the miserable character of such work in general – that it would be well that all modern decoration in old churches should be moveable?

In reading your amusing notice of the kind of architect often employed on the renovation of churches, some members of the Com: thought that you were rather hard on the half educated masons, and others, as they have not done a tenth part of the mischief that the educated architects have, and the Committee feels sure that you will agree with ~~them~~ it in this.

The Com: w^d also suggest at the part of your address where you speak of the walls of old churches being too often considered ruinous when they are not necessarily dangerous, ~~that~~ you might add that, constant attention to ~~such~~ old walls with the necessary repairs to the foundations would, in many cases, save the churches from being "restored", and at greatly less cost.

The last part of your address struck sharply at the ~~mischief caused by the~~ ignorance & laxity ~~of~~ so often shewn by the superior ecclesiastical authorities, and the Committee can hardly express its relief at such a clear and ~~manly~~ forcible ~~acknowledgment~~ exposure of ~~such~~ this unfaithfulness. The Committee feels deeply the helplessness of the English people with regard to their rights over their public buildings.

The Committee knows that, in cases where the majority of opinion is against a scheme of restoration, ~~that~~ the faculty is obtained in an obscure way, and too often under the influence of a gift of money; all the more then does the Committee rejoice that you should have found yourself impelled to put into such decided language what other people in like position ~~with~~ ᵗᵒ yourself are afraid to acknowledge.

[*pencil*] July 6 1882

Sent to Wardle to trim & send on to Boyce for him to bring to meeting tomorrow.

SPAB

---

1 William Greenwell (1820–1918) was a minor canon at Durham Cathedral and its librarian for many years, in which role he pursued his antiquarian researches, but his principal interest was in the excavation of burial mounds. His collection of artefacts at the British Museum is central to its early British holdings. A fellow of the Royal Society, he was President of the Durham and Northumberland Architectural and Archaeological Society from 1865 until his death.
2 Greenwell gave his Presidential address to the Durham and Northumberland Architectural and Archaeological Society on 16 May 1882.
3 A comprehensive report, essentially a transcript of Greenwell's address, was eventually printed in the Society's *Transactions*, III (1890), pp. xl–xlix, but Greenwell chose not to amend his remarks. Had it been published as a paper rather than a record of what had been said, perhaps he might have tweaked it, but he probably felt unfairly harangued, irritated that his commitment to building protection was being picked over, and chose to resist the idea of pushing a party line.

191 • To James Simmonds, 14 July 1882

Draft/copy

[1, Raymond Buildings . . .]
July 14. 1882.

To Mʳ James Simmons. C of Works.
Clouds Hˢᵉ East Knoyle. Salisbury
Dear Sir.

(Clouds Hˢᵉ)

Will you be so good as to direct that no sand of less finely ground quality than that done for me by the mill next the main block, be used for the cavity filling-in. It is of the utmost importance that this filling-in should be accurately & scientifically done ᵗʰᵉ ˢᵃⁿᵈ ᵃⁿᵈ ᶜᵉᵐᵉⁿᵗ ᵇᵉⁱⁿᵍ ᵐᵉᵃˢᵘʳᵉᵈ.

I ~~should~~ wish you to go to the place mentioned by Mʳ Howell, where there is a store of drift sand belonging to Mʳ Wyndham, on Monday morning (if you have not already done so) and send me a sample of it in a letter by post ᴹᵒⁿᵈᵃʸ ᵉᵛᵉⁿⁱⁿᵍ'ˢ and direct Mʳ Hibbins to have a few loads carted on ᵗᵒ the ground at once, at all events.

I am a little disappointed at ~~finding~~ ˡᵉᵃʳⁿⁱⁿᵍ that I am sometimes the first to find out that things are not being done as they should be. Your time should be employed in watching each kind of work as is goes on, and at once correcting mistakes and directing change of proceedings, when necessary.

You are aware of the kind of Chilmark stone I most want used and, in case of doubt, ᵃˢ ᵗᵒ ᑫᵘᵃˡⁱᵗʸ, you had better go again to the quarry and find out ~~where~~ what bed the stone comes f'm, wh' is being sent to the works – the "Pinney" bed being the one decided on.[1] Please also to agree with Mʳ Hibbins as to measuring ʷⁱᵗʰ ᵖʳᵒᵖᵉʳ ᵇᵒˣ ᶠʳᵃᵐᵉˢ the proportions of lime & sand put into both mills. And, 'till we can decide as to the drift sand, Mʳ Hibbins must use the sawing grit for the cavity filling, unless he can grind some gravel to that fineness, but even then it is ~~of the greatest importance~~ ⁿᵉᶜᵉˢˢᵃʳʸ that the quantities of sand and Portland cement should be exactly measured. I am very anxious as to the successful filling of the cavity between the two walls, and it can only succeed if ~~it is~~ the rules of materials & mixing are followed.

I think you quite understood what I wanted done with the damp course over the window & door heads – namely, that over the thin coat of asphalt a thin coat – chiefly of tar – should be brushed while hot.

Yours truly | Ph': W

LB-1, pp. 244-5

---

1 Of the different geological 'beds' of Chilmark stone, 'the Pinney Bed is more crystalline than the others and is harder at the bottom; its colour is yellowish-brown; it works freely and is said to weather well.' John Allen Howe, *The Geology of Building Stones* (London: Arnold, 1910), p. 252.

192 • To General Augustus Fox Pitt-Rivers, 17 July 1882

Draft/copy

[1, Raymond Buildings . . .]
July 17 1882

To Genˡ A: Pitt Rivers.[1]
4 Grosvenor Gardens. S.W.

Dear Genˡ Rivers.

(Rushmore Lodge)

In answer to your letter of the 14ᵗʰ insᵗ. I shall not myself be able to go to Rushmore before the week after next, but with some notes of the dining-room taken by my assistant, and with my recollection of the room, I can give you my opinion as to the finishing of it, as follows.[2]

The room is 32'.0" long by 24'.0" broad, and is 15'.9" high. It is rather a gaunt room, from my recollection, and from the dimensions it is too broad in proportion to its length – therefore, anything done to it should be in the way of giving it parts. For the hanging of valuable pictures it is not satisfactory, as they would (I suppose) have to be opposite the light. Would it not be possible to hang these pictures on the two end walls of the room so as to give them a side light?

It is always unsatisfactory to colour walls as a background to pictures. Either the walls should have a proper toned and patterned paper or, which would be ~~better~~ best, the~~y walls~~ should be hung with tapestried stuff. I think at present, that the best way would be to divide the walls in their height, namely, with dado, hanging, & patterned frieze on a light ground.

If you thought well of this scheme I would consult with Morris & C° as to the hangings, painting, and patterning of frieze & cornice, and, perhaps, you could send me the clear outside sizes of the frames.

Yours truly | Ph: W:

LB-1, pp. 245-7

---

1 The archaeologist and anthropologist, Augustus Henry Lane Fox Pitt-Rivers (1827–1900), married Rosalind Howard's eldest sister, Alice Margaret Stanley (d. 1910), in 1853. His work was influenced by that of Canon William Greenwell (see above, Letter 190, note 1). He became vice-president of the Society of Antiquaries, and his collection of ethnographic items formed the basis of the Pitt Rivers Museum at Oxford University. The results of his significant archaeological excavations in Cranborne Chase were given to Farnham Museum, Dorset (now an inn).
2 PSW oversaw interior alterations to Rushmore Lodge, Pitt-Rivers's eighteenth-century house at Tollard Royal, Wiltshire (1882–3). See *Kirk*, pp. 186–7 and 300.

193 • To General Augustus Fox Pitt-Rivers, 20 July 1882

Draft/copy

[1, Raymond Buildings . . .]
July 20. 1882

To General A: Pitt-Rivers.
4 Grosvenor Gardens. S.W.
My dear Sir.

(Rushmore Lodge)

Before answering your letter (with its inclosure of plan) of the 18th inst, I thought it better to see Messrs Morris on the subject of the hangings & painting for the dining-room. After going into the matter we decided that it would be quite impossible to prepare & get the work done in a month's time.

The best way would be to prepare ~~all~~ the designs and material ready for executing the work when the house was vacated for a month or six weeks. Messrs

Morris agreed with me that the hangings would make the best ground for the pictures, but that it would [be] well for us to go and see the room before deciding upon the details, & this we could arrange to do in the week after next. Green[1] has promised to send me drawings of the 4 sides of the room in a few days.

Yours truly | Ph: W:

LB-1, p. 247

---

1 A.H. Green, of Blandford.

194 • To General Augustus Fox Pitt-Rivers, 18 August 1882

Draft/copy

[1, Raymond Buildings . . .]
August 18. 1882

To General A: Pitt-Rivers.
Carlsbad Austria.
Dear Gen.ˡ Pitt-Rivers.

(Rushmore Lodge)

I duly rec.ᵈ your letter f.ᵐ Carlsbad of August 8, and since then I have set ~~the~~ going the work of ~~cleaning~~ decorating the dining-room according to the more economical estimate wh' I sent to you on August 5, and I have since heard f.ᵐ M.ʳ Green that he is advancing rapidly with the works. I have not found occasion for changing the scheme, except that the curtain stuff ~~will be~~ is being made up with a little handsomer stuff.

I have spoken to Morris & Co about a carpet for the large corridor, and they tell me that they could make one of the proper width ~~of~~ with <u>negative coloured wools</u> to go well with the Persian rugs you may have (Morris's understand the character of these) and which rugs would be set on the floor occasionally right & left of the long strip down the ~~centre~~ middle of the corridor. I do not think the long carpet need be more than f.ᵐ 4 feet to 4'.6" wide, and this would give room for Persian rugs, cabinets &c at the sides.

There ᵃʳᵉ 16 brackets on the top of oak panelling on each side of corridor – 32 in all – which would make good standing for various objects, such as bronzes, china bottles &c, there being a space of white frieze between the top of the brackets and the underside of plaster cornice of 2'.9" in height.

LB-1, pp. 251-2

195 • To Albert Estcourt, 28 August 1882

Draft/copy

[1, Raymond Buildings . . .]
August 28. 1882.

To. Mr Albert Estcourt
Builder. 1 Barton St Gloucester
Dear Sir.

(Clouds House)

I was at Knoyle on Friday and I am glad to be able to report that I found the works going on rapidly and in most ways satisfactorily but, I was greatly annoyed at finding that – beyond the damage by the railway to the Hopton Wood stone columns for the hall[1] – the stones had been inaccurately bedded, and in setting them plumb the bed joints came so irregularly as to make it quite impossible ^for me^ to pass this work.

There is nothing to be done other than to have the work ^lifted and the beds of the stones^ re~~bedded~~^cut^ perfectly truly. Also, to have ~~such~~ ^the^ bruises and injuries ^to the arrises^ cut away at the same time. I must leave it to you to settle when & how this sh^d be done, but w^d suggest that the Hopton Wood people sh^d send a man or men to Clouds to do this work themselves. I have consented that to one of the broken capitals ^it^ should have its broken string cut out and be pieced according to my directions to Mr Simmonds, but I must beg you to insist that all damaged arrises be cut down to and removed and that the settled total height of shafts be kept; ~~and~~ to do this, one ^or more^ of the stones will have to be worked anew, of increased length to make up the loss of height. The bedding joints should not exceed 1/12th of an inch and should be equal in thickness all round the shafts. Now, in some cases, the thickness of the bedding joints varied from 1/16 on one side to 3/16 on ^the^ ~~an~~other. Mr Wyndham noticed this work, and I told him that ~~the work~~ ^it^ was not yet finally set.

I had to complain to Mr Hibbins that his bricklayers, at times, <u>will</u> use ordinary mortar for pargetting the flues, in spite of my re-iterated directions to use only cowdung mortar, well made with lime & cowdung and applied thinly and carefully.[2]

Howell produced some roof tiles of much better character than those he shewed me last time and though they are not the right size, still I would agree to them being used for the stables ~~so as~~ to avoid hindering the work (the first load of ^inferior^ tiles sh^d be sent back) which will shortly be ready for tiling. The tiles for the offices and the main block sh^d be 6" x 10" when burned, and I am doubtful if Howell will be ready ~~for~~ ^with^ til~~ing~~^ing^es ^for^ the offices this year. Would it not be well to get a sample of this size from Donhead or elsewhere? I understand that they had good tiles at Donhead and would be accommodating there.[3] We shall also want hip & valley tiles to fit the pitch, and tile & half wide tiles for ^bond to^ verges and ⅔rd tiles for eaves course and ridge course – also ridge tiles.

The ch[imnely] pot Mr Hibbins shewed me was a good one, but the finish at the top would not do. I will send you a section for this so that you can get them made for the stables & offices. The pots to the main block will have to be oval on plan.

I complained to Mr Simmonds that the oak posts to stables had been painted! I do not know for what reason this had been done, but the paint will have to be scraped off.

Mr Wyndham was much pleased with the work generally, and with the progress made.

I enclose tracing of a ridge tile, wh' tiles sh^d be made ab^t 15" long, also a section of the upper edge for ch^y pots.

Y^{rs} truly | Ph: W.

LB-1, pp. 253-5

1 Hopton Wood limestone was quarried in Derbyshire and transported by rail and road to East Knoyle.
2 The traditional technique of including cow dung in mortar is still employed in parts of the world where farm animal dung is readily available.
3 The 1881 census records several brick makers in Mill Lane, Donhead St Andrew, Wiltshire.

196 • To Gertrude or Constance Astley, 29 November 1882

Draft/copy

[1, Raymond Buildings . . .]
Novr 29. 1882.

To Miss Astley
Arisaig H^{se} by Fort William N: B:

Dear Miss Astley

In answer to your letter of the 17th instant. If you should fail in getting whinstone of sufficient size to do the memorial¹ from stone got from your own ground it would seem to be hardly to the purpose to get that sort of stone from elsewhere – unless it could be got from somewhere nearby? Still I think, in that rude little churchyard with its ancient ruins standing by, the native stone would look more congruous than any imported stone would; but, if the whinstone is not to be come at I think <u>un</u>polished granite would be the next best, though, in that case, I should have to make a fresh design as the design you have is quite unsuited to the working of granite.

I enclose you a letter I have had from Mr Ramsay in answer to my request as to what rooms he had taken as wanting new paper &c. Would it not be well for you to come and see me when you are in London? I would have a book of Morris's & Co^s papers here and from this you could choose any variations from the papers now on the walls and, as I have the plans of the house, we could easily determine on the best for each ~~purpose~~ ᵣₒₒₘ? Also I could get patterns of the different paints made to suit the papers settled on, and the painters could match the colours from the patterns.

Believe me | Yours sincerely | Ph: W:

LB-2, pp. 1-2

---

1 See above, Letter 186.

197 • To General Augustus Fox Pitt-Rivers, 11 December 1882

Draft/copy

[1, Raymond Buildings . . .]
Dec[r] 11 1882

To General A: Pitt-Rivers
Rushmore Lodge by Salisbury
Dear General Pitt-Rivers.

(Rushmore)

I sent my assistant to measure the fire-place woodwork at Penywern Road on Friday[1] & I went myself in the afternoon and met the Cabinet maker there & directed him how & what to remove, ᵖᵃᶜᵏ and send to Rushmore. He told me that you had some old marble mantels which w[d] replace the woodwork. Will you be so good as to write to him & tell him where they are? I told him he had better not disturb the tile settings or remove the dog grates.[2] These latter are of no value to remove & to refix others would cost more than those removed were worth. My assistant was there again on Sat: and completed his measurements.

In answer to your letter of the 7th ins[t]. I have no objection to your proposed collaborated conceit but if Brer Jackass should saddle, bridle, and ʳⁱᵈᵉ to the devil ᵒⁿ Brer Fox please do not blame me. Something might be made of your A & your R but the P, as you have it, will not do at all. In any case I think the jest had better be cut in the oak cresting which is to come just under the coving of the roof of the wood canopy to the fireplace of hall.[3]

Yours very truly | Ph: W:

LB-2, p. 4

---

1 Pitt-Rivers's London residence was in Penywern Road, Brompton, until he moved in 1880 to 4 Grosvenor Gardens, Belgravia. He may have continued to own or to maintain an interest in the Penywern Road house.

2 Simple free-standing fire grates, which stand upon supports called dogs.
3 Pitt-Rivers seems to have been wanting to incorporate above the hall fireplace at Rushmore Lodge some kind of crest or motto, to his own design, incorporating his initials and middle name by illustrating the Fox and Stork fable of Aesop. PSW was less than convinced: see also next letter.

198 • To General Augustus Fox Pitt-Rivers, 15 December 1882

Draft/copy

[1, Raymond Buildings . . .]
Decr 15 1882

To General A: Pitt-Rivers
Rushmore Lodge by Salisbury
Dear General ^{Pitt}-Rivers.

(Rushmore)

Since receiving your letter of the 12 ins^t Mr Toten has called upon me and explained his case. He said that he had specified in his estimate that nothing was allowed for refitting the back room at N° 21 Penywern Road after the panelling tapestry &c were removed. As you, most likely, have a copy of his estimate you can see if what he says is correct.

I did not propose that the P, or central character of the Fox and Stork story should be "omitted"; what I meant was that, decoratively, the sketch of it, as it stood on your paper, would not do, as the bird and bottle would topple over and the Fox would lap-up the liquor. I do not say that the P is an impossible letter but, as a designer, I sh^d say it would be a "twister".

To get such a design $^{(altogether)}$ made would be something, in the way of $^{thought\ \&}$ care; but to get it carved in marble and set just in the front of all beholders would be more than difficult, and its obtrusive presence, trying. It seemed to me that it would be easier to get ^{it} done in wood, and that a good place for putting it ^{up} would be as part of the cresting just under the coving of the hood of the fireplace. [*sketch*] The scroll-work could be left in uncoloured oak and the story ^{be} gilded.

Your special admiration for the design of the middle letter put me in mind of the artist & critic. The artist asked his friend the critic what he thought of the central figure $^{in\ the\ artists\ picture,}$ and the critic said 'don't you think the legs are a little short?' on which the artist ~~said~~ ^{returned} 'too long you mean, too long; yes, they are a little too long'!!

Yours very truly. | Ph: W.

LB-2, pp. 5-6

199 • To John Henry Middleton, 13 February 1883

1, Raymond Buildings, Gray's Inn,| London.
Tues: Feb: 13. 1883

Dear Middleton[1]

Would not you be able to prepare a resolution, to be agreed to on Tuesday, in answer to the Dean of Peterborough who is to say that the tower is to be broken down?[2] Would not the points be

> The present lantern is a good example of one of the mediæval changes wh' have occurred in the history of the cathedral –
> That its height & character are well fitted for the indifferent foundation on wh' the church stands
> That it has for 500 years given ~~the~~ a marked character to the building so that its loss would be missed & regretted in future by all thoughtful people, &c &c

The Soc^y would urge upon the authorities to take the best precautions in removing the tower to meet the forces wh' will be in activity all round when the pressure now exercised by the tower on the 4 arms of the church at the Crossing is withdrawn, &c &c.

Yours | Ph: Webb.

P:S: No one on earth except, perhaps, Pearson,[3] would care two straws for what any modern arch^t w^d put in place of the present tower.

SPAB, Peterborough Cathedral file

---

1 John Henry Middleton (1846–96) was distinguished both as an art historian and archaeologist, though a long period of debilitating depression whilst an undergraduate took its toll on his long-term health. His expert knowledge of Roman antiquities resulted in specialised studies in 1885 and 1892. He was elected Slade Professor of Fine Art at Cambridge in 1886, awarded honorary doctorates from Cambridge (1893) and Oxford (1894), appointed director of the Fitzwilliam Museum in 1889, and became art director of the South Kensington Museum in 1892. The pressure of this final appointment threatened a recurrence of his former depression, and his death in 1896 was the result of an overdose (probably accidental) of morphia. PSW admired Middleton's erudition, and valued his membership of the SPAB.
2 See next letter.
3 For John Loughborough Pearson, see next letter, note 2.

200 • To John Perowne, Dean of Peterborough Cathedral, probably late February or early March 1883

Drafted on behalf of SPAB

S.P.A. Buildings to the very Reverend the Dean of Peterborough.[1]

The Committee of this society having seen the notices in the public newspapers as to the state of the central tower or lantern of Peterborough Cathedral ventures to address ~you,~ on a matter so momentous as that of the proposed rebuilding of the tower.[2]

The Committee wishes to express ~their~ ^{its} satisfaction that instant steps hav~ing~^e been taken under the direction of a skilled Architect to meet the danger hanging over one of the noblest buildings in England. As it will, evidently, be necessary to erect under and around the tower a shoring and scaffolding of ~enormous~ ^{immense} strength, the Committee would suggest that when this and other precautions have been taken to avoid collapse in this part of the fabric, a consultation should be held in the building under the direction of the Cathedral authorities and the architect, with the assistance of an engineer ^{or engineers} of great experience, to see if it would not be possible ~to~ so to ~support~ underpin, support and stay the tower that the necessity of taking it down and rebuilding it might be avoided.

SPAB, Peterborough Cathedral file

---

1 John James Stewart Perowne (1823–1904) was Dean of Peterborough Cathedral from 1878 until he was appointed Bishop of Worcester in 1891.
2 The poor condition of the central tower at Peterborough led the architect John Loughborough Pearson (1817–97) to condemn it as too dangerous. In 1883 it would be demolished and rebuilt, with argument focussing on how it should be replaced. 'Some people wanted the pointed east and west tower arches to be replaced by round Norman ones, while others suggested heightening the tower by one stage of work in the Norman style, using original stones . . . where possible and placing the Decorated stage above it.' Gerald Cobb, *English Cathedrals. The Forgotten Centuries. Restoration and Change from 1530 to the Present Day* (London: Thames and Hudson, 1980), p. 98.

201 • To Reverend John Perowne and Chapter of Peterborough Cathedral, 24 March 1883

Drafted on behalf of SPAB; an earlier pencil draft also survives

Peterborough Cathedral

<u>March 24 1883.</u>

To the very Revd The Dean and the Chapter of Peterborough Cathedral
Gentlemen.

The Committee of this Society fearing that its suggestions with regard to sustaining and repairing the lantern tower of the cathedral, as opposed to the proposal to pull it down and rebuild it, have not received the attention which such a proposition deserved, begs leave to reiterate its opinion that before one stone of the tower is ~raised,~ ^{lifted} a competent committee, aided by one or more civil engineers of acknowledged skill, should be formed to report upon the possibility of keeping the tower standing as it is save, only, with the necessary renewal of one or more of the piers, the strengthening of the foundations on which they stand, and the repairs of the superincumbent structure.

That it is within the power of English scientific skill to compass the safe preservation of so valuable a part of the ancient fabric this Committee fully believes and, if ^(this is) so, the public would not be fairly treated if this Society did not earnestly press on the guardians of the Cathedral the necessity there is for the assurance that all possible plans for securing the tower have been honestly canvassed before giving in to an acknowledgment of defeat & pulling it down.

[*added*] I have the honour to be | Gentlemen | Your most obedient Servant Thackeray Turner | Secretary[1]

SPAB, Peterborough Cathedral file

---

1 See below, Letter 208, note 6.

202 • To Reverend William Henry Metcalfe, April 1883

Drafted on behalf of SPAB

The Society for the Protection of Ancient Buildings

To the Rev^d W:H: Metcalfe
Vicar of Ottery St Mary: Devon.[1]

Dear Sir

Your letter of the 31^(st) of March last was ~~duly~~ laid before a Committee of this Society and received the attention due to a matter of so much importance as the preservation of the well known church of your parish.[2]

I am directed by the Committee to say that, after careful consideration, it is unable to express any sorrow for ignorance which has not been successfully laid to its charge save, perhaps, that the Society may, happily, have been misinformed as to any further proposition with regard to alterations to the building.

The Church of Ottery St Mary is so exceptional in its general character and particular features that~~, for many years~~ it has been visited ~~by~~ ^(very constantly) ^(by) archæologists and art students with both pleasure and profit and, though it suffered severely when it was scoured almost at the beginning of the, so called, restoration movement still, up to within a few years, its general ~~aspect~~ ^(appearance) had not been tampered with. The decorations applied to the ^(interior of the) south tower-transept have been done with the well known skill of one of the ablest of modern architects[3] and, no doubt, the intention of the munificent donor of the work was most praiseworthy; but this committee, and it is persuaded ~~that~~ a great majority of those people who are skilled in historical and artistic matters, have seen with dismay the disastrous effect upon the ~~original~~ perfect balance, ~~and~~ breadth, and simplicity of this, one of the delightful examples of English originality and beauty in the list of its mediæval monuments.[4]

This Committee cannot agree with you that such decoration in such a building is a mere matter of taste; ^surely it is rather a matter of fact that before these decorations were applied the building was almost unaltered in its mediæval appearance and that, now, one part of it is very markedly and unnecessarily modernised. Unhappily this work is done, & can hardly be undone, but this Committee would ask you, in all sincerity, to add your ~~influence~~ ^persuasion to what influence it has in protesting, in season & out of season, against any further change ^beyond the necessary repairs being made to a building which, ~~beyond the necessary repairs,~~ should be spared from any kind of experiment whatever either in surface decoration or structural alteration.

SPAB

---

1 William Henry Metcalfe (b. 1838/9) was vicar of St Mary's, Ottery St Mary, from 1874 until 1890.
2 St Mary's was consecrated in 1260.
3 William Butterfield oversaw the restoration in 1849–52, a report from the Exeter Diocesan Church Architectural Society in 1841 describing the church 'as having a degraded and neglected appearance'. The choir screen had been taken away earlier in the century, 'and Butterfield completed the process of opening out the building into one parochial church. The floor of the transepts and of the western part of the chancel was lowered to the level of the nave . . . In 1878, the walls of the south transept were tiled in mosaics, out of the keeping with the mediaeval work, but considered "beautiful" by the Victorian "restorers".' John A. Whitham, *The Church of St. Mary of Ottery* (Gloucester: The British Publishing Company, 1979), pp. 15–16.
4 This pinpoints the essential irreconcilability between the views of the SPAB conservationists and even the most well-intentioned of restoration architects. For PSW, Butterfield's work at Ottery St Mary could not be anything other than wrong-headed, and the fact that it can be held to typify one phase of Butterfield's use of colour captures everything that was objectionable about it. '[Butterfield's] churches of the 1840s are the simplest. White walls, brown seats and dark roof timbers always set the tone. . . . Perhaps the supreme example of this first phase is the wonderfully light and creamy brown stone interior of Ottery St Mary, where Butterfield picked out the medieval vaulting in blue, red and gold, and the windows glow with the same primary colours.' Paul Thompson, *William Butterfield* (London: Routledge & Kegan Paul, 1971), p. 272.

203 • To Percy Wyndham, 1 May 1883

Draft/copy

[1, Raymond Buildings . . .]
May 1. 1883

To Hon' Percy Wyndham M:P:
44 Belgrave Square. S.W.

Dear Mr Wyndham

(Clouds H^se)

I rec^d your letter on Saturday evening but decided to wait a day or two before answering it. I am exceedingly sorry that any of the work at Clouds should have been so contrary to your pleasure that you should have felt obliged to make up your mind to have it removed ᵃⁿᵈ ᵃᵗ ᵍʳᵉᵃᵗ ᶜᵒˢᵗ.[1] It is certainly true that, if the buff glazed bricks in the stables have to be replaced by another facing, it would be better done before any other work is fixed there, but I feel that now is not a good or safe time in which to judge of the effect of the said bricks. When the boxes and stalls are made up, the walls whitened and the rack & manger fittings in place the whole thing will have a quite different appearance.

As these bricks are built-in solid and are part of the substance & strength of the walls, if they must be removed I shall have to make build up a half brick lining instead in addition to fixing the coloured tiles you are in favour of: added to which the tiles are in themselves never so secure as the solid glazed bricks. I am going down to Knoyle this evening and will consider the matter there.[2]

I am obliged to you for the pleasant expressions of approval of the great body of the work at Clouds given in the former part of your letter but I am afraid I re-read them of rather as sops to Cerberus[3] and the pleasure was somewhat qualified. Will you be so good as to make an appointment to go with me to the Pancras Iron Company's rooms to choose the stable fittings as I should like to have settled which mangers racks &c you would wish used before giving Estcourt drawings for the work which will be in combination with them.[4]

I shall be back here tomorrow night, but I have to see Rogers Field as to the drainage &c on Thursday, but I could go with you on Friday or on a day which would suit you in next week.

Yours very truly. | Ph: W:

LB-2, pp. 10-12

---

1 After visiting Clouds on 21 April, PWY wrote of his reactions to the work in progress, expressing a reservation about the stables. "'I was ... very much pleased with the house. ... I realized how much bigger the rooms look now the house is nearer finished ... I cannot get over my dislike to the buff colour at the horses' heads and am determined to change them. I have given myself plenty of time and have tried to convince myself but cannot do it." He spoke to [Estcourt] and discovered that the glazed faces could be cut off the bricks and replaced with a facing of grey glazed tiles. The work would cost £175.' *Dakers*, pp. 67–8.

2 In fact, nothing was done about the bricks. A year later, PWY had begun to shift his ground, perhaps as much to please PSW as anything else. 'I was at Clouds yesterday and liked what I liked before as much, and disliked what I disliked before perhaps rather less' (25 June 1884). By December 1884 he had given way altogether. 'I took my coachman over to Clouds the other day and he was much pleased with his quarters, and not having a sensitive eye does not mind the yellow glazed tiles.' *Dakers*, p. 68.

3 The multi-headed dog of ancient Greek and Roman mythology, who guarded the entrance to the underworld.

4 The St Pancras Ironwork Co., describing themselves as 'Engineers, Ironfounders, and Smiths', was based in Old Saint Pancras Road, opposite Old Saint Pancras Church.

204 • To Salisbury town clerk, 12 May 1883

Drafted on behalf of SPAB; a first draft also exists

The Society for the Protection of Ancient Buildings
12th May 1883

To the Town Clerk of the Corporation of Salisbury

Dear Sir

The Committee of this Society, having received very valuable assistance from you, at the time when successful efforts were made to preserve the historic fabric of Audley House in Salisbury,[1] ventures again to ask your ~~assistance~~ help with regard to the ancient bridge, called Crane Bridge, which spans the small stream adjoining Audley House.[2]

The Committee learns that the small scheme for widening this bridge is again under the consideration of the town authorities, and that it is proposed to take away one or more of the piers and to cover the space of two or three arches with an iron construction in combination with what may remain of the ancient stone bridge.[3] Anyone who has noticed this way of dealing with old bridges – many of which in late years have been so maltreated – will be aware, at once, that this interesting remnant of mediæval Salisbury, if so treated, will not only be ruined, but will be treated with gratuitous contempt.

The bridge has evidently been widened at some former time and, with such skill that, the more ancient part of the bridge is still to be seen faithfully serving the purpose for which, so many years back it was built.

If it is now necessary to make any alteration to the bridge (this Committee has received no information of such necessity) surely it cannot be quite out of the power of modern science to do this work without such a bungling contrivance as a piece of common railroad disfigurement?

If, Sir, you can assist the Society by bringing this matter before the Town Council, or other proper authority, or in any other way helping this Society to press upon the town's-people the necessity there is to scrutinise very ~~carefully~~ closely all dealing with their antiquities, this Committee will be much indebted to you.

I am Dear Sir – On behalf of the Committee – | &c &c

SPAB, Crane Bridge Salisbury file

---

1 In 1880, Audley House in Crane Street, Salisbury, the oldest parts of which date from the fifteenth century and which from 1634 had served as the Workhouse, was threatened with demolition. A campaign to save it resulted in the building being purchased by a member of the cathedral chapter. It is now the administrative centre for the Salisbury diocese.

2 Although there was a bridge as early as 1300, the present Crane Bridge, over the Avon, dates from the fifteenth century.
3 This had been brought to the attention of the SPAB by Margaret Hussey, of the Close, Salisbury (9 May 1883, *SPAB, Crane Bridge Salisbury file*).

205 • To Jane Morris, 16 May 1883

1, Raymond Buildings, Gray's Inn, | *London.*
May 16. 1883

My dear Janey

Your letter did not come to me as quite from the dead, for I had been, a many times, living with you in thought over your great trouble. Morris has always put aside his nervousness when I asked him to tell me how you were getting on.[1]

Your letter came to me on Monday after my return from Welwyn and, as I shall not see my brother for a fortnight now, I will write to him. When I got your letter I wrote to Morris to ask him for a doctor's description of the complaint so that I might put more clearly to my brother what was wanted: of course I am not sure that he may know of such a place but, if he does not, he may know someone who does. As soon as I get his (my brother's) answer I will let you know what he says.[2]

I have always thought it lucky that, for the time, you were able to go to such a fresh scene as the place you are staying at and, remembering what the weather has been for so long a time, the place could hardly have been a better one for you all – and now the weather looks as if it meant to trifle with our feelings no more, for a while; and even smudgy London looks as fair as such a monstrous wen can look.

I went yesterday evening to see the working man – Tinworth's – terra cotta models of new Testament story.[3] They are really interesting, having a character which can only come of freedom from convention. I sh^d like you to go and see them when you come to town.

With kindest love to Jenny & May. | Believe me
yours affectionately Philip Webb:

BL Add 45342, ff. 59-60

---

1 Jane had been unwell through the winter, spending time with a carer first at Bournemouth and then at Lyme Regis, which is probably where she was still when PSW wrote. See *CLJM*, p. 127, note 1.
2 Presumably he was hoping that Harry Webb would suggest either a healthy location for Jane's symptoms, or some kind of specialist clinic. WM mentioned Jane's health when sending birthday wishes and some money to his mother. 'Janey is not so well as when she first came back from the country [*probably Kelmscott Manor*].... I would have sent [money] before, but I have had so much to pay with Janey's illness & all that to say truth I have been somewhat pressed.' WM to Emma Shelton Morris, 23 March 1883, *CLWM*, II.

3 The ceramic artist, George Tinworth (1843–1913), after a childhood of exceptional hardship, worked for the Doulton ceramic factory in Lambeth from 1867 until his death. In addition to producing pottery in the familiar Doulton salt-glazed stoneware, he also made larger terracotta pieces which were displayed annually at the Royal Academy and which had won JR's admiration. PSW attended an exhibition devoted to Tinworth's terracotta panels on biblical subjects at 9 Conduit Street, Regent Street. The subjects included *The Release of Barabbas*, *Entry into Jerusalem*, and *The Descent from the Cross*.

206 • To William Thomas Tate, 13 June 1883

Draft/copy

[1, Raymond Buildings . . .]
June 13. 1883

To. W: Thomas Tate Esq[re]
Stranton Green Hartlepool[1]

Dear Sir.

I had hoped to have answered your letter of June the 7th by sending my memoranda for ~~your~~ assisting you in building your house, but, imperative work intervened and delayed me and I could not get done by deputy what I wanted to express. I now send you a carefully considered arrangement of plan to enable you to go into the matter with your architect.[2] In so far as I am concerned, you are at liberty to use the plan in any way that may suit your convenience. I also send a sheet of memoranda to help you in advising with your Architect as to what you want done in detail.

I need scarcely say that you would do well to insist that no ornament should be applied to the house. If all ornament were omitted in modern houses they would be much less offensive. Unfortunately, ill understood and therefore bad ornament is much cheaper than good construction. In the matter of fine grates, "Mess[rs] Longden, Phœnix Foundry Sheffield" would supply you with casts from any of my patterns, which you will be at liberty to use.[3]

Yours truly. | Ph: W:

LB-2, p. 13

---

1 William Thomas Tate (1843–1921), bank accountant.
2 PSW designed Hill House in Greatham, near Hartlepool, for Tate, but pressures of work led him to entrust the working drawings and oversight of the construction work to the Hartlepool architect, James Barry. PSW refused any fee. See *Kirk*, pp. 226–7 and 300.
3 PSW often used Longden and Co. of Sheffield as suppliers of cast-iron fireplaces, stoves and other kitchen apparatus. 'Tate followed Webb's advice to avoid ornament on the exterior – and indeed also in the interior, which has characteristic Webb fittings, including fireplaces with bracketed mantelpieces and grates by Longden to Webb's design.' *Kirk*, p. 227.

207 • To Canon William Greenwell, 22 June 1883

Drafted on behalf of SPAB, and dated in a different hand. Amendments in pencil.

22 June 1883

To The Revd Canon Greenwell

Dear Sir.

The Committee of our Society has ^{since my last letter to you} seen in the "Architect" newspaper of the 9th of June 1883 a report of certain remarks made by you at a meeting of the Durham and Northumberland Archæological association, on Langley Castle, Northumberland.[1]

The Committee was pleased to have its attention ^{again drawn} to so valuable a remnant of a north country stronghold before any work had been undertaken in alteration of its present condition.

In Parker's Domestic Architecture of the Middle Ages, there is a paragraph noticing the neglected state of the building under the care of the trustees of Greenwich Hospital;[2] and it would be satisfactory to all students of historical architecture in England if they could be assured that the present possessor of the fabric would give skilfully directed attention to its preservation. ^{Evidence of this neglect is seen in the diversion of Stream into the main building where it forms a pond.}

On turning to page 332 of Parker's book – Vol. II, it will be seen that this building is a massively constructed border castle of great strength, evidently built, chiefly, for purposes of defence, when the comfort and convenience of even those days were subordinated to the special purpose of the work.

You most satisfactorily state your strong views against "restoration" but you are reported to have said that Mr Fowler (the Architect into whose hands the building would be entrusted) "would not destroy anything he could help, and would not put into the Castle any work of an ambitious or pretentious character". Now this Committee thought that it fully understood what was in your mind when so expressing yourself, but it also thought that both the proprietor, the Architect, and many others might consider that no ^{real} injury would come to the building from the adaptation of its ancient and peculiar accommodation to the requirements of a modern English gentleman's house.[3]

At our Committee meeting there were several members of large experience both of the characteristics of such strongholds as Langley Castle, and of the accepted necessities of modern house requirements of even the ruder type, and they were aghast at what would certainly happen to this noble building in refitting it (even with the best intentions as to respecting its present completeness of example) for modern use.

The Committee believed that if the building were simply roofed in, roughly floored, and used as farm storehouse and cattleshed, it would suffer less serious injury than would surely happen to it from the proposed transformation; and the Committee also wishes me to ask you if you could ~~not~~ communicate with the proprietor and the architect and get clearly stated information of what was proposed to be done, before any stone of such a splendid specimen of mediæval England were touched in the way of alteration?

SPAB, Langley Castle, Northumberland file

---

1 The Society had visited Langley Castle on 31 May, the guest of the collier and archaeologist Cadwallader John Bates (1853–1902), who bought the Castle from the trustees of Greenwich Hospital. In 1890 he served as High Sheriff of Northumberland.
2 'It is now the property of Greenwich Hospital, and much neglected by the trustees of that establishment. The interior has evidently been destroyed by fire.' John Henry Parker, *Some Account of Domestic Architecture in England, From Edward I to Richard II* (Oxford: John Henry Parker, 1853), p. 334.
3 Cadwallader John Bates was vice-president of the Society of Antiquaries of Newcastle-upon-Tyne. After his death, the Society noted that Langley Castle was, 'with the assistance of Mr. Hodgson Fowler, architect, of Durham, converted into a stately dwelling-house, sufficiently furnished with all modern comforts'.

208 • To Reverend Francis Browne Newman, 7 August 1883

Drafted on behalf of SPAB; an earlier draft also exists

The Society for the Protection of Ancient Buildings

To the Rev^d F: B: Newman.[1] Burton Latimer Rectory.
Hon' Secretary to the Northants and Oakham Architectural Society.

Sir

The present state of the Steeple of Irthlingborough Church, Northants' having been brought under the notice of a Committee of this society it was decided – after receiving the report of the Secretary of the Society who had visited the Church – to send to Irthlingborough two members[2] who were experienced in old buildings to examine into the condition of the structure of the tower and to report upon it. This visit was made in last month, and the gentlemen were kindly assisted in their examination by Mr Joseph Peacock, the architect,[3] who conducted them over the building and much assisted them with his experience and local knowledge. The members of the society were also aided by a gentleman who was there engaged in measuring and making drawings, and who most willingly answered questions and gave ^{much} useful information.

Undoubtedly the tower is in a very critical condition and must be the cause of great anxiety to the custodians of the Church. It appeared to the surveyors after close examination that the foundation itself of the steeple had not given way. This seemed to be corroborated by the fact that, about the year 1807, a buttress of great bulk, height and of enormous weight had been added to the Eastern face of the tower and, apparently, without further depressing the foundation.[4]

The cracks in the walls which were, most likely, the cause of this buttress having been built were evidently stayed by its support, but the cracks through the walls of the other faces were too surely in an active state. All round the tower at its base the faces of the ^walls shew signs of being crushed between the weight from above and the resisting foundation below, so that it appeared certain that the bulk of the walling was becoming disintegrated, and the upper stage of the tower below the lantern was spreading outwards, tearing the walls of the base of the lantern apart.

The lantern itself, of much originality in design and of great beauty, seems to have been built with greater care and with better mortar than the rest of the tower and is, practically, in a sound condition.

That this steeple of Irthlingborough should, if possible, be sustained there can be no two opinions, as to pull it down and reconstruct it – apart from the great cost of such a work – would destroy its value: added to which, before it could be taken down, it would have to be shored and strutted to make it safe for those engaged on the work.

In any case this Committee supposes that the tower will not be allowed to fall as, in falling, it would probably do untold damage to the adjoining church, fine vaulted crypts &c and would endanger life.

As, Sir, your architectural Society, which has so wisely undertaken the cost of making careful drawings of the tower as it at present stands, would be able to influence people in the county and others interested in such a valuable remnant of unmutilated Northamptonshire art, I am therefore directed to appeal to you to urge upon the attention of all so interested the necessity there is of at once taking steps to put up a scaffolding around the tower, and afterwards to apply in the most careful way a large mass of bonding, shoring and strutting, the most important part of which would be this banding or cradling. This banding should be done at several stages, bolting timbers completely round the walls, filling out between the buttresses, and sustaining with perpendiculars to keep the cradling from sliding; adding on the inside occasional stiffened floors or stagings with the necessary planking and strutting to the faces of the walls. As soon as the cradling with its supports is secured a perfect system of diagonal shoring should be applied.

If this temporary support to the tower should be determined upon and the risk of sudden collapse of the fabric met, there would be time and security in which to consider what should be done permanently to sustain the weight and support and repair the walls.

If, as this Committee believes, the foundation on which the tower is built is a sound one, it also believes that the tower could be permanently sustained. Though this work should be schemed out by an engineer or other expert accustomed to deal with great weights the Committee would suggest, as one opinion only, the principle of building up on the inside from the foundation to the lantern a complete tower of hard brick in cement, octagon on the inside, and to the outline of the inside of the tower against its walls. At certain points to lay across the new brick tower iron girders or joists projecting into the old walls, vaulting each girder stage with cement concrete between the joists, banding the tower on the outside with iron and tieing through from wall to wall with strong iron ties resting on the top of the concrete floors. In addition to this, solid brick blocks with a short iron joist in each of them should project at intervals from the internal brick tower into the old walls beyond, and the whole thoroughly grouted with liquid cement. If such a work as this were well done, it would secure the tower from collapsing or spreading, would sustain part of the weight of the tower itself, and the whole of the lantern on the top, and would give a core of great rigidity for applying any other safeguard.

The Committee [thinks] that the question before the guardians of the building is this: That it cannot be entertained that the steeple should be allowed to fall; That to take it down a strong and safe scaffolding would be necessary; That as this scaffolding was being fixed particular examination could be made as to the weakest parts of the building which could be at once secured, and that afterwards, [at] a comparatively small cost, shoring cradling could be added so as to make the work safe while the workmen were engaged in preparing and executing [carrying out] any scheme which might be resolved upon for sustaining the tower in a substantial way.

I am directed, Sir, by this Committee, to ask you to give the matter your consideration and to lay this letter before the authorities and others interested, as an outside expression of opinion formed on the necessity of considering at once how to <u>save</u> Irthlingborough steeple.

[*pencil addition to first draft*] Sent to Middleton[5] for him to overhaul & send to Turner for copying & sending off.[6]

August 7 1883.

SPAB, Irthlingborough file

---

1 Francis Browne Newman (1826–1901), rector of St Mary the Virgin, Burton Latimer, 1872–95.
2 The survey was made on 27 July by PSW and John Henry Middleton. See above, Letter 199.
3 The Scottish-born architect, Joseph Peacock (1821–93) undertook his training in Worthing, Sussex.
4 St Peter's, Irthlingborough, of twelfth-century origin, was renowned for its lantern tower. Despite the earnestness of the SPAB's campaign for its careful repair, the tower was pulled down and rebuilt in 1889–93. The new tower, lacking its original sloping buttress, was rededicated in 1893, and its peal of bells increased from six to eight.
5 See above, Letter 199, note 1.
6 Hugh Thackeray Turner (HTT, 1853–1937) had been appointed part-time paid secretary of the SPAB on 13 December 1882. From January 1883, all letters sent on behalf of the Committee carried his signature; he was doubtless the author of many of those concerning individual projects, but PSW drafted a significant number of others. For an account of HTT's own career as a church architect, which ran concurrently with his work for the SPAB, see Robin Stannard, 'The ecclesiastical work of Hugh Thackeray Turner', in Geoff Brandwood, ed., *Seven Church Architects 1830–1930* (London: The Ecclesiological Society, 2010), pp. 121–46. I am grateful to Robin Stannard for information on a number of matters relating to HTT.

209 • To George and Caroline Boyce, 8 August 1883

1, Raymond Buildings, Gray's Inn, | London.
Aug: 8. 1883

My dear Boyce, and Madame also.

It was kind of you to write so soon, and I hardly expected to hear of you for a fortnight or so. They accused you of all sorts of malignity at New Place for not taking it on your way, but I pacified them by saying how unwise it w^d have been for you to stop on your journey with the inevitable lumber, and they gave-in to the reasoning of the wise-one. Yanwath rejoiced you more than you allowed yourself to express, I am sure;[1] though, considering the fearful peril ~~of~~ from the ring nosed bull I can hardly wonder at your caution. How I should have flown out of the field, and my wits at the same time, I know too well. Heaven save me from a bull, even an Irish one. I fancy your point of view of Yanwath must be from the back – i.e. with your back to the iron way looking to the S: W: with the beck somewhat fronting you on the right hand; but I may be wrong, wh' w'd be strange indeed. Brougham Castle gatehouse is a noble tower and – from Parker – not so horridly ruined as to be useless f^m a reasonable point of view: added to which, a castle should be in ruin if any building can look satisfactorily in a picture in that state – a castle in ruin is a peaceful looking object.[2] How about the mill, attached to the Castle, wh' Parker mentions as still having some of its wheels? Brougham Hall is, I suppose, still used as a house and therefore will be for having flunkies in the foreground, plush breeches all complete or, may be, they would be ruined too under the coat tails! When you get settled, either you or Mrs Boyce will be good enough to tell me more of the sweet antiquity you must have about you: but no more of bulls I beg ^of you, – my very flesh did creep when I thought of the ring in his nose and his long swinging trot.

Middleton and I went down to Irthlingborough on Friday last, and found the Ch' tower there even finer than we had expected and also in worse condition.[3] The arch^t who met us and is, strange-to-say, anxious to save it, has "restored" the church itself – wh' he was proud in shewing us – in such a way as to have put both of us in high fever. He was absolutely unconscious of what he had done and, tho' a good-natured fellow, was incapable of understand^g the matter of old art in any way. Also, I'm afraid his constructive or engineering power is far below what is wanted for dealing with such a crumbling mass as the tower is. I believe the tower could be saved, with care, and some notion of cause and effect, and I should like to try, but the work would be taxing and somewhat costly. I think the only effort that will be made will be to get money enough to pull it down & rebuild it – say at a cost of £5000: but they can't get enough money to keep it standing – say at a cost of half that sum. Tis a bad lookout I'm afraid, as the landlords about there are all very rich and profoundly careless as to what will happen – and that shortly, unless it be looked to at once – namely, it <u>must</u> fall. I felt some spice of fear lest it should come down while I was on its parapet under the lantern.

On our way by train we had two Irish – man & woman – going to Liverpool on way to America, and it was a curious thing to hear them, & their friends on the Euston platform, cursing the English, with a mixture of whole Earse[4] and broken English, finishing with a shout of joy with, "Carey"! as much as to say that that made amends – his death – for a good deal.[5]

I found the Welwyn folk all right on Sunday, but it was misty-wet all day and I got not other walking than continual pacing of the garden, wh' was lovely enough. It has been a hot bath of moisture here ever since & today there has been heavy rain. I hope you are better off, but am suspicious of the neighbouring mountains supplying you with more than enough of water.

Wallis looked in here last night and he wanted to know of you, as you were not at the meeting,[6] he said, (I suppose there must have been a meeting of the O.W. ^{Colour} Society)[7] and he did not know you were gone. There, blessings on you both, and much luck do I wish you, and freedom from the horns of such a dilemma as those of the ringed one.

Yours always sincerely | Philip Webb.

BL Add 45354, ff. 187-8

---

1 GPB and his wife were staying at or near Eamont Bridge, in Cumbria, GPB sketching and painting. Yanwath was the neighbouring village.
2 The thirteenth-century Brougham Castle is situated on the south bank of the river Eamont, about two miles south-east of Penrith, in Cumbria. The ruins were painted by Turner, and also inspired Wordsworth (in *The Prelude*). The owner in 1883, Henry James Tufton, first Baron Hothfield (1844–1926), a member of the Cumberland and Westmorland Antiquarian Society, was sensitive to the historical value of his possession. 'As far as the castle's structure was concerned . . . he wished above all to leave well alone.' Henry Summerson, 'The History of the Castle', in Henry Summerson et al, *Brougham Castle, Cumbria*, Cumberland and Westmoreland Antiquarian and Archaeological Society, Research Series, VIII (1998), p. 72.
3 See previous letter.
4 Meanings and spellings vary: here, either Scots Gaelic, or Irish.
5 The Irish nationalist, James Carey (1845–1883) had been shot dead days earlier, on 29 July. He had been complicit in the murders of Thomas Henry Burke, Permanent Undersecretary at the Irish Office and Lord Frederick Cavendish, Chief Secretary for Ireland, in Phoenix Park, Dublin, in May 1882. After arrest, Carey gave evidence against fellow conspirators, and whilst on the run was killed on board a ship travelling from Cape Town to Natal by an Irish republican who discovered his identity.
6 The usual Thursday-night meeting of the SPAB committee. For Henry Wallis, see above, Letter 96, note 12.
7 The Old Water-Colour Society, of which GPB was a member.

210 • To Lord Crewe, about 12 August 1883

Drafted on behalf of SPAB

The Society for the Protection of Ancient Buildings

To. The Hon' Lord Crewe[1]

My Lord

As honorary Secretary of this society I beg leave to inform you that we have received a report from a skilled Archæologist and trusted correspondent – a member of our Soc[y]: - informing us with regard to Astbury Church[2] near Congleton in Cheshire, that some steps are to be taken during the putting up ~~a~~ new organ in the North aisle of the Chancel of this Church ~~of a new organ~~ which may involve the removal of a parclose screen,[3] a fine carved oak pulpit, and the cutting into and destroying the completeness of one of the few remaining perfect examples of English Rood-screen work.[4]

That such ~~ruthless~~ destruction of ~~work~~ ancient art of exceptional value should be ~~entertained~~ contemplated for a moment by the custodians of the church, this Society can hardly believe, as Architects, and other advisers of Rectors & Church Wardens are daily becoming more aware of the priceless value of our national monuments ~~of ancient art,~~ and particularly of the rarer specimens of original fittings preserved in our Churches. It is probable therefore that the Rector & Church Wardens of Astbury have not been fully ~~cautioned~~ informed as to the irreparable injury which would arise from displacing or truncating any ~~portion~~ parts of the items of furniture above named, and I feel sure that your Lordship will consider that this society is only doing its duty by calling the attention of yourself, and other persons of cultivation and responsibility in the County of Chester, ~~as~~ to any danger which would seem ~~to be approaching~~ to threaten injury to any of the fragments ~~remaining in the Country~~ of those works of artistic beauty and invaluable historical fact which may, by rare good fortune, still remain in this Country. I ~~would~~ ask your Lordship therefore if you would, in a friendly way, use your influence to urge upon the custodians of the Church at Astbury,[5] the wisdom of reconsidering, before it may be too late, any scheme which may be ~~under consideration~~ contemplated for putting up in such a position in the church a merely modern piece of furniture which would in any way involve the destruction or disturbance of parts of the building which should, surely, be sacred in the ~~minds~~ eyes of all thoughtful and educated people.

Copied on to Society's paper and sent to Morris for his amendment or signature, and to be sent to Lord Crewe, 23 Hill Street Berkeley Square at once.

Dated Aug 12. 1883. | Ph.W.

SPAB

---

1 Hungerford Crewe, third Baron Crewe (1812–94), of Crewe Hall in Cheshire, was a fellow of the Society of Antiquaries.
2 St Mary's, Newbold Astbury, Cheshire. There was a church in Saxon times: the present building is of Norman origin. Some restoration work had taken place in 1862.

3 'A screen or railing in a church enclosing an altar, tomb, etc, or separating a chapel, etc from the main body of the church.' (*OED*).
4 'The chief glory of the church is the Rood Screen of fan-tracery, of 15th century construction; the Choir Stalls and Parclose Screens are of the same date. The Rood Screen . . . suffered much from the paint and whitewash of the Puritans . . . [The Pulpit] is of the Tudor period, though it is evident that it was only placed in its present position after the removal of the "Three-decker" in the 19th century.' J.E. Gordon Cartlidge, *A Short History of the Church of St. Mary of Astbury, Cheshire* (Congleton: rev. edn., 1970), [p. 9].
5 The rector was John Edmeades Colyer (d. 1888).

211 • To Kate Faulkner, 20 August 1883

1, Raymond Buildings, Gray's Inn, | *London.*
Monday Aug: 20. '83

My dear Kate[1]

It was kind of you to write and let me know how "the mother" and you were getting-on, and all you said pleased me except as to the scraping of S[t] Peter's Ch:,[2] and your determination to come back to London so soon as the 28th! Are you bound, in the way ᵒᶠ lodging or anything other than a virtuous resolve, to be back at work so soon? The wisdom of the mother would tell you that to get the benefit of a change, time must be allowed to work.

Of course I cannot say but that it may be necessary for you to come back so quickly, but, if your intention is only governed by virtue, you had better take honestly to vice and stay where you are for another week at least. Be guided for once by my superior intelligence and matured judgment and stay longer, unless it be really impossible for you to do so.

Last ~~week~~ ᵐᵒⁿᵗʰ I had to borrow some money to carry on with, but this month I can let you and your mother have some to "have a fling" with, and cast care over the North Foreland into the vasty deep.[3] Be advised and – who knows – but I might come down and have a drinking bout with you both in another week? I am sorry to say I can't manage it this week, for my work has me by the leg, as people, during their holidays, have time to provide me ʷⁱᵗʰ occupation in turning the mill for their fancies.

I hope Charles got off pleasantly and that, between the spasms of S.S,[4] he is laying siege to the heart of the lovely US female.[5] She <u>must</u> be lovely, single, and free from all bonds except scrip, which – for all I know, may be no bond. This is nonsense, so I will leave off.

I saw Jenny Morris yesterday and her father too. Jenny is much stronger and will, I hope, do well in her quiet farm home. She seemed more cheery and herself, in all ways, than I have seen her for a long time, which made me, metaphorically, to skip with joy.

If you can find time and inclination to tell me more of your doings, and if you hear any news of Charles and let me know it also, I shall be glad.

With kindest love to the mother – Believe me
Yours every sincerely Philip Webb.

V&A, AAD

1 PSW was extremely fond of KF (1841–98), the younger sister of Lucy Orrinsmith and Charles Faulkner, 'a designer of fabrics, wallpapers and ceramic tiles produced by Morris & Co., and Jeffrey & Co., best known for her gesso-work'. Emma Ferry, '"The other Miss Faulkner": Lucy Orrinsmith and the 'Art at Home Series'", *JWMS*, XIX (Summer 2011), p. 51.
2 KF was staying in or near North Foreland, a headland on the Kent coast at the easternmost point of the Isle of Thanet. The church of St Peter-in-Thanet is twelfth century, with a Norman nave, Early English chancel and later Perpendicular features. It was extensively restored, beginning in 1860.
3 'I can call spirits from the vasty deep.' *1 Henry IV* III.i.53.
4 Seasickness.
5 This refers to CF taking a sea voyage to Italy, via Gibraltar, PSW imagining a shipboard romance for him. See below, Letter 227.

212 • To Mary Anne Ewart, 14 September 1883

Draft/copy

[1, Raymond Buildings . . .]
Sep: 14 1883

To Miss Ewart.[1]
The Peacock Hotel Rowsley, Bakewell.

Dear Miss Ewart

I duly received your letter of the 8th inst with its inclosure of Mr Bray's letter, and also yours, this morning, of yesterday's date.[2] Since I saw you I have been engaged on the plans, sections &c in trying to bring the house into shape and convenience at a lower cost. After trying several ways the plans have resolved themselves into the number and disposition of rooms &c as shewn on the accompanying tracing. You will be able to lay the new tracing over the old one and see at a glance how, in going over all the parts, I have made the reductions.

With regard to the estimate: I have gone into this as carefully as is possible at the present time, and I think I am safe in saying that the house as indicated on the new tracing can be built (not including the papering and final painting, which should not be done for a year or two after the house is built) for £4,300. I do not think the house could be built for less money (soundly), without beginning the design again on a different scheme. I am really anxious that you should not spend more money than you would consider to be wise on your part, therefore I should be glad if, between now & when I see you again, you would consider whether it would be better to throw over the present scheme and begin again, or not?

It seems to me that if I should meet Mr Bray on the ground it would be well for you to be with us, as many things could be settled at once which would, otherwise, be deferred. I could arrange to go to Ewhurst on Tuesday the 25th of September and, if this would suit you and you could send me an answer at once, I would write to Mr Bray and let him know. He said in his letter that he could meet me in "this month" if I gave him a few days' notice.

It would be quite convenient to me to see you here either on Thursday or Friday the 20th or 21st between 10 and 12 o'clock in the morning, if you could let me know which day you would call. I have noted your remarks about fencing and would speak to you about the same.

Yours truly | Ph: W:

LB-2, pp. 16-17

---

1 Mary Anne Ewart (1830–1911), daughter of William Ewart, Liberal MP, was a supporter of educational and training opportunities for young women. She was a founder member of the SPAB.
2 In the next letter, Bray is described as Mary Ewart's 'landlord' – presumably the owner of the land on which she wished to build at Ewhurst, in Surrey. PSW designed Coneyhurst for her, consisting of a five-bedroom house, with cottage and stables. See *Kirk*, pp. 227–9 and 300.

213 • To George Price Boyce, 26 September 1883

Annotated 'rec^d at Eamont Bridge'

1, Raymond Buildings, Gray's Inn, | London, W.C.
Wed: Sep: 26. 1883

My dear Boyce

Your letter was a surprise to me this morning; I had thought that you were given over to perpetual silence in order to avoid having another letter full of bad jokes from me.

I cannot think the beginning of your letter was rose coloured, but rather that it was liver coloured, and I think therefore that you are not very well, for I much doubt what you say of your work: some painters are over-nasty; you I think are a little over-nice with regard to your pictures and that, as every artist worth anything makes his aim higher than he can attain-to, you are put out a bit that you have not reached your ideal – faith, my friend, I cannot trust you on the subject of your work, and I will believe only when I see for myself. I <u>can</u> trust that critic, tho' you cannot. The picture I have in my bedroom is always a solace to me and is, to my judgment, a very serious and skilful piece of pure painting come of a keen perception of reality, with a fine sense and delicate imagination. This was done only 2 years ago, and I see no reason for your sorrowing quotation of "the night cometh" &c.[1] If it hadn't been that I could not move from here, I believe I should have put shoes & stockings into a bag and have come to Eamont Bridge in person,[2] as a yellow devil to have turned your blue devils to a laughing autumn green colour. I have many bad jokes on hand ready for such a service. Perhaps you may thank your star that I couldn't come.

I was at Ewhurst yesterday with Miss Ewart and between whiles of interviewing her landlord ^(Mr Bray) and scratching my head as to how I should be able to least mar the site with the coming house, I enjoyed the fine breezy Surrey landscape; pure bright with heaven's own sun between small showers. There is a very pleasant little Inn there at wh' we put up, and as at my former visit I admired some blue-black pigs of the landlord's which were "coming on" – knifewards. I asked after their healths and went with Luff (the landlord) to the stern of his premises and certainly to the leeward of the pig stye, and there were the beauties! We cut them up, weighed them, hung them up to smoke and partly eat them, all in a fine frenzy of anticipation. I longed to give Miss Ewart the slip and let her get back to the station alone, while I stayed & fed with the pigs like the "prodigious" son.[3] I did not: hence these tears of regret.

As Mrs Boyce will, naturally, dislike to read this brutally English letter, please to tell her that the Mathurins nectarines came soundly to mouth this morning.[4] I always delighted in nectarines, even so far as over peaches; partly because one has not to wait & take off a great coat before eating them. 'Tis an ill wind that blows no one any good, and the kind folk of Etampes will be consoled by the knowledge of the pleasure we have had from their heavy blow: all we can hope is that the trees were not permanently damaged.

I can find nothing in Turner & Parker's books[5] of the "Catterlens Hall" you mention.[6] Cartmel Church I have not seen, but Morris has told me several times that it is a very fine piece of work and, unless it has been pulled about by restorers, I think you sh{d} get to it if you can.[7] I well remember the impressive rings of ancient stones near Keswick:[8] my New Place brother and I walked by them one fine Sunday morning more than 20 years ago, and stayed on our way some quarter of an hour in their company.

Chipping Ongar Church is past praying for.[9] Other antient buildings (we ought to spell ancient with a (c) my lord) are in our orisons[10] to the devilish powers that be; but I am sorry to say that our committees are small as yet – last Thursday there were the sec{y}, and Vinall & myself as dictators, alone. I too never saw the like of the projecting vous[s]oir to the chancel arch at Newton Regny[11] (save in the photograph you brought me of the aq{u}aduct in the S. of France) but I think it must have been intended for the support of the rood beam. I have no Murray's guide to Cumberland & Westmoreland. I went to buy it once, but found almost all the book taken up with flowery descriptions of Lake scenery, and came away in disgust. The Ordnance maps, I am afraid, are done in an inferior manner, wh' is a great pity, as the one inch scale is quite large enough to allow of much more and accurate completeness. Cockermouth Castle, I believe, belongs to Percy Wyndham's brother – Ld Leconfield – but I did not know that it was all in ruins: I suppose there must be a house there besides?[12] You will be staying in the north as long as the weather is bearable I fancy, and will do something in the way of a drawing of Dacre castle? I have it in my head that the place has the making of a picture in it, though the church which I had reckoned on as a part of the subject has been mauled by soulless thieves.[13]

My sister writes me that she has had a pleasant letter from Mrs Boyce therefore I suspect that New-Place will reply, as in duty bound. At all events I shall carry your

1864–1887

good wishes when I go on Saturday evening. I have lately got a lot of Cobbet[t]s books, and among them is his French Grammar which I must attack "one of these days", but as there is an English Grammar as well I must go through that first as you will be sure that I should, from this letter.[14] I've read the "Legacy to Parsons" with much amusement. Indeed Cobbet[t] was outspoken & clear spoken and simply funny without meaning to be so.[15]

Kindest remembrance to Mrs Boyce, and joy be with you both.
Yours sincerely | Philip Webb.

BL Add 45354, ff. 189-90

---

1 'I must work the works of him that sent me, while it is day: the night cometh, when no man can work.' St John, 9.4.
2 See above, Letter 209, note 1.
3 In the Biblical parable of the prodigal son, the profligate younger son spends all the money his father has given him, and is close to starving. 'And he would fain have filled his belly with the husks that the swine did eat: and no man gave unto him.' St Luke, 15:16.
4 GPB's wife often sent fresh fruit to PSW from France, when she visited. Her parents lived at the convent of Les Mathurins in Etampes.
5 Thomas Hudson Turner, *Some Account of Domestic Architecture in England, from the Conquest to the End of the Thirteenth Century* (Oxford: Parker, 1851). For Parker, see above, Letter 207, note 2.
6 He means Catterlen Hall, in Cumbria, an early fifteenth-century fortified tower.
7 The twelfth-century Cartmel Priory is the parish church of Cartmel, in Cumbria.
8 The late Neolithic or early Bronze Age stone circle at Castlerigg, two miles from Keswick.
9 The SPAB were opposing imminent restoration at the eleventh-century church of St Martin's, Chipping Ongar, in Essex. 'Their objections were answered in a vigorous letter by the architect, C. Rolfe. This correspondence shows that the old south wall of the church contained two "ancient" windows and a doorway of original Norman work, an injured 14th-century window and a piscina at the south-east corner of the nave.' http://www.british-history.ac.uk/report.aspx?compid=15630 [accessed 27 July 2014]. The changes went ahead in 1884. For Clapton Crabb Wolfe, see also Vol. III, Letter 779, note 1.
10 'Nymph, in thy orisons / Be all my sins rememb'red.' *Hamlet*, III.i.88–9.
11 The twelfth-century church of St John, Newton Regny, about three miles NW of Penrith. A voussoir is a stone forming part of an arch or vault, 'usually having the sides inclined towards each other'. *OED*
12 The earliest parts of Cockermouth Castle, in Cumbria, are Norman, but since the Civil War much remains in a ruined state. It has been long associated with the Wyndham family, following the marriage of the sister of the first Earl of Egremont in the eighteenth century. In the mid-nineteenth century, owners of the castle took the Leconfield title. Henry Wyndham, second Baron Leconfield (1830–1901), was the eldest brother of PWY.
13 The fourteenth-century moated tower house, Dacre Castle, is situated four miles south-west of Penrith. The twelfth-century church of St Andrew's, Dacre, largely untouched since the fourteenth century, was restored in 1874–5.
14 William Cobbett, *A French Grammar, or, Plain Instructions for the Learning of French* (London: Charles Clement, 1824) and *A Grammar of the English Language . . . more Especially for the use of Soldiers, Sailors, Apprentices, and Plough-Boys* (London: Thomas Dolby, 1819).
15 Cobbett, *Legacy to Parsons* (London, 1835).

214 • To Reverend Henry Whitehead, 27 September 1883

Draft/copy

[1, Raymond Buildings . . .]
Sep 27. 1883

To The Rev.d H. Whitehead[1]
The Vicarage Brampton. Carlisle
Dear Sir

In answer to your letter of the 24th received by me this morning.[2]

The manufacturer of the patent wood flooring used in Brampton Church is M.r Thomas Gregory, Station Works, Clapham Junction London S:W: and as his men laid the flooring I think the best plan would be for your churchwardens to write to M.r Gregory and ask him to send an experienced man to Brampton to examine the wood flooring laid by him which requires some attention. When an appointment is made for this man to be at Brampton I would advise the Churchwardens to get M.r Court, of Carlisle, the joiner who made the seating, to come to Brampton and meet M.r Gregory's man and together with the Churchwardens consider the state of the flooring and the ~~reason~~ cause of the decay in the material.

I enclose an authorised prospectus of this system of flooring and in it you will see that M.r White the inventor of the flooring stipulates that the timber should be "properly Burnettized"[3] and I suspect that ~~much~~ the resistance of the wood to decay would much depend on this preparation having been properly applied. Upon your report as to the result of the proposed meeting I should be better able to advise the Ch' Wardens.

Yours truly. | Ph: W.

LB-2, pp. 17-18

---

1 Upon his arrival as vicar in April 1874, the Broad Church reformer Henry Whitehead (1825–96) had supported GH in his wish to replace the dilapidated Brampton church with the new one by PSW, together with its Morris & Co. windows. The Naworth estate also commissioned PSW to build a new Vicar's House with parish room for his use (1877–80). See *Kirk*, pp. 223–4 and 300.
2 Whitehead had written about evidence of decay to the patent wood block floor at Brampton.
3 A process named after the naval physician, Sir William Burnett (1779–1861), who served at Trafalgar. His independent commercial interests involved patenting 'a solution of zinc chloride for use as a preservative and disinfectant'. http://www.oxforddnb.com.ezproxy.londonlibrary.co.uk/view/article/4077?docPos=17 [accessed 28 July 2014].

215 • To Christopher Benson, 29 October 1883

Draft/copy

[1, Raymond Buildings . . .]
Oct.r 29. 1883

1864–1887

To Christopher Benson Esq[re][1]
Cumberland Union Banking Co | Brampton by Carlisle
Dear Sir

(S[t] Martin's Ch' Brampton)

M[r] Gregory ~~called~~ came to me on Saturday, and I called on M[r] White on Friday but he was not at home, so I wrote to him & rec[d] an answer this morning. I explained fully to M[r] Gregory the character & construction of the church, and shewed him that it was separated from the "bank" of earth by a gangway of considerable width: That the church walls ~~was~~ were carried down to an admirable foundation, with an intercepting damp-proof course, and that there were no "vaults" under ~~it~~ the building; also that this – the bank side of the church – was on the south or sunny side: That the church was specially & carefully ventilated, and that in a letter to M[r] Tho's Richardson (a churchwarden) of June 11th 1880 I had explained and insisted upon how the airing the church was to be seen to.[2] M[r] Gregory could in no way account for the decay in the floor, except that the sand used ~~with~~ in the concrete must have held some material which was injurious to the wood.

M[r] White tells me that he has known two or three cases of wood block paving decaying either from moisture or the presence of loam or some other objectionable thing in the concrete, and that in almost all positions there should be a damp course under the wood paving. Such a plan as this suggested by M[r] White must be an improved way of laying these floors, as M[r] Gregory at that time did not suggest to me that it would be well to do this, as it could well have been done.[3]

I told M[r] Gregory that I should still advise the Churchwardens to ask him to send an experienced man to examine the state of the flooring, and he said he would send such a man upon request. ~~and~~ I now express again to the Churchwardens my opinion that this should be done, and I would also advise that M[r] Gregory's offer to do any work in rectification of the mischief at "cost price" be accepted. My own opinion is, that the whole of the wood paving should be lifted, ~~that~~ all decayed or tainted wood be removed and that in relaying and renewing, all the woodwork should now be set on "hot Stockholm tar" as he suggests.[4]

I am, Dear Sir, | Yours truly | Ph: W.

P.S. It w[d] be well I think for M[r] Court, of Carlisle, or his representative to meet M[r] Gregory's man when he goes to Brampton.

LB-2, pp. 20-1

---

1 Benson was churchwarden and former organist at Brampton, the son of the previous vicar (also called Christopher Benson). His father's infirmity meant that for about three years before his retirement in 1874, and the appointment of Henry Whitehead as vicar, a curate, William Miller, was placed in charge. Miller attempted to introduce a more High Church mode of worship, opposed by many, including from the younger Benson as organist. 'Miller mentions "Persistent attempts at disturbance by gestures and noises of contempt and ridicule from the singing gallery". At length Miller

persuaded the churchwardens to threaten Benson junior with a charge of brawling in church if he did not resign. He did so, but when he died 25 years later he was a much respected churchwarden, bank manager and justice of the peace.' *Penn*, pp. 10–11.
2 See above, Letter 153.
3 Distressed that the flooring was already in need of remedial treatment, PSW decided to meet the cost of the extra work. 'He later sent to Mr. Stephenson, the agent of the estate, a cheque for £25 to cover this, saying that he was sending it to him rather than to the churchwardens, as the latter would probably ask why it was not £100, and would think him a fool for doing such a thing voluntarily. The cheque was later returned to him, presumably on the instructions of George Howard.' *Penn*, p. 24.
4 High-grade pine tar used in Scandinavia as a wood preservative is often known as Stockholm tar, a single company once holding the monopoly for its export from Stockholm.

216 • To editor(s) of Bristol newspaper(s), 1 November 1883

Drafted on behalf of SPAB

To the Editor of –

Sir.

The notice in ^(the London newspaper,) the "Building News" of October 10, of an attempt to work upon the feelings of the Citizens of Bristol so that contributions may be drawn towards a scheme for the "restoration" of the Abbey Gate-House on College Green,[1] calls for notice from this Society, for it would seem that the Ecclesiastical authorities are not ashamed to beg ^(of the public) for subscriptions ~~for~~ ~~towards~~ ^(to a fund for) restoring ancient work ~~on~~ ^(with) one hand, while they pull down valuable historical records with the other, and that in opposition to the earnest appeal of local and other ~~authorities~~ ^(thoughtful people) against the wanton destruction of The Prior's Lodging or "Minster House"! What does this anxiety for saving in one case and destroying in another mean? Let the Citizens of Bristol look to it, or the precious abbey Gateway will ~~as~~ ^(be) ~~as good as be~~ ^(practically as much) destroyed as the Prior's Lodging was really. How can the English public trust such people?

The Abbey Gate House called for watchful attention so that no ~~stone should become loose~~ accident should happen to it without protection being applied at once in skilful manner. Instead of this, the noble relic has been grossly neglected and the result is, in the words of the Dean, that "it was notified to me that portions were so ready to fall that it had become necessary, for the sake of safety of those passing through the gateway, that they should be removed. This was accordingly done". ^(Now Sir,) this is this usual thing! It must ^(be) "notified" to the caretakers ~~of~~ ^(that) a piece of antiquity is likely to break a citizen's head, before they understand that they have in charge a valuable possession, ^(the neglect of) which, ~~to every one else the neglect of the charge~~ has been ~~patent~~ ^(known) to every ^(other) passer-by. ~~And now~~ ^(Then) comes the second and consequent movement; 'let us "restore" this wilfully injured monument of ancient art and make it as good as new, or perhaps better, and no one shall know ^(that) we have slept over our watches'. Architects will be called in, estimates of cost made, & the hearts of the faithful ~~torn~~ ^(wrung) with descriptions of quick coming dissolution, which can only be met by the generosity of the toilers & moilers[2] of the city of Bristol, whose property the Abbey Gateway is not.

This is no over coloured picture of events, and the Citizens who are asked to give should, before giving, demand an explanation of what is going to be done. If it be proved that only repairs, ~~and~~ support, and strengthening are ~~done~~, to be undertaken well & good; & the citizens ~~will~~ would, no doubt, respond with their money; but, if "Restoration" is to be the outcome, not a farthing would be given by men of commonsense, and the city would let ~~it be known~~ the reason why be known.

Sir, there are, no doubt, ~~many~~ educated people in and about Bristol who will come forward and, ~~by~~ through the aid of your columns, let the people know ~~of~~ what they have lost in the past and are likely to lose in future, and thus ~~aid~~ help this Society in doing what little can be done ~~and in trying~~ to save ~~if only~~ one, if only one piece of what remains to England of her genuine ancient art.

[*pencil*] Thursday Novr 1. 1883 and taken to the Committee meeting. | Ph. W.

SPAB

---

1 The Great or Abbey Gatehouse on College Green, with its two distinctive Norman archways, was the main entrance to the original monastic precinct of St Augustine's Abbey. Its earliest parts date from the late twelfth century. Above the arches is a two-story tower with mullions and niches for statues, dating from about 1500. These later portions would be restored by John Loughborough Pearson in 1888.
2 Thankless work (archaic). 'To toyle and moyle for worldly drosse' (Edmund Spenser). (*OED*).

217 • To George Price Boyce, 13 January 1884

1, Raymond Buildings, Gray's Inn, | *London, W.C.*
Sunday 13 Jany 1884

My dear Boyce

Since I left you last night I have been considering some of my follies, one of which yesterday was my jestingly insisting on your going to France this year whether you would could should ought or not. You are too wise, I take it, to be taken in by my fun, however real-looking from its boorishness. Those two fine works I saw must not run the risk of being unfinished, from any whim bred in my unthatched head.

I am really trying so to arrange my affairs as to get to Italy this coming winter and, when I first seriously considered this uplifting of myself from deeply ingrained home-keeping habit, I had calculated that you might be going to France in 1884 and that, if so, it would be pleasant if I could be with you for a little time in that lovely country, of which I know so little. Added to which it was borne in upon my mind that as the French were so absurd as to use a language that I did not understand I should have the advantage of your parler-vousing in getting bed, board and liquor without blushing; hence my jesting scheme and these tears.

Your being unable to go to France will not stop my main business, wh' is to get to Italy this winter or never; and I can do this by going directly to Florence a little later on without so much as stopping in France.

You see? In the first place, your order of work must not be put out on my account. And in the second, <u>you</u> are not bound to go [to] France because <u>I</u> bind myself to go to Italy.

I really pine to see those two fine drawings by daylight. The more finished one – the Brougham Castle – struck me strongly. The Yanwath one having no sky or foreground gave no chance to me except in imagination and I think such a foreground as you will put in may make it one of your best works.[1]

All these words merely to say that you must not let your good nature lead you astray in listening to my jesting gabble!

Yours sincerely | Philip Webb.

BL Add 45354, ff. 193-4

---

1 GPB exhibited these two watercolours in 1885. See below, Letter 258, note 1.

218 • To Percy Wyndham, 30 January 1884

Draft/copy

[1, Raymond Buildings . . .]
Jany 30. 1884

To Hon' Percy Wyndham M.P.
Wilbury House by Salisbury
Dear Mr Wyndham

(Clouds H^{se})

In answer to your letter of the 27th inst^t. I saw Howell when I was last at Clouds and he wanted to know what bricks might be required this year so that he might turn over the clay for them at once. Of course I cannot ^{now} say how many bricks will be wanted for the garden walls and for Slades[1] but you surely may safely say that Howell should make <u>this</u> year as many bricks as he can burn, and I think you should tell him that the price for ^{the} different qualities ~~must~~ ^{should} be the same as paid for Clouds, delivered, and that no inferior bricks would be accepted, and that all bricks ^{tiles} and other material must be subject to ^{the} approval of your Architect.

I think you would run less risk by ordering as many bricks for this year as Howell can make than you would if they ran short and you had to buy a haul from Gillingham or Donhead. Supposing you changed your plans the bricks would keep, or you would surely be able to sell them in detail.[2] Howell will not be able (according to former experience) to turn out any bricks till the middle of May.

I must of course see you about Slades and the garden wall before I can do anything myself in those matters ^{and if we could meet shortly at Knoyle so much the better}. I also should wish to see Mrs Wyndham about the baths for Clouds as soon as she comes to London.

I will put your S.P.R papers in my pocket so as to ask friends for their experiences and note the answers[3] – for <u>myself</u> I answer this, after careful consideration.

1   "Hallucinations" – NO.
2   "Dreams" – NO.

Yours very truly | Ph: W:

LB-2, pp. 27-8

---

1 Existing cottages on the Clouds estate which were converted into the head gardener's cottage. See the illustrations in *Dakers*, p. 71.
2 To sell off a few at a time.
3 The Society for Psychical Research had been founded in 1882 in order to investigate human experiences not susceptible to explanation by empirical evidence. PWY was an active member, and gave financial support to its Research Fund.

219 • To Mary Anne Ewart, 28 February 1884

Draft/copy

[1, Raymond Buildings . . .]
Feby 28. 1884

To Miss Ewart.
Grand Hôtel | Grasse Alpes Maritimes. France

Dear Miss Ewart.

I only got Messrs King's tender for your house[1] on Tuesday morning last – 26th – just as I was starting for my work in Wiltshire. However, I saw Mr Goodman the "quantities" surveyor before I went and directed him to telegraph for Messrs King to come to London and see him ^{at} once.

The cost of the works estimated for by King is unsatisfactory, in so far as it comes out £456 higher than my estimate. ~~This sum~~ ^{King's tender} does <u>not</u> include the Porch – which is incorporated with the ^{gardener's} cottage – <u>nor</u> the Engineer's work for grates, ranges, heating apparatus &c. Messrs King came up to see Mr Goodman yesterday and on my return I had his report. After going all through the estimate and prices of the different items Mr Goodman could find no mistake and the prices generally were reasonable but he also found that many things had helped to swell the total. Bricks w^d be 45^s/- a thousand ^{on the ground} instead of 40^s/- as I had calculated. Lime & other things equally high ^{in proportion} chiefly on account of the cartage.

Also the drainage as planned, is ^a heavy item, partly on account of the improved pipes ^{and laying} I proposed to use. Also, I had specified that the water pipes should be treated with the "Bower-Barff" process to guard against the action of the water on the metal.² (The water ~~there~~ is soft in that part of the country and eats into the metal flaying the pipes and choking with rust. It does not ~~make a~~ deposit like hard water ^(does).) Again, the fittings throughout the house – cupboards, shelves &c – are very numerous for the class of house, so the surveyor tells me; therefore, though the prices are not unreasonable, the causes above named and others have brought up the total in a disappointing way to me, as I had hoped after my careful estimate that the tender would have been within the sum of £4,300 – whereas it comes to £4,756 without including the afore-named items.

The ^(builders & other) estimates stand thus –

Messrs King's tender, for the whole of the house ^(without the Porch)	£4,756.00
" Longdens ^(engineer's) estimate for grates, Ranges, hot water supply, heating apparatus &c –	250.0.0
	£5,006.00

From this I can deduct say £70 for a slight change in some of the work, and if the fencing by the cottage and along the west boundary of the ground were not done now £66 more could be saved.   ded^t 136.0.0

£4,870.0.0

Though it is a <u>real</u> advantage to employ a ^(known responsible) builder of the close neighbourhood it always results in ~~a~~ higher prices being charged than would be the case if the work were put out in competition before several builders, and I warned Messrs King of this, but they say they have been very careful in their prices (they took a fortnight to make up the tender) and have left no margin on which reductions could be made.

There are now 3 courses open ^(to us). First, to have the quantities lithographed and put before several builders ~~for~~ ^(in) competition?

Second, to make some reduction in the size of the house? and Third to accept King's tender as it stands?

I am ~~exceeding~~ ^(quite) unwilling to ask you to spend more money than you have considered right, so that I should be glad to learn what you think of the first & second courses.

Believe me | Yours faithfully | Ph: W:

LB-2, pp. 29-31

---

1 William and George King of Abinger Hammer would be awarded the building contract for Coneyhurst.

2 The Bower-Barff process was a recent commercial application to prevent iron from rusting, established by Frederick S. Barff and improved by George and Anthony Bower, who bought the Barff rights.

220 • To George Price Boyce, 16 May 1884

1, Raymond Buildings, Gray's Inn, | *London, W.C.*
May 16. 1884

My dear Boyce

The doctor was got away on Monday and I had a letter from him from Dunster yesterday morning.[1] They enjoyed the place & surroundings very much – walked about, saw Dunster castle and Cle[e]ve Abbey, but having some 50 dozen of flies and other tackle, became restless to the extent of moving to Dulverton yesterday, where they mean to expose their flies & themselves. I fancy that place will not be bracing enough. It is greatly beautiful I believe, but is in a blind alley of the hills. Wardle – who is a fisherman – knows that country and strongly advises their going to Exford, right up in the moor, where there is Exe in its smaller state, and quiet quarters. The doctor writes in good spirits, and that they are living freely on four square meals a day and, though he doesn't mention it, I hope sleep in proportion.

The sister writes from New Place that she is getting on very well in the present order of things and as she wishes me to go there on Saturday I shall do so, when I hope to find out for you the name of the plant of which you send me a slip. The plant was not too far gone to be seen, but I don't remember it (seldom do remember plants, except the crab stick which had been laid on the <u>outside</u> of my head) or its kind – added to which I have lent some vols: of my Baxter:[2] but I'll let you know from Welwyn.

Dillon came to the meeting yesterday,[3] and <u>he</u> also gave me an admit to the Burlington.[4] I sh$^{\underline{d}}$ be glad to go with you there on Thursday if it may be.

I've had a pretty satisfactory letter from Middleton in Rome. If things went well he w$^{\underline{d}}$ be still there when I should hope to be able to get there & under his wing.

With best remembrance to M$^{\underline{rs}}$ Boyce | I am sincerely yours | Ph: W:

BL Add 45354, ff. 199-200

---

1 For reasons either of ill-health or exhaustion, Harry Webb had decided to take a fishing trip to Somerset, accompanied by a friend – probably the Reverend Henry Jephson (see below, Letter 329, note 2), with whom he took a similar expedition in May 1885.
2 William Baxter, *British Phaenogamous Botany: or Figures and Descriptions of the Genera of British Flowering Plants*, 6 vols (Oxford: Baxter, 1834–43). PSW's copies of volumes I and V are now at the Emery Walker Library, both with his signature and the date July 1881 in his hand, in Vol. I. See *CAGM*, p. 133.
3 The landscape painter Frank Dillon (1823–1909) was a committee member of the SPAB.
4 This was an exhibition of drawings of 'architectural subjects by deceased British artists' at the Burlington Fine Arts Club, and included works by Turner, Joseph Nash, David Cox and Thomas Girtin.

221 • To Percy Wyndham, 1 July 1884

Draft/copy

[1, Raymond Buildings . . .]
July 1. 1884

To Hon' Percy Wyndham M.P.
44 Belgrave Square. S.W.

Dear Mr Wyndham

(Clouds Kitchen Gard^n)

I have made designs for the kitchen garden walling and sent them to Estcourt for estimates.

The ^(digging, concrete,) walling & buttresses all round the garden will cost ^about £1550. The difference in price for the mediæval buttresses ^(that you said you w^d prefer) over those which I had arranged for, does not come to much, about £12, and if the cost ~~was~~ ^were the only consideration you would probably ~~agree~~ ^wish to have those you prefer. Over and above the advantages which my buttresses give for practical purposes, of casting less shade and permitting fruit trees to be trained against them, there is another. The mediæval buttress shapes represent an appearance of counter-pressure against thrust at individual points, and they would look more reasonable if there was a roof over them whereas those I would prefer merely look as ^if they were ^meant to steady the wall. I have designed some decent buttresses on your plan, but I would still much prefer to use those I had proposed.

Will you let me know as soon as possible if ~~I shall direct~~ ^(you wish me to set about building the walls, and your decision as to buttresses) as the ~~time of~~ year is getting on, and we shall have to get the copings made at once? The digging, concrete and plain walling could go on directly.[1]

Yours very truly | Ph: W:

LB-2, pp. 38-9

---

1 'Percy was completely outmanoeuvred and replied with one of his shortest notes: "This is to authorise you to set about building the walls. You can put up the buttresses recommended in your last".' *Dakers*, p. 70.

222 • To Albert Estcourt, 19 July 1884

Draft/copy

[1, Raymond Buildings . . .]
July 19 1884.

To Mr Albert Estcourt.
1 Barton Street Gloucester

Dear Sir.

(Clouds H^{se})

When I was at Knoyle on Tuesday last I directed Mr Simmonds as to building the kitchen garden walls and told him to see that the bricks were well picked over to select the best for facing.

In a letter from Mr Simmonds rec^d this morning, he writes "Mr Estcourt says you struck the facing price out of his estimate – and he cannot afford to have them picked now – but the men shall pick them when building the walls".

As I am anxious that there should be no mistake on this point, I write to say that in allowing 10^s/- a rod ^{extra} for this brickwork, that would include for picking the bricks for facing; what I had cut out was for special facing with handmade bricks. It would not do to trust to the bricklayers ~~picking~~ ^{selecting} the bricks as the work went on, as they would certainly take those which first came to hand. Added to which, if the bricks were picked over properly, to have it done by a man or men ready for the bricklayers would save time to you rather than lose it.

Will you be so good as to send me an answer to this before they begin laying any bricks?

Yours truly | Ph: W:

LB-2, pp. 40-1

223 • To George Price Boyce, 28 July 1884

1, Raymond Buildings, Gray's Inn, | *London, W.C.*
July 28. 1884

My dear Boyce

I think your determination is a sensible one as, from conversations with you, I know your outlooks pretty well. As far as being able to foresee what weather will happen in the North of England, this year seems as good as any other, and your work there would be easily caught up without any other delay than accidents of flood & bulls. Mrs Boyce, merely going to and from Etampes, w^d not be troubled with quarantine, and it is not likely she would be inconvenienced by the sickness in the South.[1]

I mean – if possible – to get into Italy in October, but how, it is not possible to say at present. In any case I sh^d not start before the end of the first or second week in October, and if I did not propose to stop in France I need not leave here before the end of October, when things choleraic [*sic*] may have passed away ~~by that time~~ so as to leave the Brenner pass open, at least, by that time.[2] In any case I beg you not to let this prospective state of affairs in any way hamper your movements.

I feel anxious that you should try hard to complete that magnificent subject of Brougham Castle, as it is so far advanced and, with moderate weather, you would be able to attain the end of the Yanwath one also; the more so that you can counter-bellow from the safe side of the hedge![3]

Please let me have your address when you have one, such as, G: B: Esqre in front of the bull, England!!

Yours sincerely, with best wishes to Madame (who, happily, is not afraid of Mounseer) | Philip Webb:

BL Add 45354, ff. 206-7

---

1 An outbreak of cholera in Toulon was reported on 23 June, causing delays to shipping and the introduction of quarantine measures. Marseilles also soon reported cases, and travel restrictions to the south of France were put in place: P&O suspended its service to Marseilles early in July. During August, there were incidences of cholera in parts of Italy.
2 The Brenner Pass gave access to Italy from Austria, and a railway link had been completed by 1867.
3 See above, Letter 217, note 1.

224 • To Mary Anne Ewart, 31 July 1884

Draft/copy

[1, Raymond Buildings . . .]
July 31. 1884

To Miss Ewart
Broadleas. Devizes.

Dear Miss Ewart.

I beg to acknowledge receipt of your letter of the 28th. I expect that the ^{present quick} demand for certificates[1] will partly fall off after the building is roofed in. I was at Ewhurst on Tuesday and found the works had ^{been} got on with very rapidly, but I was ~~also~~ glad to find that they were being very well done also. I had no fault to find with either materials or workmanship. Some half dozen pairs of rafters of the main roof were already set up, and the Kings, for their own sakes are alive to the wisdom of getting the whole covered in before the autumn rains set in; the rains we have been having lately have been good for the work.

I don't think there is much risk of the water failing, indeed Holt thought there must have been some error in measurement before – as, from Saturday at 3. oc ^{p.m.} to Monday at 6 a.m., 6 feet of water had come in, which is about the ordinary supply in such time.

I can hardly by letter explain what I propose to do with the outcome of the drainage and, probably circumstances ~~will~~ ^{of ground &c may} make it better to defer a settled scheme 'till later on, but in no case would the emptying and disposal of solid & subsided matter be a serious difficulty, such as that in the case you mention.

As it is customary to give the workmen some present when the roof is getting on I asked King what would be the best way of doing this; he said that all his men were going for an outing to Portsmouth on the 16th of August and then w^d be a good time for you to give help if you felt so inclined. I w^d suggest that half a crown a man w^d be ~~appreciated~~ sufficient and as there are some 34 or 36 men on the ground and others working for you in the shop at Abinger Hammer, if you gave £5 that w^d meet the occasion. Of course you need not do this, but I thought you w^d wish me to let you know of anything that occurred to me as reasonably customary. I find, as a rule, that workmen appreciate such thought of them.

Yours very truly | Ph: W:

LB-2, pp. 41-3

---

1 As supervising architect, PSW was responsible for approving any claims for payment from the contractors engaged on a building project, which would then be presented to the client.

225 • To George Price Boyce, 29 August 1884

Annotated 'rec^d at Newton Reigny'

1, Raymond Buildings, Gray's Inn, | *London, W.C.*
Sat: Aug 29. 1884

My dear Boyce

Your letter really distressed me for the time, but on reading again & again I feel that you cannot be well and, if your liver is out of order I know, from experience, that the ill going of one's work is positive torture. With my knowledge of your work I am much more inclined to condole with you over the unlucky spots in the sky of the Yanwath drawing than in the rest of your clearly described state for, however doubtful positive failure in your work may be to me, the spots are, liver or no liver, there to confound you. You say "do not refer to it", your doleful letter to wit; but how the devil am I to pass by unnoticed a letter from my friend so coloured with real trouble?

I think I can sympathise with you, for 'tis some years past now that I gave up all hope in my own work and was sad in the extreme for some time and, indeed, great sadness has possession of me in whiles even now, but I ceased to be troubled with my disappointment at finding I was not what I at times thought I was and, barring the times when my soul is in the pit, I am merrier mostly than I used to be for, I have not yet ceased to believe that I have within me what I shall certainly never be able to bring out: and then I take infinite interest in the life of my fellow poor, & chiefly all those who have heart. Intellect is a great thing but it must, for my joy, have heart or I prefer only the company of beauty and the beasts. The world – away from the suburbs of our old towns – is full of exquisite beauty and thousands of lovely beasts – truly, when one forgets oneself the outer world becomes more lovely still.

If you are not well – as I must suppose – clearly nothing I can write will be of any service to you but, should you be taking too much to heart some real failure in your work, and that is your only real cause of distress, I would say 'I don't care, there still remain beauty, history, love, glorious appreciation of all that noble souls have conceived, and I'm not too old to wallow in those infinite joys'. You are a social being and have never been thrown on your own solitary companionship as I have ('till it has grown upon my shoulders like a comfortable old coat) and the company of your wife will be a relief to you. I presume that Mrs Boyce is on her way to you now, for, did she not kindly call this evening and leave me a box of delightful fruits of the earth? Peaches, pears, grapes, plums &c and, an egg! laid, no doubt, by the partner of a real Gallic cock; none of your miserable barn door Dorkings, but a true bred, never-to-be-improved French hen, born & reared in the navel of the world. I was sorry when I came in to tea to find from my housekeeper that Mrs Boyce had been here while I was away from home (been to see some failures of mine in foliage sculpture). Mrs Long said that her daughter, who took the parcel, said that a 'French lady brought it'. I wonder if Mrs Boyce parlervoused – or was it a lady's maid that your wife has captured in Etampes?

I should have so liked to see the French country bloom on Mrs Boyce's cheeks that it was too bad of fate not to have telegraphed that she was coming. Please give her my kindest thanks, not only for the beautiful gift but for the kindness ~~of~~ ^{in} bringing, with such trouble, the present to me herself. There, that is all the bad grammar I'll use about it.

Surely I will go to West House as soon as I can and have a look round your garden, though I fancy Mrs Boyce must have herself gone there and will tell you what the hot sun has done to the garden, as is ~~she~~ sure to have been the case, viz, to burn it up. Still that will do it good in one way, though in another it may have killed some of the plants, but it will have strengthened others.

[Fairfax] Murray writes me word from Basle that he fled on learning that he might creep through the alps (by the St Gothard pass I suppose) and escape quarantine at Luino if he was lucky, but if unlucky it was the best frontier to be shut up in.[1]

Turner is away for his holiday so that I know nothing of anti-scrape matters. We meet again on the 4th Septr. Morris's paper read at the meeting is now published in the report and is good reading, but you will get that.[2] He himself is see-sawing weekly between London & Kelmscott and has got over a strained ancle which he had come by, & which laid him up for 2 or 3 days.[3] I know nothing of Holm Cultram Ch' – go and see it when you can, for the Society.[4] When I last inquired about the variation of the compass it was 19° or thereabouts west of true North.

Come, you must write me again shortly or I shall be anxious.
Yours sincerely, | Philip Webb.

BL Add 45354, ff. 208-9

1 See above, Letter 223, note 1.
2 WM addressed the annual meeting of the SPAB on 1 July 1884. He covered familiar themes, extolling the skills of the medieval craft guilds, in contrast to the present 'time of barbarism': 'you cannot doubt that in one way or other the surface of an ancient building, the *handling* of the old handicraftsman that is, is most valuable and worthy of preservation, and I am sure also that we all feel instinctively that it cannot be reproduced at the present day; that the present attempt at reproduction not only deprives us of a monument of history, but also of a work of art.' *SPAB Annual Report, 1884*, pp. 53–4.
3 'I have been seedy: slipped on the grass & strained my ancle and obliged to lay up for two days; then a touch of gout, not over yet.' WM to Andreas Scheu, 13 August 1884, *CLWM*, II.
4 The former Cistercian Holm Cultram Abbey, founded in the twelfth century, in Abbeytown, Cumbria. By the nineteenth century it was much ruined, the stones quarried by local people for farm buildings. In 1883 some restoration occurred, including the lowering of the floor by two feet to its original level and the removal of the galleries.

226 • To Madeline Wyndham, 30 August 1884

Draft/copy

[1, Raymond Buildings . . .]
August 30. 1884

To Hon' Mrs Percy Wyndham
Wilbury House by Salisbury
Dear Mrs Wyndham

(Clouds H^{se})

In answer to your letter of the 28th instant. You are, of course, perfectly free – so far as I can be concerned – to alter and rearrange the plan of the East ~~or~~ ^{and} kitchen gardens. I have done neither of these works professionally and should not have suggested any arrangement except that things ^{were} required to be done at once when they were undertaken. With regard to the East garden, I should naturally have an opinion, as the whole surroundings of the house have been under my consideration for some years, and as I have had ~~some~~ experience of many failures happening from want of careful ~~examination of~~ $^{attention to}$ all circumstances I arranged my plan with such knowledge & taste as I had. It was a pretty piece of ground and required delicate handling and doubtless you saw this in your dealing with it.

Would it not be well to defer fitting up the little garden house in the south wall at the bottom of garden 'till things are more settled? It should be a handy neat & tidy place and ^{wd} be very convenient. I say this because of the rather wild suggestion to turn it into a dirt hole of a mushroom house. The kitchen garden would be the place for such things where proper heat will be supplied.

Surely the house plant greenhouse sh^d not be attempted this year as many things will have to ^{be} thought of with regard to it and the other glass houses in [the] kitchen garden. Mr Brown[1] could rig up some frames for his plants this winter without difficulty.

As to makers of glass houses, they are legion. There is Weekes of Chelsea,[2] Smith of Ipswich[3] &c but care would have to be used in dealing with them or you will be fitted with work at great cost ^& which would ruin the appearance of the most lovely place in England. I send you a plan of the ground on which the greenhouse is to stand, and as there is plenty of room there w^d be no reason for removing the sycamore tree. Of course it w^d not do to put the greenhouse on the East side of [the] gardener's house as it w^d be in full view of all who came up ~~the hill~~ ^to Clouds. I daresay you have noticed the pretty look of that corner as you pass the stables towards the house?

I will write to Mr Simmonds and tell him to send you an accurate plan of the kitchen garden with the roads &c as laid out. Veitch is I believe the best nurseryman for rare plants (costly in proportion)[4] Rivers for vines and other fruit trees,[5] but as the Salisbury man seems to have supplied you with a good lot of apple trees he might also be able to do the same with other fruit trees, and at a less cost than Rivers, ^though vines had better come from Rivers. Ware of Tottenham is a good man, I hear, for all herbaceous plants.[6]

Believe me | Yours very truly | Ph: W:

LB-2, pp. 43-5

1 Harry Brown, the head gardener at Wilbury, who would take on the same role at Clouds.
2 John Weekes & Company of the King's Road in Chelsea were described as Horticultural Builders.
3 The Horticultural Engineers, W.G. Smith & Co., specialised in the manufacture of glasshouses, conservatories and greenhouses.
4 Established by John Veitch (1752–1839) in the early nineteenth century, the Veitch plant nurseries at Chelsea and Exeter were well-known for their skill in growing exotic plants.
5 Established in 1725, the Rivers Nursery in Sawbridgeworth, Hertfordshire specialised in orchard fruits.
6 Thomas S. Ware of Hale Farm Nurseries, Tottenham were suppliers of young plants and seeds. In consultation with Brown, Madeline Wyndham undertook some initial planting before Clouds was finished. She limited herself 'to slow-growing yew hedges, and the chalk-walled garden was planted with bulbs and magnolia trees'. *Dakers*, p. 74.

227 • To Charles Fairfax Murray, 2 September 1884

1, Raymond Buildings, Gray's Inn | London, W.C.
Sepr 2. 1884

My dear Murray

I did not think you could hang about 'till I was ready to go to Florence but thought you would surely run for it as soon as you thought you saw a hole in the Alps which you could creep through. As the cholera seems to be active in some parts of Italy I fancy you may have been caught on the frontier and clapped into quarantine, and this letter may get to your home before you do. If you should write again, tell me how you did on the way as it might be a pleasant route for me. I suppose – after looking at the map – that you went by the St Gothard pass,[1] as that is north of Luino a place you mentioned in your letter from Basle. I suppose they have modernised that town which people used to tell me was a delightful old one?

Faulkner went for a sea voyage in his holiday by goods steamer from Liverpool, by Gibraltar into the middle sea and landed for 2 days at Genoa, from whence he went on by [the] same steamer to Naples, where also he landed and stayed, I believe, some days. He is now on his way home again. I may hear from [him] what chance there is for me, but as I shall not be able to get away before the end of October there is some hope that the cholera may by then have expended itself, and rules will be relaxed.

I hope you found your womenfolk and childer all well and merry or, if you have not yet got to them, that they will be so when you do. I suspect that the English-ish-ish-man, Stanhope, has gone into the country here somewhere, to wait 'till he can get into Italy with due dignity.[2] I'm sorry to say that I have been too busy to buy my dictionary and conversations book, and may be, it will end in my not knowing a word of Italian when I start – alas! I can see myself sitting down on my trunk (not my nose) at the stations, watching for what next I shall be done with, for no doubt they will have their way & will torture me. I'm afraid that the name of Mazzini[3] would not now be a name whereby I might conjure myself into a bed in Florence? I meant to have had another talk with you and get many passwords to help me, before you left: however, you can write 'em. Here, now, we have sunshine and shower, and really delightful cool & warm weather.

Adieu | Yours very truly | Philip Webb.

Fitzwilliam 24

---

1 The St Gotthard Pass in the Swiss Alps is on the route from Zurich to Milan. The first Gotthard rail tunnel opened in 1882.
2 See below, Letter 229, note 3.
3 See above, Letter 132, note 9.

228 • To Percy Wyndham, 26 September 1884

Draft/copy

[1, Raymond Buildings . . .]
Sep 26. 1884.

To Hon' Percy Wyndham M:P:
Wilbury House. Salisbury

Dear M[r] Wyndham

(Clouds H[se])

I beg to acknowledge receipt of cheque with thanks – I enclose a regular receipt.[1] I will write to M[rs] Wyndham about meeting her at Clouds on the 7th of October.

Your good-natured advice to me to keep my temper with the dagger-drawing Italians will not be disregarded. I will be "wery careful of that there suit of clothes", my skin to wit.² However, I shall only associate with the lower orders of people when in Italy – Sacristans, Gravediggers and other poor folk, and a Communistic or other sign will, no doubt, make us all but kin.

Yours truly | Ph: W:

LB-2, p. 47

1 'If convenient to you I should be glad if you would let me have £1,000 further on account of my work. I had £1,000 in Aug: 1881 and another £1,000 in August 1883.' PSW to PWY, 24 September 1884, *LB-2*, p. 46.
2 'Hereupon there was a general laugh; and the little judge, looking with an angry countenance over his desk, said, "You had better be careful, Sir." "So Mr. Pickwick said at the time, my Lord," replied Sam; "and I was wery careful o' that 'ere suit o' clothes; wery careful indeed, my Lord".' Dickens, *Pickwick Papers*, ch 34.

229 • To Charles Fairfax Murray, 5 October 1884

1, Raymond Buildings, Gray's Inn | London, W.C.
Sunday October 5. '84

My dear Murray

I had your letter of Sep: 5, written just after you escaped from quarantine and, last night, I got yours of Oct: 2. It is very amiable of you to spare time in trying to lug me out of my shell. I fancy that a good cracking, such as thrushes give to the "hodmandods",¹ would be sufficiently persuasive with the doubtless, and peradventure Wardle may perform that operation. I went with him, nearly a month ago, into Wiltshire – or rather he came to me when I was at my work there – and we went on to see some old English buildings and, during our talks over victuals at the bad English Inns, he rashly said he would go as far as Basle with me, at the end of October, on my way to Italy, by way of Bruges, Liege, Strasbourg &c. If he keeps to his promise I shall be well content as he is a good companion among antiquities, holding his own in a dogged fashion which provokes closer examination of objects and though, as you know, I am always right (!) still its well, even for genius, to be stimulated. I had with me your former letter which I shewed to him and I fancy that set him afire to see some of the places he has seen before. The weather here has been so splendidly fine all through Sep: up to now, that it cannot be long before the rain comes down in force which might damp his ardour before we could start: however, he is courageous and will probably hold to his promise.

If you hold to the suggestion, in your last letter, of meeting me on the border, that w^d be better than well also, as I shall shiver on being left alone with my tongue fast tied. I have bought a kind of Italian grammar and a dictionary, but they drive what few wits I have into my slippers. I've heard it said that the natives are very shy of a foreigner who talks their tongue so that there may be some chance for me. Still I should welcome your appearance at a station in the land when you can untie the label affixed to my collar, otherwise I should flee through Milan without stopping, unless there were a dog like that of Norcia who would take charge of me.² I have got some money set apart to pay for our journeys if you should find time and inclination to pilot me anywhere. I could tell you lies about buildings and you w^d do the same about pictures to me. A relative of the "British gentleman" was here yesterday and he said that the latter had got back to his rest. I was told that if I journeyed to Villa Nuti I should be taken in charge by a regiment of beggars as a shield to them on approaching his door.³ A ragged lot of that kind would be a good joke to pass on John Bull at his home.

I am busy licking my business things into such shape that they may be left in a not too embarrassing condition to the colleague left in charge.⁴ It w^d be a good thing for my clients to find out that the work had not gone on of itself before. Wallis came in the other night and played the part of a Job's comforter, sitting upon my travelling suggestions and proposing ways for me which are not likely to be followed if I sh^d go by my nose. Among others he said I sh^d go to Turin at once as, afterwards, I sh^d not be likely to do so, which seemed reasonable; but my stomach will not be able to take ^in all the pictures I shall see in any way I may turn, even if they were taken out of their frames and rolled into smallest baggage compass.

I saw Morris for two days with his "fambly", at Kelmscott in Oxfordshire, last week and took a lesson in Italian from his daughter May, who only failed – for a reason – to pull my hair when I was too stupid.⁵ Faulkner got back all safely from Naples and enjoyed his sea journey.

Yours sincerely | Philip Webb.

I shall write again, of course, before I leave the lawyers here.

Fitzwilliam 25

---

1 Dialect: from 'dodman', a snail. (*OED*).
2 Probably PSW is picking up on a detail in one of CFM's letters, relating to a visit to the Umbrian town of Norcia.
3 Spencer Stanhope bought the Villa Nuti at Bellosguardo, on the outskirts of Florence, and for health reasons moved there permanently in 1880.
4 During PSW's absence of five months, GWJ oversaw the ongoing building work at Clouds and Coneyhurst. The two were in constant communication.
5 The 'reason' was PSW's baldness.

230 • To William Morris, 8 November 1884

Year added by SCC

1, Raymond Buildings, Gray's Inn, | London, W.C.
Sat: Novr 8. [1884]

My dear Fellow

You left your bottle and Oliver Twist last night. The former I shall throw to the dogs and the latter I shall put in my bag. I hope the foot is mending.¹

I have told almost all people interested, that I am going away. Should you see anyone who w^d care to know it, please tell them.

Your affectionate | Philip Webb.

V&A, NAL MSC/1958/687, f. 9

---

1 A return of the gout from which WM had been suffering in mid-August?

231 • To George Washington Jack, 22 November 1884

Florence
November. 22. 1884

My dear Mr Jack

I got away <u>really</u> on Sunday the 9th, and have come through Dover, Ostend, Bruges, Ghent, Brussells, [*sic*] Basle, Lugano, Como & Milan to this place. Mr Wardle left me – or rather, I left him – at Brussells, and I got here last night, having had most beautifully fine weather all the time, but very cold. It now rains for the first time since I left.

I have seen many fine things – mostly in a state of decay – but many of them quite beautiful and exciting, perhaps too much so for me for I feel rather like a fish out of water, wanting the support of my daily work which has become so much of a habit to me that I do not feel quite at ease without the stay of it. This feeling will perhaps go off and I may get more elastic in mind ^and less strained in it.

You will readily understand that I have not touched any of my home work, and it may be that some days must pass before I can do so, but I mean to do what I can, and as soon as possible, to help you out so that you shall not fancy yourself deserted by me.

Will you write and tell me of anything which it w^d be well that I should know, and also let me know how you yourself are getting on? The Slades alterations and new building are rather important, as the washing women will have to be at work there in May or June next year.[1]

Your going to Clouds and personally looking into things will help you and set my mind somewhat at rest, but I think you understand what we considered together as best to be done for Clouds and Ewhurst. Mr Buckle will I think help you in this latter.[2]

With much kindly feeling, believe me | Yours sincerely | Philip Webb.

Address me
"Al Signore Philip Webb | Presso Il Signore C.F. Murray
106 Via de' Serragli | Firenze" | <u>Italy</u>

V&A, AAD

1 After much deliberation and expert consultation, the decision had been made in 1884 for the water supply to be pumped up to a newly-built water tower, to the west of the house. This was the last of PSW's major designs for Clouds; that work, as well as the completion of the laundry and alterations to the head gardener's cottage, were continuing under GWJ's supervision.
2 Buckle must have been one of PSW's assistants.

232 • To William Morris, 25 November 1884

Florence
November 25. 1884

My dear Fellow

I am not quite sure as to the date, for time with me has rather given way to space. Everything is large here and about, and the walking of the moon seems rather to belong to the little tidinesses and handful beauties of the small fatherland away than to this spot on the world of huge decay.

Wardle will have told you of how ill he was used by his impatient companion and how we parted at Brussells a week ago.

The good natured Murray picked me up at Lugano, on this side of the St Gothard, and like his forerunner puts up with my dreaming, very faithfully. He who goes abroad with^{out} the tongues has his punishment always with him, ~~and~~ ^{but} his home friends are relieved, no doubt, from a dreadful penalty. The antiscrapers must be in a state of blessed relief!

He who has all his senses should not travel – much – for the whole 5 of them are terrible torturers of the imagination, giving pleasure and pain too fully. That the things I daily see, hear, and in other ways suck in have not been killed by universal babblement, is proof of their high piled-up power. Some are less and some are much greater than I had heard of, and disappoint and please ~~by~~ ^{with} perverse surprising. I'll tell you nothing of them, so as to vex you as little as may be. I merely write to you that you may not suppose I am lost to you and your surroundings.

The weather has been fine and very helpful, only part of Saturday & yesterday ~~be~~ having been wet. Today is splendid again, but with sharp white-frost and keen low wind streaky with warm bright sun.

I have not yet had heart to touch my work – some which must be done – but shall turn to in a day or so as a relief. If you have an inclination, send me a note of your well being and of that of the women folk.

Give my love to Janey and the girls and believe me
your affectionate | Ph: Webb.

address
Al Signore Philip Webb | presso Signore C: F: Murray
106 Via de' Serragli | Firenze.

V&A, NAL MSC/1958/687, f. 10

233 • To Kate Faulkner and Mrs H. Faulkner, 26 November 1884

Florence
Novr 26. 1884

My dear Friends

You may have been reproaching me – in your kindness – for not having sent a word to you before this, and I hope you have, for I should be pleased at your wish to know whether I had been lost on the way or not. I have had several letters to write and have been much disinclined to write anything from my crowded head. I fancy that my head is the more overwhelmed ~~that~~ by the tongue in it being more or less disused: the good-natured Murray being the only one to whom I can remark anything, either in jest or earnest.

I left London on Sunday morning the 9th and went from home to Dover, across to Ostend, then to Bruges, Ghent and Brussells, all with Wardle as companion – a very good one – who watched and guarded me in the most kindly manner. I left his shielding arms on Monday the 17th in the evening, and travelled alone by night-train to Basle: I did not stop there, but went on in the morning to the St Gothard pass: from Basle and upwards there was snow and complete winter, both in appearance and coldness up to the mouth of the great tunnel: after passing through which, and shooting out into the Italian side, I came into clear bright sunshine again – another world – with no snow; one of the greatest reliefs I ever had, for I much dislike snow except – may be – on the far away mountain tops. Continuing, I came in the late afternoon to Lugano, and stopped there for the night, my present good host, Murray, arriving there also at about 10.20 at night, a very great relief to me as my tongue was a most useless & wooden one. Beside the splendid and quite lovely scenery of this Italian Switzerland and the pretty town there was one of the noblest frescos in the world to see – in wonderful condition, & as wonderfully lighted with a perfect sun.[1] We journeyed together to Como and stopped, then to Milan and stayed there, afterwards to this place where we came on Friday night the 21st.

Murray's home having many rooms, he has very kindly put at my disposal two of them in which I can be solitary after my manner and do some work, which I began this morning.[2] I shall not attempt to tell you of the wonders of the land, as I can better amuse you with my account when I come home again. My spirits vary, but I am never depressed for long together, though I confess to finding such a dim waste of glory and beauty, at times, really oppressive; this however will wear off, no doubt, and ruined beauty and deserted space will come to look natural. You must not think that I do not enjoy the wonders, for I do so, but they are piled-up, and are apt to set me musing in a rather melancholy way.

If, my dear Kate, you should feel inclined to send me word of yourself and the dear mother, I should be very glad of the news indeed. I would like you to tell me all about yourselves and Charles.

My address is
Al Signore Philip Webb. | presso Il Signore C.F. Murray
106 Via de' Serragli | Firenze. | Italy

> With kindest love to you both, believe me,
> very sincerely yours | Philip Webb.

V&A, NAL MSC/1958/687, f. 88

---

1 On the interior wall dividing the two parts of the late fifteenth-century church of S Maria degli Angoli in Lugano is a very large fresco of scenes from the Last Supper and Passion, executed in 1529–32 by Bernardino Luini (c. 1480/5–1532).
2 This work mainly related to further internal design details for Clouds, as his letters to GWJ show.

234 • To George Price Boyce, 27 November 1884

Florence
November 27. 1884

My dear Boyce

That I have not written to you and your wife from Italy, or even from Flanders, is because there has been too much for me to see and dream over and altogether a too distracting time for anything like friendly writing: added to which I was obliged to bring some work with me, and as soon as I got sat down in Florence I had to take up that. I shall reduce it to the smallest possible quantity but any work takes time. I cannot say that I find work worrying, for it rather saves me from becoming savage and moody under the impress of staring at and wondering over the vast wreck of ancient art strewn all over this country.

Wardle went with me as far as Brussells and kept things from eating too deeply into my consciousness and now, the good-natured Murray, with whom I am staying, helps also to temper wonders to my vexed soul.

How wise it was of me (!) to refuse to come to Italy for a month – say – for I find that, go to the study as slowly and carefully as I may, I am driven almost to desperation with the multitude and variety of things which cannot be passed by hastily without intense folly. The days also are so short that little time is left to go backwards & forwards over things that should be knawed [*sic*] at and not bolted. I thought to pay but general heed to pictures, but I find that they lay hold of me irresistibly and as what the knowing ones have told about the Italian architecture is ʷᵃˢ but little to the point I have to make up my mind all afresh.

I was ˢᵒ caught in the net of a tremendous Luini fresco at Lugano, on my first stepping into Italy, that I have barely recovered from the surprise of that capture now, after more than a week has passed by. I need scarcely say that things are getting muddled up in my mind in spite of my utmost care and patience.

I came here last Friday night and have as yet (partly on acc[t] of work) seen but here and there a sight. Murray is a fine sleuthhound, scenting out many hidden things that, without his aid, I sh^d surely have missed. My tongue is quite useless except in its own way of wagging, so that I have been obliged to add to my business by taking some lessons, the first of which I broke my shins over this evening, and the governess who is so good as to bear with me must have gone home with hands upraised at the folly and stupidity of the English. If she had known enough English herself she w^d have cursed me, surely, by all her Italian gods, from Bacchus downwards.

I was very glad to have your letter from Wrenbury before I left home,[1] but such was the haste with which I had to get my things together before leaving, I am not sure if I even answered it, ever so briefly? Please forgive me if I did not. If you should be willing to write me a word of the well being of yourself and Mrs Boyce, of which I should be very glad to learn, please do so and to the address given below. I heard from my sister this morning and she says she wrote to you in the north (somewhat lately) and not having heard from you is unaware of where you are. I think they w^d have real pleasure in getting you and Mrs Boyce to spend one of my usual times with them at New Place, if the cold is not too much for such an outing. Please do not consider from this that you are to go as a duty; there is no such need whatever.

My address at present is –
Al Signore Philip Webb. | presso Il Signore C: F: Murray
106 Via de' Serragli | Firenze | Italy.

Sincerely the friend of both of you | Philip Webb.

BL Add 45354, ff. 212-13

---

1 The village of Wrenbury, in Cheshire, is situated on the River Weaver.

235 • To George Washington Jack, 27 November 1884

Florence
Novr 27. 1884.

My dear Mr Jack.

I have your letters of 20th & 24th the former last evening, and the latter this morning. The first letter went round by Brindisi, by accident I suppose. I will here answer your questions.

The stable fittings ^{Clouds} to be enamelled – see Mr Basset when you can, as he is familiar with this work.[1]

If Mr Hensley writes to me I will answer him, but you can write to him & say that I shall be home in April of next year and I could, no doubt, set to work at once, then, to design his house, but it is not likely that things w^d be ready to begin building 'till the autumn of 1885, if even then; it being more likely that we sh^d be ready to work about the early spring of 1886.[2] I must see the ground before I can do anything, as the position of house depends upon circumstances, and is <u>most</u> important. You can make any arrangements you like to go and see the ground and take notes with M[r] Hensley (his address is 51 Norfolk Square Hyde Park)

Before leaving, I wrote to M[r] Wyndham and told him that I had arranged with Goodman that he should certify for all payments to Estcourt and others during my absence. Wyndham must have failed to let Rawlence & Squarey know of this. I enclose a note for you to forward to R & S in Salisbury.

Please remember me kindly to M[rs] Long,[3] and tell her to have the carpets cleaned, but to be careful to whom she goes, as some cleaners wear a carpet out in one cleaning, – do more mischief than 10 years of wear.

I send with this a drawing for the plaster enrichment in the spandrils of the dining-room beams for Clouds.[4] I think you had better faintly square this drawing in pencil and draw out full-size – as accurately as possible – the <u>outlines</u> and <u>particular curves</u> of the design in pencil, <u>not</u> putting in any shadows. Send my drawing and your outline to Estcourt with directions, first putting (in the space I've left on my drawing) the height from floor. The modeller who has done the former works will be quite able to do this work from my drawing and directions. I will do next a piece of the enrichment to run along the beams at A and send it as soon as possible, to keep the men going. After this, I will make more clear some of the parts of the drawing-room frieze. I feel quite safe in your hands as to all the works, but I should like to help you as much as possible, but depend on your using your own judgment as you think fit.

I cannot sufficiently thank you for the care you are using on my behalf. I will write to M[rs] Coronio.[5] If M[r] Buckle has come back he might go and see Ewhurst to save you, but I leave it to your direction. I suppose you have my letter written, I think, from <u>here</u> on Sunday last. You will send me what notes you can for Longden's work on the Clouds fireplaces, as I am anxious about the fitting of ironwork. Rough bits of tracing and pieces of details will be enough.

In case my last letter has not reached you, my proper address is, at present.

Al Signore Philip Webb | presso Il Signore C. F. Murray
106 Via de' Serragli | Firenze | <u>Italy</u>

Yours very sincerely | Philip Webb.

It is admirable weather here, but very cold.

V&A, AAD

---

1 PSW's former assistant.
2 The barrister, Charles Ernest Hensley (b. 1845), appears to have left an enquiry (perhaps through the recommendation of Sir William Bowman) at Raymond Buildings in PSW's absence. Nothing would come of this, probably because Hensley was wanting to proceed more quickly than PSW's schedule allowed.

3 The housekeeper for the various chambers at Raymond Buildings.
4 Spandril: 'The triangular space between the outer curve of an arch and the rectangle formed by the mouldings enclosing it, frequently filled in with ornamental work' (*OED*).
5 Aglaia Ionides Coronio (1834–1906), elder daughter of Alexander Constantine Ionides, was a member of the lively Anglo-Greek community in London and, with her cousin Maria Zambaco and Marie Spartali, one of the 'Three Graces' of Pre-Raphaelite imagery (she was a model for both Rossetti and Burne-Jones).

236 • To George Washington Jack, 6 December 1884

Florence
Dec.r 6. 1884

My dear Mr Jack

I send off this evening a detail of the smaller division of the frieze for the drawing-room at Clouds. I sent off by post, a detail (3" scale) drawing for the ornament to the curved beam for the dining-room, on the 27th Nov.r, and a full-sized drawing of the pattern to run along beams, either on the 30th Nov.r, or the 1st of Dec.r; will you let me know if you have received these? Mr Murray tells me that it is not wise to post drawings without registering them, so I send this in a different way so as to be sure that it has the best chance of getting to you. The drawing cannot go to Mr Estcourt 'till the rest of the frieze drawing is ready, but the work on it may assist in getting on with the rest of the plaque. I will now set about the Crown Imperial Lily,[1] which comes on the right hand centre-line, as that is a part less settled than the rest, and wants clearing up.

I heard from my sister yesterday, and she told me you had been to see the Ayot Green building,[2] and had called at New Place. I am very glad of this, as I fear in your anxiety for me, you may overwork yourself. I get on pretty well but find that the wonders to be seen are legion, and require a great deal of time to digest them, so that they may remain by me in time to come.

I went to Pisa on Wednesday and returned on Thursday, and found there another mine of wealth, altogether too large to be rightly assimilated. The want of the Italian language much bothers me, and though I have laid on a Governess (!) I still make but little way in it, as the things I have to do do not give me time to work long enough together at the vocabulary and grammar. When trying to measure parts of a fine 13 cent: Baldac[c]hino at a church,[3] about 4 miles from Pisa, I fell off a high stool, grazed my ankle and shook myself, but had no other mischief. A couple of workmen and 5 or 6 mischievous boys enjoyed this mischief under cover of commiseration for my disaster, and they reaped all the copper money I had, as guerdon for their sincerity. The weather is broken, and there have been 2 bad days together which has let me work steadily, with a better conscience, but again comes a fine day and I set to work to see as clearly, as my poor wits allow, those things which I have thought about for many years.

When you write, please tell me of yourself, and how you get along, and if people worry you too much. Please to remember me kindly to Mrs Long, and tell her that I often wish myself back again, but that as I am out here I must stick to it.

I have not yet heard from Sir W: Bowman's friend about his house.[4]

Believe me, Dear Jack | Yours sincerely | Philip Webb.

My address is as I gave it correctly in one of my letters.

V&A, AAD

---

1 Fritillaria Imperialis. This design survives amongst the Wyndham papers, and is illustrated in *Dakers*, p. 93. The finished plasterwork frieze is illustrated in *Kirk*, p. 141.
2 In 1884, PSW designed a 'small timber-framed pump house, for drinking water, on the village green' at Ayot St Peter, a hamlet close to Welwyn. See *Kirk*, p. 300.
3 A baldacchino (*It*) is the canopy covering the high altar, either suspended from the roof or projecting from the wall. From the next letter, the church seems to have been San Piero a Grado, four miles to the west of Pisa, and best known for its extensive fresco cycle in the nave.
4 See above, Letter 235, note 2.

237 • To Kate Faulkner and Mrs H. Faulkner, 7 December 1884

Florence.
Decr 7. 1884

My dear Friends

I had your kind letter from the hand of Kate – dated Novr 29 – and the reading of it gave me much pleasure, all except that part of it where you tell of being disappointed at not hearing from me sooner. Truly I have been busy, more so since I have been in Florence as, added to seeing, dreaming, trying to learn, going about &c &c, I have had work to do which has occupied me much. I cannot say that I dislike this work as it makes the wide-mouthed-wonder of my life in Italy seem life-like, human to me. My tongue is sadly tied, so much so as to make the time somewhat tiresome to me, as I like to talk to people wherever I meet them, & this I cannot do. In spite of 3 good lessons from a Governess (!) I make so little way that it seems almost as if I went backward, even in my baby like efforts, and I fancy that I shall, practically, have to hold my tongue almost all the time I am away. I sometimes say that it will take a strong rope to draw me away from England again.

I liked Bruges very much indeed and, I fancy, much as you did. Wardle and I were quite active in going about, and saw much. St John's Hospital[1] and the Jerusalem Ch'[2] impressed me most, perhaps, but the Belfrey [*sic*] was always a pleasure.[3] Of course I went to see the "Adoration of the Lamb"[4] and, luckily, the guide went to his dinner and left us alone there for some time.

What with the pictures there and at Brussells I thought there were more than enough to get through with attention, but here they are by the thousand and, do what I may, many, very many only just get looked at, which is a shame, or w^d be if it could be avoided. I had 2 days at Pisa last week and found that place crammed in like manner! Like an embarrassment of friends, one has to pick out those most to one's heart and mind and stick to them, so I do with the pictures. Tomorrow (I write this on Sat: night) I go again to the Uffizi gallery in the morning to try and lay hold of the greatest works there, but after all, the frescos remaining on the walks built for them are most to my content. Consider an old building of the 13th or 14th cent:, all dreary and half forgotten, having the walls more of less covered with the works of busy and skilful minds and hands of the time that the walls were ready for the painting, and all the life that has gone on and been touched by these works for 5 or 600 years! This was the case in a ch' about 4 miles out of Pisa (San Piero in Grado) lying in the fields, only a farm house adjoining it.[5] A large old ghostly church of the 13th cent: with the walls above the arches all covered with stories; the painting dim mostly, and in spaces nearly gone but yet wonderful in its diminished splendour. This ch' was not lighted up by bright sun, for it rained, but in spite of this gloom I got used, after a time, to it and came away with regret. Pisa itself is also full of wonders but they are almost deserted and neglected except in the Duomo, where worse has happened, in the way of scraping and touching up.

Your description of the going to the S. D. Federation gathering, interested me much, the more so that it was the first news of active life at home that I had heard of (I see no newspapers, except Italian ones, wh' I can't read) and the activity in such a cause cheered me:[6] here, if I could read, I do not think I sh^d find much socialistic news, as all of that kind of thought is damped down, partly by force, and partly by the anxiety to make money, which last is not of much use to the hard workers, as the taxes descend on them with dreadful weight, in order that the navy and the army may be kept at a high pitch to match those of the 'great powers'! I can tell you that what I have seen of the land in the plains of Italy – (here there is a great deal between the ranges of mountains in the val D'Arno, and a great deal more in the vast plains of Lombardy) makes me stare with amazement at the laborious care with which the tillage is carried on, labour upon labour, so that the whole place is as closely dealt with as a garden; indeed the ground looks as if it were one vast garden, clean and neat & tidy as such. This patient labour of man and beast is very touching to me.

I think I know – or rather feel – what Ruskin means with his beating down of Shelley and raising up of Keats for I have had some of the feeling of distaste for the former wh' I can hardly explain, except that I think Shelley wrote more from the head than the heart.[7]

I am sorry to learn, Kate, that you have been somewhat sleepless of late, as that wears one away and leaves nothing in repayment for the waste; I can only beg that you will take exercise, for I really believe that air and exercise is are the only help for such evil. Also, I am sure the work you did would be easier to you in the doing. I smile while writing this, thinking of my own determined opposition to any way but of my choosing. I feel almost inclined to come away home, if only to see your piano-case before it goes from your hands and is no more thoughtfully seen, for I was greatly interested in it.[8] However, I shall have the pleasure of seeing what you are about after that piece of work is done. My sister wrote to me from Welwyn and asked for your (Mrs Faulkner's) address, as she would like to send some winter flowers when they come out: I think it likely therefore that she will have the pleasure of sending some to Queen Square, as I cannot bring them to you.

You will be good enough, I am sure, to send Charles my love & any cheery word from me you can think of. I feel that it would take 50 years for me to be able to make – even a bad joke – in Italian. My last English one was at Stanhope's grand old villa, ½ a mile from here,[9] where I dined last Monday with Murray, and had rather to keep the table alive. On being pressed to eat some more after having done well in that way I said "I am half an artist myself, and must draw a line somewhere" the 'somewhere' being very much like half an artist. Murray, my host, has gone on business to London, and will not be back for some 10 days I fancy, so that his family here, who only talk Italian, will not be bored by my jests!

The weather today, after 2 days damping rather than raining, has been quite foggy this afternoon, so that when I went to the post and walked on into the middle of the town I could not see the top of Giotto's tower when standing near it.[10] This is different to what it was last Monday when I went up to its top and saw a world of splendour all round it, the day was so bright. I am intending to go into the construction of Brunelleschi's dome if I can find time and opportunity, as that is very interesting from a builder's point of view.[11] I did make a note of the preparation at the top of Giotto's tower for the lantern, or pinnacle stage, which was never built & would have been such a perfect finish for it.

Now I will tell you that I am very well in health indeed, nothing really ailing me but the universal man-cry of 'I want'. My address, for some weeks yet, will be the same at to that [sic] you last wrote to, and I shall always be glad of a letter (you must not make a point of writing) from you telling me of yourselves and what you have at heart. My kindest love to you dear Mrs Faulkner, also Kate, and I beg you to believe me

Sincerely yours | Philip Webb.

If you are in want of any books, you had better go to 1 Raymond Buildings and see if you can find them in my cases. I am sure Mrs Long would be glad to see you and give you some tea. This would be an excuse for going out!

V&A, NAL MSC/1958/687, ff. 90-1

---

1 The twelfth-century St John's Hospital in Bruges was extended during the middle ages, with the addition of a monastery and convent. Part of the building now houses the Hans Memling Museum.
2 Built in the early fifteenth century as the private chapel of an Italian merchant family, and to commemorate a pilgrimage undertaken to the Holy Land, the building was modelled on the Church of the Holy Sepulchre in Jerusalem.

3 The thirteenth-century bell tower, located in Bruges's market square, features a distinctive octagonal upper section, added in 1483–7. It originally supported a wooden spire and a figure of St Michael, but this pinnacle was destroyed by lightning in 1493. PSW recalled this visit towards the end of his life. See Vol. IV, Letter 1117.
4 The twelve-panelled polyptych of *The Adoration the Lamb* (c. 1423–32) known as the Ghent Altarpiece was made for St Bavos Cathedral in Ghent. Begun by Hubert van Eyck (c. 1385/90–1426), the work was completed by his brother, Jan van Eyck (b. before 1395, d. before 1441).
5 See previous letter, note 3.
6 Early in 1883, WM committed himself to the socialist cause, becoming an active member of the Social Democratic Federation, founded by Henry Mayers Hyndman (1842–1921). However, with others such as Andreas Scheu (1844–1927) he grew increasingly uncomfortable with Hyndman's leadership. In *The Historical Basis of Socialism* (1883), Hyndman revealed himself 'motivated by a conception of imperialism, whereby the English speaking and perhaps Teutonic peoples would lead the way to Socialism'. Moreover, he tended 'to flirt with representatives of the ruling class, and [held] an optimistic view of the possibilities of parliamentary democracy'. Martin Crick, *The History of the Social-Democratic Federation* (Keele: Ryburn Publishing, 1994), p. 33. By December 1884, factionalism in the Federation was reaching a crisis point, and would result in WM's resignation and the formation of the Socialist League. See below, Letter 241.
7 Catherine Maxwell suggests that Shelley's perceptible influence upon JR's own early writing may account for a sometimes aggressive counter-reaction in later life, such as in his 1884 Oxford 'Lecture on Patience', almost certainly the source for PSW's comment: 'read as much Keats as possible, and no Shelley. Shelley, with due admiration for his genius notwithstanding, is entirely mischievous'. Cited in Maxwell, 'Sensitive Plants: Shelley's Influence on Ruskin', *Durham University Journal*, LXXXVII (January 1995), p. 39.
8 KF had taken on the decoration, in gold and silver-gilt gesso, of the piano made in 1883 by John Broadwood & Sons for Alexander Constantine Ionides. The decorative design was prepared by EBJ, to match Ionides's interiors at 1 Holland Park. The piano was exhibited in 1888 at the first Arts and Crafts Exhibition, and was given by Mrs Ionides to the Victoria and Albert Museum. KF completed the decorations in 1885.
9 For Villa Nuti, see above, Letter 229, note 3.
10 The campanile designed by Giotto (1266/7–1337) stands adjacent to the Basilica di Santa Maria del Fiore and the St John Baptistery, all of which are situated in the Piazza del Duomo. Begun in 1334, the tower was not completed until 1359, more than twenty years after Giotto's death.
11 The Duomo of the Cathedral was designed by the architect and engineer, Filippo Brunelleschi (1377–1446), to crown the Basilica di Santa Maria del Fiore, designed by Arnolfo di Cambio (c. 1240–1300/10). Construction of the Basilica began in the late thirteenth century and was completed in 1436. The bold façade of pink, green and white marble panels, a deliberate attempt to combine aspects of the Gothic with the newer Renaissance style, is actually the product of nineteenth-century restoration, and was commissioned from Emilio de Fabris (1808–83) in 1871.

238 • To William Morris, 9 December 1884

Florence.
Dec[r] 9. 1884

My dear Fellow

I had your letter of 29 Nov[r] on the 5th Dec. and was mighty-glad of a word from activity in the region of the whistling winds; here, I doubt if there be much activity in the Cause. I am hardly able to be a judge, however, as not knowing the tongue I am mostly shut into the cell of myself. This alone therefore w[d] make any news you could give me of the working of the S.D.F as interesting as the name of the 'Derby' winner to a City clerk. You know that I am not bursting with hope of instant advance (as I say when doing my Italian primer with my Governess) but the future success is certain to my mind, but most surely only in the future.[1] From ^{what} I can see and learn here of land cultivation and labour, the system w^d be against agricultural movement, as the farming folk have a pretty tight grip of the land – leading landlords a dance – that that is enough to keep them from hazarding anything. Landlords get half of the fruits, and let them look to it that the wine be not "measured in oil barrels" as they say; the oil barrels being the smaller. The landlord must up with the light to see what is being done or the early bird will assuredly have the worm. By this it comes that "factors" are much employed, when it is "pull devil pull baker"[2] and, as a rule, the agent gets rich so quickly that the class is looked upon with envy and admiration. I hear tell that the taxes are the very devil on the top of the factor-imp,[3] and all classes have to smuggle, in one way or another, the amount they make by their labour, honest or rascally.

It is amazing to look at the cultivation of the soil, all so close and careful that a London market garden looks rather slovenly in comparison. I am drinking the good common wine of the country and I find it capital stuff: however sharp it may be it is not rough. Well, on my journeying to Pisa – say 50 or 60 miles – ^{I saw} the whole vale – plain is trellised (in plan) with vines hung to trees, and the rest of the growth is carried on in between; that is, the lines are the vines and the corn, cabbages &c are the spaces.

I see no newspapers, but now & then Murray reads a snatch of news out of an Italian print. He did this one morning at Pisa, when I heard that the English Government were on the redistribution bill, and I had heard nothing of the franchise settlement, neither do I know now![4] I think you might make it plain what should not be done to Westminster Hall if you give evidence – make an effort for this.[5] You have not seen what they have done to San Ambrogio at Milan – one of the most interesting churches in the world.[6]

What touched me most in Florence? Well I can hardly say – perhaps the view from Stanhope's Villa, overlooking the skirts of the city on one side and the val D'Arno on the other, this broad valley bounded distantly on both sides by the mighty and beautifully outlined & gradated hills. In the midst, one mass of splendid cultivation: tree'd for use mainly but plenty of such branched growth. The city itself looked mighty lovely one day when I got on to the top of Giotto's tower. Arch^{ly}, the outside of the Duomo is not so bad as English arch^{ts} & others have thought they made ^{out}. Inside it is dull as I knew it must be from plans of it. Still the dome is simply wasted – it really is a noble one. Of paintings, wall work is my pleasure; 'tis quite new to me, and the sight of Luini's great picture across the screen-wall of a plain early church at Lugano was quite compelling. It was in perfect condition lighted by the west window (so called by me) in early morning, so that all the plain of coloured light of the picture was quite and completely touching: on turning away from it the beautiful hills about the place there were all in keeping. I've had no such slap on the soul since I saw that. Indeed, as soon as the train ran out of S. Gothard tunnel the sweet hills had me at their mercy, I had no will of my own. Occasionally – say once or so in a day – I am dull; at other times I rise sufficiently to wish to stay out of my time. I find not being able to talk is a beastly nuisance, which I will not easily incur again. You will smile when I tell you that my work, which occupies me some good part of my time, is not looked upon by me as an evil! The days are very short and I sometimes work 'till it is too late to see anything inside a building.

I gave a pinch of snuff to one of the "dogs of the Lord" at Santa Maria Novella, the other day,[7] who kindly waited past his dinner time talking with Murray while I had undisturbed looking at the pictures in the 'Spanish Chapel' there, & he then opened the door for us to go – it was past the time. It was meagre day & perhaps his loss was not great. I shall surely not go to Rome 'till after Xmas, and my address at present will still be 'presso Sig: C. F. M.' as before.

Give my kind love to Miss Meadows[8] and the girls and think of me, when you do, in our 30 years way. | Your affectionate | Ph: Webb.

V&A, NAL MSC/1958/687, f. 11

---

1 PSW's willingness to commit himself to an active part in the Socialist cause is moving towards some kind of decision, and would be triggered when WM left the Social Democratic Federation. See below, Letters 241 and 248.
2 Now archaic: each man should do his best in his line of business and not interfere with that of another.
3 Meaning is allusive here, unless 'factor-imp' itself is a kind of tax (imp[osition]).
4 The principal reforms brought about by the 1884 Representation of the People Act (commonly known as the Third Reform Act) extended the franchise to all men paying rent or owning land valued at £10, and redefined boundaries, so that in future each constituency (with just a couple of exceptions) would return only one member of Parliament. Women remained wholly excluded from voting.
5 The House of Commons had established a select committee to consider a report from John Loughborough Pearson for the proposed restoration of Westminster Hall. WM's statement drawn up on behalf of the SPAB (?November 1884) argued for the careful protection of recently-discovered parts of the wall of archaeological interest, and that no more than repair and preservation of the Hall itself should be contemplated (see *CLWM*, II, p. 335, note 3). There had apparently been a response from the select committee, indicating that WM would be invited to testify to the select committee: not only must his (lost) letter to PSW of 29 November have alluded to this, so did another of 25 November, probably to George Somers Clarke: 'My evidence will be of the shortest & simplest kind, and will merely be a protest on the part of the Society against <u>any alteration at all</u>; except perhaps a petit house to guard the stones in the lower part of the wall'. WM to Clarke, 25 November 1884, *CLWM*, II. On 11 March 1885 he testified to the select committee.
6 Originally founded by St Ambrose in 279–86, the Milanese basilica of Sant'Ambrogio survives in its twelfth-century Romanesque form.
7 Alludes to the medieval pun on 'Dominicans' (*Domini canes*: 'dogs of the Lord'). The cloisters of the monastic portion of the basilica of Santa Maria Novella, the most important of the churches founded by the Dominicans in Florence, contain the fourteenth-century Cappellone degli Spagnoli (the Spanish Chapel), in the former chapter house. The walls are decorated with frescoes by Andrea da Firenze (d. 1379?), including scenes of the Passion and Crucifixion, and a large *Allegory of the Church Militant* and the *Church Triumphant* (executed 1365–9).
8 Not identified.

239 • To George Washington Jack, 9 December 1884

Florence
Dec.r 9. 1884

Dear Mr Jack

Your letter of Dec.r 4 – rec.d this morning – was comfortingly assuring. I had set to work to do another piece of the drawing-room frieze at Clouds when I got the tracing of the small dining-room arches at the end. I will now do this first, and let you have it when done. You do not mention it, but I fancy you had received the 2 separate drawings I sent for the ~~D.~~ dining room ceil.g? and, as I wrote to you on Saturday, I have sent another drawing, registered, so as to be more sure that the work is not lost by the way. Perhaps, when you next write you will say what things you get from me & letters.

They will be wanting to lay some drains at Ewhurst I fancy shortly, and the laying sh.d be carefully looked-to either by you or Mr Buckle; and perhaps he might help you with this as he knows much about the levelling &c. Each length of pipes laid should be tested before they are covered up.

As to Ayot parish room.[1] The builder has nothing to do with levelling of ground or putting gates. Mr Jephson must settle this or leave it 'till I come home;[2] but my brother tells me that Jephson is going to write to me.

Clouds. I am very glad indeed that you like the hall, as I feel sure you w.d not say so, if you did not feel it. Plasterer is vain, well, a little conceit in a workman is often a good sign, as men are seldom vain of scamping their work.[3] I am surprised that the carvers have not finished the 4 cap[ital]s in the hall: if they had been of granite they could hardly have taken longer. I am really disappointed with this length of time in their doing and shall probably think it right to pay a part of their cost myself – however, it can't be helped. I hope the lobby at foot of private stairs won't be quite as dark, as it seems to have struck you as being, when all is finished. In any case it is the private stair and people using it will know its ways.

I quite agree with you and Mr Goodman about mending Slades roof, this sh.d be done as suggested, keeping in mind repairing simply, and economically – good also as to your intention about the ivy.

In answer to your list of questions. (1) the W.C. seats at Clouds only to be of clean Honduras mahogany, not stained, and French polished with clear uncoloured polish – the rest of the W.C. fittings, oak, untouched with anything. (2) I must depend on Mr Longden for saying if I ordered a cistern for still-room boiler. I rather thought I said that it might be hand fitted, and I still rather think it might so be. (3) Cedar-wood fireplaces not to be polished or oiled – if anything be done it will be waxed, but I sh.d wish this to wait till I see it. (4) About these tiles which Longden has in stock of Morris & Co.s ~~des~~ work. I was not anxious for them, but if you think some of them will go well in the rooms, use them as you like, but Longden ought to keep the price down, as I sh.d not have used such costly ones otherwise, please to let him know this. (5) I sh.d use deal boards to garden wall, but I think the gardener had better supply these when he wants them for the trees, which will not be yet awhile. (6) I think the well in middle of garden might wait a bit, or 'till I come home, unless the Wyndhams' – either of them – ask to have it done now. (7) The boarding to covered way to laundry to be deal, and tarred, but the tarring not to be done till they have been up some little time and been dryed [sic].

How are you getting on with this work? I mean, is it in Howell's hands to begin any work about it? and has Goodman got his schedule of prices &c. I think the new building should be begun and carried on when weather allows.

I will do the necessary work to the iron fittings to the large fireplaces of house, directly I can. I should like to do this carefully, and will therefore think of it at once, & send to you when done.

I thought when doing the spandril [sic] pattern to the dining room beam, that it was hardly worthwhile to make any change for the opposite side: but, as it will [have] to be separately modelled, if you could see your way to making a drawing with some slight variation, to guide the modeller, please do so. I thank you much for your care for my work wh', poor as it is, I am always anxious about myself.

Yours very sincerely | Philip Webb.

Please give my kind remembrance to Goodman when you see him. I am getting along pretty well but find my memory very poor. I heard from Welwyn that you had been to New Place, and I was glad you did so. I have a number of letters to write so that I should be glad if you mention me kindly to Vinall. I hope Mrs Long and her people are well. I suppose you have more water than we have, the Arno is so low that it could almost be waded – quite perhaps – in parts. Address to me as last letter.

V&A, AAD

---

1 See above, Letter 236, note 2.
2 The Reverend Henry Jephson was rector of Ayot St Peter, 1872–1911.
3 'Scamping': negligently or hurriedly. (*OED*).

240 • To George Washington Jack, 26 December 1884

Florence.
Decr 26. 1884

My dear Jack.

I have had no letter from you since yours dated Decr 12. I merely mention this that you may know if your letters have reached me. There is no necessity for you to write unless there is something demanding attention. I send you by this same post a drawing of the cactus-like flower of Clouds frieze. I rather suspect that the plasterers will be pressing you for this frieze very shortly, and therefore I hasten to send you all I can to enable you to make up the whole of the detail. I think I have given enough now to allow of you and the modeller doing the rest between you. However, I shall send you one more note of this detail viz. the branch-end which falls over the top of the Solomon's seal boughs, and I will do this as soon as possible. In the drawing I now send I am not satisfied with the character of the flowers indicated at (A) on the Sⁿ seal boughs, but I think you will be able to give some character to these (in another place on the panel) from the drawing – which is of good size – in the green-bound books of botany which I left with you, with a mark at the page of the Solomon's seal.

I wish the modeller to be impressed with the importance of giving the character shewn, in my later drawings, to the arching boughs of leafage, such as those marked (B) (C) on this drawing, and all leafage referable to the same ᵏⁱⁿᵈ ᵒᶠ plant in the panel. These boughs to be well raised above the ground, but to be kept flattish at the upper surface or top plane, giving sharpness &c to the veining and general character of the leafage proper. I have noted on my different drawings that the work is to be modelled to suit the distance of the work from the eye. The exact height of this I have not by me, therefore I should like you to specify it to the modeller. You will readily understand what I mean when I say that I want the whole panel brought well together, to be modelled boldly but not heavily or with great relief to catch dust. Also, that the panel should have variation in its relief according to the disposition of the different parts of the design.

I hope my last letter of explanation gave, with sufficient exactness, my answer to your reiterated question as to Slades.[1] What sort of weather are you having? Open, or closed with frost?

Yours very sincerely | Philip Webb.

V&A, AAD

---

1 PSW had written to GWJ on 13 and 16 December, with further instructions and clarifications about the work in progress on Slades, the gardener's cottage at Clouds.

241 • To William Morris, 28 December 1884

Florence
Decʳ 28. 1884

My dear Fellow

I had your letter of the 11ᵗʰ Dec: and found it good for me. Snuff, and a letter now & then of yours will gan [*sic*] me live in this home of lovely graves, for a while. You conjured up for me a set of scenes which have cropped up now and again as I have mooned about. You have the hive about your ears and you should be more hairy all over than a bear to live tolerably thro: it. I would that you could have moderated that interesting fire-brand in Auld Reekie, but I doubt the power of water on him.[1]

The ^(want of) "no man wanting to get anything out of it for himself" will be, always, in the strife for right, the devils cross buttock in social life. Over, the combinations of men must go, time after time: well, patience. I am much afraid that I see too much in front and behind and too little in the middle to be a really useful companion.[2] Willing but unable – in fact. If only the people would but appear on the field with questions to be answered I sh^d be more hopeful of the present. I think that the best of us English, if we were without money, could be "got at". We ^(even we,) who are well off ~~can't~~ ^(could not) be sure of ourselves if the pinch came to us. The English cannot live on a little, when food fails them, spirit fails also. Here's a Job's comforter: I didn't mean it! As for the 'Gentlemen', they are as blind as bats and will go on pigeon shooting 'till the day of judgment. When Capitalism is really at its wits end for markets something may be done in England, and as soon as I read newspapers again that will be what I shall look for. Still no one must think that when capitalists are down on their marrow bones ~~that~~ they will be for the people, they are a bad-bred lot, and the ill gotten race must die out, for no good can come of them.

I should be glad to hear if, between the acts of politics, something could be done to save Westminster Hall or any other good thing remaining to us. Shaw Lefevre is bent on dishing us,[3] but he can turn tail on occasion and I should dearly like to make him, in this one matter at all events. Micklethwaite is a student, and nothing therefore can be done with him in a living world, of things tangible I doubt if he has the ghost of an idea.[4] In the whole of the small antiscrape society there are only 2 or 3 who have ever seen an old building.

I have a little got used to this place and shall feel when I move to Rome somewhat stiff and awkward again, but I dare say I shall get away ^(there) about the end of the first week in Jan: stopping at Siena on the way. I went to Prato, Pistoja and Lucca on the 3 first days of ~~this~~ ^(last) week and found much to gape at. Lucca has the wonderfullest hills round it possible and, as it was a very fine day, the sides and grooves of them shone again all in their deep green-brown. Tis only the towns that look old, the country looks as young and fresh as a 15 years old girl. All the old architecture about, before the Renaissance, I like better than I expected, but I have mixed feelings while staring at it. Strange enough to say, I can still go on with my own trumpery work without too much disgust – perhaps the reason is that I only see it on paper, where it looks real. I make next to no way with the tongue, nor shall I, that's certain – In the first place I've too little time to learn in, and in the second and worse I have no turn for learning languages, and my memory is worse than words can say. I may see a working man – a mason – at or near Siena, who talks English, and I shall try and see if he is shy on serious matters.

How are Janey and Jenny & May doing this winter? Tell Janey that I think I like the very small England as much as ever but I also have real delight in this different looking country, and the only thing which at all jars on me is the sight of a well to do Englishman. Of course I see now other than the well to do. There is a shoddy-fortuned American here who drives 7 or 8 horses in a string – has driven 16 – 2 x 2 – 'till an accident blocked the streets and the Lord Mayor of the place restricted him to 6 or 8. He uses all his horses by making his coachmen follow with separate teams, and be damned to him.

Don't you put yourself to writing me a letter 'till you have time & inclination, but I shall always be glad of a few words.

Your affectionate | Ph: Webb.

V&A, NAL MSC/1958/687, f. 12

---

1 'Auld Reekie' (Old Smoky), the colloquial name for Edinburgh. WM delivered his lecture, 'How We Live and How We Might Live' to the Edinburgh branch of the Scottish Land and Labour League (founded by Andreas Scheu) on 13 December, and the next evening lectured in Glasgow on 'Art and Labour' to the Glasgow Sunday Society. On 29 December he resigned from the Social Democratic Federation, and with other dissidents announced the formation of the Socialist League. Its manifesto was drafted by WM, as one might have supposed from the rhetorical sonority of its opening sentence: 'Fellow Citizens, We come before you as a body advocating the principles of Revolutionary International Socialism; that is we seek a change in the basis of Society – a change which would destroy the distinctions of classes and nationalities.'
2 PSW seems not to have been a member of the Federation, but clearly was influenced by WM's own recent history, for he quickly agreed to WM's wish that he might join the Bloomsbury branch of the Socialist League. See below, Letter 248.
3 George John Shaw-Lefevre (1831–1928), created Baron Eversley in 1906, was at this time MP for Reading (1863–85). He was a member of Gladstone's government, serving as Postmaster-General and First Commissioner of Works, in which role he had hired John Loughborough Pearson to report on the restoration possibilities for Westminster Hall. See above, Letter 238, note 5.
4 The architect John Thomas Micklethwaite (1843–1906) was an antiquarian and liturgical scholar by inclination, whose publications up to this time included *Modern Parish Churches: their Plan, Design and Furniture* (1874), and a scholarly paper on Westminster Abbey, which were perhaps the grounds for PSW to consider him a 'student' rather than a practitioner. Nonetheless, the SPAB had an excellent professional relationship with Micklethwaite, 'one of the few architects they did not hesitate to recommend in their early days': Chris Miele, '"English Antiquity": Historic Buildings Culture and National Identity in the Nineteenth Century', in David Crellin and Ian Dungavell, eds., *Architecture & Englishness 1880–1914* (London: Society of Architectural Historians of Great Britain, 2003), p. 98. PSW would himself canvass 'the erudite Micklethwaite' about Westminster Abbey when acting as an intermediary for Giacomo Boni. See Vol. II, Letters 447 and 460, and his letters to Micklethwaite written during July and November 1893.

242 • To George Price Boyce, 5 January 1885

Florence
Jan: 5. 1885

My dear Boyce

I had nearly given M[rs] Boyce & you up as 'gone coons',[1] when your looked for letter came and stayed all further maledictions and indeed changed the tone to blessings. I have not written so many letters of [the] personal & friendly kind for years as I have within the last 8 weeks, but well I know the kind of delay which besets one at home and delays the writing of a letter which w̃ be a pleasure, after all, to write. I've no doubt you said when yours was written, that it was not such a terrible matter ~~after all~~ when it was <u>done</u>.

I am glad you screwed up courage to go to New Place[2] as I am sure the folk there would be very glad to have the change of the company of both of you in the house, and I don't fancy the journey is much of a trouble or the place much of a bore to you; the country, even so near London, being real country and the physic real nasty! 'snasty' is the older form of a very trenchant word. When I am there, I make the doctor my conscience keeper, and eat & drink whatever he sets before me, laying any consequences on his shoulders. I hope you & Madame did the same.

I have not seen Dering's pictures for 15 or 16 years and I am afraid those left to him have been turned face to the wall for most of that time.[3]

You do well to attend at the antiscrape meetings, as so many of the half or quarter hearted members take no interest in the object, probably because they do not know or care anything about ancient work. I believe that [they] are really a little more careful in Italy than they were, but much mischief still goes on. To shew the kind of stupidity in the Italian mind as to buildings, I will instance a thing I noticed the other day. I was going into Santa Croce again one afternoon,[4] and found masons at work rubbing down the marble work of the new front there, which was only finished a few years ago, to make it look quite white again; some tone of time was actually improving the look of the dull modern work, & it was too much for the neat & weak modern mind, so they set themselves to grind it off. However, there is but little spare money in the country, and things are not being done here on the large scale they are in France. I believe that S.t Marks at Venice is safer now than it was before we made the row.[5]

I have seen the North western towns ~~of~~ Lugano, Como, & Milan, and the mid Italian towns of Pisa, Lucca, Pistoja and Prato, and I have worked away here pretty steadily, but I have almost too much to see to find time to make many notes, & what notes I do make are of the roughest – Helps to my own bad memory more than anything else: the pictures are a great hindrance, for I have found them so many & so good that I have been unable to resist looking hard & long at them. I had a sudden burst of fresh enjoyment over the Benozzo Gozzolis' in the small chapel of the Pal: Riccardi on Saturday, and they took my breath away. I like Benozzo immensely, & his work there is in such good condition.[6]

There is a good deal to be seen in Florence if you poke about for it, but I can see that one suffers less pain than others do who saw Florence 20 or 30 years ago. The loss of the walls is immense, as I have gone the ring of the place and counted the towers & bits of wall remaining & found the dulness of the boulevards which have taken the place of the walls.[7]

My work, as you note, did follow me here, and though it was a loss of time to me in one way it was a gain in another, as it made me feel less like an idle man amusing himself while the poorer were working for him. However, I have done one fit and another meets me in Rome so that friend and assistant Jack, at home, be not left too heavily taxed. If, when I come back, and we find opportunity and you inclination, we will go together to Knoyle and see the mess I have made there.[8] If there be any part of it bearable no one will be able to say that the good of it came of my seeing Italy.

How different the English and Italian landscapes are and yet how equally beautiful. Morris's first lecture put this difference on the right footing and any thoughtful person can readily know the reasons why.[9]

I have heard from Wardle, but hardly in a hopeful way, as to the energy of the anti-scrape committees. I have read no newspapers, and have only gathered what I know of this and other English things from what friends have written to me.

I thank you for seeing my beautiful Halton Castle in its place again, ready to meet me on my return.[10] I hope Mrs Long offered you civilities, as she w^{d} hardly look upon you as a thief, having brought something instead of taken something away.

Our weather has been broken, but of late more dry and cold, the last few days having a kind of English March touch in them. I take onions and oil here in moderate fashion but, as I sleep alone – yes, I do – this does not matter. I hope when this reaches you that both Mrs Boyce and you will have thrown off your colds.

I start for Rome on Wednesday, taking San Gimignano & Siena on the way, both of which places I am looking forward to seeing. I shall stay in Rome somewhere about a month, I fancy, and then return by Perugia Assisi &c to Florence again & then almost directly northwards to Bologna, Verona, and other towns to Venice, at which time it will be more spring like; but things may change my course.

If you sh^{d} wish to say anything before I again write, and you have not my address, you can send a note to Mr Jack & he will enclose it. With kindest remembrance to your wife.

Believe me | Yours sincerely | Philip Webb

I am afraid that Mrs Boyce w^{d} hardly be able to spell out this letter.[11] (My Italian goes very badly)

I gave Murray & wife the kind message of you and yours.

BL Add 45354, ff. 214-5

---

1 Slang (*USA*): a hopeless case.
2 Harry Webb's house in Welwyn.
3 This probably refers to the inventor, George Edward Dering (1831–1911), who inherited Lockleys, an early eighteenth-century house in Welwyn, from his father, Robert Dering. Something of an eccentric, Dering based himself in Brighton, only visiting Lockleys once a year until finally settling there in his final years. He inherited some fine pictures, including Conrad Faber von Creuznach (c. 1550–52), *Portrait of a Man with a Moor's Head on his Signet Ring* (c. 1535, Metropolitan Museum of Art, New York).
4 The Basilica of Santa Croce is the principal Franciscan church in Florence. Doubtless PSW was drawn to make repeated visits not just for its Giotto frescos, but in the knowledge that it was the burial place of Michelangelo.

5 For the SPAB campaign against restorations to the façade of San Marco, and the resistance experienced, see Frank C. Sharp, 'Exporting the Revolution: The Work of the SPAB outside Britain 1878–1914', in *Miele*, and also below, PSW to GBO, 18 September 1886, note 8, and Vol. II, 15 December 1889, note 6.
6 The subject of Gozzoli's cycle of frescoes, commissioned by Piero de' Medici, and which cover three walls of the Magi chapel in the Palazzo Medici Riccardi in Florence, is *The Procession of the Magi* (1459–61).
7 In 1865, Florence became Italy's capital until it was replaced by Rome six years later. During this short time the city saw much modernisation, involving the removal of many medieval houses and the demolition of the ancient town walls, leaving only the gates, as well as the introduction of a widened street system and public squares. The architect in charge was Giuseppe Poggi (1811–1901).
8 He means Clouds, at East Knoyle.
9 Writing from memory, PSW probably means WM's lecture 'The Lesser Arts', delivered before the Trades' Guild of Learning on 4 December 1877, in which he dwelt on the English countryside: 'beyond that smoky world, there, out in the country we may still see the works of our fathers yet alive amidst the very nature they were wrought into, and of which they are so completely a part: for there indeed if anywhere . . . was there a full sympathy between the works of man, and the land they were made for.' *Hopes and Fears for Art* (London: Reeves and Turner, 1889), p. 22.
10 GPB's 1881 watercolour of Halton Castle, in Northumberland, was given by PSW to the Victoria and Albert Museum in 1911.
11 The writing is small and the pages crowded.

243 • To George Washington Jack, 18 January 1885

Rome.
Sun: Jan: 18. 1884 [*sic*]

My dear Jack.

I have received your letter of date Jan: 5 and also the roll containing the tracings notes &c for band in hall at level of cap's, and the figured dim[ensio]^{ns} of drawing [-room] ceiling for Clouds.

I left Florence on Jan: 9 and was just a week ^{in} getting here, stopping at 2 or 3 places on the way, and since I have been here my time has been so fully occupied, and in a way intermixed with other peoples time, that I have been quite unable to set apart any for particular work. Also, I have not the same convenience here for work that I had in Florence, but I think I shall be able to manage the necessary details to keep you going without your being overtaxed with indefinite work.

I will now take the items of your letter as they came and answer the questions. Drawing-room frieze. You are right I think as to sending what you propose in the way of drawings for the modeller, added to which it is well that you should have the original drawing by you. I am really glad of your opinion as to the probable effect of the pattern if it is well done. Plasterboard in great hall. I will do this pattern, but it may be a week before I can get anything satisfactorily done to hand to you as, my seeing, so constantly, work of the utmost nicety in Italy makes me even more "fidgetty" than ever in doing my poor work, added to which, when I really do the work, it must <u>not</u> be a reflection of any antiquities I am studying. It <u>must</u> stand on its own weak legs. I will keep the scale of the ornament as large as you wisely suggest.

Hot water service for Laundry. Yes, Longden should do this, and I explained to him what I should want, but I sh^d wish you to impress upon him that careful economy was very necessary, as Mr Wyndham has been accustomed to very rough work at Wilbury, & was quite satisfied with it. He is also beginning to do other things about Clouds under the direction of Rawlence & Squarey in a cheap way – as a warning to me, ^{I fancy,} that he does not want to spend much more money ~~I fancy~~. However, there is no need whatever for the laundry work to be done in a fancifully perfect way, and Longden should be made to understand this.

Ironwork to large fireplaces. You must stick to it that the work to all these fireplaces should be done on the principles I have laid down and any variation sh^d only be allowed if you yourself see that it is really necessary. Longden's are very mechanical people, and so long as they can get steam engines and unskilled labour to do their work at a good profit to themselves they will care for nothing else. Anything like useful ingenuity – which w^d tax their brains (?) or reduce their profits – is out of their bargain. Unless Longden is successful at Clouds with his work – where he has already had too much his own way – I shall look to put any future work into other hands. He disappointed me too about the Ewhurst prices.

Certainly, let the dining-room chimney piece be set up ^(fixed) to take templates accurately from,[1] and I think all the other fireplaces will have to be done in the same way, but they can easily [be] protected when fixed.

I am afraid young Mr Turner has – beyond his nervousness – been a little wanting in energy; however, Macculloch should now get the carving done straight off without more ado.[2] He is wrong in saying that the matter was only between Mr Turner & myself. I applied to Macculloch once or twice for estimates &c, wh' he promised me – even by letter – but never let me have. I suspect I shall have to pay, myself, for the waste of time.

Area on N. side of offices. I think this might remain 'till I return, as, sh^d it be unfinished when Wyndham gets into the house it w^d not matter.

Ewhurst. Mr Buckle's report is good – but all the drains should be seen to and tested either by him or by you – and none covered up 'till they have been so tested. Have you heard at all from Miss Ewart? If she w^d like to meet either you or Buckle at Ewhurst you c^d arrange to do so.

I thank you for telling me your wishes as to taking your young friend to study in Raymond B^{gs}. I can see no objection to the proposition whatever, but you will readily understand that I sh^d like it to be your affair and that your cousin sh^d be under your control, not mine, subject of course to my decision on certain points.[3] I sh^d be very glad to be the means of giving a helping hand, but w^d not like in any way to be fettered. At all events the thing might be tried by you to see what comes of it, and if the young fellow can, in time, make himself useful, I sh^d be very glad to pay for all assistance according to the necessity for help and its value. I feel sure that I can leave myself in your hands in this matter. ^{Will you kindly make a note of this kind of agreement?}

I enclose the Income Tax "Demand note"; will you be so good as to pay it for me and get the proper receipts? If you sh^d be short of money before my return, will you ask Mr Wardle for some, showing him this letter, as I am sure he will kindly do it for me at the risk of Mr Morris, as the latter would wish to help me I know. A letter to my bankers w^d be enough, but the thing would be easier done in the way I here propose.

Will you be so good as to go to Archbutts', the mathematical instrument makers in Bridge Street Westminster[4] – opposite the east end of the Houses of Parliament – and get a small ^spirit level, like that I had, which has a small reflector inside it; ^the instrument is for taking levels as you walk about, thus. [*sketch*] It is of brass, about 6 or 7 inches long. I think you saw the one I had.[5] The thing costs 21/- exactly, I believe, and I sh^d like you to get Archbutts' to pack it in cotton wool in a thin light wooden case, to send by post, and you should have it registered and very clearly addressed to

Al Signore
Il Signore J: H: Middleton | 29 Via Babuino | Roma. | Italy

The thin wooden box sh^d be put into a paper wrapper – paper of a tough kind, or cut up a canvas-lined large envelope to gum to size and form. It is quite likely that Archbutts' are accustomed to send things abroad, and will know how to send it properly packed; but, at all events, it should be <u>registered</u> so as to be able to trace it in case of it's mis carriage.

I have rooms here in the same house and ^on the floor in which Mr Middleton lives, and I think it would be better for you to address your letters to me, "presso" Il Signore J: H: Middleton, as your last letter &c came all right.

I came from Florence by way of San Gimignano, Siena, and Orvieto and found much to interest me and, with their decayed wonders, also to distract me. Rome is a monstrous city which is embarrassing in more ways than one, as it has great beauties, great ruins, great uglinesses and vast discordancies [*sic*] and, though extremely interesting is, in itself, not so beautiful as many of the smaller towns of Italy; added to which, a large amount of time is necessary to allow of properly sifting the good from the bad, and a memory as long, as mine is proportionately short. The Vatican, alone, is one vast heap of wonders, beauties, extravagant and monstrous pomposities all muddled up together. Mr Middleton is a very able and experienced antiquary and, when he can get away from his laborious studies, he guides my steps through ^the vastnesses of ancient Rome. Sometimes I feel inclined to run away from the place at once, at others to stay 'till I can disentangle the multifarious objects spread over square miles of a closely packed town. I sometimes wish myself back in dingy Gray's Inn where decay – if real – is not so terrible in its self-assertion.

If my writing is not very clear, I must ask you to lay it to the account of my being cold for, even in Italy towards the South, the rooms in which one has to work or sit are not so warm & comfortable as in sooty London.

Yours sincerely | Philip Webb.

I duly received a paper kindly sent me by Mr Boyce.

I think I am likely to be here for 3 weeks or so longer, so that you can give my address to anyone.

V&A, AAD

1 PSW's design of a bird returning to the nest, symbolic of 'the central importance of Clouds to the Wyndham family' (*Kirk*, p. 139) would be carved in the centre of the drawing-room mantelpiece. See illustration in *Dakers*, p. 93.
2 This relates to PSW's irritation at the slowness with which the carvers were working on the hall capitals. See above, Letter 239.
3 This may have been the brother of Annie Christian Gray (1861–1942), the cousin whom GWJ married in 1888.
4 J. & W.E. Archbutt, of 201 Westminster Bridge Road, Lambeth, founded in 1796, manufactured scientific measuring instruments.
5 He intended this as a gift for his host in Rome, John Middleton. See below, Letters 245–6.

244 • To Kate Faulkner and Mrs H. Faulkner, 24 January 1885

Rome
Jan: 24. 1885

My dear Friends

Since I last wrote to you I have been on the move and, as I think, in my last letter I said I was about to leave Florence, I have not expected a letter from you. I have been here for 10 days, and took a week to get from Florence. The post has been stopped altogether for some days, and I believe even now it goes by the St Gothard pass instead of the Mont' Cenis route,[1] the heavy snow in the mountain region having blocked the way. It has been partly on this account, partly because I have been busy with my work, and at other times getting about to make myself as well acquainted with this city as possible in the time that has caused me to almost cease writing to England for a little while, save that I have been obliged to write to Mr Jack who is working for me still in Gray's Inn. I hope you have not been vexed at my silence or accused me of forgetting you? Truth to tell, Rome has been very cold indeed since the storms & rains which lasted 3 or 4 days after I got here; so cold has it been, that my fingers had to be thrust into pockets to keep them useable at all. I ought at once to have written when I got here, to give you my address, as I want much to know how the good mother is, and it will take at least 8 days before I can learn; however, perhaps I could not have heard from you, the post being out of gear. Will you kindly send me some word as soon as you get this letter – if you do get it.

I left Florence on the 7th of Jan: and went direct to Siena, which is nearly half way to Rome.[2] I spent some 5 days there and found the place full of interest: that is a walled town after your hearts, the streets all uphill down dale: the middle of the place being on a hill and the rest on hills which radiate from the centre, like fingers from a hand; the valleys being between the fingers. Of this place too I shall be able to shew you some photographs when I get back. The Cathedral and the town hall are the great buildings of the place, the other Churches, though huge & noble in scale, are mostly almost bare. The cathedral is extraordinarily full of fine work of a strange kind, one of the most interesting being the floor, all over which are graven, & inlaid in marble, many fine pictures.[3] You can see an example of this work in a rubbing of one design which hangs in the S. Kenⁿ Museum in the great hall on the right-hand side ~~after~~ of the one you enter by. One of the chief delights of Siena, to me, is the number of large mediæval houses still standing; some of them almost untouched.

I went one day to San Gimigno [*sic*] but was only there long enough to see its strangeness and general, but rude, beauty.[4] From Siena I went to Orvieto, a noble & most ancient city on a rock, overlooking and high above the river Pallia [*sic*], which, soon after, runs into the Tiber.[5] It was very rough, stormy weather while I was at Orvieto and, as the stupid authorities have been blundering over their repairs of the roof, a very considerable part of the ^{Cathedral} church was drenched with rain, even frescos (luckily not the best) being heavily wetted.[6] Of this place too I shall have some photographs to shew you.

I am somewhat indurated[7] with sight-seeing, but I confess I do not like it, and shall hardly be sorry when my time is up and I can pretend to earning an honest living, for as it is now – in spite of the work I do – I feel somewhat of an idle man, living on the sweat of the labours of poverty.

Rome to me, is almost a terrible place. Very wonderful it is and it has many beautiful things in it, but apart from its appearance, the very memories it stirs give it a grim cloudy look to the mind. I often think of Andrew Fairservice's "Muckle hure that sitteth on the seven hills."[8] The place is full of the remains of palaces of the rascally rich, both lay and priestly, which give it a devilish cast. Now, also, the people generally are given up to making money with the hope of becoming as rich as the envied English, and Socialism, at present, is not here, or it is so damped down that none appears. I am luckily and most kindly helped in my study of the less unworthy part of the remains by ^{my friend} Middleton, who is very hard at work upon a history of ancient Rome;[9] and as I live in a room on the same floor as his, and he likes to see a good deal of me, I pick up ~~a good deal~~ ^{something} of true information which I other-wise should miss. Amongst thousands of other wonderful things M: Angelo's ceiling of the Sistine Chapel in the Vatican is the most beautiful and comforting. The ancient ruins are wonderful, truly, but also terrible indeed. Man, in Rome, has surely shewn what a curse he can make himself. To cap past iniquities, the people are now active in building, under Mr Jeremiah's most able guidance.[10]

Just now I went for a walk, a couple of miles or so out of Rome, in to the Campagna and back by Tiber's side. This country too has a terrible look, softened here and there by some grace of beauty. I think that ^{the} most gentle things I have seen here are the happy Jackdaws, which I see playing about in the air and settling on the wind vanes, while I lie in bed before rising-time in the morning. These dear creatures have their myriad homes in the towers, and the ruined walls of the Colosseum, and Palaces of the C[a]esars. They makes this dead-alive place human to me with their active flight and their clattering talk.

If you should feel inclined & of to write to me again, and after you have told me how you both are, I should be glad to know how the new "League" is getting on. I heard from Morris just after the break up had happened, and as some time has passed since then I should like to know if things are going pretty well in the new form.[11]

I shall be here, I think, 'till about the 15th of February and my address 'till then will be

Signor Philip Webb
presso Il Signore J: H: Middleton | 29 Via Babuino | Roma. | Italy

I hope you have been able to get to your work again Kate, and that the mother is able to watch you and perhaps read to you a little at times out of the pleasant books you have pleasure in. I hope the post will serve to take this letter to you, as I should like you both to know that I often think of your kind ways to me and of the pleasure I have in your friendship.

Believe me, both of you, | Yours very sincerely | Philip Webb.

If my writing is hard to read, please to lay the cause of its badness to my ink rusting my pen & to my fingers being cold.

V&A, NAL MSC/1958/687, ff. 92-3

---

1 Now located entirely within French territory, in the second half of the nineteenth century the Mont Cenis pass formed part of the Alpine border between France and Italy, the ancient route through to Turin and on to Rome.
2 He may be measuring by journey time, rather than distance: by road, Siena is 44 miles from Florence, and Rome 149 miles from Siena.
3 The thirteenth-century Sienese Duomo is dedicated to Santa Maria Assunta, and is visually striking for its use of marble, both for the façade and the interior. The marble mosaic floor (fourteenth-sixteenth century) features 56 panels illustrating Biblical scenes and representations of the sibyls, allegories and virtues. There is notable fresco work, including examples by Pinturicchio (Bernardino di Betto, 1454–1513), in the adjacent Piccolomini Library.
4 The 'strangeness' of the Tuscan walled hill town of San Gimignano rests in its unique group of mediaeval tower houses, visible from afar.
5 The Paglia joins the Tiber to the south-east of Orvieto.
6 See also Vol. II, Letter 369. Much of the Duomo at Orvieto, dedicated, as at Siena, to Santa Maria Assunta, was completed during the fourteenth century. The most important frescoes, by Fra Angelico (c. 1395–1455), Gozzoli and Luca Signorelli (c. 1445–1521), depict scenes of the Apocalypse and Last Judgment, and decorate the vault and walls of the fifteenth-century Chapel of the Madonna di San Brizio.
7 Hardened.

8 In Walter Scott's *Rob Roy* (1817), Andrew Fairservice rejoices in the survival of the Orkney cathedral of Kirkwall. "'Ah! it's a brave kirk. . . . It had amaist a doun-come lang syne at the Reformation, when they pu'd doun the kirks of St. Andrews and Perth, and thereawa, to cleanse them o' Papery, and idolatry, and image worship, and surplices, and sic like rags o' the muckle hure that sitteth on seven hills, as if ane wasna braid eneugh for her auld hinder end".' (ch 19).
9 John Middleton, *Ancient Rome in 1885* (Edinburgh: A and C. Black, 1885). He wrote a sequel in 1888, and then a revised version of both volumes appeared as *The Remains of Ancient Rome* in 1892.
10 The Old Testament prophet Jeremiah condemned the Israelites for their sins, warned of the destruction of Jerusalem and foresaw the period of Babylonian captivity.
11 His desire for news is revealing, for the Socialist League was barely a month old.

245 • To George Washington Jack, 25 January 1885

Rome
Jan: 25. 1885

My dear Jack.

I rec[d] your letter this afternoon and I at once write to notice one or two things in it which should not be delayed. The spirit level has not yet come, but the parcel post is often a little later than the letters. You were quite right in sending the bronzed one, and I thank you for taking this trouble for me at once.

I am really sorry that the plasterwork for the dining-room has not been modelled with <u>spirit</u> and on my return, if I find it not up to the mark of that done for the hall, I must have the work taken down & redone. As to the frieze for the Drawing-room, this <u>must</u> be done with spirit, and I do not see why Estcourt took it [(the modelling)] out of the hands of the man who did that for the hall, as I expressed my satisfaction with that. Please write to this effect to Estcourt, and ask him to call and see you about it when he is in town. The drawing-room frieze is so important a part of the room that it should be modelled in the best way it can be done, and in no case should it be a <u>lifeless</u> rendering of the designs, on which we have spent much time & trouble. The man who did the modelling for the hall was a Gloucester carver, but I have forgotten his name.

I am now at work on the drawing-room ceilings, but the larger one will take me some time to do. I will send the one for the East drawing-room first, as I am making that simpler, & it will take me less time.

M[rs] Wyndham must, of course, do what she pleases with the things you mention, but if she sh[d] turn things about in a ridiculous way, I sh[d] wish you to point out the reasons for not changing my arrangement, and you sh[d] let her know that you keep me informed of what is being done. As to the Laundry, I pointed out to her, when she met me at Slades, where & what I thought of doing in this work and she agreed as to the reasonableness of my scheme. However, I am not very anxious about this work, though the supposed saving [in labour of servants &c] is a myth.

Please to write to M[r] Jones, and refer him to Mess[rs] Wing & Du Cane, solicitors, of 1 Gray's Inn Square, who have the money (£32/10/0) ready for him when the difficulty about the chambers is properly settled.[1] Will you go round and see

M^r Du Cane, and tell him of Mr Jones's application. In no case should you pay Mr Jones. I have told him it is in Messrs Wing & Du Cane's hands.

Nothing can be done for the Mrs Kohl who calls begging.² I have told her so before.

I have no objection whatever to your giving Mr Basset tracing to do when it helps you on, but I suppose you have come to some agreement with him as to payment by piece-work? I say this, as it would be better for him to work in that way now.³ I am glad you are satisfied with what I said about your cousin: I really hope he will get on and be able to help us.

I sent off to you on Friday the detail for the enriched band in hall.

Yours sincerely | Philip Webb.

My address same as given on your letter just received.

V&A, AAD

---

1 PSW's payment for the lease of 1 Raymond Buildings. It is not clear what issue required resolving.
2 Not identified.
3 Basset, PSW's former assistant, had now retired, but his experience clearly made him the obvious candidate when extra help was needed.

246 • To George Washington Jack, 26 January 1885

Rome
Jan: 26. 1885

My dear Jack.

Your letter of the 23rd came this morning also the spirit level, quite safely, for wh' I am much obliged. You were quite right to send it at the cost of the postage, as it would have been absurd to risk it more than necessary. Mr Middleton is much pleased with it, and it will be useful to him in his labours amongst the ruins of ancient Rome.

I have nearly designed the ceiling for the East drawing-room, and I will finish that first as it will not take long. If they have not run the cornice to this drawing room, let them wait 'till you have written to me to say so. Also, do not let them cast any of the design for the plaster frieze of the long or west drawing-room for this room, as I think I might arrange something cheaper & simpler; but at all events they need not make casts of frieze yet for this small drawing-room. I will go on next with the details for carving of ^main staircase.

By the way, if you can manage that the fireplace for the small or East drawing-room shall come opposite to the centre of the pier between the 2 south windows, I sh^d be glad, as in my design for this ceiling I have kept this line as the cross centre line – an inch or so out would not matter.

I am surprised that Longden should raise so many difficulties about the chimney hoods. Casters of iron must be in a bad way if they are not up to such simple matters. The Carron comp^y would have done it easily I am sure,¹ and the Coalbrookdale company could, even now.² Why should there not be another flange or two on the back of the plates to keep them straight.

I can't say I like the idea of grooving thro' the stall boards for the safety bars to stalls. You see to many of the stalls the width of gangway of stables is 10 feet from posts to wall, and the bar would have to be a large one. I think perhaps the best way would be ⁿto useⁿ a galvanized ⁿironⁿ chain strained across at night, to hang against the wall during the day, but perhaps this could wait? Would you write to Mr Wyndham and ask him if it can wait 'till I come home?

You see, highly fed & sometimes vicious horses kick their stall divisions violently, and they will sometimes lean their whole weight against the divisions, so that I should much wish <u>not</u> to weaken their present strength, which I have aimed at.

I can say nothing about the laundry as, if it <u>is</u> to be put in another place, the whole thing will have to be reconsidered, as the present <u>design</u> was made for the <u>Slades</u> position. Of course another design can be made, when I return, to suit the <u>new</u> scheme. I don't quite know where "Loader's" is.

Yes, please pay the cost of repairing bedding (£3.16.10) for me.

Yours sincerely | Philip Webb.

V&A, AAD

---

1 Founded in 1759, this very successful ironworks took its name from its location on the banks of the River Carron near Falkirk, in Stirlingshire. It made naval cannon and many cast-iron products, including fire grates and bath tubs.

2 The origins of the Coalbrookdale Company in Telford, Shropshire go back to the earliest period of iron smelting. During the nineteenth century, the company was famous for its decorative ironwork.

247 • To George Washington Jack, 2 February 1885

Rome
February 2. 1885.

Dear Mr Jack.

I have just received your letter of the 30th Jany telling me that you have had my letters, and the design for enrichment of string¹ at level of capitals in hall. I hope by this time you have got the design for the <u>East</u> drawing-room ceiling, as I sh^d not care to do it again if it were lost – but I kept a rough tracing of it.

I dare say the "liver colour" for inside of stables will do well for the painting, and the "stone colour" for harness & saddle rooms, but I hope the stone colour is <u>white</u> enough.

The door frames outside of stables and coach houses, and like work, should be <u>whitish</u> stone colour and the doors themselves <u>dark myrtle</u> green – quite dark. The rest of the work generally white, but not <u>pure</u> white, a little greenish umbre² mixed with it. I fancy we can manage, when the dining-room ceiling is painted, to make the enrichments clear. If the ^(plaster) work is done sharply and to the character of the design, I daresay I shall not be more than usually disappointed.

I send with this a design for the carving of the 4 small pinnacles to the newel-caps of main stair case – with instructions written on the drawing, for carver. I have sent this at once so that the carver should not be kept waiting. I will send the design for the carved support to the balls between pinnacles as soon as possible. I think you had better make & keep in the office a rough tracing of the carving I now send, and let the carver have the original. This would be sent to Estcourt at direct and at once.

The weather is warmer here, but is very damp. I wrote direct to Mr Mowatt.[3]

If Mr Wardle will kindly advance what money you may want beyond the £50 I left for office expenses, perhaps it w^d be better than my writing to Praeds, but if it sh^d be inconvenient to Morris & Co I will write to Praeds.[4]

Thanks for ^(your) kind questions as to my health &c. I am very well, but I do not get on with seeing things to be seen, as fast as I sh^d like, as my mornings are much taken up with this home work, and there is the large drawing-room ceiling to be designed!

Yours sincerely | Philip Webb.

V&A, AAD

---

1 String-course, or string-moulding.
2 'Umbre (also umber)': a brown earth pigment (*OED*).
3 Not identified.
4 The banking firm of Praeds & Co., founded in 1802, was named after one of its partners, William Praed. It would be bought by the Lloyds Banking Company Limited in 1891.

248 • To William Morris, 3 February 1885

Rome.
Feb: 3. 1885

My dear Fellow.

Your letter of Jan: 24 reached me all right, and was even better in its tune than the former ones. I felt quite happy, for the time, that the League had escaped the snare of sham reconciliation. Now that the cable is really cut, even if our side drifts a little, it would not matter so long as we can keep clear of the too cranky hulk of the S.D.F. I am also glad that you agree with me as to the shaky character of the new venture, but are not afraid to look in the face probabilities. I confess that my anxious nature makes me tremble a little at the work you personally have to do. I am so much afraid of the hot-bed character of such incessant work on one turn ^(line) of life. Work for Merton Abbey – when you can turn to it w^d, I think, be your safety; but how you are to manage it I cannot see.[1] If my business goes to the demnition dogs, as is likely, I might help you there, but I can say nothing certain as yet.[2] At present, 'till I come home, I am doing what I set out to do, and have my heart well in hand, which is the more easy that I had imagined most of what I find in going to & fro on the earth.

I cannot say anything clearly of Middleton, as his health is so uncertain; but I think he has (for an Oxford man, which is a doubtful quantity) some right feeling as to Socialism, but then he has not much power outside of what he has learned, which no doubt is a good deal.[3] He seems to me to be really kindly at heart (most kind to me at all events) from expressions of his now and then, which broke through the crust of his education (?). He has been really kind to me, and the more so that my qualities – if I have any – are too uncomfortable & rude, and rasp him, I am sure: added to which I laugh and make brutal jokes when customary civilization comes to the front of in him too unconsciously. I think that if his health gets stronger, and he finishes the work he is about, he will move for England and would I think be really useful. Physically he is very strong, or his ailments w^{d} have dragged him down. He walks a good deal and can tire me out, but his inwards are but badly arranged and he becomes very irritable at times, and falls to savage silence 'till the fit has passed away.

As to the Bloomsbury branch of the League, you were right to put me down for it, and you can apply £5 'till I come home, for subscriptions &c.[4] Do you think you have much hold over Scheu, & can you make him sit quiet when the fever is on him? If you can, I sh^{d} think he w^{d} be the most helpful of the companions. Charley F[aulkner] is always to be depended upon, and he is good to have in spite of his being at Oxford.[5] Sanderson is I take it, at least, a "gentleman" and can only be useful in a sort of way when hoisted by someone he is rather afraid of, so that you had better keep your eye on him.[6] By the way, I was glad to learn from Murray (who knows a man named Fisher living in Florence who married a Cobden girl)[7] that Mrs Sanderson did, after all, produce something.[8]

How did you put you acc^{ts} in order as treasurer of S.D.F when you parted company? You see, that my grocer-like nature makes me think of such things! If things go as well as they have done, I hope to save a little money from what I had put together for this journey, and the League can have it, but it may not be much, as there have been more expenses in the Gray's Inn office than I had calculated on. The Wyndhams' – at all event the female one – are rather wriggling about and upsetting the work there at Knoyle, wh' has cost me much work and money, but this don't really matter, as I did my work to amuse myself. It was not likely to interest anyone else. A good bit of my time here goes to doing work for Knoyle, but I don't dislike the interruption to seeing the battered beauties of antiquity.

The Byzantine work, and the 12th & 13 century pieces scattered about Rome and the suburbs are very interesting to me. M: Angelo is still gold to my mind, but the Renaissance is worse here, a good deal, than in Florence. Raphael comes out badly, but minor lights such as Pinturicchio tell delightfully. St. Peter's Ch' seems to have been a mistake throughout and is only a wonderful monstrosity. The big dome I think altogether unlucky[9] – expect perhaps from some miles off, the inside of the smaller domes are done very well, as architecture, but some of the decoration is lamentable enough. The Sistine chapel is altogether another thing and always holds its own, because of the great spirit of the workman who did it. The Stanza of Raphael is, to me, a waste of nonsense.[10] The mosaic covered half domes of the church apses (early) are always good and serious, even the rudest of them. Perhaps, of all buildings in Rome, the Church of S: Stefano Rotondo, a round building of great size and as bare as one's bottom – said to have been consecrated A.D. 467, but not built for a church, though I am almost sure it was.[11] The Campagna generally is quite noble and touching, ringed round as it is with fine hills and mountains. There, I've done.

I wish you could have given me better news of Janey and the girls. I can say nought, but only hope for better times. My kindest love to them, though I suppose Janey and May will be on their way to Bordighera by this time.[12] Kate tells me that her good old mother has been sadly ailing. I sh̰ think Kate wants looking in at as often as may be. I shall not leave here before the 15th or 16th of this month, after which I shall move to Perugia, Assisi, Arezzo & back to Florence for a few days. If you should happen to write after the 12th, you had better address to Murray's.

Yours very affectionately | Philip Webb.

On re-reading this, I found it a sad scrawl & must ask pardon.

V&A, NAL MSC/1958/687, f. 13

---

1 In 1881, WM had transferred the manufacturing workshops of Morris & Co. to Merton Abbey in south London.
2 'Demnition' and its shortened form, 'demd' is employed by Mr Mantalini, the employer of Nicholas's younger sister, Kate, in Dickens's *Nicholas Nickleby*. PSW favoured the use of 'deminition' in his later years, such as in 'demnition slow'.
3 WM seems to have been exploring the possibility of recruiting Middleton to the Socialist League.
4 See below, Letter 271, note 2.
5 CF was a member of the Socialist League's Provisional Council, and a co-signer of the Manifesto. He also established an Oxford branch of the League, which WM addressed on 25 February. See below, Letter 253, note 1.
6 Thomas James Sanderson (1840–1922) first practised as a barrister, meeting WM and EBJ in the 1860s. In 1882, he married Julia Sarah Anne (Annie) Cobden (1853–1926), younger daughter of the radical politician, Richard Cobden, changing his surname to Cobden-Sanderson. His interest in bookbinding began from this point, becoming his profession. In 1893 he would move to 15 Upper Mall, in Hammersmith, a few doors from WM, where he started the Doves Bindery, later establishing the Doves Press in partnership with EW (see Vol. III, Letter 741). The Cobden-Sandersons were active in the Hammersmith Socialist Society from 1890, and Annie was later a prominent suffragette activist.
7 Catherine (Kate) Cobden (1844–1916), Richard Cobden's eldest surviving daughter, had married a Sussex neighbour, Richard Fisher, in 1866.
8 The Cobden-Sandersons' first child, Richard, was born on 12 November 1884. 'Oh, that all may go what to us seems well? May he grow up strong and well, and a help for the people, and Annie strong and well, a delight to him.' Entry for 16 November in *The Journals of Thomas James Cobden-Sanderson*, 2 vols (London: Richard Cobden-Sanderson, 1926), I, p. 204.

9 St Peter's in Rome (1506–1626) replaced an older church with fourth-century origins, and which by tradition marked the burial place of the saint. Successive design plans, including those by Donato Bramante, Raphael (1483–1520) and Antonio da Sangallo, led finally to that by Michelangelo who in 1547 succeeded Sangallo as Capomaestro, superintendent of the building works. He preserved features of the designs of his predecessors whilst imposing his own authority on the work. The huge central dome was his conception, and at his death in 1564 most of the supporting drum had been built, but the dome itself was not completed until 1605. Perhaps a certain lack of architectural unity, inevitable after such a gestation in the hands of so many architects, led PSW to describe even Michelangelo's contribution as 'altogether unlucky'.
10 The four rooms in the Papal apartments of the Vatican, with frescoes by Raphael and his studio were commissioned by Pope Julius II (1443–1513), but not completed until after the painter's death.
11 The Basilica di Santo Stefano al Monte Celio is remarkable for its large number of sixteenth-century frescoes.
12 JM and MM had left London the day before PSW wrote, arriving in Bordighera on 10 February.

249 • To Kate Faulkner, 7 February 1885

Rome
Feb: 7. 1885

My dear Kate.

Your note, which came this morning, confirmed an otherwise wavering resolution to write to you in answer to it and the other kind letter of yours of date, Jan: 27. This does not mean altogether laziness or carelessness but, having a good deal to do, I take first what seems to be most urgent, and as your letter gave a rather better account of the dear Mother I rather rested on that real satisfaction. I daresay my letters, which seem so poor to me as I send them are, perhaps, in your good nature, not so trying to you to read. You see, I judge me by you by myself (partly) as I am always so happy in having a letter from Queen Square. It did not surprise me that the mother did not rise at once to usual strength, as the changeful weather is very trying, and mostly to invalids.

Please to forgive my bad writing. I am just home from a walk and my hand shakes; also, the Italian ink is made with such strong acid that the pens become scratchy at once – and decent letters & words cannot be made with them.

Morris said in his last letter that he w^d send me a 'Commonweal' but as I have not yet had it, I fancy it may have been confiscated by the police.[1] Therefore, if you will be so good as to send me a copy in an envelope, as a letter, I should like it. I fancy the postage would not be more than 5^d wh' I would repay on my return.

Next to my walks outside the city, a little way into the Campagna, and the looking into the old or Byzantine churches I have not had such pleasure in Rome as my second going to the Sistine Chapel, where I stayed for ab^t 2 hours. There were but few people there, so that the more real and familiar people on the ceiling came more home to me. This great boon of M: Angelo's to the world is a triumph of art, imagination, and beauty, and I could have comfortably spent the day there. Indeed, to use my fam common saying, I could live comfortably in this vast hall with <u>self and cat</u>, so noble & pleasant is the art of its painting. I find that 3 parts of the – so called – splendid buildings in Rome are brutal in their magnificence; whereas this greater creation than all is $^{to\,me}$ as free from offence as a small quiet room. I say 'to me' for I find few in sympathy with me on this point. Raphael's extraordinary skill, artificial, in an artificial time commands attention and much futile gabble. I am quite sick of it. I have just been to the Villa Borghesi,[2] [*sic*] where there are ancient statues by hundreds – some good, some indifferent and some bad, but the building, the fitting and marble decoration &c &c are so offensive, that I was glad to get away – even from the good things, into the open ground about, which is really beautiful in its half neglected but not ragged state. These gardens (old park rather) of great size, are a boon to the Romans, as it is free to all for 4 days in the week, where they can roam about and gather flowers, which are many: violets, making the now warmer air quite strongly scented with their own special scent. Jackdaws, by the flock, make a noise which is a comfort in this country, where the smaller birds are so killed down.

After two or three tries I, at last, got into the Pantheon,[3] which is closed to the people on account of the taking down of much theatrical rubbish, put up for the anniversary of the death of the late fat king.[4] By dexterously putting my hand into breeches pocket, the custodian let me through the gate, and I was satisfied with wonder of ^{at} the area & dome of this noted old Roman work. It is really a quite impressive vault, comparatively low down, with the big hole in the centre open, & the rain coming in as it has done since the building was set up. This is the only light into it, and it is ample. The Italian govern^t had decided to cover this light with glass, but there was enough row made to stop them; so that the meaning of the building will still remain – yet awhile! The Italians are quite reckless in destroying the smaller remains of greatest antiquity in order to set up long rows of houses of a lofty Bayswater type – though, I am bound to say, of not quite so bad a type a kind.

I rather think, Kate, that you are in want of me to tell you candidly, as I always do, what I think of your work; for I feel sure that, from long continued strain in doing so great a labour, you are not able yourself alone to make out what it is really like. However, I am afraid I shall not see it in its finished state, as I sh^d so much like to do.[5] It seems to me that such work as raising patterns with gesso must be disappointing to you, as to do it perfectly one w^d have to be brought up to it, and work at it in a traditional manner; but I felt satisfied, & more so, in the way you had done it. Added to your personal disappointment, you sh^d allow for all hearty workers being dis-satisfied with the outcome of labour which has taken some time to do. You must comfort yourself by imagining what my houses look ^{like} to me, when I see them finished, or as nearly finished as the people who are to live in them care for. My comfort is in setting about another work, to drive the taste of the former away.

I shall not be sorry to come home, when the time is up, though I hear that jinks have been played upon my work at Knoyle, but I only laugh and jeer at the stupidity. The mother and you would accuse me of brutality I am sure, but I should much like to jest in the usual way with you both, in spite of the offence I should give: never mind, but forgive me, & I shall not get better – no doubt – as I get older!! My kindest love to you both, with a petition that you will believe me, as always sincerely yours

Philip Webb.

I shall, I fancy, be leaving here in a week or ten days, but if you have a fancy to write again, please address – 'presso C: F: Murray 106 Via de' Serragli. Firenze.'

Enclosed is an Anemone, gathered just outside the walls of Rome, & is a common wild flower here.

V&A, NAL MSC/1958/687, f. 94

---

1 *The Commonweal*, of which WM was joint editor, described itself as 'the official journal of the Socialist League'. The inaugural number (for which PSW is asking) was published in February 1885, and carried on its first page the League's Manifesto, drafted by WM and others.
2 The Villa Borghese – house and substantial gardens – was designed by Flaminio Ponzio (1560–1613) for Cardinal Scipione Borghese (1577–1633).
3 One of the finest survivals from ancient Rome, the Pantheon has been in continuous use since its erection by the Roman general, Marcus Agrippa (c. 64 BC – 12 BC), probably as a private temple. In the seventh century AD it was converted into use as a Christian church, and became known locally as Santa Maria Rotunda, signifying its circular interior.
4 Victor Emmanuel II (1820–78) had died on 9 January 1878.
5 For the piano decorated by KF for Alexander Constantine Ionides, see above, Letter 237, note 8.

250 • To George Washington Jack, 10 February 1885

Rome
Feb: 10. 1885

My dear Jack.

I rec[d] yesterday yours of 6th and today yours of 7th Feb: I sent off to you, on the 2nd, detail for carving of pinnacles of newels of main stairs which you do not seem to have received when you posted your letter of the 7th instant? I now send the detail for the carving of support to balls on top of the newels. You had better make [sufficient] memorandum tracing of this and let Estcourt have my original drawing. I have think I have put sufficient notes on drawing to keep the carver right, if he attends to them and the indications of effect in the drawing.

I now answer your questions. <u>East</u> drawing (smaller) room. I think you must have the <u>cornice</u>, at present run, (of wh' I am sorry) hacked off, and the [new] design, made to go with the ceiling, run in its place. They were over-hasty in running the cornice. The moulding made <u>under frieze</u> may remain at present in both rooms, and, <u>of course</u>, the old cornice in West, or long drawing-room is to remain, as that is all right.

I should like a diagram made by Simmonds of the 4 sides of the East (small) drawing-room <u>frieze</u>, made in elevation, with figured spaces clear of inside of plaster, as I want to design a different frieze for this room to go with the ceiling. [*sketch*] This done to "½ scale will do, if accurately done. This should be done directly, and a tracing sent to me as soon as possible to my old address 'presso C: F: Murray. 106 Via de' Serragli Firenze', as I shall leave here I think in a week's time, and shall be about a week in getting to Florence.

I will do the detail for fire-place column &c, next, and send it to you. From the notes of painting work given [in] your letters, I think you will manage this all right, but I think the painting of stone work to fire places had better stand over till I return, as the surface ᵒᶠ ˢᵗᵒⁿᵉ may not please me & I might wish to have it improved.

Tiles for fireplaces in bed rooms. I think I should like one or two of the first floor rooms to have Miss Faulkner's tiles, of a pleasant quiet kind, put into such rooms as Mʳˢ Wyndham wished to have made best rooms, which you will now know her mind upon. Please to call on Miss Faulkner and consult with her about which would suit the chʸ pieces, and select a pattern (not too large) and perhaps a pale green of 2 shades wᵈ do. Miss Faulkner shᵈ supply the tiles to Longden and he only charge for carriage & not a percentage on them.[1] The other bedroom tiles I would leave to you and Mʳ Wardle's choice (if he will kindly do me this service) keeping in mind quietness of effect, and going with the marble work round them.

A plan of the loose box doors shᵈ be sent by Estcourt to the lock-maker for him to make ~~locks~~ fastenings (somewhat in character to the detail made by Basset, but of course made to suit new arrangements.) The thing to be borne in mind, is to avoid catching against horses as they pass through doors or when in boxes.

The marble recesses in W. Cˢ to remain 'till I return.

I will write to Mʳˢ Coronio.[2]

As soon as I have designed the West or long-drawing-room ceiling I will say who ought to model it. Of course Estcourt is bound ᵇʸ ᶜᵒⁿᵗʳᵃᶜᵗ to get the modelling of plaster &c done to my satisfaction. The design is difficult and will take me some time, but I shall simplify it as much as possible. The East drawing-room ceiling is easy and cheap, and the plasterer can manage all that, as also the frieze of which I am to send the design.

Fire place tiles again. Perhaps Miss Faulkner's tiles might be chosen for the one or two of the ground floor rooms in addition to those mentioned above. Any of the best fire places might have rubbed "Trough-bed" Chilmark stone hearths[3] – the hearths under grates to be in cast iron as Longden has been directed. Paving. Hall paving must remain 'till I return. The corridors might be paved with Howell's picked and hardest paving bricks laid herringbone with a strip of rubbed trough bed ˢᵗᵒⁿᵉ laid down the middle as sketched over. [sketch]

You make no mention of what Mʳˢ and Mʳ Wyndham[4] have decided about the Laundry?

Yours sincerely | Philip Webb.

Kind remembrance to Mʳ Wardle, and tell him I will write to him soon. I hope my asking his help about fireplace tiles will not inconvenience him. If it does, please settle it yourself with my indications here given.

V&A, AAD

1 This suggests that KF was herself independently supplying tiles which she had decorated, rather than that they were bought through Morris & Co. Of the known Morris & Co. designs attributed to her, perhaps a tile like 'Peony' (c. 1880) was the sort of thing which PSW had in mind. See Richard and Hilary Myers, *William Morris Tiles*, p. 96.
2 See above, Letter 235, note 5.
3 'The Chilmark Trough Bed was recorded as having been used for the renovation (1867) of the Chapter House, Westminster Abbey.' Francis G. Dimes, 'Sedimentary Rocks', in John Ashurst and Dimes, eds., *Conservation of Building and Decorative Stone*, 2 vols (London: Butterworth-Heinemann, 1990) I, p. 113.
4 The insinuation of the emphasis on 'Mr Wyndham' is that his was the opinion to be respected.

251 • To George Price Boyce, 5 March 1885

106 Via de' Serragli Firenze
March 5. 1885.

My dear Boyce

When about to leave Rome (which I did on the 19th Feb:) I was so much engaged, and since I have been here my home work has been so heavy on my hands that I had to neglect answering any but business letters, yours among the number: but I received in Rome yours of date Feb: 13, and when I got here I found yours (sent on by Mr Jack) of the 20th – both letters much worth receiving and answering. Now to note some of the contents.

I only got to Rome 2 days after the high flood of Tiber, wh' had risen in its usual way after heavy rains which bring down snow water from the mountains. The water rose and came into the Pantheon &c. When I was in that building I noted the lifting of the floor in the middle of it, sloping to the wall of circumference, and the holes under the altar steps for letting the water run off again.

I worked really at making out something of Rome, and was there 5 weeks, but out of this time had to be deducted most of my mornings which I had to use for home work, and the days were short; however I was really helped by friends, especially by Middleton, so that I saw things which, otherwise, I must have missed. After the Sistine ceiling, perhaps I was most taken by the Pinturrichio's [*sic*] in the Borgia rooms at the Vatican, to see which, quietly, some influence was used for me.[1]

I did a good deal of walking round in the Campagna for 2 or 3 miles outside the walls and, as I was not bitten or throttled by the herdsmen's dogs, I enjoyed this much. On my way back here I stayed at Assisi, Perugia and Arezzo. Assisi particularly interested me – of the very few notes I have had time to make, those made there are most useful to my understanding of what I saw, but they wd be quite unintelligible to anyone else.

True – it is hardly a loss to me that I missed the 'old masters' this year in London,[2] for my head won't hold half of what I have seen and thought over in the way of pictures in Italy. After work time I have rushed out to refresh my memory of frescoes in Florence. My time is drawing towards a close, and Mantegna, Giotto, and all the Venetians loom before me, among which Carpaccio is one that I much want to look to, there being only one fragment of him in the Uffizi here. I saw a good deal of Giotto in Assisi.³ The Pietro della Francescas', in the Francescan ch' at Arezzo, were a great gain to me⁴ – and also the Luca Signorellis' at Orvieto.⁵ Benozzo Gozzoli is ~~also~~ too one of my close friends. The good and great Fra Angelico will, I think, even with my worst of memories, never be forgotten. His work really did surprise me, in spite of what I knew of him. Mantegna is great of the great and I look forward to him.⁶ Of Giotto & M: Angelo I need say nothing.

By the way, the Pantheon was also rather of a surprise to me to the good, as Sͭ Peter's was to the bad (speaking broadly). This Church was, evidently, a mistake from first to last, and even M: Angelo could not lick [it] into satisfactory shape. The work of his there bears no relation to his well known work at San Lorenzo (the library) here, & which much interested me.⁷ It is very much a test ᵗᵒ ᵐᵉ of how much of the detail of S: Peters at Rome was his own work. But I can safely say that I have not seen a really ᵍᵒᵒᵈ Renaissance ch' ᵒʳ ᵒⁿᵉ which has in any way pleased me since I have been in Italy. Brunelleschi's San Spirito here is not really Renaissance.⁸

I thank you for your useful hints for Venice; I shall of course not be able to see all, but I ˢʰᵃˡˡ keep the notes by me as reminders of things to be looked for. I think Murray is likely to go with me to Venice, as he has business there & which may keep him there for a while, but Mͬ Darvall's address is very welcome.⁹ Murray says he knows him & he speaks well of him, though your recommendation was enough for me.

If Murray goes with me I shall go at first to an Inn he frequents, which will give time for fixing where I shall abide for the 3 weeks I think of spending ~~there~~ ᵃᵗ ⱽᵉⁿⁱᶜᵉ. I wᵈ rather take some places in Italy quietly, than a great many in a fuss of hurry. I would not have missed the time I gave to Siena, the Campagna of Rome, Orvieto, Assisi &c, for any amount of hastily looked-at places, and I must spend some time in Verona, and a couple of days in Ravenna – taking some of the places on the northern border on my way home.

I am sorry to say that my good friend Middleton had to rush home to England only to see his father die, after a stroke of paralysis. I fancy you may see Mⁿ in London before he returns to Italy. I am looking forward to his coming book on Roman antiquities. His articles in the new Ency: Britannica (I suppose the Burlington Club will have a copy) are well worth reading, and he is to write a number more if he keeps well enough. I got on capitally with him, & he is a 'kittle creature to shoe behind'.¹⁰

Your or Mʳˢ Boyce's violets from Etampes are in front of me now, and they reached me quite fragrant. The grass was nearly full of violets in the park of the Villa Borghesi [*sic*] at Rome, where the people roam to pick them. The Carnival was rather a bore to me, but the folk enjoyed it ⁽ᵒᶠ ʷʰ ᴵ ʷᵃˢ ᵍˡᵃᵈ⁾ and I could manage to slink about down back streets, & avoid the press and racket.

I hope you will get your drawings sent to the Society's gallery all right,[11] if it is only to take you off them & set you going on other work. I had better news from New Place, and I hope you & Madame will be going there to moan together over your several ills, and cheer up Giddens[12] by eating his cabbages. The birds, wherever there are secure gardens here, are singing away – particularly blackbirds – but in the open they are mercilessly slaughtered for the market, and the country is far too silent of song, in consequence.

I am afraid that the scare from last year's cholera will make the authorities here throw down what still remains of the old town wall. They propose to do this, I fancy, because it is easy and will attract attention, but it will do as little good as burning my hat would.[13] They won't sufficiently do the things which are really urgent, but would not be seen when done.

With kind remembrance to Mrs Boyce. | Believe me sincerely yours,
Philip Webb.

If your colds still stick to you, get into the fresh air!

I leave here on Mon: 9th Mr Jack will have my address sooner than anyone else – but "Albergo del Vapore" w^{d} find me.

BL Add 45354, ff. 216-7

---

1 The Borgia Apartments in the Vatican, created for Rodrigo Lanzol Borgia (1431–1503) when he became Pope Alexander VI, were elaborately decorated in 1492–4 with frescoes by Pinturicchio. The rooms were little used for many years, and only in 1889 reopened to the public.

2 The sixteenth annual winter exhibition of Old Masters at the Royal Academy had opened on 5 January.

3 The principal Franciscan church in Assisi – the town in which St Francis was born and died – is the thirteenth century Basilica di San Francesco, which features an important cycle of frescoes on the life of St Francis. Though traditionally attributed to the early part of Giotto's career, this work is now believed to have a more complex authorship, and relatively little can now be assigned with complete certainty to Giotto.

4 The mainly fourteenth century Franciscan Basilica di San Francesco in Arezzo contains some of the very best work of Piero della Francesca (c. 1415–92) in his fresco cycle on *The Legend of the True Cross* (c. 1447–65).

5 See above, Letter 244, note 6.

6 Andrea Mantegna (1430/1–1506), born near Padua, worked from 1460 in Mantua, where he became court artist to the Gonzaga family.

7 When Giulio di Giuliano de' Medici (1478–1534) became Pope Clement VII in 1523, he commissioned Michelangelo to design the Biblioteca Medicea Laurenziana, the library adjoining the Basilica di San Lorenzo in Florence. Begun in 1525, work was interrupted when Michelangelo left for Rome in 1533, but it was completed to his design by about 1562, and was regarded from the outset as a masterpiece for its innovatory use of space.

8 The Florentine Basilica di Santa Maria del Santo Spirito was built by Brunelleschi on the site of a thirteenth-century Augustinian priory. He began work in 1428, and it was completed after his death.

9 Little is known of the English painter, Henry Darvall, who appears to have been resident in Venice for some years, and was active c. 1848–89.

10 Apparently a variant of an old Scottish saying, 'kittle cattle to shoe behind', used here to mean that Middleton had the reputation of being awkward.

11 On his return from Italy, PSW bought GPB's watercolour of Catterlen Hall as a gift for his brother. See below, Letter 258, note 1.
12 Giddens was the gardener at New Place, Welwyn.
13 See Vol. II, Letter 333, note 11.

252 • To Kate Faulkner, 8 March 1885

Florence.
Mar: 8. 1885

My dear Kate.

I daresay, if you had been quite sure of where I was at this time, you w^d not have had time to write. I should have written before this if I had done rightly but have excused my neglect by saying that I was too busy, wh' w'd have been mostly true. Mr Jack sent me work here which has kept me well employed since I returned to Florence. As I leave for Bologna tomorrow (the 9th) I want you & the mother to know where I am likely to be and I use this broken day for writing.

I duly received the 1st n^o of "Commonweal" at Rome, and the 2nd, or March n^o, here; for wh' I thank you very much.[1] I am deeply interested in the progress of this new venture, and no one except Middleton, whom I have seen, cared at all for such matters. I met a very pleasant Oxford man in Rome, Bradley by name, step brother I think of the Dean of Westminster,[2] who did not dislike talking of English Socialism, but he was afraid of the sweeping character of the "Commonweal"; but as he is much less prejudiced than Oxford men generally are, I don't think he will altogether drop the subject again. He is now a professor at Liverpool, is suffering from broken health and trying what change of air & scene will do for him. I rather expect to meet him again in Venice, as he was to go from Rome to Naples & then to Athens, taking steam boat from there to Venice. He says he wants not to miss seeing me there.

Morris's poems were, both of them, a great delight to me, and I altogether liked his tone compared with the rest of the paper, which I think rather weak.[3] I suppose it must be so. I think I told you that good friend Middleton had to rush home to England to his father who was stricken with paralysis. M^n got to Wales before his father died, but he never rallied (fortunately) I think, & was quite unconscious. I had a letter from Mid^n the other day, and he said he had been in Oxford and met Charles & Morris at Bywater's rooms,[4] & had had a pleasant talk with them.

When I left Rome on the 19th Feb: I went first to Assisi – a beautiful town pitched on the top of a high hill, with a fine valley & mountains in front, and other high hills behind & close to it. San Francesco, the chief ch' is a double one, one under the other, & both covered with paintings by Orcagna, Giotto and other early Italian men. The church, beside the paintings, is also a beautiful one, and I was all busy during my stay in trying to understand what I saw there. Other churches there are, & a ruined castle, but the churches (except Francesco) have been much mutilated. I went from Assisi to Perugia, the chief interest of wh' place is its Palazzo publico: the churches also are fine in spite of terrible transformations wh' they have undergone. This large town is also on a hill. From Perugia I went to Arezzo – another hill town, but not so high up. This place had, in its Francesco ch', a series of Frescoes by Piero della Francesca, a paintinger much to my mind. There are two framed pictures of his in the National Gallery, wh' you could look at if you turned in there. The chief is a baptism of Christ, which gives his characteristics very well indeed.[5] Great purity and simplicity are the main. I am much fonder of Frescoes than framed pictures as they are there for good or ill, and permanently beautify a building – whereas the separate pictures become too much objects of mercantile exchange, of which over reaching is the chief element. Of course all noble framed pictures should be in public galleries, and not to be continually passing through the hands of cheats.

After Arezzo I came on here, and while here I have been mostly at my home work. I go, as before said, to Bologna tomorrow, from there to Ravenna: from there back again to Bologna and then on to Venice, perhaps stopping at Ferrara. I expect to be in Venice on Sat: or Sun: the 14 or 15th and to be there about 3 weeks; after which, I propose taking the remaining places I shall have time for, on my way to Milan – from Milan I shall probably come direct home.

The spring is now shewing it[s] effect here, many things are quite green and the almond trees in full bloom. The weather is fine now after some cloudy, damp & then windy days. Still, on sunny days, one gets to the shady side of the street, foretelling what it will be in May and June. I do not think the winter is a bad time in wh' to be in Italy except for the shortness of the days. In country towns the long evenings are something tiresome, and caffès [sic] only amuse for a while. In Venice they may be better, if the weather be warm, as one could sit outside in the evenings.

If you should be able to write to me, please tell me all you can about yourselves and Charles and Morris. I hope the mother is now stronger, and that you are at your work again, and of that not so despairing as when you last wrote. 'Commonweal' is the only English paper I have looked into since I have been away, and I know nothing really as to affairs in Egypt,[6] or politics generally – sometimes people tell me scraps of things about these, but in an uncertain way, as if the sources of their information were not to be depended upon. My last news from Welwyn was rather better, my brother & sister had been in a lowish sort of way and their former letters were of that complexion. The numbers of travellers' inventions which I shall have to tell when I come back, to cure lumbago rheumatisms &c, will be frightful.

Unfortunately, for the Italians, I have not been able to make them understand my brutal jokes, and I shall be out of practice when I have the pleasure of seeing you again. If you should see Morris, please tell him I have gone on to Venice, as I shall not have time to write from there here. My address there will be

'signor. Philip Webb.
Albergo del Vapore | Venezia.

    Believe me my dear Kate and mother | Yours very sincerely | Philip Webb.

V&A, NAL MSL/1957/697, f. 23

1 See above, Letter 249, note 1.
2 Andrew Cecil Bradley (1851–1935) was appointed to a chair in literature at the University College in Liverpool in 1881, subsequently moved to the University of Glasgow, and eventually was elected to the Professorship of Poetry at Oxford. There he wrote his best book, *Shakespearean Tragedy* (1904). He had a commitment to improving women's education and to egalitarian causes, but his own career was tinged with a morbidly self-critical outlook. For his half-brother, George Bradley, see above, Letter 168, note 7.
3 WM's poems in the first two numbers of *The Commonweal* were 'The March of the Workers' (February 1885), and 'The Message of the March Wind', the first part of a longer poem which became *The Pilgrims of Hope*, (March 1885). 'I have written a poem for the next number, not bad I think.' WM to JM, 10 February 1885, *CLWM*, II.
4 Ingram Bywater (1840–1914), Reader and later Regius Professor of Greek at Oxford, was a committee member of the SPAB from its early days. CF and WM were old friends. 'Though he rarely spent a night in Oxford, Morris was often to be seen in Bywater's rooms.' William Walrond Jackson, *Ingram Bywater. The Memoir of an Oxford Scholar* (Oxford: Clarendon Press, 1917), p. 41. The occasion described by Middleton occurred on 25 February, when later that evening WM addressed a socialist meeting in the Holywell music room. Bywater was in the audience (Jackson, pp. 42–3). See next letter, note 1.
5 The National Gallery in London bought Francesca's *The Baptism of Christ* (1450s) in 1861. There are two further pictures by the artist in the collection, *The Nativity* (1470–5), bought in 1874, and *Saint Michael* (1469), bought in 1867.
6 He has in mind the shockwaves in the aftermath of the Siege of Khartoum (March 1884–January 1885), defended by the British-backed Egyptian forces in the Sudan under the command of General Charles George Gordon. The capture of Khartoum by the Mahdi, Muhammed Ahmed, resulted in many of the defenders being killed, including General Gordon. There was a national outcry in Britain, for the government had refused Gordon's requests for further aid, though many regarded him as culpably stubborn.

253 • To Kate Faulkner, 28 March 1885

Albergo del Vapore. Venezia (Italy)
Mar: 28. 1885

My dear Kate.

I had your letter of Mar: 8; it was sent on to me here from Florence. I rather think I wrote you a letter which must have crossed this one of yours, but I am not sure, as I can find no note of it – but I have an indistinct recollection of having (at last) acknowledged the receipt of the Mar: "Commonweal" you were so good as to send. If I did not write this letter I am indeed sorry, as I have rec$^{\underline{d}}$ yours with so much pleasure that it w$^{\underline{d}}$ be shameful indeed if I did not make efforts to write to where I so much wish to be remembered without reproaches. I never was a good letter writer, and here, between work of various kinds and natural indolence, I am too weak in the matter. I was greatly pleased with your note of the kind mother's being about again, it makes me ashamed to be away, as I should be at home helping all I could those friends who like to have such poor aid as kindly face can give – my kindest love to her. I left Florence on the 9$^{\underline{th}}$ Mar: & went to Bologna, from whence to Ravenna, then to Forlì and on Friday the 13$^{\underline{th}}$ I came here.

Bologna is a pleasant and still much of a mediæval town, mostly built on open arches to the streets, so that one can walk all about & from end to end under vaulted cover. Ravenna is a wonderfully underline{interesting} place but, as a town very poor in character, the only ~~interest~~ ^beauty^ being in the ancient churches which, not only are old but have an air of very great age on their faces. The place is also really gloomy, perhaps more so to me then, as the weather changed from good to bad there. Forlì (accent over the i) is a pleasant place but not of great ~~moment~~ ^interest^ in architecture.

I can only tell by word of mouth of Ravenna, as it is so peculiar. Of Venice I would first say that having heard much talk of it since I was a boy, nothing in that way had spoiled it to me when I came to walk in and about its strange ways. I have been here a fortnight and am still untired of it. Added to the deep interest of its history &c, it is still very lovely to look at and, there being no hoofs & wheels to trouble one (always extraordinary in effect) the getting and standing about in it is so comfortable. To push or be pushed about in striking looking boats is a never failing pleasure, especially after being tired of walking the narrow alleys – everywhere some pieces of admirable arch^{re} turn upon one singly or in connected numbers – wait a little and then move and others front you as pleasantly. These are the gentler delights – the greater & more terribly lovely, such as the St Marks Ch' & the Ducal palace, meet one on return and are always touching. I cannot say that I like travelling, after all is said, but Venice gives me less cause for regret that I am not at home & at work or sympathising with my friends at their labours. I must try and not be dull to you & the mother when I do come back, as there will be no excuse then for my talking of myself, that dull fellow!

I really hope you will be driven into the country for a while as soon as it gets warm enough, & I shall force myself not to regret your absence if you sh^d be away when I return. I have all sorts of vain regrets and longings myself but, when I write to you, I feel inclined to say that you must take heart and be of good cheer, as if my only saying it w^d or sh^d be enough to clear your way of anxieties.

I rejoiced from what you said & from what Morris also wrote to me, that the meeting at Oxford – with Charles in the chair – was a successful one in spite of difficulties.[1] I am so with our friends in heart that I blush that I do or can do next to nothing to forward the cause. However you know how cheery I can be when picked out of myself by the companionship of those I love, that I even look forward to claiming my place with them on my return though ^in myself^ of so little strength for helping. Never mind, I still hope to cheer you with honest laughter – none of the crackling-under-pots-kind.

A. C. Bradley, of Balliol (of whom I think I must have written word) is here. He is going on to other places and I go with him tomorrow as far as Padua, where I shall stay 2 days and then return here for a few more days – perhaps a week. Murray came here to do some work, wh' he has done, and he is now at work on a study from a St George by Carpaccio for me, wh' will still take him some time[2] – he has been hindered by bad weather & would be stopped by Easter festas, so that I am anxious that he sh^d get on or I shall not get my memorial of a delightful work by a painter who pleases me so greatly. I don't like to think of possible delays as I might then fail to get what I much want.

When I leave here finally, I go to Verona, to stay as long as my now nearly ended time away will allow, but in any case I can stay but a short time in any other place than Verona. If you should feel inclined to write again, & be able to do so, send your letter here if it can arrive here before the 4th of April if you sh^d write before the 6th or 7 (letter arrived) please send it to the Poste Restante Verona; but, <u>please</u> don't write unless it be quite easy to you. I only make these notes to avoid my losing a letter when moving on.

I did <u>not</u> smile when you told me the piano was not yet gone, as I felt quite serious over your wish to make it as perfect as you could[3] – all art-work sh^d be done in that spirit. I shall hope to be able to see it when the owner has it: I shall try to get to see it.

The weather here has been very wet for some days, but happily with no snow; snow was heavy as nearby as Ferrara.

Yours very sincerely | Philip Webb.

V&A, NAL MSC/1958/687, f. 95

---

1 Although WM's letter to PSW is lost (PSW's reply follows immediately below), we may assume that he had reported on the Oxford meeting held in the Holywell music room on 25 February, at which he and Edward Aveling (1851–98) addressed a rowdy gathering, in a similar tone to that he adopted when describing the occasion to GBJ. 'Well, we had a fine lot of supporters, town and gown both . . . but the "enemy" got in in some numbers, and prepared for some enjoyment. Charley was in the chair and led off well, and they heard him with only an average amount of howling. . . . I was rather nervous before I began, as it was my first long speech without book, but the noise and life braced me up, and after all I knew my subject, so I fired off my speech fairly well I think . . . Of course they howled and stamped at certain catchwords, and our people cheered, so that it was very good fun.' WM to GBJ, 28 February 1885, *CLWM*, II. The 'joke of the evening' occurred during questions being asked, when a stink-bomb was let off. For more on Aveling, see the next letter, note 5.
2 PSW commissioned from CFM a copy of Vittore Carpaccio's *St George and the Dragon* at the Scuola di San Giorgio degli Schiavoni, in Venice. See below, Letters 257, 262, 264, 270, 272 and 273.
3 See above, Letter 237, note 8.

254 • To William Morris, 3 April 1885

Venice
April 3. 1885.

My dear Fellow.

Your letter of Mar: 19 was very pleasant to me, the more so that it had in it just what I wanted to know of your goings-on.[1] Kate Faulkner sent me the April n^o of 'Commonweal', so that when I get back I shall not be quite in the dark as to how things are with my friends. I was heartily glad of the continuation of the poem which was the best of reading for me here of elsewhere.[2]

I was on the scaffolding at the Ducal Palace this morning, & while at work I lent 'Commonweal' to the director of the works there who reads & speaks English.[3] He wanted permission to translate such pieces as the "Workers' share of art,"[4] which I gave him, and I promised to send him that piece and any more of the like kind of yours. He thinks the Italian workmen will be interested in it. This young fellow is well read in French, German & English poetry, and I mean to send him a volume of yours on my return, in recognition of the help he has given me in looking into the construction of buildings &c here. He is coming to dine with me on Sat: evening when I shall have more talk with him on this and other matters. He is a rather excitable fellow working much too hard, having the necessary vanity to stimulate his natural cleverness. He is certainly not likely to let his masters be in ignorance of the mischief if they propose anything in the way of scraping to Venetian works. He has already been threatened by the engineers, who direct all works here, that they will put him on the dredging boat in the lagoons if he is not more reticent. He is poor, & w^d have to put up with that, but he will get the sack soon I fancy unless he bends to what is really very ignorant authority.

I hope you didn't think I meant to infer, in my last letter, that you w^d neglect your Merton work? I thought, and still think you may overtax yourself, and hasten the business of the 'separator of companions'. I am always nervous as to possible health accidents from overwork, such as paralysis &c!

I am not afraid of Aveling, though I don't think I sh^d like him,[5] but I understand that it may be, & probably is, absolutely necessary for you and other serious members to use any ability you can lay hold of. I thought so even with Hyndman, who was of very inferior stuff in comparison with Aveling. I met a very good natured fellow (a friend of Middleton's) at Rome, & who came on here for a week or so, by name of Bradley, a late fellow of Balliol & now a professor at Liverpool. He is half brother of the Dean of Westm^r. I talked socialism with him & he was not afraid, but goes ~~but~~ only a short way. If he comes to London I will ask you to come to dinner & meet him. He is poor as a rat, and in very weak health.

Charley Faulkner is, of course, a capital fellow and his want of facility is small in conjunction with his heartiness & faithfulness. I <u>have</u> just heard of "rumours" of wars, but I didn't give heed, as I doubted the information &c.

I was at Padua on Sun: Mon & Tuesday in this week and looked at the big town hall there & thought of your efforts for Westminster.[6] Wardle sent me the pamphlet,[7] and I still hope some shrill yell may get to the ears of the first fool of a minister of works, before things are quite settled. Padua is an interesting town, but the hall there – barring the amusing paintings on the walls – is not equal, inside, to that of Westminster. Venice I like also, & if I were in love of impure idleness could spend or waste my time here, but I shall really be glad to get home to do what I can in the way of honest work.

I go on to Vicenza on Sunday on my way to Verona, where I shall stay as long as I can (2 or 3 days I'm afraid, only) and from thence to Brescia, Mantua, Modena & Parma to Milan whence I shall leave direct for London, on or about the 16th. Don't, therefore, write to me again as, in moving about, I should lose the letter.

I hope Jenny is stronger and that I shall find her cheery on my return. I suppose Janey & May are still in the Riviera.

Your affectionate | Philip Webb:

V&A, NAL MSC/1958/687, f. 14

---

1 'Webb is not back yet, nor have I heard from him, nor to say the truth written to him.' WM to MM (in Bordighera), 11 March 1885, *CLWM*, II.
2 WM was sufficiently pleased with 'The Message of the March Wind', in the March number of *Commonweal*, that he decided to continue it, calling the longer poem *Pilgrims of Hope*, the story of three English people – two men and a woman – who fight for the Paris Commune in 1870–1. See WM to JM, 10 February 1885, note 3, *CLWM*, II, p. 386.
3 This was PSW's first encounter with Giacomo Boni (GBO), whose friendship was to be of such profound importance in the years which followed.
4 WM's 'The Worker's Share of Art', *The Commonweal*, I, no 3 (March 1885), pp. 18–19.
5 Though he cannot have known Edward Aveling well at this time, PSW's instincts about him were perhaps surer than those of WM. Aveling's 'free marriage' with Eleanor Marx, daughter of Karl Marx, together with his intellectual brilliance and scientific background, gave him a commanding presence in the socialist movement. But he was essentially untrustworthy. MM is harshly realistic in observing that he was 'spewed out of every Socialist and Secularist Society because in money matters and sexual relations he was almost incredibly shameless, conscienceless and heartless'. Cited in *MacCarthy, WMLT*, p. 508.
6 For WM's efforts on behalf of the SPAB, relating to the planned restoration of Westminster Hall, see above, Letter 239, note 5. WM had given evidence to a select committee on 11 March.
7 In early 1885 the SPAB published the committee's views as an appeal to the House of Commons, in *Remarks on the Proposed Restorations of Westminster Hall*. It went out as from the secretary, over HTT's name.

255 • To George Washington Jack, 4 April 1885

Venice.
April 4. 1885.

Dear Jack.

I had your letter (with the enclosed letters) of the 23rd Mar: but have been too busy to answer it 'till now, and I thought there was nothing of instant importance to be said. I winked and smiled at your cutting down the drawing-room frieze pattern at Clouds – however, I am getting old and should hardly kick if you shortened my legs, both pattern & myself might be improved by your shears!

Damn the gardener and his employers, I say: for cutting down that sycamore tree where they have put their stupid greenhouse – there, I've done! We must try some 'dodge' if the beams in the dining room look as if they <u>sagged</u>. Simmonds & the plasterer <u>ought</u> to have seen to this as, after I had over & over again spoken of this matter for the drawing-room ceiling, it never occurred to me to waken them up for this one. Simmonds is not worth his salt.[1]

I think Mr Goodman should make an agreement with Howell for <u>all</u> his work.

Yes, it is in the Contract that Estcourt shᵈ keep the roads used by him in constant repair. Simmonds knows of this.

Kind remembrance to Mʳ Goodman. I wrote direct answers to the letters you sent me – Wyndham, Pitt Rivers &c.

I leave here tomorrow for Vicenza on my way to Verona. I must try & stay 2 or 3 days in the latter place – then I shall take 2 or 3 more towns on my way to Milan which place I think I shall leave direct for England on the 15ᵗʰ or 16ᵗʰ.

As I shall be more than busy for the rest of my time in Italy I shall not be able to do any more drawings for Clouds 'till my return. If there shᵈ be anything of moment for you to write me, send to "poste Restante" Milan.

I ~~will~~[2] ʰᵒᵖᵉ you will manage to do the things necessary 'till my return, and that I shall find you well then.

Yours sincerely | Philip Webb.

V&A, AAD

1 See above, Letter 174, note 1.
2 Not crossed through, but PSW surely meant to do so.

256 • To Kate Faulkner, 4 April 1885

Venice.
April. 4. 1885

My dear Kate.

I had your kind letter of the 29ᵗʰ of March with the 'Commonweal'. It was really very good of you to think of sending it to me, as it is the only paper I care to look at just now. And as it had 2 of Morris's things in it, I the more rejoiced that you sent it.[1] I am very anxious both for Morris and Charles, as they will be both of them very earnest in their labours and neither of them wanted any added work on their shoulders. Still, there is a certain~~ly~~ kind of obstinacy which one gladly puts up with in one's friends, even though they ᵃⁿᵈ ʷᵉ may suffer by it.

The note you gave me of your going away in to the country was the most pleasant news I have had for some time; let nothing short of impossibility stop you. As you say you do not go before the 8ᵗʰ or 9ᵗʰ, I send this to Queen Square. I fancy it will be the last I shall write to you from Italy, as I shall be moving about so much that there will be scanty time for writing anything more than business lines.

I leave here tomorrow morning for Vicenza on my way to Verona, where I shall hope to be able to stay for 2 or 3 days, after which I shall make my way to 2 or 3 other towns and leave Milan for England – I think – on the 15ᵗʰ or 16ᵗʰ. I shall also come home quite direct, in a through train, as I must not delay any longer getting to my home work.

Venice I have found a pleasant enough place as, over and above its great monuments of beauty, it has so many old houses remaining that, perhaps, more of a mediæval town is to be seen here than elsewhere. I need hardly say that the cold and formal arch^re of the Renaissance looks duller here than in other places.

Venice is also blessed with many pigeons, and they make alive even a stupid & pompous piece of building. The canals and shallow seas are also a continual pleasure and the absence of wheel traffic, a boon beyond comparison. Still, with all the aid of my having much to do in the way of study (without it, I w^d not have stayed away half as long) I do not really care for travelling, though I sh^d be more ready to travel if I knew the language of the people I was in the midst of. I really like to speak to all I meet, the more so as I get older.

I also wish to get back, to avoid the daily reproach that my friends are without even my small backing in their efforts for the mass of mankind. I shall be able to do very little indeed, but I can say & look some heartiness to them. The good mother's kind remembrance to me was a real pleasure and I hope she will be strong enough to pick up some good from the change into country air. Please give her my kindest love and beg her to remember all my bad jokes if she should be inclined to wisdom too severe for her health.

Bless me! After all, I may be able to see the piano before it goes from Queen Square, and I shall look to have that ~~pleasure~~ surprise. I was at Padua the first 3 days of this week, and found it a pleasant and very Italian looking city, full of streets built with arches on each side to carry the houses. Even now, when there has been more or less cloudy weather, the pleasure of the shady walk was real. The weather, on the whole, has not been bad, and a good many days have been splendidly fine. I was lucky in having bright weather for the day I went to Torcello, which is a place all too sad by side of its ruined & injured splendours. Its two strange churches stand side by side as if they were the last of the place, as they very nearly are.[2]

Now I must give over, and beg you and the mother to keep yourselves as well as you can to bless me with your friendly kindness on my return. Don't forget to remember me to Charles.

Yours very sincerely | Philip Webb.

V&A, NAL MSC/1958/687, f. 89

---

[1] In addition to 'The Message of the March Wind', the March 1885 number of *The Commonweal* carried a paragraph from WM as treasurer of the Socialist League, appealing to members to pay subscriptions regularly, to offset the expenses of 'pamphlets and leaflets setting for the principles of Socialism', and so that the League might 'engage in organising Socialism in the provinces'.

[2] The two churches on the now quiet island of Torcello in the north of the Venetian Lagoon are the Cattedrale di Santa Maria Assunta, and situated immediately on its right side, the smaller and simpler Chiesa di Santa Costa.

257 • To Charles Fairfax Murray, 30 April 1885

Incomplete

1, Raymond Buildings, Gray's Inn | London, W.C.
April 30. 1885

My dear Murray

I found your letter of "Sunday" here on getting back from my work in Wiltshire, where I was yesterday and the day before, undergoing the pain of seeing the translation of the drawings I sent from Italy, into modelled & carved plaster & wood!

I don't wonder that you thought ill of my delay in writing. You might so easily have guessed that I was caught & robbed in a bawdy-house in Paris or elsewhere when I was out of reach of your guarding self. You did well to give me a lien upon you.[1] Fawcett sent me the prints today,[2] and his bill, wh' I paid: the bill came, in exact figures, to £49.19.5 wh' was near enough for me to consider right, when your figures were 48.19.0. You must fight Fawcett for the odd shillings of difference after adding 8^s/5^d for telegrams.[3] In any case I am determined not to lose by you, though, unless I get the Carpaccio St George – done with your finest touch (and go) – I shall consider myself ill-used, though I have these Mantegna & other prints (including a Beccafumi) in my hands or strong box. Mind, you take all risks of fire or burn bailiffs!

I have ~~just~~ looked into the National Gallery here for ½ an hour; some goodish pictures, no doubt, but the 70,000er Raffaello was a mistake,[4] like the building of St Payther's at Room[5]. However, poor Burton[6] serves "ower many maisters" "as the paddock said to the harrow."[7] While looking at this Raffael I thought of the little one of his in the Louvre, with the lovely hill & treed background, wh' you may remember as having some interest in it beyond refinement of manner.[8]

Do you know anything of an <u>English</u> painter (of the end of last cent^y I fancy) named Agas? I've seen 3 or 4 of his pictures of ^{very} well done animals,[9] in landscapes worthy of Old Crome,[10] which surprised me into admiration. I know nothing of the name, but relished work which had some real soul, $^{though\ in}$ a lowish form of art. You had better look in the newspaper from Godalming and see if there is not a paragraph describing some bad work done by a Gray's Inn arch^t who has been bungling in Surrey lately. I know of no other cause for such a paper been [*sic*] sent to me in Italy except this friendly or Job's-comforting sort. I have no 'separate establishment' in Surrey.

If I did not well know the extreme caution with which you mount and ride a scaffolding, standing some 3 or 4 feet above the floor, I should be somewhat anxious as to your life when you are at work again in the Schiavoni Chapel; bewitched, may be, by the rattling of the money box. Don't 'stint' the Half Hannikin[11] when your [*page missing*]

Fitzwilliam 30

1 Lien: to give a right of possession.
2 Probably the woodblock colour printer, Benjamin Fawcett (1808–93), who produced engraved colour illustrations for works such as the six-volume ornithological handbook by Francis Orpen Morris, *A Natural History of British Birds* (Groombridge, 1850–7).
3 Evidently, PSW carried out a commission for CFM on his return to England, and had paid Fawcett on CFM's behalf for prints which he had ordered. A final settling of the debt occurred when CFM sent PSW his Carpaccio copy. See below, Letter 273, note 3.
4 In 1885 the National Gallery bought Raphael's so-called *Ansidei Madonna*, one of the paintings from the Ansidei Altarpiece made for San Fiorenzo, Perugia, from George Spencer-Churchill, eighth Duke of Marlborough, for £70,000, three times the amount previously paid for a painting.
5 St Peter's at Rome.
6 For Frederic Burton see above, Letter 26, note 2. Some of the National Gallery's finest works were acquired during Burton's tenure as director, including not just the *Ansidei Madonna*, but also *The Ambassadors* by Holbein, the *Virgin of the Rocks* by Leonardo and Botticelli's *Venus and Mars*.
7 '"Ower mony maisters – ower mony maisters, as the paddock said to the harrow, when every tooth gae her a tig".' Words of grumbling complaint by Andrew Fairchild in Scott's *Rob Roy*, ch 27.
8 Almost certainly he has in mind the *Virgin and Child with the Young St John the Baptist*, known as *La Belle Jardinière* (c. 1507).
9 The Swiss-born painter Jacques-Laurent Agasse (1767–1849) settled permanently in London after 1800. He is best known for his paintings of horses and rarer animals (leopards, tigers, lions, etc).
10 The Norwich painter and engraver, John Crome the Elder (1768–1821), whose landscapes influenced nineteenth-century English painters such as Turner, Constable and Cotman.
11 An old English dance tune, included in John Playford's *English Dancing Master* (1651), and the nickname which PSW and CFM gave to the sacristan at the Schiavoni chapel.

258 • To George Price Boyce, 4 May 1885

1, Raymond Buildings, Gray's Inn, | *London, W.C.*
Mon: May 4. 1885

My dear Boyce

I like the "Catterlen" drawing in a "more" degree.[1] Am never "rash"; ~~the~~ my nearest approach to that human weakness is a rasher.

I know a great deal about pictures, neither Burton nor Wallis[2] nor Murray can hold a candle to me in that respect. Such is my decided opinion! The above named b---y swells might <u>consider</u> me 'rash' in this assertion but then, I <u>know</u> them to be rash in urging to & giving £70,000 for a picture, merely because it is rare,[3] & there are other fools in the picture bourse.

I confess it <u>is</u> a serious thing to buy a modern picture, requiring more & better judgment than for an ancient one! But I have this advantage in the case in question, ~~as~~ I know that <u>you</u> painted it and that it is a good example of your work. Also, and this is a great point, no damned middleman has fleeced me of 4 or 500 percent in getting it.

I had spent less money in Italy than I expected & arranged for, and I could manage, when I saw – unexpectedly – an opportunity of getting another piece of honest & beautiful work for New Place, to do what I did.

My brother was greatly pleased at my "rashness", but he raised so many horrid yells at my making him a present of it that I don't know yet if he will allow me to have the pleasure of giving it; all I can do at present is to say 'let it remain, we shall see' &c, but this point is unimportant – whether I or he finally pays for it. The picture is secured for our intelligent delight and nothing more need be said.

As to your doing anything more to it *the Catterlen drawing* when it comes home, & you may have time, that is your affair, I cannot suggest anything except, perhaps, that you alter the colour & the disposition of the house and trees, tone down the foreground & heighten the background &c, and which said alterations w^d, in my opinion (a good one, as aforesaid) resolve themselves into removing a crumb of discomfort wh' has crept in between the drawing & the glass, and which looks like a bit of supernaturalism.

I looked at other pictures in the Gallery, but was much disheartened at the state of the 'pot boiling' grooves into which most of the painters' wheels do visibly run. The painters do mainly wear financial spectacles, I am afraid, and nature gets denaturalized through these lenses. Grass is not grass to them, trees not trees, and the human figure element becomes like bad novellists' [*sic*] dreams of what simple country folk are like. Mrs Allingham seems to be getting quite ridiculous in this & other ways.[4] Albert Goodwin looks to have found out how to do things with a 'go', to save thought & work. One of his drawings N° 197 was less bad in this respect.[5] Smallfield's N° 242 has some nature in the landscape & it is somewhat interesting & beautiful, but is wanting in composition, so that it is hardly a picture.[6]

Yours sincerely | Philip Webb.

BL Add 45354, ff. 218-20

---

[1] The exhibition of the Royal Society of Painters in Water Colours opened in Pall Mall East on 27 April. GPB had entered several works, including *Yanworth Hall*, *Brougham Castle* and *Catterlen Hall*, worked up from sketches made in the autumn of 1883, when staying in Cumbria. See above, Letter 213, note 6. PSW bought *Catterlen Hall* (now in the V&A) as a gift for his brother, Harry. As *The Times* put it, 'Mr. Boyce has been wandering, as usual, among the old houses of Westmoreland and Cumberland' (1 May). *The Athenæum* liked the picture, though expressed caution: 'a grand group of old grey towers in pure light, very solidly and beautifully painted. Yet much as we admire Mr. Boyce's work, it is not to be denied that he repeats too often a favourite effect of light and scheme of colour.' (2 May).

[2] Henry Wallis (see above, Letter 96, note 12) was represented in the exhibition by *Oriental Glass Merchant*, which *The Times* described as displaying 'a wealth of colour that will be a revelation even to his admirers' (1 May), as well as by *Going to Market, Bruges*.

[3] See previous letter, note 4.

[4] Helen Allingham (1848–1926) was represented by *A Basket of Clothes*, set in a cottage garden, and *Lessons*, showing a family schoolroom, works which, for *The Times*, were 'faultless and most covetable' (May). See also Vol. II, Letter 331, note 1.

[5] This was *Ilfracombe* by the landscape watercolourist, Albert Goodwin (1845–1932). The exhibition also included his *Porlock Pier* and *Clovelly*.

[6] Frederick Smallfield (1825–1915) painted in oil and watercolour, his work revealing a distinct Pre-Raphaelite sensibility.

1864–1887

259 • To George Price Boyce, 23 May 1885

1, Raymond Buildings, Gray's Inn, | London, W.C.
Sat: May 23. 1885

My dear Boyce

I have had a little anxiety lest you should have made your cold worse in the journey and umbrellaing we had together: unfortunate weather it was for us.

The little 'account' I promised to send you is this.

When I asked you to go to Knoyle with me, to cheer me in my disappointment over the work there, it was as my guest and not as a professional adviser: no doubt you thought your advice so valuable that, rather than I should not get it, you would even pay for the pleasure of rubbing it in!

However, this would never do, as you would be "bad to hold" if I in any way lent myself to encourage so preposterous (fine long word) an imagination as that anything you could say would improve my future efforts in the way of house building.

Apart from the inevitable jesting, I was – in spite of the weather – made much more comfortable in my mind by your good natured attention to what I had been able to do at Clouds, and so, peace be upon all work which I had done, and better hope for the future.

I go to Welwyn this evening, when I will give your and Madame's kindest remembrances. I have not yet heard from the doctor, but my sister tells me he has – as was to be expected – had bad weather.[1]

With kind regards to Mrs Boyce | Believe me | Sincerely yours | Philip Webb.

BL Add 45354, ff. 221-2

---

1 See next letter, note 2.

260 • To George Price Boyce, 26 May 1885

1, Raymond Buildings, Gray's Inn, | London, W.C.
May 26. 1885

My dear Boyce

Let it be so then – though I sh^d have been easier in mind if I had borne the cost of the journey, it being an unprofitable one for you. The money-order pays too much, so that I shall pay you, when I think of it, at our meeting, 4^s/9^d! and you go to Sheol!![1]

The plant journeyed safely on Sat: and I stood him on the bed (to be taken in if weather threatens frost) on a S. E aspect, & secured against falling. H.S.W will tell you what he thinks of it and you, on his return.[2] At all events my sister was pleased with it, but <u>she</u> will not transplant it, leaving that for the more botanically learned doctor. I have heard from him from the top of Dartmoor – he & Jephson are doing their best to catch fish & health on those wild knolls.

The garden at Welwyn has been considerably touched by these cold winds I noted an Arbutus[3] gone the way of all vegitables, [*sic*] and other bushes pinched and unhappy looking. Still, the place looked lovely on the whole, and the birds were miraculously wonderful in movement and song. Nightingales only turning up here & there – evidently waiting for a milder time.

I thank you for your notes on the painter, Agasse[4] – which will make me learned when I next meet General Pitt-Rivers at Rushmore.

I will try to go to the Pastoral Symphony next Monday, but am not now sure that I shall be able.[5]

Yours sincerely | Philip Webb.

My sister certainly would have written about the Illicium[6] had she not been too much put upon with house & professional labours (& headache) while the brother is away. Still, she desired kindly remembrance to you & Mrs Boyce, wh' I now deliver, as I did yours to New Place.

BL Add 45354, ff. 223-4

1 The underworld (Hebrew); the abode of departed spirits from which none return.
2 Henry (Harry) Speakman Webb was repeating the fishing expedition of the previous year. See above, Letter 220, note 1.
3 A family of shrubs with edible red berries, commonly called the Strawberry Tree.
4 See above, Letter 257, note 9.
5 Hans Richter conducted Beethoven's sixth symphony (the 'Pastoral') at St James's Hall on 1 June, in a programme which also included music by Liszt and Wagner.
6 An evergreen shrub.

261 • To Percy Wyndham, 25 June 1885

Draft

1 R.B. Gray's Inn
June 25. 1885

Dear Mr Wyndham

I thank you for your note, which was enigmatical and amusing. I fancied that, if I had been sent to $^{the\ parliamentary}$ school ~~in parliament~~, it w^d have been no enigma to me and I sh^d have read between the lines easily enough. How delighted I was to learn from a safe source that the Conservatives had nobility of heart, even at the cost of being fools,[1] and ~~that~~ if they do the bidding of "auld Nickie-ben"[2] it is he has gifted them with a knowledge of his better qualities, and a power to touch pitch on its clean side only.

I was at Clouds yesterday and Tuesday. Things are smoothing down there. One of the men ~~there~~ said you had already got a fence for the south side of house, and another that you would like a "white" fence. If you have not yet concluded as to this ~~fence~~, I would say (if you w^d care to know?) that a white fence w^d, I think, ~~perhaps~~ be the better, ^(round the stable land opposite the house,) and about 3 feet 3 inches high. The spars should be close enough to keep out a young rabbit and, perhaps, something of this kind, with a top bar that you could lean on. [*sketch*]

They have now got the panelling up in the entrance hall, & this place looks very well. I also think the great hall and main stairs look ~~very~~ well, & the high panelling in the dining-room to be a great gain.

Yours very truly | Philip Webb.

The Hon' Percy Wyndham M:P:

V&A, AAD

---

1 PSW and PWY were exchanging comments about the new Conservative caretaker administration under Lord Salisbury. Gladstone had resigned on 9 June after a defeat over Irish home rule, and Salisbury agreed on 23 June to form a government until an election under the terms of the extended franchise and revised constituencies could be called.

2 The devil, taken from the Robert Burns poem, 'Address to the deil' (1785): 'But fare you wheel, auld Nickie-ben!' (121). For PSW's more telling use of this poem, see Vol. II, Letter 388, note 3.

262 • To Charles Fairfax Murray, 30 June 1885

1, Raymond Buildings, Gray's Inn | *London, W.C.*

June 30. 1885

My dear Murray

It is with deep grief, tempered with high pleasure, that I condole & rejoice with you that you are once more perched on the swaying scaffolding in the beautiful chapel of the Schiavoni. Please to refrain from taking snuff, when you are on this tottering stage, or you will certainly sneeze and bring yourself & my picture to the ground, and your admiring patron (what a delightful position to hold in this wonderful world) to a premature grave. If I could but jabber, passably, in the Italian tongue, I would send my clients to il diavolo[1] (their own proper home) and come at once to the Schiavoni, take the place of the "Half Hannikin" of a Sacristan,[2] and watch over you with my best air of patronage. In one hand I should hold a birch rod, proper, and in the other a bag of lollipops, applying one or the other to you as occasions required and, now & then, setting you on your perch again when the scaffolding collapsed.

   If you were to think of my work, of trying to find out what my clients want, and really finding out that they don't want what I can give them, you would enjoy your work of crooning over the colour, texture, and fancy of Carpaccio, shewn in the picture you are perpetuating the fame of, instead of malignantly writing that "it was too bad of me to give you this to do". If you tumble off your perch, now, you will know the reason why.

I think Ruskin went to the wrong man for his triplicate of the Tintoret donkey's head! surely R: should have applied to me, as I know the animal well from studies at home.[3] I think I shall make an enlarged study from the photograph of one of Benozzo Gozzoli's mule heads, and send it to Ruskin as a specimen of my work of the kind, taking care to leave the study unfinished, so that the thing sh^d not look to have too much work in it. Putting in some touch and a great deal of go, but it would be touch-& go if R: would stand it, eh?

All right of Alinari[4] to photograph the minarets or double campanile at the choir end of S: Antonio: $^{at\ Padua}$.[5] I also sh^d like a photograph or two of one or two of the cloisters there: perhaps you pointed this out to him? True, the museum at Padua is a wonderful effort of Sig: Boito's genius.[6] I remember holding forth upon it loudly to Bradley when we went to see the things there.

If you should see Alinari in Venice, suggest to him the making of goodsized photographs of ^{the} triple shafted "tree" capitals in the Ch' of S:S: John & Paul.[7] He might do it, if only to spite Naya.[8] These capitals are quite beautiful and are also fresh in style. There also sh^d be a good large photo: of the sharp pointed pedimented doorway in the Campo San Luca. I have measurements of it but want a photograph.

This puts me in mind that I did not take the exact size of the S: George ^{picture} you are copying. Will you kindly do this for me? You will surely cry out against the number of tiresome and unremunerative commissions I give to you. There will be nothing for it but for you to strike and sturdily refuse to listen any more to my prayers. However, for all these and many other mercies you have bestowed on the cussedness of your friend, receive my hearty thanks.

I see in today's paper that Watts has had the grace to refuse his Baronetcy. I shall begin to look upon him with some respect again.[9]

Just now I was writing of the "cussedness" of friends. Surely it must have been 'friends', so called, who teazed [sic] E:B:J into the Academy. The thing is too stupid for one mind to have grasped the ^{whole} folly alone.[10]

My kindest remembrance to the Signora & the little maid. Entreat them from me to take a black water-gig and go to the Adriatic side of the Lido, often. I expect you to spend at least 5 lire a day in gondolas while you are at work for me.

Greet the Signori Boni & Barnaby[11] for me, and also the taxed Allesandri, [sic] and say something pretty to Darvall's long legged good natured gondolier.

No more orders at present, nor bad jests either, but sincere good wishes | from
your kindly befriended | Ph: W.

I posted a letter for you to the Serraglio[12] on Friday last, I think.

Fitzwilliam 31

---

1 The devil (*It*).
2 See above, Letter 257, note 11.
3 In 1885, the Italian painter Angelo Alessandri (1854–1931) made a watercolour copy for JR of Tintoretto's *Flight into Egypt* (1582–7) at the Scuola Grande di San Rocco in Venice, which is now

in the Guild of St George collection maintained by Museums Sheffield. The donkey is placed in the foreground, in front of Mary, with head lowered, and for JR it was the making of the composition. 'I have never seen any of the nobler animals – lion, or leopard, or horse, or dragon – made so sublime as the quiet head of the domestic ass. . . . The painter seems to have intended that everything should be subordinate to the beauty of this single head.' *The Stones of Venice*, 3 vols (London: Smith, Elder & Co., 1851–3), III, p. 328.

4 In 1852, Leopoldo Alinari and his two brothers established in Florence the world's first commercial photographic firm, which specialised in images of historic buildings, works of art, and portraits. Its archives are now at the Museum of Multimedia and History of Photography, Florence.
5 The Basilica di Sant'Antonio di Padova was completed in the early fourteenth century. The two nave bays each support a dome, with minaret-like belfries.
6 The Italian architect, Camillo Boito (1836–1914), elder brother of the composer and librettist Arrigo Boito (1842–1918), designed the Municipal Museum in Padua (1879).
7 The Basilica di San Giovanni e Paolo, one of the largest Venetian churches, completed in 1430.
8 Based in Venice, Carlo Naya (1816–82) photographed many of its buildings and art works, and also documented the restoration work on the Giotto frescoes in the Cappella degli Scrovegni, Padua.
9 G.F. Watts was offered a baronetcy by Gladstone in 1885 (as was Millais, who accepted), and again in 1894. He refused on both occasions, believing that he did not have the financial means necessary for the position. Had PSW known this, he doubtless would have mingled contempt with the soreness he still felt over his experience in building the Briary for Watts. See above, Letter 67.
10 PSW's puzzlement over EBJ's election as an Associate of the Royal Academy in June is well-founded, as it was 'an institution from which he had deliberately kept his distance and which he had very often ridiculed'. *MacCarthy, LPR*, p. 364. When the news of the election came by messenger, even GBJ assumed it was a mistake. EBJ went to see Frederic Leighton, president of the Academy, who persuaded him to accept. However, he was passed over when it came to full membership as an RA, and in 1893 resigned the Associateship.
11 Not identified.
12 CFM's address in the Via de' Serragli, in Florence.

263 • To Editor of *The Times*, 17 July 1885

Drafted on behalf of SPAB

To Editor of the Times re "Refacing of Westminster Abbey"[1]

As a ^being supplementary to the letter you were good enough to publish in ^your issue of Oct: 15 1884, ^we beg that you will ^again aid the Soc^y for the Prot^n of Anc^l B^gs by giving this letter in as early a number of your paper as may be convenient. We ask for its early admission, as the case of Westminster Hall having roused the attention of the public to the fact that one ^the few remaining great historical buildings in London are in utmost danger of destruction, under the present lamentable system of treating them as official or private property to be dealt with in the least possible public way, we think this newly created interest should not be allowed to die away without ^before calling attention ^is called be called ^to the activity at this moment displayed ^shewn in continuing the wholesale refacing of the clerestory on the south side of Westminster Abbey ^Church. Slowly, and almost imperceptibly this replacing began at the western end, next the south west tower, but during the last nine ^eight months a much greater force of workmen ^labour has been engaged, and the work of removing all traces of the original Abbey walling is being gone on with only too much actively. In a twofold way, is this, in our opinion, ^this is disastrous. In the first place

299

a ~~great~~ ^quick^ change in ^the^ settled forces of the old walling more certainly acts on the fabric than a slow & piecemeal one; and secondly, the sooner the work is done the less chance is there for the public mind to be~~come~~ ^come^ aware of the mischief, ~~being done~~ before it is too late. We beg, even now, ~~that~~ all those interested in this ~~noble historical fabric~~ ^wonderful Church^ to go into the cloisters and, with an opera glass ^from the opposite side^ examine what has been done, while there is still ~~time, to see~~ ^a chance of seeing^ the two or three bays of the work ^left^ which have ~~remaining~~ their original Godstone or Reigate stone facing.² The beautiful colour of this green-grey stone will be easily recognised, with its varied coursing and fine jointing. ^It must be acknowledged that^ The transformation in appearance is lamentable, ~~as may be seen,~~ but we speak with some knowledge when we say that the action of the fabric is equally mischievous. We can decidedly affirm that the ~~work~~ ^repairs which are were^ necessary, could have been ^done in a^ better & cheaper way, and the ~~aspect~~ ^appearance^ of the walling scarcely changed when the proper security had been obtained. Such is the haste with which the work is now being carried on we can hardly hope that even a righteous outcry against it could avail for what remains of the old facing on the south side of the nave; ~~But as~~ ^but^ the public through their sluggishness ~~have~~ ^having^ lost this deeply interesting old work ^should be made aware at once^ there is still the north side of the nave to ~~be done~~ ^ruin in the same way^ and ^this at least^ should be stopped if there is any care whatever remaining in the people for their great Abbey Church. Almost all intelligent observers agree that the church of Notre Dame in Paris has been made one of the dullest and least interesting of the mediæval historical fabrics in France; surely therefore that sharp fact should not be lost upon us with regard to Westminster Abbey.

[*pencil*] Wrote & sent this to Hon' R. Grosvenor for him to make a letter out of it to be sent to the Times.³

July 17. 1885

SPAB

---

1 This letter did not appear in *The Times*.
2 Stone from quarries at Godstone in Surrey were used in the Abbey construction.
3 The barrister, the Hon Richard Cecil Grosvenor (1848–1919), became a Progressive Party member of the London County Council, and at this time was one of the SPAB's Honorary Secretaries.

264 • To Charles Fairfax Murray, 22 July 1885

Incomplete

1, Raymond Buildings, Gray's Inn | London, W.C.
Wed: night 22nd July 1885

My dear Murray

The effect of the brick & a half on my head was somewhat softened by the news of the finishing of the S: George. The crocodile tears you have shed over my stomach and other aches really fell, no doubt, on account of your sorrow at having to leave the Schiavoni after so many days of happiness spent there. All people like doing what they can do well, and the pleasure you must have had will hardly be compensated by the payment. The pain you have suffered cannot be paid for at all, and therefore it will do you no good to remember it. I hope you behaved liberally to the Half Hannikin, whose plaything has been taken from him as ^{well as} the pleasure of seeing <u>you</u> at work while <u>he</u> was idle. When I see the work you have done I shall look narrowly at S: George's nose. As I learned from Maddox Brown's pictures the power of reflected colour, I fancy the "Venetian Burgundy" must have got into your nose & then canted off on to the George's.[1] 'Tis a pity I was not with you to take the better half of each bottle, in my usual way. If I should find fault with what <u>I</u> might consider the <u>under-finish of your</u> work you will have to lay the blame on that simple creature, good red wine! Still, I anticipate no disappointment whatever, and in spite of your oleo-margarining me as to the want of the value of my stimulating presence while you were at work, I fancy it was better done than if I had been by you; as your natural "antagonism", (as a well-known celebrity of a taskmaster has allied with your name in good sized print)[2] would surely have cropped up to the damage of the red cross knight, his girl, his horse, his toads, his ships, his city and his sky!

Perhaps I should have liked to have seen how you drew the whole picture together, when the detail was done, with the masterly touch of which you are so proud though you don't talk of it. I sh^d have ^{been} somewhat delighted if you could have told me that the great white waistcoated Liard[3] had made you come down from your perch, & that he had mounted the scaffold to get a nearer view of the work, & that that unstable pyramid had collapsed and the hoary old vagabond had broken his head on the Schiavoni pavement, and that Checco[4] & you had danced round the insensible scoundrel to the tune of the money box. How you ^{two} could have brought him round with a liberal supply of July ditch water from the neighbouring canal & toned down his white waistcoat in fine artistic style. Still I am glad for your sake he was civil & let you have a study of his pictures.

I see in my notebook that there are 3 steps to the big Campanile above the present pavement of the Piazza, so that there must have been a series of 7 or 8 of these steps to the base of the tower, originally? I forget how many Bellini shews.[5]

Certainly, my good friend, keep the drawing for a reasonable time to make any copy you like of it. I sh^d be sorry to be the cause of the loss to the world of even one more faithful copy of Carpaccio's delightful picture. However, don't let the young Nero[6] jump through it ^(my drawing) like the clown at the circus. As part punishment for my delay in getting the work, I should be glad if you would get me the whole series of [*page missing*]

Fitzwilliam 33

1 See also below, Letter 273, note 1.
2 CFM was never reticent in expressing his opinions about Italian painters, for they were usually well-founded. In this sense his relationship with JR was different in kind from that of the several other men employed to copy paintings or architectural details; as JR admitted, CFM did such work as well if not better than most, but their occasional disputes could be quite fiery: 'another of my young helpers, Mr. Charles F. Murray, – one, however, whose help is given much in the form of antagonism, – informs me of various critical discoveries lately made, both by himself, and by industrious Germans, of points respecting the authenticity of this and that, which will require notice from me: more especially he tells me of certification that the picture in the Uffizi, of which I accepted the ordinary attribution to Giotto, is by Lorenzo Monaco'. 'The Shepherd's Tower', from *Mornings in Florence* (Orpington: George Allen, 2nd edn., 1883), pp. 153–4.
3 Variant of lyard or lyart, now obsolete: grey, approaching white (*OED*). One can only assume that PSW refers to the custodian of the chapel, whose permission had initially been sought for making the copy of the Carpaccio.
4 The sacristan?
5 Gentile Bellini (c. 1429–1507) painted his *Procession of the True Cross in Piazza San Marco, Venice* (now in the Galleria dell'academia) as one of three (1496–1501) which he contributed to a cycle of eight pictures on the story of the True Cross for the Scuola di San Giovanni Evangelista. Carpaccio also participated in the commission. The steps of the campanile are not distinguishable as it is thronged by people.
6 One of CFM's young sons, either Giovanni (b. 1880) or Eduardo (b. 1883).

265 • To George Price Boyce, 14 August 1885

1, Raymond Buildings, Gray's Inn, | *London, W.C.*
Friday Aug 14. 1885

My dear Boyce

I have tried to find an evening either to get you & Mrs Boyce here, or for me to come to you before you have fled, but have failed. Send me a note to say when you are off as, if you were <u>obliged</u> to stay over Monday, perhaps you could, both of you, come here on that evening. I am disappointed at having seen so little of you of late.

My room, for the last week, has been lighted up by the Catterlen drawing, and I shall miss it when it has gone to New Place as it will ^{go} on Saturday – however, I shall see it there in better position with less disturbing surroundings than here. The Welwyn folk are looking forward to having it.

I must ask either you or Mrs Boyce to write to me from France so that friendliness may be kept up.

If you go to look at the pictures in the Louvre, don't forget to look at the Raffaello, N<u>o</u> 365 in the Salon Carré – I think it one of the pleasantest of his pictures.[1] Also, note N° 162 Jan Van Eyck!!![2] – a minute Memling – no number.[3] I need scarcely say that you should refresh your memory of the Mantegnas' in the 7 metres gallery.[4]

I wish you both good voyace, [*sic*] unless I sh^d see you before you go.

Yours sincerely | Philip Webb.

BL Add 45354, ff. 227-8

1 Raphael, *Holy Family* (c. 1518–19).
2 Jan van Eyck (c. 1390/5–1441), *Virgin and Child with Chancellor Rolin* (c. 1430–4).
3 Hans Memling (c. 1430–94). Either the *Mystic Marriage of St Catherine* (c. 1480), or *Donor Presented by St John the Baptist* (c. 1490).
4 Mantegna, *Parnassus* (1495–7), *Madonna of Victory* (1495–6) and *Pallas Expelling the Vices from the Garden of Virtue* (1499–1502).

266 • To George Price Boyce, 16 August 1885

NEW PLACE, | WELWYN, HERTS.
Sunday 16. Aug: 1885

My dear Boyce

The doctor has been good enough to pay attention to my case (the shell of my spirit) and, he having ordered me to be quiet today, here I am on my back, a pattern patient.[1]

If I am as well as I hope to be, I shall come up tomorrow by my usual train, but if not so well I may delay return 'till an evening train; but at all events if you <u>can</u> come in and see me about 7. oc I shall be very glad.

The Catterlen drawing has been properly rejoiced over. I seem to think that it w^d go best over the side board – where the Puy de Dome drawing now is[2] – as it would have a left hand light. The new picture also should I think go on the darker ground of the paper in the dining-room. I suspect the 2 old people here will rather grumble at my changing the place of the older picture, but they will get used to it after a while.

Wardle came in to my rooms yesterday and he was much pleased indeed with Catterlen hall, congratulating you on your luck in having the light shewing through the later wing. He said "Boyce must have asked the occupier to pull up his blinds"![3]

This is as lovely a summer's day as we have had this year. The garden looks very well having had some showers the week before last.

I will ask Mrs Long to do you a bit of stake [*sic*] at 7. oc.

Yours sincerely | Philip Webb.

I am very sorry indeed to miss seeing Mrs Boyce. Very kindest remembrance to her.

BL Add 45354, ff. 229-30

1 He was at his brother's house.
2 GPB's landscape *In the Puy-de-Dome*.
3 See the image at http://www.vam.ac.uk/users/node/19188, where this effect through the windows in the left wing is evident.

267 • To George Price Boyce, 18 August 1885

1, Raymond Buildings, Gray's Inn, | London, W.C.
Tuesday 18th Aug: 1885

My dear Boyce

It was well I refrained from saying anything about the Rossetti drawing last night, as I was too much surprised; a state of surprise not being good for well considered speech.[1]

I have been comforted by this expression of your kind feeling and sympathy, shewn so certainly by an act of unmistakeable generosity and goodwill.

I should be more at a loss what to say under all the circumstances if I were not dealing with you, a friend of many years standing through sometimes good but mostly (and deservedly) ill report.

To start freely on the aforesaid assumptions, I cannot (that is the word) accept this gift from you; though, perhaps, I could have done so from one less a personal friend.

The preparation (see note on back of picture) for leaving this wonderful design permanently in my hands ~~makes~~ marks the assured hope you had that I should accept it;[2] therefore, putting it somewhat paradoxically, I do accept it with abundant pleasure, and though I shall bring it back to West House one of these days, it must remain there – as mine if you will – but still so to remain till fate settles things in a way that it should actually come to ~~you~~ me, or abide with you as the survivor. I do not feel much anxiety from this half rejection of your spontaneous act of kindness but, from my knowledge of you, I am sure you will understand what I intend by these poor words and will not be hurt, no my friend, not disturbed or wounded by what I have felt constrained to do.

I have great pleasure in remembering that Mrs Boyce added her goodwill to the gift.

Yours very affectionately | Philip Webb.

A pleasant voyage to you both.

From one, either, or both I shall expect intelligence of your doings, and I shall rejoice or be sad with you as time may deal it out.

BL Add 45354, ff. 231-2

---

1 On the previous day, GPB had given PSW Rossetti's watercolour, *The Meeting of Dante and Beatrice in Paradise* (1853–4). PSW would in turn later present it to SCC, on the understanding that its final resting-place should be a national collection. The provenance is recorded on two labels on the reverse: '(a) "... The property of George P. Boyce (since April 1854) now of 33 Glebe Place, Chelsea, who at this date August 17 1885 presents it to his good friend Philip Webb whose property it now is. G.P. Boyce '85."

(b) "I, Philip Webb of Caxtons Worth, Sussex (formerly of Raymond Buildings, Gray's Inn, London) did on the 17th December 1900 give this picture to my friend Sydney C. Cockerell assured that, when he had to dispose of it, the picture would finally be placed by him in a 'National' English Gallery of Paintings."

"Given to the Fitzwilliam Museum by Sydney C. Cockerell above named, 3 June 1937. This picture is in a frame designed by the artist".' Virginia Surtees, *The Paintings and Drawings of Dante Gabriel Rossetti (1828–1882). A Catalogue Raisonné*, 2 vols (Oxford: Clarendon Press, 1971), I, p. 72. See also Vol. III, Letter 730.

2 See label (a) in previous note.

268 • To Ewan Christian, 10 September 1885

Drafted on behalf of SPAB

The Society for the Protection of Ancient Buildings

To Ewan Christian Esqre Architect[1]
Dear Sir.

A notice in the "Building News" of August 28 ~~of~~ ^on the present state of Arreton Church in the Isle of Wight and ^of some ~~proposed~~ repairs ^proposed to be done under your direction, has been brought ~~under the~~ before the Committee of this Society, and I am directed to write to you and express its satisfaction ^(if the report is correct) that no sweeping changes are under consideration.[2]

The extreme simplicity of Arreton Church and the beauty of many of its details ~~must be the cause of some anxiety to you~~ ^would make any change in its character a lasting ~~cause of~~ regret to those who have had the pleasure of seeing this ~~building before~~ ^characteristic example of an Isle of Wight church; and ~~our~~ ^my Committee would hope that you will be able to restrain ~~any intention on the part of~~ the promoters of the reparation ~~from~~ should any sign be made that the usual "restoration" be added to the necessary repairs.

In the notice, mention is made of removing the colour wash from the stonework and ^that the bases & capitals of the pillars sh^d be repaired.[3] The Committee would suggest that the colour wash be only removed so far as brush & water will take it off, and that unless the ^injuries to the pillars are dangerous to their stability any broken portions may not be pieced. It is specified that plain red tiles are to be laid for the new flooring, and the Committee hopes you will be able to use native or other plain tiles and not those of the usual mechanical kind ^so much in vogue.

I am ^Dear Sir &c

Copied & taken to Buckingham S^t | Sepr 10. 1885. | Ph. W.

SPAB

---

1 See above, Letter 147, note 4.
2 St George's, Arreton, on the Isle of Wight is mainly of twelfth and thirteenth century construction, with later additions. In 1886, the nave ceiling and box pews were removed.
3 The short report in *Building News*, XLIX (28 August 1885), p. 347, summarised Ewan Christian's judgment that 'The stonework of the arcades and windows should be cleansed from colour wash, and the bases and capitals of the pillars, needful, repaired, and the whole area refloored on a bed of cement concrete, and the bricks replaced by plain red tiles, the sound stones being relaid.'

269 • To George and Caroline Price Boyce, 11 September 1885

1, Raymond Buildings, Gray's Inn, | *London, W.C.*
Friday Sep: 11. 1885

My dear Friends.

I had your letter of the 4th written by George, yes, by George it was written within & without. No, I do not think any robbery went on with the box of fruit from Etampes, as the box was very full and the beautiful Tamarisk sprays were there, flat & uninjured. I fancy all the injury the fruit suffered from was perhaps that it was thrown for a catch and was missed by a "butter fingers". The fruit was delightful, & we all partook – New Place, my clerks, M[rs] Long and myself – praising the Mounseers & Madames who so kindly thought of perfidious Albion.

I have no books from wh' to give you the botanical names of plums, except Gerard.[1] He gives 2 specimens of Damson. One he calls the "Damson Plum tree – Prunus Damascena" and the other "The Damson tree – Prunus Domestica". I rather think, from the woodcut, that the Damascena is our common Damson. The Sloe is Prunus Sylvestris. I ~~rather~~ think the larger damson you mention is known as the Shropshire Prune – much used in the Midland counties. Miss Faulkner & I always quarrel on that point, as she, being a Birmingham person & having been brought up upon the larger damson, swears (if she could do such a thing) that *it* is *the* damson, and that my little blue black fellow is not worthy of consideration by any one born in the land of pots & kettles. I need scarcely say that my friend Miss Faulkner has been grievously imposed upon. I need [also] hardly say that I have poetic authority ~~on my side~~. The author of the Earthly Paradise[2] swears horribly on my side – need more be said?

And so the French devils are still at their work at the old buildings in France, and tho' you don't exactly say so, I am afraid the west or nobly sculptured front of Sens Cathedral has been served as the rest of the ch' had been when I was there some 19 years ago. The front was then untouched.[3]

I am really glad that you have got into fairly good quarters at Vézelay. I wish there was a merry fiddle or two in the town to strike up on Sundays, & give the boys & girls a dance. I rather expected to find some cheerfulness of that kind in Italy, & was disappointed. If the weather has mended you have set to work, and either you or Mrs Boyce (when inclined) will tell me on what you are engaged. If I recollect rightly, you have the old castle to finish?

Our weather has turned wild, with deluges of rain at intervals, and occasional brightness, as to day, after half a day & a night of open sluices. Grass well green again: weather really pleasant when one is not being drowned.

I have been down to see Tangley Manor, & found that the pleasant garden maker has been dancing a pas d'orticulture there – playing old gooseberry there in fact, and something must [be] done to remove his or some of his miserable handiwork.[4]

1864–1887

The old house is really beautiful, but I have no recollection of your taking me round to see the wooden front, ~~but~~ though I remember your shewing me the back. M̲r̲ Jack has been down to measure, and I am going to try & get a little more offices accommodation without injury – if possible – to the rest of the house. I see that the house is 15th c – altered in 1582.

Miss Ewart has got into her house, and seems to like it well enough, & when she gets some pretty things to grow against & veil the brickwork, I shall like it better.[5] Did I tell you that one of the pomegranite [sic] bushes at New Place has blossomed one bloom, & that another is coming out & may complete itself before the sun is gone south. I am a little surprised at the fact, considering how cold Welwyn is. I fancy the dry weather did the business.

The New Place folk are well, and I will deliver your message when I next go there – they will be glad to learn that you are comfortable. Your new drawing is now a part of the house & helps to make that comfortable. The doctor has been good enough to pay me much attention and has succeeded in mending me, I hope & believe, nearly to the extinction of the trouble. When he put me on the rack and I made a horrid noise, he said, 'if anyone else did it for you he would have given you a deal more pain' so I was obliged to grin & bear it – at all events now I can sit upon my injuries.

I have some more photographs for you to see – The virtues & vices by Giotto from the Arena Chapel & 5 of the coloured frescoes[6] – also a pho: of Piero della Francesca's virgin from the Milan Brera – one of the most lovely pictures in existence.[7] Murray talks of bringing my Schiavone S. Georgio over to England in November.

I wish you both a kindly time and that beautiful France will be still pleasant to you. Your work will, I know, go all right if you will but go right at it.

Yours very sincerely | Philip Webb.

BL Add 45354, ff. 233-4

---

1 The Tudor herbalist, John Gerard (c. 1545–1612), published *The Herbal*, or *General History of Plants* in 1597, with hundreds of woodcut illustrations. Perhaps PSW learnt of the book through WM, who as a child had studied a copy in the family library.
2 WM, of course.
3 One of the earliest French Gothic cathedrals, that of Saint-Etienne at Sens in the north of Burgundy is mainly twelfth century, although the building was not completed until the early sixteenth.
4 Great Tangley Manor, near Guildford, Surrey, was bought in 1884 from the estate of Lord Grantley by the solicitor and antiquarian, Wickham Flower (?1835–1904), who at his death would leave incomplete an *Early History of England*. PSW undertook various modification and enlargements of the house, in two phases, 1885–7 and 1891–4. See *Kirk*, pp. 187–9 and 300–1. 'During Lord Grantley's time the place was used as a farmhouse; the moat was choked with earth and rubbish, and overgrown with brambles and wild brushwood . . . Orchard and cabbage-patch came right up to the house . . . [Webb] set his face entirely against any renewal that should be in direct imitation of the old work; and when, later, another sitting-room and more bedrooms were required, and he built the library at the eastern end, it was done in such a way that it assumed no effect of competition with

the timbered front. It is perfectly in harmony, but gives the impression of voluntarily effacing itself in order to enhance the value of the older work.' E.H. Kennard, *History of Great Tangley Manor*, privately printed (1908), pp. 42 and 44.
5 See above, Letter 212.
6 The Cappella degli Scrovegni in Padua (also known as the Arena Chapel, as it was built adjacent to the site of a Roman arena) features Giotto's earliest known frescoes (c. 1303–5), cycles on the Life of the Virgin, events in the Life, Passion and Resurrection of Christ, the Last Judgment, and Allegorical scenes of the Vices and Virtues.
7 Piero della Francesca's *Virgin and Child* (mid-1470s), known as the Brera Altarpiece, and commissioned by Frederico III da Montefeltro, Duke of Urbino (1422–82), is in the collection of the Pinacoteca di Brera, Milan. PSW must have been struck by the striking architectural context, typical of contemporary Urbino building, beneath which the figures are placed. See also next letter.

270 • To Charles Fairfax Murray, 13 September 1885

Incomplete?

1, Raymond Buildings, Gray's Inn | London, W.C.
Sunday Sep: 13. 1885

My dear Murray

As I wrote last only to cross yours, I write now to be beforehand with you. I shall expect you in Nov: with the George under your arm, unless your bluggy swell carries it off under <u>his</u> arm, when the above adjective will be spelled with a D. I hope you have got your copy all clearly laid down from mine as, when I once clutch the watercolour, 'twill be hard to whistle it away again. Cole[1] has now sent me all the phot^s with the account for all except the 3 which you gave him to send, the value of which I shall have to hang on George's horse's tail. I thank you much for your trouble and, as reward for this graceful acknowledgment on my part, please to tell me if there is any reasonable doubt that the delightful blue virgin and attendants and kneeling Montefeltro is by Piero della Francesca?[2] I looked at it very closely the last time I was at the Brera, & found it full of signs of Piero's workmanship as well as faces, posing of figures, tag-ends of hair &c but, on the back of photo: is writ the name of B: Corradini and the bluggy Murray also gives it to that, to me, unknown painter.[3] Who was Corradini & where is his work to be seen? You <u>must</u> know all about the matter but, if you do not, don't profess that you do. I have not yet picked up the 3 other vols of Cavalcasselle [*sic*] and cannot look for myself,[4] and I have been too indifferent to gaining knowledge to go and get a Bohn's Vasari.[5] The Montefeltro is quite as good a photo: as I expected, but the print generally is black, and the flesh as black as your new felt hat. I w^d like to see what Braun could make of it.[6] He has made a very good one of the red baldechinno'd Mantegna in our Gallery.[7] I have not yet run against Burton, consequently I have not again trodden on his coat tail. I bought the small new catalogue of the foreign pics: in the Nat: Gall:[8] and see on the cover that the larger book is to be out <u>shortly</u>. Burton will be shorter I suspect when it is out and some one politely contests any points in it: <u>I</u> shall <u>not</u> for one.

1864–1887

What do you think of your violin player picture? a success?[9] You may as well say, as I can't contradict you. Boni has not sent me his paper on the Piazza diggings at Venice, probably because he knew I could not read it: my vocabulary gets shorter day by day except in English expletives, the pure well of which is in Billingsgate near here. Wardle, when looking at photographs here, sometimes asks about a [Tuscan] word; when I either coin an answer or refer to the Italian dictionary, but he knows his customer. I think he looks forward to see the George nearly as much as I do, with the difference that it is not for him particularly. I have sent to Cole for some more things as he is so admirable in attending to business. I hope he prospers.

If Edward[10] only finds cracks in himself, he could hardly guess that other things would break in two or 20 pieces when they tumble down. I remember his "ways & his manner" with regard to things on the table: bless his roars & his bellows. [*page missing?*]

Fitzwilliam 35

1 Not identified.
2 See previous letter, note 7.
3 The painting, with a traditional misattribution to Fra Carnevale (Bartolomeo di Giovanni Corradini, c. 1420/5–84), came into the collection of the Pinacoteca di Brera in Milan in 1811, not identified as being by Piero until the mid-1860s. See Keith Christiansen, ed, *From Filippo Lippi to Piero della Francesca* (New York: Metropolitan Museum, 2004), pp. 267–71.
4 Joseph Archer Crowe and Giovanni Battista Cavalcaselle produced several collaborative works. PSW presumably was wishing to consult volumes such as their *A New History of Painting in Italy: from the Second to the Sixteenth Century*, 3 vols (London: Murray, 1864–6), and *A History of Painting in North Italy*, 2 vols (London, 1871).
5 Giorgio Vasari, translated by Jonathan Foster, *Lives of the Most Eminent Painters, Sculptors, and Architects*, 5 vols (London: H.G. Bohn, 1850–2), published in the Bohn's Standard Library series.
6 The French photographer, Adolphe Braun (1812–77), who in the later part of his career photographed many art works in European public collections.
7 Presumably the *Virgin and Child with the Magdalen and Saint John the Baptist* (c. 1490–1505), in the National Gallery.
8 This would have been the latest edition (there were many) of the *Descriptive and Historical Catalogue of the Pictures in the National Gallery . . . Foreign Schools*.
9 *The Violin Player*, the original work which CFM had been working on in Florence since at least 1875, is now at the Walker Art Gallery, Liverpool.
10 Eduardo, CFM's eldest son.

271 • To Charles Faulkner, 9 October 1885

1, Raymond Buildings, Gray's Inn, | *London, W.C.*
Friday. Oct 9. 1885

My dear Charley

Both good luck & good nature got for me the fine books of the blessed Plato. I've looked in two or three places between the covers & it seemed as there would be fine times for me when leisure & resolution should come, but now I must needs join Avelings classes. I made for Geology, & Wardle seniors piled on me chemistry for which I've about as much bent as an archbishop of Canterbury has for directness – I did not intend the pun. These lectures mean an evening in the week & some other time for consideration, so that 'chemistry' must go by the board before long I sh^d think, as my earning work is to hand.[1]

I missed you last evening at the Old Compton Street branch, as Aveling must keep away without notice and so I had to make a meeting go, pretty well all on my own lifting, and I am not very handy in making people understand what is not quite clear to myself[2] – but I'll take to Plato & his philosophy to mend myself for occasions.

I don't see my way just yet for dropping on you in Oxford as I have things to do. I should have liked to come while the boys are away, but things must be as they are; wh' saying seems somewhat Platonic!

I thank you very much for these books and will have the money for payment when I next see you, which will be a pleasure to

Yours affectionately | Philip Webb.

Texas

---

1 Edward Aveling was well-known as a public lecturer, from 1879 having undertaken much educational work for the National Secular Society. He also published textbooks on a range of scientific disciplines. By 1884 his subject matter was increasingly on socialist themes. PSW attended Aveling's weekly classes on Geology, which began on 13 October 1885, the twentieth (and last) being on 23 March 1886. By contrast, he appears to have gone to very few on Chemistry. The small book in which he made notes during these classes survives (*V&A, NAL MSL/2000/11/2*), and on the first page he notes recommended text books: 'Lyall's Student Geology (the smaller book) 7/6. Copy of Aveling's Chemistry non metallic . . . Roscoe's small chemistry. Jago's chemistry out of print'. The notebook also contains some of his sketches (of fellow students?), presumably done during classes.
2 The Bloomsbury branch of the Socialist League, which PSW had joined *in absentia* when he was still in Italy, organised talks 'in a meeting room above the Eagle and Child Coffee-House on Old Compton Street'. Rachel Holmes, *Eleanor Marx: A Life* (London: Bloomsbury, 2014). p. 236. As his local branch, it was natural that PSW should sign up for Bloomsbury. It came to contain some of the most high profile of the early socialists, including Aveling and Eleanor Marx, and acquired a reputation for itself as 'the most politically formidable of the Socialist League branches'. MacCarthy, *WMLT*, p. 575.

272 • To Charles Fairfax Murray, 28 October 1885

1, Raymond Buildings, Gray's Inn | *London, W.C.*
Wednesday 28th Oct. 1885

Scene – own room: fire & light
Time – 9.45: pm:
Dramatis persona, the lean P:W: with a placid smile on his face as, when not at the moment writing, his face is turned slightly to the left & his eyes rest on a - - *

My dear Murray

Your welcome letter of the 22nd refreshed me as usual. The comfortable note in it of rich – and I may say – titled folk visiting your studios reflected a graciosity on me, even here, and made me think of the world as a delightful place for some one in 10,000 people basking in the sunshine glints from the fair white waistcoat of the Assyrian bull.

I conceive also, your glib tongue newly oiled and applied to the tenderest feelings of the director of the gallery of that nation on which the sun never sets. Let us hope the sun does not wink at robbery![1]

You are now awake, & rubbing your eyes after a quarter of an hour's nap brought on by the paragraph above, and I proceed *Yes his eyes rest on a picture set on an easel turned to proper angle of a good light. I had note of its arrival last night, from McCracken & Co, with a 'stand & deliver' if payment of expenses of transit were forthcoming. I forthwent myself this aft^n into the City and brought my George home in my arms; ^{then} shredded him of his wood box, zinc case, and brown paper foldings and sat to get back my breath, which had fled up the chimney as the colour of the horse housings[2] flashed on my unutterable gaze. I'm now an older, perhaps a wiser, yes, certainly an older man, and am as one possessed of a. . . . . downright good copy of Victor Carpaccio's S: George of the Schiavone. I don't wonder at your keeping it by you for a while, and even Edward must have felt defrauded when it left the Serragli.[3]

When dusk put an end to examination of the picture by Jack & myself, I posted off to Watson's of Wardour S^t to find a suitable ragged old frame, <u>as</u> suitable as <u>might</u> be,[4] and I picked out two which come here tomorrow for me to try on the picture itself; when it $^{(the\ frame)}$ will be cut to fit, and regilded, and the hoped for possession will be complete, all but #

As yet, I've seen none of the defects of the copy and only a hundred or so of the beauties, so that I cannot write you much more now of the soporific kind save, briefly thus. It is better than I expected, and the beginning I saw raised my hopes. Hard-to-please-Jack also murmured praise, 'till I kicked him back to his work. Now, there is peace & contentment, so far, & for the rest you must lend further aid.

Make out the account between us to the uttermost farthing and send it me directly, so that I may look on the picture with less of the glance of a thief. The bill for drink may be heavy, but who would grudge a cask of wine or two, when the colour of it has been turned to such good account on a quarter of the surface of the picture, not including George's nose, which is not too gluggy?[5] I'll say no more now, but send me the memorandum, so that I may remain the friendly Philip Webb.

If the family is yet out of bed, tell them of my joy over the picture, & give them my kindest greetings.

Fitzwilliam 37

1 PSW's meaning in these opening sentences is obscure, but if it does not refer to visitors viewing the Carpaccio copy in CFM's rooms in Florence, it may allude instead to CFM completing his own painting, *The Violin Player*. See above, Letter 270, note 9.
2 'The leather fastened at a horse's collar to turn over the back when it rains.' *OED*. PSW uses the term more generally, to describe the harness and other tackle, which is a clear feature in Carpaccio's *St George and the Dragon*.
3 'Edward wasn't troubled by its disappearance – at present his soul is occupied with boiled chestnuts – for these delicacies he would renounce his mother grandmother & all his belongings.' CFM to PSW, 1 November 1885, *V&A, AAD*.
4 Edward F. Watson, the picture dealer and restorer, operated his business from St James's Gallery, 201 Piccadilly.
5 See next letter, note 1.

273 • To Charles Fairfax Murray, 5 November 1885

1, Raymond Buildings, Gray's Inn | London, W.C.
Not posted till Friday. Nov[r] 6. | Thursday 5th Nov: '85

My dear Murray

I was glad to find from your letter, wh' came last night, that you were "set up" by my last sleight of hand; though glad, as I say, I am rather surprised, as you are seldom cast down. You will not fail to remember that I remarked the care with which you guarded against such accident when you were on the (as I should consider) preternaturally secure scaffolding in the Schiavoni chapel! I can understand your looking upon my expression of genuine admiration of your copy of the S[t] George, as "flattery", as you would naturally look upon my capacity for understanding a picture as too novice like to be worth more than a smile of 'professional' contempt, tempered with a cutaneous pleasure at the application of amateur butter somewhat ignorantly applied. There, I've done with that lantern jawed paragraph!

The S[t] George gives me more and more pleasure to look at as my enthusiasm settles into clearer vision ~~and~~ [upon] more certain examination; the first effect though is the best test of permanent satisfaction. I have found a pretty enough, but commonplace frame for the picture which I think will aid but not in any way destroy the lovely simplicity of the colour and modelling and, in a fortnight or so, I shall have my friend clothed & in his right mind with myself [in breeches and] still sane. Maybe, when you come over to us, I shall have to get you to put a touch or two to hide a sixpenny thickness of light at the edge, as I have been careful not to cover a 27000th of a centimetre more than I could help.

The beautifully drawn bill you sent me has rather put me to the blush, without the aid of wine: what was I to do?[1] I knew that the picture, according to modern commercial practice, was worth a good deal more than the £50, and to me it is worth much more than commercial villainy could make of it; but then I could not pay you its value, but I can and must pay you a little more to cover expenses, without considering the consumption of Comet wine![2] I therefore send you £11; £10 for fee and £1 for some 17 francs you have paid to 'Barnaby' for me. I also send you Fawcett's bill for prints, which is ^{for} £50, within a dirty copper or two, which will make up the £60 for the picture. ~~which~~ ^{This} I know is all too little for it, but I must console myself with the knowledge that I am sure you have the pleasure of doing me an unpaid good turn.³ Now, shall I <u>send</u> you the Mantegna & other prints, or will you be coming over here so shortly as to make sending a mistake? If you tell me to send the prints, tell me also how best to do it, and whether I should take any extra precautions against damp? The agent, through whom I got the St George, said that the tin-case was a superfluity, though I did not agree with him, considering that the parcel was a water-colour.

The weather here is 2 days of deluge to one of fine, with temperature varying from cold to warm, wh' keeps my sawbones brother on his legs from morning to night & sometimes lugs him out of bed too. The highest consideration to you & yours from

Philip Webb.

Fitzwilliam 38

---

1 To his receipt, CFM added: 'The artist deeply regrets that he is unable to charge less, but the fact of the money being spent & the expense incurred in covering St Georges nose with the purest wine to be procured in Venice for money will he trusts plead in his favour'. Characteristically, PSW had insisted on paying more than the £50 agreed, recording beneath CFM's remark: 'Threw in another 10£ to pay for the expensive wine colouring of S: George's nose'. CFM to PSW, 1 November 1885, *V&A, AAD*. See also above, Letter 264, note 1.
2 Vintages coinciding with a significant astronomical event, such as the appearance of a comet, have traditionally been regarded as offering exceptional quality.
3 See above, Letter 257. In effect, PSW was offsetting the cost of what he had already paid on CFM's behalf for prints from Benjamin Fawcett, against the cost of the commissioned Carpaccio copy, whist insisting on making up the difference to £60 as an expression of his pleasure with CFM's work.

274 • To George and Caroline Price Boyce, 23 November 1885

1, Raymond Buildings, Gray's Inn, | *London, W.C.*
Monday 23rd Nov: '85

My dear Friends

I am sure you must have given up all expectation of getting any information from me as to the state of your garden at West House. Indeed I had myself almost given up hope of getting there before your return. However I did manage to go on Saturday aft: last, was joyfully received by the maid who knew me, and permitted to walk the garden for a quarter of an hour. I really think the plants, as well as the garden generally, are looking satisfactorily; better than I had expected, as we have had some 6 or 7 sharp frosts, day after day. The gardener has been using the pruning knife pretty freely, but, so far as my little knowledge of that operation will allow me to judge, I should think it was done with judgment. There were 3 or 4 Chrysanthemums (doubtful spelling!) in blossom, one of wh', a dark red one, looked particularly beautiful. Patches of the bowling green grass had failed outright, but the rest of it looked sound, and I fancy that it would now bear taking up and relaying so as to cut the long roots and fine it down as turf – that is, to relay it next year.

I did not see Polly,[1] but heard that he or she was in good condition. The pigeons I saw, and the maid said they were all to be counted, the cats having been unsuccessful in their raids. You will be glad to know that the bell pulls at the front door were so clean and bright that I could settle the cock of my hat in their reflection, wh' means that the house did not look deserted. I asked the maid when she expected you home, & she said 'about the end of this month'. Well, as you too have given no sign I shall send this note to Vèzelay [sic], with the hope of its finding you still there.

I took back to Chelsea with me the Rossetti drawing, with many sighs and some moans, but I shall get over this dolefulness, as the drawing will still be in your hands.[2] My hands have been very full, with too many small things, to keep me active, without much to shew for my trouble. But I have got the clients into their house at Knoyle, though it is still unfinished. I slept in the house one night myself, to help them to understand their surroundings which are so different to what they expected. When they get used to finding things on their right hands, which they expected to be on their left, they will be more at ease![3]

I have set to work at Tangley Manor,[4] and I shall hope that you will, both of you, approve of what I am doing – at all events, the old house is not being knocked about, and the garden arrangements are being made somewhat more decent in appearance. However, I will say nothing more about it now, & you will be able to judge for yourselves when you go there next year.

The Welwyn folk always ask after you and perhaps the sister may have written, so I need say no more than that the housemaids have been dropping away – seemingly by the half dozen. They just come for a week or two and look round, after which, as I suppose, finding no marriageable young fellow about, they skip off again. This is rather like, I see, an old bachelor's way of looking at the fun!

You will be pleased to learn that I have my S: George by Carpaccio. Murray has made an admirable copy, and it is to me a 'speaking likeness', as they say.

I hardly like to worry you with any question about the work, but I must hope the weather has been better for it lately. We have had it very cold here, and Murray said that when he was in Paris last week it was as cold there as it is here.

With kindest remembrance to you both. | Believe me sincerely yours,
Philip Webb:

BL Add 45354, ff. 235-6

1 A pet parrot?
2 See above, Letter 267, note 1.
3 'The Wyndhams moved into Clouds on 23 September 1885, even though the plasterwork was unfinished in the drawing room, the baths were not working efficiently and there were no chandeliers in the hall.' *Dakers*, p. 81.
4 See above, Letter 269, note 4.

275 • To Archdeacon Alfred Earle,[1] about 9 February 1886

Drafted on behalf of SPAB, later signed by HTT and dated 9 February 1886. Some of the amendments in pencil.

~~This is what I would say to the Ven: Archdeacon on the Philology of the English tongue~~.

(Dear Sir)

Before replying to your letter of the 25th Jan. I took the first opportunity of laying it before the Committee of the Soc: This will I trust excuse the unusual delay.

I am now directed by the Committee to express its regret that the expression in my letter of the 22nd Jan: should have been interpreted by you as conveying a condemnation of anything you had done. It was intended to convey the opinion of the Committee that it could only usefully interfere in a work which seemed already far advanced & was clearly being conducted by principles quite at variance with ~~our its own~~ those of the Society.

Your letter of the 17th Jan. described the ch: as of great antiquity, with many alterations & the "restoration" of it as "line for line", all the mutilation being "fully & accurately restored".

On those expressions the Committee founded its opinion. It did not however "condemn" what we feared you might be doing – it expressed no opinion except that one as to the wide difference ~~that was~~ between ~~our deliberations~~ our several views of what ~~was & was~~ is and is not possible in regard to the preservation of ancient buildings. Feeling that ~~the Committee considered~~ difference & considering the work as well nigh completed, the Committee thought the only useful thing it would do was to submit to your consideration ~~criticisms & advice we have offered in cases which have come under the inspection of the Society.~~ some of the Society's printed papers.

You blame us severely for not giving timely advice. We admit you would have done so justly, had we known of the restoration of Milton Church sooner & had allowed it to go on to the present point in order that we might find cause for concern. My letter however said that the Committee had seen the notice of the proposed restoration which surely implies that the Committee had seen it for the first time & that it believed the restoration was only a proposal. If your reply to that letter had shown that the help of the Society might have been offered with a chance of usefulness, the usual step might have been taken by us. We should have proposed to make a survey of the building with a view to preparing such a series of suggestions & cautions as are found in the letter to ^(the Rectors of Wolferton & Tadmarton copies of wh: I now send you). The Committee much regrets that this opportunity did not occur.

As regards the canons on which the Soc. acts, ~~we think you have formed an must be allowed to say you have formed an incorrect opinion. The papers submitted as samples of the advice we give on the preservation of ancient Buildings are not general statements intended to comprise all cases. They do not therefore contain canons but only the application of some canons to the particular cases.~~ we cannot ~~understand how~~ ^(think) after reading the Tadmarton report you ~~should have~~ ^(will no longer) ~~accuse us of~~ ^(suppose that) we should not have accepted your canon as to the retention of the western gallery. It is possible the Committee would not have opposed – it might have recommended the removal of the galleries. Its advice would have depended upon all the circumstances. We do not include all galleries in a general clause either of destruction or preservation. We must also ask you to believe that we should not have condemned much that ^(you say) by implication we ~~did~~ ^(should) condemn. ~~Perhaps you expressed your opinion of the work Soc. before reading fully the papers which we intended as illustrations of our work. Surely the illustrations are too plain in most cases to be misinterpreted.~~ We do not condemn, for instance, we strongly encourage & plead for the retention of old floors, the careful taking down & reseating of unsafe pinnacles, the careful underpinning of old walls the proper drainage of buildings, the retention of old roofs, of old iron bars to windows & of all such like works of preservation & protection.

We oppose to the best of our ability the "reproduction of ancient features", of old tracery, old screens, old carving &c. We protest in general against the assumption that anything can be reproduced or restored which once bore on its face & has lost the impress of former modes of thought, or of artistic feelings now utterly changed or nonexistent.

The assumption that such things can be restored is ~~unfairly~~ founded on a view of the nature & capabilities of Art, which reason & experience show to be untenable. The view has worked much mischief & will always do so. It has been the ruin of many of the noblest works of art that ~~remain~~ had escaped every other danger & it is still destroying those beautiful ~~&~~ ^(but) homelier works of which at one time every English village could boast ~~at least one &~~ its own peculiar example.

You call our views on this point absurdly inconsistent. We fear you have failed to notice the name of the Society which is not for the restoration of ancient buildings but for their Protection.

SPAB, South Milton Church, Devon file

---

1 Alfred Earle (1827–1918) had a long career in the church, including periods as vicar at All Saints, South Milton, a small Devon village (the church about which PSW here writes), whilst also serving as Rural Dean and Archdeacon of Totnes (1872–87). He was subsequently a canon at Exeter Cathedral, rector of St Michael's, Cornhill, rector of St Botolph's Bishopsgate and canon at St Paul's Cathedral, suffragan Bishop of West and North West London, and finally Dean of Exeter from 1900 until his death.

1864–1887

276 • To membership of The Socialist League, ?spring 1886

Draft, damaged

The Socialist League | 113 Farringdon Road. E: C[1]

Comrade

I have been instructed by the "Ways & Means" Committee of the League to remind you that subscriptions are due from you, and to draw your attention to article N° 111 of the Rules, under the heading "Contributions".[2]

I am also to suggest that, if you do not belong to any Branch of the League, you would do well to give in your name to the ^(Clerkenwell Branch now forming at) the central ~~body~~ ^(office) or, which would be better, that you should join the nearest Branch to your place of abode, so as to aid in strengthening as much as possible the branches. They also point out to you that as the forthcoming Conference is to be a delegate one, you ~~will~~ may not be represented there unless you belong to a branch.

As Treasurer, I should w<*damage*> consider that ~~as~~ the <*damage*> is fixed for Ju<*damage*> at most <*damage*> membership should be ~~made up to~~ ^(shewn at) its full strength, ~~by~~ which can only be honestly done by the names representing paying members, and those alone.

Yours faithfully | Philip Webb. | Treasurer.

I shall be glad if you will claim my attention personally at the meeting on Monday ^(evening,) or, if you are unable to be there, that you will give me an answer, in writing, to this appeal.

Amsterdam S.L. 3186

---

1 113 Farringdon Road had been the headquarters of the Socialist League since the summer of 1885.
2 PSW had replaced WM as Treasurer of the Socialist League by early February. 'Webb has taken my place, as on all hands it was thought necessary to pull up as to money matters.' WM to John Mahon, 7 February 1886, *CLWM*, II. Sadly, MacCarthy is probably right to conclude that PSW was 'an inept choice for a post in which communication skills were of the essence', even though his wish to relieve WM of some of his burdens was laudable. *MacCarthy, WMLT*, p. 554. Nevertheless, he was re-elected into this position by the annual League meeting on 29 May 1887 and again in 1888.

277 • To Percy Wyndham, 4 June 1886

Draft/copy

[1, Raymond Buildings . . .]
June 4. 1886.

To Hon' Percy Wyndham.
Clouds House | East Knoyle.

317

Dear Mr Wyndham

In answer to your letter of 30th May. The cost of the drawing-room ceiling as originally designed would have been £645. The cost of the ceiling as executed is £289 – a reduction of £356; ~~which is very satisfactory to me~~.

I thank you for your kind expression of satisfaction with the house, and which I accept with much pleasure. I have sent Estcourt by this post a certificate, for further payment on account of his balance, for £2,000.

Mr Rogers Field asked me to see him so that he might tell me ^the result of his visit to Clouds ~~to~~ ^when he inspected the drainage. I saw him on Wednesday, and he gave me a full acc^t of the examination of the working of his system as laid down. On the whole, subject to some trifling accidents, he seemed to be ~~much~~ ^well satisfied, but he was evidently disappointed with what had been going on at the outflow in the dell. You will readily understand that the getting ^well rid of the effluent from drainage is the most difficult thing to manage successfully in all sanitary science – so called.

Rogers Field knows, I believe, as much about ^house drainage matters as any sanitary engineer in England and, though I carefully considered with him each part of his proposed system for Clouds, I have throughout carefully avoided interfering with his arrangements and their execution, as these sort of works depend so largely on the exact way in which they are done. I gathered from Field that, one of the ^most necessary points was to spread the outflow of foul water over as large an area as possible on the upper surfaces of the dell, and that this intention, since his foreman Dodman left, has been somewhat disastrously departed from.

Field has sent me a copy of his letter to you of yesterday's date, and I am decidedly of opinion that it would be best for him to send his assistant to remedy the evil as soon as possible, and that this assistant should ^have some labourers under his own directions, entirely free from any interference ~~from~~ ^by other authorities. I feel this to be important, as the warm weather will soon be here, and though there would be no danger to health from the ^present state of the dell, the smell would probably be extremely disagreeable.

Believe me | Yours very truly | Ph: W.

P.S. I hope to send you the plan for hot house wall &c tomorrow.

LB-2, pp. 52-3

278 • To Henry Halliday Sparling, 25 June 1886

1 Raymond Buildings, Gray's Inn, | London, W.C.
Friday 25th June 86

Dear Sparling[1]

I have to be at Kensington on business at 10.30 tomorrow (Saturday) morning. Can you use the money you have in hand for payments till Monday at 10.30, when I would come round to Farringdon Hall? If this plan would do, you need not answer this.

Yours truly | Philip Webb.

Amsterdam S.L. 3185/1

---

1 The son of an agricultural worker, Henry Halliday Sparling (1860–1924) was appointed secretary of the Socialist League in July 1885, co-editing *Commonweal* with WM, of whom he was a fervent admirer. He and MM married in June 1890, rather against the wishes of her parents. They separated four years later and were divorced in 1898, whereupon MM reverted to her maiden name.

279 • To George Washington Jack, 1 July 1886

1, Raymond Buildings, Gray's Inn, | London, W.C.
Thursday. July 1. '86

My dear Jack

Your letter was a relief to me, as I chose to amuse myself with the fancy that nothing but the Kilt and Bagpipes country would be stimulating enough to make you take a real holiday! Also, you might have been fearful that, as I myself w^d like to see your part of Somerset, I might turn up one evening and spoil your fun with some grim suggestion of the loveliness of mediæval architecture.

Rest in peace for your allotted time, and come back well in health and I will forgive the imagined insult, set forth above.

You did not mention a sum, so I have only sent you 5£. If you want more let me know. I have made the order payable to your Xtian and surnames in full.

Porteous is working kindly with me, but he was not very well this morning and had to go back home.[1]

Should you feel anxious towards the end of your time to throw a sop to this Cerberus,[2] you could take half a dozen notes with dimensions of that vaulted way at Cleeve, which w^d interest the "fidgetty" old man.[3]

Yours very truly | Philip Webb.

My best wishes to your mother.

V&A, AAD

---

1 Porteous was the junior assistant at Raymond Buildings between 1886–8.
2 The multi-headed dog of ancient Greek and Roman mythology, who guarded the entrance to the underworld.
3 Cleeve Abbey in Washford, Somerset is a late twelfth-century Cistercian foundation. After the dissolution of monastic houses under Henry VIII, the surviving buildings became a manor house.

280 • To Percy Wyndham, 9 July 1886

Draft

Friday. 9th July 86

Dear Mr Wyndham.

I am sorry you ^{your family & guests} should have been discomposed with the noise of hammers. I should have thought, however, that the clattering rush of the election winnowing-vans[1] would have drowned the noise of such hammering as went to laying the edging to floor boards at the hall door, and putting in the plain panels to door heads! Nevertheless, the tone of your letter was not – seemingly – very malignant. Perhaps ~~the~~ ^{your} joy ~~of~~ ^{at} having rushed in at Field's drainage – maugre the Angels[2] – counteracted the disturbing element to your temper? From what I gather from your letter to Field of June 22 (of which he sent me a copy) I, at all events, am not much disturbed at the way you have gone to work to get rid of the effluent ^{water} from the drainage, and I sincerely hope the plan may succeed as I think perhaps it might.

There may be a short delay in Estcourt's getting the dark marble (Derbyshire spar,[3] the same as that in the hall paving) to cover the coil cases, and I have told him to ask you when he could fix them at the least inconvenient time for the household.

I am afraid I cannot accept your kind call to come to Clouds and be lectured, as I have Ramsden's and other bits of work to attend to.[4] The former goes but slowly at present, and certainly has not yet advanced to that stage when he will call me "Coxcombe." It will probably arrive at that comfortable ~~stage~~ ^{point} when I am about to send him in my bill!

Yours very truly | Ph: W:

V&A, AAD

---

1 Winnowing-vans (more commonly, winnowing-fans) were the machines used to separate the grain from the chaff. Campaigning was under way for a general election. On 25 July Lord Salisbury became Prime Minister once more, leading an anti-home-rule coalition of Conservatives and Liberal Unionists.
2 'For fools rush in where angels fear to tread', Alexander Pope, *An Essay on Criticism* (1711).
3 Derbyshire Spar, otherwise known as Derbyshire Blue John, is a semi-precious mineral which in the nineteenth century was mined at Castleton in Derbyshire. It typically features a purple-blue banding.
4 PSW was engaged in making and re-making designs for a house for John Charles Francis Ramsden (1835–1910), a former army officer, which would become Willinghurst (initially called Lapscombe), in Shamley Green, Surrey (1886–9, with later additions). See *Kirk*, pp. 143–9 and 301. See below, Letter 293 and later letters.

1864–1887

281 • To Percy Wyndham, 17 July 1886

Draft/copy

[1, Raymond Buildings . . .]
July 17. 1886.

To Hon' Percy Wyndham
Clouds. East Knoyle. Salisbury

Dear Mr Wyndham

I thank you for your ~~temperate~~ ^good tempered^ letter of July 12. I do this ~~the~~ more especially as I am afraid these unlucky baths have bothered you and the rest of the family. As I also thought that no diaphragm or other contrivance would serve the purpose of moderating the pressure of cold water for any length of time, I did, on the 27th of March last, get an estimate from Longdens' for putting in an intercepting ^cold water^ cistern for the baths with separate supply to each bath, and the amount of ^their^ estimate is £70. I propose now, to direct Longdens' to proceed with this alteration at the same time as they are at work on the boilers' business, I myself undertaking to pay the cost of the former.

I did my work to the baths with the best of intentions but, unfortunately, without the aid of Dodman (Field's man) Longden's man, or Moncrieff's man,[1] who should have warned me ^at the time^ of the too high pressure of the cold supply. Still, I am pretty cheerful under the circumstances. I do not see why "good intentions" should not take the skin off one's tail as well as "pave Hell"!

On re-reading your letter, I think I would make another suggestion, before ordering Longdens' to proceed with the baths, and it is this; that I direct Moncrieff to change all the present complicated bath apparatuses for the <u>ordinary</u> system of hot and cold supply, and this also I w^d do at my own expense. I have not made so very many blunders over the rather difficult works of Clouds House that I should hesitate to clear myself of ~~the~~ ^any^ reproach ~~of~~ ^on^ this bath affair, and one or two other items of which I have made note. Will you therefore, send me word at once if you would like the bath apparatuses changed for the ordinary system?

Now, for a matter of <u>taste</u>; the paling on the south side of house. I am glad of your report ~~as~~ that it looks "cottag[e]y", for this I wished, as it would add much to the apparent size of the house. The greater part of our 19th century architecture is ruined in appearance for want of attention to a knowledge of the laws of proportion. Again, to have put up a stone balustrade would have cost as least four times as much as the wooden one, and would have taken ~~away~~ ^something^ from the house of what I consider its best quality – namely, its simplicity.

Will you answer at once the question asked above, as to whether I shall direct that the bath <u>apparatuses</u> ~~shall~~ be changed?

Yours very truly | Ph.W.

LB-2, pp. 56-8

---

1 Moncrieff appears to have been a contractor involved in plumbing work. See also below, PSW to Bowman, 10 October 1887.

282 • To Wickham Flower, 20 July 1886

Draft/copy

[1, Raymond Buildings . . .]
July 20. 1886.

To Wickham Flower Esqre
Old Swan House Chelsea. S.W.

Dear Mr Flower[1]

I am exceedingly sorry to have been obliged to keep you waiting for the stables' design. I now send you a tracing shewing what I propose should be done.

    On the ground plan you will see that I have made the stable-yard of just sufficient width to allow of 2 ^{pairs of} coach-house doors at the end of it, and to give room enough for the projecting ^{horse} doorway to stable and the man's entrance to Coach-house harness room &c so as to allow of going in and out without necessarily opening the main stable door, an important point. I put this horse stable door in the way shewn to avoid awkward opening of door and to keep it from being repeatedly blown-to by the wind. As shewn, the door will open <u>inside</u> in its own recess and thus avoid its awkward opening into the stable itself, or having it to open out on the yard.

    The coach-house I merely make a shed which will join on to and not interfere with the old granary. The harness-room is so placed as to communicate with stable & coach-house and also to get a separate entrance to stairs to loft, man's-room, hay shute &c. I propose putting a brick foundation and on the greater part of 3 sides a ^{framed &} black-weather-boarded superstructure.

    Will you kindly consider the plan & let me know what you think of it?

Yours truly | Ph: W:

LB-2, pp. 58-9

---

1 See above, Letter 269, note 4.

1864–1887

283 • To Percy Wyndham, 20 July 1886

Draft/copy

[1, Raymond Buildings . . .]
July 20. 1886

To Hon' Percy Wyndham
Clouds East Knoyle Salisbury

Dear Mr Wyndham.

I had your letter of the 18th, yesterday, and I saw Longden in the afternoon, when I gave him directions to proceed with putting in the intercepting cold water cistern &c to reduce the pressure on the baths. As Mrs Wyndham's suggestion, to supplement the present bath water appliances with two separate ~~draw~~ supply taps, seemed to me a very good one, I consulted with Longden, and we thought it could easily be done, and by him when he was doing the other work; so I ordered this ^{also} to be ~~done~~ prepared ~~for by him~~. I shall most likely ^{be} writing to Mallett[1] about these works of Longden, but I should be glad if you would direct him to make himself thoroughly master of these alterations and keep me informed of any difficulties which may arise.

I had a hearty chuckle over your pleasant jest of a probable crowd ^{of "influential people"} hastening to Gray's Inn to obtain the modest services of a "lean P.W"! No, my friend, there will be no ~~such~~ rush such as to make the police put me in "Quad" for obstruction. I must differ with you as to the joke that Clouds "is the house of the age"! There are two classes of houses, which would rightly come under that title ^{in England}. The first is the majority one, the natural style of a "shoddy period" ^{of which the houses in} Tyburnia,[2] Belgravia, Victoria Street &c ^{and their kind in the country} give the type. ^{It might be called Victorian after the last, and hang-dog style after the first.} The second is the ~~artificial one~~ ^{non-natural class} of which the mediæval style, ^{is} represented by – say – the Law Courts[3] – the scholastic, by the British Museum,[4] the showy, by the club-houses &c and the Dilettante-picturesque, by the (so-called) Queen Anne style.

All these ^{styles} are exceedingly artificial ~~styles~~, and have been worked and run to death by lively fashion. Where they are least annoying or disappointing ~~it has been~~ is, when they have been ~~built~~ ^{worked on} by really able men.

As to my "keeping people at arm's length" (if what you hint at thereby, is true) it would merely be that I do not want to lay myself out to do work for people who do not in any degree want what I could honestly do for them.

With a begging pardon for this essay | I am | Yours truly | Ph: W:

LB-2, pp. 59-61

---

1 'In July [1885] William Mallett was appointed house carpenter; he was to become clerk of works for the [Clouds] estate until his death in 1923.' *Dakers*, p. 78.
2 'Tyburnia was a name used in the early 19th century for the south-eastern corner of the [Paddington] parish, the first part of the Paddington Estate to be built up. It was adopted presumably because

323

"Tyburn" was already well known, as a reference to the gallows at Tyburn tree.' http://www.british-history.ac.uk/report.aspx?compid=22664 [accessed 11 August 2014].
3 The Gothic style of the winning design for the Royal Courts of Justice (the Law Courts), which had opened in 1882, was by George Edmund Street.
4 The British Museum was built to a Greek revival design by Sir Robert Smirke (1780–1867), and the main building was completed in 1852. In the following year it received the RIBA Gold Medal. The White Wing, matching Smirke's main building for the quadrangle, was completed in 1885 to a design by Sir John Taylor (1833–1912).

284 • To Percy Wyndham, 16 August 1886

Draft/copy

[1, Raymond Buildings . . .]
Aug: 16. 1886.

To Hon' Percy Wyndham
Clouds H^{se} E: Knoyle Salisb^y

Dear Mr Wyndham.

I rec^d your letter this morning, inclosing cheque for £1,000, for which ~~latter~~ I am obliged. The money was a convenience to me, ~~the~~ ^{but your} pleasant expression of complete satisfaction with the house at Clouds was very cheering, and will continue to be a help ~~at times~~ in my work when a sense of hopelessness ~~will~~ at times creeps upon me, that all one's efforts to make modern architecture in some ^{way} genuine seem~~s~~ to be futile.

As to your report of the red coloured matter found in the water supply. After your first use of the house I had a report from Simmonds that the water was distinctly reddened, and when Dodman – Field's for[e]man – went again to Clouds to finish his work I directed him to go carefully into the matter, to empty the water tower cistern and make ^{general & particular} examination to settle as to the cause of this redness. He told me that [he] found everything coated with an exceedingly fine precipitate, including the sides and bottom of the main reservoir, and that he was satisfied that it came from the well, and was not caused by the rusting of the pipes.

When Rogers Field and myself were considering the scheme of water piping we decided to use <u>cast</u> iron pipes for the main systems, coated with "Dr Angus Smith's composition" which he had found ^{to be} a better protection to the pipes than galvanizing.¹ He had often found galvanizing give way in patches and the water penetrate between the iron and the galvanizing. I have also elsewhere largely used the Angus Smith coated pipes ~~elsewhere~~ & have never found them rust. For the branch supply pipes, of smaller bore, where cast iron cannot be used, we decided (after testing pieces of pipe down the well for about 2 months' time) to use wrought iron drawn barrel piping, submitted to the "Bower-Barff" ^{steam chamber} process.²

You will understand that the difference between the action of water on <u>cast</u> and <u>wrought</u> iron is very great.

One of the ~~dangers~~ ʳⁱˢᵏˢ of using the Bower-Barff process is, that if any of the pipes are cut or bent after the process ~~that~~ ᵗʰᵉʳᵉ is a danger of rust. Well, all this piping was fitted in its several positions ready for use and was take[n] down again and then put through the Bower-Barff system; and this was done with the greatest precision by Dodman.

For the <u>hot</u> water supply, I used tinned copper piping, wh' has only one drawback, that of being very costly – so costly in fact that I could not entertain the idea of using it for the branch <u>cold</u> supply which has a great length of piping. The use of lead pipe for such <u>soft</u> water as yours was out of the question, and tinned lead, which has sometimes been used, has proved ᵗᵒ ᵇᵉ a failure.

I still think the reddening of the water is from a precipitate, and that ~~that~~ ⁱᵗ will use itself out, and the great rush of water through the pipes will keep them from choking.

I sincerely hope that this will be the case as, if the Bower-Barff process fails I shall ~~hardly~~ ⁿᵒᵗ know what to use in many places where the expense of tinned copper ᵖⁱᵖᵉˢ makes ~~them~~ ᵗʰᵉⁱʳ ᵘˢᵉ impossible. I have used the Bower-Barff pipes elsewhere and have not yet found them to rust, and that with very soft water.

Roger<u>s</u> Field's (not Roger) address is, 4 Westminster Chambers, Victoria Street ᵂᵉˢᵗᵐⁱⁿˢᵗᵉʳ S: W. I will see Field as soon as I can, but when you send him your cheque, perhaps you would ask him to see his foreman Dodman upon the point of the reddened water.

Yours very truly | Ph: W:

LB-2, pp. 62-5

---

1 In 1848, the chemist Dr Robert Angus Smith (1817–84) patented a method by which the interior of water pipes were coated in a prepared coal tar, to protect against corrosion.
2 For the Bower-Barff process, see above, Letter 219, note 2.

285 • To Percy Wyndham, 24 August 1886

Draft

1 R B Gray's Inn
Tuesday 24ᵗʰ Aug: '86

Dear Mʳ Wyndham.

Your ~~box of~~ boiler deposit is very interesting and may be useful. I am still inclined to believe that the red matter is <u>not</u> from rusted pipes, but from a precipitate. I hardly think that a <u>small quantity</u> of water resting for 24 hours would be enough to give ~~a~~ ᵃᵖᵖʳᵉᶜⁱᵃᵇˡᵉ sediment, but we shall see. I think the best way wᵈ be for Mallet, when the house is empty, to clean out the water tower tank and see what deposit there is there.

The well was deepened, and tunnelled at the bottom at last, to give greater storage of water and I thought it likely that a vein of fine iron sand was cut into, and that after a time (some years perhaps) this vein might be pumped out.

As you say that I am mad on the subject of trees, I hope those in the dell won't die from the effluent which went in there. If I <u>am</u> crazy, I do not think it can be timber rabies, as I do not bark like a tree! Your punishment to the yew-tree-trunks is too sad: surely if Hellfire is not enough the ~~perennial~~ perpetually being sat upon by conservative backsides is more than enough of purgatory.

Yours very truly | Ph: W:

V&A, AAD

286 • To Giacomo Boni, 18 September 1886

Photostat. Postmark LONDON. W.C. SP 18 86 *Address* Al Signore | Il Signor Giacomo Boni | Palazzo Ducale | Venezia. | Italy

1, Raymond Buildings, Gray's Inn | London W.C.
Saturday. 18th Sep^r '86

My dear Signor Boni

I have sent you today, by book post, the "Correspondence respecting the imprisonment of M^r <u>Worth</u> by the Prussians".[1] I have not yet been able to get you the other information, either at the place for the sale of Parliamentary acts, or at Hansard's for parliamentary papers, but I hope to be able to do so, and as quickly as possible. I am trying to find a trustworthy agent to search for and read up the papers and copy the same. I hope your friend will be able to wait a little. You may promise him (the Professor of International Law) that I will get the information – if I can – as quickly as possible.

I heard from Mr Hebb[2] that the Institute of British Architects (whom I called ugly names when I wrote to you before) had agreed to publish your paper and drawings on the Ca' d'Oro, and I have no doubt if the Institute does not present you with enough copies I shall get <u>one</u>, at least, from Mr Hebb.[3] I am looking forward to reading your paper and seeing the published drawing. I remember your telling me you had found out, from a scaffolding, what the old cornice was like, and as I went past the building in a gondola, I thought I recognised the pendentive character of it; but perhaps I saw this through the mind's eye, guided by what you had told me. No, I have not seen your account of the Cloaca Veneziana[4] of the x c. or that of the bronze lion on the column in the Piazzet[t]a.[5] Believe me, I have not lost my enthusiasm for these things, though I am getting on to be 2 years older since I had the pleasure of being stimulated by the fire of your springtime of life. Here, I am "tugging at the daily oar" in my ordinary work of supplying people with houses in the style of the 19th c by Ph: Webb, and the incongruity of attempting any reasonable art in this year of (un)"redemption" is almost too much for the muscles of laughter in one's face to resist! PAZIENZA.

About the Ducal Palace:[6] This building is better imprinted on my mind than any other in Venice, for I had the benefit of your attention, and a scaffolding from which I rubbed my mind and fingers well into the visible, touchable work of the mediæval Venetians. Whenever I look through my rough note book I wish to be back there, to work all day at the pretty builded story, and talk over my thoughts with you in the evening. It is not likely that I shall ever get to Italy again, but I have enough stored within me to interest my walking thoughts for the rest of my years. Added to which sentimental reflection, comes another more serious still. The <u>peoples</u> all over the world are awaking to the fact that they have been horribly cheated of their rights and I, who have enough food, clothing, and house roof must throw in my lot with them, and spend no more on myself than is reasonably necessary.[7] I began with the Ducal Palace and have drifted.

I wholly agree with you that it is a pity the authorities should have been drawn into a "frenzy" about the otherwise unimportant matter of the filled-in arches at the end of the building next the Ponte della Paglia: surely ~~that~~ there are a good many of the arches that are open? However, I also think with you that, as they have renewed the more important work of the capital, the filling-in of the arches is not much worth fighting for.

Have the engineers enough intelligence to know, if the opening of these closed arches will in <u>any</u> way affect the present settled equilibrium of the building? We, in England, find that the element of curiosity outweighs commonsense and, what is worse, no sooner is their curiosity satisfied on one point, than they forget all about the thing they were so frenzied upon a few weeks before!

Now, about S: Marco. Some little time since, the society for the Protection of Ancient Buildings addressed a modest letter to the Prefect, about some notice of a proposal to take up and relay some <u>more</u> of the pavement in the church. There have been certain letters in the "Times" newspaper from authorities in Italy ridiculing this letter of our society.[8] This does not matter in the least, but our Society wants to know if there is anything further likely to be done to the beautiful old church, in the way of <u>restoration</u>, so called? There seems to be some proposal also, to turn round some of the marble columns, so that the side which has been protected from the weather shall now be exposed to it. The society wants to know what, out of a number of doubtful stories, are the facts as to impending mischief? If you can tell us anything, without violating your trust as superintendent of some of the Venetian buildings, we shall be thankful to you. You will easily understand that, till the Italians take up the protection of their ancient buildings for themselves, outsiders will be in a state of fear for the buildings, and <u>out</u>siders of any nationality are liable to being misled by false report.

Believe me, with much delightful recollection of you | Yours sincerely
Philip Webb.

Courtauld 9a-g

1 On 10 September 1886, GBO wrote on behalf of Giulio Cesare Buzzatti (1862–1920), a professor of international law seeking information about the case of a British national, F.G. Worth, arrested in Prussian-occupied Paris in October 1870. Having been refused permission to leave Paris, Worth was captured whilst attempting an escape by balloon.
2 See above, Letter 124, note 1.
3 The Palazzo Santa Sofia (the Ca' d'Oro), is an early fifteenth-century Venetian palazzo on the Grand Canal, built for the Contarini family by the architect Giovanni Bon (1355–1443) and his son, Bartolomeo Bon (d. after 1464). On 6 December 1886, 'the Ca' D'Oro, Venice, and its External Colour', 'the work of Signor G. Boni . . . written in English by himself' was read on his behalf at RIBA by George Aitchison, and was illustrated with drawings and photographs. An abstract together with the resulting discussion (to which Hebb contributed) was published in the *RIBA Proceedings* (9 December 1886), pp. 61–5.
4 Venetian sewers (*It*).
5 The Piazzetta is the area linking the main Piazza of San Marco with the waterfront (the Molo), where the column surmounted by the winged lion of San Marco stands. See Vol. II, Letter 358, note 7.
6 The Palazzo Ducale in the Piazza San Marco was the residence of the Doge, the chief magistrate and governor of the Venetian republic. The current building is mainly of fourteenth and fifteenth-century design, with later additions and restorations. It was on the scaffolding supporting works in progress that PSW first met GBO in March 1885.
7 PSW's most explicit statement to date of the extent of his conversion to the socialist cause.
8 The letter sent by the SPAB to the Prefect of Venice, expressing concern about plans to relay the mosaic floor of San Marco, was also published in *The Times* on 21 September, prompting an attack from a British correspondent, 'mocking the society's efforts as fighting change because "the touch of a broom might injure the 'tone' of the dust" in the cathedral'. Frank C. Sharp, 'Exporting the Revolution: The Work of the SPAB outside Britain 1878–1914', in *Miele*, p. 197.

287 • To Edward Augustus Freeman, 20 September 1886

Drafted on behalf of SPAB; later signed by HTT and dated 20 September 1886

The Society for the Protection of Ancient Buildings
9 Buckingham Street Adelphi. WC.

To Professor E:A: Freeman
The "Saxon" Chapel at Bradford on Avon.[1]
Dear Sir.[2]

At the last Committee meeting of this society, attention was called to notices which have lately appeared in the public papers respecting the venerable remains of this Church or Chapel.[3]

The building is, of course, well known to many members of the society, and some of them have noticed from time to time that various repairs have been undertaken, and the Committee is bound to confess that some of them have been done with more zeal than knowledge or discretion. From this it will be inferred that my Committee is heartily glad to learn that your valuable advice is at the disposal of the present guardians of the building.

My Committee directs me to express to you a doubt it has, as to the wisdom of the proposal (seemingly sanctioned by you) to remove the comparatively modern building which is at present attached to the South side of the Nave. With all respect, my Committee would urge that further consideration should be given to this proposal before it is carried into execution.

Practical architects are aware ^that^ risk is often run in removing from an ancient building any structure which has for some time been attached to ~~an old building~~ ^it^, and they are convinced that unless such attached work is certainly injurious it is much safer to leave it standing, for, its weight has been brought in contact with the more ancient work and, in course of time, has settled to its present state of equilibrium: the removal of which force will assuredly be felt by the main structure.

<~~We would~~> It also appears to my committee, that the more modern building is far from unsightly, and if carefully repaired would not really be damaging even to the appearance of the little church, as it noticeably gives it scale. Also, the more modern floored building gives facility for students to examine closely some of the interesting instruction and other character of the blank arcading. It might also be suggested that, if the attached building were strongly repaired, it would serve for storing and arranging ^for examination^ any fragments of interest discovered from time to time.

I remain &c.

P.S. My Committee would ask you (if you have not already done so) to give the weight of your name to any appeal which could be made to the owner of the beautiful 14th c Barn, in the outskirts of Bradford,[4] ^to protect it from unnecessary injury.^ Some time back, by some carelessness, ~~that allowed~~ the smoke from a steam engine ^had been allowed most unfortunately to^ blacken one side of the walls.

T.T.

---

1 See above, Letter 123, note 3.
2 The historian Edward Augustus Freeman (1823–92) had argued that the earliest surviving parts of the chapel dated from the time of its putative founder, St Aldhelm, and read a paper on the subject to the Somerset Archaeological Society in 1874.
3 The SPAB file includes cuttings from *The Architect* (10 September) and *The Saturday Review* (11 September).
4 See above, Letter 125, note 4.

288 • To George and Caroline Boyce, 30 September 1886

Annotated 'rec[d] at St Donat's'

1, Raymond Buildings, Gray's Inn, | *London, W.C.*
Thursday. 30th Sep. '86

My dear Friends

I have your united and, on the whole, unconscionable letter of the 26th. How to pacify an irritable man, living amongst the lawyers, will occupy your time of enforced seclusion from the intelligent world (?) for the rest of your stay abroad![1] I am not sure that I have said all, on this point, which has been stored up in my breast for the last month. I should be sorry if these bitter reflections on my part should destroy the appetites of one or both of you, but that must be as it may; still – but perhaps I had better say no more, or perhaps a hat & bonnet may be found on the St Donat's shore as the only [*word obliterated*] ^relics of a faithless pair! It is really difficult to tear myself away from this distressing subject, but I will make some effort.

I carry with me this afternoon, George's memoranda on Llantwitt [*sic*] Church,[2] to the anti-scrape meeting of a few responsible and dependable persons giving their intelligence to the preservation of the memorials of the dead art of architecture. The photograph received is accepted as in some small way expiatory of[a] shocking sin, (slightly touched upon above) and will be looked at with a dashed pleasure.

According to Madame's note, "landscape painters have always difficulties" in the way of their work and, according to an interscription of Monsieur's, it is from incompetency in the painter. I should say it is rather from an over nice sense of the tremendous character of nature, in combination with ancient art, that makes the painter take refuge in dallying over his coffee and cigarette and thereby getting late to work, and then leisurely considering that, if the arrangement of the mechanical contrivance of the world (whereby hills are steep and are hard to climb) had been so modified, that, when the top of creation was at the bottom of the hill, it did then tilt up and allow the forked radish, called man,[3] leisurely to walk down to his object, things would have been easier. I grant that, but the reason (according to my way of thinking) why nature did not stop at the gorilla and made the aforesaid forked radish was, that the last & worst-and-best animal was intended to set things straight & make them plain, out of pure enjoyment of the exercise of the faculties he is said to be endowed with. It may be altogether a mistake, and man is not endowed with exceptional faculties beyond the brute beast; well, considering the present state of human affairs I am, at times, inclined to doubt if the forked creature is anything else than a strutting, gibbering sham.

I am glad to learn that Madame has turned to reading that classical piece of English literature in which Signors Quilp and Swiveller are embedded in a perfect mass of egg, jelly and juicy gravy with which the rest of the precious book is made up.[4]

I see that the inimitable (perhaps happily so) Voltaire, has had ashes sprinkled on his head by a performance lately put on the stage in Paris (in a more or less reasonable way) of the play of Hamlet by the British "barbarian", the "immortal Williams".[5] Tears seem to have flowed freely, and the Parisians to have forgotten the perfidy of Albion when considering that of Hamlet's mother. Peace be with the ashes of Shakespeare, Voltaire and England (for it looks as if this 'geographical expression' were coming to an end) and may the shade of Hamlet's father never be less!

When George likened the lovely turmoil of the sky, the birds, and the sea roaring and rattling through the pebbles of your beach, with that subdued but sadder and more terrible roar of the outraged peoples now going on within the rings of all the beaches of the world,[6] I felt inclined to flit from my present engagement with the latter, to the stimulating sounds of the former, but, patience, all things are good for those who can see into them. George may rest assured that I have not missed his words of sympathy with those who feel drawn towards a tragedy which is neither written, not acted, but is.

And now I must give over, asking if I have not worked out your expiation for you, by laying on you this tangled hair-shirt of stuff contained on these sheets?

I did a ~~hare~~ Peacock, then a Hare, then a Lion in watercolour for Morris's people to do in tapestry: I do not know if you saw either [*sic*] of them. I am now engaged on a Fox, and am looking forward to Sunday holiday to finish him, or get well on to making him round.[7] The Welwyn folk are pretty well, & I shall carry your words to them next week, as Carry[8] is on the look out for such news. She is getting on <u>pretty</u> well with household matters.

Yours very truly | Philip Webb.

Do you get "Commonweal"? There are some good things in it, and w$^{\underline{d}}$ be good reading by sounding shore.[9]

BL Add 45354, ff. 237-9

---

1. GPB and his wife were staying in St Donat's, near Llantwit Major in the Vale of Glamorgan, about 19 miles west of Cardiff.
2. The church of St Illtud, Llantwit Major, founded by Illtud in the fifth-sixth centuries, was an early centre for learning. The present church is mainly thirteenth-fifteenth centuries, with earlier survivals including ancient Celtic crosses.
3. 'When 'a was naked, he was for all the world like a fork'd redish, with a head fantastically carv'd upon it with a knife.' *2 Henry IV*, III,ii,310–12.
4. The malign Daniel Quilp and good-naturedly feckless Dick Swiveller are characters in Dickens's *The Old Curiosity Shop* (1840–1). PSW's copy (London: Chapman and Hall, 1856) is now in the Emery Walker Library. See *CAGM*, p. 136.
5. i.e. Shakespeare: an in-joke, presumably. PSW had evidently seen that day's report in *The Times* of a well-received performance of *Hamlet* by the Comédie Française, a revival of the abbreviated translation made by Alexandre Dumas père (1802–70) and Paul Meurice (1818–1905), with Jean Mounet-Sully (1841–1916) in the title role. The mention of Voltaire alludes to the dismissal of Shakespeare's importance by this most famous of France's Enlightenment figures, who considered the English stage to be 'in a grossly infantile state'. Cited in John Pemble, *Shakespeare Goes to Paris. How the Bard Conquered France* (London: Hambledon and London, 2005), p. 3.
6. This seems to allude to both the language and theme of Matthew Arnold's poem, 'Dover Beach', first published in 1867.
7. The 'Forest' tapestry (bought from Morris & Co. by Alex Ionides for 1 Holland Park, now at the V&A), was designed by WM and John Henry Dearle and woven in 1887, embodying PSW's animal and bird designs (peacock, hare, lion, fox and raven, now at Wightwick Manor). It is generally regarded as the Firm's 'most successful tapestry'. Linda Parry, *William Morris Textiles* (London: Weidenfeld and Nicolson, 1983), p. 111. For PSW's recollections of drawing the creatures, see Vol. III, Letter 786. The tapestry is illustrated in *Kirk*, p. 54.
8. Caroline, PSW's younger sister.
9. Pope, *An Essay on Criticism*: 'But when loud surges lash the sounding shore'.

289 • To Hugh Thackeray Turner, 5 November 1886

1, Raymond Buildings, Gray's Inn, | *London, W.C.*
Friday. 5th Nov: '86

My dear Turner

If I go to Oxford at all I must go, I think, next Thursday;[1] as I should surely be asked at Brazenose College as to the Society's informant abt the chapel &c I should either have permission from Parson Mitchell[2] to give his name or refuse to answer the College people this question.

Will you be so good as to write to Mr Mitchell and tell him that there is a grievance against the society, at Brazenose, and that a member of our come had been deputed to go to Oxford to try and make peace – and would he, Mitchell, object to his name being given as informant as to what was proposed to be done to the chapel. Mitchell's name would not be mentioned unless it was found impossible, without further mischief, to withhold it.

Yours truly | Ph: Webb.

SPAB, Brasenose College, Oxford file

---

1 'I write to inform you that Mr Philip Webb proposes to visit Oxford next Thursday the 11th inst: and he will then take the opportunity of calling upon [you] as arranged.' HTT to Alfred John Butler, 6 November 1886, file copy, *SPAB*. Butler (1850–1936), was Bursar of Brasenose, and had recently resigned his membership of the SPAB, writing on 9 October that 'I cannot pretend to agree with the principles of a Society which forbids the addition of a memorial tablet to any ancient building: which disapproves the replacement of a common glass window by stained glass (in a case like the present): which considers a really infamous tile pavement dating from some 20 years ago so sacred that it must be for ever better than a good mosaic pavement of today: and which actually pretends to reverence the varnished deal case of a new organ to such an extent as to censure the proposal to put up a fresh organ-case of possibly some artistic merit.' *SPAB*.
2 Not identified.

290 • To Henry Wallis, 8 November 1886

Copy of draft

1 R.B. Gray's Inn.
Mon: 8th Nov: '86

Copy

My dear Wallis.

You are as difficult to draw as a Badger. There was no wish to bait you, as if you were the Lord Mayor!

I cannot say anything formally in answer to your letter to me, as I shall not see my colleagues until Thursday; but, as an individual member of the S: Mark's Com: I can say that I know there have been various suspicious-looking proposals made by the Italian functionaries which ought to be looked into by the S: Mark's com:;[1] and, unless we, who are in town, can get our secretary to meet us with his evidences we might have some difficulty in giving authorities for statements.

Your time I know is precious, and Morris's and mine and that of others is not of much account, but if you feel, as naturally you might, that our opinion is not of weight sufficient to stir you to call a meeting of the S.M. Com: I, as a mere individual, would ask you to come down and cross examine us and, if necessary, charge us for the loss of your time.[2]

I don't wonder at the Italians making a mistake as to the particular Com: they should thunder at, as it was the S.P.A.B who first brought the wasps' nest about their ears, and stayed their defacing hands, before the S.M. Com: "first saw the light", born of the above named lesser light.

Perhaps you could come to Buckingham S^t on Thursday at 4 o'c, letting the S.P.A.B. Sec^y know, so that he might urge other members to meet you. After which we might consider whether it would be worthwhile to summon Street (no, you can hardly get him to ~~attend~~ come) & Poynter & other big-wigs to attend a meeting. But in no case ought we, I think, to offer to pay their expenses or the expenses of any R:A; who would ruin us altogether if they were paid the value of what they estimate their time at.

Yours very truly | Ph: W:

V&A, AAD

---

1 See above, Letter 286, note 8.
2 If Wallis is being accused of prevarication, in his defence it needs to be said that his report to the SPAB's Foreign Committee in 1879 had provided on-the-spot information to assist its campaign against the earlier planned restoration of the West front of St Mark's. At that time he had managed to examine behind the protective screens erected by the workmen. But the force and tone of SPAB's consequent opposition under WM's leadership was received as arrogant and patronising, resulting in a perhaps predictable reaction from the Italian authorities as well as from some voices closer to home. Wallis feared that any future campaigns could be counter-productive, and had written in December 1879 to warn WM that if the wider public in Britain registered the force of Italian protests, this would 'prevent us getting support on another occasion'. See Sharp, 'Exporting the Revolution', pp. 188–94, and next letter, note 1.

291 • To Henry Wallis, 10 November 1886

Copy of draft

1 R.B. Gray's Inn
Wed: 10th Nov: 86

Copy

My dear Wallis,

Thanks for your letter rec^d this morning. I agree with you that it would hardly do to summon the magnificent and foreign members of the S. Mark's Com: to dingy

November London to meet half a dozen or so of nobodies ^(you are not included here) in a dirty street off the Strand. If the President ~~were~~ of the R:A: were a member of S:M: Committee (is he?) it might be different; as he, with his shiny-pot-hattedness and grease-pot eloquence might make some amends for the want of the signs and seals of respectability, so lamentably deficient in some members of the S: Mark's Com:[1] I am sincerely glad of your assurance that nothing "serious" is contemplated in the way of improvement to the Basilica.[2] When I was in Venice last year I felt somewhat uncomfortable ^{on this point}, I assure you; but as my hands ^{and eyes & mind} were so full of the ^{still} wonderful things about me, I had to stick pretty closely to making up – what I am pleased to call my mind – on many things connected with my inner life, that I probably failed to get ^{much} information on controversial matters which ~~would,~~ perhaps, ^{might} have helped in the future. However, I did get hold of some unfiltered Venetian information, and have, luckily, been in touch with it since my return.[3]

Naturally, I cannot tell you "what business is to be transacted at the meeting", as I fancied the suggested meeting of the London members of the S Mark's Com: was to see if it was necessary to <u>set about</u> transacting some! But if you cannot come, you cannot, and thus an end of my unofficial movement in the matter. I will therefore merely send <u>your</u> unofficial letters to Buckingham Street, and hope for the best to come to the top in this "best of all possible worlds".[4]

Yours very truly | Ph: W:

V&A, AAD

---

1 It seems hardly credible that these remarks were simply to be regarded as 'good-naturedly chaffy' (see next letter). The bitterness of PSW's sarcasm suggests a real sense of anger at Wallis's reluctance to enter into another dispute with the Italian authorities.
2 'I suppose you have some letters, or papers respecting the "suspicious circumstances". Can I have copies of them? I will then make enquiries at Venice. I know there are things done at the Church that you & I w^{ld} not approve of, but they are not serious. If we are constantly "nagging" about trifles we shall destroy our influence, & then will not have public opinion with us in any really serious matter.' Wallis to PSW, 9 November 1886, *V&A, AAD*.
3 He means GBO.
4 The words of the German philosopher Gottfried Leibnitz (1646–1716), that 'we live in the best of all possible worlds', were satirised by Voltaire in his novella *Candide* (1759).

292 • To George Wardle, 10 November 1886

1 Raymond Buildings, Gray's Inn, | London, W.C.
Wed: 10th Nov: '86

My dear Wardle

As I have – as you know – to go to Oxford tomorrow, on the Brasenose Coll: business, I send you two letters I have rec^d from Wallis about the S. Mark's Com: matter &c. I have made a copy of my rough draft of first answer to Wallis, as I thought you would hardly decypher [*sic*] that scrawled on the back of Wallis's own letter.

Wallis is not a bad natured chap really, but his "cussedness" is amazing. Also, it seems to me that he may have tipped a wink to his friends in Italy as to his (Wallis's) opinion of the S.P.A.B or, why this close reserve on his part and steady refusal to give us any information?

I thought it well to be good-naturedly chaffy in my letters to him, as I know of no other physic for cussedness.

If Morris is at the meeting tomorrow, try and get at his <u>second</u> thoughts after he learns of Wallis's tactics. For, any stiff standing against Wallis will only make him stiffer than a telegraph pole.

Of course that is all nonsense about his being desired to summon all members of the S.M: Com:, foreign & other, as, at several times, he (the Sec^y) has called a few members together in the way we proposed, though, in dealing with Wallis we should be most punctilious as to wording any request.

I am to meet Butler at Brasenose Coll: tomorrow between 12 & 1 o'c: and shall do what I can (honestly) to smooth matters, so as to avoid breaches new or widening of old.[1]

Thanks for sending me the engravings of ventilating apparatus from old Newgate. I shall want your aid to set the mousetrap, as the principle is unexplained, there being no letter press.

Yours | Ph: Webb

Will you kindly send me back Wallis's letters & my answers when you have read them on Thursday? | Ph.W.

V&A, AAD

---

1 See above, Letter 289.

293 • To John Ramsden, 17 November 1886

Draft/copy

[1, Raymond Buildings . . .]
Nov: 17. 1886.

To J: C: Ramsden Esqre [1]
Busbridge Hall, by Godalming

Dear Mr Ramsden

I have taken a little time to consider how I might best advise you on the matter contained in your letter of the 14th ins^t. I will at once answer your particular questions.

My estimate ^(of the probable cost) of the present ^(design for the) building at Lapscombe, according to my letter to you at Manchester of the 6^(th) July last, was £9,332 but in working out the glazed corridor at the West end of house some little addition ^(was incurred & an allowance) should be made – say – of £100.

This estimate <u>does</u> include for the drainage, water service <u>inside</u> the house, bell-wires, and two or three speaking tubes and the ~~cost of~~ ^(surveyor's charge for) taking out the quantities. It also includes for all grates, ranges &c unless in the kitchen some further apparatus is required than I have considered necessary for the size & character of the house. Preparation is made for the heating apparatus & <u>i</u>ncluded in the cost, but the cost of the apparatus itself (boiler, pipes &c and such covering to coils as I usually adopt) is not included, but I think you can safely put this cost at £175.0.0.

<small>The cost of any decorative painting and papering is not included, as that w^d probably not be done for 2 or 3 years after the house was built.</small> My own charges as Architect are fully given in a mem^m attached to my letter to you of March 17, 1886.

If a clerk of the works is employed you would have to pay him, according to his class, from £3.3.0 to £4.4.0 a week. If it should be considered that the builder was so trustworthy that a resident clerk of the works would not be necessary, ^(or only necessary for a time,) I could arrange that one of my assistants should spend an occasional week or month on the works and only charge you half his salary, and his expenses of living, for the ~~time~~s he was at the works.

You will easily understand that with my experience I ~~can~~ ^(am) aware how easy it is, when a house is being designed, for the client to, almost <u>un</u>consciously, increase the extent of the house, and when conscious of some addition it seems so natural when building a house to put in what might prove to have been unwise to leave out. I think your recollection will bear me out that, all along, I have been very anxious to keep the extent of the house within bounds? Upon looking at the plans you will see that a large amount of accommodation and a number & variety of rooms have been grouped together in a compact and workmanlike way and, though the house is extremely simple and unostentatious it is, nevertheless, substantially designed?

If you should think, after having completed your calculations, that it would be unwise to build so large a house, I would advise you to begin again on a smaller scale, and not attempt to modify the present plan which is well arranged as it is, but w^d be ill arranged if its scheme ~~is~~ ^(were) disorganised.

Again, if you should think that another architect would give you a ~~better & cheaper~~ ^(house more to your mind & at a) less cost, I would advise you to put yourself in his hands, as it would be better to sacrifice ~~3 or 4~~ ^(a few) hundred pounds now & save ~~say 3 or 4~~ ^(a few) thousand pounds in the end.

I find that Mr Goodman the surveyor has completed about half of his work in taking out the quantities, and if the works are <u>not</u> carried out his charge for the work done would be £107.0.0 but, as I said before, if the works are carried out this charge and that for the completion of his work would be a part of the estimate of the house, ~~and~~ included in the builder's tender, and paid for by him.

Believe me | Yours very truly | Ph: W:

LB-2, pp. 65-7

---

1 For Ramsden, see above, Letter 280, note 4.

294 • To Mary King-Milbanke, Lady Wentworth, 19 November 1886

Draft, incomplete

1 R.B. Gray's Inn
Nov: 19. 1886

Dear Lady Wentworth[1]

In answer to your request that I would give you my opinion on the practicability of repairing and so far refitting some of the houses in Cheyne Walk Chelsea, that they might be made habitable under changed ^{sanitary} conditions, ~~of sanitary science~~ I would say ~~in ans~~ that I took the opportunity of going over two of the houses the other day and just looked into a third, and from my personal knowledge of the construction of two other houses in Cheyne Walk – namely, that inhabited by Mr Rafe Leycester,[2] and another west of Manor Street which was the residence of the late Mr Gabriel Rossetti – I am able to speak with more confidence than if I had merely ~~been able to~~ judged of the houses from the outside and not ^{in addition} from professional experience of two of those above mentioned.

Mr Leycester's house, N° 6, is, no doubt, less injured by modern alterations than the houses between it and Manor Street, but I suspect that the materials of construction would practically be nearly the same. And as I found, when I directed the repairs to N° 6 some 10 or 12 years ago, that ^{the timbers of} the floors were heavy and sound, it is probable that the main timbers of some if not all of the other houses in question would be sound also.

Now, if any of the buildings had to be repaired and partly refitted, it would probably be found that the roofs and the basement floors would require the more considerable attention. At N⁰ 6, I had to lift all the paving in the basement and take out the earth below down to the footings of the walls, and as [*page missing*]

V&A, AAD

1 Mary Caroline Stuart-Wortley (1848–1941), second wife of Ralph King-Milbanke (1839–1906), thirteenth Baron Wentworth and later second Earl of Lovelace.
2 PSW had undertaken alterations and the refurbishment of 6 Cheyne Walk, Chelsea in 1869–72, for Rafe Oswald Leycester (1844–1929), of Toft Hall, Cheshire. See *Kirk*, p. 298.

295 • To John Ramsden, 26 November 1886

Copy/draft

[1, Raymond Buildings . . .]
Nov: 26. 1886.

To J: C: Ramsden Esqre
Busbridge Hall by Godalming

Dear Mr Ramsden

Before answering the letters of yourself and Mrs Ramsden, dated respectively the 20th & 21st of this month, I wished so to consider the matters contained in them that there should be as little ~~possibility of~~ misunderstanding between us as possible.

On referring to back drawings I find that my first design, ~~a tracing of which was sent to you~~ of the plan was submitted to you here, and is dated Mar: 18: 1886, on this plan was based a fresh design, a tracing of which was sent to you April 13. 1886, and since then there have been 3 other arrangements of plan, the last one of which, after various modifications, ~~has marked on it several more modifications~~ in detail in different parts of the house and several more alterations marked on it is dated July 6. '86. From this last plan, to $\frac{1}{16}$th scale, the ⅛th scale plans were made, and as these ~~plans~~ latter were proceeding several variations in detail were suggested, and agreed to by me.

It will thus be seen that from March to November of 1886 I have been closely engaged on the designs for your house, and I can safely say that I have never before taken as much time & trouble in sifting the arrangements of a house before the definite plans were proceeded with, as I have in this of yours. I do not in any way complain of this, indeed I congratulated myself in thinking that whatever time & trouble had been bestowed upon the plans before the final drawings were made, so much time would be saved in the long run. Now, as the ⅛th scale plans exactly represent the settled arrangements arrived at between us on the preliminary plans wh' accurate first plans were considered by us in detail at interviews, and by letters, I confess I was disappointed at finding the questions of the arrangements completely unsettled by your last letters.

I would like to guard against a possible supposition that I should think ~~that,~~ even now, some better scheme ~~might~~ could not be arrived at, and which would be worth the trouble and expense; but I certainly feel ~~that~~ the probability is, that any further designs made by me would only leave the thing in ~~an~~ a still unsettled state, and myself in a more uncomfortable position as architect. No architect, worthy of the name, ever matures a set of plans without understanding as he proceeds that the work shewn on the drawings is practicable & workmanlike, & to be sure of this, I always carry on at the time of making out the working drawings, others drawings to a large scale, so that all construction &c may be clear to myself, and the surveyor who takes out the quantities. For the house for Lapscombe this has been *properly* done, and *it* necessarily ~~caused~~ occupied much time, so that it was imperative ~~that~~ the work should be in [a] form ~~for getting~~ from which to get tenders from builders as soon as possible, ~~so~~ that the works might be begun in the earliest open weather of 1887.

When I put the drawings in the hands of the surveyor on the 13th of October, it never occurred to me that any important variation from the *agreed upon* plans would be contemplated.

To prepare a fresh set of drawings embodying such radical alterations as are proposed in your last letters would occupy me for so considerable a time, that, with the best hope for mutual & settled agreement on such plans, ~~would~~ the time at which the works could be begun after obtaining tenders ~~would~~ must be later in the *coming* year than would be satisfactory.

I do not, as I said before, think that it might not be better to incur such delay, but I feel very doubtful whether your confidence in me as an architect is such as to make it reasonable for me to undertake fresh plans for you; for, from several criticisms on my character of design made verbally here & some note in your letters with regard to my having run into expensive roofing for insufficient cause, make me hesitate in any way to lead you to repose ~~any~~ further confidence in my experience and ability as an architect.

It would ~~be~~ hardly *be* worthwhile I think for me to enter now on further detailed explanation, but perhaps I had better just say that the second staircase is 2'.9"¼ wide in the clear: That the greatest value of the third staircase is from the ground floor to the first floor: That the first floor *main block* water closet is advisedly placed where it is for sanitary reasons: That there would be no difficulty in my modifying the windows to the main stairs if a change was really a wise one: That the arrangement of the main stairs was arrived at, after much consideration, to make the hall a pleasant place to sit in: That there would certainly be a saving in cost if the south wall to yard were stopped *at the s. end of main yard* and did not continue as a screen, but the loss of it would, *I am sure,* be felt as much both by the servants and those using the garden: That the bay window to the drawing-room is <u>without</u> a pillar dividing it, as the window was expressly designed to avoid ~~the~~ *using a* pillar *here*, and I had no intention of departing, in a side way, f^m a settled arrangement. With regard to your expression of opinion as to the drawings beings "beautiful", I would merely say that they are only plain straightforward "working" drawings, made without the waste of ~~any~~ useless ~~work~~ *labour* on them whatever.

In conclusion I would say, that I do not wish to carp over small things, ~~&~~ which are really unimportant from my point of view; but I would seriously urge upon you whether it would not *be* better that the proposed re-disposition of the arrangements of the house were undertaken *for you* by some other architect, before other cost was incurred which, too, might not be a satisfactory end of preliminary expense?

Believe me | Yours very truly | Ph: W:

LB-2, pp. 68-71

296 • To James Havard Thomas, 13 December 1886

Draft

1 R.B. Gray's Inn
Decr 13. '86

Sir[1]

I beg to acknowledge ^{the} receipt of your circular letter ~~of~~ accompanied by two other papers regarding the matter of a proposed "national exhibition of the arts" &c.

Having carefully considered ~~as to~~ whether it would be well ~~for me~~ to accept the offer made ^{to me} by the signatories of the letter of invitation that I, as an architect, should agree to serve on the committee referred to therein, I beg to say that I have concluded not to accept the invitation.

I am well aware of the evils of the present mercantile monopoly of art exhibitions ^{in England} generally, and should be well pleased if some more honest way could be found as a remedy to the present restricted and prejudiced ways of exhibiting works of art.

As I am not myself an exhibitor, and as my time is fully occupied even now by serving on committees in addition to my daily work I am certainly not a fit person to serve on your committee, the more so, that the work to be incurred by the movement entered upon will require much energy and perseverance on the part of all ~~concerned~~ ^{engaged,} to carry it to a successful issue.

I am Sir, | Yours faithfully | Ph. W.

J: Havard Thomas Esqr

Cheltenham 1991.1016.658

---

1 The sculptor, James Havard Thomas (1854–1921), moved to Italy in 1889. In 1886 he was a founder member and secretary of the New English Art Club, but in 1889 'he destroyed the contents of his studio and moved to Italy.' http://www.oxforddnb.com.ezproxy.londonlibrary.co.uk/view/article/64509 [accessed 11 March 2015].

297 • To Percy Wyndham, 24 December 1886

Draft/copy

[1, Raymond Buildings . . .]
Dec[r] 24 1886.

To The Hon' Percy Wyndham
Clouds House by Salisbury

Dear M[r] Wyndham

Inclosed is a revised summary of M[r] Estcourts acc[t] for his work at Clouds, which I hope you will find clear. As to Longden's acc[t], the £22 for coil case wire guard sh[d] have been sent direct to me, but the mistake is of no importance. It can be paid by you to him along with your own acc[t] with him and the balance of his acc[t] of 233.12.9. By the reduction of £66.13.4 on Estcourts acc[t] and the addition of the £22.0.0 of Longden's it will give a reduction of £44.0.0 on the amount on which my own charge is made – therefore, if, when you pay my balance, you deduct £2.4.0 from the £215.0.0 ~~it~~ the error will be corrected.

I am indeed glad that you find ~~the~~ your house fairly satisfactory as, in these days of rottenness in the arts, that is as much as can reasonably be hoped for. The Master of Balliol must have given you the smooth side of his tongue, than which there is nothing more oily![1]

When you decide upon doing any "whitewashing", as advised by William Morris, please let me know, as there is a way of doing even *this* properly. I will give my advice as an amateur in the whitewasher's art.

Please accept my thanks for the brace of pheasants. If you could have but persuaded them to come here on foot I w[d] have painted their portraits for them, whereas now, I shall have to eat them.

Believe me, | Yours faithfully | Ph.W.

P.S. I presume M[rs] Wyndham has not returned to Clouds? I sent to her there two sets of drawings for fittings, and have a third ready. I hope her sister is better. Ph.W.

LB-2, pp. 73-4

---

[1] The reputation of the classicist, Benjamin Jowett (1817–93), rests on his authority as a highly influential Master of Balliol College, Oxford. He was committed to college and university reform, and although this brought him opponents, generations of undergraduates were shaped by his powerful influence as a tutor. Perhaps Jowett had visited Clouds.

298 • To John Ramsden, about 27 December 1886

Draft/copy

Decr 17. [*sic*] 1886

To J: C: Ramsden Esqre
Busbridge Hall. Godalming
Dear Mr Ramsden

I duly rec^d your letter of Dec: 21 inclosing a tracing of a suggested new treatment of the entrance, hall space &c for ^(the house at) Lapscombe.

I can understand that you were not satisfied with the space given ~~for~~ ^to hall in comparison with the arrangement in the finished plans. Nevertheless, the plan I sent you on the 17th Decr had its qualities, which perhaps may not have weighed with you as much as they did with me.

The tracing of suggestion you sent me can hardly be accepted by me as ^in ^(any way) satisfactory, and for the following reasons among others. (1) There is no head room at entrance under half-landing of stairs. (2) The entrance into the hall cuts across the window recesses, and delivers the cold air almost directly on to the fire place (3) The hall itself would certainly be an awkward shaped space ^(and in serving the hall door it w^d be rendered uncomfortable). (4) The landing ~~by~~ ^(of stairs) on corridor under skylight comes too close into one corner, and the entrance to ^the W.C is ~~very uncomfortably exposed~~ ^(too openly exposed) to the corridor. (5) The W.C apparatus working over the hall itself would certainly be felt as a nuisance, and no "deafening" would sufficiently deaden the sound. (6) The necessity for another soil pipe to W.C and an increased length of drain, extra ventilation shaft ^manhole &c would be, as I explained to you when you were here, ruinous to good sanitary arrangement.

Having let the matter rest for a few days, I turned-to once more to see if it would not be possible ^yet to arrive at some more or less satisfactory arrangement of this part of the house, ^and to which we could both agree. I now send you a plan which certainly gives more hall space than the 17th of Decr plan, and ~~to~~ ^in which I have been able to attach a bow window in combination with the porch. The porch itself is enlarged so as, in some ^small way, to make up for the want of an entrance hall, and I have arranged that the entrance door can be served without first coming into the hall.

The arrangement on the landing is satisfactory, in so far as it meets those requirements, ^in which my experience of the working out of house plans enables me to be sure of ^what the result will be. I believe the plans will sufficiently further explain themselves.

Y^{rs} very truly | Ph: W:

LB-2, pp. 76-7

299 • To Percy Wyndham, 28 December 1886

Draft/copy

[1, Raymond Buildings . . .]
Decr 28. 1886.

To Hon' Percy Wyndham
Clouds House East Knoyle

Dear Mr Wyndham

On the other side I send receipt for cheque &c. I am exceedingly glad that the drawing-room pleases you. I looked that it should do so, as it is planned for a long south room, having the fireplace towards one end, and heating coils at the other, so that when in use for one or two persons only there would be a pleasant place by the fire, not exactly in the middle of the room, and yet the other end of room would not be cold. For a drawing-room, when filled, it would also be good: as the philosophers – male & female – may generalise at one end, and the rat-catchers (general name for the sporting fraternity) enter into particulars of prowess at the other, and both may be out of ear-shot.

Will you get Mallett to makes notes of his observation of the effects of the very soft water, as it might be useful in future. I need hardly say that all evidence sh^d be sifted! Please tell Mrs Wyndham that there is no necessity for her to write. I was merely desirous of knowing if the plans reached their destination.

Yours faithfully | Ph: W:

LB-2, pp. 74-6

300 • To Frank Faulkner, 24 January 1887

Draft/copy

[1, Raymond Buildings . . .]
Jan 24. 1887

To Frank Faulkner Esqre
Croswell's Brewery Oldbury

My dear Frank Faulkner[1]

Your letter of the 21st ins^t was addressed to E: Webb instead of Philip, and went to N° 6 in these buildings, where there seems to be established another person with the surname of Webb, but whether he is an iniquitous arch^t or unjust lawyer, I cannot say; however, he forwarded the letter $^{to\,me}$ this morning.

You may be assured I should be very pleased to be in any way of assistance to you, but, as to professionally, I had better ^{first} send you a note or two from my experience, for your guidance before entering on the proposed work of house building.

The success of investment of money in house building depends ~~so~~ much upon circumstances. As a rule, the better the house, the poorer the investment. If a house is carefully built, with some attention to the scientific parts of its construction &c, the less likely is it that, on being sold, it will fetch the consequent price. Again, as to the art part of the matter; if it be fairly good from that point of view it will be less likely to sell well, as the popular idea is ᶠᵒʳ much shew at little cost, whereas the art value depends upon considerations which have no market value. Then, again, would the person who is to live in the house be disappointed if it were not of the ordinary kind?

The foregoing applies to a small as well as to a large ~~building~~ ʰᵒᵘˢᵉ. If after considering these questions, you would still wish me to help in the matter I ~~will come~~ ʷᵒᵘˡᵈ ᵍᵒ to Leicester to look into the surroundings and other matters at such time as would suit you.

Yours very truly | Ph: W:

LB-2, pp. 79-80

---

1 Brother of Charles, Kate and Lucy Faulkner, Frank Faulkner 'was a pioneer in modern brewing methods . . . [and] a prolific writer on brewing matters with much of his work appearing in the *Brewers' Journal*'. Amber Patrick, 'Beeston Maltings . . . ', *Brewery History*, no 136, Summer 2010, p. 59. Although the proposal came to nothing, Faulkner's family relationship to CF and KF made PSW willing to help. See also Vol. III, Letter 850, note 10.

301 • To Frank Faulkner, 10 February 1887

Draft/copy

[1, Raymond Buildings . . .]
Feb: 10. 1887

To Frank Faulkner Esq^ʳᵉ
Croswells Brewery, Oldbury.

Dear Frank Faulkner.

I went to Leicester on Tuesday (the 8ᵗʰ) and examined the site on which ᵗʰᵉ Messʳˢ Bates', the Eagle Brewery stands,[1] and also the additional piece of ground adjoining on which the proposed house for the brewer is to ~~stand~~ be placed. The proposition, thus far, seemed to me to be a good working arrangement. At first I had the assistance of Mʳ Bates, the younger, and afterwards of Mʳ Saunders in explaining the ᶜⁱʳᶜᵘᵐˢᵗᵃⁿᶜᵉˢ, requirements, and collateral necessities.

At lunch (which I took with Mʳ Saunders) I arrived at ᵗʰᵉ particulars of requirements from Mʳ Saunders' point of view. At my suggestion, an appointment was made for me to meet Mʳ Bates, the elder, Mʳ Bishell and Mʳ Bland (a local builder who had done much work ᶠᵒʳ ᵗʰᵉ ᶠⁱʳᵐ, including the brewery buildings) at 3 o'clock. Mʳ Saunders' wish was to have 2 moderate sized sitting-rooms and one small one, with kitchen, small washhouse &c and upstairs 2 bedrooms ~~&~~ ᵃ bathroom, and servant's bedroom, with a water closet for the house, and another in ~~the~~ ᵃ ˢᵐᵃˡˡ ᵇᵃᶜᵏ yard for the servant, a general cellar underground, and a coal cellar.

This proposal seemed reasonable enough to me, but I should have preferred that there should have been one <u>considerable</u> sized ˢⁱᵗᵗⁱⁿᵍ room and a small alternative ~~sitting~~ ʳᵒᵒᵐ instead of the 3 ˢⁱᵗᵗⁱⁿᵍ rooms.

On meeting Mʳ Bates senior and the rest of the firm & the builder I carefully went into particulars of contrivance, cost, materials, drainage, ʷᵃᵗᵉʳ ˢᵘᵖᵖˡʸ, &c, and I found that Mʳ Bates was strongly averse to so large a house as that above described. He was somewhat (though good humouredly) sarcastic on the amount of accommodation specified by Mʳ Saunders. I mediated as well as I could, and promised, if I undertook the work, to reduce in every way possible. I obtained useful information from the builder, but found that his ideas of a <u>substantial</u> though exceedingly plain & simple house, were rather different to mine, but not so much so but that a medium might have been struck.

Mʳ Bates insisted that the house should, practically, be of the rental of £25 a year, and he considered Mʳ Saunders' proposition wᵈ turn out to be one at £50 and, if so, it would be an unwise proceeding on the part of the firm merely for a "brewers" house. I did not combat this opinion, and said I could say nothing myself on this point but would lay the matter before you exactly as the case stood ᵃⁿᵈ ʷʰ' ᴵ ʰᵃᵛᵉ ʰᵉʳᵉ ᵈᵒⁿᵉ.

On my return journey I rather thought of suggesting that it would be better that Messʳˢ Bates should employ the architect at work on the brewery, for the sake of economy, but on further consideration yesterday, I thought I would offer to make a plan of what I considered would be a satisfactory arrangement for a small house for the purpose ⁱⁿ ᑫᵘᵉˢᵗⁱᵒⁿ, and submit it for your and Messʳˢ Bates' approval – but I received this morning the inclosed letter from the firm, which practically puts the matter at rest as far as I am concerned, however, I must beg you to be assured that if I can aid <u>you</u> in any way farther, I shall have much pleasure in doing so.

Yours very truly | Ph W.

<u>Copy inclosed</u>

Eagle Brewery. Northampton Sqʳᵉ & Lower Charnwood Street. | Leicester.
Feb: 8. 1887

Dear Sir.

On looking at Mʳ Faulkner's conditions we saw a reason for seeing our solicitor. We have done so and find the house cannot go up on those lines. Please, therefore, do not go into the matter at present. We fear it will have to drop, or if it is done we shall ourselves have to do it. It would have been best had we seen our solicitor at first.

Yours truly (signed) | Bates Son & Bishell

P. Webb Esqʳᵉ

LB-2, pp. 80-3

1 The Eagle Brewery in Leicester was founded in the 1820s in Northampton Square, and in the 1870s took on additional premises in Charnwood Street, where there was also room for expansion. The business later became known as the Leicester Brewing and Malting Co.

302 • To Sir Isaac Lowthian Bell, 23 February 1887

Draft/copy

[1, Raymond Buildings . . .]
Feb: 23 1887

To Sir Lowthian Bell Bart'[1]
Rounton Grange Northallerton

My dear Bell

I am really sorry to have been obliged to keep you so long without the drawings of the memorial but it was unavoidable.[2] The design was somewhat tiresome to work out in a clear way for the mason, and I found it necessary to do some of the work twice over. I now send the drawings which I hope you will like.

In dealing with the mason (the same one, I suppose, who did the other family memorials?) I think you should send the drawings to him and that he should understand he was to estimate for doing and fixing the work, and the whole in exact accordance with the drawings and the directions thereon written, and that you should urge that the stone used should be carefully selected.

You will see that I have ordered your shield to be cut[3] as, it would be difficult at some future time to cut it without moving the stone and, indeed, the 2 shields should go together. It w^d be easy ^{enough} to cut any further inscriptions without moving the stone.

Believe me | Yours very truly | Ph: W:

LB-2, pp. 83-4

1 See above, Letter 73, note 5.
2 Lowthian Bell's wife, Margaret Pattinson, had died in 1886.
3 He means the space on the memorial where Bell's own name would eventually be added.

303 • To Charles Faulkner, 8 March 1887

Postmark LONDON W.C. MR 8 87 *Address* Charles Faulkner | University College | Oxford.

1 Raymond Buildings, Gray's Inn, | *London, W.C.*
Tues: 8th Mar: '87

My dear Charley

I saw Kate last night and found her better, certainly; so that I hope, as soon as the wind changes and milder weather comes, she will get round again. She showed me your last letter which interested me much (I hope if this freedom is not to your mind, you will say so?).

It is, perhaps, a good thing you cannot come up this week as I feel sure that the less excitement she has, the better chance there is for her, and you know that the "strong meat" conversation which goes on between us when we meet, and which interests her more than ordinary talk, also excites her. I have taken round to her photographs and drawings to pass away the time which hangs rather heavily on her hands. I think Mrs Lewis is a great help, at present, and I trust it will last, as seems likely.

The next book which I shall say I want – before you – will be, say, Beate Virginæ Maria c. 1320, illuminated & pictured on all its leaves, bound by Grolier[1] &c &c, price £860 as, perhaps, that price might stop you from lending it to me. Now I have Cæsar's Commentaries from you[2] (wh' I mean to pay for on purpose to vex you) and a host of other books which my present dynamite studies do not even allow me to look at for more than 5 min: at a time. I cannot say that my intellect is allowed to rust for, last night at our Council meeting[3] there was more cantankerous criticism than enough and more angry answer than would serve for a board meeting of a Vestry.

Nevertheless I thank you kindly for the "Omnis Gallia" book.

Your affectionate | Ph: Webb.

We shall probably see you on Friday week?

WMG J551

---

1 Jean Grolier de Servières, (1489-90-1565) was French Treasurer-General and an eminent bibliophile. His collection favoured elaborately decorated book-bindings, now much valued.
2 Julius Caesar's *Commentaries on the Gallic War*. Amongst the several editions which CF could have acquired for PSW is that edited by Dr Giles in 2 vols (London: Cornish & Sons, 1886).
3 Council of the Socialist League, of which PSW, as Treasurer, was an elected member.

304 • To William Morris, 20 March 1887

1, Raymond Buildings, Gray's Inn, | *London, W.C.*
Sun: 20th Mar: '87

My dear Fellow

I have John Glasse's £5,[1] and have sent mem^m to Debney.[2]

I thought we were fairly well delivered by the Commune and as well as could be expected afterwards. I saw you were dog tired and hoarse as a raven – added to which there was not much more to be said on the theme without careful thought as to how to ring a change.[3] I believe at the ^{first} commemoration of your death I should be obliged to say, 'we will drink to his memory, and in silence'.

Things are being brewed, I fancy, for a one-sided conference, which would be a misfortune if so ruled, never mind, patience!

Yours, | Ph. Webb.

I think Charley may come up on Mon: or Tues: Kate is certainly better, but is very slow on the way, a S.W wind would be a help to her. This persistent wind is whiggish.

V&A, NAL MSC/1958/687, f. 15

---

1 The Christian Socialist, John Glasse (1848–1918) was an Edinburgh clergyman, and a member of the Democratic Foundation. PSW records here Glasse's membership fee for the Socialist League, which WM had encouraged him to join when he spoke on 14 March at the Edinburgh Branch of the Scottish Land and Labour League. A note in his diary records that 'Glasse proclaimed himself a socialist and active . . . and said he was going to join the League'. *CLWM*, II, p. 628 note 2.
2 Lawrence Debney worked for Morris & Co., and was an active Socialist League member.
3 On 17 March at the South Place Institute, Finsbury, WM spoke at the annual commemoration of the Paris Commune, organised by London socialist organisations. Like PSW, WM felt that 'one has by this time said all one has to say on the subject'. WM to JEM, 17 March 1887, *CLWM*, II. He reflected ruefully in his diary that 'I spoke last, and to my great vexation and shame, *very* badly . . . I tried to be literary and original, and so paid for my egotism.' *CLWM*, II, p. 628 note 3.

305 • To Henry Barker, 26 March 1887

1 Raymond Buildings Gray's Inn W: C:
Sat Mar: 26 '87

Dear Barker[1]

I have rec^d f^m you the Commonweal bills but <u>not</u> the weekly ways & means sheet: as I cannot enter anything in my book without this I should be glad if you could manage to make it out. I believe Charles is still in London;[2] could you not get him for half an hour just to aid in putting last Thursday's business into the usual form?

Yours Ph. Webb

Amsterdam S.L. 3180/1

---

1 Henry Alfred Barker (1858–1940), appointed General Secretary of the Socialist League on 29 May 1887.
2 Probably Frederick Charles. See Vol. II, Letter 337.

306 • To Mitchell Brothers, 30 April 1887

Draft/copy

[1, Raymond Buildings . . .]
April 30 1887.

To Messrs Mitchell Bros
Builders Shalford Guildford

Dear Sirs.

(Mr Ramsden's Hse)

Mr Ramsden has decided to accept your tender for building ~~the~~ his house, and that the works should go on at once. I will prepare the specification and agreement for signature with the drawings. This work will take me some little time, but you can, of course, at once proceed in making preparation for the works by ordering bricks &c.

Mr Ramsden seemed to think there would be some spare room in the Cottage adjoining the site which might possibly be of use to you, and if you will call on me the next time you are in London I would speak to you about this and other things.

You will understand that I am taking it for granted that you will do your very best in all ways to make the building satisfactory to Mr Ramsden and a credit to me & yourselves.

Yours truly | Ph: W:

LB-2, pp. 90-1

307 • To John Hardy, 3 May 1887

Draft/copy

[1, Raymond Buildings . . .]
May 3 1887.

To Mr John Hardy – Clerk of Works[1]
Mr Gilbertson's. Market Place Guisboro: Yorks'.

Dear Sir.

The building of a House in Surrey of wh' I spoke to you ~~about~~ when you were last here is now to go on and as my client (Mr Ramsden) has decided to have a resident clerk of the works ~~on the ground~~ I now write to ask you if you are disengaged and able & willing to undertake the work under my direction? The house is somewhere abt the size of Major Godman's. The builder is a satisfactory person who has done work for me before, and he undertak~~inge~~s all the trades; ~~and~~ I believe you would only have to <u>help</u> him properly to carry out his work, and not be troubled in any way with obstruction.

Will you be so good as to let me know if you could come within a week, and what salary you ask? There is a comfortable Farm House on the estate (within 10 minutes ^walk^ of site) where I believe you could come to terms with the tenant, with Mr Ramsden's consent, for use of bed-room, ^small^ private room for your papers, ~~&c~~ and general room ^with tenant^ for ^your^ meals &c.

As the year is already ~~far~~ ^much^ advanced I am anxious to get things forward at once, and I shall be glad of an answer directly.

Yours truly | Ph: W:

P.S. I believe you are able to use the surveyor's level?

LB-2, pp. 91-2

---

1 PSW held John Hardy in the highest professional regard. See above, Letter 135, note 1, and also below, Letter 311.

308 • To Henry Barker, 4 June 1887

1 R. B. Gray's Inn Sat: June 4 '87

Dear Barker

Your plan for cash acc^t^ seems promising and [1] shall be glad to fall in with it if nothing better turns up. I think, at all events, we can try it till Faulkner comes to London in 2 or 3 weeks' time.

Cannot you make out a black board acc^t^ for Monday to be taken as only <u>moderately</u> accurate?

Perhaps Turner[1] will be able before next Thursday to have another wrestle with the transfer of items from you to me and, as he will not now have to learn the office ledger, he can give more time to the unsolved problems.

Yours truly | Ph Webb.

Amsterdam S.L. 3180/2

---

1 William Turner was appointed Financial Secretary of the Socialist League on 29 May 1887, providing administrative support to PSW in his role as Treasurer.

309 • To Editor, Stratford-on-Avon Herald, 28 July 1887

Second draft, on behalf of SPAB[1]

To the Editor of the Stratford on Avon Herald.

Sir. The letter published in your paper of July 8 [1887] calls aloud for a protest from the Society for the Protection of Ancient buildings.

The letter in question, signed by G.E. Bell, is one of those the point of which should be met with persistent opposition from all English people, and more particularly from those in the neighbourhood of Henley in Arden where a wayside-cross is still actually standing in, ~~as far as the several members of the cross are concerned,~~ a ^{singularly} complete condition.[2]

We have photographs by us giving this fact clearly, and by the use of a lens it is also as clear that to "restore" it would be to lose at once, for this and coming generations, the inestimable value of this relic of mediæval England which has escaped that doom up to the present time.

It is probable that Mr Bell is both sincere and earnest in his proposal, but how mistaken only those who have watched for the last 30 or 40 years the ceaseless destruction by "restoration" are able to appreciate.

It is certain that our descendants will be more intelligent in such a matter than we are, but unless what intelligence we possess is whipped into activity there will be nothing ancient left standing for our children to take care of.

Now, many of us know, only too well what calling in the "eminent architect" means. It will be, that he comes to the place, shakes his busy head over the iniquities of ruthless time, and decides to send an assistant to measure the antiquity for its new suit of clothes, after which, certain drawings will go through the mill of his many handed office; books of antiquities will be searched for "examples"; many and wide differences of opinion will go the round of vivacious pupils, as to whether such and such a detail from some other ancient building is of the exact date of the miserable patient to be operated upon. At last things are settled so that a sparkling drawing is made which carries by acclamation the vote of ignorant people: the works are set about, and a venerable fragment is made a jest of till time also shall soften the severity of just opinion and one more piece of concrete dishonesty.

Now Sir, this Henley in Arden way-side-cross can only be saved for an indefinite time by one way of treatment, and this is to prop, stay, band, tie and secure in every honest possible way so that no part of the work shall fall or be thrown down by the wind. Then time will gradually crumble it to dust, and it will never be an object of scorn and ridicule as in a "restored" state it certainly would be. Its still remaining years of existence would be of some use to students and other sincere people, and it might be said for years to come that one town cross remained which had power in it to compel respect if it did not afford personal glorification.[3]

[*pencil*] July 28. '87

SPAB, Roadside Cross, Henley-in-Arden file

---

1 A first draft also exists in PSW's hand, as well as a file copy as sent on 30 July, signed by HTT. It was published in the *Stratford-on-Avon Herald* on 5 August 1887.

2 The likely condition of the cross in 1887 is captured in a handbook published in 1863, which also included an engraving. 'In the centre of the town, which is called the Market-place, stands one of

the few Crosses remaining in this country, which is traditionally related to have been preserved from destruction in the seventeenth century by a shed which was built over it. This Cross is now much injured by time. The base, shaft, and capital are composed of three separate stones; the base being mortised into the shaft and capital. At the beginning of the present century there were niches on the four faces of the capital, containing the Rood, the Trinity, St. Peter with his key, and another subject defaced, all of which have now mouldered away, not a trace of the sculptured figures named being visible.' John Hannett, *The Forest of Arden, its Towns, Villages, and Hamlets* (London: Simpkin, Marshall, and Co., 1863), pp. 44–5.

3 In fact, no restoration occurred. Only the base of three steps and a small portion of the shaft now remains.

310 • To H. S. H. Jones, 1 September 1887

Draft/copy

[1, Raymond Buildings . . .]
Sep 1. 1887.

To H.S.H. Jones Esq[rel]
Bragbury by Stevenage.
Dear Sir.

(Datchworth Ch')

In answer to your letter of yesterday's date. It seems to me that nothing need (since the receipt of this letter) stand in the way of my surveying your church, with regard to some apparent defects in the structure, supposed to ^be active, and requiring immediate attention.

My time is wholly engaged till Monday next, the 5th instant, on which day I could come to Knebworth station by the 1.25 train from Kings Cross, getting to Knebworth at 2.17, I believe.

As I have heard separately your Co-Churchwarden's acc[t] of the building, ~~separately~~ I should prefer to hear yours also alone before meeting the Rector[2] & M[r] Lawrance,[3] and this you could probably give me on your way to the Church?

I told M[r] Lawrance last Monday that he should at once put some shores against the building in the best way he could, and I think it would be well if you directed him to provide ladders of such length in the church ~~for~~ ^as would allow me to examine the cracks when I am there on Monday.

I am sorry to be unable to accept your & M[rs] Jones' kind invitation ^to lunch or to stay to dinner as I must return by the 5.54 train from Knebworth station.

Yours very truly | Ph.W.

P.S. Of course I should wish to see both M[r] Wardale & M[r] Lawrance at some time during my visit.

LB-2, pp. 96-7

1 Jones was one of the churchwardens of All Saints, Datchworth, Hertfordshire. PSW undertook some repairs and remedial work (1888–90).
2 The Reverend John Wardale, rector.
3 William Lawrance, the local builder who undertook the work under PSW's instructions.

311 • To Mr Edwards, 3 September 1887

Draft/copy

[1, Raymond Buildings . . .]
Sepr 3. 1887.

To Mr Edwards. Foreman of Works
Lapscombe. ^(Cranleigh) by Guildford

Dear Mr Edwards.

For some ~~little~~ time I have been aware of a little difference between you and Mr Hardy, my clerk of the works, and yesterday I endeavoured to get at the bottom of the difficulty for, as you will readily understand, any serious increase of misunderstanding between you and Mr Hardy would oblige me to act decisively, and probably injuriously to one of the parties to the difference.

In questioning ^{Mr} Hardy and Mr Mitchell, ~~I think~~ I found out enough to guide my judgment in deciding what should be done if a better feeling did not arise at once. Of course I know there is something to be said on both sides, and shall allow for that, but I would wish to impress upon you in a friendly way that I have <u>not</u> put a clerk of the works at Lapscombe who is a hasty inexperienced man, but one I have known for years, ~~and~~ who has always done his duty fairly and honestly under the circumstances, and I have a respect for his judgment and experience. Now, I must ask you, for your own good, for the good of the works, and out of respect to me as Architect having heavy responsibility, to carefully consider whether you cannot manage to work with Mr Hardy in such a way as to modify, if not altogether do away with hastiness and ill feeling?

Please to remember that it is a rule ^{with me} as well as a pleasure ~~to me~~ to work to the utmost of my ability in a perfectly friendly way with all classes of working men with whom I have dealings.

Yours truly | Ph: W:

P.S. I have also written to Mr Hardy on the same subject.

LB-2, pp. 97-8

312 • To John Hardy, 3 September 1887

Draft/copy

[1, Raymond Buildings . . .]
Sepr 3. 1887

To Mr John Hardy – C of Works
Shamley Green Guildford

Dear Mr Hardy

(Lapscombe works)

I had a talk with Mr Mitchell yesterday, after leaving the works, as to the uncomfortable relations between Mr Edwards ^{as foreman} & yourself as Clerk of the works,[1] and I explained to him what I thought was the chief cause of the difference namely, that Edwards was a young and rather inexperienced man & that he did not sufficiently submit to your greater experience and the necessity there was for you, as clerk of the works and my assistant to decide upon how things should be done. Mr Mitchell seemed to think that the chief cause of Edwards' irritation was that you sometimes gave direct orders to the workmen without doing so through Edwards.

Of course you will know, ~~that~~ with my limited knowledge of how things go on between you, that it ^{would be} almost impossible for me to be quite fair to both parties if I hastily decided upon sharp measures. I particularly wish to avoid this, and as I have written a clear letter to Edwards, though in a ~~very~~ friendly spirit, I am in hopes that he will now more easily defer to your wider experience and greater age.

If you can help me to narrow the causes of difference in any possible way I shall be obliged. If I had taken severe measures, you will readily understand that Messrs Mitchell would then be put out, which in the long run would act injuriously to the works they have in hand for Mr Ramsden.

Yours truly | Ph. W.

LB-2, pp. 98-9

1 Mitchell ran the local firm to which PSW had awarded the Lapscombe/Willinghurst building contract at Shamley Green (see above, Letter 306), and for which Edwards worked as foreman.

313 • To Henry Barker, 19 September 1887

1 Raymond Buildings Gray's Inn
Mon: Sep 19. '87

Dear Barker

I have caught a sharp chill ^{with sore throat} and can do nothing more than just poke at my work here a bit. As I shall not be at Committee tonight[1] will you be so good as to book up the 6 pences &c of the weekly donations for me – I shall have here the C. J. F[aulkner]. Oxford Br[anch]: E. B. B.[2] P. W. and "Langley" so that you can advertise them & what you get, in the 'Weal. Lane[3] or Morris would take round the hat in an impressive way.

I hope to be well enough for the Ways & Means

Y^{rs} Ph: Webb.

Amsterdam S.L. 3180/4

---

1 Meeting of the Council of the Socialist League.
2 Ernest Belfort Bax (1854–1926) was a close associate of WM, having help found the Socialist League after their departure from the Social Democratic Federation at the end of 1884. They collaborated on some articles for *The Commonweal*, and were its co-editors for a time.
3 Joseph Lane (1851–1920), a founder-member of the Labour Emancipation League, later affiliated with the Social Democratic Federation. His working-class origins gave him a special credibility when, like Bax, he too left the Federation to found the Socialist League with WM.

314 • To Henry Barker, 9 October 1887

1 R B Gray's Inn
Sun: Oct 9. '87

Dear Barker

I looked for Commonweals' and, lo, none! I looked for salve to my depressed mind from reading the "dramatic sketch"[1] and my spirit has sunk lower from want of cheering aliment.

No reproach intended – nothing covert – all above board. My throat is rather dogged but I hope to be well enough to meet comrades on Monday.

Y^{rs} <u>Ph Webb</u>.

Faulkner sent me a Comm^h but I found no advert^t of the 7/6 subscr^{ns}!! <u>no</u> reproach, still

For Council meeting October 10 '87

Philip Webb. To ask a question as to what course the Socialist League will pursue with regard to the "unemployed", during the coming winter.

Amsterdam S.L. 3181/2

---

1 He may mean the introductory 'Notes' of current matters, over WM's initials, or the short piece on 'Free Speech in America' in which WM deplored the capital sentences passed in Chicago on seven men who had demonstrated against a police attack on striking workers. Both items appeared in *The Commonweal* on 8 October.

315 • To Sir William Bowman, 10 October 1887

Draft/copy

[1, Raymond Buildings . . .]
Octr 10. 1887.

To Sir William Bowman Bart'
Joldwynds, by Dorking

My dear Bowman

I have been unwell for some 3 weeks and have done comparatively little work, but I am now able to send you some tracings of what I would propose to do to stay the spreading of the billiard-room roof.[1]

In a letter ⁿᵒᶠ ʸᵒᵘʳˢ to me of Aug 28, you suggest to run a tie rod across the roof midway of the room. The plan had ᵒᶜᶜᵘʳʳᵉᵈ ᵗᵒ ᵐᵉ ᵃⁿᵈ returned again and again as the simplest resource, but I have been obliged to put the idea on one side ᵃˢ ᵒᵘᵗ ᵒᶠ ᵗʰᵉ ૧ᵘᵉˢᵗⁱᵒⁿ. It would be certain, when using the billiard table that the cues would be constantly ~~knocked against~~ ᶜᵒᵐⁱⁿᵍ ⁱⁿ ᶜᵒⁿᵗᵃᶜᵗ ʷⁱᵗʰ the rod, which would be exceeding annoying to the players and provocative of bad language: injurious to cues and morals at the same time.

From the tracings you will, I think, readily understand my plan, which is the simplest ~~and~~ I can think of, having in view to disturb the room as little as possible.

The east wall at the plate level is now slightly bowed outwards as shewn and the applying the 2 steel joists running the whole length of room, secured at ~~each~~ ᵇᵒᵗʰ ends with tie rods ᵃᶜʳᵒˢˢ ᵗʰᵉ ʳᵒᵒᵐ ᵃᵍᵃⁱⁿˢᵗ ᵗʰᵉ ² ᵉⁿᵈ ʷᵃˡˡˢ and also bolted through the plates at distances ᵃᵖᵃʳᵗ midway, ʷⁱˡˡ ˢᵉᶜᵘʳᵉ ᵃᵍᵃⁱⁿˢᵗ ᶠᵘʳᵗʰᵉʳ ᵉˣᵖᵃⁿˢⁱᵒⁿ. The <u>steel</u> joists allow of less size for the amount of strength ᵗʰᵃⁿ ⁱʳᵒⁿ and they would, I believe, secure the roof ~~from spreading any more,~~ and yet ~~allow of~~ ᵏᵉᵉᵖ ᶠʳᵉᵉ the clear ~~height~~ space over the billiard table. Will you kindly let me know what you think of the scheme?

The works at 25 Young Street are now drawing to a close,[2] and both Sanders and Moncrieff[3] would be glad of another instalment of payment on acc^t. I therefore certify for £500: (£400 for Sanders and £100 for Moncrieff, which the former will pay to the latter). Sanders has had £1200 and Moncrieff £150. Sanders would be glad of the cheque – if convenient to you – by Thursday morning.

Yours very truly | Ph: W:

LB-2, pp. 99-101

---

1 PSW had built Joldwynds for Sir William Bowman in 1870–5 (see above, Letter 73, note 4). These subsequent works, including a library extension, were carried out in 1888–93. See *Kirk*, p. 298.
2 Bowman paid for alterations, enlargement and redecoration of Felday House, 25 Young Street, Kensington (1887–8), the house of his younger son, Frederick Bowman and his wife.
3 The building work for Felday House was undertaken by Francis Sanders of Dorset Square, Marylebone.

316 • To George Price Boyce, 11 October 1887

Annotated 'rec^d at Llantwitt [*sic*] Major'

> 1, *Raymond Buildings, Gray's Inn,* | *London, W.C.*
> Tuesday. 11th Oct: '87

My dear Boyce

I thank you for your good letter, though I am not happy with the bad news you give of the treatment of the church of Llantwitt [*sic*] Major. It all but drives one to despair.

Perhaps you could not have done better than make for the place so as to better finish your fine drawing of the Ch', though I am afraid it may be very cold for you, as the paper of this morning said there was snow in Shropshire. Perhaps the neighbourhood of the sea may keep you free of that trial.

Last Saturday fortnight I went to Welwyn with the hope of being cured by Monday to return and go on with my work, but getting worse I did not get away till the next Monday. I hate being ill in another's house, but I was hardly my own master and the doctor & the sister nursed me as if I were a Saint, which is odd, considering that I belong to a profession which points ancient churches with <u>black</u> mortar! However, I am better now, though feeble – able, happily, still to laugh at a joke, even a bad one of my own. I've had a bad throat that is all.

If socialists have throats they sh^d be of cast iron.

I go on Thursday with Wardle to examine Staple Inn, for which building we are in a state of doubt & anxiety.[1] I don't think any fellows understand what the society means.

Let me hope that you have a comfortable lodging, and that both you and Madame will enjoy the good Welsh air and wild sea. After you have been seated for half an hour at your work, take a turn round the ch' yard to quicken your blood, and . . . and . . . don't be obstinate. Mrs Boyce will dish you up a dinner after your work which will make a new man of you. I w^d like to be with you and make merry over a bottle – even of Gilbey's reflection of Bordeaux.

The Welwyn doctor looked in here today, and I gave him your & Madame's greeting. He said he expected you both to go to New Place on your return. Confound that nuisance Wallis; what with his impudence and stupidity, he will do more mischief than enough.[2]

With kind remembrance and thanks to both of you I remain as before, till I hear from you again, | Sincerely | Ph: Webb.

BL Add 45354, ff. 245-6

1 On 13 November 1886 the SPAB had presented a formal petition to 'the Lord Mayor, Aldermen, and Commons of the City of London, in Common Council assembled', appealing against the forthcoming sale by auction of Staple Inn', and asking that the whole site 'be acquired by the Corporation to be held by them in trust as memorials of the history of the City of London, and as an open space and garden'.
2 See above, Letter 290.

317 • To George Washington Jack, 24 October 1887

1, Raymond Buildings, Gray's Inn, | *London, W.C.*
Monday. 24th Oct: '87

My dear Jack

Of course I have made a hundred & one jokes over your faithfulness. You say that writing in holiday time is a luxury, & so it seems to be, & only to be partaken of <u>very</u> sparingly! Never mind, you can make up for your studied silence by telling me long travellers' stories of the wonders you have seen on your way, that is, on your return, for I cannot expect you to do more than you have done in the way of letter writing.

I see that New Abbey, in my list, is also called "Sweetheart"! perhaps because of the use to which the ruins are now put by lovers.[1] I see that you are not far from the estuary of the Nith, and have much notable ground (to say nothing of water & perhaps whiskey) to soak your mind with. Please don't forget to make yourself acquainted with the proper pronunciation of the names of places, not forgetting Annan, and all other names connected with the immortal Nanty Ewart.[2]

If you spot any characteristic pieces of work in photographs (odd and unfashionable beauties) please bring them back say, to the amount of 5/- or so. I shall want something by which to correct your tremendous enthusiasm for N.B.[3] I take it for granted you will somehow manage to get across & see what Hackston [*sic*] is about[4] – remember me to him [*word deleted and illegible*] with all proper civility due to himself, & as the pupil of the invaluable madman of Coniston.

News is rough here – the town & people's heads being under the rule of policemen's batons.[5] I see in this morning's paper they have tumbled the erratic Wilfrid Blunt off a platform in Ireland.[6] They are putting more power into their elbows, and revolutionists must look out for their knowledge boxes.

I am getting on single handed, pretty fairly. Have to go to Datchworth Church this afternoon and, I hope to be able to get to Lapscombe on Friday, but I'll not name any more of these horrid things.

I am not yet as strong as I shd like to be, but the doctor does not seem to be anxious about me so I look forward to coming out strongly in a little time.

I send you by book post Morris's amusing "Interlude" which will make you laugh and, perhaps, forget things you wd rather not remember.[7]

Yours very truly | Philip Webb.

V&A, AAD

1 About eight miles south of Dumfries, the Cistercian monastery which came to be known as Sweetheart Abbey was founded in 1273 by Dervoguilla of Galloway as a memorial to her husband, John Balliol.
2 Antony (Nanty) Ewart is master of the brig, 'Jumping Jenny', in Scott's 'Waverley' novel, *Redgauntlet* (1824).
3 North Britain.
4 The Scottish watercolourist William Haxton (1855–1921) started life as an architect. JR encouraged his painting, as well as commissioning drawings of French cathedral towns, suggesting also that he change his surname to Hackstoun. His fiery temperament was not best suited to JR's somewhat imperious demands. He spent some years in St Andrews, landscape painting.
5 The autumn of 1887 saw increasing civil unrest, with high unemployment and ongoing frictions over the unresolved issue of Irish home rule. Processions of the unemployed were routinely stopped by the police. PSW was writing before the crisis of 'Bloody Sunday', on 13 November, when 'Trafalgar Square was the scene of the most ruthless display of establishment power that London has ever seen'. *MacCarthy, WMLT*, p. 567. A well-planned operation, involving large numbers of police, cavalry and foot soldiers broke up a procession of the unemployed, supported by Socialists, Radicals and Anarchists. Many were injured.
6 The poet and maverick aristocrat, Wilfrid Scawen Blunt (1840–1922), JM's lover and PSW's future landlord, was arrested on 23 October at Woodford in Ireland for inciting tenants to resist arrest for the non-payment of rent. He subsequently served a prison sentence of two months with hard labour.
7 *The Tables Turned: or Nupkins Awakened, A Socialist Interlude*. WM's dramatic satire was performed in the hall of the Socialist League headquarters in Farringdon Road on 15 November 1887, as a fund-raising event for *The Commonweal*, WM himself taking the role of the Archbishop of Canterbury.

318 • To Charles Fairfax Murray, 6 December 1887

Dictated to GWJ

1 Raymond Buildings | Grays Inn WC
Dec[r] 6th 1887

Dear Murray

Sorry that the exigencies of sacred sickness obliged my nurse to drive you from my door this morning. She was just strapping me down to my board to perambulate the streets, when you called, so there was nothing else to be done.[1]

Apart from joking I should like to have had a few words with you though the doctors make it a very hard and stiff rule that I should keep away visitors. The doctors say visitors introduce all sorts of maggots into my brain, religious, revolutionary, artistic, & what not that is dangerous to the foundations of society. When you next call, purify yourself of anything more dangerous to this community than that of money getting honestly or dishonestly, as the case may be.

The best time to call will be perhaps between one & two, for a few minutes

Yours sincerely | Philip Webb | by Geo: Jack

Fitzwilliam 48

---

1 PSW described his illness as 'rheumatism of the knees' (PSW to HTT, 17 November 1887, *SPAB* archive). He was seriously incapacitated for months, and even at the beginning of February 1888 he was still required to keep indoors.

319 • To Giacomo Boni, 21 December 1887

Pencil; dictated to GWJ

Dec[r] 21st 1887

My dear Giacomo Boni

By the hand of my friend & colleague I send you a few words in answer to your delightful letter of Dec 14th. It was my greatest surprise during the whole time of my sickness, as I had almost forgotten everything else in the world, than a bed and a sick fool in it. However I am better now[1] and able to think of your rhapsodic idea of the lagoon & Torcello. It was very good of you to chime in with my present sentiment which is almost childish.[2]

Your notes on what you and others have done towards saving for a more reasonable generation some small fragments of beautiful things – done also by a less foolish generation than ours – demands my respect and hearty congratulations. Go on as long as there is any breath in your body and earn honest thanks.

After I left Venice with Sig Murray, we went eastward, and I staid for a day and a half in Vicenza – and after having been made melancholy by the skilful but dismal representatives of the skill of the great Palladio[3] I turned to the beautiful bits of remains of that Mediæval work of which you speak with admiration.[4] Your photograph of the Casa Pigafetta[5] interests me greatly though of course the Renaissance had already begun to tell disastrously on the imaginative work of the middle ages. If you can get your book of 20 plates together of these Vicenza remains I, and some of my friends shall be glad of some copies – at 20 f [each] & at all events for your present purpose of collecting subscriptions to enable you to publish you may put down the following names as subscribers *** for which money you will hold <u>me</u> responsible, and I will send you the money when you write for it.[6]

The pamphlet on ca' D'Ora interests me exceedingly and your beautiful drawing of the original cornice and parapet finish most satisfactory.

I hope shortly to become a human being again and able to do something for myself once more – when I will write to you, and tell of things unmentioned in this letter.

Yours sincerely | Philip Webb | by George Jack

***

William Morris	5 copies
Charles Faulkner	3 "
George Boyce	1 "
George Wardle	2 "
Philip Webb	5 "
	----------
	16 "

Courtauld 17a-f.

1 'Better' than he had been, perhaps, but he was still having to dictate his letters, either because he was bed-bound or otherwise incapacitated.
2 GBO had heard that PSW was ill. 'You will recover soon, that is my heartiest wish, and take a long rest, here, as you deserve after such a laborious life, and we will build a little sandolo [*a flat-bottomed Venetian rowing boat*], with a pointed sail, of a dark yellow colour, and with its upper point darker, like the wings of a swallow – and we will go to Torcello and touch with our fingers the basket-work of the XI century capitals, and see how the little cristals [*sic*] of the Greek marble glitter.' GBO to PSW, 14 December 1887, *Courtauld* 16a.
3 The work of architect Andrea Palladio (1508–80), infused by the influence of Greek and Roman models, can be found throughout the Venetian Republic. He spent much of his life in Vicenza, where there are many Palladian buildings.
4 '[D]uring last autumn I spent twelve days at Vicenza, and studied its mediaeval antiquities; so beautiful, and yet so unknown, and neglected.' 16b.
5 The Casa Pigafetta in Vicenza, dating from 1440, was the birthplace and home of the navigator Antonio Pigafetta (c.1492–c.1531) companion of Magellan during his circumnavigation expedition of the world (1519–22).
6 '[T]o preserve some record of these precious remains I have photographed the most characteristic examples, of which I propose to print a certain number of copies on <u>Bromide</u> paper. . . . These prints I desire to publish by private subscription at the price of 20 francs for the collection of 20 sheets.' 16c.

320 • To Jenny Morris, 29 December 1887

Pencil

1, Raymond Buildings, Gray's Inn, | London, W.C.
Thursday. 29. Dec: '87

My dear Jenny

It was very good (of course) of you to send so quickly the photographs of the great man – on the whole he comes out pretty well. Unfortunately not one of them gives the best known side of his character, namely, that of "volcanic" rage. The serious side-face portrait gives the tragic of [*sic*] an ill spent life, and says to <u>me</u> as much as, Well – 'there <u>is</u> a devil after all then'!![1]

Excuse freedom of thought & ~~speech~~ writing.

And so the mother is keeping me company in the dismal shades of sickness. My love to her and best wishes that she may soon touch the firmer ground of ordinary well being – as I am doing.

Good will to May also. For yourself, I'd like to have a talk with you, to shew you how egoistic a sick man (either in England or Turkey) can be.

Charley & Kate are to touch their lips when (in time to come) I pass the bounds of honest breeding in the line of chattering.

I'm apt – now that I'm out of <u>recognised</u> delirium – to talk of things far too volubly – Things wh' ordinary folk wood [*sic*] say were barely on the sane side of life!

My love to you my dear. | Y[rs] sincerely | Philip Webb.

BL Add 45342, ff. 63-4

1 This set of pictures may include the 'side-face portrait' from the late 1880s, taken by Elliott and Fry and illustrated in *MacCarthy, WMLT*, black-and-white plate 85. 'I send herewith a photo: the artist has done his best in it I *do* believe. But what would you have?' WM to John Bruce Glasier, 21 December 1887, *CLWM*, II.